ALSO BY CLIFFORD IRVING

A True Tale of Vengeance, Betrayal, and Texas Justice

Clifford Irving

DaDDY'S GIRL

THE CAMPBELL MURDER CASE

SUMMIT BOOKS
New York   London   Toronto   Sydney   Tokyo

for Moish te adoré

DADDY'S GIRL

DADDY'S GIRL

Contents

Contents

Preface

Murder is a universal human obsession. Few of us, fortunately, deal with it in our daily lives. But when we do, our vision of reality on the planet is changed. We become even more aware of human frailty, more grateful for whatever harmony and love exist in our lives.

Every lawyer involved in the Campbell murder case believed that it was the most bizarre and psychologically complex case he had ever dealt with. My own involvement is detailed in the pages that follow. I started out in Houston as a writer on assignment, in theory an observer—but I became an investigator, a friend to many of the dramatis personae, and a trial witness. As a result, to my surprise and mild horror (for it was never my conscious intention), I helped to determine the outcome of events.

In the course of my inquiries I took detailed notes and used a tape recorder whenever possible. Nearly every phrase quoted in this book was said to me, or to someone else whose recall I trusted, or is a matter of public record. Most of the described thoughts are what people told me they were thinking at the time. Were they being truthful? I used my judgment.

Everyone whom I have written about helped me in one way or another, and it would require an index to list the names. I am grateful to them all—in particular, Dan Grothaus, for his research, and also (in alphabetical order): Judge A. D. Azios, Roy Beene, Rick Brass, Ginger Casey, P. M. Clinton, Frank Cooper, Maureen Earl, Melanie Edgecombe, Russell Hardin, Jr., Allen C. Isbell, Peter Justin, Jerry Lane, Jim Leitner, Lyn McClellan, Randy McDonald, Sgt. J. C. Mosier, Eugene M. Nettles, Brenda Palmer, Kent Schaffer, Nancy Schaffer, Max Schaffer, and Clyde Wilson.

My friend and lawyer, Maury Nessen, and my publisher and editor, James Silberman, annotated the manuscript with perception and patience. Thank you again.

Was justice done in Texas? I will let the reader decide.

C. I.
November 5, 1987

The courtroom oath—"to tell the truth, the whole truth and nothing but the truth"—is applicable only to witnesses. Defense attorneys, prosecutors, and judges don't take this oath—they couldn't! Indeed, it is fair to say that the American justice system is built on a foundation of *not* telling the whole truth.

ALAN DERSHOWITZ
The Best Defense

The law protects us from barbarianism, but gives us the barbarianism of the law.

JEAN LE MALCHANCEUX
A Crusader's Journal

PART I

EXECUTION

EXECUTION

I

A humid June night slowly melted toward the stillness of a Texas dawn. No breeze blew, and the house set back from Memorial Drive was silent. A hazy quarter-moon glimmered through pin oaks and pines. The house seemed becalmed in the forest.

Upstairs on the second floor, two small boys burrowed among blankets strewn at the foot of a king-sized bed. The older boy, Michael, was nearly nine—his brother Matthew was seven. They had watched *Star Wars* on the VCR until past midnight, but they knew the movie so well they no longer needed to watch the ending, and they drifted to sleep long before the rescue of the dark-haired princess and the final battle against evil Darth Vader. Weaponry still sizzled even as Michael's head slumped into his pillow and Matthew's eyes closed.

And now the blank television screen hummed quietly, casting a pearl-gray light throughout the bedroom. The central air conditioning had been turned off many hours ago. The air was damp and lifeless.

On the bed above the two boys their grandparents slept. The grandfather, James Campbell, a fifty-five-year-old lawyer, lay flat on his back atop the covers. He wore a mauve golf shirt and blue boxer shorts. The grandmother, Virginia Campbell, curled on her side, sweating lightly, her short nightgown pulled high over bared plump buttocks. She had black hair and very white skin. She tossed in her sleep. All day she had been uneasy and short-tempered; she had even cried.

The Campbells had come back only a week ago from three weeks' vacation in Austria, Germany, and Czechoslovakia, where they had played golf in Salzburg and gambled at the casino on Lake Konstanz. The boys called their grandparents "Papa" and "Mama," although their real mother lived a few miles away in another part of Houston. Their mother was becoming a stranger to her children.

The glowing numbers of the digital clock-radio on the grandmother's bedside table said 3:30 A.M.

From far away, downstairs, came a light crash—as if a window had fallen or rudely been thrust open. The grandmother cried out in her sleep. The grandfather stirred but didn't wake. The boys dreamed on of demons and tigers, creatures from uncharted worlds. They heard nothing.

Silence once again . . . and then the carpeted stairs creaked a few times.

Jagged noises penetrated Michael's sleep. He had heard such sounds many times on television, but these were louder, and they cudgeled his eardrums. Confused and frightened, pajamas soaked with urine, the eight-year-old boy peered up from the sticky quilt on the floor. In the light of a ceiling lamp he saw a figure standing by the door that led to the hall. Then the figure vanished.

Michael quickly shook his brother awake. The two boys wriggled out of the damp bedding and clambered to their feet. They stared at the bed, where blood glistened cherry-red in the lamplight.

"Papa had one eye open," Michael said later to Maria, the maid. "He looked at me. He was all red. I tried to talk to him, but he wouldn't say nothing. *I got scared!*"

Teeth chattering even in the heat, the two boys ran down the stairs, out the back door, and across the dirt of the yard. Silvery light had begun to puncture the blackness and seep through the pines on Memorial Drive. Clattering up the outside metal staircase to Maria's little apartment over the garage, Michael and Matthew pounded their knuckles on her door.

Maria opened the door, gaping at them. *"Que pasó?"* she demanded, for the boys spoke Spanish with her. Michael screamed what he'd seen.

Unclutching her bathrobe with one hand, she made the sign of the cross.

"Tengo miedo! Yo no voy allá." She was afraid, she said. She wouldn't go over there. Trembling, she pressed the boys close to her bosom.

At 4:25 A.M. the dispatcher's office of the Houston Police Department received a telephone call from a man identifying himself as J. W. Campbell. Campbell said, "My brother and his wife have been murdered."

The dispatcher calmly jotted down the address Campbell claimed to be calling from—8901 Memorial Drive—instructed him not to touch anything, and then called a patrol unit cruising somewhere in the darkness of residential West Houston and ordered them to investigate. Ten minutes later Officer M. E. Meaney called back on his car radio and confirmed: "Double homicide, 8901 Memorial."

The dispatcher summoned a Fire Department ambulance—just in case Meaney was wrong and a flicker of life was left in one of the assumed corpses, or a wounded person came crawling out from behind a bloody bush—and then punched out Homicide's telephone number on the third floor of Police Headquarters.

The duty lieutenant took the information and immediately yelled down the corridor to the cubbyhole that housed the next-up team of Homicide detectives on the rotation list, Carl Kent and Mike St. John. Kent and St. John just happened to be there on the third floor at that dull, black hour on June 19, 1982.

St. John was in the midst of reading that day's edition of the Houston *Chronicle*. Israeli troops and armor had rumbled through East Beirut to the boundary of Yasser Arafat's enclave. John Cheever had died. The Houston Astros, twelve-and-a-half games behind Atlanta in the National League West, had been beaten again by San Diego in the Astrodome. *Porkys, Das Boot,* and *E.T.* were playing at local cinemas, and Queen Beatrice of the Netherlands had visited with Houston cultural leaders at an early morning Croissant & Strawberry Reception at the Museum of Fine Arts. Major crime in Harris County, the *Chronicle* reported, was down 2.9 percent for the previous year, but homicide was up 7.4 percent.

St. John and Kent hustled out the back door into the parking lot and started to earn their pay. It was their job to travel to where the murder had been committed, record any statements by witnesses, describe the gore, supervise the crime scene unit that would hunt for evidence, and do all the routine things that usually solve a murder, if it isn't already solved by the presence of a hysterical man waving a bloody kitchen knife or a still-loaded .38, yelling, "Yeah, I did it! And I'd do it again!" Most murders in Houston—anywhere, for that matter—involve friends and family and are perpetrated in provoked rage, at night, in hot weather,

17

while drunk, and there is little mystery about who is dead and who killed them.

This one seemed different. A double murder in the expensive Memorial area smelled like a case that would haunt the five o'clock news until it was solved or HPD quit on it. A big case, from the police point of view, but not a good case.

The two detectives drove out in an unmarked four-door Chrysler sedan, each carrying a .45 in a waistband holster with a few extra clips in a jacket pocket. They wore jackets and ties; that was regulation. Outside the car the temperature at dawn had dropped to a relatively welcome eighty-two degrees, but it was a metal-gray early morning, and it would get hotter. Mike St. John was excited because this was only his third week as a Homicide detective. He was twenty-six years old; he was studying to be a lawyer, going to law school at night. Carl Kent, his partner, an eight-year Homicide veteran who chewed tobacco and smoked cigars, stood three inches over six feet and weighed 275 pounds: a robust man of forty-one who seemed friendly to everyone but made you feel relieved that he was *your* friend. He was unfamiliar with the Memorial neighborhood as a quarter for homicide scenes and he made the mistake of whipping the Chrysler onto westbound I-10, which forced him to circle round and head back toward downtown on the forested curves of Memorial Drive before he reached the house.

Several HPD patrol units had heard the dispatcher's call on their radios and were out there now. They would monitor their radios—if they got a call, they would scoot. Back on the grassy shoulder, the red rotating flashers of the patrol cars illuminated the tall trees along Memorial Drive and turned the green thickets a bizarre shade of crimson. The neighboring houses were what St. John would call estates, with lights that glowed now like big, curious, rectangular yellow eyes. A hundred yards away some groups of people in bathrobes stood in the fog on clipped lawns, watching.

Only one of the patrol cars and a civilian Cadillac were parked in the driveway of the Campbell house, where flashlight beams swept eerie trails in all directions. One of them blinked into St. John's eyes, a drawn pistol in the wavering shadow below and behind it. He and Kent showed their shields. They entered the house through the open front door and instantly noticed a single thin, whitely transparent, surgical glove just inside the door on the carpet. They walked carefully around it, knowing that when the time came the crime scene unit would tweezer it up and work on it for prints.

A clue straight out of Sherlock Holmes. It seemed too good to be true. *The Case of the Surgical Glove*, St. John thought. Now he was even more excited.

18

The house itself—sand-colored brick, with a partial flagstone overlay—was not as large as he would have expected at that address on Memorial Drive. There was one bedroom downstairs and only two upstairs, and in all the rooms a minimum of furniture, most of it scuffed, plain, and old: a leatherette recliner in the den, a sofa and one lumpy easy chair in the living room, a drooping green plant, a spinet, a bookcase featuring an outdated set of the *Encyclopedia Britannica*. The walls were settling, the paint cracking. Hardwood floors were covered with a turquoise-green carpet, here and there torn.

St. John decided it looked like a house that had been bought by a moderately wealthy man who at some point lost most of his money and had become a recluse, an oddball.

Chewing on the stub of his cigar, Kent growled, "Tobacco Road, man. Who lives here?"

One of the patrol officers said: "A lawyer named Campbell and his wife. Bodies are in the bedroom to the left at the top of the stairs. Seems like about three or four shots each, killed them right off. Campbell's brother is here, in the kitchen—he's the guy who made the call—and there's a maid, and two little kids, the grandsons. Whoever did it must have got into the house through a window in the den. The window's stuck, and we haven't touched it. Want to see?"

"Sure do," Kent said.

They sauntered round the house through brambles and scattered brush, following a blurred flashlight beam and marveling aloud at what a mess the grounds were. St. John reckoned that no one had cut a branch here for years or mowed all summer. Couldn't this guy afford a wetback gardener twice a month? Didn't he own a lawn mower? A machete?

"Don't get too close to the window," Kent cautioned, waving at the damp earth beneath their shoes. "Might be footprints, and we can get a mold."

The HPD officer laughed nervously. "Hey, if there are any footprints now, they belong to six or seven cops." Then he remembered: "There's a locked bedroom upstairs. Some of the guys think the killer may be in there."

Kent said cheerfully, "Well, how about we go up and find out? Maybe break the case!"

It seemed a wonderful possibility, and now that the two Homicide detectives were here to bear the responsibility, four police officers with drawn guns edged cautiously upstairs toward the locked bedroom. They would happily have kicked the door down, but Maria the maid materialized, wringing her hands and moaning in Spanish, and produced a key that spoiled their fun. Kent twisted the key into the lock, then prudently stepped aside to let the uniformed officers, moving fast even in that confining hallway space, rush through the door with their guns sweeping round the room, which turned out to be empty except for a bed and a dresser crammed with a large-sized young woman's casual clothes.

Kent grumbled, "We got to go to work after all."

Lights cast a mellow glow in the master bedroom. A half dozen gleaming brass shells, what police call hulls, were scattered all over the floor near the open door. Everyone was being careful not to kick them out of place or step on them and dent them, as sometimes happens in the bustle of the moment. St. John could see they were hulls from a .45, and since a .45 ejects to the right and behind, he reasoned that the hulls must have bounced off the wall to the right of the door as you faced into the bedroom. The king-sized bed was on the right, a glass-enclosed gun cabinet stood against the back wall, and rumpled bedding lay thrown on the carpet at the foot of the bed. There was a .45 automatic in the gun cabinet but it had not been recently fired. A loaded shotgun stood against the wall by the bed. A Magnavox TV and a VCR hookup sat on a chest of drawers against the wall facing the bed. Nearby a man's brown trousers had been carelessly tossed over two suitcases, as if the owner was habitually messy or in a hurry to consummate a sexual passion. An old straw hat lay on the floor, and a single iron barbell with forty pounds of weight, and a pair of woman's pink flipflops. It all screamed of normalcy, except for the blood.

Blood was spattered on the ceiling, the flower-patterned white sheets and pillowcases, the headboard of the bed, the yellow drapes behind the headboard, various lamp shades, a mirror, and a coral-pink pillow that had been thrown on the carpet on Virginia Campbell's side of the bed. Virginia Campbell had been shot through the face and breast, and from the way she curled in her shortie nightgown, head nested in the pillow, mouth slightly open, eyes closed, white arms dangling over the side of the bed, it looked as if she had not awakened for even a second. Her sleep had just become permanent.

Her husband, James Campbell, in his pastel-colored golf shirt and underpants, lay flat on his back, fists clenched, shot through the left eye and under the jaw. One bullet had exited the back of his head, so that blood and gray brain and pink-flecked bone tissue stained the pillow. The right eye was open, staring with what a romantic might have interpreted as mild puzzlement; but really there was no expression at all. He had died almost instantly.

Policemen as a general rule are paranoid, more affected by the practical and philosophical implications of what they see than they're willing to let on. When he stopped for a moment to consider what had happened, and to whom, the flesh on St. John's arm rose in cold goose bumps. It was the kind of murder that frightened him, because the dead couple looked to be anybody's mother and father, and anybody's mother and father can be asleep in the house when some lunatic breaks in and starts blasting away.

On second thought, no—not a lunatic. There were no open drawers, no sign of a search. The wife was still wearing her big diamond ring and gold earrings. No burglar had been surprised and then panicked. Six shots had struck home in vital areas. None had missed.

"This was an execution," Kent said quietly. "Someone knew his way around well enough not to trip over a lamp or make any noise and wake them. Didn't say 'Gimme your jewelry,' or even 'Your time's come, motherfucker.' Just pumped away with the old .45—got the job done. Shot her first, killed her in her sleep. Looks like Mr. Campbell heard the sound, jumped up in bed, turned to the door. Then he took one in the left eye."

"Good shooting," St. John said, out of professional respect.

"No powder residue on these people, " Kent went on. "The perpetrator wouldn't want to get blood all over his clothes. Had to be standing six to eight feet away."

A .45 wasn't the big cannon, didn't have the enormous kick of a .44 or a Magnum, but still there was considerable recoil. The bullet is a fat, short shell that travels relatively slowly, has little penetrating power and doesn't make a big hole, but hits with the power of a hammer swung hard by a 200-pound man. It often creates a grotesque jerking motion in a human target. You had to be an experienced pistol shot, Kent meant, to put six straight rounds from a .45 in the center of a human target at six to eight feet. You had to be nearly nerveless. You couldn't do it if you were angry, or in combat of any kind. It was not simply a matter of skill. It was a matter of *attitude*. No lunatic shot like that. Or else—a special kind of lunatic.

St. John whistled soundlessly. "Are you saying it's a hit? A contract killing?"

"Could be," Kent said.

The two detectives were near the end of their ten-to-six night shift. A long day stretched before them—plenty of overtime to punch into the computer, which is why some cops battled to get into Homicide—but they weren't tired and the adrenaline was banging through the bloodstream.

"Let's talk to the brother," Kent decided.

J. W. Campbell sat in the kitchen at a Formica breakfast table. St. John glanced around the room and noticed black and white tile, metal cabinets, and some kind of preformed metal ceiling, as if the kitchen had been built in the 1940s and nobody had remodeled it since.

J. W. Campbell was composed, but pale beneath his summer tan. He was in his late fifties, wearing rumpled trousers and a white golf shirt. Two of his upper front teeth were partially missing, which gave him the look of a yokel. When the detectives asked him a question it took him a while to focus and work up an answer, and sometimes he didn't seem to realize the question had been asked. He was into his own thoughts. His brother had been killed—it didn't happen every day.

Of course in the eyes of the detectives he was only peripherally a grieving brother. He was first of all a source of information that might lead to the killer. He was also a suspect. In the Bible, and in Houston, brothers killed brothers. So the condolences were brief. Kent thumped onto a kitchen chair, straddled it, and muttered, "Mr. Campbell, I'm real sorry what happened to your brother"—and then, scarcely missing a beat—"So do you have any idea who did it?"

J. W. Campbell had no idea. "A client," he suggested vaguely.

"Your brother—?"

"—was a lawyer."

"What kind of a lawyer?"

"Personal injury cases, and he did some criminal work. It could have been an angry client—"

But he didn't have any particular one in mind. He would have to go over the list back at Jim's office. Jim and Virginia had just come back from a trip to Europe; he hadn't been in close contact with them recently. He was a lawyer, too. Same field of practice. Yes, sometimes they worked together. Yes, of course they got along fine.

"What about other family?"

"They've got four daughters. Two live over in Austin, one's up in Tennessee, one's here in Houston." J. W. Campbell looked up warily.

St. John dutifully wrote down the daughters' names and J. W.'s seemingly loose knowledge of their ages. Michelle and Betty Ann, the two in Austin, he thought were about thirty-one and twenty-nine. Betty Ann, the younger of that pair, was married and had a child. Cindy, the mother of the two boys who had been sleeping at the foot of the bed upstairs, lived here in Houston, and she was twenty-six. The baby of the family was twenty-one-year-old Jamie, a student at some little tech school in Knoxville.

"I have to call them," J. W. said woodenly, nodding to himself, obviously dreading it.

Meanwhile the crime scene unit had arrived. In the noise and the flow of traffic, cops were beginning to trip over each other's feet. St. John had also called out a new unit with HPD that was videotaping the entire house, outside and inside, room by room.

On the way over to the maid's apartment above the garage, where the two little kids were holed up, big Kent dug an elbow into St. John's ribs. In the whitening shadows of dawn his voice boomed. "You hear what he said? *'My brother was a lawyer, so it could have been an angry client.'* See what it means to be a lawyer? Every goddamn client is a potential assassin! You still want to bust your chops in law school? That's how you could wind up one day, like that guy upstairs in the bed." Kent laughed cruelly. "One eye open, man."

That was cop humor, death humor. Most cops had no love for criminal defense attorneys. They had been grilled on the witness stand too often by the best and the worst. They could understand why you might want to creep up on one of those scumbags in the middle of the night and put a bullet in his miserable heart.

St. John didn't believe that this dead lawyer and his wife were scumbags. And he kept mulling over what a good shot the killer was. That kind of skill and control, such deadly purpose—they were rare. Like a scene from *The Godfather*. What could these middle-aged suburban people, he in his violet T-shirt and she in her white nightie, have done to deserve this kind of death?

The maid, a squat, thickly built, Mayan-looking sixty-year-old woman in a cotton nightgown, with a huge flat plane between her nose and upper lip, had limited English. Kent sent out word to call in an interpreter from Homicide.

In the maid's quarters the boys still wore their pajamas. The younger one, Matthew, the seven year old, was crying and on the verge of hysteria. And who could blame him? This wasn't TV. The blood wasn't ketchup. So where was his mother? Why were the kids living here and not with her? St. John kept wondering about that, but it wasn't his job to dig into personal matters that had nothing to do with the homicide.

The older boy, Michael, jabbered at them. He was nearly nine, he told them. Earlier, when one of the officers had asked him a simple question, he'd said, "We can't talk to you until we've seen our lawyer." Their grand-uncle, J. W., after he heard about it, smiled sadly and released Michael from that self-imposed directive. He also told the boys not to confuse the police by referring to their grandparents as "Papa and Mama."

Michael couldn't stop now: *"My grandmommy and granddaddy got blood all over them! There was all this blood! Blood everywhere!"* It was obviously the most exciting thing that had happened to the kid since he'd squirmed out of the womb, St. John thought. He and Kent had to calm the boy down.

Putting together what J. W. had told them with what they could unscramble from Michael's ramblings, and with what they could understand of his breathless translation of Maria's mile-a-minute Spanish, this seemed to be the sequence of events. . . .

Maria was roused from sleep by a crash. Not a shot. She was positive and specific: a big noise, like a crash. That may have been the stuck den window, Kent decided, the one the killer seemed to have used to get into the house. "Did it sound like a window slamming?" he asked. "One of the downstairs windows?"

"Yes!" Maria said. "The downstairs window, yes, that must have been it!" The thought excited her. She rattled on some more, but too fast for translation.

"Slow her down," Kent ordered the boy, realizing he had made a mistake in prompting her. "Get her to tell me what happened, what she saw and what she heard. Not what she thinks happened, or what she thinks I want to hear."

That may have gone over the boy's head. After hearing the crash of the downstairs window, Maria said—she was emphatic about it now—she turned on her radio to a Spanish-speaking station. A minute later she heard the deejay give the time as 3:40 A.M. She didn't know what to do. She went to the bathroom. She sat down on her bed and waited.

After the boys had raced over to give her the news, she tried to calm them down with a glass of sugared water. She was terribly frightened: if the Señor and the Señora had been murdered, who was to say the murderer wasn't still lurking outside, waiting for *her*? Matthew knew the telephone number of his Uncle J. W. He dialed, and Michael snatched the phone.

Michael said, "Papa's been shot, and he's all red."

J. W. had already told Kent, "I got dressed in a hurry, and on the way over I kept thinking, well, maybe there's a misunderstanding. Jim loved a certain red hot sauce, and maybe he'd had one Scotch too many and spilled the sauce all over him before falling asleep, and the boy had imagined the rest."

No, Michael hadn't recognized anyone. He had seen a figure by the door. He didn't know who it was. Matthew hadn't awakened in time to see anyone at all.

Maria was trying to tell the detectives a story. Out it gushed, they couldn't stop her. The boys' absent and unemployed mother, Cynthia Ray—Maria called her "Cindy"—was divorced. The boys were Cindy's only children, but they had lived with their grandparents since they were small, in fact ever since Maria had been working there. For the last three years they had spent nearly every Friday and Saturday night in their grandparents' bedroom; it was a ritual treat. Last week, a day or so after the Campbells got back from Europe, the daughter Cindy had come over to the house. The Señora went shopping with Cindy and there was a big argument. After that the Señora was nervous.

Well, that's no big deal, St. John thought. He remembered again how good the shooting had been. This was no daughter getting pissed off at something Mama said and coming back with a cannon in the middle of the night.

"And a while ago," Maria meandered on, through Michael, "when she had no business being there, I saw Cindy at the window downstairs— the same window that made the big crash last night! She may have been fooling around with the lock on that window. Yes, now I realize she *was*."

St. John drew Kent aside, speaking softly. "This is the kids' mother the old crow is talking about. I don't like this. It's just going to upset them."

"The kid is lapping it up," Kent pointed out.

But then word came that the interpreter, Sgt. J. T. Mosqueda, had arrived. J. W. Campbell took the boys into the kitchen and fed them milk and a bag of Oreo cookies. The Homicide team escorted Mosqueda through the yard and sat down again with Maria in her cramped kitchen above the garage. It was growing light now, and hot. Maria was agitated, sighing nonstop.

Mosqueda's brown brow glistened. The droning air conditioning unit was old, pumping air halfway between warm and damp cool.

Mosqueda turned to the detectives. "Maria says that the argument last week between the mother and the daughter, this Cindy, was a real shitscreamer."

"She told us that already," Kent said. "I thinks she's really got it in for this particular daughter."

"Well, she wants to tell you again. I don't know if I can stop her." Mosqueda listened some more, while Kent shifted his thighs and scratched his nose and sighed. Mosqueda translated: "She says she heard that the Campbells were going to file some sort of court action to get custody of the grandkids. That's because their daughter Cindy was such a neglectful mother, and they were also going to cut the daughter off from her monthly allowance. There's your motive."

"Love it," Kent said. "Mama threatens to cut off your allowance, so you put out a contract and hire two guys from the local Mafia to come round a week later and blow her brains out. Daddy's, too. You promise 'em half the allowance to do the job. Hey, it would make a great movie. Dan Aykroyd as the killer. Who's the daughter? Madeline Kahn?"

Sorrowing eyes afire, the maid began to talk again. Her old white teeth clicked. She went so fast that even Mosqueda had to tell her to slow down.

Kent said, "This woman's off the wall. I guess you can't blame her, but it's not helping us. Is she telling you again about the daughter and the window in the den?"

"Wait a minute," Mosqueda said, raising his hand toward Maria. He told her forcefully to stop, to wait, there was too much to translate in one go. Out of breath, she puffed like a spent old dog. Mosqueda turned to Kent and St. John, who were straddling two chairs, both of them playing Sam Spade.

Mosqueda said, "This woman has been working for the Campbells for more than five years. She's from Monterrey, in Mexico. She's a loyal servant—it's a special Mexican mentality you have to understand. She says that the little boys' mother—Cindy, the one daughter with all the problems—has a boyfriend. The Señor and the Señora, which is what she calls the Campbells, didn't like this boyfriend, whose name is David. (Kent had heard her say the name several times angrily in Spanish: *Dahveed.*) Maria says she saw him hit little Michael a couple of times, in the po-po, and he always called the kids stupid and spoiled. Once, about a year or so ago, the boyfriend insulted Maria. The Señor and the Señora weren't home and the boyfriend was upstairs roaming through the house without permission. Cindy was downstairs with the kids. So Maria goes up and tells David to get out of the house, and he calls her a stupid fat old whore—he speaks some Spanish, at least good enough to say 'stupid fat old whore.' Maria yells back at him that he's a no-good bum, get out. Then in the midst of this Mrs. Campbell comes home, and naturally Maria right away tells her everything that's gone down. Mrs. Campbell orders David out. So he calls Mrs. Campbell some bad names, too. That results in Mrs. Campbell telling him don't ever come back. Told Cindy later that if she saw him here she'd call the police. After that, whenever David brings Cindy over, which he has to do because Cindy doesn't drive, he waits in his car in the driveway. Maria says that Cindy— sometimes she calls her *la pobrecita*, 'the poor little one'—would come over to get money from her mother, or food from the refrigerator. A while ago she'd wanted to move back into the house, but Mr. Campbell wouldn't let her. She says Mrs. Campbell was afraid of this one daughter. Thought she might be crazy and have to be put in an institution."

Kent thought all that over for a while. He had been scribbling notes in his pad. He took a fresh cigar from the breast pocket of his jacket and began to peel the cellophane. Then he clucked his tongue a few times, almost regretfully.

"Ask her to tell us again," he said, "about the poor little one playing around with the den window."

26

2

Night shift detectives rarely conduct ongoing investigations, and on Sunday, June 20, 1982, the day after the murders, Carl Kent and Michael St. John, although they are destined to return to this story, left the case. They were succeeded by Gil Schultz and Paul Motard, two day-shift detectives.

Schultz was forty-four, a twenty-year HPD veteran who had once been described in *Texas Monthly* magazine as "the archetypal homicide detective—paunchy and rumpled, with haggard eyes and a brave smile." Schultz liked the second half of that description and often quoted it to friends and nosy journalists. His face was round and owlish and his eyes were pale blue without much expression. He had two great passions. One of them was his hobby, wallpapering: he liked to wallpaper houses and was constantly asking his friends and relatives if they weren't ready for a new wallpapering job on their bedrooms or bathrooms, which he would do free of charge, or at cost. His other passion was his work. He once said, "Homicide is so exacting. Two people know who did it. One ain't talking, and the other can't." He liked that challenge.

Motard, at twenty-nine, was lean, dark, and handsome, and generally uncommunicative. So was Schultz. They were both good detectives. They just weren't in the public relations business.

––––––––––––

In the first few days, following the leads given them by J. W. Campbell, Schultz and Motard had no lack of suspects. The victim, James Campbell, had been a plaintiff's personal injury lawyer; he represented people who sued companies, stores, communities, the State of Texas, or the federal government for injuries sustained at work or in public places. The worst of such lawyers were called ambulance chasers. The best were highly paid and nearly always worked for a contingency fee, gambling that they would win, preferably out of court in a settlement, but if necessary in trial. Their fee was one-third to 40 percent of the settlement or award.

Throughout the Houston legal world James Campbell owned the eloquent nickname of "Dirty Jim." The Houston Bar Association reported, "We had several complaints by clients against him. But nothing really serious. Nothing that resulted in a public reprimand or suspension of his license." In 1963, in a losing case, he had been fined and held in contempt of court for kicking another lawyer in front of the judge's bench. A former Harris County assistant district attorney, Don Lambright, said, "His reputation was that of a liar. He often posted bonds for his own clients, especially if they were from out of town, and if those clients jumped bail and forfeited, Campbell did his best to avoid payment. A sheriff from St. Augustine once had to chase him through downtown Houston, and eventually found him hiding behind a parked car. He was a slippery customer."

But the investigating homicide detectives soon discovered that there was no one who hated Dirty Jim enough to kill him, and if they did they were either in prison, or out of state, or dead.

For a short time the brother, J. W. Campbell, was a suspect, because of something odd that had happened on the night of the murders. When J. W. arrived at Memorial, Maria and the boys had told him all they knew. But J. W. had refused, or at least declined, to enter the bedroom where his brother and sister-in-law lay dead. He had sent his wife instead. Was he squeamish? Frightened? Wasn't it possible that his brother was still alive and might need help? Or did he already know what was in the bedroom? And when Michael first called to say that "Papa's all red," why hadn't J. W. called an ambulance or at least a doctor?

Schultz pondered that. Brother Jim, he found out, had always pushed J. W. as a lawyer, somewhat to the annoyance of his friends, who characterized J. W. as "ordinary" and "not terribly bright," and "nowhere near the man that Jim was." When he would find a client J. W. would often turn the case over to Jim and share the fee. The strong feeling was that J. W. needed Jim a lot more than Jim needed J. W. A dead Jim seemed no advantage to J. W. Campbell.

And so, willy-nilly, the detectives were thrown back on the maid's insistence that she had seen Cindy, the second youngest of the Campbells' daughters, hanging around a downstairs window a week or ten days before the murder. And there was the reported shouting match between Cindy and her mother.

Pretty thin, Schultz thought.

He talked to the other three sisters: Michelle, Betty Ann, and Jamie. Yes, yes, yes: they all agreed that Cindy didn't get on well with their parents. The trouble went back a long way, and the reasons were obscure. Yes, Cindy was difficult, and you might even call her the black sheep of the family, but she'd gotten plenty of love and attention.

"Our parents were very good to her," Michelle said. "They always supported her."

"They just didn't get on well," Betty Ann said.

"No more than that?" Schultz asked.

"That's all."

"Daddy has—well, I guess he *had*," Jamie said, "this little apartment house near River Oaks. He let Cindy live there and she didn't pay rent."

Family squabbles. An old argument didn't make motive, and motive didn't make opportunity. The Campbells' murder was no crime of passion or sudden retaliation for wrongdoing or neglect, real or imagined. It had been skillfully planned.

But Cindy was still the best suspect. Without much heart or conviction, the detectives tried to focus on her. What might have been her motive?

"Money," Motard declared, trying it out.

Robert Harris, a lawyer, Jim Campbell's closest friend, was the executor of the estate. He estimated that its value would be between $1.5 and $2 million, but mostly in hard-to-sell real estate in Waco and Brownsville. Surprisingly there was only $200,000 in life insurance, and that was under a policy provided by the state bar association. Not much cash. All told, substantially less than you'd expect for a highrolling fifty-five-year-old lawyer with a house on Memorial Drive. But it wasn't a shabby sum if you had nothing and were in line for a quarter of the total.

The two older sisters said their mother had told them that their Daddy was in the process of writing a new will, disinheriting Cindy in favor of her two sons. On the day after the murder, both of Jim Campbell's safe deposit boxes that J. W. Campbell opened were empty, so J. W. claimed.

Schultz didn't know what to make of that. A lawyer without a will? He wondered a lot about J. W.

The estate would now be divided equally among the heirs, the four Campbell daughters. And they were *all* poor. Jamie, the youngest, was a student at the Professional Academy of Broadcasting in Knoxville, Tennessee. Daddy paid all the bills, always had. Michelle, thirty-two, the oldest, was studying photography in Austin; she supposedly lived with a young woman called Teresina. Daddy subsidized Michelle. Good old Daddy. The only married daughter was the second oldest, Betty Ann Hinds, thirty, whose husband was a systems analyst for Nash-Phillips-Copus in Austin. Betty Ann also had taken money from Jim and Virginia over the past years.

All four sisters had sucked at Jim's ready tit. If greed was the motive, why single out Cindy?

"Still," Motard said.

" 'Still' ain't evidence," Schultz observed. "Look, assume she did it. She didn't do it alone, right?"

The killer had squeezed the trigger of a heavy .45 automatic six times, with all the bullets hitting vital areas of two separate human targets.

29

Cindy Ray was a fat, unathletic young woman with no known experience in weaponry.

"A hired gun?" Motard said.

"Hired with *what?*"

Motard sighed again. Hired guns, unlike personal injury lawyers, didn't work on contingency fees.

"What about the boyfriend?" Now Schultz played the role of devil's advocate. Could the boyfriend, this David who had that little spat with the Señora, have been the trigger man?

He and Motard put together what little they knew about David, whose last name was West. Father was an engineer and West Point graduate, grandfather a federal judge (deceased), mother a former set designer at the Alley Theater. David West himself was a young ex-marine who owned a dilapidated two-story house in Montrose, a trendy but rundown inner-city section of Houston which its residents liked to compare, at least in spirit, to New York's Greenwich Village and SoHo. Like Cindy, David West was currently unemployed.

Jamie, slim and doe-eyed, the youngest Campbell sister and the prettiest, had been a casual girlfriend of West's even before Cindy. She had been to his house a few times. "Not to his bedroom," she stressed. "But when he was drunk or doing drugs," she said, "he used to shoot a gun into the air, right out the living room window, or into the ceiling."

"You saw that?" Schultz asked. "How many times?"

"Well . . . once, I guess."

"What kind of gun? Was it a handgun?"

"I guess so," Jamie said. "It was black. It looked like this." With her hands she drew in the air a thick L-shaped pattern.

"Was it a .45 pistol, Ms. Campbell?"

"Gosh, I don't know."

But then, from several sources, the detectives discovered that David and Cindy had ended their love affair at least a year ago. No one had even seen them together during that year. West had had several girlfriends in the interim. If he and Cindy had resumed any kind of close relationship, it had only been in the last week or two before the murders. The impression was that even now they were not passionately involved. For auld lang syne and because it was the decent thing to do, he was taking care of her during a period of mourning and travail.

"So the problem still is," Schultz said grumpily to Motard, "*why*. I mean, even assuming Cindy needed the inheritance money so badly and wanted to murder her folks, how does she get *him* to go along with it? He pops back into her life after a year away and just says, 'Sure, honey, whatever you say'? These kids don't strike me as Leopold and Loeb. This murder was not an intellectual exercise."

"How do you know?"

"Gut feeling." It was one of Schultz's favorite phrases.

"The kid sister says West is a survivalist," Motard pointed out.

"Guy sleeps in a hammock and shoots a couple of bullets out the window when he's smoked a joint. Big deal. He's got no criminal record, there's no known violence. What is it, he misses target practice in the Marine Corps? Well, let's not give up on it," Schultz said, more or less because he had already given up on everything else. "Let's talk to him, if he wants to talk."

On June 22, during the funeral, the detectives babysat the two little boys out at Memorial. They played with them for two hours and learned nothing. After the funeral, Gil Schultz invited the entire Campbell family down to Police Headquarters on Reisner Street to make statements and provide elimination prints, so that if HPD ever found any fingerprints they would know which ones were foreign to the household. David West was at the funeral, too, and he escorted Cindy to Reisner Street. That was serendipitous, Schultz thought.

Homicide, with its acoustic tile ceilings and tan linoleum floors, overlooked the police parking lot and a tangle of freeways. Betty Ann, Michelle, Jamie, J. W. and his wife Brucene, went up to the Latent Print Lab on the fourth floor, and then the two oldest sisters returned to Memorial to argue over who would get their mother's jewelry and the carpets and the piano. After Cindy Ray's prints were taken, Schultz invited her and David West down to the third floor. His office, and all the offices, were sparsely furnished in government metal, with paper strewn on every available surface, the inevitable calendar hanging crookedly on the wall, and a faint smell in the air of old sweat and recent fear. If you were not a cop, the faces that peered out at every turn in the corridor were unfriendly. You had done wrong just by being here. If you hadn't murdered somebody, maybe you were thinking about it. You were certainly capable of it. If not murder, some other crime. The point is, you were on the wrong side of the badge.

Cynthia Ray had mentioned to the detectives that she had gone by 8901 Memorial on the evening before the murders to talk to her mother and borrow a few dollars.

"Ms. Ray," Schultz said blandly, "except for the killer, you were the last one to see your parents alive. We have to consider you a suspect. Would you give us a sworn statement, please? And Mr. West, since apparently you were with Cynthia that evening, and you're here, would *you* mind . . . ?"

David West was a bushy-haired, bearded, but nonetheless clean-looking man, just turned twenty-six, who wore a dark blue suit and somber tie. He wasn't big, although he lifted weights, flexed rock-solid biceps, and showed well-rounded pectorals. Probably a weak chin under the beard, Schultz decided.

He was polite, friendly, and appeared respectful of authority. He told Schultz he didn't mind making a statement. He went into another room while Cindy Ray settled calmly into a chair in a corner office in front of the battered desk. She didn't seem frightened or upset by Schultz's casual accusation that she was a suspect. But she didn't seem overcome by grief, either. She was a plump young woman, also twenty-six years old, with long fingernails, good skin, and an uptilted ski nose a bit like Richard Nixon's. Her dark brown hair was parted in the middle, and she wore heavy blue eye makeup. She had a clear and pleasant voice. An attractive woman, Schultz thought.

Cindy talked softly while Motard typed, and then she signed a statement that said: "The last time I saw my parents was around 10 P.M. Friday night. I went over there for money. I had called earlier and talked to my mother and she said come on over. David lives with me and he brought me over in his Cadillac. We drove on over there and I went into the house alone and met with my mother. I think that my father and children were home, but I didn't see them. I followed my mother halfway to the bedroom and she brought down some money. It was ten dollars. I thanked my mother, told her that I loved her, and she asked me if I wanted to see the boys. I told her that I was in a hurry and left. That was the last time that I saw them."

She then related the tale of how she and David West spent the evening, winding up at "Rudyard's club, which is a punk rock place on Waugh Drive." They stayed until closing, "went on home and slept for a while and got up around 3:30 or 4 A.M., I think," and then got out of bed to go to a party in the neighborhood.

Motard then interviewed David West, who had a wholesome air about him despite the fact that he supposedly slept in a hammock and lived in the gay and cruddy part of town. West corroborated the visit to Memorial and the time spent at Rudyard's club. "We left at closing, 2 A.M.," and then home, and later to "a party at Gennessee and Fairview. It was around 3:30 A.M. when we got to the party. The party was breaking up when we got there. I saw Paul and Riley, who play for a group called the Bounders. I found out that they were going to breakfast at Perky's, at Kirby and Richmond. Cindy and I followed them over there. I talked to them a little bit. After breakfast, around 4 or 4:15 A.M., Cindy and I left and went home. I got up around 9 or 10 A.M. We went by her apartment . . . the place looked ransacked."

Their stories dovetailed without being exact duplicates of each other. That was in their favor.

But there was one noticeable gap in the alibi. If Maria's semi-hysterical recollections were accurate, the Campbells had been murdered between 3:45 and 4 A.M. Both Cindy Ray and David West, in their separate statements, claimed to have left Rudyard's bar at 2 A.M. According to David they then went home, and "when we got up, it was somewhere after 3 A.M." Cindy's accounting for the time—they "went on home and slept for a while"—was only a shade less shy.

Gil Schultz shrugged his round shoulders. Nothing wrong with a quick roll in the hay. The only thing that puzzled him was why they crawled out of bed afterward and went out partying again. But they weren't married, and they were young. They had energy that his bones had forgotten about a long time ago.

Both had been to college, Schultz knew. They weren't dummies. If they had committed a carefully planned pair of murders, it would have been no trick to cook up a story that accounted for their whereabouts during the vital hour between 3:30 and 4:30 A.M. But they hadn't done that. Instead they'd left themselves open to doubt and questioning.

Schultz smiled at this irony. If their alibis had been airtight, that would have made him suspicious.

He let them go home.

_____

The following day, on the recommendation of a friend, Cindy called a lawyer named Ellis McCullough. She made an appointment and went to McCullough's office with her two children in tow. She also brought David West.

McCullough said later, "They didn't present themselves as boyfriend and girlfriend. There was no such affection between them. I thought their community of interest was that the police wanted to talk to them both. He was quiet—I figured he was just along for the ride. I had no specific impression. Not weak, not strong. She wore jeans and flat shoes, and I considered her attractive. She was stoned, wired, I thought. Completely disconnected. The kids were spooky—weird kids. I asked what they'd seen. No one they knew, they said. They'd got up, they told me, seen their grandparents' bodies, with bullet holes and lots of blood. They weren't upset—it was like a little joke. They seemed detached. I talked to them and their mother for a while. The background of those kids was the kind that's filled our juvenile and adult penal institutions."

Cindy denied any involvement whatever in the murders. McCullough counseled her not to talk to anybody unless he was present. A fee was set, never paid. Cindy never called him again.

On Friday, June 25, a hot day with the sun bouncing in waves off the metal of parked cars, Schultz and Motard decided to talk to Cindy one more time to find out if she remembered anything she'd forgotten before. They dropped by David West's old house on Vermont. But West was tightlipped and seemed annoyed at the intrusion, and he walked off down the street with his pit bulldog.

Cindy came to the door but wouldn't let them in the house and wouldn't talk to them. "I'm in contact with a lawyer, and I have nothing more to say."

On balance, Schultz thought, that was also in her favor. People with something to hide are usually glad to talk, to cover up, to convince you they're on the side of the angels.

But where did he go now?

In late July the increasingly frustrated Gil Schultz was making a routine check with Jamie, the youngest Campbell daughter, about a woman's wallet and coin purse supposedly missing from 8901 Memorial. He didn't get anywhere. And Jamie was an odd duck, he thought. She was the only one of the four sisters who sounded as if she'd been raised in back country Texas. The other three were sophisticated, whereas Jamie came on like a hillbilly. And yet she was a college student and had even spent a year at school in Switzerland.

During their talk, she recalled a conversation with Cindy that had taken place about a year before the murders.

"She was real upset with Mom and Dad about something or other," Jamie said, "but I can't really remember what it was. Maybe it was that she smoked a whole heck of a lot and they were always on her back to quit. Or it was some dang argument they had. She told me that one day she was gonna kill him . . . my father. She was gonna wear gloves and big boots and leave footprints and then, when it was over, throw Marlboro cigarettes all over the yard."

"I don't get it," Schultz admitted.

"Y'all must've seen those ads," Jamie said, "where the cowboys always smoke Marlboros. It's a *man's* cigarette, see? So she'd make it look like a man done it."

"Oh . . . sure. I see."

He thanked Jamie, but there hadn't been any Marlboro cigarettes in the yard at Memorial, and no footprints, and no one knew what the killer had worn. Could have been gloves and big boots—could just as easily have been a tuxedo and tennis shoes. No evidence. No witnesses except those piss-drenched kids.

Using the hunt-and-peck method, Schultz punched the data from the interview into one of the Sperry Rand computer terminals at HPD Homicide. But even as he did it, he knew that it didn't fit into the category of evidence. It fit into the category of gossip.

Or maybe even bad blood.

He began to wonder a little about Jamie's motive. She was in for a quarter of the estate too, wasn't she? She seemed dumb, but could anybody from that background and with that much college education be *that* dumb?

He stared at the thickening HPD offense report that contained all the interviews, the Harris County coroner's report, and the facts as laid out by the crime scene unit. Here's a case, he thought, that may never be solved unless Sherlock Holmes comes back to life. And fast.

3

The investigation meandered along through the sweltering Houston summer. Motard found the grassy area off Memorial Drive where apparently the getaway car had been parked. The tire prints seemed to be those of a compact car. Schultz discovered that on the night of the murders Cindy Ray's boyfriend, or caretaker, David West, had been driving a big Cadillac. Another point in his and Cindy's favor.

The detectives talked to all the neighbors on Memorial Drive, queried all Harris county pawnshops for recently pawned .45s, checked back over burglary arrests for the past three years. In September they took young Michael Ray to the zoo and the aquarium. They ate jumbo hot dogs with him at James Coney Island restaurant. At the end of the excursion Michael thanked them and said he'd had fun. But he still didn't remember anything he hadn't already told them.

Schultz learned that Cindy Ray and David West had split up again. The investigation, already drifting, began to stall.

Then, late in the afternoon on October 15, nearly four months after the murders of his brother and sister-in-law, J. W. Campbell received a phone call at his law office from a woman who identified herself as Ms. Gwen Sampson.

A little coyly, she said, "I was a friend of your niece."

Gwen Sampson explained on the telephone to J. W. that some five years ago she had taught a photography course at the Houston School of Commercial Art. Cindy Ray had been her pupil. Cindy had also taken a painting course.

"She was very talented," Gwen said, "and later on we became friends. Well, let's put it this way . . . she fascinated me. She was just like a lost puppy. I became her confidante, and we saw each other once or twice a month."

Tapping his fingers nervously on the paper-strewn desk, J. W. listened to her story.

After he hung up, he called Gil Schultz at Homicide and repeated what he had been told. And so at eleven o'clock the following morning of October 16, 1982, Schultz and Paul Motard drove over to the Billie Funk Insurance Agency on Merwin Street, where Gwen Sampson now worked. Gwen was a hefty but moderately pretty blonde in her midforties, blowzy and a little too affected for Schultz's taste. But he didn't need to like her, he had only to interview her. They sat down together in a back room for two hours. Schultz punched the *record* button on his tape recorder.

"Cindy was goofy," Gwen said, "but I always wanted to help her . . . maybe because she was such a talented painter. Last June we weren't in touch. I first found out about the murder of her parents from some mutual friends. I took a day off from work and went over to see Cindy to find out how she was holding up. And after that we talked on the phone at least every other day, and I got a lot of two and three o'clock in the morning phone calls, boo hoo hoo. Then about two weeks ago she called me. She was staying at Dave West's parents' house in Montrose. She'd broken up with Dave, but she was still friendly with his mother. She said she needed my help. My husband Don and I discussed it for hours. I said, 'Cindy's always had a drinking problem, a drug problem, and if we can do something to help her—I mean, we're not professionals—but if she just has *one* friend who'll stick by her . . . '

"So we took her in. She was in a terrible physical state. She was diagnosed as having scurvy. All I know is her teeth were falling out, her hair was falling out in clumps, she had a black growth on her tongue. I thought, dear God, she's going to bring the *plague* over here with her! The whole time she was in the house she went to bed drunk, she woke up drunk, she stayed drunk. She was drinking a fifth of gin, a fifth of rum, whatever we had in the cabinet. She took booze with Valium. The only time she was quiet was when she passed out."

Two things happened, Gwen claimed, that forced her to get rid of her new house guest. A few nights after Cindy's arrival Gwen was awakened at 2 A.M. by cries from her fourteen-year-old son, Jeff. Rushing into his bedroom, she threw a hand to her heart.

Cindy was in bed with Jeff.

"And he's going, 'Get this weirdo out of here, Mother, *please!*'" Which she did, pronto.

"And then I came home the next day and Cindy said, 'Your husband dropped his drawers in front of me.' I told Don about it, and he said, '*What?*'"

Feeling that she'd been invaded by some alien swarm in the person of her former pupil and good friend, Cindy Ray, Gwen went into action.

She said into Schultz's tape recorder: "I took her out to dinner at Felix's restaurant on Kirby, while Don and Jeff put her stuff in our van and took it back to her apartment. After dinner I was going to take her there. During dinner she didn't eat. She drank, which was the whole purpose. I wanted her to get calm so that when I dropped her off she wouldn't have a screaming fit. She kept calling me 'Mommy,' and said she needed a mommy, and out of the blue, for no reason, and out of context in the conversation, she just said, 'I was there, you know.'

"I looked at her, and tried to stay calm, and said, 'I always kind of wondered if you were.'"

This was what Gwen had told to J. W. Campbell when she'd called him, and what J. W. had relayed to Homicide. So Schultz was not surprised. But he was certainly interested. There was something about this woman that he didn't take to, but nevertheless she was pointing a finger at the perpetrator of a brutal, unsolved double murder.

"What brought that on?" he asked Gwen.

"She said she couldn't live with it, that she was too afraid they were going to get her, whoever 'they' are, and she talked about Mafia connections. She looked me straight in the eye and said, 'This is how it happened. I stood beside him, with my children on the floor. I didn't look when he shot my father. I didn't look when he shot my mother . . . but I felt that her body must have shook some.'"

"Did she describe how they got to the house? How it was set up?"

"Just that he knew the floor plan of the home better than she did."

"Did she use his name?"

"Salino," Gwen said. "She said that he was with the Mafia out of Vegas."

The name seemed familiar, but Schultz didn't know why. And the business about 'the Mafia out of Vegas' made him feel, this is a woman I don't trust, and it's turning into a story I don't believe.

"How did she happen to meet this guy?"

"She picked him up somewhere, maybe Birraporetti's—someplace she hung out."

"And how did he know the floor plan of the house?"

37

"I don't know. It didn't occur to me to even ask her, because from what she told me she was with David that night—David West."

That's more like it, Schultz thought.

"My mind was more on the need to get rid of this lady," Gwen went on. "I didn't want something to happen to my children, my husband, or my dog. But she said she took a glove off and left it on the floor. . . . "

Much more like it. Schultz remembered the surgical glove that Kent and St. John had found on the living room carpet by the front door. HPD hadn't been able to pull prints because of the talcum powder inside. They had sent it to the FBI lab to be laser-printed. No luck.

He asked Gwen, "Why would she do a thing like that?"

"She told me she left the glove so that there'd be some evidence and perhaps they could trace it back, because she said that Salino held a gun to her head and said that if she ever opened her mouth she'd be next."

If that's true, Schultz thought, it would absolve Cindy of criminal capability.

"And what was the motive for the killing?"

"He wanted to cure her."

Schultz frowned. "Of what?"

"So that she wouldn't feel badly that her parents had abused her. They were like the root of all her troubles, and if they were eliminated, she would have no more troubles."

Schultz decided this terrain was swampy and dangerous, and he veered off to firmer ground. "Was she going to pay this man any money for what he did?"

"No, she didn't mention that."

"Did she say what kind of gun he used?"

"No, and it never occurred to me to ask. I just kept saying, 'Shhh, not so loud—*shut up*.' We were in Felix's, and she was talking rather loudly, and every now and then tears would come to her eyes. She said, 'Do you think I would have done anything like that if I knew my children were in the room? But *he* knew that my children were in the room! Supposedly that night, every Friday, they got to sleep with their grandparents in the same room. *And he knew that.* He went straight to the bedroom, he took out the gun, went *blam blam*.' "

Gwen shook her head slowly. She seemed to savor the drama.

"So I said, 'And you stood there, Cindy . . . *and you let it happen?*' She said, 'Well, he held the gun on me! He said if I ever said anything he would kill me, too!' Then she told me about leaving the glove."

"What did she do that for?" Schultz asked a second time. Leaving the glove still made no sense to him.

"The story ended there," Gwen said. "I didn't want to push it any further. I was trying to get rid of this person and keep her calm enough to dump her body back in her apartment without having a scene. I just said, 'Fine, I don't want to know anymore, don't tell me anymore.'"

After dinner Gwen took Cindy back to her apartment at 2301 Kingston. She told Cindy that her husband and son had brought her things over and put them upstairs.

"What was her reaction?" Schultz asked.

"Rolling around on the bed with her eyes open and screaming, 'Oh God, now I'm really in for it, I've lost the only friend I ever had!' I said, 'I'm sorry, you did it to yourself. I have children and they come first. Goodbye.'

"Then, after I left, I thought, dear God, if what she told me is all true, what do I do from this point? I was concerned about my kids. I wanted to make sure they could come home from school and not be mowed down. And so, yesterday, finally, I called her uncle."

This woman could be a nut, Schultz realized, but she seemed genuinely frightened. He thanked her. They would like to talk to her again, and they'd call her. Would she consider wearing a body mike sometime and visiting her friend Cindy again for a little chat?

Gwen said she'd have to think about that.

Schultz and Motard talked about it on the way back to Reisner Street, and then Schultz made some telephone calls. He wondered what Gwen had meant when he'd asked about the possible motive for the killings and Gwen had said, *"He wanted to cure her . . . so that she wouldn't feel badly that her parents had abused her."*

What sort of abuse? This was no backwoods Texas family where Pa had his way with li'l Liza Jane. These were normal, decent people. He thought about it for a long time before he went over to the Harris County District Attorney's Office at 201 Fannin and discussed it with Russell Hardin, Jr., his favorite assistant district attorney.

Rusty Hardin was a cocky, compact, bright-eyed North Carolinian who knew more law than most Harris County judges. Schultz thought he was about the most dedicated prosecutor he had ever met, and most of the Texas legal community shared his opinion. Criminal defense attorneys didn't like him: he was too ruthless, and too righteous. And he won cases. Despite a certain dapper air—he bought his clothes almost exclusively at Sakowitz and Neiman-Marcus, the best shops in Houston*—Rusty was tough and markedly masculine. You felt his intelli-

---

* In the early 1980s, at Neiman's, you could buy his and her submarines for only $37,400 each, and Sakowitz offered a Texas-shaped swimming pool (filled with Perrier water) for $127,174.

gence right away, and he had an easy smile, a quick gleam firing out of hard blue eyes.

What Schultz liked most about him was his lucidity, his passion to explain. Schultz, who was a cynic about most things, believed that if there was a case that could be made of what Gwen Sampson had related to him, Rusty Hardin would make it.

But the forty-one-year-old prosecutor only confirmed Schultz's pessimism. "Is there anything of what she said that checked out?" Rusty asked.

"The glove. That's about it."

"The glove is fine, unless J. W. Campbell told Cindy about the glove —because he saw it lying there, you remember?—or told one of the other three sisters and they turned around and told Cindy. What about this guy Salino? Is he real or a figment of her imagination?"

"We can't find anyone by that name in Houston."

"How about what the younger sister told y'all?"

"Well, we didn't find any Marlboro cigarettes at the house, and no one can describe the killer as being a man or wearing boots or anything."

"The kids?"

"They still say they didn't see anyone."

"You didn't come in with the first load of watermelon, Gil. What's your gut feeling about the Sampson woman?"

"Sincere, but an actress. Afraid of the Mafia. Kind of kooky."

"Keep working on the kids," Rusty Hardin said, "but don't upset them. Sounds like they've been put through more hell than a good preacher can pray 'em out of. A witness, Gil—that's your hope. This Sampson woman won't do the trick. Even if she turns out to be reliable, all she's told you is that Cindy confessed to having been there under duress while someone else murdered her parents. That's not even conspiracy. Legally, it couldn't even crawl into court with crutches, much less stand up when it got before a judge."

Schultz hesitated. "You agree with me, Rusty, that the Ray woman probably did it?"

Rusty Hardin nodded. "Keep at it."

Schultz left the meeting feeling that he was throwing rocks at phantoms. Motive was not something a prosecutor had to prove at a trial; he had only to prove that the accused did whatever he or she was accused of. But it was something a homicide detective needed to guess at, or he lost faith and a sense of direction. And lack of motive was the cul-de-sac in this case. *To cure her.* Cure her of what? He wasn't aware that Cynthia Ray had any disease, physical or mental. She had impressed him as a normal and attractive young woman. David West hadn't struck him as a nut or a crusader. It made no sense.

He called Gwen Sampson again. Yes, she'd thought about being wired, or allowing HPD to tap her phone, but she had decided against it. The Mafia, she said, had long arms. Could HPD guarantee her round-the-clock protection?

"We're not really equipped for that," Schultz said.

"And besides," Gwen said, "my mother has cancer."

"Oh," said Schultz, "I'm sorry to hear that." He didn't quite see what it had to do with tapping a telephone, but he was in no position to argue. A crabbed rage rose within him. The daughter had killed her parents, and she was going to get away with it.

Fall became winter. Cold winds struck at Houston from the northern plains. No one lived now at the house on Memorial. The heirs of the dead Campbells—the four daughters and J. W., the brother—began to scrap about the inheritance. Cindy wanted to liquidate: sell the house and the parcels of land and get cash. Her older sisters, Michelle and Betty Ann, voted to wait. Jamie, the youngest, vacillated. Michelle, Betty Ann, and J. W. banded together to fire the probate attorney, Robert Harris, who had been Jim Campbell's closest friend. The administrator, appointed by the sisters, was J. W. Campbell.

"You're all against me," Cindy accused, "and J. W.'s stealing everything he can get his hands on."

She hired a lawyer to fight the rest of her family.

And fired him when he couldn't produce results. And hired another . . . and another.

No unsolved murder case is ever removed from Homicide's files on Reisner Street. It stays there not only in a cardboard folder in a gray metal filing cabinet but also in the memory of the mainframe Sperry Rand computer, waiting patiently for fresh evidence, a confession, a parallel murder . . . anything that will cast new light into the fog and shadow.

To the two older Campbell sisters in Austin it didn't seem possible that a sophisticated police force couldn't come up with a single serious suspect, a single illuminating clue, assemble a valid case and turn it over to the District Attorney's Office for an indictment that would stick.

41

On January 7, 1983, more than six months after the murders, articles appeared in the Houston *Post* and the Houston *Chronicle* announcing that Richard Hinds and Betty Campbell Hinds—the son-in-law and second oldest daughter of the murdered couple—were offering a reward of $10,000 to anyone supplying HPD with information leading to an indictment. Anonymity was guaranteed.

But there wasn't even a single crank call in response. Gil Schultz up at Homicide shook his head, amazed. Not one!

Then in February Schultz received a blistering call from Cindy Ray. She was convinced that her telephone was bugged. There were funny clicks on the line.

"That's not so, Ms. Ray," Schultz said politely. "That would be illegal without a court order."

"You can bug my toothbrush if you like," Cindy said, laughing harshly, "but you won't learn anything, because I've got nothing to hide." And she hung up.

Dead end, Schultz thought.

But that spring one man decided to take action, and the first link was forged in a chain of absurd events that would end in three of the most unusual murder trials in Texas history.

———————

In March 1983, Walter Hinds, Richard Hinds's father, put in a call from Austin to the Toyota Corporation in Houston. He spoke to the director of corporate security, P. M. Clinton. Hinds had written down Clinton's name as the result of a recommendation from an Austin lawyer for whom Clinton had done some investigations on malpractice suits. "P. M. Clinton is a good private eye," the lawyer told Walter Hinds, "and he has excellent connections in the Houston Police Department. He can find out what you want to know."

Clinton, when Walter Hinds finally met him, turned out to be a congenial, pleasant-looking fellow of thirty-three with thinning red hair and an orange-colored mustache. He had been a small-town Baptist boy who graduated from Southwest Texas College in San Marcos, where he fell in love with the daughter of a Houston private investigator named Clyde Wilson. By 1975 Clinton was a lieutenant of detectives for the Harris County District Attorney's Office, in charge of criminal investigation for ten trial courts.

Walter Hinds, a retired factory manager, a Texan, ergo a man of action, laid it on the line to P. M. Clinton. Hinds wanted to know why in hell HPD hadn't been able to find out who had killed his daughter-in-law's parents over one year ago. What did HPD know, and what didn't they know? Were they just plain incompetent? If not, why were they stalling? Just what in the goddamn hell was going on?

"In defense of HPD," P. M. said, "they're overworked. You know, we're not New York, where you're talking about 20,000 police officers. Here in Houston there are only 2,000. When I was a lieutenant in the D.A.'s Office, Mr. Hinds, we were handling an average of 43,000 criminal cases at any given moment. You don't have time to be creative. As far as Homicide's concerned, you've got to have a smoking gun in some black guy's hand with his common-law wife and her boyfriend laid out over the pool table bleeding into all the pockets. If it's not like that, they don't mess with it too long. Last year there were more than 650 homicides. That's close to a record."

"I want to know what they know," Hinds said stubbornly. "My daughter-in-law's parents were professionally gunned down in the middle of the night. We don't know by who, and the law's given up on it. Who's to say the killer's going to stop with Jim and Virginia Campbell? If there's an inheritance involved, there are other people in line for it, including my daughter-in-law. If it's not the inheritance and there's a maniac out there, he may have it in for Betty Ann and my son, too. So that's my reason. Danger to the family. Is that good enough?"

P. M. checked with the right people and soon afterward sent a report to Hinds in Austin in which he set forth pretty much all that HPD knew, including the statement made by Gwen Sampson. His contact had said, "But, P. M., we got a hundred suspects, not just the one daughter. This guy Jim Campbell was not well liked."

P. M. added to the report his own opinion, which was that the most probable suspects were still the black sheep daughter, Cynthia Ray, and her ex-boyfriend, David West. The gap in the alibi was the reason—the unaccounted-for crucial hour between 3:30 and 4:30 A.M. on the morning of the murders. Schultz had thought it bespoke their innocence. P. M. Clinton thought just the opposite. It was clever, he said. It was a kind of reverse double-think, and it didn't smell right.

But, he added in his report, the other prime suspects were the three remaining Campbell daughters—Michelle, Jamie, and even Betty Ann. There was an old principle in law investigation that went back to Roman times. *Cui bono*—who profits from the crime? They all had, P. M. pointed out. He had found out that Betty Ann had called her parents a week before the murders, just after their return from Europe, complaining that her savings account was low, and asking for money. Her mother said, "Daddy hasn't settled any cases lately. Fifty dollars is all I can spare."

Betty Ann had been annoyed.

How annoyed? P. M. wondered.

4

The town of Houston was founded as a land speculation by two brothers, Augustus C. Allen and John K. Allen, marauding scoundrels from New York who envisioned a protected inland port only an eight-hour steamboat ride from Galveston (then the largest city in Texas) and the Gulf of Mexico. They bought the original site for $5,000—$1,000 of it in cash, the rest in notes. Today most boosters of the city decline to see the Allen brothers as scoundrels, but if you read the New Yorkers' advertisement about "Houston town" printed in Southwestern newspapers in August 1836, you might be swayed to that opinion.

"There is no place in Texas more healthy, having an abundance of excellent spring water, and enjoying the sea breeze in all its freshness . . . it is handsome and beautifully elevated, salubrious. . . . "

In fact the drinking water is brackish and bitter, although Houstonians consume 400 million gallons of it on an average summer day; the city's elevation is perfectly flat except for the flyovers on the freeways; there is no suspicion or even rumor of a sea breeze; and if oil hadn't been struck in 1901 on a wildcat derrick near Beaumont at a place later known as Spindletop, and air conditioning installed in 1923 at the Second National Bank downtown, the whole place might have regressed to the green swamp it once was. As for salubriousness, in 1964 an English correspondent for *The Guardian* visited Houston, and took understatement to its farthest frontier when he wrote of the brash city on the bayou: "Everything is so new, clean, fresh-looking, as compared with the cluttered, grey life in England. But . . . it's rather warm outside, isn't it?"

Jim Campbell's parents came from Tennessee. His father was what J. W. Campbell termed "a traveling druggist"—a nice euphemism for a medicinal pitch-man. One of ten children, Jim was born near Abilene in what he liked to call "a sparsely populated wide spot on State Road 36 called Cross Plains, Texas."

Virginia was from Monroe, Wisconsin. They met in Los Angeles in 1948 on a blind date, while she was working as a legal secretary and Jim, a navy veteran, was getting his B.A. in psychology at UCLA. He had often said, "I'm going to marry a blue-eyed blonde." Virginia's hair was raven-black.

The coroner's report stated: *"The body was that of a well-nourished and well-developed white female, consistent with the stated age of fifty years,"* but that last detail was not true. They were both fifty-five when they died. Virginia had always lied about her age, and Jim had approved.

After they married Jim went to law school at UT—Austin, and then in 1952 the young couple settled in Houston. Virginia became Jim's legal secretary, taking time off only to give birth to four daughters, and until her death she still worked with her husband as a full-time paralegal assistant and bookkeeper. In 1972, after twenty years of trial experience, Jim was serving on the State Bar Grievance Committee and was a nominee for director of the Houston Bar Association. He had once run as a Democrat for state representative, and then for judge in the 179th District Court, losing both elections. Brother J. W., on the other hand, lived in Hollywood for twenty-seven years, winding up in the sales end of television distribution—he had come relatively late in life to the practice of law, moving back to Houston at Jim's suggestion. He became a bail bondsman; and then, under a grandfather clause in the Texas statutes, Jim certified that J. W. had worked in his law office for three years and reached the required level of competency to take the bar exams without having been to law school.

Jim, a Shriner and a Mason, was known as a tough lawyer. The insurance companies with whom he dealt often resented him. He carried strong grudges and hated for anyone to get away with anything. Other lawyers called him not only "Dirty Jim," but "Snake." They called his brother "Slime."

In 1962 the Campbells bought the house on Memorial Drive. Their best friends were two couples: Bob and Sue Harris, and Tom and Hattie Thurlow. All the men were lawyers. Bob Harris and Jim Campbell officed * together for nine years in the Houston First Savings Building and then later in the Houston Bar Center Building at 723 Main Street.

The men called him Jim. The women, in a somewhat more intimate manner, used James, giving it the Texas pronunciation of Jay-ums. He liked women, and women always felt he liked them.

Bob Harris and Jim Campbell traveled together, golfed together, and gambled together. Jim wasn't what Bob would call a big gambler, but he was a passionate one. He loved Las Vegas and Lake Tahoe, flying there three or four times a year on weekend gambling junkets where the hotel paid for the air fare and provided free rooms and drinks.

The big Nevada hotels—the MGM, Sands, Caesar's Palace, and the

---

* *To office:* in Texas, a verb used by independent and/or maverick lawyers to describe sharing premises, receptionist, xerox facilities, and telephone with other independent and/or maverick lawyers.

Sahara Tahoe, all of which at one time played host to the Campbells and the Harrises—calculated an average drop per gambler of 20 percent. But Jim Campbell, whose line of credit grew to $10,000, had a way around that. Smoking his Travis Club cigars, he would bet heavily when he first took up his stance at the craps table, make a fuss about how much he was losing, then gradually reduce his bets. It was not a sophisticated scheme, and it was detectable if the house cared to look carefully. They didn't care.

If Jim went with Bob Harris they sometimes worked together in a simple scam, each setting up shop at opposite ends of the table, and each buying $5,000 worth of chips. Jim would bet the "Pass" line, Bob the "Don't Pass." When one threw the dice, the other would bet against him. At the end of a few hours they would be roughly even. Time to quit, meet in the bar, have a good laugh about it. Jim Campbell could afford to lose, but what he liked almost as much as winning was the thrill of getting away with something. Getting a freebie. He would rarely win or lose more than a few hundred dollars, but he would bring home one or two bottles of Chivas Regal that the hotel management had sent to his room. That was something to chuckle about on the flight back to Houston.

Harris in 1982 was a quiet, balding man of fifty, a former professor of oil and gas law at South Texas Law School. "Jim had a pool table in his garage," he said, "where he practiced. He won money in pool halls, in small amounts like ten or twenty dollars—fifty dollars at the most. I wasn't as good as he was, but I could give him a game. He was skilled at con games, at con work. We'd play for five or ten dollars, and if I lost, I paid. But if he lost he'd say, 'Bobbie, I'll pay you later.' He often didn't. So after a while I had to tell him, 'Hey, big fella, we'll put up the money ahead of time.' "

But Bob Harris thought of him as "a likable rogue." And added, "I miss Jim every day."

Jim was a pleasant-looking man, six feet four inches tall, in good shape. "He wasn't shy," Harris said. "He was healthy, vigorous, with what I gathered was a good sexual appetite. I never saw him fool around, but he liked to flirt. In Vegas he always talked and joked with the hookers. One of the guys on a junket told me once that Jim had taken one of the hookers to his room, the friend's room, and screwed her. Virginia was there in Vegas on that trip."

Virginia was a gambler, too. She drank Brandy Alexanders and she played craps. She told Sue Harris, "I've been to Europe six times, but if you give me a choice to go anywhere, I'll take Las Vegas."

No two people describe Virginia quite the same way. Sue Harris called her "plain but lively . . . witty, happy, always fun . . . always talking, with a wonderful sparkle in her eyes." Bob Harris considered her quiet and unassuming. "Almost dowdy . . . and kind of humped over." Her oldest friend in Houston, Hattie Thurlow, remembered Virginia as having a slight hunchback. "But she looked as if she might have been beautiful when she was young. She wore a lot of diamonds. She had very white skin. Too much makeup. Not plain at all! She looked as flamboyant as James acted. She wore expensive clothes and she was proud of her jewelry, the gaudier the better. I liked her and trusted her. She would never hurt anybody."

In 1969 Virginia and Hattie bought oils and canvas, and sometimes on weekends they painted together. Virginia liked to copy postcard scenes of European cities she had visited. "They were awful," Hattie Thurlow said. Virginia had never gone to college, but once her children were grown she took courses at Houston Baptist University. She wanted a degree, but that required courses in physical education, and she was too shy about her slightly bowed body to go to the gym and suit up with the younger women. She quit the school.

Virginia and Sue Harris gambled anywhere they could. They had been on junkets to Yugoslavia and Monte Carlo. During their final trip to Europe in May 1982, in the casino at Konstanz, Virginia ran out of chips and was kibitzing, rooting for Sue at the roulette wheel—"Come on, Sue! Go for it, Sue!" Their husbands had been denied entrance to the casino because they weren't wearing jackets. Virginia was annoyed at that. "She was hollering," Sue said, "and the casino people came over —'Shhh, we don't allow noise here.' So we waltzed out, and then right at the door of the casino Virginia hollered in the street at James and Robert, who were standing by the lake. They were embarrassed; they pretended not to know us. It was always fun to be with Virginia . . . to be with Virginia *and* James."

"He was an attractive man," said Hattie Thurlow, who now worked as a technical writer for NASA. "And a big tease. He liked to shock us. He'd bring bizarre people into our social circle, like a private detective named Dudley Bell who's in the penitentiary now.* James, for such a rapscallion, was also a student of psychology. He spoke good Spanish, and Virginia always had to ask him to give instructions to their maid, Maria. Virginia was his stability. He adored her, and he'd give her whatever she wanted. I got the idea that once they'd been without money and now they enjoyed spending it."

But there was something odd about their lives. All their friends sensed

---

* For solicitation of capital murder, and serving a sentence of thirty-eight years.

it. None liked to define or even characterize it, except to say that in their personal lives James and Virginia were "private people."

"I always thought they were hiding something," Hattie Thurlow said. "But I couldn't begin to guess what it was."

In all the years of their friendship, Bob Harris, Jim's closest friend, visited the Campbell home only once. He had been in the yard a few times, waiting for Jim to come out with his golf clubs, but he and Sue had never been invited in for a drink or a meal. Similarly, the Campbells had declined all but a single invitation to dine at the Harrises.

Hattie Thurlow knew all the Campbell girls—Michelle, Betty Ann, Cindy, and Jamie. They were all shy, although Betty Ann was the most assertive and often the only one who would talk when adults were present. After producing three daughters the Campbells had waited five years; then James decided he wanted a son, who was to be named James Jr. The genetic deck was stacked. He had a fourth daughter. That was Jamie, tall and thin.

Neither Jim nor Virginia, in Bob Harris's opinion, was close to their children. Bob never liked any of them, although certain events after the Campbells' death colored his attitude. Spoiled rotten, he thought. Jim bought them cars and clothes and installed a complete soda fountain for them in the garage. He spent his money freely—if they asked, they got.

Early in the friendship the Campbells and Harrises went to Mexico City on a holiday, and one morning, walking about at the base of the pyramids of Teotihuacán, Virginia was prattling on about her children. Sue Harris, who had no children of her own, realized something.

Sue was an easily excitable woman. "You always only talk about *three* children!" she cried. "But you and James have *four!* What about the fourth? The second youngest . . . is it Cindy? Virginia, do you realize you never even mention her *name!*"

"I forgot to put one of those pills in our water bottle this morning," Virginia said. She hurried off to find a bathroom.

Hattie Thurlow made the same observation: "Virginia would rarely speak the name of her third daughter. If I asked after Cindy, Virginia would be evasive. There was something she didn't want you to know."

Cindy was the shyest, a little plump. She was always dieting and became more attractive as she grew older. A strange girl, Hattie Thurlow thought. Hattie had heard that for a time they had to send her away to live with James's mother in a distant Houston suburb best known for a bar with a mechanical bull. Other than the family flake, Cindy was its mystery. Sue Harris said later, "We never even heard from James or Virginia about Cindy's getting married. We heard it from someone else. And there was something odder still to come. . . . "

Sue Harris drove to 8901 Memorial one chilly December day in 1976 to pick up Virginia. They were going shopping at Sakowitz. Sue was waiting at the back door when she heard the sound of babies crying. The new maid, Maria, was trying to calm them in Spanish.

Virginia came out into the cold morning, flushed.

"What's going on here?" Sue demanded. "I hear *babies*."

"My grandchildren have come to live with me," Virginia said.

"*What* grandchildren?" Sue cried. She was Virginia's closest friend but she didn't know about any grandchildren.

"Cindy's two boys. Their names are Michael and Matthew. Can we please go now?"

It took a while before Sue realized that Cindy and her husband were living in the house, too.

But afterward Virginia talked all the time about Michael and Matthew, and so did James. They had legal guardianship of the children, James said. Cindy had no job, no money. She and her husband finally moved elsewhere in Houston. The husband vanished, but the little boys continued to stay at Memorial. Cindy could come visit them and take them home for a while, to wherever she was living, whenever it suited her. Of course Sue Harris thought that was a peculiar arrangement. It wasn't her idea of how a mother should behave. And what was it doing to the poor little kids?

"No problem for them," Virginia said tersely.

Bob Harris saw that a hostile relationship existed between father and daughter. Cindy would come up to the office and sit stolidly in the waiting room, sometimes for hours. Jim would refuse to see her. If he had to pass through the waiting room, he would ignore her. She was there to mooch money from her mother, Harris realized.

During her thin years Harris thought she was attractive, in a frightening way. She wore heavy makeup, which he didn't like. Cindy, he decided, was exactly the opposite of the sweet, loving girl you'd like for a daughter. Already at eighteen she had the look of a ruthless woman.

The Houston Shriners announced a three-week charter trip scheduled for late May 1982—to Switzerland, Germany, and Austria, with a stop in New York on the way. The Campbells and the Harrises decided to go. They paid $2,495 per person, everything included.

One night in May, at about 2 A.M., when Jim Campbell woke in the early morning blackness he sensed that something was wrong. In his bedroom he stocked what Mike St. John later described as "an arsenal."

Grabbing his shotgun, he padded across the carpet to the bedroom door, which he opened into the semi-darkness in time to see a figure moving quickly down the stairs. Jim didn't fire. The intruder fled out the open front door. Jim didn't pursue. Later he described the figure as "probably a man," and "he was wearing sneakers."

It was a mildly frightening incident, but not all that uncommon in Houston, where the burglary rate was high. The Campbells assumed that before going to bed they had forgotten to flip the lock on the front door, although Virginia, who usually did it, didn't recall *not* doing it.

Jim was busy clearing up his court calendar and reassuring his clients that he wasn't falling off the edge of the world, only flying to Europe for three weeks. Virginia was on the telephone four and five times a day with Sue, talking breathlessly about the right clothes to take for Vienna and the casinos. They drove off to Houston Intercontinental Airport on Friday, May 20, 1982.

From every city the Campbells called home to check that the children were all right. Michael, during one call, boasted that he had destroyed two wooden dining room chairs with karate blows. All was well.

In Zurich the two couples rented a car, driving to Colmar and through the Moselle wine country of France, then into Germany to gamble at Konstanz, and then back to Basel to rejoin the tour bus for the trip to Innsbruck and Vienna. In Vienna Bob had a yen to dent the Iron Curtain. Jim was leery. But Bob hauled him off to the Czech Embassy, and in the afternoon, in a hired car with two other American tourists and an Austrian driver, they crossed the Danube and drove to Bratislava. The driver was nervous, and it seemed to infect Jim Campbell. "Jim never said a word out of line the whole trip," Bob recalled, "and he was a man who would crack jokes with the devil."

They flew back to the United States on Thursday, June 10, 1982, arriving in Houston that evening. Running in the front door, they hugged and kissed their grandsons.

Matthew's seventh birthday was on June 12. Cindy brought a chocolate birthday cake. On Thursday, June 17, Virginia called Sue to chat. She was about to take eight-year-old Michael to a karate lesson. She had just finished Danielle Steel's *Crossings,* and she was out of best-sellers and wondering what to read during the hour she would have to wait for her grandson. "Buy a book of crossword puzzles," Sue suggested.

"God, I've done 'em *all,*" Virginia said.

The next afternoon, Friday, June 18, a torrid day, Sue called Virginia at the law office. Virginia took the call and blurted, "Can't talk honey . . . James has a big trial on Monday in Beaumont . . . we're working on the case all day. . . . " And then she said a curt goodbye and hung up.

Sue was annoyed to the point of being aggravated. Especially in hindsight.

At six o'clock on Saturday morning, June 19, the telephone rang, waking both Sue Harris and her husband. Bob answered. It was the police, announcing that James and Virginia Campbell had been murdered.

Bewildered, Bob said at first, "You must mean J. W." When he told Sue, she shouted, *"It can't be!"* Impatient and not quite awake, she punched out Virginia's familiar telephone number. A police officer answered. Out of control, Sue began shouting at him until Bob pressed the button that broke the connection.

Hattie Thurlow, who lived nearly an hour away in Clear Lake, near the NASA complex, heard about it in the midmorning from Tom Thurlow, her ex-husband. The day passed; she was unable to do even the simplest of tasks.

"I was so *offended*. They were such harmless people. Why would anyone murder them?"

The four daughters—Michelle, Betty Ann and Jamie from Austin, and Cindy—gathered at the house by noon on Saturday. Michelle and J. W. searched James's office that afternoon, looking for a will. They found none, J. W. said, despite the fact that Jim had drafted more than 300 wills for clients and had on his desk a sign facing the seated visitor that asked: "HAVE YOU WRITTEN YOUR WILL?"

On Monday morning J. W. and Michelle opened Jim's safe deposit boxes at the bank. Nothing of value, J. W. reported.

———————————

For a time Bob Harris represented the Campbell estate. Cindy was living in the apartment on Kingston, and since she had always received a monthly stipend from her father, Harris continued to dole out cash to her and pay some of her bills with the estate's money. There was an element of confusion regarding who was responsible for what, and in late August, as the result of nonpayment, Houston Light & Power cut off Cindy's electricity. She called Harris to complain. "I'm sorry," he said, "it was my understanding that I'd give you a fixed amount and pay the taxes, and you were to take care of the utilities."

She said, "You better get that light turned back on or you'll regret it."

He didn't like the threatening tone.

Sometimes she would visit the office to voice her complaints. She didn't know how to drive, and once she sent up what he considered an angry message: "You'd better come down and pay the taxi."

Harris thought all the sisters were a little wooly-headed, lacking good judgment. One morning he talked in his office to Michelle, the oldest, and said, "The four of you have got to do something with your parents' house. It's worth nearly half a million dollars, but it's in awful condition. Getting worse every day now that no one's living there. You should fix it up, then sell it." The sisters offered some vague talk that they were waiting for a better market and an agreement among themselves as to how to divide the proceeds.

They did nothing. Three years later the house was still vacant. In the humid South Texas climate, the carpets were rotting away.

Harris had always shared two office telephones with Jim Campbell. Virginia paid the monthly bill from Southwestern Bell, simplifying matters by sending a memo to Harris noting the amount of his share. After Jim's death, Harris wanted to keep the two telephone numbers, and J. W. had no objection. In July the first bills arrived for Harris to pay—but they were for over $2,000. After a few squawks he realized that Michelle, Betty Ann, and Jamie charged all their long distance calls to the office numbers. Thumbing back through the files, he discovered that they had been doing it for several years. There were calls to and from Tennessee, where Jamie had been going to college, and some lasted for two hours.

Harris wrote to Southwestern Bell and said, "No more third party calls charged to these numbers."

That angered the sisters in Austin, and they fired Bob Harris, appointing their Uncle J. W. the administrator of his brother's estate.

Ellis McCullough said, "J. W. did a good ole boy act. Got to if you're that dumb. He stumbled onto a gold mine when Jim got killed—all those cases and clients and referrals he inherited." At his death, according to the records of the district clerk, Jim Campbell was attorney of record for over 200 cases. The trial in Beaumont that he had been due to argue on June 21, 1982, was settled six months later by J. W. for $120,000, which included a legal fee of $40,000.

The older daughters rented a U-Haul to truck their parents' possessions back to Austin. They wanted to give Sue Harris a piece of their mother's jewelry, a gold ring that James had bought for Virginia in Las Vegas, as a keepsake. Sue wouldn't take it. She was so stricken by Virginia's death that she said, "I'll never go to Vegas again."

But she did, in September, and then again in May, when she won a blackjack tournament at the Frontier Hotel.

Almost two years passed. P. M. Clinton changed jobs. He went to work for his father-in-law, Clyde Wilson, the private investigator. A month later in Austin, Walter Hinds fell dead of a heart attack.

So slender—and so randomly parted—was the chain that bound both a murderer's destiny and the secret annals of a Texas family.

5

Throughout the second half of 1982 the Campbell sisters in Austin kept in close touch with Sgt. Gil Schultz at Homicide in Houston. Betty Ann Hinds called Schultz once or twice a week, to the point where she became a pest. Schultz told Betty Ann about the talk with Gwen Sampson.

"Does this man Salino exist?" Betty Ann asked.

"We don't think so," Schultz said.

"So it's another one of my sister Cindy's dramatic hallucinations."

"Does she have them often?"

"Oh, periodically."

"Did y'all know about the glove inside the front door?"

"I seem to remember hearing about that," Betty Ann said.

If she knew about it, Schultz thought, so might Cindy. He called J. W. to ask if he'd ever mentioned it to Cindy, but J. W. didn't recall.

Betty Ann's calls slacked off to about once a month in 1983 and into 1984, except for a flurry when she offered the reward. Michelle called, too. Those women sure loved to talk, Schultz realized. But he knew he was the connecting thread to the hope of a solution to the unsolved murder of their parents. If they stopped calling him, it meant they had given up.

On a Friday in September of 1984 Michelle called and said she and Jamie would be in Houston the following week, and could they have lunch? Schultz and Motard agreed to meet them at Dan McCluskey's, a businessman's restaurant.

At lunch Michelle said that she and her sisters had been thinking idly of hiring a private detective. "Would it hurt your feelings, Sgt. Schultz, or interfere with your investigation?"

"Absolutely not," Schultz said, trying to hide his smile. "But don't hire a sleazebag and get taken for a ride and lose all your money."

"We were thinking of P. M. Clinton and Clyde Wilson," Michelle said. "What do you think of them?"

"Never heard of them," Schultz said.

The offices of Clyde A. Wilson, Investigations, occupied an entire brick ranch house in a wooded section of northwest Houston, just off the Katy Freeway at the corner of Upland and Timberlane. Anywhere from eight to twelve cars and pickup trucks usually sat parked in the crescent-shaped driveway. A sign on the front door read: *WARNING! Property Protected by Trained Attack Cat.*

In his private office, at one time the master bedroom of the house, Clyde Wilson lolled in a big swivel chair behind an oversized walnut desk. Despite his high blood pressure he smoked fairly steadily, but he said to visitors, "Don't tell Mama. That's not my mother—Mama is Agnes, my wife. We have seven kids and fourteen grandchildren." He indicated the cigarette, whose smoke had been curling up into his right eye, which was made of blue and white glass. "I promised Mama I'd quit."

Clyde in late 1984 had just turned sixty, and was exactly how you would imagine a seasoned Texas good ole boy: six feet two inches tall, rangy, gnarled, dressed in denim, cowboy-booted, salty in speech, bone dry in wit. His office was furnished with a ship's wheel, a walnut conference table and a working fireplace, a caged parrot named Roberto, and a wooden cigar store Indian wearing a gaudy Mexican *rebozo*. The walls were filled with news clips detailing Clyde's exploits throughout the past decades as a private eye. During a ten-year stint as chief of security for Tenneco, the Houston-based oil and gas company, Clyde had recovered more than $13 million of stolen money and materiel, and in 1974 he flew to Ethiopia to effect a rescue of four Tenneco employees held for ransom by guerrillas. His only known comeuppance had occurred in 1969, while working an undercover assignment for Dallas oilmen Nelson and Herbert Hunt. Clyde was accused of illegally wiretapping six Hunt employees suspected of embezzlement, and he was asked, in front of a grand jury, "Have you ever tapped into telephones, sir?" Clyde replied, "I never have in my life. If I get out of this, I never will again." That guaranteed the indictment, but he pled guilty and walked out of the federal courtroom with a $1,000 fine. Within ninety days, in the select company of Tokyo Rose and Richard Nixon, he received a pardon from President Gerald Ford.

He had mellowed since then, but he liked to say, "We've been called

54

the Cadillac of investigative agencies. Fifty bucks an hour is what we charge, per operative, plus expenses. May not sound like a hell of a lot when you figure those three-piece-suit downtown lawyers are making triple and quadruple that, but when we put our people on an eighteen-hour-a-day surveillance job, meter running all the time—pardner, that adds up."

On November 15, 1984, P. M. Clinton marched through a kitchen where fresh coffee was brewing, past offices, secretaries, and glowing computer terminals, to bang on his father-in-law's door. Invited into the inner sanctum, he settled into a chair and lifted his boots up to rest on a comfortable surface. "Here's a good one," he said. He told Clyde the story of how in 1983 he had come to submit a report on the Campbell murders to Walter Hinds of Austin, and what had been in the report. "So yesterday Betty Hinds, old Walter's daughter-in-law, calls me. 'Hello, how are you,' I say, kind of feeling her out, 'and how's your Daddy doing?' And she goes, kind of icily, 'Mr. Clinton, I guess y'all in Houston didn't know, but my father passed away a few months ago. Among his private papers, although I had no idea it existed, I found—' "

"Jesus Christ!" Clyde yelled, clapping his hands. "She found your report saying you thought her sister Cindy had probably killed her parents! And if her sister hadn't done it, then she and the other sisters were next in line as suspects! Ain't life sometimes a weird mother!"

"Sure is," P. M. said ruefully. "She wants me to do an investigation. Find out who killed her parents."

"Well, do it," said Clyde. "Find out!"

"A murder case?"

"You can't handle it?"

"I got a lot of other things on my plate, Clyde. A homicide investigation, in case you haven't ever noticed, tends to be a full-time job."

Clyde gave him a level look. "Let me ask you this. Do you *want* to take it on?"

"Sure I do. It'll be just like TV. My only problem is the time, the billing, and the personnel."

"Get Denise to help you. Check in with me when you get some leads or if you have problems. I'd take it on myself, except I'm too busy with the Hermann Hospital case. Can these people in Austin afford us?"

"She says so."

"Then go for it, hombre."

A few days later, at P. M.'s request, Betty Ann Hinds asked the Clyde Wilson Agency to "develop information leading to the persons responsible for the murders of James and Virginia Campbell on June 19,

1982," and also to "conduct an investigation to locate and document the activities of Cynthia Campbell Ray."

Denise Moseley, another operative in the agency, drove up to Austin and met with Betty Ann Hinds, who was a Trinity University graduate with a degree in zoology, working now as a hydrologic technician with the U.S. Geological Survey. She talked with Denise for four hours in her living room, with a break for lunch. The chief subject was her younger sister, Cynthia Campbell Ray.

Part of the inheritance had been settled, Betty Ann said—P. M. guessed that was where she had found the money to hire "the Cadillac of investigative agencies"—but a war of attrition had broken out between Cindy and the family over the major portion of the estate. Cindy was remarried now to a young Syrian, Talal Makhlouf, a former student who worked as a waiter in a downtown Houston restaurant. It was rumored that he married her in order to get American citizenship. Cindy had become a semi-recluse—if the rest of the family wanted to talk to her they had to go through a lawyer named Steve Simmons, who was handling her claims against the estate. Occasionally Cindy would call her sisters to complain about the slowness of the settlement, but she always called collect from a pay telephone or from someone else's house. Neither Betty Ann nor the other sisters were able to call back, other than to leave a message at Steve Simmons's office. And nobody knew where Cindy lived.

Settling back in her chair in the Hinds's living room, Denise said, "Tell me everything about your sister Cynthia."

Well, Cindy had been married twice before—the first time, at seventeen, to a tugboat worker named Michael Ray who grew up, Betty Ann thought, in Oklahoma. He was the father of Cindy's two sons, but she had left him, Betty Ann said, because he fooled around with other women. After the divorce she gave the children to her parents to raise, and the father never saw them again. A terrible mother, Cindy was not the least bit interested in her children. She married a second time with a young man named Philip Sanford, whom she had met at a meeting of Parents Without Partners. A divorce followed almost immediately. "Cindy claimed he flashed schoolgirls."

Then: "It seemed that she had a lot of quick affairs, mostly with Arabs." And then came a live-in boyfriend, a construction worker named Maurice Lambert, known as "Moe," whom Betty Ann described as "the most normal of the long line of men in Cindy's life." He began beating her, Cindy said, and she left him, too.

"She moved back into Memorial with our parents. They paid for her to go to college, to St. Thomas, to study art. My sister Jamie was a student there, too. And that's where Jamie met David West and introduced him to Cindy."

Betty Ann leaned intently across the coffee table in her living room. "Cindy once tried to convince me that a Moslem doesn't feel he'll lose his soul if he kills a non-Moslem. She made a big point of that. It seemed to fascinate her."

The next words were not easy to say.

"I think she had our parents killed. Not by this man David West, but by one of her Moslem friends . . . maybe even this Arab she's married to now. I want you to track her down. Find out if she did it. Put our suspicions to rest," Betty Ann begged.

"What leads you to think she killed them?" Denise asked carefully.

"Maybe it's her *attitude*. She never seems to miss Mother and Daddy, and that disturbs me. It's like . . . a complete lack of sentiment and feeling. Plus what this Gwen Sampson woman said to Sgt. Schultz. And then what I read in Mr. Clinton's report to my father-in-law."

"How did Cindy get on with your Mother and Daddy?"

"Real good with Daddy. It was a good relationship, as far as she had a good relationship with anyone. I mean, she always had trouble in school, because she was overweight and made poor grades, and she was a real selfish kid. With Mother it wasn't good. Mother was fed up with her because she'd abandoned her two babies, just dumped them on the doorstep, so to speak. And she just refused to ever work or earn money in any fashion."

"Still . . . why would she do such a thing as murder them?" Denise asked. "Isn't that . . . *overreacting?*"

"I don't know," Betty Ann said quietly. "We're a normal family. My mother and father never hurt her. In some ways when she was younger she was Daddy's favorite. She was a difficult child, and not happy, but . . . that's no reason, is it? I don't know." She ended on a plaintive note. "And I hope it's not true. But we have to find out, don't we?"

"From now on," Denise instructed her, "tape all your sister's calls."

Denise Moseley was Clyde Wilson's expert at finding people who didn't want to be found. A slender brunette in her early thirties, Denise looked like a thin-lipped schoolteacher or bank teller, which is one of the reasons she was a good private detective.

She was a dogged seeker, and she traced Cindy through four different residences: a series of evictions and fumigations. In September 1983 Cindy and husband Makhlouf had been thrown out of an apartment on

Walnut Bend. The landlord said, "They still owed me a few hundred dollars rent and damages, but I had to get rid of them—I couldn't stand it anymore. I'm talking about the stench. After they left, the place had to be aired for two full weeks. Not pets—they didn't have pets. They just never bathed. They never cleaned the kitchen, and what they did in the bathroom was *disgusting*."

In late November Denise, through their marriage records, finally discovered them in an apartment at 5710 Glenmont. Cindy was unemployed, and Makhlouf was waiting table at Fat Ernie's restaurant downtown. Surveillance was initiated, but Cindy's movements were minimal. She didn't drive and Makhlouf didn't own a car. They took taxis. Cindy led a normal life, even if she rarely went out except to buy junk food.

P. M. decided to make contact. "To run on Cindy," as they said in the investigative trade. One cool evening, when they were sure she was home, he and Denise rang her doorbell on the second floor of the Glenmont apartment complex. They had with them a local free shopper, the Greensheet, in which they had placed an ad for a Zenith TV, listing Cindy's address. The purpose of the exercise was to get a foot in the door, literally, and then establish a relationship.

But Cynthia wouldn't allow a foot in the door. She wouldn't open the door more than an inch. It was on a chain lock, and P. M., with Denise at his elbow and nudging the small of his back to shove him forward, kept waving his copy of the newspaper. "This is the address, this is the number! You have a Zenith color TV and we want to buy it. Here, look in the paper if you don't believe me!"

Cindy screeched through the door, *"Get away!"*

"But it says here—"

"Go away!"

They held their ground. A low male voice murmured from inside the apartment.

"My husband's coming out," Cindy said through the one-inch opening. "Just go downstairs and wait."

P. M. and Denise obeyed. A minute later Makhlouf, short, chunky, and black-haired, wearing chinos and a blue sport shirt, marched down the stairs into the courtyard. He was formal and polite. He said, "I believe you have made a mistake."

"We drove all the way across town to buy this darn TV," P. M. explained. "Are you sure y'all don't want to sell it?"

They could hear the upstairs apartment door unlatch and bang against the concrete outer wall. Cindy yelled, "Don't talk to those people! Run them off!"

"I'm sorry, please forgive this," Makhlouf said. "My wife is not feeling well."

P. M. said, "Look, I realize there's some kind of error. But could we just come in for a minute and use your telephone?"

"We have no telephone, sir."

"Well, my wife needs desperately to use the bathroom. Could we just—?"

"*Get lost! Get the fuck out of here!*" Cindy yelled.

"I'm sorry," Makhlouf said.

P. M. sighed and took Denise's arm. They walked back to the car. "That was genuinely comical," Denise said.

"It was also a genuine waste of time."

P. M. reported to Clyde the next day. "If she had let us in and we'd been able to bullshit for a while," he said glumly, "we would have become her best friends. She has no driver's license. We would have taken her around town, been her slaves. But that woman is truly paranoid."

That same week Betty Ann mailed Denise a package of tape-recorded telephone calls. Cindy had made all the calls from unknown numbers in Houston. Denise took out her Panasonic and clamped on the earphones.

For the most part the conversations seemed to be the inane chatter of bored young women with no apparent purpose in life other than getting through the Christmas season without undue stress. They discussed hairdressers: "My hair looks like Dolly Parton," Betty Ann said—and their mutual hypochondria: "We're old friends, kidney infection and me," Cindy said, "and lower back pain. I perspire when I have it . . . and my blood pressure's high." Dieting: Betty Ann weighed 144, Cindy at least 50 pounds more than that. Movies they had seen: Betty Ann was pushing *Terms of Endearment,* while Cindy cited old loves, *A Clockwork Orange* and *Young Frankenstein.* Cindy hadn't seen *Terms of Endearment,* she said, because she was "on a tight budget."

And with a droning regularity, as though it was just another dreary topic to wile away the darkening winter afternoons, they chatted about the unsettled inheritance and Cindy's pending lawsuit against the family. "Kingston's only worth 210. . . . I should go ahead and keep Kingston and you take Memorial." . . . "I don't want to keep Memorial." . . . "I'm not about to take land in Podunk or Jasper with a low appreciation and give all the good stuff to you guys." . . . "I'd want the law library—you could sell it for two, three thousand dollars." . . . "I want cash and maybe a bit of Jasper. . . . "

Like the game of Monopoly. But the properties were real. They had belonged to their murdered father.

Astonishingly, considering that one sister suspected the other of ordering the death of their parents and had hired a private detective to prove or disprove it, their conversations were warm and often loving. They reminisced about the past and their parents.

"There are mechanical elves in a window on Westheimer," Cindy said, "like the ones that were in Foley's when we were little. The craftsmanship, the detail, that they don't do anymore."

"Remember how I used to go down there every year?" Betty Ann asked.

"And stand on the ramp," Cindy remembered. "And Mother would be one of the few adults that would stand there as long as we did. We'd stand there half a day."

"Mother enjoyed it as much as we did. . . . I think downtown Houston is deteriorating."

"It's depressing," Cindy said. "They haven't torn down those downtown movie thee-ay-ters, but they're all boarded up. Winos are there now. Remember the Metro, how gorgeous it was? It's a shame that so many things were discarded in the early sixties. They didn't know that craftsmanship would be gone. But throughout history, it always comes back. . . ."

Cindy said, "They're building a multi-million-dollar mansion next to Memorial, and that'll bring up the value. It's worth between one and one-point-five, what they're building—"

Betty Ann said, "You were never good at math before."

"I was good at math all my life."

"Don't you remember me helping you with your homework? Remember when they had New Math?"

"When I decided to work at it," Cindy said wistfully, "I did it in five weeks. I'm a whiz at math. Daddy used to cram me with check stubs when I was little, and have me check them."

"Good old Daddy. . . ."

Betty Ann's tone was nasal, with a Southwestern twang. Cindy had a more cultured and sensuous voice, although her laughter was harsh. Now and then Cindy rose above the banality. Betty Ann asked how her art work was going. Cindy said, "The people who are good work twelve to fourteen hours a day. They mess up their relationships. I've never bled over anything in my life, and good artists bleed over every piece. They're degraded if they don't. I couldn't have that determination and obsessiveness. I think for a little while Michelle did. But didn't she have migraine headaches from putting everything into it?"

Betty Ann said, "I have to really strain—it doesn't flow out like it does with you and Michelle."

"In real life," Cindy said, "things don't flow. They didn't flow for Beethoven."

"I'm glad you called," Betty Ann said, at the close of that conversation. "I was worrying about you."

"We're not getting anywhere," P. M. said. "The surveillance is a waste of time and money. The telephone calls make it sound like she loved her parents and she's not trying to hide anything."

"She has no Moslem friends now?" Clyde asked.

"Far as I can tell, she has *no* friends."

"Does she ever visit David West?"

"That's all finished. Been finished for a couple of years."

"Take a crack at West," Clyde suggested. "He may know something."

Cindy's former boyfriend owned a home at 1409 Vermont, * in the Montrose section of the city. The clapboard wooden house was run-down and dilapidated. Some of the windows were broken or missing. West lived there in December 1984 with two roommates: another young ex-marine named Robin St. John (no relation to HPD's Michael St. John), a weightlifter and motorbike enthusiast; and a twenty-five-year-old long-haired carpenter and ex-U.S. Army Ranger with the improbable name of Wickie Weinstein.

Wickie Weinstein later described the life style on Vermont: "I never ate anything cooked in that house. Everything David owned was filthy. He used to throw all his clothes in the closet—wasn't even a closet! He moved to a different room, and it had been a bathroom there for God knows how long. A complete bathroom that worked—it was just that he'd packed up all his stuff in there."

Up for sale, the house had an asking price of $79,000. Posing as investors hoping to renovate crummy old properties, P. M. and Denise, with Mike Manela, one of Clyde's other investigators, met on December 10, 1984 with a Montrose realtor. They described what they were looking for.

---

* In common usage, both oral and postal, many addresses in Houston are not given surnames such as "Street" or "Avenue." Vermont was one of these.

"I have just the place for you." The realtor pulled the card happily. "It's over on Vermont. Bunch of hippies live there."

Once inside West's house, Denise took out her tapemeasure, got down on her knees in the dust, and occupied the realtor. Neither David nor any of his housemates was home, and P. M. began to search.

The peeling walls were covered with shiplap and army camouflage netting. The pipes and the wiring were exposed, and often without insulation. Fleas jumped up from tattered rugs where wet dogs had slept. Crusted dishes were piled in the kitchen sink and on the kitchen table. Texas-sized cockroaches ran track meets along every surface.

P. M. penetrated upstairs to what he assumed was David West's bedroom. An army hammock, draped with mosquito netting, sagged from one wall to another. An olive drab U.S. Marine Corps trunk stood in one corner, open and filled with carelessly flung male clothing, most of which looked like it needed a morning at the laundromat. Downstairs P. M. had already noticed a riot shotgun propped against the wall by the front door, and there was another riot shotgun here in the bedroom. He checked the second one, and it was loaded. No crime. This was Texas. A man's home is his castle—he can defend it with bazookas and machine guns if he knows where to get them. He can blow away anyone who enters the premises without permission and the law will not punish him.

A small cigar box stood on a shaky white-painted table next to the hammock. P. M. tipped back the lid. No cigars inside, but among some old foreign coins, mostly from Morocco, and other souvenirs, an object dully gleamed.

A bullet.

Picking it up, P. M. rolled it back and forth across his palm . . . heavy and cold and sinister. He was not a ballistics expert but he knew bullets. This one was a .45 silver-tipped hollowpoint. Silver-tipped hollowpoints weren't rare, but neither were they commonly used. They could be bought at any gun store at about double the price paid for an ordinary bullet. They spread upon impact.

P. M. remembered the HPD Offense Report on the Campbell murder. Silver-tipped hollowpoints from a .45 were the bullets that had torn through the hearts and brains of James and Virginia Campbell two and a half years ago.

Finding the bullet was proof of nothing at all. It wasn't as if he had found the weapon that had fired its mates. The weapon was what he was really looking for. I was a fool to think he'd just leave it laying around, P. M. realized.

But who keeps a single hollowpoint except as a souvenir? This must be our man, he thought.

Just as they were leaving the house, a key scratched in the lock and the owner of the house let himself in the front door. The real estate agent introduced them. David West wore a combat jumpsuit; he looked to P. M. as if he might have just come back from hunting. He was friendly and well spoken, although his voice was slightly high-pitched. Blue eyes? Brown eyes? Consciously trying to memorize a description, P. M. couldn't decide. Later he understood the reason. David West had one hazel-brown eye, one blue-gray one.

West apologized for the messy condition of the house. "But it's a good old house," he said. "I've had some good times here. I'll be sorry to leave it." Then, with a little theatrical bow, he bounded up the stairs.

In the street, after they parted from the realtor, P. M. told Denise about his discovery of the .45 hollowpoint.

"I think that's the one bullet he didn't fire. He's the trigger man."

"That's hard to believe. He seems like such a nice guy," Denise murmured.

And why would he do it, she asked herself, for what boiled down to an ex-girlfriend? That was always the baffling element in this case—the *why*.

————————

Betty Ann Hinds, in Austin, began calling the office. "She's driving me crazy," P. M. complained.

Denise lifted an eyebrow. "What about me? Sometimes I have to give her hourly reports. And sometimes we've talked for hours, literally."

"We can't run a business that way," P. M. reminded her. "I know you're not logging that telephone time. That's the kind of thing that really pisses Clyde off."

The billing mounted. By the end of the affair it would cost the Hinds family just over $30,000, not including legal fees. Denise knew that Betty Ann was consumed with it. How could you help but be if your parents had been murdered, and you believed your sister had done it?

But Denise had the feeling after her visit to Austin that the Hindses didn't have a lot of money, despite the inheritance, and that whatever they were spending was a kind of blood sacrifice. She began trying to poorboy the investigation. She told Betty Ann, "I'm afraid we're wasting your money. We're not getting anywhere." But Betty Ann would ask for the surveillance of Cindy to continue just one more weekend . . . then another few days . . . and most of her telephone calls were to beg the investigators not to lose interest.

P. M. understood that Cindy Ray and David West hadn't been living together for over two years and no longer even saw each other. But if

West did it, a bond of some kind must still exist, P. M. believed. If West wasn't the actual trigger man, maybe he knew who was. Maybe he arranged it for her. Maybe he recruited the trigger man—one of his paramilitary pals in Montrose. Maybe he just made the introduction and she did the rest.

"Let's do one more thing," he suggested to Denise. "Let's go in the back door. Let's run on David West to get to Cindy."

"How do you propose to do that?"

"Send someone in on him. Like a mole. Spy stuff. This guy may live in Montrose where all the faggots live, but he seems to like girls. So let's do the 'I-want-to buy-your-TV' scam with some pretty girl. She can get close to him and find out what he knows."

"Are you kidding?" Denise's lips flattened out to a pencil line. "He's going to meet some sexy dish and then blab to her about how his ex-girlfriend knocked off her parents? He's not crazy. And this isn't the KGB, you know. We don't have any good-looking whores on tap for that kind of operation."

P. M. thought, I could be all wrong. I could waste our client's money, and our time, on nothing more than a gut feeling. It's like rolling the dice in Vegas.

But it had become a minor obsession with him. "Let's do it," he said fervently. "I know I'm right about this guy."

"Who do you have in mind?"

Denise herself was the agency's most experienced undercover operative, but she had blown her cover by pretending to be a buyer of West's house on Vermont. And there were no other young women working for Clyde Wilson except Penny, the new receptionist, and Clyde's daughter, Mary Wood, their resident polygraph expert.

"Mary's too straight," P. M. said immediately. "Penny's good-looking enough, but she hasn't had any undercover experience." He let it bubble for a few moments, and then realized he'd known all along who he had in mind. "What about this girl Kim Paris? The one who works backs for Mike Manela?"

"Kind of seedy," Denise said, curling her lip.

Mike Manela, a young employee at the Wilson Agency, had brought Kim Paris into the office that past August. While Kim waited outside, Mike explained to Clyde that she was a navy veteran just come up from the base at Corpus Christi, broke and looking for work. She'd moved into Mike's neighborhood, he said, and he met her. She was twenty-three years old. They were friends.

"You screwing her?" Clyde asked.

"Nope."

"You never lied to me yet. Bring her in."

Mike needed her help in some workmen's compensation cases. Clyde talked to her and looked her over. Sexy, he thought, and good-looking —pretty sharp, not scared to speak up. He said to Mike, "Okay, why not?"

A workman's compensation case was one where an employee had claimed injury on the job—usually a crippling back injury that was difficult to diagnose, which is why it was called "working backs"—and was suing his former employer for damages. The employer would hire the Wilson Agency. Kim Paris, clad in tight blue jeans and clinging sweater, parked her car near the injured plaintiff's house. Using the tip of a ballpoint pen she let the air out of one of her tires. When the man hobbled out, Kim blinked her startlingly blue eyes and asked him if he could give her a hand with the flat. "I'm just so helpless," she crooned, "when it comes to mechanical stuff."

Clyde chuckled whenever he told the story. "Poor dumb sonofabitch got down on his hands and knees, changed the tire for her. Mike Manela was across the street with a zoom lens. Shot a video of the whole thing. End of lawsuit."

After a while Clyde viewed his new part-time employee as a con artist. Sometimes, he realized, I can't stand her, and sometimes I love her. He was partial to her because she reminded him of a pair of his own children who had given him ongoing trouble. The wild ones receive special dispensation.

After Kim had done her bit in a few cases working backs, a Houston lawyer named Marian Rosen, an old friend of Clyde's, hired the agency's services for a doctor who was in the process of divorce and suspected that his wife was a lesbian. The wife was vacationing at Esalen, a spa near Big Sur in Northern California, and the doctor wanted someone to spy on her. Kim received the assignment. She flew out there with her camera. "Got friendly with the lady, took some pictures, and made the case," Clyde said later.

After that P. M. Clinton believed that Kim could take care of herself. She was a manipulator who knew how to use people to her advantage. "And she can bullshit," he said to Denise. "She's like Clyde—she could sell you a dead horse and you'd drag it away with a smile on your face thinking you just made the buy of a lifetime. That's a real plus, especially in a deal like this. Because if this guy West is really the trigger man, there's risk."

"Why not use Mike?" Denise said. "He was out in the car that day when we saw the house. West never met him."

65

"A man tends to confide the big secret things in his life to a woman, not to another man."

Denise wasn't so sure of that. But in the end she agreed. If Clyde approved, they would offer the job of getting close to David West—in order to find out if Cindy Ray had murdered her parents—to twenty-three-year-old Kim Paris.

6

Tall and robust, with a lean face and mildly prognathous jaw, Kim Paris was not quite beautiful. Her blue eyes seemed a size too small for her face, and they often had a chilly light that was at odds with a façade of little-girl exuberance. What was genuine and what was faked was hard to say. Perhaps all of it was real, if we accept that we are creatures of multiform deep contradictions. Kim certainly was. There was something of the actress about her or she wouldn't have been able to work backs and win the confidence of the lesbian wife out at Esalen. But she was quick-witted, barbed-tongued and intelligent, and ambitious, and often jolly, and she said laughingly, in her throaty voice, "I have to be careful that my crocodile mouth doesn't run away with my hummingbird mind." She liked to drink, and to drive quickly, and to party, and sometimes she liked to do all three of those things at the same time. Born in Minnesota and christened Kimberly Ann, raised in suburban St. Louis by her mother and dentist father, Kim wore the blue and gold of the cheerleading squad at Francis Howell High School for two years. After graduation she sailed Dad's sloop on Carlyle Lake in Illinois for a summer and then joined the navy to become an air traffic controller.

Discharged from the navy in Corpus Christi, Texas, Kim wandered up to Houston with a slim, attractive Cajun girlfriend named Sandra Smith. Sami, as Sandra called herself, had various talents. Like Jim Campbell, she was a crack pool player. "We hung out for a while," Kim later said, "and hustled in the pool halls. Made a few mistakes. . . . You know how it is when you're new in town."

Then Kim met Mike Manela, who lived just a few doors down on their street in Montrose. She began working backs for Clyde Wilson. The resourceful Sami, who could type as well as bank a nine-ball into a corner pocket, got a job as a secretary for Marian Rosen, the lawyer who had employed Kim to fly to Esalen. You scratch my back, I'll scratch yours.

P. M. Clinton went to Clyde Wilson to ask if he could offer Kim Paris the assignment to get friendly with David West.

"She's a little squirrely, isn't she?" Clyde asked.

"I think she can handle it," P. M. said.

Clyde shrugged. "Okay, it's your deal. Just keep checking in with me. I don't want anything to go wrong."

P. M. talked to Kim that afternoon. "Sure," she said, "I like it. Sounds exciting. I never turn down a challenge." And, not quite as an afterthought, "I can use the money."

The Wilson Agency would bill the Hinds family for Kim's expenses plus fifty dollars an hour. Kim would keep half the fee.

P. M. and Mike Manela prepped her on the murder of the Campbells and the family background. "You have to be careful," P. M. warned. "Denise doesn't think this guy is the killer, but you wouldn't want to bet your life on it. Because, literally, that's what you might be doing. Just become friends. If you can work on him to trust you and confide in you, then maybe he'll introduce you to Cindy Ray. She's the target. How you get close to him is up to you. Whatever you're comfortable with."

Kim stared at him with uncertainty, and then her expression darkened. "What are you saying? Are you talking to me about *sex?*"

"No way," P. M. said quickly. "Clyde would have a fit!"

"No hanky panky *at all*," Denise emphasized. "The last thing we want our clients to think is that we're running some kind of whore service."

Kim pouted, twisted her lower lip between thumb and forefinger. "Well, is this guy normal?"

"We think so."

"Then he's liable to want to do a tad more than hold my hand and enjoy my scintillating intellect. I better come up with some story. Is he the aggressive type? Is he sensitive at all?"

"He seemed pleasant," Denise said, remembering her brief meeting with David West at the front door of his house. "Not a nut. I'd say no, he's not aggressive. But you never can tell."

"What if I tell him I was raped a while ago, and I'm still having nightmares about it? Then if we get friendly and he wants to take friendship to its logical culmination, I can go, 'Hey, no, give me a break—in my psychological condition that'll freak me out, man!' And he'll understand why I'm not jumping into the sack with him or letting him paw me."

"Great," P. M. said. "That's what I mean. Whatever you're comfortable with."

Kim asked how she should meet West in the first place. P. M. explained the TV ploy, but Kim didn't like it. She pointed out that if West ever compared notes with Cindy Ray, it would smell from here to Galveston. Mike Manela, by then in on the discussion, suggested the "stranded person" scenario.

"What's that?" Kim asked.

No Charlie here? Whoops! Well, what happened was, a guy down in Corpus Christi, a guy named Charlie . . . nice guy, a friend, no more than that . . . gave me this address and a phone number, told me to look him up when I got to Houston. I lost the piece of paper, but I could have sworn this was the number. . . .

Kim said, "Sure, I can do that. That's *me.*"

"Let's move on this," P. M. said. "Otherwise this case will die on us. We give it a couple of weeks, and if it doesn't work, dump it."

Kim thought about it for a day and then made her plans. West was from Montrose, she reasoned, and everybody in Montrose seemed to have an act. Using a vegetable dye, Kim gave her hair a pinkish-burgundy cast, so that she looked like a punker, and at two o'clock on the Monday afternoon of December 17, 1984, down she went to 1409 Vermont in Montrose, looking for the elusive nonexistent Charlie. Her heart beat a little faster when she knocked on the door. Any problems and she'd fly away quicker than hell could scorch a feather.

No one answered her knocking. A neighbor walked by and told her that he knew the owner of the house, Mr. West, who worked at the A1 Blueprint Company, and that he usually got home about 6:30. But that night neither David West nor any of his housemates returned until after eleven. By then Kim was gone.

The same thing happened on Tuesday. This time Kim stayed until one in the morning. Bored and a little discouraged, she went home.

So far, at $50 an hour for the logged hours of Kim's surveillance, P. M.'s brilliancy had cost Betty Ann Hinds $525, plus sixty miles' worth of car expenses at 35 cents a mile, and not a word had been exchanged with the peripatetic David West.

On the third evening Kim began surveillance at 6 P.M. Ten minutes later Robin St. John, David's young housemate—curly blond hair and glasses, wearing a black T-shirt that hugged bulging pecs—cruised round the corner and thrust a key into the lock of 1409 Vermont. Kim waited five minutes and then knocked firmly on the door.

" . . . well, what happened, see, was, a guy down in Corpus Christi, a guy named Charlie . . . I lost the piece of paper, but . . . "

An interested and self-congratulating Robin took her in and an hour later escorted her to the Park Lane Tavern around the corner on West Alabama, where, as he explained with a hint of regret, he had a date to meet his buddy and landlord, Dave.

68

Once Kim was introduced to her target, she homed in like a heat-seeking missile, and Robin was left to find solace throwing darts at the cork board beside the bar.

A few weeks later in a written report to the Wilson Agency, Kim described her first impressions of David West:

" . . . about 28–30 years old, 5'10" tall, medium build, dark blond hair that he wears cut over his ears, kind of long in back, not an Afro but kind of kinky. He has a goatee and is missing the little finger on his left hand and his eyes are two different colors, one green, one blue. David, as a person, I have found to be very, very intelligent . . . so intelligent that I wonder why he's living like he does. He was in the Marine Corps for a while, never saw Vietnam. He found a way to get out of that. I'm not sure how he did it, but he said he doesn't like to fight. He's very articulate; he has an immense vocabulary, very impressive. He is very familiar with American and European history. He can sit down and spout all kinds of facts. . . . "

Kim was astute and determined. She was also beautiful, or nearly beautiful, and David West in his life thus far had enjoyed scant success with women who fit either of those descriptions. He was a trier—everyone gave him credit for that—but he rarely succeeded. Maybe he tried *too* hard, and in too quaint a manner. His housemate Wickie Weinstein said of him: "No manner, no tact, no couth whatever. It was a big joke around all of us that if you wanted to get laid, you just didn't go out with Dave."

Women who knew him or had dated him said, "He's a nice guy, but . . . "

One described him as "nerdy. Once a friend of mine came into this bar wearing a wig, a kind of pink hairpiece, and Dave didn't like it and poured a glass of beer over it. I said, 'My God, Dave, haven't we learned anything from the sixties? Be cool.' But he wasn't cool."

Mary Hooper was an actress with Stages, a Houston repertory theater. She had blue hair and she drove a pink Cutlass—an eccentric and sensual young woman. David courted her when her actor boyfriend, Scottie, was away on location in North Carolina in the movie *Firestarter*. David telephoned her and came by several times to the facial salon where she worked: "To the point," Mary Hooper recounted, "where my boss told him to stay away." One time when she had the flu he brought food to her house. When she was well he bought her an expensive gold necklace. "It made me uncomfortable," she said. "He acted obsessed. I was lonesome, but I was in love with Scottie. What Dave and I had in common was that we both lifted weights and both loved cars. When I explained that I thought of him as a friend and didn't want to date him, he told me details of how Scottie had been fucking around with some of the other girls in the neighborhood. Dave was saying, 'This guy screws around, why don't you do it with me?' That offended me. It was making me acknowledge something I didn't want to know about. I never encouraged Dave sexually, but who's to say? Maybe just the fact that I wore tight pants would be encouraging someone like Dave. The only girl I ever heard him talk about was Cindy Ray. He said he really cared for her, but she was crazy and he had to end the relationship. I didn't think of him as a latent homosexual, but more as in the adolescent sexual mode where girls were still some other kind of creature, 'icky,' and the guys were 'buddies.' He had that idea of the sexes."

He must have been on top of the world, Mary Hooper thought later, when Kim Paris entered his life. He must have thought that his ship had come in.

Another young woman, Lindsey Wilson, met David in late 1982, when he was tending bar at the Ale House, a British-style pub in Montrose. She was then a nurse-consultant to insurance companies, giving rape-crisis training at the Houston Area Women's Center. She had been interviewed on the PBS station as a rape survivor, and David recognized her in the Ale House and said, "You're the woman on TV. You're very brave. You've been through a lot."

"He was a plague in my life" was how Lindsey Wilson put it. "He dogged me. Wherever I went, he was always there. I had a car wreck and hurt my back, and Dave found out. He showed up, bringing flowers and magazines. He sat by my bed for hours. I knew that if I had once said, 'Okay, we'll date,' he would have proposed marriage. The puppy dog, moon-eyed thing—he was too willing, too ready. He was always trying to pick up good-looking girls, but without success. He would smile and laugh and giggle, but it wasn't truly there. There's a classic glaze that psychiatric patients have in their eyes. He had it. He told me he wasn't from here, that he had been born on another star. He talked a lot about his parents—he loved them a lot. When his dad had a heart attack, he was devastated. And he did a lot of drugs when I knew him. He offered me speed, cocaine, mushrooms, and he always had pot. He and his survivalist buddies."

David told her that rapists and violent criminals needed to be killed. "What would you do, Lindsey, if you found the guy who raped you?"

"I don't know, Dave."

"Wouldn't you want to kill him?"

"It was a long time ago," she said.

A woman named Cathy, David's hairdresser, said, "He was always the butt of jokes. Everyone took advantage of him. Amber, my nine-year-old daughter, didn't like him. He believed in too much discipline—children should be seen and not heard. He loved dogs, but he was really into discipline with them, too. He liked to help women in trouble. It was his way of getting close to them."

Shannon Shea, a full-lipped, good-looking young woman who was assistant manager at Pearl's Oyster Bar in Montrose, knew him, too. "He used to come in here. He liked me and tried to date me. He told me that he was going to come into a lot of money. I asked him, 'From what?' and he said, 'I'll tell you some day.' He took me out, and we tried to go to the Prince concert at The Summit. We stood on line but we missed getting in by only a few people, so he said, 'Let's go to my house.' We went there, and it was dirty, scummy, and I didn't like it. We went to my place instead. We started kissing. But suddenly he got very rough. Adolescent boys sometimes try to dry-hump a girl, and that's kind of what he did." She was repulsed and didn't hesitate to tell Dave. "That ended our sex. What's really odd is that he wasn't angry or terribly disappointed. It was as if he was used to rejection."

Mary Hooper, the actress, echoed that thought and took it one level deeper. "He had that kind of mentality where there are good girls and bad girls. He would have to put a girl on a pedestal in order to marry her . . . and also to cope with the lack of confidence he must have had in his own lovemaking skill and ability to seduce her."

Not cool. A nice guy, but. This was the target, the man that Kim Paris was meant to befriend in order to discover if Cynthia Campbell Ray had murdered her parents on that June night more than two years ago.

Kim, her hair dyed pink, wearing red stockings and black pixie boots, sat down next to David West in the booth at the Park Lane Tavern. He thought she looked as if she'd bought her pseudo-military jacket and pants at Banana Republic. But he liked what he glimpsed underneath.

"I'm Teresa," she said. "Call me Tee."

By the end of the first meeting, at 1:30 A.M. when she drove off into the dark December morning, she had given him the rudiments of a story that provided her with the freedom she needed to keep her physical distance. She told the truth up to the point of her discharge from the navy; but that was only a week ago, she said. Now, after the navy, she was at a crossroads. She was here in Houston living with her sister and brother-in-law, hanging out, looking for a job, not quite sure what to do next in her life.

"The next important thing you're going to do in your life," David West said masterfully, "is meet me here tomorrow night at eight o'clock for dinner."

Thus began a most curious relationship whose heart was masquerade and whose soul was seduction. Kim, as Teresa Neele—she chose the name because Agatha Christie had used it during the mystery writer's famous disappearance in England in 1926—saw David West in bars, in restaurants, and in his home, but never invited him to her own home, never even gave him her telephone number. She couldn't, she explained. Her brother-in-law, Buddy Rosen,* in whose house she now lived, was a tyrant, obsessed with keeping her apart from men. He was a Vietnam vet, a real psycho. He sometimes dealt cocaine. She suspected he had Mafia connections. He had made a pass at her at his wedding reception. He beat her sister Sami regularly, had once cracked her cheekbone and broken her leg by pushing her down the stairs. Teresa didn't dare offend Buddy for fear of the repercussions that might land on Sami.

She went so far in this story—and it was so key to erecting a barrier against sex and preventing David West from discovering her true identity—that at a midpoint in their two-month courtship she produced a friend, a thirty-nine-year-old painter named Emil Lewis Bocz (he pronounced it Boats), to play the part of Buddy, the psycho brother-in-law.

Lew Bocz had been living in Panama City, Florida, where he painted, etched on glass, and ran a head shop, which he sometimes described as "a boutique." He was a tall, slim, dark-haired man, so softspoken that it was often difficult to hear him. His voice seemed to be mired in mud, and he had a tendency to speak by rote in convoluted phrases. He wore gold chains, hand-tooled boots, and designer jeans. He used phrases like, "What are you talking about, timeframewise?"

When he met Kim she was working at a club called Reflections, one of several typical Houston nightspots often called titty bars. These were flash establishments where attractive young women worked as topless waitresses, platform dancers, and hostesses. Wearing only high heels and a pelvic thong, the hostesses circulated and accepted invitations to crouch over the laps of the male customers and gyrate erotically to a disco beat. After the event—more likely, nonevent—it was customary for the gent to slip at least a ten-dollar bill into the thong.

Bocz became friendly with Kim and tried to impress upon her that there were other jobs with better potential. There was no lasting romance between them, but later, when she had a problem, she would call.

---

* Kim chose that surname in honor of Marian Rosen, the lawyer. She called him Buddy, she said, "just for the hell of it."

She was close enough to Bocz in early January of 1985 to have dinner with him and tell him the tale of her involvement in the David West investigation.

"It's my first big case." Even as she used that worn phrase, she laughed merrily. "All the rest of the stuff I did for Clyde was nickel-and-dime. This is *murder*."

"Then you'd better not take it lightly," Bocz warned. "You're in a potentially dangerous situation."

A week later they talked about it again. One of the problems, Kim said, was that she wasn't getting sufficient backup from Clyde and his staff. She would file her report, and Denise or P. M. would just nod and say, "Okay. Good work." The agency just wanted the case to go on, she claimed, so they could collect the fees. She needed somebody to help her with direction.

Lew Bocz became that somebody. She was the star, he the director. He thought he understood David West, and he told Kim how to handle him. He met with Kim perhaps five times during the course of the operation, but they talked several times a week on the phone, at length. Kim brought him an interesting document—about twenty-five xeroxed pages of computerized dot-matrix printout in a nine-by-twelve manila envelope. The pages were each labeled "Original Information Report Non-Public, Houston Police Department Offense Report, Incident No. 036787082." That incident was the murder of James and Virginia Campbell.

"Where'd you get this?" Bocz asked. "This looks like classified material."

"You think so?" Kim asked, wide-eyed.

"I guess from Clyde Wilson," Bocz said.

Kim laughed, but didn't confirm. Bocz read all the pages carefully. They gave him new knowledge and insights.

He made a proposition to Kim. He knew that she was ambitious, and already she had begun to sense this was the big opportunity in her young life, if she could wring a confession out of David West. "Let's write a book about it together," Bocz suggested. He claimed to have three books in the works: two children's books, "one of them about 95 percent complete," and "10,000 actual words" of a science fiction novel. A fifty-fifty split, he proposed, and Kim agreed.

The lie about "Buddy's" role as the bad guy in her life led easily to the second lie that was vital for Kim in keeping up the relationship with her target. She had been raped in Corpus Christi, she told David. It was brutal and traumatic, and she didn't want to talk about it. She still had nightmares. And therefore, for the moment at least, she wanted no sex with men.

There was some truth to that, and to the rape story too, except that the rapes—there were two—had occurred in Houston. The first time, December 3, 1983, Kim returned to her apartment at 2 A.M., "very much intoxicated," she stated to the police. At 4:30 A.M., "still intoxicated," she was assaulted by a stranger who somehow climbed up a ladder, broke a window, and clambered in. The second time, six months later on June 24, 1984, after having had "four or five mixed drinks," she was returning from a party at an unknown address and walking down an unknown street at 12:15 A.M. She explained to the police that she wore a "two-piece swimsuit" and a loose blouse covering it. When two black men offered her a ride she accepted, and they drove to another unknown dark street and raped her, one after the other. They took what little money she had and dumped her behind the Warwick Hotel.

She told the tale of the second rape to David West, setting it in Corpus Christi, and he believed her.

He believed everything she told him. As Mary Hooper had guessed, he thought his ship had come in. Or it was close by, nosing into port, flags flying, whistle hooting, bow wave purling. It was Kim's dream to be famous; it was David's to win the heart of a beautiful woman.

He liked to talk to her; she was such a good listener. On one arm he had the tattoo of a black eagle with spread talons: a souvenir of the Corps, he said. The little finger on his left hand was missing, and she asked about it. "Happened back in high school," he said, "in the Shop class. Chewed off by some machine that cuts metal. I tried to pull my hand back—too late. My finger was just hanging there by a couple of red threads, utterly fuckin' ground up. I waited for about thirty seconds for the pain to hit, and it didn't. Then I willed myself to feel no pain. While I was waiting for the nurse to put antiseptic on it, I still kept waiting for the pain, and there was none. I think I was able to block it out by sheer will power."

As early as their second meeting in the Park Lane Tavern he confided that he was planning on opening a Montrose bar of his own. Financial independence was the goal. He had a backer who would be a silent partner. After a few pitchers of beer he admitted that the backer would be "an old girlfriend." No name, yet. "I'm her Svengali," he said—they were just friends now, but she still depended on him. Funny relationship: when he'd first met her she couldn't even look people in the eye, just hid behind her long hair. He had met her younger sister first, and then been introduced to the family and the older sister, who later became his girlfriend.

At that point Kim realized that he was talking about Cynthia Campbell Ray.

"She's unstable," David said sadly. "She had a terrible upbringing—the family scapegoat. She lives like a recluse now. She's mentally ill."

Kim probed gently. "But she wasn't always like that, was she?"

"Oh, no, of course not. When she was with me she was fine. She was beautiful. Now she's gotten fat and paranoid."

"Why'd you split up?"

Personal problems, he said, and their friendship became . . . "well, let's just say, strained." He hesitated. There were some "awful things" that she had involved him in, and they came between them.

Awful things? Almost breathlessly, Kim asked, "What do you mean?"

But it was a subject he didn't want to discuss. "Tell me about *you*, Tee. . . . "

Before the evening was over he again mentioned the bar that he was soon going to own. Understanding that he was trying to impress her, Kim widened her eyes and parted her lips, nodding her head sympathetically as he talked. He said, "I pick up jobs to take me through the hard times, like this shitty job at the blueprint company I've got now, and I tend bar. But that's all marking time. I already own my own home—you'll see it soon, although it's pretty messy, it needs a lot of work. I have to be my own boss. And it will happen, as soon as . . . " His reedy voice trailed off.

"As soon as what?"

"The money that this old girlfriend's going to invest is coming from an inheritance, but it's not settled yet because the will's still in probate. She's got these three sisters—the youngest one and the oldest one are lesbians—and an uncle, and they've all ganged up to try and screw her out of her share. Wicked people. They still have to go through all kinds of shit before she gets it."

"Both her parents died?" Kim asked.

"Yeah, in an automobile accident."

Kim's heart began to pound. "That's awful," she said.

"No, it was the best thing that ever happened to her," David West said.

She continued seeing him over the Christmas holidays and into the new year, calling him at work or at home, making dates to meet at the Park Lane or another bar called Rudyard's. He could never call her. Often she would bring up his plan to become a bar owner, and he finally attached a name—Cynthia—to the old girlfriend and future patron. No last name. "I'd just rather not jinx it by telling you," he explained, with that endearing melancholy smile he had.

David was in love. It had happened twice before in his life, once with Cindy Ray and then later with a woman named Jerry whom he'd met in Rudyard's, a woman with two small children and more problems than David felt he was able to handle. But with Kim it was different. For one thing, it was sexless. Not *his* choice. She'd never had an orgasm with a man, she told him. She wouldn't say more. He wasn't quite sure if that meant she'd only had them by herself or with women, but he didn't want to probe and hear an answer that he couldn't cope with. He understood the trauma she'd been through with the rape, and he was determined to be kind, sympathetic, patient, so that she'd know he really cared, and could trust him and be brought back to life by him.

He couldn't even kiss her. When he moved close to her he felt her stiffen. He swore that if he could ever find those bastards who did that to her, he'd beat them to pulp, kill them.

She begged him to be patient. In time, all would be well.

"Tee, I want to marry you," he said. "Make a life together. Do you understand that?"

"I know, David. I want that, too. But you have to give me space. Give me time," She smiled a little sadly. "Meanwhile, let's get to know each other."

———————————

On January 7, 1985, Cindy Ray signed a final settlement agreement with her sisters and J. W. Campbell, the executor of her parents' estate. Represented by her baby-faced lawyer, Steve Simmons, Cindy received the ownership of the apartment building on Kingston where she had been living rent free for the past year—it was worth somewhere between $200,000 and $250,000—plus an agreed sum of just over $58,000. Although most of that money had already been doled out to her in dribs and drabs during the two and a half years since the Campbells had been murdered, there was a final payment of $25,000 when Cindy signed the papers. She gave the check to Steve Simmons.

Betty Ann Hinds informed Denise Moseley about the settlement and the payment, and Denise told Kim Paris.

Kim was pleased with her progress. She felt in no danger. In her January 15, 1985 report to the Wilson Agency she wrote: "David, at this point, is not aware of Cynthia receiving the money for the inheritance. Their relationship is strained because of 'something in their past.' Every time we speak of Cynthia, David makes a point of how emotionally disturbed she is, and getting worse all the time. He feels a great deal of pity for her . . . [her] suicide would not surprise him. We got into David being a violent person. He denies being physically violent, but does admit to having an extremely bad temper that, at times, affects his better judgment. I've personally seen, when I'm with him, if another gentleman looks sideways at me, he's very ready to put up his fists, very possessive, and I can see where he would have a bad temper. Sometimes he'll look at me and just grit his teeth, which is kind of spooky. . . . He also made a point of telling me that he could have just about anything he wanted from Cynthia. He knows which buttons to push, and I have no doubt, him being as strong as he is, that in their relationship, she was manipulated. She would do whatever he wanted her to do. . . . "

One night he fixed a Mexican dinner for Kim in his house and showed her his sawed-off 12-gauge shotgun. He pointed it at her and said, "How'd you like to be looking down the barrel of this bad boy?" No, he had never owned a .45. "I love to shoot," Kim said, and they made tentative plans to go to a range in north Houston. She asked him to come up with a .45—it was a handgun she'd never used and she was just dying to try one out.

"He has a few *Soldiers of Fortune* [magazines]," she reported, "although he does not embrace their philosophy. He said he used to be into it a lot more, but now that he's matured he's realized that it's a bunch of garbage. Although he does have a friend that he called 'Wickie' —supposed to be the mercenary type who has a lot of weapons."

She met Wickie Weinstein in late January and found him "a braggart, and considers himself quite a tough guy." He was a theatrical carpenter, she was told, but at the moment he had a job laying TV cable.

That month Wickie and David were arrested and jailed overnight for outstanding traffic tickets. The police came to the door of 1409 Vermont with the warrants and—so David said—Wickie greeted them there with a shotgun. David told Kim that he'd had to use the money he had saved for his monthly house payment to bail himself and Wickie out of Harris County Jail. He sold his TV set. His Trans Am had a ruined tire and he couldn't afford to fix it. To save money he began to drink Everclear, a brand of 180 proof pure alcohol, with tonic. (In her notes to the Wilson Agency Kim drew a little round face with down-turned mouth and tongue sticking out: her way of saying "Phooey.") "Tastes just like vodka," David said, and joked, "I'm so broke now that I can't even pay attention."

Kim would drop in to the house and find him lifting weights and smoking a joint at the same time. She had picked up most of the tabs in the Park Lane and Rudyard's, courtesy of Betty Ann Hinds; now she did David's grocery shopping and took him out to dinner at a club called Fitzgerald's and to the Bavarian Gardens restaurant. They used her little VW Jetta when they went out. He no longer wanted to stay with her at home—he was embarrassed by its shabby condition. But he didn't want to roam the streets and bars of Houston interminably. "Why can't we go to your house?" he kept asking. "I can handle your brother-in-law."

No. So they went out. He was a pussycat.

By late January she felt that he was ready to confess something to her. She always fell back on the devious statement he had made when they first met, that his old girlfriend's parents had been killed in a horrible car accident.

"That's a lie, and so it's proof of *something,*" she said to P. M. Clinton. "I mean, I can't figure out why he couldn't just say, 'Her parents were shot and killed back in 1982,' can you?"

"I don't know," P. M. said. "There might be some kind of weird reason. Maybe he doesn't want you to know who Cynthia is, and if he tells you her parents were murdered you'd remember the incident and figure it out."

Kim shook her head. "David didn't kill those people. I'm positive of that now. I know him too well—he's too sweet, and he has a real moral attitude about things, so he couldn't have done that. But I think he knows who did."

Payday came at the blueprint company where he worked, and on Saturday night, February 2, David insisted on taking Teresa to Fitzgerald's to hear the Fabulous Thunderbirds.

He was in good spirits and they stayed out the entire evening, partying. Kim had been pursuing a theme that she was telepathic to a certain extent, and that night she told David that although she had grown very close to him, she also *physically felt* something standing between them—like a barrier. Leaving Fitzgerald's, a little tipsy, she said, "I can't pinpoint exactly what that 'something' is, but it feels like something you're hiding from me. Something big."

"No—"

"Shit, it's *there!* I can feel it! I can almost see it! It's like—well, like a big dark barrier." She grew mournful. "I can't ever trust you as long as that stands between us—"

"Tee, listen—"

"No, don't interrupt. Don't fuck with my mind. This is what you've got to understand. Whatever it is, it won't destroy our relationship. Whatever it is, I wouldn't be afraid to hear it, and I won't think less of you. Do you understand that?"

Later they were sitting in her car outside David's house. It was chilly, and she clung close to him. She began to shiver.

"What's the matter, honey?" David asked.

In a low voice she said, "I haven't told you the truth."

"Tell me."

"I've been having these dreams. I know what the barrier is. I know what you're hiding."

David drew away from her. "What is it?"

He didn't sound nervous, but she knew he *had* to be.

"It has to do with Cindy."

After a minute, he said quietly, "Yes, that's true. There's something, and it has to do with her."

Suddenly he began to sob, and his head dropped to her lap. She comforted him like a child, stroking his hair, murmuring his name. "It's okay, it's okay . . . it's okay, baby. . . . "

"I want to tell you," he sobbed, "but I'm afraid. You don't understand! My whole goddamn life hangs in the balance."

He cried for ten minutes while Kim patted him on the head, soothing him, whispering, "Everything will be okay. . . . "

Then he disengaged from her and said, in a broken voice, "Please don't ask me anymore now. Please give me time. I'll tell you when the time is ripe. But not now."

She let him go and watched him shamble into the house in the darkness, hands stuffed into his pockets, head bent. She thought she heard him sob again.

She was shaken, but she was also thrilled. She was close.

The following morning, on Sunday, she called him to find out how he was.

"I feel relieved," he said. "Relieved that I told you what I did, and real relieved that you called. I feel so close to you now. I was scared that after what happened you wouldn't ever call me again, wouldn't want to see me. Men aren't supposed to cry like that. I thought you'd just drop out of sight."

"But I love you, David."

She wrote in her report that evening: "I feel a confession is imminent."

On Monday morning she told Denise Moseley that she wanted to carry a tape recorder on her next date with David West. "You know, the kind that you can stick in a handbag. But I don't have one. Can I borrow yours?"

Denise, who didn't like or trust Kim, wasn't keen on lending her Panasonic to her.

"Are you kidding me?" Kim said.

"No!"

"Jesus! I'll ask Clyde if I can borrow his."

Clyde Wilson mulled this over for half a day and came up with a slightly different solution. He called his good friend J. C. Mosier, a former homicide detective whom he had met when they were both investigating the kidnapping of a little girl in Katy, Texas. Mosier had just been named spokesman of HPD's Public Information Office. He was a cordial, open-faced man with none of the suspicious reserve usually associated with homicide detectives.

J. C. Mosier had been in Homicide when the Campbells were killed. A dedicated detective didn't want a beer joint killing with a smoking gun that could be solved and cleared after five minutes interrogation. He wanted a challenge, a good whodunit. No longer in the field, Mosier felt a certain nostalgia for it, and he had kept up with the Campbell case.

Clyde called him on Thursday, January 31. After a few minutes of gossip he got to the point and explained what he knew of Kim's situation with David West. "She's in with the guy, she has some sort of fake relationship with him, whether it's boyfriend-girlfriend or what. There's a possibility that she could get some information out of him. I want her to come down and talk to you, so you can evaluate what she's done and see if it's any good. J. C., it might be a bunch of shit—I don't know. See what you think about where she could go with it."

Mosier was interested—he knew that Clyde wouldn't call him if it wasn't serious business. "I'll talk to her," he promised, "but I can't run an end run around Gil Schultz and Paul Motard. Tell her to come in anytime Monday."

On Sunday Mosier was in a barbecue circuit tournament at the Bear Creek golf course. With his mind trapped in a memory of the Campbell case, he missed a four-foot putt and bogeyed the fifteenth hole. Maybe, he thought, I should never have quit Homicide.

7

On Monday morning, February 4, 1985, J. C. Mosier glanced up from his desk as Kim Paris edged hesitantly into the room. He raised his eyebrows. Say, that's not bad . . . not bad at all. Clyde never mentioned she was *that* good-looking.

Clyde, you dirty old devil!

J. C. liked Kim from the start. She had courage and frankness, and a bubbling enthusiasm you rarely saw in cops and private eyes. Sharp kid, he decided.

She finished her story. "J. C., I really don't know if the guy did it or not. I don't want to believe he did, but I'm not sure. What I *am* sure of is that something's got to pop, and I need help, because it's getting to the point where he's itchy. And I am *not* going to screw him, you hear?" Passion appeared in her voice when she said that. Then she giggled. "He's creepy. I just couldn't do it."

"Relax," J. C. soothed her, "you won't have to."

"Well, I've got an idea," Kim said, and set forth a plan that she reckoned would speed things up. She would get some of Clyde's people to drive by David West's house on Vermont, just as she and David were coming out the front door. They would play a scene out of *The Godfather* and fire a shotgun at him—"I mean, don't worry, they'll *miss* him!"—and that would make him think that Cindy Ray was trying to kill him in order to shut him up.

Mosier's face grew less pink and warm, more gray and stony.

"I'll put that idea in his head," Kim continued, "and he'll be so discombobulated he'll spill his guts to me. What do you think?"

"What I think," Mosier said, "is that I don't want to be part of this deal, and neither does the Houston Police Department." He leaned forward instructively. She was a kid. He had to remember that. "In the first place, Kim, it's illegal to fire a gun at someone, even if it's a blank. And what happens, let's say, if you and Clyde's people pull this stunt and just then a patrolman turns the corner? Things could get a little tacky, right? And what if West fires back at your people with his *own* shotgun? And what if the day after he believes so strongly that Cynthia Ray's out to snuff him that he panics and flies off to darkest Mexico? We'd never see him again."

"I didn't think of that," Kim admitted.

Now he thinks I'm a jerk, she thought. *I've blown it.*

"We don't want to lose the guy," Mosier said, "and you've got him where you want him. You're doing good. So listen to me."

By then he had evaluated her and, never mind the idea to pump lead à la Al Capone through the streets of Houston, he thought she was probably level-headed enough to take directions.

It was a dead-end case at this point, he explained. No physical evidence. The file was as fat as the Manhattan telephone book, but it had cobwebs hanging on it. HPD had worked hard and got nowhere. They had given up, and you couldn't blame them. Homicide cops can't ride losing horses forever.

The only way to make the case, he said, was for her to put on a wire, a hidden microphone, and get West to confess.

"In no uncertain terms, either. If he says, 'I killed these people,' that's not enough. We can't take that to the D.A.'s Office and ask for an indictment—they'll laugh at us. West has got to say, 'I took my .45 and walked into the upstairs bedroom where they were sleeping at such-and-such an hour of the morning, with the two kids on the floor, and shot both of them twice in the heads and once each in the chest.' Left a glove on the floor, and so forth. We need him to admit to the facts of the murder *that only the murderer would have known.* The more he can tell you about it, the better it is. Not just where he shot them, but where he was standing, what he wore, how he got in the house, how he got out, and what he did with the gun. *Details.* And it's got to be on that tape recorder."

And when West confessed—*if* he confessed—"Kim, you can't freak out. You've got to be cold and callous and not be shocked. At least not *too* shocked. . . . I'm sure he'd expect you to be a little bit shocked. It's a fine line to tread. Can you do all that?"

"I don't know," Kim said frankly. She was remembering a movie called *Prince of the City,* where Treat Williams, playing a crooked cop turned snitch, had a wire taped to his stomach in order to get the goods on drug sellers, and how he was nearly killed at a table in an Italian restaurant when the wire was suspected and almost discovered. It was a frightening memory. Could David West kill her if she fouled up and he found out what she was up to? If he was the murderer of the Campbell family, yes, he damn well could. No trick to do it a second time. Defend your territory. He loved her, he said, but any fool knew with what blazing rapidity love could turn to hate.

For the first time, Kim was worried. Not a game anymore.

"How can I get him to confess?" she asked, sidestepping any decision about the wire.

Mosier explained that she had to kick something off in his head that made him feel he was safe in telling her his deepest secrets. "You have to assume that on some unconscious level he *wants* to confess, because if he doesn't want to, you can serenade him till the cows come home and you might as well sing to a clam. You just have to tap in on the right level." As a homicide detective, Mosier said, he had done that often— sat in a quiet, bare room and talked to a suspected murderer—"And you know he wants to tell you, is about to tell you, and the scenario you play on him is: 'You're not a bad guy just because you killed somebody. Hell, they probably *deserved* killing. World's better off without 'em! I've wanted to kill people—shit, man, once or twice I came *that* close. It doesn't necessarily make you a bad guy if you do it.'"

82

Did she grasp it? Could she handle it?

Well, she thought so. But was that really enough?

You never knew. They refined it further. They worked out two scenarios. One: she'd always wanted to snuff her crazy brother-in-law, Buddy, because of the nasty things he'd done to her sister. So she was capable of murder, of understanding the *need* to murder. Two: she knew someone in her past who had in fact killed someone, and this trusting person had told her about it, sworn her to secrecy, and in all these years she'd never breathed a word of it to a living soul. Never would, never could. Don't ask me for names and details, David. This man's life depends on me.

"And remember," Mosier said, "one of the main things is, no matter what he tells you, don't be negative! If he tells you he hung up two babies on a clothesline in the noonday sun just to find out what temperature they'd boil at—don't express shock. Because you want him in a frame of mind where he's not ashamed to tell you *anything*. You want to unlock the fact, if it's a fact, that he murdered two people, shot them in the head while their two grandchildren were sleeping not six feet away. That's a terrible thing. So be cool. *And get the details.* Remember, without them, we can't take the case to court. It won't be easy, and you can't grill him and pump him. But just keep all that in mind, and do your best."

They had spoken for nearly two hours. Tired and giddy, Kim was glad when Mosier looked at his watch and stood up. He took her down the windowless and dully lit yellow vinyl corridor to Detective Gil Schultz's cubicle of an office. Paul Motard was somewhere else, delayed on his return route from the men's room. At his desk, hands resting on his paunch, Schultz blinked his cool blue eyes, listened to an outline of the story, and was not impressed. Kim got the feeling that he was looking up her dress the whole time. He took Mosier aside, but he spoke so that Kim could hear.

"What is this, J. C.? Is this for real? Is this amateur night in Dixie? How do we know the Ray woman and David West didn't send this bimbo down here to find out what we know? Even if this woman's really working for this Clyde Wilson, who you say is good people but I never heard of, that doesn't make her legitimate. She could have pulled the wool over Wilson's eyes the same way she says she did over West's. Have you checked this woman out?"

There was nothing Mosier could do. It wasn't his case. He got the accused bimbo out of there. He told her to do what he'd suggested and said, don't worry, he was sure that Sgt. Gil Schultz would change his mind. He thanked her for coming down.

"You're doing just great!"

A disheartened Kim drove back in her VW to the tree-shaded office at Upland and said to Denise Moseley, "Schultz thinks it's all a load of crap. What a cold fish that guy is!" Her depression grew. She didn't know if she could really take the enterprise any farther. She didn't believe that David West was really the murderer, only that he would lead her to the murderer. She called Lew Bocz to talk it over. He had some interesting ideas.

———————

Kim was stubborn and resilient. That evening she stopped by David's house to reinforce his positive feelings about confiding in her. She couldn't stay long, she protested. But she had to talk to him, she said, about *that*.

"About what?"

About her recurrent dream, about the thing he was hiding from her, the thing with Cindy, whatever it was. Otherwise, like an incubus, it would claw its way up from the blackness of her nightmares and blot out the light of their relationship.

"Listen," David said, "I've been thinking a lot. You've got to make some moves, too. You've got to meet me halfway. What I'm saying is, move in with me. Live with me."

Kim's heart seemed to shrink in her chest. Moving in with him would certainly bring her to the closeness she wanted. But it had to mean sex —she couldn't hold out in that sort of situation.

It wasn't only that her restricted life style was driving him crazy, David went on. It was no good for *her*. It was a little sick, he dared to say. Her brother-in-law, Buddy Rosen, the coke-sniffing Mafioso, was clearly a maniac. If she moved into the house on Vermont, it would be the first big step toward freeing her of what he believed was crushing part of her spirit. And then he, David, would be able to talk to her, to bare his past and lift the weight that crushed *him*.

Kim's time was up. She had told him she could stay only twenty minutes, and that was long gone. She had to be consistent. She had to be able to say, "I never exaggerate, I never lie to you. I always mean what I say. . . ."

"I don't know," she said coolly. "Jesus, you're too much . . . here I am talking about never seeing you again, and you come back with asking me to move in with you."

"What do you mean, *never seeing me again?*" He was shocked. Had she said that? No!

"What I said."

"You didn't say—"

"You don't *hear* me, David. You don't fuckin' hear what I'm really saying! I'm saying I'm so upset that you're holding things back from me that it's *hurting* me. That's where it's at, man, and you don't even *see* it! I have to go." She bustled off toward the door again.

"Will you call me?"

"Let me think, David."

"Wait a minute." He clasped her arm more strongly than he intended. "Don't do this."

She shook loose. "I have to go. I told you that!"

She stayed away for three days. She could afford to be cruel. On Thursday morning, February 7, she called him at work and asked to see him that evening. He all but meowed his pleasure over the telephone. They met in the Park Lane and through four hours of conversation drank—according to her expense account—eight pitchers of beer.

She began a campaign now and continued it on Saturday evening when they met again. Life was hard, Kim said. You can't trust anybody. Well, hardly anybody. Wasn't it ironic that there was nothing more important in a human relationship than the concept of trust and loyalty, and yet that was the first thing that rotted, if it even existed in the first place? She knew. She'd had bad experiences, man. She'd trusted, then been zapped, been hurt. Now she was wary of people. She hungered for trust, but where could you find it? When she did, she was elated; it was like finding the most precious diamond. Christine DeLorean, for example, who had stood by her man when all the world was against him: "That's the kind of woman I admire above all others. That's the kind of woman I want to be. I think I *am*, but I've just never really had the chance to prove it."

And it was what she wanted out of a man, too. Total trust and confidence. Someone who would really stick by her, never be disloyal, never rat or snitch *no matter what*.

"I guess I come from the old school," Kim said, pouring more beer into David's mug, "which is probably the result of my growing up in a rough neighborhood in St. Louis. You know, there we were, just young punks running the streets, but if any single one of us got busted—and it happened, man, let me tell you!—the others knew, without a doubt, that they could count on him not to snitch you off. Or count on *her*."

"Yeah," David said, "they just don't make kids like they used to."

She laughed. She liked him. He could be sincere and witty at the same time. She told him that.

"Well, I feel very close to you, Tee, in what I'd call a psychic sense. I know I can trust you. We're cut from the same cloth."

In her notes the next day to P. M. and Denise, she wrote of this meeting: "It was *very* productive."

But now he begged her for more. Sexually, he was being driven nuts. There was an old Texas cowhand's expression: "I hear you cluckin' but I cain't find your nest." Hadn't he proved he could be tender and understanding and patient? There was a limit on patience that was imposed by nature and biology. "Let me meet your brother-in-law," David said, "so he sees I'm not an ogre, and we can become friends, and then you and I can see each other like normal people. Damn, you *owe* that to me!"

He was so upset that at this point Kim made a decision to produce Buddy in the flesh.

"Okay," she said, "I'll see if I can talk him into meeting you."

"Let's have a drink at the Park Lane."

"No, he hates bars. I'm telling you, he's a real nut." She was afraid that Bocz, to whom she had already assigned the part, might bump into someone who would say, "Hi, Lew!"

"Will he come over here?" David asked. "I'll cook a dinner. I'll get the place cleaned up."

"I'll ask him," Kim said.

With her roommate Sami acting as the persecuted sister, Kim and Lew Bocz arrived for dinner at David's house on Saturday evening, February 9. David cooked a lamb stew. Bocz was silent and glowering. He and Kim and David argued politics. David contended that we had backed the wrong regime in Saigon and were doing it again now with Marcos in the Philippines. Kim said no, America's historical destiny was to fight communism no matter who we had to lug along as an ally. Bocz contributed a tight-lipped monologue about manifest destiny and the domino theory which nobody really could hear properly.

Later David said to Kim, "Your brother-in-law isn't as nasty as you painted him to be. But he sure is weird. And *grim*. Did he like me? Will he let me come to his house?"

"David, things take time."

She saw David once again, and then, on the afternoon before Valentine's Day, without calling to say goodbye or letting him know that she was going, Kim said to hell with it and flew to Acapulco.

It had come up suddenly: Mike Manela was going with one of her friends, a woman named Anita McCartney who had originally tried to pick up Sami in a bar and later become romantically involved with Mike. Anita said to her, "Why don't you and Sami come, too? We can sit on the beach and work out nutty new things for you to tell your killer boyfriend."

"Jesus!" Kim blanched. "Don't you ever let Mike know that you and

Sami know about David West! If that got back to Clyde, the old boy would kick me out on my ear!"

But couldn't she lead a normal life? Couldn't she have fun? The foursome flew down to Acapulco on Wednesday, February 13—Mike and Anita shared one room on Condesa Beach, Kim and Sami another—and they were back on Sunday. By then she was worried: had he written her off? She discussed it with her guru.

"Don't make him jealous," Bocz warned her. "Show him the Polaroid shots you took on the beach but tell him that *I* took them. You're with your sister and me. Tell him it was a business trip—Mike and Anita work for me, you can say. How could he guess what your real relationship is with Sami? Tell him I wouldn't let you call to say goodbye."

She called David that evening. He screeched, "Where the fuck were you?"

A worried Kim blurted out the story she'd worked out with Bocz. And she was back, wasn't she?

"I've got to see you," David said strongly.

At the office the next morning, February 18, Kim told Denise Moseley she was ready. She thought he would talk.

"Should I call Gil Schultz?"

Kim knew the risks, but she wanted this badly. (Bocz had said, "There's not just a book in it. There's the distinct possibility of a TV movie.")

"Call him," Kim said.

Denise reached Gil Schultz at Homicide and identified herself as an operative at Clyde Wilson's office. "You saw Kim Paris recently, about the Campbell murders? I'm supposed to get together with you and Sgt. Motard, so we can orchestrate this deal on Kim and David West."

Schultz laughed thinly. "Right, okay, I remember. I gave your friend a hard time, didn't I? Where do y'all want to take us to lunch?"

It's playtime for these guys, Denise realized.

That afternoon, on the off chance that something might come of it, Schultz dropped in on Officers Ray White and Ron Knotts of HPD's Criminal Intelligence Division (CID), and together they worked out a tentative plan for Kim to carry a hidden transmitter. (Schultz was all for the wiretapping of private citizens: "*I* got nothing to hide," he liked to say. "Do *you*?")

The next day Denise Moseley took Schultz and Motard to lunch, with Kim, at Foley's restaurant in Greenway Plaza. The detectives smiled and smirked. "Is it like *Charlie's Angels,* Ms. Moseley?"

Kim's risking her ass, Denise thought, and these guys think it's a joke.

And here I am, another woman, vouching for her credibility. Fuck you, you slob.

"Whatever you say, girls. Just tell us what you want us to do."

"I told you," Denise said calmly. "I want you to set up a way to tape Kim's conversation with David West."

"That's already taken care of," Schultz said. "When do you want to do it?"

Denise turned to Kim.

"Right away," Kim said.

"Tomorrow night suit you, Ms. Paris?"

"Tomorrow night will be fine."

"Well, honey, remember, if you don't get a confession the first night, don't worry about it. I mean, you're gonna do the best you can. Just try again."

They figure it's going to be a good party, Denise decided, and they'll put in a lot of overtime.

Kim went to see Lew Bocz that evening and asked him how he thought she should handle it.

Go for broke, Bocz counseled. He had had some frustrating experiences in his life with women and he thought he knew how David West felt. By now his balls were probably turning a dark shade of blue. "So get hysterical. Walk out on him. He's a wimp, he'll try to stop you—you can bet on it. Tell him that with you, life's all or nothing. You're ready to give your all. Tell him you need a gesture of trust on his part. A big one, Davey darlin'. *The* big one."

On a cool Wednesday evening, February 20, Ray White of CID and Gil Schultz drove out in the CID van to Clyde Wilson's suburban office. A second police car, an unmarked red Camaro, followed. P. M. Clinton was sick with the flu, at home, and Mike Manela took his place. Ray White and his partner, Ron Knotts, wired Kim by putting a small compact-sized Nagra transmitter in her purse under a wad of Kleenex. White was attentive to her, and worried.

He's the only one gives a damn, Kim thought.

"Don't drop the purse," White said, "and don't leave it behind when you go to the powder room, because if he gets snoopy and looks inside it—"

"I get the picture," Kim said, remembering the terror of Treat Williams in *Prince of the City*.

Knotts installed a tracking device in Kim's VW—"So we'll always know where you are," he explained. Kim felt better. She had faith in hi-tech, and hi-tech was now on her side. Denise and Mike Manela climbed into the van with Schultz and White, while Motard and Knotts slid into the Camaro.

"So long, guys," Kim said, grinning nervously. "Have a nice evening."

The three-vehicle caravan took off for Montrose. Twenty minutes later Kim knocked on David's door.

The van and the Camaro were parked at the corner of Waugh Drive and Nevada Street, one block north of Vermont. In the van Schultz kept yawning. The reel-to-reel Nagra tapes whirred above his head as the CID team listened to David West's futile attempt to seduce the woman he knew as Teresa Neele.

"I'm a very sexual person," David said. "I want to hold you and kiss you and love you. . . . I'm giving, I'm not taking. . . . I'm pouring my guts out to you. . . . What I'm trying to say about sexuality is that I, God, I can wait, I can wait, but—"

"This is pitiful," Schultz said.

White agreed. "What an asshole."

"Here's a guy couldn't make out in a whorehouse. Oops"—Schultz turned to Denise—"Excuse me."

Kim then told David, "I'm taking you out to dinner at Tony's."

"I've never been there," he said. "I can't afford it."

"Neither can I," Kim said, "but I'll tell you what. We'll go to dinner at Tony's, and then halfway through the meal . . . "

By now they were out the door of the house and in the car. Schultz, at the wheel of the van parked around the corner, turned the ignition key and kicked the engine into life. At that moment the tape broke. Nothing but static.

Kim's VW vanished around the corner.

"Shit!" White howled.

"Don't worry," said Schultz. "What are we missing?"

The Camaro, with Motard as wheel man and Knotts sitting beside him, kept them in view. At one point Kim made a sharp and illegal left turn from the righthand lane.

"What would she do," Knotts asked, "if a cop pulled her over and gave her a ticket?"

"You're a cop. Find out," Motard said, laughing.

Kim stopped her car not at Tony's in the Galleria area, but a mile short of there in the parking lot of a sushi bar called Yako's.

The van caught up and pulled into a parking spot across the street. Ten minutes later the police and the two private investigators were treated to the following discourse by David West.

"You can't get this fish here in America. It's caught in Japan and packed in ice and flown by Japan Airlines directly over here . . . and you mix in the teriyaki sauce with a little bit of the wasabi and what you have is a hot teriyaki sauce, and then you take it with your chopsticks, you know how to use chopsticks?"

"This is starting to give me an appetite," White said in the van.

"Raw fucking fish?" Schultz was shocked.

Most of the conversation in the noisy sushi restaurant was unintelligible to the listeners. At 10:05 P.M. Kim and David left. Driving back to Vermont, the van had difficulty keeping up with the VW, and that conversation was lost, too. Inside the house David discovered that Wickie Weinstein and a friend were in the living room. They had just finished a joint and had begun smoking another. David and Kim sat down with them. The conversation ranged from a debate over the ownership of a Batman button to being stoned once upon a time in Connecticut.

In the van, with the tapes running, Denise Moseley let her head sink into her hands. She ground her teeth. This is a farce, she thought. No, *worse* than a farce. It's not funny, it's not interesting, and it's not getting us anywhere. You can't understand half of what they're saying.

She didn't dare look at Gil Schultz. His boredom seemed to stream out of every pore and fill the van like poison gas. She heard him rock his chair back and forth on the floor. Denise peeked at her watch. It was 11:42.

"Go until midnight?" Ray White whispered to Schultz.

Schultz nodded very slightly.

Just as Schultz's head dipped and his eyes began to glaze into sleep, David West kicked his friends out.

Go for it, Denise thought. *Now.*

"I have to go," Kim said. "I probably won't see you for a while."

Denise was afraid to look at Schultz or White.

David slid into the front seat of the VW, next to Kim at the wheel. And they began to argue. The argument went on and on until Denise was hardly paying attention. Kim was yelling, David was protesting. The words blurred, made no sense. Kim was hysterical. This is all wrong, Denise thought. This is the end of the relationship.

90

Denise felt her own eyelids drooping. She willed them to stay open. She could barely understand Kim's words blasting over the loudspeaker in the van. She thought she heard Schultz begin to lightly snore. Ray White reached up to turn the volume down.

For a while Denise barely listened.

At two minutes to midnight David West said quietly to Kim Paris, "Okay, I'll tell you. . . . I killed both of Cindy's parents."

"And you could have heard a pin drop in that van," Denise told Clyde Wilson, in his office the next morning. "Schultz's eyes popped open so hard they nearly jumped out of their sockets. I've never known a silence like that in my life. You didn't hear a breath. That was the *neatest* thing! And then David West started talking about Cindy Ray, with all these details that only the killer would know, like *'She begged me to do it, and I wanted to do it. She offered me a lot of money. She stood there with me and I shot each of them three times.'* And after that, Clyde, those policemen just couldn't do enough for us. They had their evidence. They had their confession to take to the D.A. They were so happy they wanted to hug and kiss me. Their case was solved, they thought."

When the night was over, an exhausted Kim went back to drink a few beers with Mike Manela at his house. She was thrilled. She felt a sense of accomplishment she had never known before.

"I did it, Mike! I showed them."

"You certainly did."

She was thinking about Lew Bocz's book, and the movie. Did she need Lew Bocz? Was he the right person? Probably not. She would have to talk to someone about that and make some solid, farseeing plans.

"You better go home and get some sleep," Mike said.

Kim drove off happily into the 3 A.M. darkness.

Early in the morning Gil Schultz hand-delivered the tapes to the District Attorney's Office. That afternoon, after he had listened carefully for the better part of two hours, Assistant District Attorney Rusty Hardin went before a grand jury. He asked for and received a bill of indictment against David West.

The case against Cynthia Campbell Ray was not quite as solid. The best that HPD could do was a probable cause warrant, which meant that the district attorney of Harris County had filed (or was about to file) a complaint with the court stating that an officer of HPD Homicide believed that she had committed murder.*

"We need more," the prosecutor said, and Schultz relayed the message.

That Thursday evening Kim went back for more. David was drinking beer at the Park Lane on West Alabama when Kim honked her horn and picked him up. They went to the Café Moustache to drink wine. David prattled on, while the tapes in the police van whirred. *Details,* Mosier and then the D.A.'s Office had asked for. Amid the clatter of dishes and background music, punctuated by occasional discussions with the waitress about the proper wine to order, David offered up details in profusion.

"*Pow pow pow.* That loud a sound, but nobody heard anything. The maid that lives in the back of the house didn't hear it. The kids had to go wake her up and bring her in to call the police. That always amazes me. I thought the fuckin' neighbors and everybody would be running out of the fuckin' houses. . . . I was using another person's car, and I switched plates. So even if somebody saw that car, it wouldn't have the same plate. . . .

"Cindy was wearing a mask, too. She didn't actually stay to see it, but she was there. She's the one that fuckin' planned it. And we trained each other, we sat there trying to think of everything the cops could ask. . . . She pointed out all the emotional shit that they had done to her. She's going to give me $25,000. I don't feel any remorse. All I did was administer justice."

The gun could never be found, he said. It was buried somewhere under water. By now it would be "a big hunk of rust."

At 11:30 they left the Café Moustache and drove back along Westheimer. "I'm out of cigarettes," Kim said, veering the car into a Circle K convenience store. This was all arranged; she jumped out, in enough of a hurry that she forgot to put the car in gear.

The police van bumped up next to the VW. Gil Schultz and Ray White hurtled out, .38s drawn.

---

* Dated February 23, 1985, the complaint listed a felony charge of capital murder and stated: "Before me, the undersigned District Attorney of Harris County, Texas, this day appeared . . . Sgt. Gilbert C. Schultz, HPD, who under oath says that he has good reason to believe and does believe that . . . CYNTHIA HELEN RAY . . . on or about June 19, 1982 . . . intentionally and knowingly caused the death of VIRGINIA CAMPBELL, hereafter styled the Complainant, by shooting the Complainant with a gun, and the Defendant committed the murder for remuneration and the promise of remuneration, namely, money . . . AGAINST THE PEACE AND DIGNITY OF THE STATE." Against David West there was an indictment using the same language.

"Police! Freeze!"

A drunk standing by the door of the Circle K heard the cry and raised his hands. The VW was starting to roll backward into the street. A shocked David reached over to jam it into reverse. Schultz's finger tightened on the trigger. . . .

———————

Down at Reisner Street they held him overnight in the fifth-floor city jail. They waited for a further confession, a corroboration of what he'd told Kim Paris. David West didn't offer it. His face looked bleached, deathlike. It wasn't until early in the morning that he said, "I want to make a phone call."

At the same time J. C. Mosier telephoned all his media contacts, announcing that "an unidentified man, age twenty-eight," had been arrested in the Campbell murder case. The story went out on news broadcasts and morning TV, so that Denise Moseley heard it at 5:30 A.M. on KPRC radio.

Promptly at 7 A.M. Kim Paris picked up the telephone and began dialing Cindy Ray's number. With Schultz and Motard she had prepared the following script.

"I'm David West's new girlfriend. They've just arrested him, and he says he's got to have that $25,000 you owe him for killing your parents, or he'll confess and you'll both go down the drain. We've got to meet. . . ."

And at that meeting Cindy Ray would say something stupid that would implicate her, and Kim would tape *that*, too.

Great idea. Except that when Kim called, a dozen or more times, there was no answer.

Schultz began to fidget. Cindy still had most of the $25,000 she'd received in early January, Schultz wrongly assumed. Certainly enough of it, if she heard about David's arrest, to finance a bus trip south and a disappearance into the mountains of Mexico. She'd abandon the house. What good would the house do her if she was wanted for murder?

Late in the afternoon of February 22, with some shaky foreboding that if they waited any longer the case would collapse around their ears and HPD would look like nincompoops, Schultz made a decision. Carl Kent and his new partner, Jerry Novak, parked their car in front of Cindy's apartment at 2301 Kingston, between Montrose and River Oaks, and set up surveillance.

Rarely did Cindy Ray go out and stay out, but this was one of those times. The detectives waited two hours; then a car drew up and a fat young woman squeezed from the front seat and entered the front door. Must be her, Kent thought, although she didn't look much like the photograph he'd seen. The detectives waited another hour; they had no warrant yet for her arrest. A young neighbor noticed the police stakeout and, possibly motivated by some form of honor among neighbors, knocked on Cindy's door to warn her.

"If she'd taken a walk out the back of the house," Kent said later, "she could have been long gone."

But she came out the front door, a bulky presence. Within minutes, bewildered, weeping with frustration, she was arrested for the murder of her parents 978 days ago.

After all, they had David West's word for it. West's admission was against self-interest, so it had to be true.

All of it had to be true, didn't it?

———————————

Nothing appeared in the Houston newspapers until Saturday morning, February 23, more than thirty-six hours after the arrest at the Circle K. But then the Houston *Post* bannered it across page one: "2 ARRESTED IN DEATHS OF LAWYER, WIFE," with the subhead: *"Daughter, alleged triggerman held in execution-style killings."* Accompanying the story in pink-tinted full color were two photographs, one of Kim Paris, and one of Cynthia Campbell Ray with her new attorney, Roy Beene. One story recapped the two-and-a-half-year-old murders and discussed the case and the arrests in general, and another story profiled Kim Paris, with the edifying headline: "I don't feel sorry for him. . . ."

On Sunday, February 24, the Houston *Chronicle* ran a page one full-color photograph of Clyde Wilson seated at his desk with a dazed-looking Kim and a bland Denise Moseley hovering over his shoulder, and the headline proclaimed, "Daughter, 28, Held in Mom's Hired Murder." A second headline under the photograph quoted Clyde on the subject of Kim: "This was her chance to earn her spurs."

The focus was clear: the two women—the blue-eyed private eye and the fat brown-eyed alleged murderess of her parents—were the stars of this show. David West, who had admitted to *"pow pow pow* . . . all I did was administer justice," was odd man out.

The only thing missing from all the newspaper accounts was any attempt to say *why* David West and Cynthia Ray had murdered her parents. No one knew. Or if they knew, they weren't saying. It seemed at the time as if no one even cared.

8

The room had that peculiar stale smell caused by cigarette smoke mixing with artificial cold air pumped through ducts. Cindy Ray had given Motard a crumpled dollar bill, and he had gone to the machine in the hallway and come back with a pack of Benson & Hedges Lights. Freed from the restraining handcuffs, she smoked steadily.

Gil Schultz, in his small office at the rear of the third floor down at Police Headquarters, said to her, "You have the right to remain silent, and anything you say can and will be held against you"—and then finished reading aloud the rest of her rights, including that of legal counsel.

Her face gone milk-white as she inhaled the cigarette smoke and barked a steady cough, Cindy said softly, "Can I make a telephone call?"

She made that call to a thirty-two-year-old man who had once worked as a security guard in the building where a lawyer named Roy Beene officed. Roy Beene, with mild glee at the eccentricity of the supporting cast in this murder mystery, always referred to him as "Queer Bob." Beene said later, "I suppose when he worked in my building I treated Bob like a human being instead of a simple faggot, and he remembered that, and that's why, out of the 250 full-time criminal lawyers in Houston, he picked me."

Roy Beene was unmistakably a Texan, but he had spent seven years as an assistant U.S. attorney in Newark, across the river from the pleasures of Manhattan, and by the time he returned to private practice in Houston he was an aficionado of sophisticated decadence. Sartorially, however, he was a mess: his tie barely reached his collar button and his shirt all too often managed to hang out of his trousers under his open suit jacket. His trousers were an inch too short or long. He was a bachelor in his early forties, with a graying beard, thick glasses that hid surprisingly kind, pale blue eyes, a protruding round belly, and a high vulgar laugh.

On February 22, 1985, an agitated Queer Bob called him and asked: "Will you represent a friend of mine? She's just been arrested for murder." Bob at the time shared Cindy's apartment, although, one tended to assume, not her bed.

"Maybe," Beene said cautiously. "What's her name?"

"Cynthia Campbell Ray. And I'm sure she's innocent of what they say she's done."

95

"They always are, Robert," Roy cackled, "until they're proved guilty."

Roy had read the newspapers with some interest, for he had known Jim Campbell professionally. He once described the older lawyer as "chickenshit, nasty, and unethical."

He asked Bob, "Does she want me, or does she want a court-appointed lawyer?" In other words: can she afford to pay?

"She wants *you*," Bob insisted.

Roy jumped into his car, a computerized steel-gray Cadillac with empty Mexican beer bottles clinking on heaps of newspapers on the floor in the front seat, and drove down to Reisner Street. He arrived to discover his prospective client in a little room on the third floor in the Homicide Division. Sgt. Gil Schultz was interrogating her, with Carl Kent looking on.

". . . Ms. Ray, don't you feel bad about your children being there, seeing all that blood?"

"Hang on there," Roy Beene said. "I represent this little girl."

"You do? Bullshit." Carl Kent took Roy aside. "You're just trying to get money out of her. You probably want this brick building she owns over on Kingston."

Gil Schultz, according to Roy Beene, was "a decent human being." That was one of Roy's favorite phrases, always spoken with a tremor in his voice, and with a widening of watery eyes behind thick lenses. "He's a *decent* human being!"—as if Roy's faith in humankind's goodness, if it was to survive in the Texas legal world, needed not only replenishing from external sources but also periodic affirmation from some hardy fount within Roy himself.

He meant in this instance that Schultz could have kept the invading defense attorney at bay in an anteroom, could meanwhile have dug for a confession, probed for a slip of the tongue that might prove a wedge to be hammered on in court—but, because he was "a decent human being," Schultz let Roy into the little room with a brave smile and no delay. And in the space of no more than three minutes, for paperwork, not advantage, Schultz released Cindy Ray into her new lawyer's custody within the confines of Police Headquarters.

Roy sat down with her in another of those dreary and chilling little rooms. Silently, although he himself was no lean hunk, he marveled at her size. Often he wondered, how did a young woman *get* that big? You'd have to work at it, he decided, or be utterly uncaring, or be physically ill with a thyroid condition . . . or worse. She wasn't physically ill. But upon entering the Houston City Jail, Cindy officially weighed in at 264 pounds. She was swollen, full of creases, nearly double the width of a normal woman her age, which was twenty-eight. Her legs were solid enough to support a butcher block.

And yet on top of this awkward and unaesthetic structure was the face of a pretty girl. Buried in flesh, but clearly there.

She told Roy Beene that she was innocent, that David West was a very sick young man.

Roy heard her out. He didn't ask her if she did it or not. A criminal defense lawyer never asks a client that, not even if the police catch him standing over a corpse with a smoking gun. If the client *tells* you . . . well, that might be your bad luck. But you never ask. At best: "Tell me what happened."

She squeaked: *"Mr. Beene, help me! Save my life!"* He thought, you poor, fat girl . . . you sad creature . . . you dumb cunt.

But he said to her, "Yes, I can help you. But first you have to shut up for a while and listen to me."

Roy suspected already that the state had a flimsy case, for Texas had an unusual legal concept called "the accomplice-witness rule." The federal system of justice didn't have it, and few other state judiciaries were required to enforce it in so strict a form. It held that the State of Texas could not obtain a conviction on the uncorroborated testimony of a party to a crime. Before the courts would allow such a conviction, there had to be other independent evidence that tended to connect the defendant to the offense.

Johnny Holmes, the flamboyant multimillionaire district attorney of Harris County, explained it this way to a visiting writer from New York. "Let's say you and I rob a little old 7-Eleven. I drive the car, you go in with the pistol. You get identified, caught, and the cops tell you they're gonna prosecute. 'Goddamn Yankee pen-pusher, we'll teach you to fuck around with us redneck cowboys!' You say, 'Look, I want to cut a deal. You won't believe who the wheel man was! A public official in Houston shared in this endeavor, and for a little consideration, I'll finger him for you.' "

In a federal court, that might work. But never in Texas, where, more than most places, a man is entitled to scratch his own itch. "The problem is," Holmes said, "we tell too many tall tales in Texas . . . we're naturally skeptical when a person involved in a dark deed wants to improve his position by making a deal. We are so skeptical in Texas that we won't allow a conviction without corroboration from another source."

Roy Beene had already heard through courthouse gossip that there were no witnesses to the Campbells' murder except two scared little kids whose heads were buried in sleeping bags. No murder weapon or fingerprints found. David West's surreptitiously taped confession, naming Cindy as the author of the murders and his accomplice in carrying them out *("She begged me to do it . . . she stood there with me and I shot each of them three times"),* could never be used against her unless West vouched for its accuracy. West, as far as Roy Beene knew, to date had said no more than, "Hey, I'm not crazy! You think I was telling the truth to Kim Paris? No way!"

And the sonofabitch might not be lying, Roy Beene thought.

But above all, the accomplice-witness rule shielded Cynthia Ray like a steel suit of armor. Not even an indictment was possible unless additional independent evidence existed; she was being held only under the probable-cause warrant. Because it was capital murder, punishable by death, the court had refused to set bond. Under Texas law she would either have to be released or indicted within 60 days. If Roy Beene at any time demanded a speedy trial, the state would be required to prosecute within 120 days or drop all charges forever.

As lawyers often do, usually to the chagrin of their clients, Roy decided to bide his time. But he remembered Shakespeare writing that "there was never yet philosopher that could endure the toothache patiently." The toothache was Cindy's, not his.

"They're going to put you in jail," he said, facing her in the gray-walled little room at Homicide, which he had inspected for a minute or two in a hunt for bugs other than cockroaches. "You'll be in a big cell—it's called a tank—with six or seven other women. Most of them will be black. Most of them will be scumbags. After all, let's face it"—he giggled evilly—"that's the sort of people you find in jails, my dear. And you can be sure that at least one or two of them are snitches. You can also be sure that you're not smart enough to figure out which are the ones. *So don't talk to anyone.* You hear me? I'm going out to investigate. That is, as soon as we settle on the fee."

"How much do you want, Mr. Beene?" Cindy timidly asked.

"This is a capital murder case. Rusty Hardin's the best they've got, and a man who never gives up. If they try you for the murder of your Daddy and we get a not guilty, they'll want to try you then for the murder of your mother. Of course if we win one trial, we can win two. Let's say about $200,000."

Cindy gasped.

"You're looking at half a year of trial work," Roy explained. "I'm going to hire an appellate lawyer named Will Gray. He's one of the best. His fee's included. And an investigator. I pay his costs, too."

She was broke, she whined. The police were speculating that the lump sum payment of $25,000 she had received from her parents' estate was the payoff money for David West, or that she'd squirreled it away for hard times, but they were wrong. The $25,000 had been disbursed by Steve Simmons, who had handled the lawsuit against her sisters: $3,500 to Simmons; $14,700 to Allied Bank (repayment of a loan, cosigned by

Simmons, the purpose of which had been to pay off Cindy's $11,000 debt to her former civil lawyer, Bill Estes); and the remaining $6,800 was in the bank but under Simmons's care. She couldn't get at it. Her husband, Makhlouf, the expatriate Syrian, was an impoverished student who worked as a waiter. They were separated, she wept, and he no longer cared what happened to her. All she had left from the inheritance was her tiny little house at 2301 Kingston.

The house was what Texans call a fourplex: a two-story red brick building with four small rentable apartments. Her father had acquired it some years ago in lieu of a legal fee. He had let Cindy and his mother-in-law live in it while he was alive.

"I'll go have a look at it," Roy said.

That evening he drove over to Kingston, a block between fashionable River Oaks and the trendy Montrose area. The brick building was square, shabby, poorly cared for, an unaesthetic box. Like Cindy Ray, Roy mused. Still, the dirt it stood on had to be worth something.

Lawyers were in the habit of taking property in lieu of cash, but there was always risk: a thorough title search took too long. Roy had been burned before.

He went back to the jail the next afternoon and told Cindy that he would gamble and make a deal with her. He would accept the building as his fee, no matter how long it took for him to win her case. If she didn't want to do that, she should file an affidavit of indigency and ask for a court-appointed lawyer. That would be free. Roy would retire gracefully, as of now. No charge.

"Will the lawyer they appoint for me be as good as you, Mr. Beene?" Cindy was always overtly respectful to her lawyers; she never called them by their first names.

"Maybe better, maybe worse," Roy said truthfully, and added—fatefully, as it turned out—"but if you don't like him, you can usually get the judge to fire him and appoint you another one. Of course, you'll have to give up Kingston first, because as long as you own property you're not considered indigent."

"I can't do that!" Cindy alternately glared, wept, and yelled. Her voice was brassy and petulant, and then suddenly she would whimper, turn syrupy like a begging child. But finally she agreed to Roy's proposition. Her property didn't do her any good while she faced a capital murder charge.

Papers were signed and notarized. Roy filed the deed that afternoon.

In the nick of time, as it turned out, for the next morning the civil court froze all of Cindy's assets. But those assets were now zero, for Steve Simmons had already closed the account at Allied Bank and spirited away the balance of $6,800 in a bank check made out to his client (but destined never to reach her), and Roy Beene had the deed to Kingston. Presto-chango, within twenty-four hours Roy had transferred it to a Panamanian corporation in exchange for fishing rights off the coast of Chile.

Duval West III—David West's father—quit smoking cigarettes in October 1984. Four months later, when his son was arrested for murder, he started again, finishing off two to three packs of Carltons a day. His teeth were already yellow. His hair, his clothes, and especially his breath, exuded the smell of stale tobacco. Most people who spoke to him tried to keep a few feet away.

Duval was a sixty-eight-year-old electrical engineer, born in Muskogee, Oklahoma, but raised in Austin, Texas. His ancestors, the Duvals, had emigrated from France to Virginia in the eighteenth century. Just before World War II Duval transferred from the University of Texas to West Point, where he was graduated a second lieutenant. Although he was shy and often seemed evasive, on this issue he never equivocated: he would not have gone to the Point if it hadn't been the Depression and if World War II hadn't been looming. He spent that war in Persia and Iraq with the Signal Corps. Now, in 1985, he was a mild-mannered, myopic man, semi-retired, an amateur historian and collector of 78 rpm jazz records. In the cluttered darkness of the living room of his house on Kipling, only a few blocks from where David lived, stacks of records gathered dust along an entire wall. It was a gloomy house that he had bought in 1956 and shared with his second wife, Cecilia, a former fashion designer for the Alley Theater.

Duval West's telephone rang at 6 A.M. on Friday morning, February 22. At first he couldn't understand what his son David was saying. He was conscious of babbling: "You're in jail? You've been arrested? *For murdering Cindy's parents?*"

Duval felt his forehead and his extremities go cold. Then his heart seemed to soar toward his throat and he thought he would choke and die. He almost vomited, but he made an effort to control himself, until slowly the warmth returned to his head and the nausea subsided. His heart still beat rapidly but it seemed back in its place.

"I'll be right down."

This whole story couldn't possibly be true. His son and his son's old girlfriend were normal people: they didn't murder anyone. Duval made a pot of coffee and some buttered toast before he dared wake Cecilia, who had much the same reaction as her husband. But those were the worst moments and nothing ever equaled them. After that the Wests were remarkably calm and efficient.

Duval left Cecilia at home and drove alone to Police Headquarters—the city jail occupied its fifth floor. Downtown he was delayed almost an hour; he had to sign forms, trudge from office to office. Finally he was allowed to see David. But there was a thick glass plate between them, and they had to talk on a greasy black telephone with terrible static.

Duval said to his son, "Be very careful what you tell me. This phone is almost certainly bugged."

Bearing that in mind, a quick decision was made. David needed a lawyer. His father would go out and get one.

America is a nation with a complex tradition of violence, and we love the trappings of a good murder. As one Houston lawyer said, "If it had been a forty-five-year-old male detective who had broken this case, after a while it might have been just another case." But it was an extremely attractive twenty-three-year-old female detective with a name that might have been conjured up by a Hollywood press agent. One headline from a California newspaper summed up the media's general attitude. The Torrance *Daily Breeze* proclaimed: "Sexy Sleuth Sets a Super Love Trap To Snare Suspect."

A few days later Kim Paris said to a friend, "If I hear the phrase 'power of the pussy' one more time, I'm going to scream!"

Instead she kept her voice modulated. Guided by Clyde Wilson, her employer, and Marian Rosen, now her lawyer, she aimed her statements at maximum national exposure. Houston was instantly fascinated; then Texas; then, in a matter of twenty-four hours, the nation. Phyllis George, in an interview for a segment of *CBS Morning News*, introduced her guest as "Kim Paris, the private eye who trapped a murder suspect with love." *Time*, and then *People*, did a story. Said Eric Hanson, a Houston *Chronicle* reporter: "Just think of it! When I got to work on Friday no one had heard of her, and by that evening she was a celebrity!"

Since Carroll John Daly's creation of Race Williams in *Black Mask* magazine in 1923, through Dashiell Hammett's Continental Op and Raymond Chandler's Philip Marlow, right up to Travis McGee and television's bickering duo on *Moonlighting*, America had always loved private eyes. And now, in young, five-foot-nine-inch Kim Paris, it had one in the flesh. Female flesh! Within days of the investigative triumph her story and a photographic portrait became front-page news in France, Germany, and England, while in Kim's own country the talk shows were wooing and the telephones ringing with inquiries from publishers and film producers. Andy Griffith was going to play the part of Clyde, and Kim would be portrayed by Valerie Bertinelli. "No way," Kim said. She had her own ideas as to who should play her part. "I want control on how the story comes out. If they Hollywoodize this and make me into a South Texas tramp, I don't want to have to live with that." She contracted with Luce Press Clippings of New York for clippings at seventy five cents each. By the time she terminated the arrangement she claimed that her bill had come to $600, and she had received articles from as far away as Australia.

Prompting and censoring, Clyde Wilson stood by her side for every newspaper interview. He orchestrated her TV appearances and included his own mandatory presence in the package. "If I don't," he said to P. M. Clinton, "the law of self-preservation will prevail. She's got a big mouth, and she's more interested in herself than our agency." Beyond that he worried that she might say things in front of the television cameras that would endanger the State of Texas's case against David West. Clyde couldn't afford that kind of gaffe; he intended to keep on doing business in Texas long after the fuss over Kim's derring-do was over.

As a team they did *Good Morning America* and then the *Donahue* Show. In New York Kim, Clyde, P. M. Clinton, and Denise Moseley stayed at the St. Moritz Hotel on Central Park South. (Kim was broke again; she asked P. M. if she could borrow his credit card so that she could go to Bloomingdale's and buy a dress. P. M. said, "I can't do that, Kim. My wife would *kill* me.") Clyde paid for the air fares and the rooms —he didn't want charges of impropriety to compromise his firm's testimony in the case. And if the questions on either program grew hostile, he figured, he could walk off the show and be within his rights. He owed the networks zip.

Before the *Donahue* interview began, the host told Kim and Clyde that he wanted them to call him Phil and he would call them by their first names. Clyde drawled, "With your permission, I'd like to call you Mr. Donahue, because down in Texas we don't call a man by his first name until we've decided whether we like him or not."

Donahue started to argue but didn't get far. Clyde had paid his own way.

That set the tone for the hour. A bright-eyed Kim, a stubborn Clyde, and an impassive Denise Moseley went on camera in company with Robert Blecker, an NYU Law School professor who commented, generally favorably, on their recent activities. Clyde appeared in a gray suit and cowboy boots, and Kim was all sweetness despite her heavy black eye makeup. Phil Donahue, bounding up and down the aisles to thrust his microphone into the faces of his primarily female constituency, compared Kim's exploits to those of television's *A Team*. He called Kim "brave and beautiful."

But then he asked his audience if they would approve of private eyes taping *their* conversations. And what if they were only *suspected* of some wrongdoing? After all, David West hadn't yet been found guilty, hadn't even been indicted by a grand jury the night Kim Paris got him to blurt, "I killed both of her parents." The Supreme Court's *Miranda* rulings had taken away some of the treasured tools of police officers and district attorneys, presumably for good reason. Why did Kim Paris have the right to use those tools?

"It used to be called a deposition," Donahue said. "Now it's a tape recorder in a purse in a fancy restaurant!" He then took Clyde to task for being "a good ole boy" from Texas not only willing but proud to string up cattle rustlers from the nearest cottonwood tree.

Clyde shot from the hip. "So far this 'good ole boy' in front of you—that you don't want to quite trust—has gotten a killer off the streets."

The audience broke into applause, and Donahue shook his head in distress. "So the means justify the end?"

"In this case," Clyde said cordially—the last word, as it turned out—"*these* means justify *these* ends."

Kim Paris was launched, on her way to status as a national heroine. Where the rule-bound police had failed, she had succeeded. Now only two obstacles remained: the trial, where she would testify as to the validity of the tapes—and, of course, a jury's conviction of David West as the murderer.

But if they didn't convict him, Kim was thinking, and he was let free, she wondered if it would be safe for her to stay in Houston. David would never forgive her. If he killed once and got away with it, why not again?

———————

David's father had no experience with the law and didn't know any lawyers. Duval West went home from the city jail on February 22 and began making phone calls. That afternoon, through the recommendation of a college fraternity brother, he hired a lawyer named Eugene Nettles, a former assistant district attorney in Harris County who had now been in private practice for five years. In effect, Duval put his son's

103

life into the hands of a stranger, an act oddly reminiscent of what his son had recently done.

Gene Nettles met with Duval at the Heritage Club on the fiftieth floor of Allen Center. The club was cool and decorous and the cocktail hour pianist played "I'll Take Manhattan." From the six high windows in the lounge you could see Houston's intertwined freeways pretzeling toward all points of the compass, with cars that seemed to move silently, like mechanical toys on tracks. In a westerly direction Memorial Drive curled toward the verdant suburbs and the flat outlands of Harris County. An anonymous wit had once said, "Texas is a place where you can look farther to see less than anywhere else on earth."

At thirty-five Nettles was an exceptionally handsome man, with straight black hair, dark liquid eyes that snapped and glowed, a prosperous mustache, and smooth cheeks that promised to become pudgy with age. But what struck others most forcefully was his pure Texas baritone (He said "ah cain't" for "I can't" and "doh-er" for "door"), sharklike when it needed to bite, silky when it needed to cajole, loud whether or not he liked it to be loud. It was a dominating voice and definitely not one you would want to have directed against you if you were in a witness chair testifying for the opposition. It was the kind of voice that seemed to exemplify what Howard Cosell had once called "Texas cruel."

A Houston boy, after private school Gene had galloped off to the University of Texas at Austin, where he put in four hell-raising years of beer, dope, women, and occasional study. In 1971, simmering down, he entered the South Texas Law School in Houston, passed the bar, and was accepted by Harris County as an assistant district attorney. In a few years he married and went into private practice. Now for the most part he handled civil litigation, but as soon as Duval West called him he made up his mind to take the case.

Up in the Heritage Club he said to the anxious father, "When you're in law school, and then starting out as a young trial lawyer, this is the kind of case you dream of. It's the zenith of a lawyer's career, to try a big capital murder case. It's exciting! It's challenging! It's a joust! I— *love* —it!"

Duval West explained: "We're going to back David all the way in this. Whatever it costs, we'll pay. His mother and I ask just one favor of you. We assume that he didn't do it, but we'd prefer that you didn't comment on that assumption. In other words, don't tell us if he's innocent or guilty. Can you agree to that?"

Gene Nettles stared at the father of his client for a long moment, and then nodded his agreement.

He hurried over to the Harris County Jail to see David, and two

104

hours later he invaded the office of Rusty Hardin, the prosecutor. They were old friends from Gene's time as an assistant district attorney; they had begun their legal careers as allies. Now they were friendly opponents. Rusty played part of the first night's tape for Gene, then handed him cassettes of both nights and a copy of the state's rudimentary transcript thus far.

"This all you got?" Gene asked.

"They're dynamite, and you know it," the prosecutor said.

"What you can hear of them," said Gene. "And even that ain't enough to convict. You can't win this one, Rusty. Don't even *think* of offering me a deal. I'm in this to the end. My boy's going to walk out of that courtroom laughing like Bugs Bunny."

Rusty smiled. He had been through such gamesmanship many times before. The two lawyers were like boxers at a weigh-in before a championship fight.

The next morning Gene met again with Duval West, and this time, at Gene's request, Cecilia West was there, too.

"Mr. West," Gene said, "it's going to be a hell of a trial. Rusty Hardin loves publicity, so we're gonna have us a real dogfight, a real stompin' show. The tapes of this so-called confession to Kim Paris are one of the two keys to what will happen. They're garbled. They're real hard to understand. And what I felt when I heard them," he added guardedly, eyes glowing with portent, "is that drugs and booze were used to get your son to say whatever it was he *did* say. So I'm filing a motion to keep the tapes from being allowed into evidence."

Duval nodded in satisfaction. He had picked the right lawyer. "You mentioned *two* keys. . . ."

"The other one is this Kim Paris woman. I want to hire a private detective to dig into her character. Fight fire with fire. ('Far with far,' Nettles said.) We'll just have to discuss whether it's financially feasible, because it's going to have to be added to the bill. But when that bitch takes the witness stand," he promised with gusto, "I'm going to cut her up so small you could put her in a jar and feed her to a baby."

"What do you think the chances are for an acquittal?" Duval asked.

Nettles covered up, like a boxer on the ropes struck in the kidneys. "I don't know, Mr. West. Hard to say. Depends on a whole lot of factors."

Like, for example, on whether David really had done it. David had *said* he hadn't, and that was good enough for Nettles. But that didn't make it true or false.

Nettles didn't say that to his client's father, or even allude to it. He knew better. In a murder trial, you can't predict. And you can't make statements about guilt or innocence. Only a jury can do that.

Gene Nettles had to know all there was to know about the young man he was defending. "I'm going to talk to David," he said, "and then to you both. And then I want to know all about this woman, Cynthia Campbell Ray."

9

David West said, "I was born in Houston on May 4, 1956. I grew up in the Montrose area, where there weren't a lot of kids to play with. I wasn't a tough kid. I had no brothers and my half-sister was much older and never lived with us, so my childhood was a lonely one. And then it became a dangerous one.

"When I was thirteen, there was no busing, but the Supreme Court had decreed you had to go to whatever school the state told you to. The zones were arbitrary. My parents told me, 'This is the law, you have to do it.' I went to Miller Junior High, in the ghetto on the other side of Main Street. The first day I came walking up and there's fifteen hundred black kids, one other white guy, and four Mexican girls. I was a skinny little scared white kid. The black kids crowded round me. 'Oooooh, look what we got here!' They reached out and touched my hair, as if they hadn't ever been that close to a white person, and said, 'Wow, it's so soft!' Then they stole my bike and beat me up. I got beat up every day by groups of blacks while the rest of them stood around and laughed.

"My parents thought I was exaggerating—they couldn't believe it was as bad as that. I saw a running gun battle on the school grounds between the police and what was known as the Freeway Gang, some kids that hung out underneath the freeway. And there was a riot. I was alone in the library that day—it was like an earthquake. You felt it before you heard it. Hundreds of kids pounding through the halls. A fight had started in the cafeteria, and everyone joined in.

"The day I finally got fed up and fought back, and busted this kid's nose, he ran off to get his brothers. I said, 'To hell with this, my mama didn't raise a fool.' I never came back—I'd lasted maybe two weeks. I left the house every morning and went over to Sears and sat in the television sales department and watched their big demonstrator console TVs. Finally I started getting the evil eye from the sales people, and I decided to leave. It took almost to the end of the semester for the school to realize I was gone and to contact my parents.

"Then the City Council changed the zone laws, so that the line zigged where before it zagged, and I got sent to a different school. It was called Lincoln and it was on West Allen, on the edge of downtown—about 60 percent black, 30 percent Mexican, and the rest white. I wasn't afraid there. I had learned at the other school that you might as well fight back, because it's just another ass-beating in a mindless game of domination and aggression. If you're weak and they can pick on you, they'll do it, so you have to let them know that they're going to get hurt, too, and then maybe they won't mess with you. There were several other white guys in my position, and they were amazed when I'd look people right in the eye and say, 'Hey, fuck you, if you want to do it, do it.' And the black kids would freak out that a white boy had enough nerve to stand up.

"The other problem in my life was that my Dad considered himself an intellectual. My Mom didn't go to college. She just reads a lot. If you know what real intellectuals are, my Mom certainly isn't. But my Dad didn't do much except work and come home and read and watch public television and listen to Louis Armstrong, and he's a bottomless pit of historical knowledge. So I didn't have an average middle-class role model for a father. Don't get me wrong—he's a very fine man. He's very intelligent, extremely honorable, and has high morals without being some kind of Moral Majority hypocrite.

"My Dad thought that the physical was not something you should accentuate. He had been forced into athletics at West Point—as a result, I never got introduced to sports or got any good at them. I didn't even know the rules of baseball or football, and I couldn't participate, it would just handicap my team. I've only played a couple of games of baseball in my entire life. I was always the last one picked. They would argue about who got stuck with me."

David's parents decided to solve the problem by sending him to Allen Military Academy in Bryan, Texas, but David, as he put it, "wanted to get on with life and girls," and at the end of his junior year—in 1975, when he was seventeen—he left Allen and joined the Marine Corps. After boot camp in San Diego and a few other postings he served in Morocco for eighteen months, guarding naval installations. In the marines he took accelerated courses that gave him a high school diploma. He didn't see any combat.

While he was in the service his mother's aunt died. David inherited $100,000 in cash and stocks, including Exxon, Levi's, and Texaco. Cecilia West, acting as executor, put a down payment of $62,000 on the house on Vermont and bought a parcel of land for her son in Iola, Texas. When David got out of the marines in 1978 he sold most of the stock, then flew to Europe. Young, eager, still with close-cropped hair from the Corps, he traveled through Germany, France, and England for three months.

That grand tour over, he jetted back to Houston and began living in the house on Vermont. "He was supposed to remodel it," his mother said, "but instead of doing that he moved in there immediately, and these marine pals of his, as fast as they got out, they moved in with him. They just roosted there."

He tried college, and he worked at various jobs: an art major at St. Thomas, then a film and video major at the University of Houston. He tended bar at night. "I couldn't do either one right, wound up with no sleep, screwed up all the time, plus my bills kept mounting." His last job was working on high-rise structural steel construction, topping out the Allied Bank Plaza downtown. (Viewed from the air the building complex looks like a dollar sign.) "I worked for sixteen dollars an hour. You're seventy stories high, walking on a piece of steel that might be six inches wide. No net. Safety belt, yes, but it's not hooked up all the time. I was forcing myself to do it. The guys who had been doing it for years, they didn't care. They were smoking dope, drinking, taking downers, they were crazy." David quit and sold the land in Iola to live.

Cecilia West said, "I dragged my heels as much as possible, but I generally capitulated and gave him money when he asked for it, whenever he was out of a job and broke. By the time he was twenty-five, in 1982, there was only $6,000 left."

Wickie Weinstein, one of the pals who roosted at Vermont, described David and his environment. "Dave would go to a party and eat everything there. He bought a Trans Am. He bent the axle, tore it up, and he'd messed up everything to do with his Mustang before that. Dave loved guns, but he had no technical sense. His guns would just sit in the corner, rusting. If you had to use them, they wouldn't work. There are people who take a wrench and they strip the bolt every time: that was Dave West. He was ten years behind everything else, way back there in the early seventies in music and in muscle cars. All of us were thinking about new light fast Japanese cars, and Dave's thinking 350 and 450 monstrous heavy engines.

"I knew his parents a little bit. His mom was a drinker, very sharp, very eccentric and outspoken. He liked her but also hated her—she was always nagging at him to clean this, clean that, complaining all the time. Dave hated his dad. He just stayed home and drank wine and read books —hardly had a hand in raising Dave. Dave's main gripe about him was that he didn't care about anything and didn't do anything for him. Sent him away to military school . . . hey, man, that's a pretty cold way to bring up a child."

108

Cecilia West was close to her son. David often took his mother to local bars and introduced her to his friends. She was also close to his girl-friend, the love of his life, Cynthia Campbell Ray.

David quickly became aware of the similarities between the two women. Both were what he thought of as submissive. Neither drove a car or could ride a bicycle. Both loved fairy tales.

"Cindy confided in me," Cecilia West said, "in a way that she didn't confide in David. Cindy has so many wonderful qualities, but she doesn't fight. If something happens, she moans about it. She was like a puppy dog toward her parents. She was almost crawling and licking their feet and saying, 'Please, please, love me. I've done everything I could to please you. Why don't you love me?' So several times I was very annoyed with her, and I started asking myself, what would cause her to act like this? In particular the way she swung back and forth in her attitude toward her father. You could tell she loved him, and you could tell she hated and feared him. And yet she was fascinated by him, and she was proud of him. Just sick. Mixed up. So I asked, and she told me. Here would be a little dribble, and a little bit on further, and a little more. And finally it was just a flood. And I would be sick to my stomach listening to her, and yet trying to help her. Until one day I had to tell her what her father would seem like to the average person if they knew about this—just how disgusting, how despicable, he would be. And she was *amazed!* This wonderful, godlike creature!

"You have to know the scrambled-up child that was inside of all that and hear the things that she took so casually for granted about her own family. They were a dung heap. She was like something that was smashed but was still holding together."

Some of this Gene Nettles already knew from his talk with David. Cindy had told Cecilia West, and then David, that her father had begun sexually molesting her when she was thirteen years old. And to Kim Paris, with the tape running, David had said: *"She pointed out all the emotional shit that they had done to her. . . . All I did was administer justice."*

"Cindy of course had two grandmothers," Cecilia continued, "her father's mother, who she called 'Big Grandma,' because she's about six feet tall in her stocking feet, and 'Little Grandma,' her mother's mother, about five feet tall, who also lived in one of those apartments at Kingston. Now this is what *I* know," Cecilia stressed. "The little grandmother is vicious as a snapping turtle. She told lies about Cindy all around the neighborhood, and to the tenants in the building at Kingston, and then confessed to another person, 'I don't know why I did it. Cindy's the only one who's ever been decent to me.'

"Cindy dearly loved 'Big Grandma,' but when her own mother found out the deep affection there, she forbade Cindy to visit her. The big grandmother found out that Cindy had no toys, and so for Christmas she bought Cindy three beautiful dolls. And they didn't last till morning of the next day. Her sisters deliberately destroyed them.

"I took Cindy to the zoo. She was hysterical with joy, although she hated the idea of the cages. She wanted to go back, over and over again, to the bird house. When I taught her how to stuff a turkey she was as thrilled as if I had presented her with a mink coat. When she had a little money, or was making a little money, she bought caviar. She'd feed it to the dog. She brought David and the dog breakfast in bed. Another time someone gave her a big Irish setter. When I looked at it, I knew immediately that the dog was terribly ill. But Cindy had no idea until I told her. Then of course she was willing to do anything that was necessary to get the dog well."

Cecilia West told a story to Gene Nettles, the man who would fight to prove her son's innocence, that seemed to shed light into a cobwebbed corner. In late 1981 Cecilia, Cindy, and David were coming home, driving down Montrose Avenue near Vermont—"sedately," Cecilia claimed, "with David driving like silk"—when they were struck from behind, several times, within the space of a minute.

"A middle-aged man with a fiendish grimace on his face deliberately accelerated his car and rammed us again and again. None of us had ever seen him before. He must have been deeply upset about something. We never knew what it was.

"David stopped the car, but Cindy went completely to pieces. Her eyes are a sort of greenish-amber, and the pupils dilated. She tried to stand up in the car, and started screaming, *I won't do it again, Mother! I don't know what I've done, but please, I won't do it again. Please, stop it! I won't do it again. . . .*" And just absolutely shuddering, like a bowl of jelly. And her eyes black, and screaming.

"I had to grab her and pull her down. The bumpers were still hitting. David jumped out. He had only jogging shoes on his feet, a T-shirt, and blue jeans, which is practically his uniform. He gave a karate kick and kicked in the driver's side of the man's car, and then the other side, and then he kicked in the whole front part of the car each time the man tried to head the car at us. David went round and round the car. By the time it was over he must have done a thousand dollars worth of damage with just his feet.

"We went home. It took about an hour to completely calm Cindy.

110

And that," Cecilia West concluded, "is a story that illustrates the nature of those two young people. Cindy is a vulnerable and sick child. And there's nothing that David won't do to protect the ones he loves."

———————

Rusty Hardin was the state's star prosecutor, "a *decent* human being," in Roy Beene's opinion, en route to becoming district attorney of Harris County or maybe even governor of Texas—unless Johnny Holmes, his current boss, beat him to it. Since the death penalty had been reinstated in Texas in 1974, following the Supreme Court decision in *Furman* v. *Georgia,* the Harris County District Attorney's Office had compiled a remarkable record: it had never lost a murder case. Every defendant who had boldly pled not guilty had lost at trial and been found guilty. That demonstrated a careful selection of cases as much as it did brilliance before the jury. If the prosecutorial brain trust of Holmes and Hardin thought they had any serious weakness in a case they would encourage the defendant to plea-bargain and settle for a life sentence, or something like thirty to forty years and the possibility of parole after serving a third of the time. Texas prisons were crowded; with time off for good behavior, life meant twenty years.

But the Campbell murder case had everything to warrant at least a degree of confrontation and ballyhoo. Pathos, tragedy, crumbled lives. The fear of every parent who had ever disciplined a child beyond a slap on the hand or the taking away of his bubble gum: *"This little kid I'm spanking is going to grow up and kill me for it."* Or, more immediately: *"If I yell one more time at this six-foot-two teen-ager to 'Do the goddamn dishes!' he'll turn around and stick a kitchen knife in me."* And beyond that: *"This crazy girl is mad at me for locking her in her room and not letting her watch TV, and just because when I was drunk a couple of times I kind of cozied up to her, she's going to tell the police I'm abusing her."*

Roy Beene decided that the David West murder trial was guaranteed to continue as page one news in Texas and, because of the presence of Kim Paris, the sexy private eye, invite national exposure. Therefore the prosecutors could not afford to lose. It might be less humiliating to compromise well in advance than go down in flames in the Crime section of *Time* magazine.

And I don't think they can convict, Roy concluded. I think Rusty Hardin's worried and Johnny Holmes is shitscared of messing up his perfect record.

Roy Beene visited Cindy Ray every day. "Be calm," he said. "Keep your mouth shut. We're winning."

A week after the arrest a pressured District Attorney Holmes admitted publicly that his prosecutor was facing a dilemma in proving Cindy's part in her parents' deaths. Yes, it was true that David West, in his confession to Kim Paris, had named Ms. Ray as his accomplice. "But," Holmes said bitterly, "it disappoints me that, if she did it, we don't have the evidence to make her answer for it." He announced that he was hoping someone in whom she had confided about the killings would step forth and speak up. He needed someone who would also name David West rather than the fictitious Salino that Cindy had conjured up for her friend Gwen Sampson. Holmes had no specific person in mind. He was just fishing in muddy waters.

And from a leaky boat, Roy Beene concluded gleefully. Immediately after the D.A.'s statement he demanded a bond hearing. State District Judge Woody Densen saw it Roy's way now, bowed to the demand, and set bond at $30,000, which turned out to be quixotic since no one could or would come up with the $4,500 needed to pay the bondsman as security.

Lawyers can see their clients in special visiting cubicles at Harris County Jail. They sit facing each other on straightbacked chairs, separated by a thick metal mesh, observed only by a closed-circuit television camera that has no recording mechanism. They talk. The lawyers look grave, but calm. The clients clench their fists and usually shake their heads in disbelief.

"With clients like her," Roy explained later, "I dance. I do a minuet. It's like a courtship. You know, I'm not going to pull my pecker out and shove it in their mouths—that's rape, not courtship—but I seduce them into telling me as much of the truth as I can bear. I have to look ahead to what might happen at the trial, and whether or not I can have them testify on their own behalf. A lawyer vouches for his witnesses when they're under oath. I'll never tell a client they *can't* lie, but if I put someone on the stand *knowing* they're about to tell a few untruths, that's called subornation of perjury. I could go to the penitentiary. And I am definitely unwilling to fill a cell in Huntsville Prison that my client should have filled."

After talking to Cindy for a few days he came to the conclusion that he didn't like her. She believed she was bright, and that may have been true; but Roy saw her as a fundamentally mean, petty, petulant person. He concluded that was the result of the way she was raised, lacking what he would call a moral education. If she'd had a decent childhood, he ardently believed, it might have been different. Bad luck. Life ain't fair. If it was, the jails wouldn't be full, and I'd be out of work.

He also found it hard to understand how anyone could have fallen in love with her. It wasn't that she was physically ugly—he could see that she had been attractive before she porked up. It was that her personality was . . . he groped for the one word and came up with *nasty*.

Her constant theme was a strident *"You owe this to me . . . you have to do this for me. . . . "*

Nasty.

Now that she'd paid him—and generously, she thought—she called him three and four times a day from the jail. Prisoners were allowed nearly unlimited telephone calls, depending on the whims of the block wardens. Cindy demanded to know what was happening. He'd taken her property from her—wouldn't *he* put up the $4,500 cash for the bail bond? How much longer did she have to suffer? When would she be out? How soon would he visit her?

"Goddammit," she yelled, "what are you *doing?*"

He danced and kept her at bay. He knew that each day the district attorney's complaint languished in infertile soil and failed to flower into a poisonous indictment, her position grew stronger. Time was a friend, not an enemy. He was only worried that after listening to the buttery inducements of Rusty Hardin (Roy once characterized Rusty as "slicker'n deer guts on a doorknob"), young David West might try to cut a deal for himself that required him to point an accusing finger at Cindy Ray. That would certainly complicate matters. Roy thought of calling Gene Nettles to suggest that they pool their information, since he and Nettles had a joint interest. Nevertheless, upon reflection, it struck him that their conflict of interest was more pronounced, and he decided against the call. It was analogous to Chinese Checkers, or the card game of Hearts, where at a certain stage the players fluctuate between common goals and direct competition. And here the stakes were life and death.

On Thursday, March 14, 1985, at the end of the third week of Cindy's imprisonment, a friend of Roy's high in the Harris County Jail hierarchy called to tip him that the District Attorney's Office had ordered Cindy's release. She was to be no-billed. An indictment ordered by a grand jury, in response to a request by the district attorney, is called "a bill of indictment," and to be no-billed is to have the grand jury vote for "no bill of indictment."

Roy clapped his hands and poured himself a cold bottle of Carta Blanca. He alerted Cindy's pal, the reclusive Queer Bob. Then, to avoid any harassment by reporters and TV cameras, he arranged with the

Harris County Sheriff's Office for Cindy to be released on the first floor of the jail rather than from the customary basement exit, where, he knew, the rapacious representatives of the media would be waiting to devour her for the six o'clock news and spit her out on a ten o'clock segment.

When Cindy appeared, stringy-haired, hunched over in some awful cotton dress, bulking in the doorway of the elevator, met there by Bob, Roy was smiling with satisfaction, as any lawyer would be whose client had just stepped from the fluorescent-lit penitential dungeons into the Texas sunlight.

But Cindy waddled past him as rapidly as she could. "I can't talk to you now," she said, and grabbed Bob's hand for support.

"Wait a minute!" Roy cried.

"I'll call you," she yelled, squeezing into Bob's car.

Later that afternoon, when a perplexed Roy reached his office, he found a messenger-delivered letter from Cindy waiting for him. "You are no longer my lawyer," she wrote. "In other words, Mr. Beene, you are *fired!*"

Three days later she hired a new lawyer, Henri-Ann Nortman, and filed civil suit against Roy Beene for the return of the property at 2301 Kingston. Then she hired Percy Foreman, the dean of Houston criminal defense attorneys, to represent her vis-à-vis the vengeful District Attorney's Office. He received as a fee the final $6,800 of her inheritance that had been held for her by Steve Simmons, whom Nortman had replaced.

The larger questions remained unanswered. Could they convict David West on the basis of a surreptitious *tape?* Wasn't that entrapment? But entrapment resulted only from an officer of the law convincing someone to commit a crime that would not otherwise have been committed. Still, most people thought the confession had a bad smell about it. What had Kim Paris done to induce it? Had West told the whole truth and nothing but the truth? And if he had, was Cynthia Ray going to get away with hiring him to kill her parents while the lovesick trigger man faced the death penalty? That surely wasn't justice.

David West still faced a charge of capital murder, with a trial likely in the summer. Fascinating case, most people felt. But something's wrong.

Soon after Cindy was no-billed for the murder of her parents, the rumor of incest and sexual abuse began to circulate through the Houston legal world. Bob Harris, Jim Campbell's friend, when he heard that tale, thought it was preposterous. And when he thought about it further, he was enraged. What a mean and contemptible thing for her to say, after her Daddy was dead and couldn't refute it!

10

I can no longer stay outside this story. Some pages back, when District Attorney Johnny Holmes talked to "a writer from New York" about robbing a 7-Eleven and the accomplice-witness rule, that writer was me. And many of the statements already quoted from those involved in the Campbell murders—from David West, Cecilia West, Roy Beene, Wickie Weinstein, the Harrises, the Thurlows—were made to me. There are more to come.

Although I was born and brought up in Manhattan, my home is in a cobbled Mexican mountain town in the state of Guanajuato. In 1985, when David West made his confession to Kim Paris, I was there in Mexico tending an unruly flower garden, learning to ride a horse in the desert, and writing a novel. My town had no airport, I didn't own a television set, and I seldom read an English-language newspaper, so that my contact with what most people call the real world was limited. But in April of that year, through the intervention of a friend, I became interested in the Campbell murder case. I was invited to Houston to meet with Kim Paris, Clyde Wilson, and Marian Rosen.

At the time I needed to see a good gringo dentist. And I liked Texas: the people were friendly and it still had towns called Poverty Slant, Cut and Shoot, Help, Harmony, Snap, Sweat Box, Uncertain, and Po Boy. The Inn on the Park, however, where I stayed, was deep-carpeted and sophisticated. I didn't know Houston at all, and superficially it seemed a convenience-oriented, plastic American town masquerading as a city. I was wrong. But I was a New Yorker; for me there was only one true city.

Marian Rosen took us all to dinner at a restaurant called Tony's, by reputation the best in Houston. When we were kids together in Manhattan, Marian and I had lived in the same neighborhood on the Upper West Side and gone to Joan of Arc Junior High School. Now she was head of her own law firm, an urbane, nasal-voiced, platinum-blond woman in her early fifties with a big two-stone diamond ring on her left hand, wearing a bright blue suit and a little red pompom hat that made her look like an organ grinder's monkey. She was there not only as Kim Paris's lawyer but as her protector and agent.

I met Kim, and I liked her. She wore a sternly tailored navy blue suit and snowy white blouse, and her dark auburn hair fell nearly to her shoulders in a shag. The businesslike effect was marred only by her eyes.

115

Surrounded by brown kohl and lilac shadow, they were so intensely blue that I wondered if she wore tinted contacts.

Brassy but intelligent, cocky but quick-witted, Kim had at least a whiff of star quality. At times, as the evening progressed, I caught glimpses of a confused little girl hiding inside the shell of a handsome and hard-bitten woman. At other times, an overt youthfulness—a husky giggle, the quick blush of an ingénue—seemed to thinly cloak a massive determination to make the most of her current chances. She listened carefully to what everyone said. She was weighing alternatives, sizing people up, sending out a clear message: *Don't tread on me.* She certainly had that right.

At dinner she touched on her relationship with David West.

"It was strictly platonic," she said, "although I had to keep dancing around the subject of sex. It wasn't that hard—David considers himself an intellectual on a higher plane than most people, even though he's a gun nut and a survivalist. We actually spent most of our time talking about history and politics and religion. Funny thing is, I liked him, even though I wasn't at all attracted to him. He wanted to marry me—he was ready to introduce me to his mother." She dropped her voice dramatically. "And now—God!—he's charged with capital murder! He can get the death penalty. . . . "

I asked, "If you were so close to him that he wanted to marry you, how will you feel if he *does* get the death penalty?"

"That's tough," she said, and a chilly light flickered in her eyes.

Quickly Marian Rosen softened it: "Kim took a hired gun off the streets. A killer who slaughtered two innocent people."

Toward the end of dinner, just as the dessert cart was wheeled round, someone brought up the subject of the TV movie that could be based on Kim's adventures, and the small fortune that might come her way.

Kim shook her head. "I don't give a fuck about the money. Pardon my French. I just want to make sure that if there's a movie about me, and what I did, it has some class. And that my part is played by some star I really like."

I asked if she had anyone in mind.

"Debra Winger," she said, with no break in stride. She had been thinking about it.

Over coffee Marian Rosen raised a finger tipped by a long, pale plum-lacquered nail and made a little speech. She represented not only Kim, but also the absent Clyde Wilson, regarding any property value in the story of how David Duval West had been bewitched into confessing to the murders of James and Virginia Campbell. At least thirty writers, publishers, and film producers had approached her, she said, including

MGM, Paramount, Universal, and 20th Century—Fox. She had an obligation to her clients to listen to every proposition and select the one best suited to their interests.

"We already have an offer from a New York publisher who offered an advance payment of $500,000. We're still considering it."

"You should grab that one," I said, "while the publisher's still in business."

Marian looked nonplussed, but only for the wink of an eye.

It was never as jolly after that, although I did promise to drop in to Clyde Wilson's office and meet once more with Kim. Marian paid the bill. I think she just nodded to a waiter and they put it on her tab. Tony's was that kind of restaurant.

The next day I met Clyde Wilson, and it was the beginning of a friendship. I told him about the reported offer of half a million dollars for the Kim Paris and Clyde Wilson story.

"Bullshit," Clyde said. "First I heard of it. Some Jew must have whispered that in Marian's ear, told her the story was worth half a million, and that's what he'd get for her. Marian's an old pal of mine, and a smart lawyer, but she's not so smart when it comes to knowing who to trust. She trusts Kim Paris—that's a proven mistake. If you don't believe me, ask David West." He leaned forward, winking at me with his one good blue eye. "Listen, son, I know you're Jewish. Did I tell you I was a quarter Jewish? Sometimes I tell people that, because for all I know it may be true." He showed me his perfectly even teeth: too even, too white. "You have to learn when I'm kidding and when I'm serious."

"I'll try," I said. "It doesn't sound easy."

In the evening I took Kim and her girlfriend Sami to dinner at a popular local restaurant called Thank God It's Friday, and they introduced me to potato skins as a main course. No longer an unknown neophyte private eye, Kim was recognized wherever she went in Houston and often asked for her autograph.

The next day I finished up at the dentist and in the afternoon flew back to Mexico to tend my garden and think about whether they would ever convict David West for what he had done, or not done, and what part, if any, Cynthia Campbell Ray had played in the murder of her parents.

Before I left Houston, Roy Beene, pale blue eyes glittering, leaned across a lunch table at a Tex-Mex restaurant and said to me, "If I was representing West and if it got as far as a trial, which I doubt it will, I'll tell you what my closing argument would be. I'd say, 'Ladies and gentlemen of the jury, what is the strongest fiber in the world?' (He had a muscular West Texas accent: fiber became *fahbuh* and world was broken into two syllables, as in *wurrold*.) 'I'll tell you. The strongest fiber in the world is a pussy hair. You catch one of them li'l thin hairs 'tween a man's teeth . . . and you can pull him halfway round the world! You can get him to do or say *anything you want.*"

Roy thumped back in the chair. "That's called the Pussy-hair Defense. Gene Nettles hasn't got any choice. He's got to use it. And he can win with it."

I thought that over for a while. If I were on the jury and I heard that argument, I said, I thought I'd vote not guilty.

That realization was probably what made me sign on for the duration. It was clear that the road to truth and justice in this case would be a bumpy one. There wasn't even a guarantee of arrival. Hostiles and venomous critters would lurk behind many a rock.

I had no idea then that I would be one of them.

In early July, after some mutual backing and forthing, Marian Rosen wrote a letter complaining that I left Houston with "confidential information secured from Kim Paris, Clyde Wilson and/or his personnel" and instructing me "to cease and desist from proceeding further with a book on the Kim Paris story and/or the Campbell murder case." That puzzled me even more than it irked me, because as a lawyer conversant with the First Amendment to the Federal Constitution, she should have known better. In August I flew out of the cool Mexican mountain summer into the sultry bayou heat to spend another week in the city that the adventurous Allen brothers had predicted would become "the great interior commercial emporium of Texas," and had, and still was, despite the drop in oil prices that made Louisianans call it, in 1986, "Death City."

The trial of David West was scheduled for September in the 232nd District Court, the court of Judge A. D. Azios. In his early sixties now, Judge Azios had a reputation for a dogged thoroughness, an ecumenical friendliness, and an attitude toward lawyers and jurors that may have been unique in Houston. Or, as Sgt. J. C. Mosier said, "He runs a bizarre courtroom." He pointed to the judge's last capital murder trial, known as "the Pickaxe Murders," in honor of the weapon used by the female defendant. When the woman was found guilty and sentenced to death, the judge called the twelve jurors to the bench and gave them each a brass belt buckle with the scales of justice for the conscientious job they had done during the eight hard weeks of the trial. In return the

118

jury gifted the judge with an ornate brass door knocker. The doomed defendant was still in the courtroom at the time, staring goggle-eyed at this camaraderie.

What still bothered me, however, as August rolled round and the David West trial loomed, was that Cynthia Campbell Ray was exempt from punishment and at liberty. That made no sense to me. I am a Jew; I believe in the culpability of those who sign the extermination orders. There were two theories as to motive if indeed she was guilty: her share of the inheritance, and revenge for the rumored sexual abuse at the hands of her father. But why then condemn the mother? And how did she get David West—no longer her lover, apparently only casually in touch with her—to accomplish her ends? Surely there had to be a reckoning and some sort of explanation. What kind of satisfying conclusion could this bloody drama reach if its Lady Macbeth sat in the audience throughout the play?

I called the various Houston reporters who had covered the breaking story last winter. I listed names and telephone numbers. I reached Cindy Ray's current lawyer, Henri-Ann Nortman.

"I'll ask Ms. Ray," she said, "but I'm positive that she won't talk to you. She's still suing Roy Beene for the return of her Kingston property. Steve Simmons is suing *her* for an interest in the property, and a realtor is suing *everybody* for the 6 percent commission on the transfer of the house. Ms. Ray can't comment on any of that."

Before I left Houston that August I had dinner again with Kim Paris. This time she made me promise that I wouldn't tell Marian Rosen we were meeting. Marian was supporting Kim and ready to make a deal, Kim said, with a writer named Jack Olsen, whose last book, *Son*, was about a rapist in Spokane. But she would talk to me provided we stayed away from the subject of the murder and the upcoming trial. I didn't see how we could do that. Nonetheless, I agreed to try.

I picked her up at her apartment on North Boulevard, a clean-looking place with parquet floors and a minimum of furniture that she told me came from the flea market and the Salvation Army. I said hello to her roommate, the exotic Sami, and then to a polite, dark-haired young man named David Borosov. Kim said, "This is my fiancé."

We ate without him in a small Thai restaurant in Montrose. "I love Thai food," Kim said. The waitress was a sweet young Thai whom I told, "Just bring us what you think we'd like." She didn't understand me and her aunt came over to take the order. The aunt, who managed the restaurant, recommended Thai egg roll as a specialty, and a beef dish, and hot and spicy shrimp.

"I hope the waitress comes back," Kim said, while we waited for our vodka tonics. She did, and Kim was pleased. When the egg roll came, Kim showed me how to wrap it in lettuce and then dip it into the sauce.

She was garrulous that evening. Whatever agreements we had made were soon dispensed with. In jeans and a blue denim shirt she looked more relaxed than when I had first met her back in April. She had a clean, neat look, and she was broader in the beam and less chesty than I remembered. Her hair was browner, not as auburn. She admitted that she wore less makeup and used less hair coloring since she'd seen herself in a video replay of the March *Donahue* show. But her eyes still glowed like Navajo turquoise. She was twenty-three years old and still trying out visions of herself in order to find out which of them were truly her, or at least which she and others could comfortably live with.

What the hell, I thought, and asked her if she was wearing tinted contacts. She laughed brightly. "Sure! They make my eyes look respectable after a hard night. Listen, Clifford, I want to tell you the truth about myself . . . as much as I can, under the circumstances. Because you're going to write about me, right?"

"Right. So tell me, first of all, if you're really getting married."

"Yes, but not right away."

"Don't you have a problem with his name?"

Another merry laugh danced on her lips. "How'd you guess? When I talk to my mother in St. Louis I have to refer to him as '*my* David,' as opposed to '*that* David.' "

This led the way smoothly to a discussion of "*that* David." I told her she had surprised me in April, at Tony's, when I'd asked her how she would feel if David West got the death penalty, and she had snapped back, "That's tough."

"That was callous of me," she said, coloring. "It's not true. If it happens, I'm going to freak out."

"You still feel something for him?"

"Not the way you mean. I did back then. Until the night he confessed, I didn't believe he was the one who did it. What I fear now is that he hates me so much he could kill me. They can't get those tapes into evidence without me, so if I had an accident, that would be the end of the State of Texas's case against David West! And he has some weird and violent friends, like this one guy, Wickie Weinstein, who may have been involved in what happened."

I thought back to my picking her up at the apartment. It had been dark in the street. There were no police around, guarding her. She was an easy target.

"If *that* David got out on bond," she said, "I don't know what I'd do. He's got this executioner's complex. He's proud of it! That's how he

120

thinks of what he did to Cindy's parents—an execution. I mean it, those were his words! *They deserved to die.'* "

"Tell me about the sexual abuse."

She looked unhappy. "I'm not supposed to talk about it."

I couldn't persuade her. I would have to find out for myself.

"Then tell me about this Wickie Weinstein. How was he involved?"

"I can't," she said firmly. "It will all come out at the trial."

No way to budge her, and she went on to subjects where she felt she wasn't betraying her team. She had met Gene Nettles, she related. She was sitting in Rusty Hardin's office the day Nettles dropped by to pick up copies of the confession tapes. Like everyone else, Kim was struck by his handsomeness, the magnetic glow of his umber eyes. Nevertheless she looked at him squarely and said, "Hey, I hear you're really going to do a full-scale character assassination of me."

To her surprise, Nettles in his deep voice drawled, "Ms. Paris, that's my job. I have to serve my client's best interests."

"I know he's been poking around into my past," Kim said in the restaurant, and a hint of distress appeared behind her eyes. "But Rusty says Nettles is hot-tempered, breaks racquets on the tennis court, that sort of thing. It'll work against him in this case. He could press me too hard and wind up prejudicing the jury in my favor. And if he yells at me, I know how to take it, because, man, I've had a lot of shit thrown at me in my time. In the navy it got to the point where I didn't even know someone was talking to me if they didn't call me 'asshole.' " She grinned; you could tell she had used that line before and got good reaction from it. "Rusty will protect me. If Nettles has me on the witness stand and tries something like, 'Have you ever taken money for sexual favors?' Rusty won't let him get away with that kind of garbage."

I wondered why she'd chosen that example.

But Rusty wasn't preparing her yet for the cross-examination, she said. He wanted her to be spontaneous. He also seemed to worry that she might be questioned as to preparation, and he didn't want her to have to say, "Yes, sure, we rehearsed this dialogue twice a week at the D.A.'s Office." And he was being prudent about being seen with her. He wouldn't even take her to lunch alone for fear that their names might be linked romantically.

"Have you met Rusty yet?" Kim asked me.

"He never returns my calls."

"He's in charge of a whole division of prosecutors. He has to clear the decks for a month before this trial starts. Just picking the jury, he says, will take three weeks."

"What kind of jury will he go for?"

"Mostly women." From the way her eyes sparkled, this seemed to amuse her. "On the theory that a man might take offense at the way I lured poor David into confessing."

"A certain kind of woman," I said, "might also take offense at what you did. A feminist might feel that the method you used was degrading to women in general."

"That's interesting," Kim said coolly, with no apparent resentment. The waitress glided over, and Kim began talking to her about the food.

Toward the end of the meal, when she was working on her third vodka tonic, she switched the subject to Clyde Wilson. "You like him, I know that. And I guess he and I have got kind of a love-hate relationship." She slurred her words slightly. "But the hate is real. He's acted badly in this whole affair. He horned in on all those interviews and TV shows. I brought him a lot of publicity, didn't I? With what result? He turns out to be two-faced and ungrateful. He won't give me another job." That stone-hard look glinted in her eyes again, and she shrugged. "Well, the fact that he's under constant medication may have something to do with it."

The "constant medication," I later found out, referred to two aspirins a day and a diuretic three times a week that Clyde took for high blood pressure.

"When I was seeing David West," Kim went on, "I lost faith for a while in what I was doing. Like I said, I didn't really believe he'd killed those people, and I told that to Denise. But she and Clyde wanted to keep the investigation going so they could keep picking up the fees from Betty Hinds. That's ironic, isn't it? Because they were greedy, I caught a murderer."

"That's hard to believe," I said.

She looked at me sharply. "You think Clyde's a saint? No one thinks *I'm* a saint. I was the one who took the risk! And now everyone acts as if I did something wrong! What have I done that's so bad? He killed them, didn't he? He and that fat pig? He wouldn't have lied to me. You don't lie about things like that." Kim gripped my wrist. "You can't be rigid. I never gave David my word about anything. I never promised him a goddamn thing, not really."

"What does 'not really' mean?"

"It means I promised him *nothing.*"

"One more question," I said. "If you didn't go to bed with him . . . how did you get him to confess to the murders?"

Kim deliberated for a while, then reached her decision.

"That will all come out in court," she said huskily, touching me on the back of the hand with the tip of a long fingernail, and smiling her warmest smile. I realized she had a range of smiles, from wicked down through naughty and youthfully enthusiastic and sweet all the way to innocent. "It will be an exciting trial," she predicted. "And I'll be the star witness, won't I? Flashbulbs popping, as they used to say, and cameras clicking, and all that. . . . "

I suppose she really meant it. If not, she was a fairly good actress; but she had already proved that with David West. A child of her time, she saw things in cinematic terms. Debra Winger in the part. Come to think of it, Kim *looked* a bit like Debra Winger.

"You'll be the star," I predicted, wrongly.

"And I have a funny feeling—I can't explain or justify it—that something unexpected is going to happen."

She wouldn't elaborate. I tried to find out more about Cynthia Ray, but Kim had made other covenants and promises. Her words were worth cash.

The manager, the aunt of our pretty young Thai waitress, brought us special filtered French coffee. She wouldn't let me use Equal in it. The waitress glided gracefully to the table and offered the bill. She spoke hardly any English, but she smiled all the time, like the petite young women I'd seen on the back streets of Bangkok and Chiang Mai, all of whom looked like they'd been delicately stamped from smooth tan dough by the same cookie cutter. "She's so sweet," Kim said softly, "I'd like to take her home with me."

That was something about her I hadn't understood before. I thought about it quite often, then and later.

Tracking down David West's former housemate, Wickie Weinstein, wasn't easy, and I didn't find him for a long time. But I found people who knew him. And eventually he talked to me, too.

Wickie was his real name—he had been born with it in New Brunswick, New Jersey, although his mother and stepfather had moved to Houston when he was a baby. He told people that his mother had called him Wickie because he was illegitimate and there was no father to name him, and the honor had gone to an uncle whose best friend was Chinese and bore that name. In Chinese, he said, Wickie meant sunlight. He was raised as a Jew, bar mitzvahed at Houston's Temple Beth Yeshurun, but it no longer meant anything to him. He considered himself a Texan.

A slim, good-looking, generally dour young man of twenty-six, he reminded some people of James Dean. He said to me, in a soft local accent, "I never fit. I was Anglo in a Semitic kind of world. Jews do

123

pinch pennies, and they do have their little idiosyncrasies. I was always a lot different than they were. I didn't care that much about money, and I wasn't that studious. I was rebellious."

The young Wickie went to Cypress Fairbanks High School in Houston, but left in the middle of ninth grade and roamed out to California, where he enlisted as a U.S. Army Ranger. His tour of service ranged from two to four years, depending on who he was talking to. He had served in Okinawa and Panama. He told some people that he had been in Vietnam, and he told some others that he had fought as a mercenary in Central America.

He shared Dave West's love for beer and weaponry, but he made his living as a carpenter and had worked backstage for a time with the Alley Theater. Before moving into Dave's house on Vermont he lived with Melanie Edgecombe, an attractive, blonde young woman from Ohio. Melanie was also a carpenter, and she had taught the skill to Wickie and got him in the union. When he and Melanie broke up during Christmas week of 1984, Wickie needed a place to bed down. He agreed to pay Dave West $150 a month rent, but he never paid. "I did drugs and drank with that money," he told me.

When Dave was arrested, it didn't take long before Sgts. Schultz and Motard rang Melanie Edgecombe's doorbell in Bellaire, an independent township squeezed into southwest Houston. She led them to Wickie, and he proved to be cooperative.

Sure, he said, he'd known Dave a long time. They'd met in a Montrose bar around Christmas of 1980, become drinking buddies. In fact, one night in the spring of 1982, on their way to a friend's house to do some drugs, talking about old times in the service and philosophizing about death and man's inhumanity to man, Dave asked Wickie, "Could you ever kill someone for money?"

"I don't know," Wickie said. "Probably not, but you never know."

Dave persisted. "What would make up your mind for you? Would it matter if they were good people or bad people?"

"No, that wouldn't stop me," Wickie said. "I mean, shit, man, if you're getting paid, you're not in much of a position to make value judgments like that. You just do the job and take the money and see if you can live with it. The money's what it's all about."

"But you wouldn't do it?"

"Like I said . . . probably not."

"It would be a lot easier for me to do it for money," Dave said, "if I thought the people really deserved it, and there was no big hassle about getting it done. I could do it on the one condition that they were evil people."

"Evil would help," Wickie agreed.

That, in any event, was his story to the police.

Dave West had a small collection of guns, Wickie told Gil Schultz, including a 12-gauge shotgun and a .22 Marlin rifle. In the spring of 1982, though, he decided he needed a .45 automatic, and he didn't want to buy one in a store, although all he'd need to do so was his Texas driver's license. "I had a .45 Colt Combat Commander," Wickie related, "which I wanted to sell, and Dave bought it for $450 cash. We went up to the firing range at Carter's Country on Treschwig Road to test-fire it. Great gun, all tuned and accurized." Schultz, playing dumb, asked what he meant, and Wickie explained: "A .45 comes either sloppy or tight. When it comes real tight it doesn't function very well, and any kind of dirt or grit will slow it down. So you put diamond dust in it, then smooth off the burrs and file it down with a diamond file, and then the bullet slides up the ramp quicker, straighter. I bought a .375 Ruger the same day, to kind of take the place of the .45. But that .45 was always my favorite."

He even had a small photograph of the gun, a souvenir. He gave it to Schultz, then took the detectives over to David West's house on Vermont and conducted them on a tour.

At the time of the Campbell murders, Wickie claimed, he was seeing a lot of Melanie and wasn't that close to Dave. "I didn't even know about the murders when they happened. Dave didn't mention it, and I wasn't into reading the newspapers or watching the news on TV. Cynthia Ray never really hung around Montrose much. I mean, she didn't walk into a bar and lay her head down and blubber, 'My parents got shot last night.' "

But after the murders, Wickie realized later, Dave seemed to change. "He used to work out—we had set up a gym in the living room with free weights—but now he stopped. He drank a lot more. He became cautious about getting arrested for such minor deals as speeding or DWI. He began to neglect his dogs, a pit bull named Max, who he cherished, and a young Rottweiler he found wandering around in the streets of Montrose and called Nana. At one time he'd started to fix up his house, built a porch and a fence around it, but all that ended after the murders."

And then, Wickie continued, at some careless moment in the summer of 1983, with more than a few beers under his belt, Dave said to him, "Hey, you know that .45 you sold me? Well, listen, man, I used it to kill someone. I have to get it off my chest. The point is, whoever it was I killed, believe me, they rated it, they deserved it."

Wickie asked, "What did you do with the .45?"

125

"Threw it into Buffalo Bayou. It's under ten feet of silt and mud by now."

"Don't ever tell anyone else what you told me," Wickie cautioned.

After Dave met Kim Paris, on the day he was arrested, he said to Wickie, "I'm going to marry her. She's the perfect Aryan woman, big-boned, strong, and blue-eyed. She'll make a good breeder. She's intelligent but she's not wimpy, she goes out there and *does* things."

"That was true," Wickie said to Gil Schultz. "He found out that night."

Rusty Hardin asked Wickie to come downtown and read the first draft transcripts of Dave's confession to Kim Paris. He showed Wickie some gruesome color photographs of the Campbells dead in their king-sized bed at 8901 Memorial. Then he brought Wickie before the grand jury to talk about the gun and what Dave had told him about it.

A few days later David West called Wickie from the jail and asked him to please meet with Gene Nettles. Wickie agreed. Up at the defense attorney's office, he repeated his story. He said, "I feel real sorry for Dave. Any way I can help him, let me know."

"We'll keep in touch," Gene said coolly. You scumbag, he thought, you'd sell your own mother for a bottle of Everclear or a dime bag.

But the price was slightly higher. Soon afterward Wickie met for lunch with a Houston reporter named Dan Grothaus and repeated his story. He told Grothaus that for $200 cash he would provide an exclusive interview of his good friend Dave West. Grothaus gave it a pass, although he did pick up the check for lunch.

When I met Wickie after that, we sat on the porch of Melanie Edge-combe's house so that Wickie could smoke—because Melanie was a nonsmoker—and he smoked steadily. He explained to me his philosophy about who he would kill and who he would not kill. "If for some wild reason," he said, "I was called up for duty tomorrow and sent, let's say, to Nicaragua, I'd kill every fucking Nicaraguan soldier that got in my path. But I would not kill every civilian. I think if another man says, 'I'm a soldier, and I pit myself against you'—fine, there's a war. A war can be that guy sitting over there in his truck deciding he doesn't like my face, and he's drunk, and he takes a shot at me, and I shoot back. In a barroom fight, if two guys pull weapons and one kills the other, aside from the harm they might have done to innocent bystanders, I don't think they should get any criminal sentence. That might be archaic, man, a jungle law not practical for this time and age . . . but that's what I believe."

11

Good newspaper reporters are fundamentally skeptical or else they would be television reporters. In February and March of 1985 two Houston *Chronicle* reporters—Burke Watson and Dan Grothaus, to whom Wickie would later offer the exclusive interview of David West—jointly covered the unraveling of the Campbell murder mystery. In early April Grothaus moved over to the competition newspaper, the Houston *Post*. A thirty-two-year-old graduate of the University of Missouri School of Journalism—intense, sandy-haired and mustachioed, and good-looking—Grothaus had taken one careful squint at Kim's changeable blue eyes and saucy demeanor and decided it was worth running a deep background check on her. Probing U.S. Navy files at Corpus Christi, St. Louis, and Washington, D.C., he came up with interesting information.

For one thing, since April 1, 1983, four months before her separation from the navy, Kimberly Ann Paris legally had been Mrs. Jay A. Monson. Like Kim at the time, husband Jay was also a naval air traffic controller. Grothaus managed to track him down at his new home in El Cajon, California, to ask if he was still married.

"I guess so," Monson said casually.

"Do you know anything about your wife's discharge from the navy?" Grothaus asked.

After a moment's eloquent hesitation, Monson said he couldn't remember anything about it. He thought it had happened after he had left.

"Any truth to the rumors that she was a prostitute?"

"I've heard those rumors but I've never seen evidence of that," Monson said. "She was too intelligent and too good-looking to have to make a living like that. Just by being herself she could get pretty much anything she wanted out of anybody."

Grothaus was keying on his other discovery that Kim's discharge from the navy was neither honorable nor dishonorable, but rather a general discharge under other than honorable conditions. The exact wording provided by the U.S. Navy was " . . . for frequent involvement of a discreditable nature with civil or military authorities indicating a pattern of misconduct." Lt. Scott Wilson, a spokesman attached to the Naval Military Personnel Office at the Corpus Christi base, said that after being busted from the rank of E-4 to E-3 she was asked to leave the navy.

More often than not, Wilson explained, the reasons for such an unceremonious farewell were morals charges.

Grothaus confronted Kim Paris with this, and she rebutted coolly, "My experience in the military was like a *Private Benjamin* scenario. I came in with three suitcases filled with clothes, my backgammon set, a hair dryer, the works. They told me I couldn't wear makeup and I couldn't use my Walkman. I thought, 'Jeez, no blush, okay, but I have to have my mascara!' I encountered a lot of sexual harassment in the military. Like, officers checking to make sure the stencil was straight on my uniform—at chest level. It was a problem of selective enforcement of rules. I had an 'attitude,' so they started leaning on me for little things like being two minutes tardy, anything to load my file with black marks. And there was a rumor on the base that I was a prostitute," she said, laughing. "I was eventually brought before Capt. Simpson, a discipline officer. I decided to get out. They wanted me out, but it was *my* choice. It was like plea bargaining—I finally agreed to leave if they'd give me an honorable discharge, or at least not what they call an 'other than honorable discharge.' "

"I see," Grothaus said.

He began to understand how Kim Paris had accomplished her mission with David West.

A map of Houston resembles a spiderweb, with freeways spinning out from the downtown center and another freeway looping around that center in the shape of a squashed circle. That circular freeway, with a radius of about five miles, is officially Interstate 610, but locally it's referred to as the Loop. Houstonians live "outside the Loop" or "inside the Loop," and inside the Loop means possibly nonconformist, definitely not bourgeois or suburban. The area called Montrose was emphatically inside the Loop, just south of the high-rise downtown area dominated by the seventy-five-story Texas Commerce Tower.

Like Los Angeles, Houston is remarkably green and geographically huge. Within its city limits you could fit Boston, Detroit, Atlanta, San Francisco, Denver, and Louisville, and there would still be room for another of the ubiquitous parking lots. But Montrose and the *barrio* are the only parts of Houston where people stroll around and socialize on the tree-shaded streets as they do all the time in New York or San Francisco. In Montrose there are straight bars, redneck bars, and gay bars, ethnic restaurants and convenience stores, boutiques and supermarkets, but none of the modern malls or drive-up shopping centers

128

that characterize the rest of the South Texas urban amoeba, now the fourth largest in the country. Most of Montrose is residential, with narrow, tree-lined streets and interesting-looking wooden houses. It's an old *neighborhood*. There aren't many left in the United States.

Two Montrose bars—the Park Lane Tavern on Alabama Avenue, and Rudyard's British Pub on Waugh Drive—figured prominently in the Campbell murder case. The Park Lane had been Kim's and David's favorite watering hole. Rudyard's, or Rud's, as it was often called by its clientele, had been visited by Cindy and David on the night of the murders.

David West was well known in both bars, and both were favorite gathering places for an eccentric inner-city club—or gang, depending upon whom you asked—called the Urban Animals.

The Animals' main activity was rollerskating. You *had* to skate to be an Animal. A nocturnal species, they leaped five-foot-high guard chains on two-inch polyurethane wheels in the darkness of winter mornings, zoomed down ten-story parking garage ramps, and played bone-busting hockey two nights a week on the plaza of the Albert Thomas Convention Center downtown. It was illegal to skate in downtown Houston, but the regulation was seldom enforced. The Animal motto, "Skate or Die," was a presumed cry of defiance against urban rigidity. "We don't mean to intimidate anyone," said one Animal, "although clearly it's hard to appear meek when you wear black and stand on two-inch wheels."*

Twice a year a score of the hardiest Animals, carrying weapons made of inch-and-a-quarter pipe and padded milk cartons, squared off on skates on a roped-off downtown street before crowds of spectators . . . and *jousted*. The police let that happen, too. Houston was still Texas, where you could create your own law if you had the courage and the presence.

Burke Watson of the *Chronicle* told me that he considered the Urban Animals to be violent young men, and Rudyard's the sort of place he wouldn't care to visit after eleven o'clock at night. "Some of the characters who wander in, you wonder how tightly they're wired." One night, he said, an Animal called Mad Military Mike had thrown a tear gas grenade inside Rudyard's while he stood outside and yelled, "If anybody runs out, I'll kill the motherfucker!" Rudyard's patrons scrambled out the back door, some on all fours. Many tripped but none were trampled.

Most of David West's pals in Montrose, including Wickie Weinstein and Robin St. John, wore the emblazoned black sweatshirts and knee-

---

* A few less skillful wheelpersons in Montrose formed a splinter group and called it the Urban Sissies. They wore pink sweatshirts emblazoned with the motto, "Trip and Cry."

pads of the Animals. But not David. He wanted to, but he couldn't skate. His physicist father had never taught him, and as a boy he'd had few friends, none of whom skated. He tried several times, as a man, but when he put on wheels and stumbled forth on the hot pavements of Montrose, he kept falling and bruising his knees. He was oddly awkward.

"Hey," David said, trying to make light of it, "guess I was meant to be a human being and not an Animal."

Wickie and Robin and Mad Military Mike grinned. Poor Dave. Nice guy, but.

Dan Grothaus of the *Post* had heard some rumors among the Urban Animals that David West was not the murderer of James and Virginia Campbell. Or else that when Cindy Ray asked him to do it, David hired a friend to oblige.

Rumors worth pursuing, I thought.

With Grothaus I began to hang around the Montrose bars. The Park Lane was small, clubby, not yet trendy, with a couple of dart boards. One evening in August I met Spike Douglas there. A baby-faced Animal of about thirty, he wore a black T-shirt with the sleeves cut off. His left hand was in a cast because he tried to hit someone—he grinned bashfully when he explained—and connected with a wall instead.

Dave West? "Real nice guy," Spike said sincerely. "Had these dogs, treated them real well. Loved kids. He always told me he wanted a family, wanted to settle down . . . so when this Kim came along, he was certainly ready. I couldn't imagine him killing anyone."

They'd said that of Hitler and Goering, too. Well-known kid and dog lovers.

"Anyway," Spike said, a beer later, "I heard Cindy Ray asked Dave to do it, and he said shit no, but he got a friend of his to take care of it."

"Where'd you hear that, Spike?" I asked.

Spike didn't remember.

"Which friend of Dave's was supposed to have done it?"

"Hey, anyone who hung out at Dave West's flophouse could have done it for him. Dave was just a guy with his nose pressed against the window pane. He ran out and got the beer. He was no mercenary like these other dudes were."

"Or like they pretended to be," Grothaus said.

"Wanted to be," Spike amended. "Wanted real bad."

Grothaus and I moved on to Rudyard's British Pub, on the narrow, crooked, poorly lit street incongruously named Waugh Drive—to me the name seemed suggestive of residential affluence—opposite a tumble-down icehouse. Outside the icehouse in the hot night steam rose from a big brown bouillabaisse pot on a wooden table, and a group of tattooed and muscled young men in sleeveless T-shirts were eating fish and pota-toes and drinking Miller Lite, and talking about getting Uzis for a trip to Honduras. Join up with President Reagan's freedom fighters. "Hang out, see what's happening, man."

Once inside Rudyard's, it struck me as the Texas equivalent of a Mexican *cantina,* with swinging doors and the hombres lined up at the scarred old wooden bar. Some of the hombres in Rud's, however, were señoritas and señoras—attractive, shapely, generally blond, and big. It was dark in the bar. I took a second look and realized the women were on roller skates, which accounted for the illusion of size.

I met Karen, an Urban Animal and an anthropology major from the University of Florida. "I went up to Dave West's place around Thanks-giving, just after the murders. He began showing his handguns to me, trying to explain the difference. At one point, with this .357 Magnum, it went off. He fired a bullet into the wall. He was so embarrassed! He said, 'Gosh, I'm supposed to be the expert, and look what happened.' That's what Dave was like. He's just not the type who could have killed anyone, except maybe in self-defense."

"Did you hear any rumor that Dave got a friend of his to do the deed for Cindy Ray?"

"I heard that. I can believe that."

If the rumor was true, why hadn't David West told the truth? He was facing the death penalty. To turn informer carried risks, but none graver than death by cyanide injection.

On the other hand, the State of Texas, with no eye witness or hard evidence, had a weak case. If West had played the role of Cindy Ray's broker and found the person to kill the Campbells, I thought, he may be figuring it's his safest bet to sit quietly in jail until the trial, and then hope he can get acquitted without having to snitch on the real murderer. If he keeps his mouth shut, Rusty Hardin & Co. may even back off first. They may not *get* to trial.

Robin St. John, the man who had answered Kim Paris's first ring of the doorbell—blond, tough-looking, with a Marine Corps T-shirt—parked his motorbike and wandered into the bar. But he wouldn't make any statement that had anything to do with the Campbell murders. "Mr. Hardin told me not to talk to anyone," he said, his face frozen in an unsmiling expression.

Mad Military Mike wasn't around. His real name was Michael Caya. Gone to California, I heard.

And Wickie Weinstein, who was supposed to be back in Houston, wasn't showing his face in public.

Grothaus and I took our beers to the back and began throwing darts at one of the pockmarked boards, while we batted various scenarios back and forth between us. Leaving out the names of any confidential sources, we had already swapped most of the information we had separately accumulated.

"Was Wickie really in 'Nam?" I asked.

"If they let them fight at fourteen. These guys just barely graduated from Dungeons & Dragons. They all have this fantasy life about war and confrontation."

Wickie was supposed to be a good shot, better than David. Ditto for Mad Military Mike. Maybe David hired one of them and did it with him, or hired both, and either did it with them or dispatched them to Memorial on their own. There were a mind-numbing amount of possibilities.

But David West was at the heart of each one, for if David hadn't been involved, how did he know all those details that he gave to Kim Paris? P. M. Clinton and Denise Moseley had heard the tapes; they said that David knew things that only the killer could have known. But what we were talking about, I realized, was access to knowledge. David West may have had access to what the killer knew, or access through Cindy and her sisters and J. W. Campbell to what the police knew. It was all in the HPD offense report. Kim had seen part of that and showed it to Lew Bocz.

As far as David buying a .45 from Wickie Weinstein, that proved nothing. There was no way to link that .45 with the vanished .45 that had killed the Campbells.

The case was weak. You could argue with conviction that the only reason David West told Kim Paris he killed Jim and Virginia Campbell was because he was crazy in love, and in heat. And something or someone put it into his mind that the only way he was going to get into this divine creature's zippered-up jeans was to tell her a sick story of what a dauntlessly macho guy he was, and how he gunned down his ex-girlfriend's parents in the dead of night three years ago. And he fell for that something or someone.

Grothaus's dart hit close to the bull's-eye. He had won the game. I paid for our round of beers. He said, "I think something's going to happen at the trial that no one can imagine. A real surprise."

Kim had said that, too. As it turned out, they were right.

12

J ury selection was due to begin on September 23, or as soon as Judge A. D. Azios could bring in another judge to handle his daily docket of cases.

The accused murderer languished in Harris County Jail while Gene Nettles filed a pretrial motion asking for suppression of the tapes as evidence in *Texas* v. *David Duval West*. If Nettles was successful in gagging West's electronically recorded voice on those two fateful nights in February, then—zap! crash!—the prosecution's case would collapse. David West would walk out of the jail and, if he'd learned his lesson, keep his mouth shut for the rest of his life concerning his relationship with Cindy Ray.

In August, through the good offices of Marian Rosen, Kim made a deal to have her story written by Jack Olsen. Olsen flew to Houston from his home on Bainbridge Island in the state of Washington. On August 24, just after midnight, Kim was driving Olsen's rented car home from where he was staying at the Hotel Meridien on Dallas Street when —according to J. C. Mosier in the Public Information Office—she nearly hit a cruising HPD patrol car. When she couldn't pass the field test, counting, she was charged with suspicion of drunk driving and driving without a license. It was her third DWI since she had arrived in Houston.

A standard twenty-minute videotape was taken of her at the police station, to judge if she could read aloud coherently and perform basic motor skills. She passed that test but refused to take an Intoxilyzer test, which would have analyzed her blood alcohol content. The newspaper reports quoted a grinning Kim as saying, "I didn't look drunk at all on the video . . . but the appearance doesn't portray my best side." Later she threatened to make a formal complaint that the female jail officials beat her up. It was never filed. The DWI charge was dropped.

The other woman in the case, Cynthia Campbell Ray, spent the humid Houston summer in a downstairs apartment at the Kingston street fourplex she had traded to Roy Beene for his services in getting her no-billed. On April 29 Cindy had brought an action against Roy to set aside their agreement, and the matter was still in the courts.

One of the upstairs apartments in the fourplex was rented in June to Terry Hasty, a young Missouri woman with a two-year-old child and heavily pregnant with another one. She had just come back from Germany, where she had left her husband. Cindy's telephone had been disconnected for nonpayment, and on occasion—but sometimes as often as three times a day—she climbed the stairs to make calls from Terry Hasty's kitchen. Terry usually had a pot of coffee on the stove, and Cindy would ask for a cup. The two women talked. Cindy's hands shook, rattling the cup on the saucer. She smoked steadily. And she smelled, Terry noticed. It was a powerful and pungent body odor, and for a while Terry couldn't, or didn't want to, define it. "She was always nice to my kids," Terry said later, when I met her, "but when she leaned over my two year old to say 'hi,' he would rear up and scream. Then after a while, I realized she smelled like someone who didn't wash after sex. One day she was angry about something and I noticed that the angrier she got the worse she smelled. A horrible body odor. Sometimes it would leave my whole house smelling."

But there was no sexual partner in Cindy's life at the time. She never talked about sex, and Terry got the feeling it wasn't very high on her landlady's list of priorities. Cindy was separated from her husband, Makhlouf. A few times when she didn't pay the gas and the hot water heater didn't work she told Terry that Makhlouf was supposed to be giving her money and hadn't done it. Her only friend seemed to be Queer Bob, who had been living with Cindy when Terry first moved in. But at daybreak, almost every day, Cindy would scream at Bob and chase him into the street. Finally he moved out.

"I don't care about men anymore," Cindy said one day, over coffee, discussing her increasing poundage. "They're more trouble than they're worth, so why worry about weight? I don't care about men, and I don't care about me."

Cindy rarely went out alone. No one took her anywhere. A few times when Terry Hasty was loading her car to go to the laundromat or shop at Safeway she offered to take Cindy along, or even buy groceries for her. Cindy never accepted. She played certain tapes—Judy Garland singing "Somewhere Over the Rainbow," and Edith Piaf's "La Vie en Rose" —over and over. If Terry knocked on the door for any reason, Cindy opened it about two inches and peered out, her bulk blocking entry. She wouldn't let Terry see inside.

She never discussed David West, never said anything about her children, parents, or family. For a while Terry had no idea about Cindy's notoriety. A few weeks after she moved in, a visiting friend said, "Do you know who that is down there? Are you crazy, living here?" After that Terry became a little nervous.

On July 2 Roy Beene went to court and formally asked that Cynthia Ray vacate the premises. Cindy protested, but in deposition before

Judge Thomas R. Phillips of Harris County's 280th District Court, she was asked by Roy if she had inherited the house as a result of her conspiring with David West to plot the murder of her parents. Under oath, she replied softly, "Upon advice of counsel, I refuse to answer that question and invoke my privilege against self-incrimination as protected by the Fifth Amendment to the Constitution of the United States and Article One, Section Ten, of the Constitution of the State of Texas."

Roy Beene argued that if Cindy was guilty of capital murder "in the form of the most detested of crimes, patricide and matricide," then surely no reasonable attorney would commit himself to her defense without adequate compensation, and therefore it was vital for the purpose of determining a fair fee to know if she was guilty or innocent, and she couldn't hide behind the shield of the Fifth Amendment. Judge Phillips agreed and dismissed the suit with prejudice. On August 20 an appellate court rejected Cindy's appeal, and she was served with formal notice of eviction.

Cindy obeyed and moved out.

"After she left and took her things," Terry Hasty said, "the odor from downstairs started seeping up to me. On a real hot day, sometimes, I could smell it on the stairwell. It was foul. I told Roy I thought there was a dead animal in there."

On Labor Day, with Makhlouf, Cindy came by the fourplex. Under a tropical afternoon sun Terry sat with her two year old in a little blue plastic swimming pool in the front yard. Cindy demanded the rent money for September. Terry explained that Roy Beene had come by and told her he was the new landlord. "I asked him for proof," Terry said, "and he showed me a copy of the deed where you signed the house over to him."

An exasperated Cindy screamed, "That issue's still in court! You can either pay your rent to me on the first or you'll be evicted! I don't care if you're having a baby or not!" She threw Terry a handwritten eviction notice.

"Keep it. I don't need any toilet paper," Terry said.

Two days later Terry gave birth to her baby, and on that same day Roy Beene forced the door and entered Cindy's downstairs apartment. He muttered, "Jesus Christ, I don't believe this." Tim Lewis, a lawyer who had represented Makhlouf before the grand jury in March, was with Roy, and later said to me, "Words cannot describe what we encountered."

Nevertheless, he tried.

No curtains or blinds covered the windows, just soiled sheets nailed to the walls. The hardwood floors and one carpet were covered with dead cockroaches and catshit. The light switches were smeared with grease. Open sacks full of several weeks' garbage filled the kitchen. A filthy mattress lay on the bedroom floor. Fruit flies flew through the apartment in gangs of thousands. The living room walls were spray-painted with indecipherable hieroglyphics. The bathroom was littered with hair and wadded Kleenex and looked as if it had never been cleaned, and the floor of the closet opposite to the sink was piled a foot high with used toilet paper. The smell was nauseating.

Roy Beene was not a neat man, but this was beyond his understanding. He arranged for a visiting sea captain named Rick Cadwallader to live in the apartment rent-free in exchange for a thorough cleaning job. Cadwallader poured eight gallons of bleach and sulfuric acid on the wooden floor to remove various stains, many of which he believed were urine.

In the garage Roy discovered about 200 pounds of modeling clay and an unfinished oil portrait of a beautiful woman. He realized that it was an idealized self-portrait of Cindy Ray. It had been painted by her three or four years ago, before she gained weight. Her hands were on her hips, her breasts were thrust forward, her glossy auburn hair fell to one side. It was the portrait of a strong and confident woman who no longer existed . . . who may indeed never have existed other than in fantasy and on canvas.

Looking at it made Roy feel uncomfortable and then melancholic. A tragedy, he thought again. What happened to this woman? She was young once, and pretty . . . and *clean*. When did it all begin?

I wondered about that, too.

Roy Beene also told a story that a few days after the August eviction Cindy called him, anxious to settle their quarrel, and offered him $100,000 for the house. "You sued me," Roy pointed out. "You don't throw the dice and lose and then ask to settle. Besides, you don't have $100,000."

If he gave her back the house, Cindy explained, she would agree to sell it and pay him the money.

No deal, said Roy.

His attitude hardened even more when he received a telephone call the following week from Makhlouf. Gino, as many people called him, wanted to see Roy on his wife's behalf. At noon on the next day, just as Roy returned to his Woodway Drive office from court, Gino appeared, sweating from the September heat. He was a short, somber man in his late twenties, with black curly hair, black brows, dark eyes, and olive skin. A boxer's face. He wore the same blue shirt and chinos that he seemed to always wear.

His English was decent, but at moments of stress it tended to become stilted. His face rarely betrayed an expression. He said to Roy, "I have these three things to tell you. First, I am serving notice on you that my wife is still the owner of 2301 Kingston and has the right to collect rent there from her tenant. Second, if you don't back down from this attitude you have, the same thing that occurred before might soon occur to you. Third—"

Roy interrupted: "Don't tell me the third thing. You'd better hit me in the heart with the first bullet, or you're a dead Arab motherfucker."

He told Gino to get out. That afternoon he filed a report about the alleged threat with HPD and with Rusty Hardin at the District Attorney's Office. "If I get killed," he said, "I want you people to know who did it."

Cindy called him on the following Saturday and sweetly asked for a meeting. "Whoa there, wait a minute," Roy said, "I didn't like being threatened by Gino. What have you got in mind this time, the rack or the Iron Maiden?"

She swore Roy had misunderstood. Her husband hadn't meant to threaten him. He was upset. Moslems are very emotional. Wouldn't Roy please see her?

Roy felt a bit badly about what he had done in extracting the house from her in exchange for only three weeks of legal representation—there was a fair amount of criticism flying behind his back in the Houston legal world—and he agreed. But he took one precaution: he insisted they meet in daylight in a public place, and he chose a little downtown bit of greenery on Buffalo Bayou called Cleveland Park.

The day was warm and muggy. Roy made sure he was upwind of her. She was fatter than ever, he estimated. And just as unpleasant. He kept trying to stuff his shirt in over his belly and peer myopically over his shoulder into the dazzling glare of sunlight to see if Gino was drawing a bead on him from afar. Such things happened, he knew.

"I'll give you $60,000 for the house," Cindy said, after the pleasantries were over, "or I'll keep suing you."

Roy blinked in surprise. But he had come here to compromise and salve his conscience. He sighed, "I'll take the $100,000 you offered me before Gino came round."

She refused. Sixty thousand, take it or leave it.

You dumb cow, Roy thought, that was your last chance. "Good luck, Cindy," he said, and bounded off to his Cadillac, happy to be alive.

A defendant facing the death penalty tends to forget that his lawyer lives in a larger world in which other clients and even a family exist. In that other world, separate from the David West trial, Gene Nettles was a troubled man. He and his law partner (they were an independent, two-man operation) had just been bought out by an aggressive Austin-based law firm, Scott, Douglass & Lutin, which was opening a new office in Houston to be staffed by at least thirty lawyers. It was too good a deal to turn down: Gene would nearly double his income. But he had not only to move offices, he had to rethink his vision of himself as a lawyer. He would now handle cases because the firm wanted him to, and justify before a weekly partnership meeting the taking on of new clients. He was not optimistic.

To add to that professional concern, his wife Corliss, a tall, beautiful, fragile-looking woman in her early thirties, was pregnant for the fourth time. The previous three times she had miscarried. The doctor had restricted Corliss's movements; she was meant to spend most of the day in bed. Gene was worried about her.

Despite these preoccupations he had cleared his caseload and was prepared to concentrate on saving the life of David West. With the approval of David's father, Gene obtained the services of Bobby Newman, a former HPD officer and now head of the Acta Detective Agency. Gene set Newman the task of carrying out a full background investigation of Kim Paris. He also hired a part-time University of Houston Law School senior to act as legal researcher on the case, and she began work by serving a subpoena on the U.S. Navy for Kim Paris's service records.

Jury selection in a capital murder trial could last many weeks; it was a nonstop, exhausting process. You couldn't pick a jury and at the same time properly prepare witnesses and evaluate evidence. What he really needed, Gene thought—and then told Duval West—was the full-time help of another experienced trial lawyer.

The bill was mounting, threatening to rise in an exponential curve. Gene, who charged $150 an hour for his services, hadn't even begun to put in the evening and weekend hours that were inevitable during trial. Duval was dipping into his life's savings, and they were dwindling. He had put his son's old house on the market, but it was a wreck; no one had leaped to buy it in a Texas economy already starting to suffer because of sinking oil prices.

Duval sighed and lit another Carlton. How could he afford a *second* lawyer? "I don't know what to tell you," he said to Gene, blinking his rheumy eyes.

As a result, Gene made a bold legal move, and one that was to have consequences far beyond what he or anyone could foresee. He put on

138

his most sober suit and in stentorian tones presented his problem to Judge Azios. The State of Texas, he argued, had two full-time lawyers working on this case—the formidable Rusty Hardin, star of the Harris County district attorney's staff, and Assistant District Attorney Lyn McClellan, a chief prosecutor. Beyond that, Rusty Hardin could command the full logistical and research services of the Harris County District Attorney's Office. "I've got only me," Gene complained, "and whoever else I can afford to hire, which at the moment is nobody except a senior from U. of H. This is a high-profile case, Judge. It's already attracted national publicity. There's one writer doing a book about it already, and another hotfooting it this way from Washington. I'm going to look pretty foolish—and so is this court, and so is Harris County—trying to act like a one-man band. Judge, do you see what I'm saying? I need help. I need a court-appointed lawyer to back me up."

The judge sympathized. He asked Gene Nettles for a list of criminal defense attorneys who would be acceptable to the defense, and they finally agreed on Jim Leitner, another former assistant district attorney who had recently gone into private practice. He was a hard-working, able, and sincere man. He and Nettles had been friends when they first started out in the District Attorney's Office. Judge Azios contacted Leitner that afternoon and Leitner agreed to take on the case as Nettles's junior partner—"to sit second chair," as trial lawyers say. The State of Texas would pay him.

Rusty Hardin, when he learned of the appointment, jumped up from his swivel chair at his desk in the D.A.'s Office and blistered the air. Had the legal world gone mad? What Nettles had requested and what Judge Azios had granted was an unprecedented judicial act. In Texas any indigent defendant has the right to a court-appointed lawyer; sometimes, in a major case, the court would indeed appoint two lawyers. But by hiring Gene Nettles and making a payment agreement with him, David West had renounced any claims to poverty. Nettles, if he needed help, could have arranged for the West family to hire and pay Leitner (or any other lawyer), or agreed to split his own fees with Leitner, or looked for co-counsel among his new partners at Scott, Douglass & Lutin. Judge Azios had agreed to pay Leitner $500 a day for pretrial court time and $750 a day when the trial began. With the court's appointment of Leitner, the State of Texas, in effect, was subsidizing Gene Nettles.

Rusty's temper simmered slowly. Then Nettles, with a smile, turned up the gas and struck a match.

Last March, for the David West trial, the District Attorney's Office had engaged the services of Professor Al Yonovitz, Associate Professor

139

of Hearing Sciences and director of the Speech and Hearing Institute at the University of Texas's Health Science Center in Houston. Dr. Yonovitz's task was to "enhance" the tapes for maximum intelligibility and prepare a final transcript that the state would offer to the jury. A draft version of this transcript had been finished in July and a copy provided to Nettles. Rusty had also given Gene what Dr. Yonovitz called a "first-generation" copy of the raw tapes. They filled nearly five ninety-minute cassettes.

Two weeks after he had secured Jim Leitner to sit second chair, Gene, with Duval's permission, hired his *own* expert—Samuel A. Guiberson, a documentary filmmaker-turned-lawyer who specialized in cases involving electronic surveillance. Guiberson had written a much-discussed article for the *National Law Journal* with the catchy title, "How To Send Prosecutors Reeling with Their Own Taped Evidence." At Gene's request Guiberson began work on an independent transcribing job of the West-Paris tapes, and it was soon apparent that the defense's version and the state's version would differ. Except at certain moments, the tapes were difficult to listen to. Kim Paris had carried the transmitter in her purse; every time she moved, or shifted the purse, extraneous noise garbled or suffocated the transmission. Much of the conversation on both nights had taken place in restaurants, with background chatter of other diners, chairs scraping, dishes and cutlery clinking, and loud music. There were gaps in the dialogue, one of them fairly long, when the van had lost touch with Kim in her racing VW.

On August 14 Nettles moved to postpone the motion to suppress the tapes as evidence until after jury selection. He wanted to give Sam Guiberson time to complete his study, and he needed more information on the possible use of drugs and alcohol in eliciting the confession. Judge Azios granted the postponement.

And Rusty reeled. He nearly boiled over. If Duval West was too broke to hire Jim Leitner, where in hell was the money coming from to pay for the time of this new defense expert? "Now the State of Texas isn't just subsidizing Gene Nettles," Rusty yelled, "it's subsidizing Sam Guiberson!"

"And why shouldn't they?" Nettles would have yelled back, had he been openly accused. "Are they afraid of a fair fight?"

But he wasn't openly accused. Rusty Hardin grasped the effect of that unspoken argument. It may not have legal merit, but it would look good in print and perhaps even in an appellate brief should David West be convicted. And so Rusty decided, for the moment, to limit his choleric complaints to the sympathetic audience of his comrades in the District Attorney's Office. If he made a public fuss, it would seem as if he was

Left to right: Hattie and Tom Thurlow, James and Virginia Campbell, Robert and Sue Harris. Las Vegas, 1974. "It was always fun to be with Virginia and James . . ."

1.

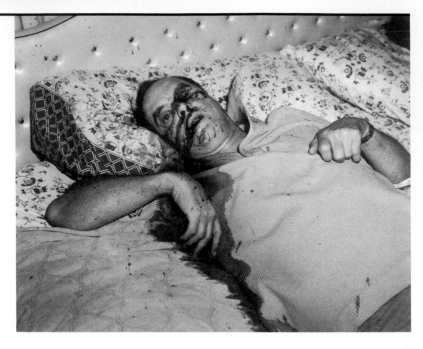

2.

James Campbell, June 19, 1982. "Here was horror . . ."

3.

Virginia Campbell, June 19, 1982. "What could these middle-aged sub-urban people have done to deserve this kind of death?"

4.

Front view, 8901 Memorial Drive. "If you come upon a bunker, assault it."

Press conference, December 11, 1985. Left to right: Kim Paris, Rusty Hardin, Sgt. Paul Motard, Officer Ray White, Sgt. Gil Schultz, Moss Thornton, KPRC-radio. "He wanted justice done, but it was so much sweeter with a bit of drama."

5.

Sgt. Gil Schultz, HPD. *"Homicide is so exacting. Two people know who did it. One ain't talking, and the other can't."*

Back view, 8901 Memorial Drive. June 1986. *"Sgt. Schultz, did you see that the trees and shrubbery had been cut?"*

Clyde Wilson at his desk. *"We've been called the Cadillac of investigative agencies."*

Kim Paris and Rusty Hardin at the December 11, 1985, press conference. "This should have been her special day . . ."

Urban Animals at a picnic in Allen Park (seated center: Melanie Edgecombe). "The Animal motto, 'Skate or Die,' was a cry of defiance against urban rigidity."

10.

11.

David West's house at 1409 Vermont. *"Those Marine pals of his moved in with him. They just roosted there."*

At voir dire, November 1985. Left to right: Lyn McClellan, David West, Rusty Hardin (obscured: Jim Leitner). "And here, too, human beings are permitted to play at being gods."

12.

13 and 14.

David West in court, June 1986 and March 1987. *"They've just been executed, is all. I didn't do anything wrong."*

Duval and Cecilia West. *"We assume he didn't do it. Don't tell us if he's innocent or guilty."* ▼

15.

16.

David West (just after his arrest). "Betrayed was too pale a word."

unsure of his case against David West and was trying to weight the odds
—in terms of manpower—too heavily in favor of the state.

He *was* unsure of his case. Drawing closer to jury selection, he began
to grasp the enormous problem of convincing twelve people to convict
a man of capital murder solely on the basis of a repudiated admission to
a scheming woman. That's how the world might well see it, he realized,
especially now that the creative mind of Sam Guiberson had joined the
defense team. But he didn't dare let Nettles and Leitner or the media
know the extent of his doubt, and so he clamped his jaw shut and
decided to move forward as if all was well.

13

Another trial postponement was announced. They would start picking
a jury, I was told, on October 14. Frustrated by the delay, I went to see
District Attorney Johnny Holmes on October 3 to talk about the case,
to ask him if he was really convinced that David West had told the truth
to Kim Paris. Holmes wasn't sure. "When you have a man by the balls,"
he said, "his heart and soul follow. I know some guys that would admit
to shooting the Pope to get a piece of ass. So . . . was West just making
admissions to placate this woman? That's a fact question. Up to the
jury."

At the close of our hour I mentioned that I'd been calling Rusty
Hardin regularly but had never reached him and never been called back.

"He's just busy," Holmes assured me, a bit too quickly.

On Tuesday evening, October 8, Rusty finally called. He had a cordial
Southern voice. He said, "I want you to know I've received all your
messages. I always return phone calls from journalists, but in your case
I made an exception. I decided I wouldn't talk to you."

"You're talking to me now," I said, with more lightheartedness than I
really felt.

"That's because I felt guilty about not trusting you," he admitted.

I took a deep breath and asked a question to which I already knew the
answer. "Why do you think you can't trust me?"

"Because of certain events in your past."

Ah. That.

He didn't have to be more specific.

The Brooklyn Dodgers' Ralph Branca will always be remembered by baseball fans as the pitcher who served up the home run ball to Bobby Thompson of the Giants in the final game of the 1951 National League playoffs. And so far in my life I was known as the man who, in 1971, conceived and engineered the Howard Hughes Autobiography Hoax.

Bored at forty, a novelist looking for a challenge, living on the remote island of Ibiza off the coast of Spain, inexcusably naive at the outset and ultimately greedy, I had pretended to the McGraw-Hill Book Company that America's famous reclusive billionaire had entrusted me with the task of writing his "warts and all" autobiography. I did a thorough research job, got lucky and gained access to previously secret files; I concocted some remarkable tales of Howard Hughes's business capers, germ phobias, love life, political shenanigans, and long relationships with Albert Schweitzer and Ernest Hemingway—with the result that the final potpourri of bizarre fiction and even more bizarre fact received the imprimatur from Time Inc., and they bought the first serial rights for *Life* magazine.

When the hoax fell apart—as it had to, considering its basic lunacy— I returned the money to the publishers (less what I had spent on research and some high living, and sums gobbled up by the IRS and the Swiss government) and for my efforts received from the Nixon administration a tax bill of $450,000 and a sixteen-month tour of various federal prisons, where I learned to lift weights, cook bootleg steaks on burning rolls of toilet paper, and be courteous to men serving life sentences for violent crimes.

Five years later, in 1978, I went on a publicity tour for a just-published novel called *The Death Freak,* and in every city, in every interview, I was asked not about the novel but about the Hughes Hoax. Had I really believed I'd get away with it? Had it hurt my career as a writer? Did I regret having done it? "Yes," I usually said to that last one, "because I've been nearly bored to death by questions about it."*

---

* One recent biographer of Howard Hughes details the following historical footnote to the hoax— which escaped the attention of journalists in the 1970s.

Not a fan of Richard Nixon, I had my Howard admit in the *Autobiography* that he had passed $400,000 in cash to Nixon when the latter was vice-president, as a quid pro quo for Nixon's fixing the TWA case in Howard's favor. On my part this was guesswork based on good sources, logic, and bias.

In *Citizen Hughes* (New York: Holt, Rinehart & Winston, 1985, pp. 421–22, 500), Michael Drosnin wrote: "The account of the Hughes–Nixon dealings in Irving's book was quoted in an unpublished Senate Watergate Committe report. [H. R.] Haldeman started getting FBI reports on the Irving affair directly from J. Edgar Hoover, and [in early 1972] the White House managed to obtain a copy of the still-secret manuscript from a source at McGraw-Hill. . . . Nixon read at least a summary of Irving's account. It came as quite a shock. The $400,000 figure [was] probably not far off the mark." In consequence—Drosnin claims—in order to discover what the opposition

"You have a reputation for being a fair man," I said to Rusty Hardin, on the telephone in Houston, in October 1985. "Let's sit down for five minutes, face to face. I'll speak my piece, and you make up your mind."

After a thoughtful pause, he said, "All right . . . nine o'clock tomorrow morning. Seventh floor, the District Attorney's Building."

Rusty had once said in a crowded courtroom: "Could I have it quiet? I'm trying to do the Lord's work here, and I'm just not getting any respect." He was smiling, but most people who knew him well thought he was quite serious. Not that he was a religious fanatic; he simply equated his role in the process of justice with order in the universe. Order and justice were God's purposes. Rusty was therefore at His right hand, doing service. He was a man dedicated to doing the right thing, and he was also a righteous man with a quick temper. He admitted it. His temper was such that once it had led to his being hit by a defense lawyer named Bob Tarrant.

Tarrant, who had been defending his own daughter against the charge of possession of a controlled substance, told me the story. Rusty later confirmed it.

"Rusty and I are in court. He's smarter than me, and he wins. But my tactics must have offended him. After the trial he leans over and whispers in my ear, 'You're the biggest piece of scum I ever met.' So I socked him. He recovered and said, 'And you haven't got much of a punch.' So I socked him again, and this time I knocked him into the jury box."

Tarrant was fined twenty-five dollars by the presiding judge. Later someone said to Rusty, "That was the stupidest thing you ever did, cursing at Bob Tarrant."

"No," Rusty chuckled ruefully, "the stupidest thing I ever did was tell him that he hadn't got much of a punch."

Born and raised in Monroe, North Carolina, Rusty had graduated from Wesleyan University in Connecticut in 1965 and then taken a job teaching history at a small private school in Alabama. The Vietnam war came along. "I was the only half-blind recruit to slip through OCS training,"

---

knew about the Hughes "loans," the Hunt–Liddy team was created to break into National Democratic Headquarters at the Watergate.

he once said. "I just memorized the chart on the side of my bad eye. When they found out, they called me Cyclops." He spent fifteen months in Vietnam and placed that experience in an interesting perspective by commenting that "I mainly distinguished myself by sleeping through an enemy mortar attack." After his discharge from the army he worked in Washington for a congressman from North Carolina, an experience that convinced him to forget about politics as a career. Rusty wanted to make his mark, but he wanted to do it cleanly, without owing favors and without compromising his ethics. He was a true son of the 1960s.

The law seemed a proper alternative to politics. A late starter, Rusty wound up in Texas because Southern Methodist University in Dallas was the only one of thirteen law schools he applied to that would have him. He confessed to a reporter, "The funny thing is that back then I envisioned myself as a defense attorney. At SMU I heard Racehorse Haynes lecture. He talked about what a great feeling of accomplishment it was for a defense attorney to walk into federal court, face all the power and majesty of the U.S. government, and beat them single-handedly. That impressed me."

Because not only did Rusty want to do the right thing, to follow the precepts of his beloved John F. Kennedy by serving and contributing— he wanted to win at whatever he did. Could you do both? He would give it a try.

In 1975, when he passed the bar, he took an offered job with Harris County as a lowly assistant district attorney in the "nonsupport" section, locating and prosecuting husbands who failed in their child support payments. A good place to begin practicing trial law, he thought. But to his surprise he discovered that he loved it. Here he found he could do the right thing *and* win. The combination was irresistible.

And he was good at what he did. Not merely good, but innovative, inspirational. Three years later he was chief prosecutor in a district court, and in 1985, at a vigorous forty-four, in the organizational structure of the Harris County District Attorney's Office he was what was known as a super-chief. At one time or another nearly everyone else in the department sat in on his trials to learn how the job was properly done. At cross-examination and final argument he had no peer in Harris County. It seemed to be a matter of the right man in the right place in the right job.

Rusty Hardin was deeply, painfully ambitious. He was ambitious the way a fine golfer is who knows he can drive the ball 250 yards every time, and dare not drive it less, and secretly aches to reach the 300-yard mark. Rusty had won ninety-four felony cases in a row in Harris County, topping former Assistant District Attorney Ted Poe's mark of seventy-four. The David West trial would make ninety-five. Rusty was like the sheriff of Dodge City, and the ninety-four wins might have been notches on his six-shooter. As a result, every gunfighter wanted to shoot him down. Gene Nettles was no exception.

Rusty looked forward to winning an even hundred. After that, he made no predictions. Even if Johnny Holmes went elsewhere, Rusty would probably refuse the promotion to district attorney, because the D.A. was an administrator and didn't argue cases in court. He would certainly never become a defense attorney, because defense attorneys, by definition, could not do the Lord's work. Their aim was to make money, and their obligation was to serve their client faithfully and walk him out of the courtroom even if he had committed the most heinous of crimes. Rusty understood the concept of the adversary system, but the idea of fighting to free a guilty man sometimes made him want to retch.

Most people believed that one day Rusty would be offered a vacant state judgeship, or even a seat on the federal bench. No one was sure that he would take it. "I don't want to illustrate the Peter Principle," he once said, "where every employee tends to rise to the level of his incompetence."

He was what they called a lifer. He might just keep prosecuting criminals until they carted him away.

————————

His seventh-floor office was cozy, warmly furnished in oak, with brown leather visitors' chairs. Rusty was a scrubbed-looking man of less than average height, compactly built, darting in movement—and when he wasn't in motion he seemed to quiver in fixed alertness like a jackrabbit. Some people radiate intelligence, instant authority, and unquestionable competence; Rusty was such a man. He had the ruddy tan and strong veined hands of an outdoorsman, the thoughtful blue eyes of a philosopher, the stubborn jaw of a middleweight contender. You would follow him, I thought, into an unmapped jungle, and you would focus on him as a force to be reckoned with if he chose to run for political office. On the day I met him he was dressed like a cross between a TV network executive and a college professor in smart navy blue blazer, yellow shirt, and yellow silk foulard tie.

He sat behind his desk with an unlit pipe clamped between his teeth. Rusty had given up smoking cigarettes one year and four days ago, he told me later. He still missed it, he admitted—he wasn't a nonsmoker, but a smoker who no longer smoked. I understood. So was I.

"I told you I have trouble trusting you," he said to me in that melo-

145

dious Carolina accent, "and that of course is because of the Hughes hoax. I wasn't even going to meet you, but Johnny Holmes likes you. He twisted my arm. The Campbell case is capital murder—what you call in New York first degree murder. A man's life or death is at stake. I can't have people around me who I have to worry about."

"The reason you don't trust me," I said, "is because of something that happened fourteen years ago."

Rusty thought that over, then smiled softly in homage to time. "Fourteen years ago? That makes me feel old."

"Me too," I said.

"What do you want from me?"

"Your confidence. This will be my first nonfiction book since 1969, and you can bet your best pair of boots my publisher's lawyers will read it under a microscope. I have to be scrupulous. And good."

Rusty started talking, and I didn't leave his office until two hours later.

"I love this job," he said, "because I've never once been asked to do anything I didn't believe in. I call myself a happy man. I get up in the morning, and I can't wait to get to work. When the day is done, which usually turns out to be around seven in the evening, I can't wait to get home." A carved wood plaque on his desk attested to that: RUSTY HARDIN, A/K/A "STILL HERE." It had been a gift from his lanky blond wife, Ann, called Tissy. Photographs of her, with their two sons, decorated the walls of the office.

I was glad to meet him. I had been looking for a hero in this drama, and Rusty seemed the prime candidate.

"What do you know about this case?" he asked.

I told him all the facts I'd accumulated, all the theories I'd kicked around in my head. Sometimes he commented; more often not. I asked him about Cindy Ray still being free. It bothered him—it bothered him a lot. He was a little surprised when I quoted Johnny Holmes as saying that he would require a lot of persuasion to ever make a deal with the trigger man in order to get the person who set the wheels of murder in motion.

"Johnny said that? Well, I don't necessarily agree, but in this case I have other reasons to focus on David West."

"You wouldn't consider a plea bargain in order to get an indictment against Cindy Ray?"

With all his heart he wanted that indictment, but not at any cost. "I don't see how we could justify that kind of barter to the public. In my view we have a responsibility to the people's perception of what justice is. I can't just say, 'Fuck what people think.' And even more importantly —you'll discover this yourself when you hear the confession tapes played

146

in court—David, not Cindy, was the prime mover in the inception of the Campbells' murder. That sick, confused girl couldn't have pushed a man to kill someone. She began to get cold feet and David said, in effect, 'You've got to take revenge, got to execute your parents for what they did to you.'"

But I pointed out that Rusty knew all that only from what David West told Kim Paris under strained circumstances. Suppose it wasn't true?

Rusty frowned and bit hard on his pipe. "I may be the only one around here who believes wholeheartedly that David told the truth to Kim, and that he deserves death for a villainous crime. I run everything by Tissy, my wife, and I've learned to trust her insights. She agrees with you in this instance. She says, 'What if he was boasting? Trying to be macho?'"

"And what if Tissy's right?"

"Let the jury decide," Rusty said, echoing Holmes. "That's what the system is all about."

"Do you mean you'd prosecute even if you had doubts that a defendant was guilty?"

His eyes turned a trifle stony at that, and there was a new cutting edge to his tone. "If I had *reasonable* doubt that a defendant was guilty, I'd drop the case and get the indictment quashed. I told you I believe wholeheartedly that he did it. I'm asking for the death penalty! Do you think I'd do that frivolously?"

"I hope not," I said. We had a little moment of tension there, a portent, but it passed. Then he smiled almost radiantly. Rusty loved to joust.

He was a fan of Kim Paris, he told me. He respected her. She'd had no experience at what she did, but she had done it with remarkable professionalism—never led David West in the interrogation, never imbedded any answer in her question. In such a scam, Rusty explained, there was a tendency for the investigator to do most of the talking, to guide the subject into the areas that would be most harmful for him, to ask yes-or-no questions when the going got rocky. But Kim hadn't done that. It had been a brilliant free-form performance. It would stand up in court under scrutiny. When I heard the tapes, I would understand.

Gene Nettles, he predicted, would be a tough opponent. Jim Leitner, the co-defense counsel, might play an interesting role. He and Rusty lived in houses that faced each other across the same suburban street in Southwest Houston near Brays Bayou. Their children were in Little League together. "The gentle giant," Rusty called him fondly, but I hadn't met Leitner yet and didn't know what Rusty meant.

"What are the odds on the verdict?" I asked.

"This is off the record, until the trial's over. I wouldn't want Gene Nettles to know how I feel about this. (I felt an inner glow. He trusted me!) Have you met David West yet?"

"They won't let him have visitors."

"He's our main problem. He's kind of a gooney bird. He'll make a good impression on the jury. It's going to be difficult for them to believe that he pulled the trigger and murdered two people in cold blood."

I wasn't exactly sure what a gooney bird was, but it was an evocative image. I said, "That's what everyone in Montrose says about him. Six shots all hit their mark. Good shooting for a gooney bird. Maybe they could have been fired by someone like Wickie Weinstein," I tried, "or Mad Military Mike."

Rusty nodded coolly. My stock was rising, but he wasn't going to buy in yet.

"Or Salino," I added.

He raised an eyebrow. "What do you know about Salino?"

"If he exists, he's a local Mafia hood, a friend of Cindy Ray's. I'm going to hunt for him. What do *you* know about him?"

"No more than you. She's mentioned him more than once as a friend, her confidant. He's probably a fantasy character. But we're looking for him. You know what's odd? That a space cadet like Cindy never confided in anyone about the murders. At least we've never found anyone."

"You found Gwen Sampson."

But again Rusty offered no comment. My warm inner glow was beginning to cool. He wasn't going to take me in as his partner in the investigation.

"If I find Salino," I promised, "I'll let you know. If I find out anything about the murders that seems important, and if it's not information given to me in confidence, I'll tell you. I'll tell Nettles, too. I won't play favorites."

"I'm comfortable with that," Rusty said. "You may very well wind up knowing more about the case—particularly the people in it—than I do. So I'll always be interested to hear what you learn."

"Can you let me see the HPD offense report on the case?"

"It's not mine to show. You should ask Gil Schultz."

We shook hands.

———————————

On a hot blue October afternoon, through what was the greenest and probably the prettiest part of the city, I drove along winding Memorial Drive. There was little traffic on the road. I was hunting for a number

148

and finally flew right by it, for the faded "8901" on the mailbox was easy to miss. I made a U-turn and pulled into the driveway.

A damp breeze blew lightly through the forest, but otherwise the afternoon was silent. Cloaked by masses of foliage from the surrounding trees, the brick and flagstone house was set back about thirty yards from the road in a wooded area of pines and small pin oaks, with just enough room for one car to nose up on the dirt driveway against the metal gates. The gates were chained together with an old padlock.

I parked my wagon in that slot in full view of the world. It struck me that if my car was out in the open it would be just a little bit easier to talk myself out of any trouble, for I hadn't asked official permission to come here and hadn't wanted to know if it was necessary.

A strong wire fence circled the property. I couldn't see far enough into the green shadows of the forest to make out if the fence line was broken anywhere. The gates were padlocked and were too high to climb, but they had plenty of give and creak, and the chain was only waist high. I slung my camera over my shoulder, dropped my note pad over the fence into the dirt, pulled the gates apart and clambered over the chain.

The house was derelict. It was the kind of comfortable, ordinary suburban brick house that could fit into almost any community in the United States, and yet in the dappled sunlight of this Texas afternoon it had the quality of a remote New England manor house that Hollywood favors for gothics and horror stories. Rain pelts down, lightning crackles in swollen dark skies, and black cats screech as doors suddenly slam. The kind of movie where, as ulcerated corpses rise from the grave, even the most world-weary among us hears himself gasp, and the palms grow clammy.

That kind of house . . . and it was apropos. The human beings who lived here had been slaughtered. Despite the heat of the afternoon, every time I thought of that I felt a chill. Their death was real, not a game to be played by curious journalists and jousting lawyers.

Behind the house a metal staircase led to the apartment over the garage. I climbed it. These had been the quarters of the maid, Maria. The glass pane of the door was broken, and I reached in and unlocked the door. It was stifling inside, and I started sweating. A few plastic kids' toys lay on the floor, and a collection of Dr. Seuss books was moldering away on a book shelf. Little Michael and littler Matthew had played here. A 1982 calendar in Spanish, with scenes of Mexican churches, still hung on the wall above a sagging brown sofa. The last month that showed was *Junio*. So, playing detective, I deduced that Maria had left within two weeks of the murders.

Her former bedroom had no furniture, but was crammed with worn

149

cartons and shopping bags stuffed with women's clothes. They were a young woman's clothes, not Maria's: faded blue jeans, dirty sneakers, piles of damp sweaters that smelled of mold. An old metal camp trunk was filled with professionally printed eight-by-ten black-and-white enlargements: people set against backgrounds that looked not only Texan but European. I guessed they had been shot by Michelle Campbell, the oldest of the sisters, who was a photographer now in Austin. The drawings were line and charcoal and ink, portraits and nudes, and they showed talent. I wondered if they had been done by Cindy Ray. Do murderers create fine art? Can you see violence in their line?

I closed that door behind me, went down the iron steps in the silence of the warm afternoon, and, sweating freely, crossed the yard to the back of the house. The yard was an untended jungle. It had been that way too when the Campbells were alive.

In the garage there was a soda and ice cream dispenser. Discarded old golf balls were festooned with cobwebs. Relics of a dead and buried past. . . .

I tried a window at the back of the house. To my surprise, it slid open with no difficulty. Then I realized this was the window to the den, the window through which the murderer had entered in the early morning blackness more than three years ago. I could look inside and see that the room was bare of furniture.

Like the murderer, I hoisted myself up and squeezed through the open window.

Inside the house it was stuffy. With the tennis sweatband on my wrist, I wiped my forehead. I padded from the den into the hallway, and then into the living room. Wraiths and shades swirled round. . . .

The green wall-to-wall carpeting extended to every room, but it was shabby and frayed, here and there torn. I assumed at the time that this was the natural result of three years of neglect and vermin; I didn't realize, because I hadn't yet met Mike St. John, that it had been like this when the Campbells lived here.

The murderer would have had to pass through the living room, then mount the staircase with its silver Art Deco banister. Tall chimes stood against the wall. If they still functioned they would ring when the front door bell was pushed. That hot June night, the chimes had not rung.

Reaching the top of the stairs, I turned left past a bathroom. I walked slowly through the open door of the master bedroom—the room where James and Virginia Campbell had slept, the room where they had died. The light switch was to the left of the door. There was another bathroom and a walk-in closet to the left, and a smaller closet to the right. The

150

king-sized bed would have been *there*, to the right. Jim Campbell's gun cabinet would have stood against *that* wall.

David West, if indeed it had been David West, would have stood exactly where I stood now, but in darkness.

Two sleeping people whom he hardly knew. What had they really done to Cindy Ray—and to *him*—to merit their extinction? I was hooked; I had to know the answers.

PART II

ABSOLUTION

14

The eight-story granite cube of the Harris County Courthouse on San Jacinto Street is the ugliest building in downtown Houston, with the nearby Harris County Jail a close second. And yet, for all their vulgarity, both buildings possess an aura of power. They need no decoration—they are bare stages for drama. Within their walls men and women accused of breaking the social contract are either granted the freedom to pursue their ends or condemned to be divided from all they hold dear. Human passions live and die here. Madness and cunning, poverty and greed, fear and hatred, suffering and deceit, jealousy and desperation, brutality and ignorance—all are common currency. The lesson we try so hard to teach our children, that all acts have consequences, becomes a stunning reality.

And here too, human beings are permitted to play at being gods.

On Tuesday, October 15, 1985, a few minutes before 10 A.M., jury selection began in the *State of Texas* v. *David Duval West*. Since Judge A. D. Azios was forced to vacate his regular courtroom (in order that a visiting judge from West Texas might deal with his daily docket), he and his entourage moved around the corner to the red brick courthouse annex at 403 Caroline, the Old Fire Station.

155

The rows of wooden spectators' benches in the fifth-floor courtroom were empty. The judge sat behind the high judicial barrier, the so-called bench, sipping from an outsized coffee mug. He was a kindly-looking man of sixty-four with a full head of dark, graying hair and a concerned manner. He wore no black robes now, just an olive-colored suit, white shirt, striped tie, and horn-rimmed glasses, so that he could easily have been taken for a bank president from the Rio Grande Valley, where indeed Arnulfo Diego Azios had been born. Without straining you could hear in his voice the lilt of Mexican ancestry. One of six children, he was ten when his father died, and he liked to say, "My Daddy left us his good name, and that was all, but it was a lot." Behind the bench, out of sight, he kept an electric heater for his feet (the courtroom air conditioning at times became arctic), a paper bag full of Fig Newtons and butter cookies, a jar of Nescafé and a small electric kettle, a well-thumbed edition of *Webster's Handy College Dictionary*, a paperback *Word Book* (which he studied, when he could, in order to enlarge his considerable vocabulary), a book called *West's Texas Cases*, copies of the current indictment, and several yellow legal pads full of notes and schedules.

A prelaw student at UT-Austin, young A. D. entered the army in May 1943 as an infantry volunteer, was wounded in Luxembourg, then spent four months as a POW in three German camps (including the infamous Alten Grabow), from the last of which he ultimately escaped. In the summer of 1985 he traveled to East Germany to visit all three camps, and on the following Veteran's Day he wrote a memoir for the Houston *Post*: *"Oh, Alten Grabow, where the lengthening starvation caused some POWs to thank the Allied planes for bombing us. . . . God was my foxhole buddy; He pulled me through."*

After the war he was graduated from South Texas College of Law and had his own law practice in Houston until he was elected to a judgeship in 1976. Now, every other year, he spent a week or two taking courses in jurisprudence at such universities as Harvard, Stanford, and Brandeis. Every spring all the criminal court judges in Texas spend several days in Huntsville, at the state's prison complex, for a judges' conference. On those occasions A. D. Azios usually visited the prison. "I need to see where I'm sending men," he said. "I go to the metalworking shop and the furniture workshop. I want to make sure they're learning a trade."

Behind the bench in the courtroom an American flag and the flag of the State of Texas drooped on their stanchions. Bettie Conway, deputy district clerk for the 232nd District Court occupied a desk to the judge's left, where she sifted nonstop through jury lists and piles of documentation. She gave the impression of a patient, pleasant, middle-aged, overweight, overburdened housewife. To the right of the judge sat his court

156

reporter, Brenda Palmer, a beautiful thirty-four-year-old woman with dusky brown skin, cheerful dark eyes, and what a woman journalist covering the trial described as "one of the best-looking pair of legs I've ever seen." Although she was unmarried, Brenda wore a fat diamond on the third finger of her left hand. A fourteen-year courthouse veteran, she was paid by the page, and she had been Judge Azios's court reporter for the last four years. "She's *chiflada*," the judge liked to say, "spoiled. That's my fault. Sometimes I even carry her machine for her."

Five men sat grouped around a large counsel table placed directly in front of the bench. Rusty Hardin wore a stylish off-white summer suit, a dazzlingly blue shirt with a white collar, and a red tie. The other four were dressed in navy blue suits, conservative ties, and spotless white shirts, so that they looked like members of a club gathered for a formal occasion such as the induction of officers.

Gene Nettles shot his cuffs and crossed his legs, showing high-heeled, hand-tooled lizardskin boots.* He often spoke of his boyhood in Houston as if it had taken place in the last century: "When I was a boy, I rode my horse down Katy Road to the grocery store." Black-mustached and solemn, he looked as if he would have been equally at home starring in a John Ford movie about the cavalry's struggle to tame the West as he was in a court of law. He looked *Texan*.

Jim Leitner leaned across to whisper in his ear. A former prosecutor, married and the thirty-six-year-old father of four young sons, Leitner was an elder in three different Lutheran churches—a dark-eyed, friendly man who had the reputation of being studiously ethical. He had once been a champion weightlifter, at twenty-one setting a national collegiate record in the light-heavyweight class for the clean-and-jerk. In 1973, already a law student, he went to the Pan American games in Guadalajara, Mexico, and won three gold medals. He almost gave up the law to work for the York Barbell Company, and he once said to me, "I often wonder if I did the right thing. It would never have fed me, but it would be something they couldn't take away from me . . . if I had gone to the Olympics and won." He still worked out regularly at the Jewish Community Center near his home, and his rounded pectorals and bulging deltoids couldn't be hidden by a three-piece suit.

The next man, Bryan Lyn McClellan—Leitner's current prosecutorial opposite, in that he was "sitting second chair" to Rusty Hardin in this case—had started his professional life as an accountant. Wearying of

---

* This was a Houston tradition. Bum Phillips, former coach of the Houston Oilers football team, owned boots made from lizard, crocodile, alligator, python, kangaroo, badger, eel, anteater, caribou, ostrich, turkey, and beaver.

balance sheets and 1040 forms, he matriculated at South Texas College of Law at the age of thirty-two, passed the bar, won the State Moot Court Competition of the Texas Young Lawyers Association, and then joined the District Attorney's Office in Houston, where he advanced rapidly to be chief of prosecutors in Division C under Rusty Hardin.

Lyn, as everyone called him, was thirty-nine years old, bright and quick, jolly and needle-tongued, and, most obviously, fat. He weighed at least 300 pounds, and the way he squeezed his heft into an ordinary wooden courtroom armchair was akin to the way you might try to jam a liter of slippery custard into a one-quart container. There was overflow, a certain amount of adjustment, and often an evanescent smile of relief at the end. With his round cheeks and jowls that pressed over his white collar, and his trousers that never quite reached his shoes, Lyn looked like a small boy grown much too quickly into an obese man. He frightened many people, for he had tiny dark brown eyes, and he looked as if he could turn mean. You certainly wouldn't want Lyn McClellan to get angry and sit on you.

The fourth blue-suited member of this temporary club, who had an urchinlike quality that reminded me of a less arrogant Jimmy Connors, the tennis pro, was paler and younger than the others, with a small mouth and a cleft chin. A casual visitor could easily miss the fact that he wasn't a lawyer, although his neck did stick out a bit awkwardly from his white collar, like football players in college yearbook photographs. On his left wrist he wore a wide plastic ID bracelet from the Harris County Jail. He was David West, the accused murderer.

They all were going to help decide whether or not to kill this young man, and he was in on the decision.

The process that leads to the selection of a jury is called voir dire, and if you get any two lawyers in a room it is a fairly safe bet that they will not agree on either the meaning or origin of the words, or, if they happen to be from New York and Texas, how they are pronounced. A New York lawyer uses the French pronunciation, *vwah deer*. A Texan says *voar dyer* if he's from Dallas and *voh-er dahr* if he's from anywhere south or west of there. The translation of the French is "to see" and "to speak," but in Old French and Latin the words mean "to say the truth."

One hopes. The idea is to get the prospective jurors to testify accurately concerning their competency to reach a verdict. In a capital murder case in Texas, with death as a possible punishment, each juror is examined individually and privately in open court; his or her history, habits, beliefs, and prejudices are laid bare for all to see and dissect and frown at. It can take a long time. The results can be decisive, even alarming.

David West was about to find out.

So was Rusty Hardin. From his point of view, for a long time, the entire Campbell murder case would turn on an act that took place in voir dire and reached its logical and bizarre conclusion only when a jury sat down to deliberate.

On the first morning, before voir dire began, Nettles rattled off several motions for disclosure of evidence held by the state, until Judge Azios raised his hand and said, "A motion for this, a motion for that. All these motions! Slow down, please, Mr. Nettles. You're making me dizzy."

David West winked his hazel-brown eye at Rusty Hardin across the table and said quietly, "The judge has motion sickness."

Rusty Hardin tried to suppress his laughter, but couldn't.

That day four jurors were separately examined, and one—Lelia Sublett, a forty-eight-year-old housewife born in Ohio—was selected. She came across as a feisty, opinionated woman; nevertheless both sides, and David West, who was consulted by his lawyers, liked her spirit. But on the following morning, before the first juror entered the room to be heard, Rusty turned to Gene Nettles at the counsel table and muttered, "I was up half the night thinking about Ms. Sublett. She's a tough lady. I have a funny feeling one of us is going to live to regret picking her."

Without missing a beat, David West poked his pale head forward from where he lolled in the chair next to Nettles, and said, "I sure hope it's me."

Once it registered, everyone cracked up laughing.

When the group broke for lunch, Rusty remarked to Nettles, "Your client is witty."

David heard that remark. He was flattered. He had always thought of himself as witty, but a trial to determine whether he lived or died hadn't seemed the right place to showcase it. Yet it made the proceedings less coldly frightening if they could be overlaid with a patina of good humor. And he was beginning to *like* Rusty.

How could you not? Rusty was so quick, so aware. You had to be careful with this man if you were in David's shoes. David realized that.

Rusty also thought about it when he drove home that evening on the Southwest Freeway. This man's making jokes, he thought, when the end result could be his death. That was interesting. Unusual. A little startling. He thought about it that evening at the dinner table, too, and after the boys had gone off to watch TV he told the story to Tissy. "This guy's a comedian," he said. "I never tried to get the death penalty for a comedian before."

"It bothers you?" Tissy asked.

"We'll see," Rusty said, troubled.

Two more jurors—Lou Shields, a thirty-five-year-old supply technician at Sam Houston Hospital, and Lawrence Stanley, forty-three, a businessman—were picked in the next three days. A fast pace. Each side, if they could not prevail upon the judge to excuse the juror for a legal reason—for "cause"—was allowed throughout voir dire a total of fifteen peremptory dismissals, or strikes. So far both the state and the defense had each used only three strikes. At that rate, Judge Azios reflected, the trial could begin on November 11 and finish before Thanksgiving. That put the judge in a good mood.

That was not to last for long.

Michael A. Brown, a shirt-sleeved, bright-looking, twenty-four-year-old black man who worked in a Firestone warehouse, took the stand. Peering down at him, Judge Azios adjusted his horn-rimmed glasses, leaned forward, and made his standard opening speech to individual jurors. He had the knack of making it sound fresh and personal, as if he had thought long and deeply about these matters and needed very badly to impart their meaning directly to *you*.

"Mr. Brown, I want to remind you of what I said to all the jurors before. The burden of proof in this case is on the State of Texas, and they must go forward to prove that the defendant is guilty beyond a reasonable doubt." The judge read the indictment, and then he explained that this was a two-stage trial. In the first stage the jury would decide David West's guilt or innocence. If they found him innocent, they could go home. Guilty, and they passed to the second stage, in which they had to vote on two "special issues": whether the murder was committed deliberately; and whether, in the future, "there is a probability that the defendant would commit criminal acts of violence that would constitute a continuing threat to society"—the so-called issue of future dangerousness. A *yes* answer to both questions meant a mandatory punishment of death. A *no* to either question meant life in TDC, the Texas Department of Corrections. The slammer for at least twenty years.

"Now I ask you, sir, do you have any religious, moral, conscientious scruples, or scruples of any kind against the infliction of death as a punishment for a crime in a proper case?"

160

Brown, after a slight pause, said he didn't.

The judge queried him as to whether or not he had formed any opinion about David West's guilt or innocence from what he had read in the papers or seen on TV, and Brown said no, he could listen to the facts of the case and dissociate himself from everything he'd read and seen.

"I'm going to pass you to the attorneys," the judge said. "They'll ask you questions about yourself and your opinions. There are no right or wrong answers. If they ask you whether the earth is flat and you think it is, say so. Don't try to please them."

Rusty Hardin took over—friendly, folksy, sparkle-eyed. "Let's visit together, Mr. Brown. Share with me your feelings about the death penalty . . . about whether you can predict future dangerousness . . . about the idea of reasonable doubt. . . . " Starting with reasonable doubt: "I drop this pen to the floor. You saw it happen, right? But if you go outside and say to a man in the corridor, 'I saw Rusty Hardin drop a pen,' how does that man know it's true? Can you convince that man beyond the shadow of a doubt? No, you surely can't. But I think you can probably convince him beyond *reasonable* doubt. And that's what we have to do with the jury. Because no one of you will have witnessed the crime, and a juror is a person who has to decide whether or not something happened based on what strangers tell him."

You could see enlightenment flood the juror's eyes. Like the judge, this bright, peppery, articulate man was *helping* him. David West also nodded. He was learning from Rusty, too. That was Rusty's calling: to illuminate. You had to be impressed.

Having noted a pause in response to the judge's question about the death penalty, Rusty asked Brown if he could vote for it in a proper case, and Brown said, "I'm not against it, but it would have to be something drastic, awful, like my mother being killed, for me to vote for the death penalty."

That made Rusty waver. He liked what he saw in this young juror so far, but now he wasn't sure he wanted him. Except, of course, Virginia Campbell had been *somebody's* mother.

Rusty asked, "Are you a happy person, Mr. Brown? Looking back on your life, what do you regret? Could you kind of just give us a two-minute biography of yourself?"

Brown replied easily that he didn't quite know what happy meant, but he wasn't *un*happy. He had been born in Houston, considered himself a loner, a rebel. He liked life—having fun, working hard. He'd been a Golden Gloves boxer. His father used to be a navy jet pilot, and then about five years ago he'd been shot in the back on a Houston street, and disabled, and now he was a preacher.

They learned more from the answer to that last question, Lyn Mc-
Clellan said, than from any other. People revealed themselves; and if
they made an effort not to, you could sense what they wanted to hide.

Rusty began to shore up any future reaction by the juror against Kim
Paris. "Can you share with me your reactions to the idea of secret taping,
if the judge said it was legal?" And: "You could have a situation in a case
where maybe you don't like the way a witness gathered the evidence.
Let's say, a friend taping a friend. What I'm after is where someone takes
the stand and you don't like his or her attitude, or life style, or personality. Could you act on believing what he's saying even if you don't like
the witness?"

"I wouldn't have any trouble doing that," Brown said.

"In Texas we have several kinds of murder, according to the law. What
makes capital murder, as opposed to simple murder, is the presence of
what we call 'an aggravating factor.' In this case, the state is alleging two
such factors. One is the promise of money from Cynthia Campbell Ray
—murder for hire. Doesn't matter if she actually paid him or not—what
matters is she offered and he agreed, if that's what you conclude. The
second is 'murder during the course of a burglary.' The law says burglary
in the State of Texas is going into someone's home, without their permission, with the intent of committing a felony. In this case, the felony
of murder. Any problem with that? Could you as a citizen follow the
law in that respect?"

Yes, Brown said, he could.

"Does the subject of wiretapping or electronic surveillance give you
some pause?"

"Well, it would depend."

"Of course it would. What our law in Texas says is: for it to be a legal
electronic recording, one party to the conversation has to be aware of
the recording. If I were sitting here with a body mike while we were
talking, and you didn't know it, that would be legal. Because one person
in the conversation had consented to the recording—namely, me. If,
however, someone put a bug in this room while you and I were talking
and neither of us knew about it, that's illegal. The idea about the first
situation is, 'Hey, I could go write notes as soon as we quit talking, so
what's the difference in allowing me fully and accurately to report it?'
Does that bother you?"

"Not really."

On the question of future dangerousness, which would arise in special
issue #2 if David were found guilty, Rusty said, "Let's assume, during
the course of the trial, you decide you understand why the defendant
did what he did, and you liked him. Could you answer yes as to his
future dangerousness?"

"Well," Brown said, "if I liked him and understood why he'd killed someone, I might be able to see just why he'd do it again."

Rusty smiled; the answer had delighted him. He knew he was dealing with an intelligent young man. But Gene Nettles frowned.

And finally, with a certain wistfulness punctuated by tamped-down anger: "In the indictment, Cynthia Campbell Ray is mentioned. You might be in a situation where you hear certain evidence and wish you could hear directly from her, but I want you to be aware right now that neither we nor the defense will be able to call Ms. Ray as a witness. So you can't hold the failure to call her against either side.* Some people might say, 'Hey, I can't decide *this* defendant's fate if I don't also have access to deciding *her* fate.' Would you be able to do that?"

Yes, the juror said, he wouldn't have any trouble doing that.

Rusty's questioning took two hours. The judge then stopped for what he liked to call a "Brenda-break." After an hour or two of almost nonstop 200- to 250-word-per-minute transcribing at her stenograph machine, Brenda Palmer's fingers, neck, and lower back ached. The judge did whatever he could to make Brenda's working life easier, and that included frequent Brenda-breaks.

After the break, Gene Nettles took over. He questioned Brown for another two hours, failed in an attempt to get the judge to dismiss the juror for cause—on the basis of an ineradicable prejudice such as a leaning toward a yes answer on special issue #2—and finally used one of the defense's fifteen precious strikes to get rid of Brown.

Rusty moaned, "Another fair juror down the tube."

He hated this process. The world in general thought that prosecutors were vengeful and cold-hearted men, whereas defense attorneys existed to protect the innocent and ensure that justice triumphed. And yet who wanted a fair jury? Not the defense. Did they want intelligent jurors? No, they wanted jurors with grudges against the system, with hidden longings to break the law and get away with it. They wanted compassionate jurors, of course. But what about compassion for the victims of a crime?

Rusty thought of himself not so much as the attorney for the state as he did the attorney for the victims. For the dead. For their families who grieved and had no recourse against the killers and the rapists and the slashers and the muggers and the assaulters of children. For the people's right to ward off evil and to cry to the assassins of peace, "You will be punished!"

---

* It is unethical for a lawyer to call a witness who intends to invoke the constitutional privilege against self-incrimination, and Cindy's lawyer had let it be known that if she were called, she would "take the Fifth Amendment."

That's my job, Rusty thought, and I can live with it. He wondered again how the criminal defense attorneys could live with *their* job.

Regarding the death penalty, he would not have been grieved for a moment if it was stricken from the statutes. But it was not; it was part of the law now. And Rusty's job was to uphold the law, to make it work, *whatever it was.*

In that he was relentless.

A truck driver born in Haiti took the stand. He spoke Creole, French, and Spanish—English a distant fourth. He was excused by mutual agreement: on Rusty's part, because "he wouldn't have understood the tapes," and on Gene's because "you think in Haiti they have anything against the death penalty?"

Judge Azios asked a middle-aged black woman, active in the Mt. Zion Baptist Church, if she had any scruples against the death penalty. "If he's found guilty, no," she replied. "But if he's found not guilty, yes, I'd object."

But after the laughter had subsided, she told Rusty that she could never predict the future probability of violence if a defendant had committed only one crime. When Rusty moved that she be excused for cause, the judge said, "Granted."

Glenn Hager, an oil explorer retired from Conoco, admitted to the court that he was prejudiced against David West "because the system isn't frivolous, and he's come this far to court." The defense was forced to use a strike.

Terrell J. Bairrington, a bearded ex-marine who had served in Vietnam, said: "I'd probably be inclined to believe a police officer as opposed to a layman, because the police officer is a trained observer."

Nettles used another strike.

Rusty shook his head in open disgust. They just didn't want a fair jury. He muttered to me, "This is obscene."

Gary D. Halepeska—thirty-four years old, a mustached Texas-born engineer in a quilted vest and wide-collared shirt—sat down in the witness chair for examination. "Everyone was glad to see the death penalty come back," he said, when Rusty took him on voir dire. "I don't think it's used enough."

Rusty then "rehabilitated" him—got Halepeska to back down on the rigidity of his position and qualify, but just barely, as an unbiased juror.

During the break before the defense's turn came, I stood outside the men's room with Rusty, Lyn McClellan, and Jim Leitner. Halepeska passed by on his way to the water cooler. I said to Lyn, "You'd like twelve of him, right?"

"He could do it with his bare hands," Lyn agreed.

Rusty then told a story—he and Leitner both swore it was *not* apocryphal—that was supposed to typify Harris County jurors, who were reputed to be advocates of extreme punishment. During voir dire at a capital murder trial the previous year, one blue collar juror was asked by the judge if he would be able to inflict the death penalty in a proper case. After thinking it over for a minute, the juror replied, "Well, yes, if it was on a weekend."

We all guffawed.

Rusty recovered first and stared down the hallway at the receding figure of Halepeska. "This is the kind of juror that strikes were meant for," he said quietly.

"We're going to have to use one," Leitner admitted.

Rusty sighed. "No, you won't. Make a motion to excuse him, and we'll join you."

Opposed to his burning desire to win and serve the victim, Rusty had a compulsion to be fair. To do it the *right* way. A stacked deck proved nothing.

A juror named Ann Welles* took the stand—a secretary for an oil company, a gentle, serious blond woman in her forties who admitted that she had a chemical imbalance and since 1978 took medication four times a day for depression and anxiety. Gene asked for a short break. When the juror was out of the room he and Rusty quickly agreed to excuse her.

"But let's voir dire her a bit more," Rusty said, "so she doesn't feel too badly. Because I can tell she *wants* to serve."

Gene, with a sigh at this gallantry, nevertheless agreed. Ann Welles was recalled. Rusty now turned on the charm, while at the same time he probed for a reason, other than medical, to have her excused. Unfortunately, he couldn't find anything. Ann Welles was otherwise a perfect juror.

Rusty choked off a grin and passed the buck to Gene.

But Gene couldn't find anything either. Forty minutes of voir dire had elapsed in the charade. Sweat sprouting on his forehead, Gene glanced at Rusty. "Pass the juror," he said, a little desperately.

Rusty jumped up and said, "Ms. Welles, if the tapes of the defendant's alleged admissions aren't played before the jury, would you remember that in fact they existed?"

---

* This is a pseudonym—the only one I have used. The reason will be clear.

165

"I guess I'd have to remember," the juror said, puzzled. "It would take a certain amount of effort, I think, to forget."

"State moves to excuse," Rusty said, and the judge immediately agreed. Juror Welles left the courtroom, bewildered. Rusty ran after her to thank her for coming down and being a good citizen.

"That was good of you," I said to him, when he came back.

"I'm just concerned that I may have depressed her even more by getting rid of her *that* way," he said.

"You did your best."

"Did I? I always wonder about that. There's always something more you can do. Or should have done. I have to live with all this when it's over."

On the fifth day of voir dire, between prospective jurors, Rusty Hardin told the court, "Miss Paris is here. Can we hear her?"

"Yes, certainly," said Judge Azios.

There was a bustle of activity, and then Kim Paris thrust into the courtroom, long brown hair bouncing, and swept confidently toward the witness chair. She carried a leather handbag and wore a tailored dark blue Brooks Brothers suit with a U.S. Navy pin in the lapel. Other than eye shadow, she used no makeup today. A couple of television reporters slid into the courtroom after her, and their cameramen jostled to position themselves and their Minicams on the other side of the glass-paneled courtroom door.

The purpose of this interlude with Kim was called "discovery." Gene Nettles wanted to probe a little, to find out if any other recorded material existed that might contradict David's taped admissions to murder. Rusty Hardin wanted to assure the court that no such material existed.

David West, sitting at the table with his two lawyers, hadn't seen Kim since he had stepped out of her Volkswagen Jetta in the Circle K parking lot on the night of February 21, and a moment later looked into the barrel of Gil Schultz's gun. Now, while he chewed on the end of a pencil, he peered at her with his hazel-brown and blue-gray eyes. His expression was calm; he couldn't grow significantly paler than he already was. But his mind was churning, and his thought, a self-assessment, could be summed up in one word.

Asshole.

Kim eyed David fleetingly. She was sworn in by the clerk, and Rusty asked her in quick succession if she had been employed by Clyde Wilson in February of 1985, if she had investigated the murder of James and

Virginia Campbell on behalf of the Clyde Wilson Agency, and if she had been with David West on the nights of February 20 and 21, 1985. To all these questions Kim responded with a throaty, "Yes, sir."

"Other than the tapes made by the Houston Police Department on those two nights, with your cooperation, do you know of any other tapes of your conversations with David West?"

"No, sir."

"Pass the witness," Rusty said.

Gene Nettles stood and introduced himself to Kim as if they had never met before. He was cordial. The bogey man wasn't so bad after all. Kim smiled at him shyly.

"Miss Paris, how long had you been working for Clyde Wilson before you got involved in this particular case?"

"Objection," Rusty said. He was determined even now to protect Kim from any badgering. "Irrelevant, and beyond the scope of this pretrial examination."

"That's ridiculous!" Gene snapped.

"If he thinks *that's* ridiculous," Rusty fired back toward the judge, "wait until he hears the rest of my objections to his questions."

Gene began to argue, and his voice rose, not in pitch but in volume. Judge Azios interrupted: "Mr. Nettles, I don't think the people outside in the street are interested in your objections. Please don't holler." He turned back to Rusty and said, "Objection sustained."

Modulating his powerful baritone as best he could, Gene asked Kim, "How did you record your notes?"

On legal pads, she said. She brought the notes to the office and left them on Denise Moseley's desk. "They're kind of sloppy in parts . . . "

"Any notes that you *didn't* bring?"

"No, sir."

Gene went fishing. "Any notes that you made at a later date, after the police department had made those two tapes of you and Mr. West?"

Rusty, confident that the pool was empty, let him troll away. He was glad for Kim to have the experience of testimony before the actual trial.

"No, sir," Kim said.

"Any tapes that you made at a later date?"

Kim hesitated. "You mean with David West?"

Gene heard the hesitation, and he pounced. "With *anyone*."

"Well, yes." Now Kim seemed upset.

Gene was elated; his gloomy dark eyes sparkled. He rode hard over Rusty's tardy objections and demanded to know with whom these later tapes had been made.

"With a writer named Jack Olsen," Kim said.

They had talked about what happened between her and David West. Olsen had the tapes—she estimated "about five hours' worth." They were his property. They had been made in his hotel room here in Houston, in September. No, she didn't have any written agreement with Mr. Olsen.

"I want these recordings with Mr. Olsen to be made part of the record," Gene demanded.

Rusty hopped about the judicial bench, his finger stabbing repeatedly in Gene's direction. "He is not entitled to review everything she's said to anyone else!" He wheeled like a free safety when a wide receiver changes direction. "A perilous path!" he warned the court. "Mr. Olsen is a member of the press, the Fourth Estate!"

"He's not a member of the press," Gene growled. "He's just a writer. And I ask this court to subpoena these tapes to look for Brady material." *

"No way!" Rusty yelped. "He's not entitled to go fishing in the files of any member of the press! No law in Texas allows this. Bring us some law, Mr. Nettles!"

"Yes," said the judge, "I'm reserving decision. Bring me some law, Mr. Nettles."

"Your Honor, I will," Gene promised solemnly, and let Kim Paris go.

Blooded now, she left the courtroom. She knew that Nettles could smile warmly and spit in her face at the same time. She was a little shaken.

The following day, from another source, Nettles discovered that Kim had a selective memory as a witness. She had signed a letter of agreement with her writer, Jack Olsen, three weeks before her sworn testimony that she hadn't done so. She also had an agreement with her lawyer, Marian Rosen, who was taking 20 percent of Kim's net from a book or a movie. And Marian Rosen had hired Alyss Dorese, a New York literary agent, who was cut in for 10 percent of Kim's gross after the Scott Meredith Agency, which represented Jack Olsen, took *its* 10 percent off the top.

"This Paris woman has turned herself into a *commodity!*" Nettles chortled in anticipation of how he would bring all this out at trial.

Everywhere, not just in Houston, 90 percent of criminal charges were traded out in advance. Deals were cut, pleas were made for lesser sen-

---

* Brady material meant any evidence that might help a defendant or impeach the credibility of a prosecution witness—so named because of a landmark case, *Brady* v. *Maryland,* where the U.S. Supreme Court reversed a conviction because the prosecutor withheld material from the defense that would have proved the defendant innocent.

tences. Not this one, Gene thought. If he could destroy the credibility of Kim Paris, he had a winner.

As the voir dire wore on into the second and then the third week, Rusty and Gene Nettles began to exchange sidebar remarks in open court. Sidebars are statements and complaints meant for the judge at the bench, beyond hearing of any jurors. Rusty was examining a juror, and Gene objected to a question. When Judge Azios overruled the objection, Gene complained angrily that he hadn't yet made his point. Rusty said, "Your Honor, would you please instruct counsel for the defense not to whine in front of the jurors?"

Gene's dark eyes zigzagged in their sockets.

Just before lunch, after Gene was forced to use yet another strike on the juror who had heard the "whining" remark, Rusty turned to Gene and told him he'd rarely had to deal with such "chickenshit objections and interruptions" during a voir dire. Brenda Palmer hadn't yet been told to stop her silent tapping at the keys of the stenograph, and Rusty's "chickenshit" remark went into the record.

At that point the two lawyers ceased being polite adversaries and became frosty antagonists. At lunch an enraged Gene said to me and Leitner, "That sorry little motherfucker! Over there at the D.A.'s Office he's a superchief, he can do what he pleases! He's not used to anyone saying, 'Whoa!' Okay . . . now we get rough."

When Gene returned he told the court that he had some remarks that he wanted to make for the record. Brenda began transcribing. Gene said, "The prosecutor has seen fit to call me chickenshit. I resent that. When Mr. Hardin says, in front of a juror, that I'm whining, I just don't appreciate that. I think *that's* chickenshit. And unethical."

The charge of *unethical* in any circumstances turned Rusty into a reckless driver. With eyes smoking behind his tinted aviator glasses, he sprang to his feet and lashed into Gene for "a clear violation of the rules. I would ask the court to admonish him," Rusty said sharply. "He is not free, in the face of an objection, to say in front of a juror, 'It's about time somebody told Mr. Hardin to sit down.' I ignored that. Mr. Nettles, for the record, thinks that's funny now. He's laughing. I'm telling you, these things are improper! And Mr. Nettles has a habit, when he wants to get up and be righteously indignant, the volume gets so loud that it actually makes people jump."

Gene would have broken more decibel records, but the judge smoothed his quills and then told both lawyers to behave.

From then on, other than in the courtroom and then only when it was necessary, Gene refused to talk to Rusty. "This is war," he said to Leitner. "We won't win if we don't see it that way. And I'm going to win."

Throughout much of this, David West, whose life was the prize in the battle—or as Gene now had it, the war—sat at the defense table, listening only randomly, like a student faintly bored by his professors. Most of the time his head was bent to two big black binders that each contained what looked to be several hundred pages of xeroxed typescript. They were the state's transcript of his taped conversations with Kim Paris. "Keep him busy," Nettles had said to Leitner. Otherwise, as he discovered during the first days of voir dire, David, brow furrowed, was constantly laying a palm on his lawyer's sleeve, whispering suggestions: "Why don't you ask her . . . " or "What if in trial we took the approach that . . . "

And so Leitner handed David the transcripts and said, "Tell us where they're inaccurate. And try to remember what it is that you *did* say."

After the first week the courtroom at 403 Caroline was requisitioned for another purpose and our little group moved to a room on the seventh floor of the main courthouse. Used primarily for voir dire, it was about fifty feet long and fifteen feet wide, with wooden benches for spectators, a single counsel table, a judicial bench, and chairs for the court reporter and witness.

The judge steered a genial course; if Rusty and Gene were at each other's throats, that was *their* problem. It was like a small boat at sea—you had to get along well with your mates or the voyage would be miserable. Kindness and camaraderie were brazen human forces demanding to fill a vacuum.

Other than for the record, Judge Azios usually called David by his first name. David asked the judge if he could share his jar of Nescafé. With a twinkle in his usually earnest eyes, the judge said, "Just make sure you use a spoon and not your fingers, David."

The next day Bettie Conway, the court clerk, called Jim Leitner to the bench, reached into a paper bag, and said, "Would you please slip a cookie to David? I can't give him one, I'll get into trouble, but you can."

Leitner asked, "Why do you want to do that?"

Bettie said, "Yesterday I was talking about jelly donuts, and he said how much he loved them. He's like my son. Please slip him a cookie, Mr. Leitner, and tell him it's from me."

"We have to get these jurors to *know* him," Leitner said to Nettles. "Then they'll *like* him. Like Bettie does."

Howard D. Burroughs, a carrot-haired Assembly of God minister, took the stand for voir dire. Yes, he remembered reading about Mr. West and the Campbell murders. "As I recall, he was supposed to have killed two people in their sleep—"

In his chair at the counsel table, David nodded his head up and down.

"And the grandchildren were there—"

David nodded again. *Yes, you've got it right so far.*

"A house in the River Oaks area—"

David shook his head, frowning. *Try again, sir.*

"—or was it Memorial?"

David smiled encouragingly. *Yes, that's it.*

Afterward, alone in the empty jury room, Leitner yelled at him: "Cut it out! Look the juror in the eye, establish some contact, but no more prompting as if you were really there!"

The pace had slowed. Another week went by and only one more juror was chosen. As the holiday season approached, the lawyers began to openly debate whether a postponement might be necessary. Rusty had plans for a ten-day family trip over Christmas to visit his parents in Florida. The trial might have to be rescheduled to begin in January. "Hey, wait a minute," David said. "I want to be home for Christmas!"

"You're home already, David," Lyn McClellan said jovially.

Another day Rusty entered the courtroom and mimed a karate blow at David, who defended himself, laughing.

All pals. But whenever they talked about him in private, Lyn and Rusty called him a sociopath. The defined that for my benefit as "a mentally ill or unstable person whose behavior is antisocial." Rusty added, "And seems to be without remorse."

"He's pleasant and funny in the courtroom," Lyn said, "because it's a structured situation. But I sure wouldn't want to meet him out on the street. Would you give him a lift if you were driving down the street and he was hitchhiking? Not me. No way to know what he'd be like."

November had been sunny and springlike, but one day heavy rain fell outside in the streets and lightning crackled above the fourteen-story monolith of the Harris County Jail. The lawyers returned and everyone stood around drinking hot coffee out of plastic cups. The atmosphere was that of a cocktail party. Prosecutor and defendant discussed the difficulties of giving up smoking; David reminisced about the loss of the old neighborhood in Montrose, and how he'd crashed the Cannes Film Festival by telling them at the door that he was an actor in *A Hard Day's Night*.

When they reconvened, but before a new juror was brought on, Rusty rose and said, "Your Honor, the defendant's informed the State of Texas that he would like a sun lamp. He's taken the position that pallor is prejudicial. I can't disagree."

And yet, an hour later, Rusty said to a juror: "You know the state is seeking the death penalty against this gentleman here"—nodding at the pale young man in the blue blazer and striped regimental tie.

Jim Leitner sighed. He wasn't overwhelmed by the jokes and the partytime closeness. He saw the danger. "David has a child's mentality," he told Nettles. "He's a sixteen-year-old boy in a twenty-nine-year-old man's body."

Gene shrugged. "He wants to be popular."

But who knew? Perhaps Rusty would grow to like David, too. Perhaps he would see that David didn't deserve to die. And who could guess what prayers and schemes bubbled up unbidden from David's embattled mind?

15

Lyn McClellan joked each morning: "Here comes the voir dire junkie." He couldn't understand why I showed up every day for the same speeches by the same actors, the same questions, nearly the same answers. The judge was puzzled, too. One fresh November day he took me to lunch at Inns of Court, a lawyers' and judges' club a few blocks from the courthouse. He said, "Clifford, I see your pen flying. You can't be taking notes on all those dozens of jurors and all the dumbass things that Nettles and Hardin and everyone says, including me. . . . "

"Just impressions, Judge."

Rusty Hardin never asked what I was writing on the yellow legal pads, but he smiled conspiratorially. Once or twice a week he and Lyn McClellan and I had lunch together, and most other days I ate with the defense lawyers.

On the first day of my presence a pallid David conferred worriedly with Gene Nettles. Who's that? A *writer*? Can't we get him out of here? One more boastful statement overheard by the wrong person, he figured, could kill him.

Nettles raised an eyebrow and said, "The idea of a public trial is to have the press in, not keep them out."

172

David settled down, and later Gene introduced us. I didn't know how to begin: I didn't glorify murderers, and this one was accused of cold-blooded murder for hire. Had he been a friend I probably would have said, "Impossible! He couldn't have done that!" But he was a stranger and we tend to believe whatever we first hear about strangers. The introductory adjectives tossed out by any authority become the standard against which all later information is measured. "Innocent until proven guilty" is an uphill battle for the mind.

During a break I talked to David about jail; it seemed a neutral subject, and I had been there, and he was suddenly garrulous. The Houston City Jail, he told me, where he'd spent thirty-six hours back in February, was filthy, infested with vermin. Since then he'd been eight months in solitary at Harris County Jail. He guessed that was for his own protection. "I'm not afraid for myself, physically speaking, but I must say I'm glad not to be thrown in with some of those guys in the general population. They're bad people. Most of them can hardly read or write. They look like they just crawled out from under some slimy rock. I have to exercise and shower with them three times a week. Not very pleasant."

I remembered Kim saying that he considered himself an intellectual on a higher plane than most people. He read a lot, he said, although limited to what was in the jail library. Mostly junk. He was currently into Robert Ludlum's *The Bourne Identity*. He had no TV: "But I can see through my cell door into the opposite cell, where they've got an old black-and-white RCA with earphones. I saw a Clint Eastwood movie the other night at long distance." He laughed shrilly. "No sound, but in a Clint Eastwood movie, does that matter?"

He was lifting weights, and probably in better shape than when he went in. I felt his left biceps: it was solid. On the nights when he couldn't exercise he had trouble sleeping. Jog in place in your cell, I suggested. Get a good heart pump going for twenty minutes. You'll sleep.

"Thanks. Good idea."

We talked about Kim Paris, which I thought would be a touchy subject, but he wasn't bothered. "An obnoxious bitch," he said. "She came on as Miss Goodie-Two-Shoes. Later she changed, and I preferred her that way. At first she had this awful punk hairdo, and she wore a blanket. I didn't like it. But I was a fool. She fulfilled my dream. I was infatuated. I should have known, because there were so many weird things. I thought she made a pass at my friend's girlfriend one night at Fitzgerald's. I challenged her on it and said, 'It's okay, this is Montrose and I understand gay people'—but she got very upset and said, 'No, no, no.' "

Later in the day Jim Leitner was trying to break down a tight-lipped

173

juror who had offered the opinion that electronic surveillance was fair because *she* personally wouldn't say anything if she was being taped that she wouldn't say in private. Leitner's questions were growing muddier and more obtuse. He began to crack his knuckles, as he was wont to do during moments of tension. From across the room, David raised a little note to me that he had printed on a strip of yellow legal paper. It said: *SEMANTICS!*

During the break he whispered across the table, "It's like chess. And they want to checkmate me. Rusty and Gene are the opposing queens. . . . " A quick grin, and then, turning swiftly toward Gene, who was studying the juror lists, "No offense intended." Gene heard, stroked his black mustache, and scowled. He leaned across to us. "Keep your mouth shut, David. If you've got to talk, talk about the weather and sports. . . . "

David tried, but it wasn't his nature. He wanted so keenly to be liked. He wanted the friendship of men he thought of as his peers and the love of women he thought of as attractive and feminine. He was no sycophant—he reached out to embrace warm bodies. Nothing sick about that: just, under the circumstances, a little saddening.

"Funny thing is," he expounded, "I'm for the death penalty. I usually lean to the right, on the side of law and order. Clean up the neighborhood! Get the trash out! That comes from being brought up in Montrose, which was peaceful and residential when I was a kid and then went to pot, literally. I got out of the Corps and I was disgusted by what had happened to my old neighborhood. All the queers. And they were so swish! We have these bull sessions in the joint, and I always say that some of the scumbags in there should never be let back on the street."

"Watch your step."

"Oh, I'm not scared." David laughed easily. "Too dumb to be scared."

I was growing to like him. I wondered what Rusty felt.

It was the small boat at sea effect—all of us stuck with each other for the duration. Best to be friendly, pliant, find out what the other passengers had to offer. Nettles and Leitner and I had lunch at a little nameless joint where we ate turkey hoagies and drank Diet Cokes. The streets near the courthouse were full of bag ladies and derelicts and tacky bail bond offices that advertised telephone numbers such as F-R-E-E-D-O-M and 4-3-2-1-OUT.

Leitner tested a theory on me. "Surely you have to believe that a man in love doesn't tell his dearly beloved how he killed two people in cold blood—not unless he's been led to believe that's what she *wants* him to say in order to keep her love."

"Or get it," Nettles rumbled. "She was wiggling her pussy in front of his face the whole time, wasn't she? The man was dazzled and dazed. He didn't know what he was saying!"

"What do you think?" Leitner asked me.

"Makes sense," I said. "Long as he didn't really kill them."

The lawyers laughed nervously; that was something the ethics of confidentiality forbade them to discuss.

Another steamy day we picked up chicken salad sandwiches and yogurts at a parking lot shack aptly named the Small Claims Cafe and brought it all back to eat in the air-conditioned jury room. Nettles shut the door and peered suspiciously through a hole in the sheetrock wall. Throughout the case he had felt uncomfortable talking on the telephone. "Even in my office! Don't forget, Cindy Ray is still out there, thumbing her nose at the D.A. Hardin really wants her ass behind bars. And with West I think that law enforcement would probably use any and all means, illicit and otherwise, to try to get a conviction."

He had been an assistant district attorney for five years; he had to know what he was talking about.

"Here's the thing about West," Leitner said, leaning forward over his vanilla yogurt, the pack of muscle shifting under his shirt. "I've repped capital murder defendants before. Guys where you say, 'If you could do your life over again, what would you do different?' And they come back, 'Fuck, man, I would've saved a bullet for the scumbag who ratted on me.' David's just the opposite. He doesn't hate Kim. If they find him guilty, I just don't think he's the kind of person the death penalty is meant for. Hardin and McClellan won't admit it, but basically they have the same feeling. You see how they treat him?"

The lunches continued. One day Nettles, Leitner, Lyn McClellan, Judge Azios, and I went to Chinatown. Over wonton soup and a heaped plate of egg rolls, Lyn said, "I've known some cases where someone stubbed out their cigarette butts on a baby. I could cut their throats ear to ear and never look back. Then you hear about one where this guy rapes a thirteen-year-old girl and drowns her in a puddle of mud. Give me a fucking break! Death by injection has to be too kind for that. I think they ought to be executed the same way they killed the victim." Lyn frowned. "I obviously don't feel that way about David West . . . although he sure didn't say, 'You have the right to have a policeman present before I blow your brains out.' "

He wagged a finger at Gene Nettles. "You guys have it made. We've got no evidence. It's a whale in a barrel—y'all don't even have to take aim." He turned to Judge Azios. "I don't want to be associated, even as number two, with the first loss of a capital murder case in Harris County. Remember that, Judge. You could ruin my career."

The judge laughed, but didn't comment.

Gene only snickered at the way Lyn and Rusty badmouthed their chances. On another occasion, in his new office on the forty-third floor of the Republic Bank Building, he explained to me that Leitner was in charge of the second stage of the trial, if David was found guilty. "I'm concentrating on freeing him," Gene said. "I'll do whatever I can to plant reasonable doubt. But the tapes are devastating." He cast a dark look out the window; he could see the Harris County Jail, Sam Houston Park, where Vietnamese children washed clothes in the pond, and Police Headquarters with its oval running track atop the annex. "That's the basic problem: how do we refute the tapes? Even if she used emotional coercion, even if she got him drunk and stoned, he still says, '*I did it.*' " Cracking his knuckles—he seemed to have picked up the habit from Leitner—Gene turned back from the window. "So, in case things go poorly, Leitner's concentrating on saving David's life."

And on converting him. Leitner, the devout Lutheran, felt a call to witness to his clients—"to let them know where I'm coming from, morally." It frightened David at first. He wasn't interested in going to heaven in return for confessing to Christ. He had been brought up as an atheist. "My father's religion is physics," he said. He hadn't done anything morally wrong, he told Leitner, hadn't committed any sins. But he enjoyed debating.

"The Bible's a lot of regurgitated garbage. There's no way all the truth can be contained in one book. There are other religions, too, and as a reasonable man, which you seem to be, Jim, you've got to give them some credence."

Leitner argued *ad hominem:* "David, everything you've done in life so far hasn't worked out too well for you. So why not try something else? Why not ask Christ for help? Gene and I are doing our best to save your ass. But if we fail, you have to think about your soul."

A little peeved, David said, "Just so long as you remember that on the list of priorities my ass is number one, and my ass is also number two. My soul's in a distant third place."

But then, discussing his life since he'd left the Marine Corps and returned to Houston, he admitted: "I was dealing with sleazy people in sleazy situations. And the state of my soul was rotten." He agreed to read the Bible, and Leitner brought him two versions: *The Good News Bible* and *The New Testament as Literature.*

The Wests came to voir dire twice a week. Duval was pale and nervous. Cecilia West had short frizzy hair of no ascertainable color, a crumpled face, a weary look. The deputies allowed his parents to talk with David as long as they kept a physical distance. During the break Gene introduced us, and the following week I sat down on a wooden bench next to Cecilia in the hallway outside the courtroom.

"This must be hard for you," I said.

Rusty Hardin strode by, eyes averted, jaw thrust forward, and Cecilia couldn't restrain herself.

"There's the villain," she said.

"Well, he believes David is guilty."

She said nothing. She'd been warned by Nettles and Leitner to keep mum, and it wasn't easy; she was a garrulous woman. I told her I'd been out and around in Montrose, asking about her son.

"I hope people say nice things."

"For the most part, they do. And most of them say he wasn't violent."

"He always acted like a knight in shining armor."

One day in the courtroom, during a coffee break, beyond earshot of Nettles or Leitner, David said to me, "This business about my being a gung-ho survivalist isn't true. I didn't subscribe to *Soldier of Fortune*. I had three copies of the magazine lying around. One was because there was an article about a new helmet, and I was interested. Another was about a new model of the M-16. So when I got out of the Corps I bought them. Big deal. But I'm worried that people will believe the worst, because who have we got to put on to contradict it?"

"Maybe you'll have to testify on your own behalf."

"I don't think so," he said. "For one thing, I'm scared of Rusty. He's supposed to be very, very good. I know he wants to kill me. I think about that all the time."

"Then why are you friendly to him?"

"If someone's friendly to me, it's my nature to be friendly back to them. But a soldier who's not scared of the bullets is a fool." He meant: apropos his testifying.

"Strange case," I said, as if I were discussing it with someone other than the defendant. "It's no longer a question of whether you did it or not. It's a question of what they can prove and can't prove."

"It's always been that," David said thoughtfully. "The real truth may never come out. But I want to tell you one thing. I could never kill anyone for money."

Beyond that revelation, what did David want? Of course to be found

177

not guilty. To regain his lost freedom. But beyond that? *Deeper* than that? I began to suspect what it was, but I hardly dared give it credence. It was too bizarre.

On another pleasant November day Nettles and Leitner and I had lunch at Glatzmeier's Fish Market on Market Square, with overhead fans and the smell of blackened redfish frying in butter. But on the way back to the courthouse—the air felt like spring—Leitner slowed his step. "I feel sick going back there," he said fervently. "It gets worse all the time. I'd rather defend a man I hated, some thug or street scum."

"I'm going to help you," I said. "I'm going to give you some expert layman's advice."

Nettles snapped his eyes in my direction like a whip. "If you want to help us, get us a witness."

"I'm going to give you the benefit of my mind."

"Fuck your mind. I need a live body."

"To testify to what?"

"That my client couldn't have done it."

"Until you find one, tell your client to get a haircut. With the bushy hair and the long sideburns and the cheesy color, he looks a bit like one of those goons in *A Clockwork Orange*."

Nettles squawked, "That disgusting movie? Are you crazy? Those guys were *brutal!*"

But I was only needling him. Like the others, I had fallen victim to David's charm. Within the limits of where we were, he was frank and sincere, and he seemed to have a moral code. He was a young man who asked questions of himself. The answers were rarely superficial. I was becoming steadily more troubled, because if indeed he was guilty, there was one thing that eluded me, and that was: *How could he have done it?*

I had climbed those carpeted stairs at 8901 Memorial. Those steps, that spooky house, the big bedroom, were not abstract to me. I could not imagine David—the David I knew—climbing them, .45 in hand, toward the second floor where a man who had never said a harsh word to him in his life, and a woman who had done no more than bar him from the premises for an insult to a maid, slept securely in their bed and would never, by his action, feel the warmth of the sun or smell coffee perking or see their family again. How could he contemplate what he was about to do? The urge to murder may rise wildly up, unbidden, in all of us, but to act on that urge, to *do,* is radically different, alien to all we are taught as semicivilized human beings. Each creak of the steps

178

brought David closer to barbarism. But David was *not* a barbarian, or a thug, or a contract killer. Except for this assumed aberration he had been —indeed, *was*—a cordial young man trying to find a way through the maze of life and time. Why didn't some voice stop him, as it would have stopped me, and you? I could not understand how he evaded the voice of his father, of his own primal ethic, or conscience, throbbing in his ear: "Enough. You cannot go further. You cannot *do* it." That voice must have spoken. Did he hear it and refuse to listen?

That was what made me believe that either he was mad or something that I didn't yet understand.

At about that time, to my amazement, David began to develop yet another relationship with a woman. I knew the woman, too; she was a friend. The previous July, Ginger Casey, the talented young anchor for Fox-TV's Channel 26 News, had become interested in the case. She wrote a letter to David asking for an in-depth interview that would be aired only after the trial. It was a guardedly cordial letter, evidencing a sympathy for how David had been manipulated by Kim Paris. David also replied guardedly, but he was moved. He called Ginger Casey from the jail, and he continued to call her throughout the voir dire, sometimes twice a day.

Larry Pollinger, Judge Azios's process server and chief bailiff, looked at David one day and said to me, "Here's a man who can really say, 'Two women ruined my life.' And I'll bet if a third came along now, he'd be just as gullible."

Ginger Casey and Dan Grothaus of the Houston *Post* were lovers then, living together in Ginger's house in Montrose. Ginger revealed that relationship to David so that there could be no misunderstandings, and she and David became—as much as was possible under the circumstances—telephone friends.

David asked her to visit him, and she did. He may have been an accused murderer, but Ginger liked him, too. Later she said to me, "He's a real pussycat. He has this cute cleft chin. And he's bright." She felt sorry for David. And she wanted the story.

During voir dire, Nettles and Leitner learned of David's new friendship. Leitner thought Casey was a beautiful and intelligent woman.

"But I trust her," David said.

"You *can't!*" Nettles yelled at him.

The lawyers forbade further visits until after the trial, and David glumly accepted that. But he kept calling Ginger. He didn't want to talk

179

about the case; he just wanted to chat and air his views on life and love and whatever book he was reading. He wanted to know that there was a human being out there, other than his parents, who cared. And he wanted her to know that *he* cared. One evening she told him she had a cold. He immediately prescribed home remedies and wound up saying, "You take care of yourself, babe."

A week later, when Ginger brought up the subject of his friends in Montrose, he mentioned Wickie Weinstein. Wickie used to brag, David claimed, about contract killings he had done. And then David said, "I'm not going to put my ass in a sling just to protect Wickie, you know."

"Wickie?" Ginger raised an eyebrow. "How is he involved that you have to protect him?"

"Forget I ever said that," David said into the telephone.

_____

Gene Nettles invited me to a weekly Sunday dinner at his parents' house in the wooded section of Memorial. His father, an industrial engineer, could have posed for *Saturday Evening Post* covers by Norman Rockwell. His Houston-born mother, although she looked and acted and cooked Italian, spoke pure Texan. After lunch we drove back to Gene's house and talked about the case; we always talked about the case. He was already thinking about summation, but he had to get his point of view across long before that, and, as he so often pointed out, he had only the state's witnesses to do it with. He could cross-examine. And boy, would he!

"That's how we can win. I can't begin to describe to you what happens in a trial when the main star gets on the witness stand and gets the shit kicked out of him, or her, as in this instance. They say in law school, 'Go out there and tear that witness a new asshole.' I'm going to keep her on the witness stand for a *long* time . . . maybe two whole days. I'm going to reorganize her whole anatomy."

"If you do that," I asked, "aren't you afraid the jury will start feeling sympathy for her?"

"Fuck her. She's a nasty slut. The jury isn't going to feel sorry for a nasty slut."

"She'll try to project just the opposite."

"She won't get away with that for very long. She's a slut. That's what I want them to come away thinking. She's a whore. She's a street person."

He glared at me. To win his case he had to destroy Kim Paris.

To that effect, after he had done the promised research into the law,

Nettles filed a subpoena *duces tecum,* demanding that when Jack Olsen appear for the trial he bring with him "tapes and other documents relating to a recorded conversation of approximately five hours with the state's key witness, Ms. Kim Paris." To Rusty's consternation, for he saw it as the beginning of the end of journalistic privacy in Texas, Judge Azios signed the subpoena. Rusty said to me—as it turned out, prophetically—"There are no shield laws in Texas. No writer or journalist is protected. You and Olsen are sitting on a time bomb."

Jack Olsen up in Washington had the last laugh. After several appeals and stays he informed the court in Houston that he had wiped out the tapes, had never transcribed them, and he had no notes.

Judge Azios said softly, almost admiringly, "That sonofabitch!" But there was nothing he could do.

Nettles grew gloomy. He was running out of time and he had no ammunition. If he didn't come up with any, his client's life was at forfeit.

Late one afternoon, after the last juror had been questioned and dismissed, when the defense lawyers had been given permission to talk to David in the locked jury room, I stayed behind to talk to Judge Azios. I sat in a chair at the defense table with my feet on another chair, and the judge sat on the table, swinging his legs.

The two uniformed deputies were waiting to escort David back through the underground tunnel to the jail, and they hovered on the edge of our conversation. They were both powerfully built Chicanos and looked like brothers. The younger, Simon Ramirez, had glistening black hair and a black mustache and smooth olive skin. He listened to us with a calm intensity, nodding now and then in silent approval or disagreement. He was a handsome man, with flat dark eyes, broody, and, I thought, dangerous.

"Is this an interesting case for you?" I asked the judge.

A. D. nodded emphatically. "I've only had one capital murder case in three years—the pickaxe murders. You ought to see my general docket. I call it at 8:30 A.M., and I have twenty lawyers crowding round. One wants a bond review, some want pretrial release, some don't want me to revoke probation—everybody wants something, and I have to listen, and the state's always against everything. I'm like a mental octopus, doing eight things at a time. But I love it. I've been on the bench eight and a half years. I have to run for office again next year. I'm elected by the whole county. Last time I won by 180,000 versus 130,000."

"What do you think of David West?" I asked.

"I can't tell you now," the judge said. "Wait until the trial's over."

"He hardly reacted the other day when Kim Paris testified about her contracts. Did you notice that?"

Before the judge could reply, or decline to comment, Ramirez, the deputy, said to me, "You're wrong. He was real nervous. It took him at least five minutes to look at her. They finally made eye contact. When their eyes met, she kept staring at him." Ramirez spoke quietly, so that we all had to strain a bit to hear him. As a result there was a dramatic impact. "I study people carefully. She feels real sorry for him. She did the job too well. She wants to tell him that she feels guilty and she can't do it. It may be years from now. She'll do it some day."

"And he hates her?" I asked, fascinated.

"No, he doesn't." Ramirez spoke even more softly. "He has very mixed emotions."

Drawn into it despite himself, the judge, his legs swinging back and forth, said, "It's a love-hate relationship. Stronger hate than love."

Established in our circle now, Ramirez spoke about the jail two blocks away, where David West lived. He used to be a receiving deputy there. The jail housed 4,500 men and it was a twenty-four-hour-a-day operation. The lights never went off, so there was no day or night there. Three, four o'clock in the morning, nine telephones jangled nonstop.

"Prisoners screaming and crying, being moved in and out. Sixty or seventy people are always waiting in the booking area on the first floor. Pumped in, pumped out. Someone's coming in, fighting drunk, two deputies trying to take his cuffs off, he's kicking them, he's going nuts. You got a young kid who's crying because he's never been to jail before and wants to call his dad, you got a guy who hardly speaks English and might be crazy, you got a woman who's ready to deliver a baby. . . . When you get out of there after eight hours, you're ready to not hear any voices or any telephones ringing ever again. It's like a movie, every night. You get burned out."

The judge nodded. "I used to go home, and the washer-dryer would make that buzz, like the buzz of the jury box when they're ready with their verdict. I used to hate it. My wife would say, 'It's only the dryer, honey.' "

Ramirez said, "In my job I get to handle most of the people who commit real hideous crimes and the next morning have to be taken to court for arraignment. The last ones we had were devil worshippers. They buried a pipe in this kid's face while he was still alive. And before that a Vietnamese, a mental case, stabbed this boy by a bus stop for no reason, seventy-two times with a small knife. I get to know these people.

And they talk to me. Like we're sitting here, talking. Because I'm the person that takes care of them."

The judge decided he had better leave or he might hear something he shouldn't hear. He invited me to a barbecue to be given that evening for 15,000 people at the Astrodome by Walter Rankin, a Houston politician. "I don't go there to eat," the judge said, "I go there to politic. If I'd thought of it, I would've had a big campaign sign and parked my truck right there."

When the judge had gone Ramirez told me he brought David West across from the jail every day, through the tunnel into the basement of the courthouse. "I walk him up the ramp, then I take his cuffs off. I can't let the jury see him handcuffed, because that's in violation of his civil rights. The first day I said, 'David, I'm taking you up to the court. If you run, I'm gonna chase after you. If I can't catch you, I'm gonna shoot you.' " Ramirez paused as if he was ruminating anew, but you could see that he had thought about this already. "If he really wants to, he could make me his executioner."

"What do you think about David?"

"He did it," Ramirez said.

"Why do you say that?"

His eyes grew even graver. "I handle convicts every day. And so does he." He inclined his head toward the other deputy, Joe Alvarado, who nodded in solemn confirmation of everything Ramirez was saying. "You're around them. You know what they're capable of."

"You think the jury will see David as a man capable of cold-blooded murder?"

Ramirez smiled delicately. "You ever look into his eyes, Clifford? Look like shark eyes. There's no affection in those eyes."

I stood up and took a turn around the defense table; I felt like a lawyer in closing argument. "Both Hardin and Nettles have said to me that this guy looks innocent. He doesn't look like he'd kill anybody. Looks like a gooney bird."

"He may to them," Ramirez said calmly.

"I think he's got a good chance of being acquitted. I'm not talking about whether he did it or not. Just the peculiarities of the law."

Ramirez looked me dead in the eye, smiled his brooding smile, and lowered his already soft voice. "Trust the jury," he said. "Trust the system."

Joe Alvarado nodded again. Clearly he and Ramirez were intimate with the secret process of justice. I said, "It's so clubby here. It's all a game. A little minuet of social revenge in South Texas on Planet Earth."

Glad that I'd understood, Ramirez nodded briskly. "It's always like that. You see how Hardin and Nettles insult each other? When they're done, they'll walk out of the courtroom, and you'll find them five or six blocks from here, eating lunch, laughing. Friends again. After the verdict. You're right, it's a game." His cool brown eyes sparkled.

16

The judge and I had lunch again at Inns of Court and then went to his chambers on the eighth floor behind his regular courtroom, a sunny office lined with books of Texas cases. Set into the window in stained glass were the gold scales of justice. The desk was a swamp of papers and letters, stacked awry. Predictably, the judge said, "But I know where everything is."

Roy Beene had told me that prior to voir dire in the West case Lyn McClellan had been prosecuting a defendant for "plain vanilla murder," as Lyn called it, and had offered him twenty years. The man turned the deal down, deciding to plead guilty and take his chances with Judge Azios rather than with the State of Texas. But A. D. stunned him with a sentence of thirty-five years.

In his chambers now I asked if this story was true.

The judge nodded. "This sonofabitch shot a woman during an argument in a bar, and when she hit the floor he bent down and finished her off with a bullet in the head. He was a Mexican-American. Lyn Mc-Clellan offered him twenty years, which I wasn't supposed to know, but I know everything that goes on. I gave that guy thirty-five years because, shit, he deserved it. He was an animal. So, Clifford, don't characterize me as compassionate. I can't win reelection that way. A lot of people think because I'm fair and very patient that I'm soft. It's not true. When I have to pass sentence, if a man's violent and I smell no remorse, I give him *la chingada*." Roughly translated, it meant, "I fuck him."

_____

On November 5 Nettles and Leitner and I were at lunch, and I remarked on the lawyers' intensity and total involvement with the voir dire. For example, I said, that morning while Gene had been questioning a juror, Rusty, sitting behind him at the counsel table, had been nodding his agreement every time the juror echoed the state's position.

"*What?*" Gene's head jerked up from his plate. "He was prompting a juror? Are you serious?"

"He wasn't prompting the juror," I said. "Just nodding. I doubt that he was aware of it."

"I saw that, too," Leitner said.

After lunch, before the first juror was called, Gene stood up in court —on the record—and told Judge Azios that "it's been brought to my attention that Mr. Hardin's been prompting the jurors behind my back while I questioned them." Gene requested that the court chastise Mr. Hardin and put a stop to it.

Rusty leaped up, yelling. "I've had enough! He'd better have a witness to this!"

"I have two," Gene said coolly. "I have Mr. Leitner and Mr. Irving."

"Please stand and be sworn," the judge said to us.

I stood with Leitner, but I couldn't believe it, and I was furious. I controlled myself and said, "I'm an observer here. I'm not involved. Do I really have to do this, Judge?"

"I think you'd better," the judge said, in a friendly manner.

I took the oath and then Gene called Leitner and asked me to leave the room. I waited outside, seething, and quite impotent.

The bailiff called me a few minutes later. I marched up to the witness stand, was reminded by Judge Azios that I was still under oath, and then turned my attention to Gene Nettles. Had I seen Mr. Hardin nodding to jurors while the defense was questioning them? Yes, I had. Had these nods occurred when the juror said something that might be construed as favorable to the state's position in the case?

"Often," I said.

Before Gene could go on, I said, "But I'd like to point out that I was observing Mr. Hardin closely, and I never once got the impression that he was trying to communicate with a juror or encourage a juror or influence a juror in any way. It was my impression that he was just deeply involved and carried away and didn't realize what he was doing."

"Pass the witness," Gene said, frowning.

Rusty took me on cross. He looked so pleased.

This is fun, I thought.

"Mr. Irving, you're sitting now in the witness chair, and Mr. Nettles is sitting exactly where he sits when he questions a juror, and I'm sitting where I usually sit when he does that. . . . Isn't that correct?"

"Correct."

"Isn't it true that if you look at Mr. Nettles now, I'm not in your line of vision, and you don't see me?"

"True," I said, "but if I were looking at Gene and you nodded your head the way you did when the juror was talking, that would catch my attention, my peripheral vision, and I would see it."

Wise guy. Rusty didn't say it, but that's what his look meant.

But I loved it.

The judge gently admonished Rusty to try not to nod at jurors, and then suggested we get on with the voir dire so that we could go to trial in this century.

Later I had coffee with Rusty and we chuckled about what had happened. Then I buttonholed Gene, and he laughed, too. He wasn't angry at all. "You know that before you testified, Leitner got up there and denied that he saw *anything*? I felt like an idiot. You saved my ass, Clifford."

Rusty and Lyn McClellan and I went to lunch near the courthouse. "Gene seems to think I have an ace up my sleeve," Rusty said, "or I wouldn't be taking this case to trial. But it's not true." He was taking it to trial, he said, because he believed David had done a terrible act and must be punished for it, but as the hour approached he felt a premonition of failure and utter frustration. He had gone on a YMCA Indian Guides camping weekend with his two young sons: "And the guys in this group all appear to be more conservative than me, by far. You know, the kind the average prosecutor would put on a jury in a New York minute. And every one of them was bothered by the way Kim got that confession." He shook his head dejectedly. "Basically all I've got are those tapes. What I need is a confirming witness."

That was a problem he shared with Nettles, but I didn't say it, just as I wouldn't tell Gene anything Rusty said. Those were the rules of the game.

Rusty discussed the process of jury selection. Bravely ignoring the presence of Lyn McClellan, he said, "I usually don't like to select fat jurors. As kids they were picked on, and so they tend to favor the underdog. I want harmonious people—there are twelve of them, they've got to get along. I like happy people, because they're at peace with the social order. I can relate to them. Cynics are out. They're antisocial, and I represent society. And it's no secret," he continued, "that I like women on the jury. Despite your suspicions, I don't consciously try to charm them, or flirt with them. My wife would disagree—she says I'm a flirt. Gene makes a lot more effort than I do in that respect. You can see him trying to win over the women jurors."

"Yes, you can see him," I agreed, "but you're a lot smoother than Gene."

186

McClellan chuckled, but Rusty shook his head. "I'm not. I just like women. I'm interested in them. They feel it."

From there he began to talk about the jury panels, how refreshing it was to see the seriousness and "ethical determination" as he put it, of the jurors. A true slice of America. "Except for doctors and lawyers and people in the arts and entertainment world, who know how to slither out of the obligation. But these people you see come in here are proud to serve. I love it! It gives me faith. And in some ways, although I didn't vote for Reagan, I see this partly as a manifestation of his regime. It's acceptable now to feel a civic pride, a patriotism. Ten years ago, when we were recovering from Watergate, it wouldn't have been."

He asked me at that lunch what I thought of the whole process. He meant not only the jury selection but the impending trial.

I told him that, despite the university degrees held by the participants, I saw it as a little ritual of social vengeance, primitive, literally older than history. The prelude to *lex talionis,* slaying with legal sanction. As a result, society felt reassured and could face the sunset without dread. Of course there were the trappings of protection in the unlikely event that vengeance proved to be inappropriate. It was a contest, a game, and for all but the defendant—although *this* case might be an exception—it was fun.

Suddenly upset, Rusty asked, "You think I'm playing a game in this trial? You think I'm not sincere?"

No. I tried to explain my point of view. There were abstract concepts of truth and justice, right and wrong, guilt and innocence. They were goals—ideals. To achieve them we had devised this adversary system where opposing lawyers battle on behalf of the state as the guardian of peaceful social order and on behalf of the accused breaker of that order. But we were not an all-knowing species. In the Dark Ages charges were often resolved by walking barefoot and blindfolded over nine red hot plowshares laid lengthwise at unequal distances. If the accused were burned, he was declared guilty. And people *believed.* Just as now they believed that two lawyers and a judge and a jury arrived at truth and justice. Perhaps a thousand years from now that would seem as archaic and random as walking on plowshares. The goals were illusory. At best we could approximate them, but not achieve them. And we wouldn't admit to that publicly.

"It's still a contest, a medieval joust," I said, "whether you like it or not. Not a frivolous test of skill, though, because if you have fact on your side and the appearance of truth, you're better armed, and you win."

"I'm glad you added that," Rusty said.

"I don't demean the process. It's all we've got, so far."

"If you think it's a contest of wills, then what's *your* objective?"

"To dig into the area of truth, if that's possible. Not just whodunit, but why. And *how*. I don't mean with what weapon. I mean morally how."

"So do I want to know that," Rusty said.

"You want a conviction. With honor."

"*And* the truth."

"What if they're incompatible?"

"Then I won't prosecute."

"That makes you judge and jury as well. In an adversary system you have to prosecute. Nettles has to defend. Otherwise we have chaos."

McClellan shook his head, convinced I was a nut. Rusty just acted as if he thought there was something suspect about my attitude. Something disruptive, and therefore *wrong*. But we were still friendly. He still trusted me.

───────────

"It's no secret," Rusty says on a Friday afternoon to one of the prospective jurors, "that Mr. McClellan and I will be seeking to introduce evidence that will convince the jury to vote yes on special issues #1 and #2, and will therefore result in the death penalty for the defendant." He goes on from there to ask her how she feels about the death penalty. This is all in front of David West.

When Rusty enters the courtroom on the following Monday morning, he smiles warmly at David and says, "How are you today? Have a good weekend?" He means what he's saying. He's not a hypocrite.

At noon that day Rusty and Lyn and I leave the courtroom together for yet another lunch. Duval West is in the elevator with us. He's always blinking and restlessly smiling, and he reeks so much of tobacco you'd think he used it as tooth powder. The elevator is crowded. Sweating lawyers and harassed bailiffs and worried witnesses push their way in. Rusty is thrown against Duval. Duval mutters something that may be "Hello." Rusty looks up a few inches, essays a tight smile, and says, "How are you, Mr. West?" He extends his hand automatically and Duval takes it. They shake.

"We've never been introduced," Duval says.

"Oh, I'm Rusty Hardin . . . as you know . . . uh . . . I guess. And this is Lyn McClellan."

Lyn wraps his paw around Duval's fingers. Then they all chat about the weather. Dry and sunny, one of Houston's brief pleasant seasons between bouts of enervating heat and the winter cold snap. They agree that the fall's been hotter than usual. And yet less rainy. Nice weather.

188

In the street, after Duval shambled off in another direction, I couldn't contain myself. "How can you chat about the weather with a man whose son you're trying to kill?"

"That's a harsh way to put it," Rusty said tautly. "What should I have done?"

I didn't know.

In the restaurant, Rusty said, "Well, the last six weeks have been awkward. But I'm comfortable with what I'm doing," he explained, using one of his favorite phrases. It was akin to the old Hemingway ethos: if it feels good, it's moral. In Rusty's case it stemmed from an enormous self-confidence in his moral correctness: if I feel comfortable with it, it can't be wrong. That kind of thinking had yet to let him down.

Tucking into a chef's salad, he said, "I don't hate David at all. He's a sociopath. I'd like to understand him, if it's possible—he's the most interesting defendant I've ever known. The other day, within his hearing, discussing the people in the case, someone said, 'That sleazebag . . . ' And David turned and said, 'Who, Campbell?' " Rusty shook his head in amazement. "After all these weeks of discussion about murder, he still thinks that way. He believes he's going to be found not guilty. He may be right"—he frowned at that thought—"and even if he's wrong and the jury votes for the death penalty, he thinks somehow he'll get a reversal. As far as life in the pen goes, he wouldn't mind that. He's the center of attention now. He loves it. He went to the door yesterday and told a juror, 'You're next.' "

"Then why are you so friendly with him," I asked, "when you think he's evil and you're out to kill him?"

Rusty flushed. "I wish you wouldn't keep saying that. I'm not a killer, and I don't think he's evil. Just dangerous and sick. I'm friendly with him so that if he takes the stand on his own behalf I'll have a relationship with him. But it's not Machiavellian. It's just more natural this way."

"You think David might testify?"

"If he does," Rusty said, "I will have to leave the courtroom first in order to have an orgasm." He mused on it; he was always able to see both sides of a dilemma. "Here's the paradox. If he wants to save his life, he shouldn't testify. But if he wants to go for all the bananas, he's got to get up there and do it."

He thought a little longer and said, "They have an excellent case. I'd lick my chops at the chance to take someone like Kim on cross. Maybe at the end of the second day her composure will start to wane. Then Gene could break her. And Wickie Weinstein! Boy, *there's* a witness who carries a lot of bad baggage! Would I love to cross-examine Wickie! 'So you say you sold the gun to David? But he was broke, wasn't he? And you were then on every kind of drug, weren't you? And who was more

189

violent, you or David? Who was the better shot? Who really owned all those guns?' "

McClellan offered a buttery laugh. "You want me to make a motion to the judge for you to switch sides, Rusty?"

"I have to get down to work on this case," Rusty said solemnly. "The truth is that when I leave that voir dire room I haven't been concentrating on David at all. I've been looking to make a case against Cindy Ray. It's just a burr under my saddle that she's out there. But I have to live with it," he said, "unless a miracle happens."

Voir dire was postponed for a week in order for Leitner, a reserve lieutenant-commander in the Coast Guard, to go on a special sea exercise to intercept drug smugglers in the Gulf of Mexico, and on the evening of November 12 I called Rusty to see if we could meet. He was too busy, but we talked on the telephone for more than an hour.

A few days ago, he said, he had eleven-year-old Michael Ray brought to his office. He had thought of using the boy as a witness, but after speaking to him for two hours he decided that Michael was too confused to be of any use, and the last thing Rusty wanted to do was unnecessarily resurrect the trauma of that bloody night. The boys were living now with Brucene and J. W. Campbell. They were in school; they were mending slowly. They seemed cheerful enough on the surface, but surely there were terrible memories that lay beneath. Rusty's two sons were of similar ages. Sometimes in the 3 A.M. darkness, when he lay awake thinking about the case, his mind drifted to what Michael and Matthew had gone through at that hour on June 19 three years ago. After that, on such nights, Rusty could never sleep.

I thought of them, too, I said. I knew they were being kept out of it by the people who cared for them, but from time to time, I admitted, I had considered making an effort to seek them out.

"Have you ever done it?" Rusty asked.

"No. They have to be left alone. Let them get over this and try to grow."

Rusty was in the mood to air his problems. How did he corroborate what David said to Kim? He was out hunting for witnesses, but none helped him. And the issue of sexual abuse kept clouding the case. Was it fact or an unconscionable fiction? There was little doubt in Rusty's mind that Cindy had convinced David it had happened, but that didn't mean that it was so. And what about motive? The state didn't have to prove motive, but it was vital to Rusty's moral stance to absorb and believe in one. His faith was slipping. Had David done the murders for the money, or genuinely adopted the role of a surrogate avenger? Had Cindy begged him to kill her parents, or had David begged Cindy's approval to *let* him do it? All dim and cloudy.

"I don't know any of those answers," Rusty admitted. "Not the way I need to know."

Rusty was dedicated and suave but under that façade drawn taut as the string on a longbow. I didn't fully understand that—I had been concentrating on Gene's expected temper tantrums—until the morning of November 22 when the tenth juror was picked. Rusty wasn't there that day for the beginning of voir dire, and Lyn McClellan took over. The prospective juror was a fat young black woman named Tracey Owens. When she balked keenly at the idea of predicting future dangerousness, Lyn moved to excuse her. The judge wouldn't allow it, not unless the state wanted to spend a strike. Gene then rehabilitated her to the point where she backed down and said: All right, in some cases, with violent people, she *could* say that future violence was probable.

Lyn finally accepted Owens as the tenth juror. He thought that what he saw as Gene's macho attitude offended black jurors, and he also said, "She'll decide that David'll throw rocks at people, and then—" With his right hand he made a stabbing motion at a vein in his left arm. David hardly blinked at that. He was still having a good time. The general impression was that he knew something that no one else knew. The cavalry was going to come pounding over the horizon and save him just as the hatchet blade descended toward his scalp.

A few minutes after eleven o'clock, while the next juror was being examined, Rusty strode in. Lyn leaned across the table and whispered in Rusty's ear. He pointed to the jury sheet.

Rusty's jaw tightened. Five minutes later he caught my eye and signaled me to leave. We met outside and walked into the adjoining empty courtroom. Calmly he said, "Tell me about the tenth juror."

I read from my notes. A vein in his neck throbbed. He darted back and forth with quick strides. "What the fuck is Lyn doing?" When he used the expletive his whole face jerked; he bit the word off so hard that he deleted the vowel, and it burst out as "fk!" Bloodless lips drew back across his teeth. "We're sitting on ten strikes! Lyn takes a fucking *filler*? I want people I can relate to! He knows that! And you say she's *fat*? How fat? How old is she? She's only *twenty?*"

He only stopped striding and barking to put his head into his hands in despair. He had been to the eye doctor that morning—he had cornea problems because of failing sight in his right eye. He was so forlorn and enraged that I tried to console him. "She's young and friendly and good-natured," I said, "and she'll follow the lead of the other three black women. The three black women are the strongest and most intelligent jurors so far. No harm done."

"You've made me feel better," Rusty said. Then his face turned pink and he yelled, "How could he *do* this to me?" A good part of the anger came from his frustration at never having seen the juror. He was going to conduct the trial, and he needed to know who he was talking to. Now he had one cipher among the twelve, one woman who had hidden buttons he wouldn't know how to press. "This juror is going to bother me right through the whole trial," he admitted, less ruffled now, but at the same time twisting the knife even deeper into his guts. "I'm like that. I'll stew over it every night. I'll lose sleep. I'll drive Tissy nuts. I'll get paranoid. A fat, young juror! At this stage we should only have jurors we *love!*"

During a break Lyn came out and tracked us to the empty courtroom. He had guessed what was going on. He didn't kowtow, and Rusty, making an enormous effort at brotherhood, pulled himself together, and in a level, even friendly voice—although I suppose Lyn was shrewd enough to hear the underlying agony—asked Lyn to brief him on the new juror.

"She's a filler, not a killer. I liked her."

"Describe her to me."

"Large," McClellan said.

"How large?"

"*Large* large."

Rusty lowered his head to bang it against a wooden chair—*clunk*—harder than he intended. "My depth perception is off today. . . . " He rubbed his reddening forehead. You could see that it hurt. He looked up sadly. "Do you mean *fat?*"

Lyn didn't hesitate. Maybe he was enjoying this moment. Maybe part of him hated Rusty because Rusty was his boss and so commanding and trim. "I'd say that, yes. Fat. Very fat. Immense. The biggest one we've got."

Rusty groaned in pain and kept rubbing the red spot on his forehead.

"No more fillers," he said, in a voice more abject than I would have believed possible. "Please."

When I went back into the courtroom Gene Nettles grabbed me by the arm. "What did he want? Don't get cute, I saw him give you the nod. You didn't go out there to wish him a happy Thanksgiving."

"He wanted to know what David is always saying to me."

"He wanted to hear about juror number ten, right? I'll bet he was just pissed off right out of his socks!" Gene couldn't have been more delighted than if he'd got David West off with five strokes of the cane and a reprimand. Jim Leitner came over and Gene said gleefully, "It kills Hardin that something happened he wasn't aware of and couldn't control. I love it!"

Gene Nettles's big break came in a way so preposterous, so *goofy*, that no one could have foreseen it. It wasn't that I was more disposed to help the defense than the prosecution. The ball just fell into that pocket—then.

In late October I had placed a classified ad in the Houston *Post*. It said: *"Anyone who knew David West, Cindy Ray, or Kim Paris, please call . . ."* and then my telephone number. No doubt an amateurish way to try to research a murder, but it led to my meeting a woman who had worked with David West when he was tending bar in Montrose, and then to a talk with one of Cindy's friends at both junior high and high school. She described a girl who was heavy but had a pretty face, rarely smiled, was definitely not popular, didn't care or try at school—"got in trouble a lot and was always in the principal's office, which puzzled me because she was so quiet"—didn't go to any of the proms and didn't come to either the five- or ten-year reunion. No boyfriends, ever.

And then on November 12 I had a call from a woman who said her name was Angie, and claimed to have known Cindy Ray when they both performed amateur theater at The Comedy Workshop in Montrose. What she had to say wasn't particularly interesting. "Cindy was pretty freaky," and "she didn't seem at all remorseful after her parents' death."

Angie told me she was from Oklahoma, but she wouldn't give me her last name or her telephone number. She asked as many questions of me as I asked of her. What did I think of Kim Paris? Of Clyde Wilson? How did I think the trial would turn out?

I gave dull answers.

She called a second time. Again I didn't learn anything of value.

On Sunday afternoon, November 24, she called a third time. This time she startled me. In an agitated voice she said, "My name is Anita McCartney. Please don't hang up when I tell you this—I'm the one who's been calling you and saying she was 'Angie.' Kim Paris put me up to it. We were roommates, and Kim wanted to get information out of you, so I made the calls for her as a favor, a joke. Please forgive me!

193

Yesterday she locked me out of my place and today I had to get the police to help me break back in. Now I want to meet with you—I want to tell you everything I know about that bitch. I know the *real* Kim."

Better believe I had a good chuckle at this backfire of intentions.

"I've got two conditions," Anita McCartney—or *was* it Anita Mc-Cartney?—said. "This information is for you and for Gene Nettles. Definitely not to get to Rusty Hardin, because Kim's boyfriend threatened my life. He said to me, 'You make trouble, and I'll have you taken care of.' "

I gave her my word, and that evening we met at a Szechuan restaurant in the suburbs. I put my tape recorder on the table. Anita McCartney—she showed me ID to prove it—was an attractive, dark-haired woman of twenty-six who worked as an accountant in a downtown Houston oil and gas exploration company.

She was agitated; she kept twisting the big ring on her finger.

She had first met Sami, she said, at a women's bar in Montrose where Sami was playing pool. She and Sami and Kim had then lived together, and Mike Manela, who worked for Clyde, became Anita's boyfriend for a while. Anita flew off to Acapulco with Kim, Sami, and Mike last Valentine's Day. The *real* Kim Paris, according to Anita, when she first came to Houston had been a cocaine user and a topless dancer at a flashy joint called Caligula (where she had met David Borosov); she had also "found" a Sakowitz department store charge card, belonging to someone named Yardley, which she'd used to buy a Christian Dior robe and slippers for Mike Manela on his birthday, and "about $500 worth of other stuff." Anita wrote down the number of the account for me. Kim's marriage in the navy, she went on, had been for financial and social convenience. She once offered "downer" pills to someone in Clyde Wilson's office.* She borrowed money and never returned it, she was a slob to live with, and she left the thermostat at 68 degrees, which ran up air conditioning bills that averaged $370 a month. She was "the coldest person I've ever met in my life."

Anita said, "When she got her third DWI, she called Rusty Hardin and told him to fix it. I was sitting right next to her. She was drunk. Rusty said he wouldn't do that, and Kim said, 'Well, then fuck you, I'm not going to be your witness!' She called Rusty's wife up and screamed at her, too."

---

* P. M. Clinton confirmed: "It was in January. She said to Penny, the receptionist, 'You look tired today. I've got something can fix that.' The pills were prescription, and Kim said she had plenty, and did anyone else in the office want them? Penny became uneasy and told Denise Moseley. Denise hated Kim and told it to Clyde, and they were considering calling in the police—at least firing Kim. I had to remind them that they were in the midst of a case, and it would be a hell of a chore to find someone else to run on David West. So they just dressed Kim down."

Anita rambled on. When she finished she said, "You'll tell all this to Gene Nettles?"

"Well . . . maybe. But I can't vouch to him that it's true."

"You don't believe me?"

"Didn't you lie to me once, when you told me you were Angie?"

"Just give the tapes you made to Nettles. Let him make up his own mind. And remember you promised not to tell Rusty." She was afraid he would tell Kim, and Kim would sic David Borosov on her. She was right; Rusty would be obliged to tell Kim.

I agreed.

Gene, when he heard the tapes, literally warwhooped for joy. The next evening he went to Anita McCartney's apartment in southwest Houston and sat down with her for two hours with his own tape recorder running. In his euphoria the following morning he said to Leitner, "This is what we needed. This will make the case for us."

That hadn't been my plan—I wasn't working for the defense. I began to wonder: What if my leading Nettles to Anita McCartney somehow resulted in David being found not guilty? Could I live with that?

Find out, I thought. Let it be.

And then, almost immediately, I righted the balance, and there was a price to pay.

17

Dan Grothaus was going to cover the trial for the Houston *Post*. Neither of us had ever satisfied ourselves as to what role Wickie Weinstein might have played in the murders beyond what he had told the police, or indeed, if what he had told the police was true. Then David made his peculiar remark to Ginger Casey, the anchor at Channel 26, about not putting "his ass in a sling to protect Wickie Weinstein." Ginger, who had become my friend, mentioned it to Dan, and then to me, with the understanding that for the moment it was off the record. But we could think about it.

We did, often.

Dan and I had agreed to swap information, and when he called one night in early November he sounded excited. He had spoken to a friend in Montrose who said Wickie was back in Houston after a two-month drying out session at Hazelden, a Minnesota clinic for alcoholics. The reported cost was $4,000, paid for by his mother back in New Jersey.

Wickie had split up with Melanie Edgecombe and become a shadow figure, a kind of rumor in the Montrose underworld. According to Dan's friend he had put the word out in the neighborhood that people should keep their mouths shut about Dave West and the Campbell murders. She said, "Wickie's not the sort of person you want to annoy. He's violent and he's crazy. He knows how to do two things—carpentry and killing people."

All that piqued Dan's interest even more. He began calling in some markers.

One warm Sunday in early November I went to an Urban Animal skate rally at Allen Parkway on the edge of downtown Houston. Wickie didn't show, but I found Melanie, his ex-girlfriend, in roller skates and black outfit proclaiming "Skate or Die!" We lolled on the warm grass with the sun-gilded skyscrapers of downtown Houston soaring into the background. Melanie had milky skin, punk-cut yellow hair, and distracting green eye shadow. She wouldn't tell me where Wickie was, but she was willing to talk about David.

"He was always protective. Sometimes in Rud's a guy would come in and start to hassle us, and Dave would go up to him and tell him in a nonviolent way that we may have looked like we were ready to whoop it up but we weren't like that at all." She frowned. "But Dave killed the Campbells. I can't tell you how, but I know he did it."

Unlike Deputy Ramirez, she wasn't talking about his shark's eyes. It had to be something Wickie had told her. What did Wickie know? And how did he know it?

Dan called again that night and said, "I found someone out there who's agreed to talk. It's a friend of Wickie's named Lynn Roebuck. She works the door at a club called Midtown Live."

Dan met with her on Tuesday evening, November 12, at a bar named Blythe Spirits. She had called him earlier at the *Post* to ask if she could bring someone who had also known Wickie and Dave. Dan said, "Sure."

Lynn Roebuck was a big and handsome woman close to forty, with a firm manner. She gave happy hour parties in different Montrose bars, trying to put together hairdressers, university instructors, psychiatrists, whoever she could find. In Blythe Spirits she introduced Dan to her friend: Paul Whitfield, a slim, black-bearded man of thirty-one. He wore jeans and a white shirt. They were going to get married, Lynn said.

Most of the time, when Lynn spoke, Paul smiled tactfully and nodded his agreement. Dan focused on Lynn. He assumed Paul was there just to hold her hand.

"You have to first promise us," Lynn said to Grothaus, "that whatever we tell you is off the record. You won't print it in the *Post* and you won't take it to the prosecutor or the defense attorney."

Dan gave his word. But unless they had an objection, he said, he would tell *me,* because we had an agreement. They agreed to that.

Lynn was an accountant, Paul an electrical repairman; they lived together in a rented house only a block from Dave West's house on Vermont. Lynn said she had been introduced to Dave by Wickie and Melanie. They'd all hung out together in Rudyard's, where they talked about dogs, animal rights, guns, politics. Now and then they smoked some dope together.

"Dave and Wickie were pretty tight," Paul said. "I'm an ex-marine too. We all used to go to pistol ranges in northwest Houston, off I-45. They shot tight groups. They went out to the range probably two or three times a month."

Now, for the first time, Dan began to focus on Paul Whitfield, who seemed a tentative man. Not so Lynn. Nothing tentative about Lynn.

"Dave had a pit bull named Max," Lynn said, "but there was a sign outside his house: 'Forget the dog, beware of owner.' And there was a gun barrel pointed at you. I hated that!"

Paul clarified: "We always just thought Dave was all blow and no go."

"And these tall tales he and Wickie told, we never believed them," Lynn declared.

"Until at one point the stories they told me were actually coming to life," Paul said. "For example, I've had both of them telling me about killing somebody, that David had shot somebody, and got the gun from Wickie, and they had to get rid of it—stuff like that. They said they had to throw it into Buffalo Bayou so it couldn't be traced."

Grothaus felt his skin tingle. He hit the brakes. "Go over that again. Who is 'they?' Who had to throw the gun in Buffalo Bayou? Do you know what kind of gun they were talking about?"

"Just a casual conversation," Paul said, "about killing some people. Like something came down and it had to be done. It was Wickie that told me it had to be. Because it was his gun, his .45. He had to throw it in the bayou."

Grothaus took a deep breath, then leaned forward across his beer to make sure his tape recorder still had plenty of running time left.

_____

On Friday, November 15, Dan gave me a computer printout of the tape transcript. Paul Whitfield's statements about the gun seemed ambiguous. A few days later I reached Paul and made a date to meet him and Lynn Roebuck on Monday evening, November 25, in the bar of the Grand Hotel at Westheimer and the Loop.

The Grand was comfortable and quiet, with plush armchairs, soft lighting, and a long table of free hors d'oeuvres. Grothaus was going to meet us but had called to say he'd be late.

Paul and Lynn were nervous. I ordered the drinks and told them I had read the transcript of their interview with Dan, but there were things that had confused me. Such as: Who had thrown the .45 away in Buffalo Bayou? What *exactly* had Wickie said?

Paul explained again. "Wickie said, 'We threw it away.' Meaning him and Dave. He told me it had really bothered him to do that because it was such a nice gun. His favorite—a pearl-handled automatic. That's what Dave said, too. He said he borrowed the gun from Wickie and—"

"*Borrowed?* Not sold?"

"Borrowed. Wickie said that, too, that he loaned it to Dave."

Now for the first time I thought I understood what had prompted Rusty's oddly inappropriate: "*Would I love to cross-examine Wickie! 'So you say you sold the gun to David? But he was broke, wasn't he?'*"

I asked Paul if Wickie and Dave told him this together.

No, Dave had told him first, one afternoon in what must have been the spring of 1983. Paul had assumed it was part of "all blow and no go," but it remained in his mind with enough sticking power so that a few weeks later, alone with Wickie on the way to a party, he remarked, "Hey, you know what Dave says . . . ?"

And Wickie had confirmed. *My favorite gun. Yeah, Dave borrowed it. And then later me and Dave threw it away.*

I asked if either of them were drunk or stoned.

"Not at all," Paul said.

"Either of them say that Cindy Ray was with them when they threw the gun away?"

"Her name never came up. The whole thing about the killings seemed more of a brag than anything else. But Dave didn't act like he was proud of it. He acted more like it had to be done, like somebody crossed him and he had to get even. I didn't tie it in with the Campbells at all."

"And when this thing happened," Lynn Roebuck said, "when we heard on TV that Dave had admitted to killing Cindy Ray's mother and father, I barricaded myself in my apartment for three days. It scared me —it just tore me up *so!*"

Grothaus joined us in the bar and we ordered a second round of drinks. I asked Paul to repeat his story. When he did, Dan and I eyed each other. Lynn Roebuck said to me, "Is this important, what they told Paul? If Paul testified, would it matter?"

I explained that it would probably prove Dave West guilty, that Rusty Hardin urgently needed a witness to corroborate Kim Paris. And it also suggested that Wickie, not Cindy Ray, was Dave's probable accomplice.

If his favorite gun was *borrowed*, it was odds on that Wickie would have demanded to know why Dave needed it. Moreover, if they threw it away together in the bayou, surely that was within hours of the murders. Wickie was involved in the murder up to his eyeballs.

"Why didn't you ever tell anyone until now?" Grothaus asked.

Paul laughed nervously. "No one ever asked me."

I wondered how many other people were out there who hadn't been asked the right question.

Lynn turned to him and said, "I think you should testify."

Paul nodded deliberately. "I think David's guilty," he said. "I wouldn't feel good if he got away with it." He meditated for a while, then shifted his gaze to me. "What do you think I should do?"

"Not me," I said. "I'm not encouraging you to testify, but I can't encourage you *not* to testify. That would be what the law calls obstruction of justice. You make up your own mind."

He had two problems, he explained. One was that certain aspects of his and Lynn's past life style in Montrose would come to light under cross-examination by a tough defense lawyer. And he wouldn't testify if the prosecutor didn't convince him that what he had to say was vital to the success of the case. He didn't want to turn the key on David West, and implicate Wickie, and then have that pair go free and come blasting after him and his fiancée with a shotgun to even the score. He and Lynn had seen David beat up someone outside Rudyard's one night because of an insult to Lynn inside the bar. David had gone home, according to Lynn, changed into what he'd called his "fighting clothes," and come back to seek retribution. And another time David and Wickie together had ambushed yet another Rudyard's habitué named Virgil Lee Johnson, who had supposedly stolen their friend Robin's tools, and brained him with a pickaxe handle. Blood flowed.

"I was a marine," Paul said. "Dave's a marine, and with marines, you're geared up to kill. I would only fight in self-defense now, but some of those guys see a shadow move the wrong way and they think someone's out to get them. They believe in preventive strikes."

He asked me to sound out Rusty Hardin.

I could have said no—I didn't recall volunteering to play the role of go-between—but I didn't. Somehow I felt responsible; if I hadn't sought them out after Grothaus had talked to them, they might have stayed out in the cold. I said, "I'll deliver the message, but I want to tell Gene Nettles about it, too. No nasty surprises."

Unlike Anita McCartney, Paul agreed, with the stipulation that I didn't mention his name.

I was going home to Mexico for the Thanksgiving holiday, and at the

Wednesday noon break from voir dire I buttonholed Nettles and Leitner in a poor little patch of shade outside the courthouse. They were on their way to the Y to run the indoor track. I said, "There's someone out there in Montrose who claims David told him he killed two people with a pearl-handled .45 he borrowed from Wickie. And that David and Wickie threw the gun away together in Buffalo Bayou. He's not keen on testifying, but he might change his mind."

"Who is this clown?" Gene said.

"He asked me to get some guarantees from Rusty. But I'm telling you, too."

"You're cute, Clifford."

"Hey, I'm trying to do you and your client a favor."

Nettles shook his head. "This person says David told him he borrowed a pearl-handled .45 from Wickie? That's how I know it's bullshit. Wasn't pearl-handled, wasn't borrowed. We have to go running, Clifford. Keep up the good work."

Later in the day I caught Rusty's eye during the voir dire. He left the room and I followed. "Let's have coffee," I said.

The basement cafeteria in the courthouse seemed like a leftover eatery from a more tawdry age. The overhead fluorescent lighting glared and hummed. Over coffee and a soggy donut, I said, "There's a man out there—no name yet. He'll swear that David West told him he killed two people with a pearl-handled .45 borrowed from Wickie. And that Wickie and David threw the gun into Buffalo Bayou together. And that on a later occasion, Wickie—sober, not stoned—confirmed both parts of the story."

Rusty's eyes bloomed with light. "Bring him down," he said.

"This fellow is shy. He wants to know a few things first."

Rusty agreed that the past life of the unknown witness wouldn't be bared; he would make a motion *in limine* (at the beginning of the proceedings) to bar any such revelation in open court. He couldn't offer any other guarantees. He certainly couldn't promise that Paul would walk away from a meeting at the D.A.'s Office with the freedom to choose whether or not he would testify. From Rusty's point of view the emergence of truth took precedence over everything.

"Bring your man down," he repeated.

He wasn't my man, but Rusty didn't know that, so I decided to try a little horsetrading. "If I bring him down, will you do me a favor? I want a look at your copy of the HPD offense report."

200

Rusty frowned. He considered it a minute, then said, "People talk to the police with the understanding that they're talking in confidence. How do you think they'd feel if they knew there was a possibility that HPD would open its files to writers? I can't do it."

Unfortunately, that made sense. But Rusty wasn't finished.

"Clifford, you should make your best effort to bring this man in as a witness. Not for personal gain. It's your duty as a good citizen."

"Fuck being a good citizen," I said. That was a stupid and brazen thing to say, and I regretted it right away. But I said it.

He looked at me as if I had spat on the American flag. All his worst early suspicions about me were confirmed. I was an anarchist. An ex-con.

"Rusty, I'm not *bringing* him. I was bluffing. He comes down, or he doesn't, on his own volition. Today I'm just a bearer of messages."

"This weekend would be convenient," Rusty said.

"This weekend I'll be eating skinny Mexican turkey and drinking margaritas. And this guy's going home for Thanksgiving to New Orleans, or maybe Albania, I can't remember. Besides, he needs time. He's scared."

"He doesn't have to be scared of Wickie. And his testimony about Wickie won't trouble me at all."

"I'll see what I can do."

Kim Paris joined us for coffee, and that ended the discussion.

I told all that to Paul Whitfield in a telephone call before I drove to Hobby Airport. Paul said he would think it over. He struck me as being on the verge of saying, "I want out of this," and I was glad.

After the Thanksgiving holiday, the day before the pretrial motion began, Gene Nettles called me.

"I told David about this person in Montrose who claims he talked to him. He says, 'No way.' It's just some publicity hound trying to get his name in the papers. Does this guy intend to testify?"

"Thinking about it," I said. "Can't make up his mind."

"You're too involved out there. Stop stirring up trouble, Clifford."

I bristled. I could think that, but I didn't like his saying it. "If I wasn't out there," I said, "doing whatever I'm doing, you wouldn't have got to your favorite vengeful hysteric and star informant, Anita McCartney. You wouldn't be able to cut up Kim Paris and save David's ass. You wouldn't have a case. Right?"

We growled at each other for a while.

201

Later I kept wondering about it. *Yes, of course I was too involved.* And was that wrong? I didn't know. I wasn't unearthing anything that didn't seem to be true or leading to truth. If Anita McCartney was lying, that would come out. Ditto for Paul Whitfield. If they were telling the truth, they deserved to be heard. Was I stirring up trouble? Trouble was anything that threatened to change people's fixed ideas. Trouble was always out there, looking for a way to get in. Maybe I was the way. I didn't like that idea, but I still didn't quite see what I could do about it.

———————

That day I had lunch with beautiful Melanie Edgecombe—she wasn't *my* idea of a carpenter—who told me, "Rusty's so cute!" She liked him, and was feeding him information.

"Dave is my friend. I like him, too. I wish I could help him. How does he feel about Wickie?"

"Hates him now," I said.

"What else could Wickie do?" Melanie asked. She meant, other than testify about the .45 and what David had said.

"He has to tell the truth."

She nodded and bit her lip. Since Paul Whitfield had been talking to me, the truth seemed more complex than we had previously imagined. Did Melanie know any part of it?

"Melanie. . . . The gun, the .45—"

"The one Wickie sold him?"

"*Was* it sold—or loaned?"

"Sold," she said firmly, "but not paid for."

"When?"

"The day before the murder! Can you imagine?" Her eyes shone.

"How do you know that?"

"Wickie told me. It really worried him."

The day before the murder. That pulled Wickie even closer to the act. If Wickie was that intricately involved, had David lied to Kim about what Cindy had really done? Or had the three of them committed the murders together?

Cindy Ray is still the key to everything, I realized. They were her parents. The grisly events of that June night turned on what she had done or not done, said or not said. *"He wanted to cure her,"* Gwen Sampson had said.

Of what?

Cindy Ray and the history of the Campbell family were the targets where the entire investigation should be focused. But she was a blur. Not in anybody's sights. Or didn't seem to be, then.

"The state calls Officer Raymond White."

With those words on Tuesday, December 3, 1985, the awesome bureaucratic machinery of the state lurched into motion because of careless words in a parked car by a lovesick man to a clever woman. Another way of looking at it was that the restless souls of James and Virginia Campbell at last stood a chance of calling their murderer to account—provided that Rusty Hardin could bring all his abilities to bear and focus, and win a case that seemed to be slipping away from him.

A feeling akin to dread filled him that morning when he edged quietly out of bed and padded to the kitchen to squeeze the orange juice. A gray morning, and his heart felt swollen in his chest. He had slept poorly. Neither Tissy nor the kids were awake yet, and Rusty was glad. He could rarely hide his emotions from his family, and he hated for them to see him in so uncertain and jangled a mood.

We could lose, he thought. It would be so easy. David could walk out of there. He'll come up to me and want to shake my hand. And what will I do?

Wish him luck, and mean it, and hate myself for meaning it.

Not a game, he thought. Not two knights jousting. The man is a murderer and we have to make him pay. Because he's the kind of man who, if he found someone else he believed deserved it, could murder again.

More than any case he had ever tried, Rusty wanted to win this one. He was more involved than he had ever been. And more than any case he had ever tried, he had less faith in the outcome. *She* was already free. One of the murderers had escaped justice.

Not two, he prayed.

The entire Sioux nation was on the warpath, and only a small band of cavalry stood between them and the unguarded fort that housed the settlers. Gene Nettles, in command, squinted into the sunrise. Having interviewed Anita McCartney, he believed he was armed with all he needed to destroy the prosecution's star witness. If he could beat Rusty's objections into the dust he would emerge a winner, and David West would throw away his plastic ID tag and walk out of the courtroom a free man.

That was a defense attorney's job. Right or wrong, guilty or innocent. Fight for your client. Free him. Worry about the consequences later.

The first order of business was the pretrial motion to suppress from evidence the two potentially devastating tapes. Gene rose confidently to ask that the press be excluded from this hearing. "It is the *defendant*," he stressed, "who has the right to a public trial."

Judge Azios stared at him balefully for about five seconds. "Motion denied. Any others?"

Undaunted, Gene made a motion to sequester the jury throughout the trial.

"Motion denied," Judge Azios said pleasantly.

The jury was led in by one of the courtroom bailiffs and seated on the twelve black cloth swivel chairs in the jury box. There were seven women, four of them black, and five white men, ranging from an engineer with a master's degree to a construction worker. The average age was forty-one, on the high side. The women typified Houstonians in that half of them had been born elsewhere than Texas. They were a solemn lot—this was a capital murder case and they had been put through an inquisition to get here. Judge Azios asked if in the last seven weeks anyone had heard or read any publicity about the case or discussed it with anyone. No one had. They were all deaf, dumb, and blind.

The judge told the jurors to go home and to return at 9 A.M. the following Monday, December 9. Until then, they were not to discuss the case or read about it in the newspapers. If they were watching the news on TV and they heard the names David West, Cynthia Campbell Ray, or Kim Paris, they were to drop their coffee cups and flee their living rooms.

The puzzled jury members left the crowded courtroom and went home. The spectators stayed.

The first row of the six pine benches was reserved for the press. Squeezed onto one of the five benches given over to the public, Melanie Edgecombe watched David West, who wore his dark blue blazer and sat next to Gene Nettles at the defense table. He looks so pale, Melanie thought. And there was a crazed look in his eyes that she had never seen before.

Officer Raymond White, tall, bearded, and burly, wearing a three-piece blue suit and striped tie, was called to the stand by Rusty Hardin. HPD's chief audiovisual expert in the Criminal Intelligence Division, he had been in command of the taping on the nights of February 20 and

21. He testified as to the details of the equipment used in the police van: a reel-to-reel Nagra that would run for three hours, and back-up one-hour Sony cassette tapes. The Nagra transmitter, "about the size of a pack of cigarettes," could easily be secreted in a purse or handbag and, in this case, was. Ray White produced the cassettes from a crumpled manila envelope.

Judge Azios ruled that for the purposes of this hearing, without the jury present, the tapes would be admitted into evidence. After further testimony, the court would make its final ruling as to whether or not, when the trial proper finally began, the jury would also hear them.

Rusty rose and said, "We will offer the tapes *and* a video, so that you can watch the words on a screen as you hear the words."

A *video?* Gene Nettles had as close to a tantrum as a man can have without writhing on the floor. He had a momentary vision that Rusty Hardin had secretly hired actors to portray Kim and David and reenact the confession. A *video?* Did they have a contract yet for a prime-time TV movie?

Judge Azios told him that wasn't what the state had in mind. "Be calm, Mr. Nettles. Let's listen to their proposal."

Rusty called his expert to the stand. Dr. Al Yonovitz, director of the Speech and Hearing Institute at the University of Texas's Health Science Center, was thirty-eight years old, wore metal-rimmed glasses and a curly black beard, and to match his rabbinical air his curly hair matted on his head in the shape of a yarmulke. Like Officer White he wore a three-piece dark blue suit and white shirt; the two men glimpsed together might have been guests at a wedding. One wondered if the state issued the suits to witnesses from a rack.

Dr. Yonovitz, with the help of his students, had created the videotape for the State of Texas. There was no charge. Part of his mandate at the Health Science Center was to provide free specialized services. The bailiff and Lyn McClellan wheeled in two twenty-five-inch Magnavox television sets on metal platforms: speakers above, VCRs below. A third nineteen-inch set was placed on the bench for the private use of Judge Azios. A world premiere.*

In a modulated, scholarly voice Dr. Yonovitz explained to the courtroom audience that the script would scroll up, screen by screen, coordinating with 'the audio. What you hear is what you see. A far better idea than handing out printed transcripts which would allow each individual juror to skim forward and backward in the written text and perhaps not

---

* Lyn McClellan stopped by the reporters' front bench, bent down, and whispered in my ear: "Clifford, this is a video of you during voir dire, behaving atrociously."

pay attention to what was being said. David West's speeches would be on-screen in white, those of Kim Paris in blue. "The tapes are full of interference and static," Dr. Yonovitz warned the judge. "A lot of what we call dropout, when an obstacle gets in the way. Range problems, some yelling, a lot of whispering." He explained that the tapes had been "enhanced"—extraneous background noise eliminated—but not altered or edited.

And so, at last, since this was open court in a free society, what David West had said to his newly beloved on the nights of February 20 and 21, 1985—and how she convinced him to say it, a matter which many of us had wondered about—was heard. Now, even before the jury had a chance to do so, we would make our own judgments as to whether David was lying or baring the true corruption of his soul.

David, at the defense table, kept his hands in his lap so that no one could see him picking the skin off his thumbs. A defensive half-smile played across his face. He didn't look at Kim at all. Who was she now to him? No one he knew. He was disassociated from her. The reality of those nights last winter had vanished.

With her profile to him, Kim sat alone in the first row of the two-tiered jury box; it might have been the royal box at the opera. (Since she had helped prepare the tapes, there was no reason for her not to be here.) She never turned her head toward David. She stayed aloof and queenly, and she looked lovely. No one else in the courtroom knew it, but she was four months pregnant.

Off to one side sat Dr. Yonovitz, basking in the blue-white glow of his creation like an audiovisual Dr. Frankenstein.

Rusty Hardin's head was about six inches from Kim's as he reclined in his seat at the prosecution's table, finger on one cheek in a pose reminiscent of Rodin's *Thinker*. Makhlouf, Cindy Ray's husband—chunky, unshaven, wearing his blue shirt and army chinos—sat in the third row of spectators, looking like every grainy black-and-white photograph anyone had ever seen of a freedom fighter for Al Fatah. His legs shook rapidly; he either had a tic or a full bladder.

Jim Leitner cracked his knuckles every few minutes.

Sixty-eight-year-old Duval West, squeezed into the second row of the wooden spectator benches, fell asleep until the engine of Kim's Jetta started outside his son's house. That woke him, and he resumed listening.

Wednesday, February 20, 1985

Kim and David sat on a lumpy and torn black Naugahyde sofa in David's living room at 1409 Vermont. Behind them was a bare wall with pipes

206

and electrical wires showing. A hammock was slung from spikes in another wall, a shotgun leaned against a wooden chair, and there were empty liquor cartons piled along the wall leading to the kitchen. A couple of lamps with cockeyed shades shed warm light.

The windows were shut, for the evening air was cool. It was approximately 8:15 p.m.*

"This is the truth," David said. " . . . I told you that Cindy's younger sister was the first one in that family that I knew. She was seventeen and just got out of high school and came to the University of St. Thomas. And she was slender and, you know, all right looking, not real pretty or anything, but she was in our political science class, and she was smart. She and I got along well and we had these little dates, and we got to be friends. And she kind of acted like a tomboy. But over a couple of years she actually developed into a full-fledged dyke, where there was no femininity left at all, and she liked women and it was really blatant. . . . "

"Goddamn!" Kim exclaimed. "That's too much."

Kim excused herself then to go to the bathroom, from where she called, "David, you have roaches on your toothpaste!"

And then, "Goddamn! David, do you have an eyeliner pencil I can borrow?"

"Yeah, right next to the mascara."

"I don't see any mascara. I see a dildo here."

"You gotta plug it in to make it work."

"The eyeliner or the dildo?"

Returning to the living room and guiding the conversation back to the subject of Cindy Ray, Kim asked, "Why didn't she go for help?"

"They all hated her," David said.

"Why?"

"Because Daddy liked her, and Daddy ignored them. They were all the failures, except for the last one. The last one was his last attempt at having a son, and he was supposed to be named James, after himself. But instead it was a girl, so it was Jamie. And that was the one that I knew."

"But what did the mother say about this? Didn't Cynthia go to her mother and . . . "

"I don't know exactly, but as soon as it started manifesting itself,

---

* What follows are excerpts from the tapes. Gaps in the text are noted by editorial description or passages in brackets. Many repetitions, as well as syntactical and grammatical errors that confuse the apparent intent of the speaker, have been deleted. Some lengthy passages have been condensed. Nothing has been added that was not said.

Several transcript versions of the tapes exist, but for the most part I have reproduced Dr. Yonovitz's final version as shown on the video monitor. On the few occasions when there was serious conflict, I trusted my good left ear and my common sense.

basically the mother started catching on, and then fuckin' resented her, you know. Listen, the mother was a *hunchback!* You know, like Notre Dame? Big hump. I can't believe this fuckin' family. The father came from some jiveass horrible sleazy hick family in Tennessee, and because he was from that poverty environment he was a real cutthroat. You know, go right for the jugular. And he made a real good lawyer."

[In the courtroom, hearing that remark, Judge Azios couldn't stop himself from laughing.]

Veering again to Cindy, Kim said, "But she needs you. It's none of my business, but there must be something that you could do to help a person like that."

"You'd think so."

"No, goddamn, I bet the best day of her life was when her parents were killed in that accident. . . . "

"A matter of emotional and mental survival. It's like . . . there's only so much shit I can put up with. I tried for two years, I got her down in weight and everything, and everybody started chasing after her ass. She was very attractive. In essence, this is part of what I was trying to tell you the other day—she still is, although she's not as much as she was then, but she's innocent. She's innocent in a real . . . it's like, as far as emotional development goes, it's retardation, because there's so much horrible shit that's happened to her. She wants to be a good girl."

"Any of the sisters know about this child?" Kim was referring to Cindy's older son, then aged ten. David had theorized earlier that the boy had been fathered by Jim Campbell.

David said, "Apparently everybody in the family at least officially kind of turned their head and said, 'Well, she got pregnant out of wedlock,' and left it at that. But the thing is, if you look at her features and you look at the father's features and you look at the son, you can see it all right there. It's there. It was just the most hateful, back-stabbing, weasely, fucked-up family I've ever seen in my life. . . . "

The two boys, he continued, were "in a private boarding school, in Austin someplace, and she hasn't seen them for years."

"She doesn't want them? But you said—"

"Oh, she wants them, emotionally she wants them. In fact, a couple of times she's—she'll call me up at fuckin' weird times at night, but I told her not to anymore."

"I know," Kim said, suddenly annoyed. "And you told me she hadn't called."

"Let me tell you," David begged. "I lied, and I didn't lie—"

"I love you no matter what," Kim said, remembering J. C. Mosier's advice: don't be negative. "David, do you understand that? Do you know why I'm interested?"

208

"Yeah, because you're interested in me," David said. "This is a very big part of my life, and I hate it, and I don't want it to be a part of my life at all. It's something that I'm trying to shitcan."

"I know. But you know that it bothers me. It's not because she's a fuckin' threat—"

"It's just because she's an enigma."

"No, it's not even that," Kim said. "You know exactly what it is. But we'll talk about it later. Are you hungry?"

There was a ten-second pause in the conversation. [West told his lawyers that they had kissed. He began to grow aroused; she then pulled away to the far end of the living room couch.]

"Listen," he said awkwardly, "there's something I want to say to you . . . about sexuality. I'm a very sexual person, and wanting to hold you and hug you and kiss you . . . I mean, I get a lot of resentment from you. And I take that as being from your last sexual experience with those —shitheads. And I can understand that, but you need to try to understand that when I want to hold and kiss you and love you . . . I'm giving. I'm not taking. But I expect it to be spontaneously reciprocal."

"I know that." Kim's voice was tender.

"I'm not demanding anything from you. But it's fuckin' me up. It's a big thing to me, but I've got patience. It's like, I want to hold, be held, and loved. . . ."

Kim said, "But I love you where it counts. You know how tired I am of these 'add-water-and-stir' kind of relationships? They're fucked. And I'm trying to deal with you on something completely different. If you don't understand, then you don't understand. That's fine. That's fuckin' fine." She had grown surly. "And then, you know, I can categorize you, and I'll be on my way."

"What you're doing is an automatic, defensive reaction," David said.

"Well, you know, everyone wants to, you know, fuck. 'Let's fuck and then we'll get to know each other.' And it's not that I don't care about you, because I do, very much. And I feel closer to you all the time . . . but you know what it is."

"Yeah, but there's shit with you, too. The thing is, listen—"

"You know what it is, David. It's that simple."

"No, no, no. Whoa! You're saying that I know what it is. Maybe I don't know what it is. I'm pouring my guts out to you, I'm trying to build a relationship based on honesty. What I was trying to say about sexuality is this—it's that I, God, I can wait. But I definitely make a big differentiation between having sex and kissing you. And you, you repel that, and that makes me feel weird."

"You're exaggerating," Kim said. "I've told you a long time ago you have a flair for the dramatic. It's not that hateful. Don't be ugly, David.

It's like when I was in high school. You know, if you kiss a boy, then one thing leads to another, then you have no right to say no."

"But I'm not a rapist, and you *can* say no, and I can understand."

"You're making me nervous," Kim said. "You know, sometimes I can't even talk to you. You cut me off cold. And then I'm supposed to feel close to you? . . . Let's go eat."

———————

In Kim's car they drove to a sushi bar on Westheimer. The dinner table discussion ranged from the proper use of the chopsticks to the taste of eel and seaweed and the macho character of Japanese society. After dinner they returned to David's house. Wickie Weinstein was there with a man named Fred, a stagehand at the Alley Theater, smoking a joint in the living room. David took a few hits. [David told Nettles that Kim had a bump or two, but Kim denied it.] They talked about the Urban Animals. David said to Kim, "I'm friends with all the Urban Animals and if I could skate well enough I'd be an Urban Animal."

[In the police van Gil Schultz wanted to quit, go home. To hell with overtime. This was ridiculous.]

David and Wickie and Fred and Kim talked about the fourth dimension, and dogs, and Tina Turner, until Kim, losing patience, coldly announced that she had to go home. "My mother called."

David said to Fred and Wickie, "Well, you guys ought to be leaving." And they did.

Kim said, "They're totally fucked up, man. I remember the first time I did cocaine and acid . . . "

"No, Wickie's drunk," David said. (And now his own voice sounded as if he was under the influence of something.)

"I have to go." Kim got up swiftly from the old living room couch. "I probably won't see you for a while."

David jumped up, too. "Why? Hey!"

She crossed the room, and he must have seen his ship, which only so recently and miraculously had come in, yawing out of snug harbor and sliding into a hole in the ocean. Kim yanked open the front door. He trotted after her into the street, where she got into her car, the Jetta. In the chilly evening David stood for a moment, perplexed, downcast on the edge of heartsick, then slid in next to her in the front seat.

"I care about you an awful lot, David." Kim turned the key and started the VW's engine. The night was colder now; she wanted the heat. "And we've addressed it before, and you just fuckin' blow it all out and it doesn't matter."

David was confused. "What do you mean?"

"I've got to go."

[In the HPD van, Ray White reached to shut off the tapes, then changed his mind.]

She turned to him and kissed him, or let him kiss her. It was not a chaste, platonic kiss, but it was nothing more—Kim said later—than a kiss. Then, cheek to cheek, her breasts against his chest, she said, "I love you, David. Come on, don't get all upset."

"You're starting to sound real final."

"Things bother me. Friday's gonna be a big step"—she was referring to a previously discussed plan for her to leave Buddy's house and move into a spare room at 1409 Vermont—"and I just don't know if I want that to happen. And you know what it is, and how I feel in the situation."

"I don't understand."

"It's driving me crazy!" Kim cried. "If you're ready to be honest and to put everything on the right track, then Friday I'm ready to make a commitment and everything. If not—"

"What do you mean, 'be honest'?"

"This is an all or nothing proposition. I'm ready."

By then David had a throbbing erection; as close as they were in the front seat of the car it would have been difficult for Kim to be unaware. "I'm ready," he said. "I've *been* ready."

She pulled away. "I do love you, David. And tonight you think about love and you think about commitment. I'm not full of shit, and I don't make this stuff up that I'm talking about."

"Look," he protested, "I'm not full of shit either. But I'm sorry, there's just some things that have to remain unsaid, and may be known, but they're unsaid, and that's it."

"Well, then," she blazed back, "that's it! I'm not about, man, to fuckin' trust you and, you know, just—"

"No, listen! There's some things—you got to give, too—it can't be all your way—"

"Give? You know I've given! And I'm not going to argue with you. And you're raising your voice. Why are you raising your voice at me?" By now she sounded hysterical; it was an acting job that fed upon itself.

"If I didn't know anything, David, it wouldn't make any difference. But the fact that I do, and you admit to me that you're holding back . . . and I don't know why you're so deceitful, man."

He spoke calmly now, and with purpose, and his whole heart. "The thing is . . . I'm sure there are a lot of things that, probably, as much as you care about me—maybe I'm being cynical, but I figured there's

things that you just haven't told me. And someday you will. And someday, maybe I will. But the point is that my ass is at stake. And I'm sorry.
Well, just like you said the other day, the perfect crime is doing something and nobody knowing about it and nobody seeing it."

[Where had that come from? What "perfect crime"? Ray White, in the
parked police van, perked up and began to pay more attention.]

"David, I love you. And I hate to argue. Don't treat me like some
punk you pick up off the street to pay to do what you want them to
do."

More confused than ever, David said, "What are you *talking* about?"

"You just quoted me."

"I quoted something that you said, which was that if someone was to
commit a crime, the best way to go about it would be not to have
anybody see it and not tell anybody about it. Now, you're perceptive,
and you've realized something's gone on, and as much as I could be, I've
been honest with you about that. I could've sat there and stared at your
face and said, 'Well, I don't know what you're talking about.' I don't
want to lie to you. But there's some things I just don't want to say,
because they don't matter to you and me and—"

"They do."

"No, they don't. This is where trust comes in. The point is, I feel like
rushing it, too, but what you're asking is something that shouldn't be
asked. It's not anything emotional. You understand the idea, the concept
of need-to-know? You don't need to know this because it hasn't got
anything to do with you and me. It's strictly mechanical. It's legal. It's
got nothing to do with emotional."

Kim's voice rose dramatically. "Yes, it does, because it's you, and I've
. . . I have to think."

He allowed that, and during the silence, her head in her hands now,
she gathered herself together, and then looked up angrily and burst out:
"You have the unmitigated fuckin' gall to sit here and tell me that you
won't fuckin' tell me and at the same time you talked about marrying
me, about loving me, about having kids and everything else—"

"One thing has nothing to do with the other."

"*It's you!*" she yelled. "It has to do with goddamn *you,* and if you don't
trust me that's fine! It's not like you have to bare your soul. I don't
expect you to sign an affidavit to everything you've done wrong in your
entire life up till now." Heading toward crescendo now, she cried, "Except this is fuckin' *different,* because you *know* it bothers me, because you
know I've been thinking about it, because you know I have dreams
about it, and you know it goddamn *bothers* me!" She still gathered pace,
like an unchecked engine on a downgrade. "And it's like I told you ten
minutes ago, David, if I didn't know a thing about it, it wouldn't fuckin'

212

matter! We've talked about it, you've addressed it, and then you hold out on me and at the same goddamn time you talk about marrying me and having goddamn kids! And I don't buy it! And it"—more subdued now, coming down to the flat off the jittery, quaking high—"it just makes me fuckin' nervous. And if you don't want to talk about it, then we won't talk about another goddamn thing. . . . "

"All right. Lighten up. . . . "

"And now you got me screaming," she said, still throttling down, "and I hate to scream. David, I love you and this is driving me nuts."

He tried a ploy: shore up your position where it doesn't matter, divert the enemy from battering at your weakness. "The thing about Cindy was, when I first told you I didn't hear from her very often, it was true. About a month after I met you, she called me up because Mom gave her my fuckin' number. She asked me to take her out to put up some signs to advertise that she's got apartments for rent. The only deception was, about that time you asked me again, and I said no, I hadn't seen her in a while, because I felt weird about it. Because I just don't fuckin' want her being part of my life at all! I don't want her affecting you and me, because she's nothing. She's just a big fuckin' problem."

"I know she's nothing," Kim said. "The problem is not Cynthia. It's you. *I don't give a goddamn about your perfect fuckin' crime!*" she yelled. *"What I care about is you and me!"* Heading up the grade again: "And you're playing these fucked up games and you don't want to talk about it! But all I know is that whatever this is, until it's cleared up, *I can't handle it!* I'm ready to make a commitment to you, body and fuckin' soul, and you're playing these fucked up games with me"—and now down— "and that's fine because . . . that's fine." She waited a moment. "You just won't ever see me again."

"All right," David sighed. "Look at me."

"I can't, I'm too upset."

"Look at me."

"What?"

"I killed both of her parents."

[And in the police van, as Denise Moseley told Clyde Wilson, nobody breathed. Kim later told P. M. Clinton, "When he said that to me, I almost pissed in my drawers."]

Kim was silent for exactly seven seconds. Then she said softly, "Why didn't you just tell me?"

"I did," he said, amazed.

"Why?"

David laughed nervously. "It's not just strict conversational everyday bullshit, you know—"

"You're fuckin' with me now," Kim said, a little angrily.

"No, it . . . why should I say it? My God, it's not something you say, especially to somebody that you don't want to drive away—"

"But that's not what would drive me away. Do you think that's something I haven't seen before?" She remembered her lesson from J. C. Mosier: she'd known a murderer in the past and had never given him away.

"All right. Do you understand why? You knew it. We've said it all without saying it."

"But you never—"

"And the other thing is, the other reason I keep in contact with her at all is because partially she owes me some money for it. Quite a large hunk, as a matter of fact. But if—"

"What happened? Back up and just help me clear all of this."

David backed up, dug in, and then, tongue wagging and propelling him through the violent and dangerous air, took off on a track that seemed to have no end: "Look, the deal was she was going down the fuckin' drain and her parents, her sisters, and everybody, was preying on her. This is at a time when I was still involved with her. I knew everything that had happened to her. The very hardest part of this is the believability of the whole thing, right? Except that I was there. I knew all the people. It was just in the context in which I was told it, I believed it. That's all I can say. And I'm not stupid. I don't take shit at face value. This is over years. And I knew that this horrible tale was real, and it was driving her nuts, and past all my efforts she had just this overpowering self-destructive thing that had been beaten into her since she was a little kid. They hated her and she was a bad person and she felt unworthy and horrible, and it was just . . . there was no reason for it, 'cause she was basically great, except that she wouldn't be. And it was just sickening. And she was really fuckin' *losing* it, and she didn't have any place to turn. And they took her in and they kept berating her and fuckin' with her while she was there. Just real . . . ganging it. It's the kind of thing that's hard to relate because I don't remember a lot of the actual details, just the general tone of the whole thing. Over years and years, it was just the same. And snotty remarks—"

Kim lit a cigarette and, in her nervousness, offered him one. "No thanks," he said, "I don't smoke."

He continued the catharsis: " . . . and just horrible shit. Just stuff you can't believe people would do to each other, especially in the same fuckin' family. And finally I was convinced that her fuckin' parents were the main cause of her problems, and she had to get away 'cause they were laying all the childhood shit on her while she was there in the house again. 'You're no good. You're bad.' And he was going, 'Aw,

214

you've been a bad little girl, but Daddy loves you anyway.' You know what I'm saying? And the kid, the kid is nine years old and he's smart, and he's starting to suspect shit. He's noticing the similarities between him and Grandpa and how Grandpa looks at Mama—it goes on and on and gets worse. And she fuckin' begged me to do it, finally. First, early on, when she first told me about this shit—it was a real reaction thing —I said, 'Goddamn, you oughta just fuckin' kill 'em. I can't believe you take this shit.' And then later on, years later, she said, 'You know, you're right.' She fuckin' begged me to do it, and I wanted to do it, frankly. And she also offered me a lot of fuckin' money. And I said, 'Yeah.' And the thing was that I made her stand there with me when I did it. I wasn't gonna have her say, 'Well, you did it. I didn't have the belly for it.' I made her go in there with me and stand there right by the bed, and I shot each of them three times. And it was in the news, on and off."

"They were in bed?"

"Yes."

"Were you living there at the time, or—?"

"No, no. She went there the day before, unlocked the window, I got in, we got in, and just walked up there and did it. And they rated it. I don't feel like I've even compromised myself morally, frankly. They've just been executed, is all. That's it. I mean, I don't feel any—there's no —I didn't do anything wrong as far as I'm concerned. The children were in the room when I did it, asleep at the foot of the bed, playing like camp-out in sleeping bags. They woke up and I had a mask on so they didn't know who I was, and so I just left. And she'd already run out the door. Actually, she'd run out the door before the shots were fired. But there it is, blow by blow. Is that good enough for you? Do I trust you? You've got my life in your hands now. Is that good enough? Is that what you want?"

"Everything will be okay," Kim breathed. "Everything will be okay. . . ."

They talked about the money. David believed Cindy was about to get $25,000 in a settlement; apparently he didn't know, as Kim did, that Cindy had already made her settlement with her sisters six weeks ago and received that money. He was going to have Cindy invest in a bar that he would secretly own.

Kim said, "What'd you shoot them with? That 12-gauge, man, that you keep in the house?'

"You out of your mind? My mama didn't raise no fool. No, that weapon's gone. Don't worry about that."

"You be careful."

215

"Yeah, well . . . this wasn't very careful now, was it?"

"No, but you're lucky."

"You needed a commitment. You got your fuckin' commitment. All right?"

They kissed again—a long kiss. Not a platonic one now. Perhaps she was a little thrilled to kiss him now. Or grateful to him for giving her the one thing she had wanted. This kiss was his reward. All of it.

Kim said, "You better go to bed, give me time to think about this. I'll call you tomorrow."

"I'm scared," David said quietly.

"Why?"

"I've never said all that to anybody."

"Hearsay is hearsay. It's all hearsay. Go to bed," Kim said, touching his cheek.

"I feel good now," David said.

They kissed good night and she drove around the corner to the police van.

19

Now and then, I noticed, David had seemed to marvel at something especially silly that he had said, and he shook his head in what seemed abashed wonderment when he heard himself admit, *"You've got my life in your hands now,"* or crow, *"My mama didn't raise no fool."*

Judge Azios took me into his chambers after the playback of the first night's tapes. He said, "Wasn't that dramatic? I got goose pimples."

He wondered how the language would affect the jurors. Sam Guiberson, the defense's electronic surveillance expert, had already remarked, "The tapes are enough to give conversational obscenity a bad name. I have the impression that their idea of whispering a sweet nothing in your lover's ear was to say, 'I'm not talking shit.' "

A gang of reporters went down in the elevator together. They were speculating about the silences and heavy breathing in the parked car before and after the confession. Dan Grothaus said, "I wonder if Yonovitz can enhance the tapes for zipper movements."

The newspapers and television carried flamboyant accounts of the videotapes. The absent jurors, of course, were forbidden to read these accounts.

That evening, because we had arranged it before the Thanksgiving holiday, I met again with Paul Whitfield, Lynn Roebuck, and Grothaus. We went for dinner to Renu's, a Thai restaurant in Montrose. I put my Sony on the table. Paul looked older and more tired than the first time we'd met. He said, "After what I heard today, I guess there's no doubt what happened. Can they convict him?"

"I don't know," I said. "Maybe not."

"I'd like to talk to Rusty Hardin," Paul said. "But I don't want him pressuring me."

"He has to pressure you. That's his job."

Paul didn't know what to do. Like Kim, he had Dave's life in his hands. And perhaps Wickie's. That seemed to be the rub. The ex-marine was frightened of the ex-ranger. And that Tuesday evening nothing was decided.

The next day in court the second night's tapes were played.

A few minutes after 8 P.M. on Thursday, February 21, David West was drinking at the bar of the Park Lane Tavern. A horn honked outside in the street. David threw a few bills down on the counter and hurried out.

In the VW he and Kim drove to the Café Moustache in the River Oaks section. Kim was apprehensive lest David would have turned paranoid, regret his admissions, try to smooth them over and back down. But he surprised her.

"God, that was the best night's sleep I've had in a long time. Just so relaxed!"

"Well, good, I'm glad you feel that way. I didn't know . . . I know that was hard for you."

"It was very hard," David admitted. "Actually, it scared me . . . a lot of fears, a lot of fears. It's given you power over me, and I don't like that at all."

"But I'm not the one who has power. The only one who has power is Cynthia. . . ."

They reached the restaurant, and the hostess seated them in a corner booth on the second level. The adjoining table was empty. In the booth, by candlelight, they discussed California wines versus French wines. Kim said she didn't like German wine—too fruity. David ordered a dry California Chardonnay.

Kim moved back on course. " . . . because I wouldn't want to have three kids and another on the way and have her turn you around."

217

"And have me going to jail."

She then dropped a verbal hand grenade in his lap. Cindy was lying to him, Kim said. Cindy had her inheritance money already. David had never actually revealed Cindy's last name—so, Kim explained, she had subtly queried Buddy, her brother-in-law, and he remembered the Campbell case. This morning, Kim told David, she went to the civil courthouse to check out the files and records, and discovered that the inheritance had already been paid out.

Predictably, David's flesh paled, his eyes bulged. How could she *do* that? How could she endanger him that way? He harangued her for another fifteen minutes. *What if Buddy*—

"He doesn't give a shit," Kim said. "Let's look at the worst possible thing. If his curiosity was aroused—"

"I'll tell you," David spluttered, "before I go to fuckin' jail, I'll kill myself. Before I get burned for something I'll end my whole fuckin' life. What do you think, I'm going to get put in there and butt-fucked by bodybuilders? You out of your mind? Not me! I'm either scot free, or I'll check out."

"David, let's not even talk about that. You're going off on some mind trip. The point is, I'm thinking of our security, and you're telling me you have this blind faith in Cindy, and I found out that you have reason not to. It *is* my business now because of the fact that I have knowledge and that I love you and we have a future together, and all I'm trying to do is make sure all these angles are covered. Because she is a crazy person. Like I said, I don't want to have three kids and another on the way and something gets all fucked up. . . . "

From there, when he began to calm down, she moved him to a description of the murders. He obliged now with no coaxing. He *wanted* to talk, to explain, to spew.

"We sat there," he said, "and planned all this out logically, coldly."

The waitress came over and said, "How are y'all doing?"

"We're doing good, thank you," Kim said.

"Fine," David said, "we're doing great. Thanks."

The waitress left. "See," David went on, "the way it originated was: 'Kill the motherfuckers. I can't believe you're tolerating all this shit.' She'd been worn down so badly when she was a little kid. Her mother locked her in the goddamn bathroom—"

"Why would her mother lock her in the bathroom?"

"Because she didn't want to see her father fuck her."

"Is that reason to kill somebody?" Kim dared ask.

"All of it, cumulatively. And I allowed for her overreaction, allowed for her emotional outlet, and everything else. But, see, I was the one who originally said, 'Well, look, just fuckin' kill those people.' "

"What made you finally trust her then?"

"Because she started talking real cold and calculating and mechanical. And then she also would bring out all the emotional shit that they had done to her. Look, how would you like to be making love with somebody and have them start calling you 'Daddy'? Makes me sick, you know? I don't feel any remorse. I didn't do anything—all I did was administer justice. Really, I don't feel that I've compromised my morality at all."

"Not to this day you don't?"

"No. It may not have been the wisest thing to do, but I told her it was not wrong. It was clean, efficient, and painless."

"Didn't they wake up?"

"The second one started to wake up after the first one was already dead." He clasped his hands together and swung them from side to side. "It went *poong, poong, poong, poong, poong, poong.*"

The waitress refilled their wine glasses. A seventeenth-century flute concerto played sweetly through the restaurant's stereo speakers.

"Merci," Kim said.

And then, to David, "What about the kids being there? Didn't that bother you?"

"You bet your life, but I'd already started—"

"You didn't know they were going to be there?"

"No. I thought they were playing camp-out, just didn't want to be in their room alone, or some crap, I don't know. I crept in and walked up the stairs, opened the door silently—"

"Cindy was right behind you?"

He nodded yes. "And I got positioned right there, and I said, 'Hit the lights.' And the lights came on and I opened fire, and then I looked down and the kids were there."

"And you went, '*Oh, Jeez!*'"

"First thing that ran through my mind was, shit, they've got to be removed also. But then I thought, no, they don't know who the fuck I am, and I don't want to kill kids."

"Did they see her, though? Their mother?"

"No, she was wearing a mask, too. But she'd run out, she didn't actually stay to see it. But she was there."

"Weren't you afraid that they might be able to—"

"No, I was wearing a mask, and a big coat that didn't reveal anything about my physique. And I had gloves on. There were no fingerprints. It was a clear, clean execution. That was it. It's just . . . they rated it. You know, I've never done anything like that, and I feel real weird about it. I don't feel bad about it. I feel bad about it *sometimes.* I feel bad about the fact that I killed somebody. . . . "

"Have you ever killed anybody else?"

"No. That's what I was trying to say. I've changed my entire opinion of myself. I am no longer . . . I know it's on my fuckin' hands, but I am a good person. I feel weird about it because I lost my innocence."

He told her he had thrown the gun away under water; it couldn't be found now, and if it was "it'd be a big hunk of rust." He described how they had concocted a joint alibi and trained each other to resist interrogation. "And trying to remember from all the detective shows and all that other crap. And we went over the dialogue, over and over again, and we tried to keep it from sounding exactly verbatim, like memorized. You know, when they put the two stories together: 'Gee, these words are exactly the same.' We tried to keep from generating too much detail, which would be something that they could pick away at. We tried to keep it flat and basic. So far it's fuckin' worked."

"Maybe you should write for TV," Kim said.

"It's no big deal. There's no weapon, no witnesses. I mean, it was pathetically easy. See, that's the deal about TV—they always fuck up, they always get caught. Because Hollywood is committed to the government, to not sponsor antisocial behavior." He chuckled at that. "They try to make it look like the cops are always the good guys. They don't show corruption and petty little sick egomaniac fuckheads as cops. The only time they ever catch people is if somebody's a fuckin' idiot or they just had real bad luck. The people that are smart—"

"It'd be my luck, though," Kim said.

A Mexican love song played in the background as David told her how he had switched plates on his car on the evening of the murders, and how, after he and Cindy had run from the house on Memorial Drive, a car had come round the curve. He was fumbling for his keys. He couldn't find them. He was aware how ridiculous that was. "Mister Professional! And we still had the masks on. I figured, well, if the goddamn car stops, I'll kill those motherfuckers, too."

But they didn't. And he didn't have to. And he found the keys in his other pocket.

Nobody had heard the shots?

Nobody.

"So it was flawless?" Kim was wide-eyed, admiring, yet concerned. "There wasn't one fatal flaw that haunts you?"

"The only flaw that haunts me is somebody fuckin' up and talking."

Hastily Kim asked about Cindy: "Do you expect her not to tell out of a love for you, or did you tell her that if you go, she goes?"

"For one thing, she knows if I go because she narced on me, I'll make it look like a cold-blooded thought on her part alone. It'd be just my word, but once it goes that far, part of it is what the jury believes and what they don't believe."

He admitted that for a while he was afraid of what Cindy might do if "she lost it," if she became irrational. She *was* irrational. And she was scared. She had looked into his eyes a month or so after the murders and said, "Are you thinking about killing me, too?" And he had replied, "I don't know what to think right now."

Kim asked, "Did you seriously entertain thoughts of killing her?"

"Yes, yes I did—"

"David, you would have been a fucking mass murderer!"

"—but I said, 'Is it necessary? No, it's not.' Of course, everything is possible."

"How long will it be before you decide to do away with me?" Kim asked quietly.

"That's not possible," he said.

The discussion continued while David paid the bill, and then on the way out of the restaurant he said earnestly, "See, what we're talking about here is two different modes. There's the person mode, and there's a soldier mode. When I did that, it was a soldier mode. But I'm a person. And you've seen how sensitive I can be, and that's the real me. And if I can't relax and love and just be right, then everything's fucked. It's like, I've got to retain that romanticism and innocence. That's what you can expect from me."

They got into the car and drove down Westheimer. "Sweet baby," David said to her softly, having purged himself. It had been so easy. He felt wonderful.

On the way home they discussed valet parking and tipping, and how when they were married David would bring her breakfast in bed, and then salmon eggs ("Ugh! Tres ugh!" Kim cried), and esoteric Mexican food such as tripe and brains. "I've always had this rule," David explained, "that I'll appreciate what somebody sees in a food whether I really end up liking it or not, but brains I just can't stand. I tried it—I don't like the texture, it tasted like scrambled eggs that are a bit on the runny side, a real mineral taste."

And then, because Kim had said she was out of cigarettes, David pointed out a Circle K convenience store on the other side of Westheimer. Kim swung into it and parked. She seemed to be in a hurry. As David peered out the front window at her vanishing figure, a van pulled in next to him.

Raymond White and Gil Schultz jumped out, guns drawn, shouting. Paul Motard and Ron Knotts were in the backup car, still taping.

"*Police officer, freeze!* Hands up! Get out of there!"

221

The car was beginning to roll backward. Kim had forgotten to put it in gear, and the emergency brake was broken.

David said, "Whoa! Sure thing, sure thing. Whoa. No problem! Yes, sir, no problem. Right away!"

He put the car into gear, then bustled out, hands above his head. Schultz threw him against the car and began to pat him down for weapons.

"What's the deal?" David demanded. "What's—what's the problem?"

On the way to the jail he felt desolated, heartsore. Schultz and White were laughing, joking, ebullient, babbling about Kim.

Kim? Who was Kim?

Kim Paris?

Who was Kim Paris? What a theatrical name.

She was one of them. A cop of some sort.

Slowly, and with intense pain, and with an even more intense effort at denial—*No, I don't believe what I'm hearing*—he gathered that Kim Paris was Teresa, the woman to whom he had offered his love and proposed marriage and children and a life together until death do us part. And she was a private eye. He also began to get the impression that these cops had somehow taped the evening's conversation. He couldn't just nervously laugh it off and say, "She's lying."

"You've got my life in your hands now. Is that good enough? Is that what you want?"

This is just a little fucking hard to believe. *Betrayed* was too pale a word. And this is not a nightmare. This is all truly happening to me.

———

David's voice on the tapes was younger and more high-pitched than it was now, and far more vulgar. Maybe he had aged. Maybe it was the pressure of dealing with Kim, who had hooked him and played him like a game fish. Once you heard the tapes you knew it had only been a question of time—of when, not if. Kim hadn't known that, just as the fisherman doesn't know with absolute certainty that he'll land the fish. And the fish knows nothing other than localized pain and the invading presence of a terrible force hauling it from briny comfort, and normality, to an alien environment, and death. But the fish can't see the air or the boat deck or that death; it feels only the force as it's whipped along.

David had felt squeezed into the envelope of Kim's power but had never understood its nature. He had no hope to hold out unless she said or did something exceedingly stupid, and she was too into her role and too immaculately concentrated on her prey to do that. Even if she *had*,

222

he probably would have made excuses for her. She told him she'd asked Buddy about the murders and then traipsed on down to the civil court to see if Cindy had received her inheritance. Some shaky non sequiturs there. And David let it go, forgave her. *My mama didn't raise no fool.*

Oh yes, she had. Every mama raises a fool. Why should he be unique, armored against love?

———————

Now at last I began to hear what David had always been trying to say to us. He had believed Cindy's father had bedded her and sired her first son. Gwen Sampson had told Schultz, *"He wanted to cure her. If they were eliminated, she would have no more troubles."*

"And she fuckin' begged me to do it, finally," David had told Kim. In the voir dire he had said to me, *"The real truth may never come out. But I want to tell you one thing. I could never kill anyone for money."* No, not for money. For his vision of justice, and for the love of a fallen woman. For the righting of a terrible wrong and the freeing of a battered soul. He believed that.

And what he wanted now was absolution. More than his freedom he wanted to be told by a very few people—in a far more personal way than any jury could tell him—that he was not guilty. That he had done the right thing. Or, since his perceptions were changing, the wrong thing for the right reasons. Absolution. Forgiveness. Understanding, and perhaps even approval.

———————

At 4:05 P.M. on Wednesday, December 4, after the playing of the second night's tape, Lyn McClellan rose in the packed courtroom and said, "The state rests on the motion."

Gene Nettles promptly moved for a delay, and the judge granted a continuance to 9 A.M. on Friday. (At that point Lyn privately decided the trial wouldn't start until January 6 of the new year, 1986, and he made his holiday plans accordingly.)

Before leaving the courtroom I stood next to David for a moment. He was staring at the bundle of videotapes tucked under Leitner's arm. The half-amused light was gone from his eyes. He turned to me and said forcefully, "Those are lies in there. Fuckin' lies."

But Leitner wouldn't let him say any more; he hustled him back to the empty jury room.

I talked to Sam Guiberson for a while. Of course he had heard the

223

tapes many times, had almost memorized certain passages. He still marveled at how an execution-style murder of a sleeping couple—an act that seemed to require as its author a moral and psychological defective—could be so casually committed. "It was a kind of indulgence," he said. "There's a tone of levity that isn't consistent with our perception of murder as a crime. The problem the tapes cause for David is the cavalier, emotionally dislocated way he details the offense."

He had an interesting theory. "David would have surrendered this knowledge to anyone with whom he developed a relationship, be they man or woman. It's not a matter of his sexual interest in Kim Paris overcoming his good sense or self-interest—it's that he was a man so isolated within himself that any bond with another human being would have outed this same admission. It's so easy to say he's sociopathic, as if that key word tells it all. Why does David want to be in a woman's power? His relationship with Cindy Ray is the one I'd like to know about."

"We all would," I said.

Guiberson also was able to recognize what he called "an agenda of prompting" that worked to lessen David's inhibitions. "I don't believe there's a moment where Kim touches or hugs him until he gives her the line that she's been waiting for. You can hear it. It might be that he enjoyed the experience of suggesting his murderous machismo to a woman who obviously was excited and stimulated by it."

That morning Guiberson had cautioned Nettles and Leitner that tapes played in court—"stripped of all context, laid bare to the public"—usually depress the defendant. "Every client has a sense of ego dissociation from what he's said. He can't accept it. He insists there was something not recorded that would have altered everything heard and put it in a more favorable light. Lawyers have a similar reaction. It's demoralizing, that first listen. Beware," Guiberson said.

I sat down on Wednesday night, alone, and tried to make some judgments.

You believed David's voice, although it was not the voice we had heard during voir dire: sympathetic, witty, interested. In the tapes it was shrill and obscene and morally crooked. You believed he killed those two people in cold blood in their sleep with the grandkids at the foot of the bed. He could have been lying, but it was improbable.

Improbable . . . but not impossible.

As a conscientious juror, could you vote guilty on a *probability*?

Rusty had talked to young Michael Ray for two hours and then let him go. Rusty wasn't going to pull an eye witness out of a hat or dredge the gun out of the Gulf of Mexico and discover one of David's hairs caught in the trigger mechanism. Even if they hauled Cindy Ray into court with a derrick, she would take the Fifth.

There was no evidence other than the tapes, and they were tainted by another factor. When Phil Donahue had used the word "erotic" to describe her undercover investigation, Kim had snapped back: "The scenario that you paint and the adjective you use—'erotic'—is not at all accurate. It was an intellectual relationship that we had. I'm not trying to fool you, but it's imperative that you understand."

Understand that there had been no sex, just the promise of it. No seduction, just perfidy. Manipulation by "I love you." The most dangerous words in the language. What we yearn for, what we'll kill for, die for, lie for.

Kim had offered herself to him "body and fuckin' soul." If not an immortal phrase, certainly a punchy combination, but hardly the foundation for the claimed intellectual relationship. Marriage, three children, love—Zorba's "full catastrophe." David must have missed the movie.

No one at Clyde Wilson's office or at Homicide had instructed Kim to make that offer. The way that Hollywood might have played it, I thought, is that Kim falls in love with David, and there's some moment of audience analysis when you wonder if her goal is going to be overshadowed by her personal feelings, and how will she choose? But in this case there was no love, therefore no conflict. David for Kim was a neuter. The only reason that anyone had paid attention to the rumors of Kim's alleged lesbianism, or bisexuality, was because it helped explain the ease with which she stayed aloof from David's pain.

If I were a juror, I decided, I could be persuaded that the confession was not sufficient to send a man to Huntsville for death by lethal injection. That was Rusty Hardin's deep worry, and it was justified. The doubt was a reasonable one. As a juror I might consider myself a moral coward for refusing to vote guilty, but I might face the lifelong nightmare of considering myself party to an unjust sentencing for refusing to vote *not* guilty. I couldn't give David the moral absolution he wanted—neither could I give Rusty the verdict *he* wanted. The Pussy-hair Defense held up.

But Guiberson had said, "Beware," and Gene Nettles either didn't listen or didn't understand.

Early on Thursday, the day after the tapes had been played in court, Lynn Roebuck called Rusty. She identified herself as "the wife of the man who wants to talk to you about David West and Wickie Weinstein." After she'd made her pitch as to why her husband needed some advance guarantees of immunity before he could come in and testify, Rusty said to her, "Look, Lynn Roebuck, why don't you and Paul come down this evening? Believe me, I want to help you."

She hung up immediately and called me.

At nine o'clock on Friday morning, December 6, I went through the door into the hallway that led to the judge's chambers. I called the area "backstage," because this was where most of the behind-the-scenes private dramas took place. There were two wooden benches with five sets of steel handcuffs on iron rings. A steel door on the left led to the communal holding cell, which contained facing wooden benches and a smelly open toilet. About eight black men were in there, and David West. David came out of the cell, and I had never seen him look that worried. Larry Pollinger, the chief bailiff, cuffed David's wrist and shackled his leg, then took him into the jury room at the end of the hallway. I wondered what was going on. When Larry came back, I asked.

"Conference with Nettles and Leitner."

Grothaus came in and we talked for a while. Then Rusty banged through the door. I had been waiting to beard him about how he'd handled the telephone call from Lynn Roebuck. But before I got halfway through my complaint he exploded, in much the same way he'd exploded about the tenth juror, except now he had the culprit in front of him and it wasn't a brother assistant district attorney. We were toe to toe, his eyes sizzling.

"Listen, Clifford, contrary to what you think—this is not a game! *I* certainly am not playing fucking games with these people! I'm going to bring them in before a grand jury! They think they can sit out there and agonize over their choices? They think they have the choice whether or not to testify? *They don't.*"

I understood his frustration, but I said, "Rusty, you spooked the woman. You want a cooperative witness, not a hostile one."

"*I want the truth!*" he yelled, so that if anyone backstage hadn't heard him before, they did now. Several reporters moved closer to listen. Rusty bit off his words like a mongoose snapping at a cobra. "Wait until they understand what's involved in being under oath before a grand jury! Cooperative or hostile, they'll tell the truth! I want to be courteous, I want to be fair, but I can't coddle these people! And I would have the ass of any assistant district attorney who relied on a fucking *author* to

226

bring in an important witness for a trial! I told Lynn Roebuck I'd give them two days to make up their minds and call me and come down . . . and if they don't, I'm going after them!"

Gene Nettles stepped out of the room where he and Leitner had been sequestered with David West. He had heard the shouting. Rusty broke away from me to exchange a few whispered words with Nettles. Neither he nor Gene looked pleased. Then Rusty turned back to the waiting reporters. He was suddenly smiling again and courteous even to me. That was his nature, to blow up in an instant like a tropical gale, then settle down with equal rapidity. I think he realized that I knew that and wouldn't hold any outburst against him.

"We're postponed until Monday morning," he said. He explained that the defense still wasn't ready with its challenges to the video.

The reporters trooped across the street to the civil courthouse, where Pennzoil was suing Texaco for billions and where a verdict was expected any hour. But I didn't go. Feeling a little battered in the ego, I went home. Not my day, I thought.

In the early afternoon Paul Whitfield called me. He had made a decision: he wanted to see Rusty Hardin as soon as possible. Could I arrange it?

Me? Why me?

Okay. . . .

I called Rusty's office but he wasn't there; he was lecturing at a special course for investigators. No doubt on the subject of how to handle uppity writers.

"Name a time," Lyn McClellan said, when he heard that Whitfield wanted to come in. "Rusty will be here."

"How about four-thirty this afternoon?"

He agreed. I called Paul to tell him. He sounded less sure of himself than before. He said, "Could you do me a favor and go down there with me? I wouldn't mind having a witness, just in case there's a problem."

Stop stirring up trouble, Clifford.

In the waning gray day I picked up Paul Whitfield near his house in Montrose. He and Lynn were standing in the street in front of a banged up Toyota station wagon with a flat tire. Lynn's face was puffy. She was crying. With a quick kiss and a mutter of goodbye, Paul jumped in the front seat of my car.

"She all right?"

"Pissed off," he said. "And scared."

After I parked downtown we walked in a chilly afternoon wind to the District Attorney's Building. Rusty and Lyn McClellan were waiting for us by the elevator on the seventh floor. In Rusty's office big drawings

227

and floor plans of the Campbell house were stacked against a wall next to blown-up aerial color photographs of the Memorial area.

Rusty was in shirtsleeves—white collar, blue shirt—pipe clamped between his teeth. Seductive, charming, and yet stern. I didn't offer to leave, and I wasn't asked. Part of the team again. Rusty did me an unasked favor by assuring Paul that I hadn't given him their names. He couldn't say who had. No, it wasn't Wickie. Then who else? I assumed he had promised Wickie he wouldn't tell. We were all caught up in these curious obligations of silence.

After some waffling, Paul explained that he was reluctant to testify because of certain things in his and Lynn's past. He explained them, and Rusty assured him he would be protected and they wouldn't be discussed at trial. "Now," Rusty said, "tell me your story."

Paul had laid a pack of cigarettes on the table. He smoked steadily, and his knees were shaking. It wasn't a game to him either: it was a murder story. Real people, real murder. Real danger. He might be next, he thought, if things didn't work out the way he anticipated.

" . . . and then," Paul finished, "Wickie said, 'We had to throw the gun away in the bayou, and I hated to do that, because it was my favorite gun.' And that's about it. . . . I didn't ask any more questions. We never talked about it again."

They went over that story in detail, as well as other tales of David West's aggression in Montrose bars.

It had grown dark outside, and the night wind was still blowing out of the Gulf of Mexico and across the Texas plains. Rusty looked at his watch—we had been there for more than two hours. It was ten past seven. He was thoughtful. He stood up and tapped his pipe. He said to Paul, "I don't think we'll need you in the first stage of the trial. Maybe in the second stage, if we get that far. And Lynn, too—those stories about David beating up those guys outside of Rudyard's are definitely material for special issue #2, future dangerousness."

That was all hocus-pocus to Paul, but not to me. Rusty didn't want him as a witness in the guilt or innocence stage? *Why not?*

He could see the surprise all over my face like a thrown cream pie.

"It's too vague," he said, waving his pipe in the air. "David didn't say to him that he killed the Campbells, just that he killed 'someone,' or 'a couple of people.' "

"Are you kidding me?" I stared at him. Wickie was going to testify to *a* .45, not *the* .45. Wickie was a witness with a lot of baggage and Rusty still intended to use him. In comparison, Paul was squeaky-clean.

"I may change my mind, but at the moment I can't use it." Rusty smiled politely, but firmly, as if he had said no to a set of pots and pans that I wanted to sell him at the back door to his home.

"Let's go," I said to Paul.

We hurried through the dark, deserted downtown streets to my car. The cold wind hacked at us, and we hardly talked. Paul seemed relieved, but I was depressed and unsettled. *What was happening?* For the first time I felt in over my head. If it was a game, I didn't understand these rules. A few days ago Rusty would have given blood to get Paul as a witness. Now he didn't seem to care. What did he know now that he hadn't known when he told me I had a "duty" to bring Paul in? Had he found another witness?

Had he found Cindy Ray?

An element was missing. Something was happening in the case that none of us on the outside knew about.

Trust the system, Ramirez had said that day when he talked about David's shark eyes. All right . . . I will. But trust it to do *what?*

20

The brief Texas winter, for which no one was ever quite prepared, had arrived early. On a gray and chilly Monday afternoon, December 9, court was called into session. The courtroom was not only no longer air conditioned; it was heated. In the great American tradition of public buildings in winter, it was so hot you felt trapped inside your clothes, and there was nothing to breathe except thick steam heat.

The jury was still absent. So was Rusty; Lyn McClellan was in charge today. The defense's turn had come to present evidence to disqualify the tapes.

Gene Nettles called Sgt. Gil Schultz to the stand.

Schultz didn't like defense attorneys. "In a trial," he had said to me a few weeks ago, "the defense gets all the information from the prosecution. The prosecution gets nothing. And just because they have a college degree, these guys get away with all kinds of shit. The legislature is all lawyers—do they ever pass a pro-cop law?"

Schultz was an experienced witness. You couldn't easily rattle him, and Nettles didn't want to try, not yet. He wanted only to find out what Schultz might say later on in front of the jury.

No, Schultz testified, no physical evidence of David's was seized, "other than a .45 bullet or something like that." No, he wasn't aware on either night that Kim or David were smoking pot.

But Gene did get from him an admission that on the second night of

taping, with his and Motard's knowledge, Kim bought a bottle of Everclear—180 proof pure grain alcohol, usually mixed with fruit juice to
achieve a zero-delay bombing—that she intended to drink with David.

"Were you aware," Gene asked, "that J. C. Mosier had instructed Kim
Paris how to deal with David West?"

McClellan heaved up, a blimp breaking its ties, to object on the
grounds that the question was beyond the limited scope of the pretrial
motion. The judge sustained his objection.

It was growing late, and Gene let Schultz go. Tomorrow he would
call Kim Paris, the state's star witness. Judge Azios said, "We'll resume
at nine o'clock sharp, American time."

Grothaus and I left the courthouse, through the revolving door into
the chill damp of the street that came as an unfamiliar shock after the
dry warmth of the courtroom.

"Something funny is going on," Dan said. "Those lawyers keep dis-
appearing into the jury room together. All this testimony seems so
pointless."

Nettles and Leitner finally came thundering through the revolving
door, and I pulled my collar up and stalked after them. Gene strode
along the pavement, clutching his big leather briefcase stuffed with documents. On the way to the two-dollar parking lot that we all used, I
unburdened about Paul Whitfield.

"So that's what you've been stirring up," Nettles said.

"I didn't stir anything—Whitfield's out there and Grothaus found
him. The girlfriend talked him into wanting to testify. I told you most
of this a week ago, without the name. You said it was bullshit." I handed
them a copy of the tape I'd made in Renu's with Paul and Lynn.

Gene thanked me, but he looked worn out. "Well, that does it,"
Leitner murmured.

In the parking lot, flailed by the cold wind, we said goodbye. Something funny going on, Dan had said. Now I believed it, too.

It had begun on Thursday, the day after the second night's tapes had
been played, and the day before a worried Paul Whitfield appeared on
the seventh floor of the District Attorney's Building. A quiet day, no
court in session; Nettles and Leitner were being given time to study the
video and list the disputed passages. They worked with David in the
empty jury room, his ankle shackled to a leg of the table.

In the late afternoon Rusty was eating a slice of apple pie and drinking
coffee in the courthouse coffee shop. Gene dropped into a chair next to

him with his own mug of coffee. Other than in court, and then only when necessary, the two lawyers had not spoken to each other for over a month. After a brief sigh, Gene cleared his throat.

Rusty instantly knew what was coming. His skin tingled. But he could hardly believe it.

Gene said stiffly, "Would you be interested, at this stage of the proceedings, in making a recommendation?" He meant for a lesser sentence than life, if David West would plead guilty.

"No," Rusty said, taking an enormous gamble. Make the other guy come to you.

Again Gene cleared his throat. "What if he were willing to testify against Cindy Ray? If he were willing to do that—and I think it's in his interest to do that now—would you make some kind of recommendation?"

"Probably not," Rusty said. He picked his words with care. "I'd have to be convinced I would never get Cindy any other way. And the Campbell family and HPD would have to be willing. And even then . . . my preference would be to have a case where I don't have to sponsor David as a witness." Satisfied, tentatively thrilled, because here now was the possibility of victory being salvaged from the dreaded defeat, he drained the last of his coffee.

There must be a catch, Rusty thought. Even if we can convince a jury to find David guilty, the chances of getting them to say *yes* to the question of future dangerousness are slim to none. The gooney bird will fly away. He can't expect to get more than life, so why then would he want to settle for that in advance? If I were David, he thought, why not gamble on walking away, or at least hanging up the jury on the issue of Kim's having manipulated him into a lie?

"Have you discussed this with Leitner?" Rusty asked.

"Sure."

"How about with David?"

"Not yet," Gene said.

Under the bland fluorescent lights of the cafeteria, Rusty's eyes glinted with something less than love. "So you're fishing around to make a deal, and y'all don't even know if the defendant you're trying to make it for would be willing!" Suddenly he didn't like the situation at all. Was he being set up for something?

"I'm just testing the waters of a muddy pond," Gene said, offering a gracious smile.

Rusty checked an angry reply. Instead he said, after some mental lip-biting, that if David could provide the state with information that would be sufficient to convict Cindy independent of his testimony—for exam-

231

ple, the whereabouts of a murder weapon with her prints on it, or a written confession that he'd got from her as an insurance policy—then the state *might* be interested. But not for less than a life sentence.

And maybe not at all.

"We'll talk to him," Gene said.

Before he left the table Gene added, "I don't want you to think I've given up. The tapes are just a little hard to take. They were embarrassing. David's a little shaken. But I still think we've got a decent chance at not guilty. And in the punishment stage, if we get that far, we've got a fifty-fifty shot at life. However, I've got a responsibility to my client to explore all the avenues. See what I'm saying? It would be irresponsible of me not to do it."

"I understand," Rusty said, more annoyed than ever. "And it would be irresponsible of me to tell you to go fuck yourself."

Gene had to swallow that. "So you'll think about it?"

"I don't promise anything." Except to pray, Rusty thought.

On Friday morning in the jury room (while Rusty and I shouted at each other outside about the way he had handled Lynn Roebuck's telephone call) Nettles asked David some hard questions.

David read right through it. Gene's panicking, he realized.

"You think I'll lose," David said.

Gene shrugged his shoulders. "Let me put it this way. After seeing and hearing how people reacted to the tapes, I'm less optimistic about our chances. It's what you said about maybe killing the kids except for the good luck that you were wearing a mask and they couldn't recognize you. And then that business about 'if the car coming round the bend stops, I'll kill those motherfuckers, too.' That was bad, David. I know none of that was true, but it made you look . . . violent, and dangerous. The pretrial was like a dress rehearsal. We were lucky to have it, I think. Got to profit from it, though."

"So what are you suggesting?"

"A deal, David."

"I plead guilty—"

"You give them Cindy, and you get life."

"Give them Cindy?" David's breath grew choppy. "No way."

"You want to die?" Nettles asked cruelly.

"I sure as shit don't want *her* to die in my place," David snapped back. "Don't you know me at all? What kind of person do you think I am?"

"Listen carefully. You plead guilty to murder, not capital murder, and you get life. You testify against Cindy—she gets tried for murder, too, not capital murder. The worst *she* can get is life."

"I don't want to cut any deal," David said angrily. "I still think we can win."

232

Before lunch Gene pulled Rusty into a corner by the bank of elevators. "He doesn't know anything to convict her independently of what he could testify to. I mean, he can't give you Cindy without being a witness himself." He didn't add any more about David's attitude.

"Then let's just forget it," Rusty responded cordially.

But Rusty didn't mean that. Since yesterday's kaffee klatch in the basement cafeteria he had thought about little else. Lyn McClellan said to him, "Do it! Cut a deal."

Rusty asked Gil Schultz at Homicide to stop by. With no hesitation Schultz said that if David was willing, why not? Schultz didn't believe they were in the business of killing people. They were in the business of finding and convicting them, and putting them away in Huntsville where they couldn't do any more harm. And this was a tough case to win.

"I can't do it unless the family agrees," Rusty replied.

"The family will fall over backwards to try and put that fat freak in jail," Schultz said.

"Maybe not." Blood ties, Rusty thought. They cut deep. Faced with the decision, the family may back off.

"She had their Mama and their Daddy killed," Schultz said. "David West doesn't mean shit to them. He just pulled the trigger. She told him to do it. She offered him twenty-five grand, didn't she?"

On Sunday evening Rusty picked up Kim Paris at her apartment and took her to dinner at a restaurant in the Rice University area. He didn't prepare her extensively for Nettles's coming interrogation on Tuesday, but he did give her the guidelines he always gave to state's witnesses. "Don't answer any questions you don't know the answers to—don't volunteer when you're not sure—don't argue with him—and don't get impatient or start agreeing with him when he goes over the same stuff."

Then he told her about the deal that had been proposed for David. And what did she think about it? She went back and forth, and finally said, "Do it."

She didn't want David to die; that would have been a burden to bear. But she didn't want him out on the street either, free. Thinking, *That bitch tried to have me killed.*

"Do it, Rusty."

"If I can. If it all falls into place."

———————————

That same Sunday evening, David West called me from the Harris County Jail. He was thoughtful; he wasn't the same man who had talked to Kim about cops as "petty little sick egomaniac fuckheads."

"How are you?" I asked, not intending it as the usual meaningless question.

"Okay, I guess, considering."

"You mean considering the video."

"It was driving me crazy. At least I kept from crying. That was a major effort sometimes. I didn't have the transcript of the second night most of the time, so I didn't really realize how horrible it is. I got the feeling a lot of people in the courtroom were laughing and kind of with me on the first night of the tapes. Came the second night, it was—'*Hey, boy, you're some kind of psycho!*' But that's not me! That's not what I'm like!"

"That's what you're going to have prove in court," I said.

"I don't know if I can. I was drinking. She got me talking along those lines, and, you know, you want to talk real crazy garbage . . . well, that's the way you sound when you do it. It could quite possibly be that I'm just plain, pardon the expression, fucked."

He didn't tell me, of course, that Nettles had proposed a deal. I was still unaware. But I realized later that he was calling me for help.

We talked about his parents and how supportive they were, and his time in the Marine Corps and then walking iron in the high wind atop the Allied Bank Plaza, and then Kim Paris. "I was lonely," he said, "and she said everything that I wanted to hear."

"Unfortunately, you also said everything *she* wanted to hear."

He sighed. "That's the truth."

"Do you blame her a lot?"

"I don't know what to think. A couple of times in court she'd look at me, and the look in her eyes was like, 'Gee, David, don't hold it against me. I was just doing my job.' So it's a whole combination of things. Like, she's a sleazy bimbo, but she's not consciously an evil person. She's going for the money, but she thinks it's right, too. Let's put it this way —if some miraculous thing happened and I got out of this, it wouldn't be some horrible burning hatred I'd be nurturing for the rest of my life. It would just be: 'Stay the hell away from me.' "

In the background a cell door clanged. There were harsh shouts. He said, "I have to go. The deputy's waving. . . ."

Whatever he had called for, I hadn't given to him.

On Monday morning, when Nettles brought up the question of the plea bargain, Rusty said truthfully, "I'm still thinking about it." He was also afraid to let Gene suspect how good a deal it seemed to everybody on the law enforcement team.

At six o'clock that evening Rusty went with Lyn McClellan to see Johnny Holmes. Holmes's office was an odd combination of cowhide and buffalo heads and wooden Indians, two-way radios and a much-used computer. Holmes sat behind the desk puffing at his pipe and stroking his big handlebar mustache. "Lyn thinks we ought to do it," Rusty said. "Homicide thinks we ought to do it. So does Kim Paris. My guess is the family will go for it, too."

"And what about you?" Holmes asked.

"I don't like it. I'm the reluctant dragon."

"Why?"

"Because I think David's the prime mover. He deserves death. He started it. He said, 'You ought to just kill 'em.' Later she got involved, maybe talked him into it, but what could she have done without him?"

Holmes said, "Let me see if I understand the situation. You've got one guy, the trigger man, who you think might get death, although the odds are against it. You don't know if you can convict him. If you don't make a deal, you could lose, and you'll never get the woman he says set her parents up, participated, and in many ways influenced the guy who did it."

"That's exactly it," Rusty said.

Holmes reversed what he had said in October—that he would require a lot of persuasion to ever make a deal with the trigger man in order to get a conspirator—and said: "I think that if the family wants the deal, you have to do it. It's not right to leave the woman out there, free. But you're the trial prosecutor. It's your decision."

But Holmes pointed out that there was another problem. He knew, because he had been a young assistant district attorney during Harris County's famous 1975 trial of Lilla Paulus for the "Blood and Money" murder of Dr. John Hill. Lilla Paulus was convicted on the uncorroborated testimony of Marcia McKittrick, a prostitute and an accomplice; but later the conviction was overturned in the appellate court. The accomplice-witness rule hung over Texas criminal procedure like a self-sharpening sword. No sense in making a deal, Holmes warned, if in spite of his testimony you don't have additional evidence. If David West testified against Cynthia Campbell Ray, who would corroborate what he had to say?

Gwen Sampson, Rusty explained. Cindy's friend, to whom she'd said, "*I was there, you know.*"

"Check it out."

Rusty called Betty Ann Hinds in Austin and asked her to round up the Campbell family and have them in his office at 12:30 P.M. the next day, Tuesday. Briefly he told her what was happening. "Don't comment or ask questions now. Think about it. Tomorrow we can talk." Then he and Lyn McClellan retired to the sixth-floor library of the District Attorney's Building. They researched case law until 11 P.M., by which time Rusty realized there was no case in the books that was exactly parallel. But there were enough precedents. If the family went for it, they could do it.

If David West agreed. The *ifs* could give you ulcers. Rusty already felt pains in his chest and abdomen.

He called Gene Nettles at home. Corliss told him that Gene was still at Jim Leitner's office, working on the tapes. When Leitner answered the telephone, Rusty said, "Listen, how serious are you guys about this deal?"

"Hey, we're very serious," Leitner said. "You must know how I feel."

Rusty realized then that Leitner, far more than dreaming of a victory in the first stage of the trial, had always been intent on saving David's life. His soul and his life together. Had not Leitner been drawn so brazenly—and illegitimately, Rusty recalled—into the case as cocounsel, we might not be talking this way now. Leitner's influence in giving up the battle-by-trial was the fallout that Gene Nettles had not been able to foresee.

Ironic. You try to pull a fast one, and at some curve down the road it jumps up and smacks you in the face. The right way is the only way to do anything if you want to avoid the ethical banana peels on the pavement. And even then, where's the guarantee? There's none. You do your best.

"What about David?" he asked Leitner.

Gene picked up the phone. "Don't worry about David."

"But I do worry about him. I want to talk to him tomorrow morning early," Rusty said, "with y'all there. I just want to satisfy myself about any other corroboration he might have tucked away in the back of his mind." What he really wanted was to satisfy himself that David understood what was happening.

On the telephone then, they cut the outline of the deal. Rusty spoke to Nettles and Leitner separately; he wanted each of them to understand the small print in the contract.

Now it's up to the family, Rusty thought. And David. And me. I can still back out. Sleep on it.

But that night, before he turned out his bedside light, he made yet another decision. If we do this thing, there's no reason not to get full value.

Tomorrow, Tuesday, he would go to the grand jury to ask for a sealed indictment against Cynthia Campbell Ray. If she was arrested by midnight she would appear on the docket of Judge Azios's 232nd District Court the following day. David could plead guilty in front of her on Wednesday morning; he could point her out in the courtroom. She wouldn't know what was happening, that he was pitching her into the garbage disposal in return for the promise of his life, until the moment that he did it. The shock would be awesome. Who could predict how she would react? If she was as emotionally unstable as everyone believed, she might fly at her betrayer and give herself away.

The hair on the back of Rusty's neck tingled. He wanted justice done, and he wanted to win, but it was so much sweeter with a bit of drama. Give them a good show, he thought. Just hope that nothing goes wrong.

21

Despite the call for "nine sharp," at 10 A.M. Judge Azios was still going through his docket. One reporter said, "In this courtroom we go by Azios Standard Time." But that was not wholly accurate. In fact the judge was on Mexican time. In Mexico nothing happens on schedule except the bullfight, and no one gets upset, for Mexicans have a fundamental belief in the doomed quality of humankind's finest schemes. Why hurry fate?

Nevertheless I entered the courtroom at 8:45 and talked for a while to Larry Pollinger about his twenty-nine-footer that he kept in the harbor of Galveston Bay. Rusty prowled in, hunting for Kim. We exchanged a few words, and he told me I looked "tired and irritable." I hadn't realized it showed. I was still thinking about his rejecting Paul Whitfield as a witness. Had I known what he knew, I would have realized that if David West was going to plead guilty, the State of Texas didn't need Paul Whitfield to testify. And if they were going to bring Cindy Ray to trial, they might prefer that the earth open up and swallow Paul Whitfield. Because what Paul had to say didn't point to Cindy as David's accomplice in the murders—it pointed to Wickie Weinstein.

"Who's at bat first?" I asked.

"The defense still wants Kim."

Still? That should have alerted me.

Nettles and Leitner had been up all night working on the video. At that moment, backstage in the privacy of the empty jury room, they were finally telling David West that there was a new witness lurking out there—Paul Whitfield. Rusty had put him on hold, but that had to be the usual prosecutorial deviltry.

"Oh, shit." David sighed. He knew what he'd told Paul Whitfield. He hadn't wanted to admit it before, even to himself. "I guess that's it," he said, echoing Leitner.

"I don't think we can win," Gene said brusquely. "Do you want the deal?"

David looked up with bleak eyes. He could still hear his shrill voice on the tapes, boasting, twisting the screw on the garrote. After a moment he nodded once. Leitner suddenly believed that for the first time David was grasping the consequences of what he had done.

Rusty knocked on the door. Leitner let him in. While Rusty spoke, Leitner kept getting up and going to the little toilet in the jury room; the strain had worked its way from his mind to his bladder.

David, face puffy with indecision, listened in a brooding silence while Rusty laid out the deal as he and the defense lawyers understood it. David kept nodding—brief and awkward jerks of his head—without committing himself. Yes, he understood. Yes, that too. And that.

"You'll get life, David," Rusty said crisply. "That's not negotiable. The judge will pass sentence right then and there. Tomorrow. You lose your right to appeal when you plead guilty. Do you understand that?"

"Yes," David said. "And what does Cindy get?"

"An indictment for murder. Just murder."

David's heart suddenly started to accelerate, an uncontrollable woodpecker tap-tap-tap against his rib cage. *Life.* To Kim Paris he had said, *"You think I'm going to get put in there and get butt-fucked by fuckin' bodybuilders? I'm either scot free or I'll check out."* But that was before he had heard his shrill and obscene voice saying, "She also offered me a lot of fuckin' money" and "It was pathetically easy," and begun to contemplate death by injection.

That wasn't me. I'm not really like that.

He had seen the faces of those twelve jurors they had so painstakingly selected over the seven weeks of voir dire. He could feel their decision creeping up on him. Good people—intelligent, righteous, right-thinking people—and all of them had said *yes, they could inflict the death penalty in a proper case.* I'll be on death row, and so maybe they'll lose a bit of sleep over it in their air-conditioned houses in the suburbs. Won't do me any fuckin' good, will it? Six men had been executed in Texas so far that year, the most in the nation. Nice as he was, Judge Azios would allow him to be killed.

He glanced down at his blue blazer and white shirt covering his beat-

238

ing heart. There had never been any evidence. That was the beauty part. He had planned it so well, leaving not a clue other than his big mouth. I loved her and that made me crazy. Told her so many things that weren't true. He wanted to scream that aloud to Rusty, carve it into Rusty's mind so there wouldn't be any doubt. *Rusty, listen to me—I have a code of honor. I know right from wrong.* I'll go, but I won't grovel! I want to cry, but I'm a man, not a child.

I was a marine.

Still, there was one thing that had to be set straight. Not just important, but vital. Rusty was his judge and jury now. And maybe always had been.

"I want to ask you one thing," David said purposefully, leaning forward to him.

Gene, weary from a night of work with only ninety scattered minutes of sleep, grabbed David's arm from behind. He said hoarsely in David's ear: "This isn't settled yet. Don't say anything. *Don't admit to anything.*"

"No, I'm willing," David murmured. He shook Gene off and turned back to Rusty. "One thing. . . ."

Gene looked toward Leitner.

Leitner couldn't help now. Leitner wanted it to happen. Gene didn't know what he wanted. He cracked his knuckles.

Rusty remained impassive.

David said to him, "You don't really think I killed them for money, do you?"

He held his breath while Rusty considered it.

Then, cautiously—and truthfully—Rusty said, "No, not really. I believe what you said to Kim. I believe that money was a contributing factor, but a small contributing factor. Primarily you killed them because you thought they were bad people."

"That's all I wanted to know." Satisfied, exonerated from the charge of murder for hire, David let the breath slide from his lungs.

After Rusty and Gene and David had left, Leitner put his head down on the table. He thought he might cry; he had come to care for David, and he was not sanguine about David's future. But no tears came. Instead he fell asleep, and slept for nearly an hour with his head on the cool wood until the bailiff brushed past him, on the way to the toilet, and knocked his elbow. Leitner woke.

Well, it was done. A murderer would be justly punished. But a life had been saved . . . perhaps even for Christ.

———————

A group of students from Willow Ridge High School in Missouri City, Texas, occupied the back rows of the courtroom. They were taking a course in business law and mistakenly they had wound up in the criminal courthouse. Judge Azios welcomed them and explained the concept of these pretrial hearings with no jury present.

At 10:30 Kim Paris took the stand, and the hearing continued. Kim wore her navy blue suit and a white shirt, and she looked pale. Her gray-bearded biographer, Jack Olsen, in dark sunglasses and a bush jacket, was in the courtroom today for the first time, flown down from Seattle. Duval and Cecilia West were there, too. They had never seen Kim.

Gene Nettles, sedately dressed in gray pencil-stripe, didn't rise from the defense table when he began to question Kim. Rusty had said to him, "You better not pull any punches with her, because we haven't got a deal yet. Not until the family agrees. Don't come complaining to me afterward."

Don't worry, Gene thought.

Gene's voice was syrupy and dark, a little suspect, like burned molasses. He had Kim describe her arrival in Houston with Sandra Smith, her roommate.

Rusty asked permission to approach the bench; he wanted certain questions about the relationship between Kim and Sami barred. After listening to his argument, the judge agreed. Kim's private life had nothing to do with her testimony at this hearing.

Frowning, Gene asked, "Who did you go to work for when you came to Houston?"

Rusty wanted that part of Kim's life excluded, too. The judge again agreed.

Frustrated, a glowering Gene moved along to Kim's assignment to meet David West. Had she seen any pages from the HPD offense report on the case?

"I had seen some things," she replied, "but I thought it was Clyde's paperwork."

Gene let that go.

Talking about how she worked at her relationship with David, her voice veering between breathy and husky, but always respectful of her interrogator—"Yes, sir" . . . "No, sir"—Kim admitted that twice she had bought bottles of 180 proof Everclear and brought them with her to their rendezvous. "I tried to appear a little intoxicated when I wasn't."

"Did you smoke marijuana with him?"

"No, sir. The guys at his house sometimes did."

"When did he propose marriage to you?"

"He gave me a bracelet on the twentieth of January. We called ourselves betrothed."

She seemed to be trying to project demure and cute.

"How would you describe the relationship?"

Smiling, she leaned back in the witness chair. "David and I became closer. There was a lot of trust there."

I wondered what she would have done on the night of February 20 if David had said, "No, I didn't do it," or, "I know that Cindy and Wickie Weinstein did it." Would she have picked up her handbag, kissed him goodbye and flown out the door? What then about having his three kids? What about body and fuckin' soul?

We broke for lunch. Rusty hurried at a trot to his seventh-floor office in the District Attorney's Building to meet with the three Campbell daughters, J. W. and his wife, Kim, and Schultz, Motard, White, and Knotts of HPD. Heart pounding, Rusty laid out the elements of the deal. David would plead guilty to the murder of Virginia Campbell and receive a life sentence. He would be eligible for parole in twenty years.

"*Will* he get paroled?" Betty Ann asked.

"Probably," Rusty said. "Texas prisons are crowded. Knowing David, he'll study, earn a degree, be a model prisoner."

In return for the life sentence, David would testify against Cindy. If he backed down anywhere along the line and refused to do it, or took the stand and didn't tell the truth, the state could still indict him for the murder of James Campbell. That was the insurance policy. Cindy would be indicted for murder, not capital murder. The state couldn't justify cutting a deal with the trigger man for life and then indicting the co-conspirator, who hadn't pulled the trigger, for a crime that carried the death penalty.

Rusty said, "I don't want y'all to think this is on the table because we haven't got a case against David West. We do. There's no desperation in what I'm suggesting. It was suggested to *me* by David's attorney. Y'all have to decide. If anyone says no, the deal's off."

"What do *you* want to do?" Michelle Campbell asked.

"You speak first," Rusty said.

One by one, they agreed to go forward with the deal. The sisters showed no malice or loathing for their sibling who had murdered their parents. They were stony-faced. J. W. projected indifference. Kim and the four HPD officers were just onlookers; they had already voiced their feelings.

"Okay," Rusty said, "we'll go forward." His heart thumped even harder against his rib cage.

He called Johnny Holmes. "Good," the district attorney said. "Just keep me advised."

Back in the courthouse, Rusty ran upstairs to the grand jury room on the ninth floor. He was red-faced, exhilarated. Earlier that day another assistant district attorney, Charlie Davidson, had put his name rather than Rusty's on the docket in the quest for a sealed indictment against Cynthia Campbell Ray. The idea was to keep the press at bay. If in the midst of the David West trial, Rusty thought, they'd seen the formidable Hardin heading in there to present a case, they would go bonkers wanting to know what it was all about.

Unnoticed, he slipped into the grand jury room. His presentation took exactly an hour. Then he hurried to his office a block away on Fannin. At 2:30 a message reached him from Charlie Davidson: the grand jury had returned a true bill of indictment against Cynthia Campbell Ray and sealed it. The secret was safe.

Rusty was hungry but there was no time to eat. He called Johnny Holmes to give him the news. Johnny wanted to know if he had checked out the law with Appellate.

"I'm headed there right now," Rusty said.

At 2:30 P.M. Kim took the stand for the afternoon session with Nettles. Rusty had been present in the morning to protect his star witness, but now he was in conference with Calvin Hartman and Tim Taft, the best book lawyers in the state's Appellate Division.

In the courtroom, Lyn McClellan sat guard over Kim Paris on the witness stand.

Gene asked her, "The relationship between you and David was platonic?"

"Yes, sir."

"And you managed to keep it that way by saying that you'd been raped and were leery of sex, right?"

"Yes, sir," Kim said. "And it was true. I had been raped."

"Wasn't that rape just a bad trick you were turning," Gene demanded, "that went awry?"

A suddenly hushed courtroom heard McClellan screech, "*Objection!*" Rusty would *kill* him, he thought, if he let this get out of hand. He cried, "What's that got to do with the admissibility of the tapes?"

Kim's eyes burned like blue neon. Gene didn't care. He may have been in the midst of trading away his coveted chance to tear a new orifice in her anatomy with what he'd learned from Anita McCartney, but he had prepared for this a long time and he wanted to dig in his nails a little bit now and show the world what might have happened. Just to let you know, folks, that I would have gone down scratching and clawing, and blood would have flowed in these premises.

242

And the deal hadn't been inked yet. It might still fall through. Anything was possible when you were dealing with a psychopath like West and a righteous sonofabitch like Hardin.

He attacked.

Didn't she try to get David West drunk on the night of February 20? If not, why did she buy the bottle of Everclear? ("To be nice," Kim replied, floundering.) Hadn't the police told her to make promises of sex and marriage in order to get a confession? Wouldn't David on that night have said or done anything she wanted him to say or do? Wasn't she directed by Lew Bocz in the hopes of making money from a book and movie about her work on this project?

An embattled Kim stood her ground. No, sir. No, sir. No, sir.

Rusty entered the courtroom at four o'clock, feeling fine. Hartman and Taft had told him that, yes, in their opinion a conviction of Cynthia Campbell Ray based on David West's testimony had an excellent chance of being upheld on appeal. Lyn McClellan told him what had been going on. Rusty gripped the edge of the prosecutorial table until his knuckles turned yellow.

"Pass the witness," Nettles said. And kiss my ass, Hardin.

Bridling his anger, Rusty rose and took Kim swiftly through the events of last winter—her employment by Clyde Wilson, her assignment to the Campbell murder case, and her befriending of David West—to her moment of triumph when David unburdened his soul. He brought out her impression of Gil Schultz's skepticism regarding her mission.

"And how did you feel," Rusty said, "after David West had confessed to you, and you next saw Sgt. Schultz? What went through your mind?"

Kim smiled and sang, "*Nah*, nah, nah, nah, *nah*, nah," the way little girls do at little boys they've bested in some street game.

"No more questions," Rusty said.

The judge had been made privy to what was happening, but he wasn't allowed to tell. He struck his fist on the bench top and announced to the press corps that he would rule on the admissibility of the tapes at 8:30 A.M. tomorrow—"because the jury will be seated at nine sharp."

A few minutes later he called me up to the bench and said, "You be here at 8:30, too, Clifford. I know you think I'm on Mexico City time, but this time I mean it."

The judge left. Like a spent runner after a long race, Rusty was leaning casually on the bar, the long wooden railing that separates the spectators' section from the privileged area. When a lawyer takes the bar exams and "passes the bar," it entitles him—and more than ever, her—to pass forward of that railing. With the court out of session, Dan Grothaus passed the bar and confronted Rusty. He slid his note pad out of his back pocket. Most of the TV newspeople planned to quote Nettles's remark about "a bad trick gone awry." The gate was open, and Grothaus, more than most, knew what lay behind it.

"Rusty," he said, "I've been told that before Kim went to work for Clyde here in Houston she was a topless dancer. Any comment?"

Rusty's face grew as flat and chilly as the polar ice cap. It was a direct question; he couldn't avoid answering. "Well . . . yes, she was some sort of exotic dancer here at some club, but I don't see how that's relevant."

She's the state's star witness in a capital murder trial, Grothaus thought. They want to execute a guy based on conversations he had with her—conversations replete with sexual promises. *Everything* about her life is relevant.

"Is it true that she was a topless dancer?" he asked again.

Rusty was boxed in. "Yes, but it's not relevant. You can write what you want, but what difference does it make?" *(We're about to make a deal, you idiot!)*

"Do you know which club she worked at? Was it Caligula?"

"We never checked it out. And I repeat, I don't really think it's relevant."

Rusty backed off. He was furious at Gene for what he had done to Kim on the stand, and now this reporter was on the scent. Opportunists and parasites, Rusty thought. Didn't they see that whatever Kim may have done in the past, when it counted she had done the right thing? The right thing in the right cause. What else mattered?

In the jury room with Nettles, David told his parents that he had killed James and Virginia Campbell, that he was about to plead guilty and would receive a life sentence. "In twenty years, Mom, I'll be out. Take away the year I've already served, it's only nineteen." The lines came out awkwardly, almost comically; he felt like Jimmy Cagney delivering them. Cecilia cried. Duval's eyes glistened. Cecilia had always suspected he was guilty. Duval had known all along there was a chance he had done it, but he had elected to believe that David was being railroaded. He wiped away his tears. The case had taken nearly all of his life's savings. He had paid for nine months of a high-priced lawyer's time and his son had never even gone to trial and now was going to spend at least nineteen more years of his life behind bars.

Fleetingly Duval wondered, did we do something wrong? And what could it have been? Nothing in his large area of knowledge afforded him an answer to those questions. We always loved the boy. We gave him what he wanted. It's the times. They're complex, and the society is corrupt. Young people just don't know anymore what they're doing.

At seven o'clock that evening, armed with a warrant for arrest and the sealed indictment, Sgts. Schultz and Motard and Officers Knotts and White arrived in two unmarked vehicles at Fat Ernie's Restaurant behind the Hyatt Regency Hotel. Makhlouf, menus in hand, spotted Gil Schultz and tried to bar the door. The owner of Fat Ernie's counseled him to step aside and cooperate. Schultz said to Makhlouf, "We have a warrant for the arrest of your wife. Take us to where she is."

They had no idea where that was. They didn't know where she and Makhlouf lived. They weren't even sure that Cindy was in Houston. Just hoping.

Black brows knitted in rage and frustration, Makhlouf muttered something that sounded like agreement. But he dug in his heels and refused to ride with the police. He would take a taxi.

With its brooding Syrian passenger the taxi moved westward on Westheimer at about fifteen miles per hour. They were approaching Kirby Drive, west of Montrose, when Knotts cried out, "Hey! There's a cellular phone in that cab! He'll call her!" Ray White hit the accelerator, pulled next to the taxi and ordered it to the curb. He leaned out the window and showed his shield to the befuddled driver. "No telephone calls!" he bellowed, and the driver, grateful for guidance, rapped back, "Yes, *sir!*"

Ten minutes later Makhlouf got out at Dunkin' Donuts at the corner of Hillcroft and Westheimer and stalked inside. Knotts and White hurried after him, with Schultz and Motard waiting in the second car. Makhlouf had coffee and a Boston cream pie donut, sat around for twenty minutes, then left. He hailed another taxi out on Westheimer. Gil Schultz jumped in with him.

"Get out," Makhlouf said. "This is my taxi. I'm paying for it."

Schultz shrugged. "I'll split the fare with you."

Makhlouf said, "I go alone, or I don't go."

Schultz let him go and jumped into the pursuit car. Knotts said, "He could have come with us for free."

But Makhlouf took the second taxi to his brother's house in West Houston. Knotts and White were about a step behind when the brother answered the repeated stab of the doorbell. A short discussion in Arabic took place, while the law waited. Jerking a thumb at Makhlouf, the brother said to Ron Knotts, "He's crazy." The distressed Makhlouf finally obliged by climbing into the back seat of the first police car and directing them to the Swiss Village Apartments, an apartment house farther out in West Houston.

A few minutes past 10 P.M. he knocked on a downstairs door surrounded by sweet-smelling shrubbery, and when he heard weighty slippered footsteps, cried, "Cynthia, the police are with me!"

"They can't come in," she yelled gruffly.

Schultz called out, "Ms. Ray, we have a warrant for your arrest. We don't want to have to break in. And don't try getting out a window— we have the house surrounded." Knotts almost broke up laughing, but Motard didn't; he had his hand on the butt of his .45.

In a minute Cindy Ray opened the door. Inside the apartment there was hardly any furniture, just a queen-sized mattress on the floor, a few wooden chairs, a dining room table, and a TV. Knotts later described it as "foul." Food was all over the carpet, some of it congealed and putrid. "She smelled as if she hadn't bathed or douched in a month."

She was a pathetically fat and greasy woman. Schultz, who hadn't seen her since June of 1982, when he considered her to be attractive and feminine, wouldn't have recognized her if they had bumped into each other on the street. He arrested her and read her her rights from his blue card.

Cindy said quietly to Makhlouf, "I love you, baby. Don't let them do this to me."

Grothaus's story in the *Post* the following morning had headlines on pages one and five: "Ex-Detective Also Ex-Topless Dancer," and "West's Attorney Attacks Ex-Detective's Credibility." The headlines were written by Glenn Lewis, the assistant city editor; Grothaus never saw them until the paper hit the pavement. The lead paragraph of the story read, "Kim Paris, the key witness against accused killer David Duval West, worked as a topless dancer before becoming a private investigator, a prosecutor acknowledged Tuesday."

Reading the newspaper at breakfast, Rusty nearly spat out his orange juice.

It rained hard that dark December morning. It was only forty-five degrees, but the wet wind cut through clothing. The freeways were slick and crowded and slow, and by the time I had splashed over to the courthouse from the parking lot on Travis and furled my soaked umbrella, it was 8:45. No matter. We were on Mexican time. But I felt uneasy. I always did when I was late; my mother had brought me up that way.

Dripping from the downpour, I hurried out of the elevator and pushed open the heavy swinging door to the crowded courtroom.

The first thing I noticed out of the ordinary was a fat young woman hunched alone in a seat in the jury box. A shapeless gray-striped institutional dress flowed around her body like a burlap parachute. Her face was piglike, her eyes and snout swollen, her long brown hair unkempt. Her head was bowed but you could see tears of misery cut into the folds of her cheeks. Her belly bulged. That was Cynthia Campbell Ray.

And the rest of the cast was there, too.

Makhlouf glowered in the back row, wearing his usual blue shirt and chinos, looking like he was ready to throw a hand grenade. Among the other spectators were Clyde Wilson with a somber Denise Moseley and a smiling P. M. Clinton, and next to them sat the unsmiling Campbell sisters. The youngest, Jamie, in black slacks and high heels, I thought was fine-boned and attractive. Betty Ann Hinds was dark-haired and pretty, but otherwise nondescript. Michelle, the oldest, resembled a human-sized squirrel. She was fat but not as fat as Cindy. On their left was J. W. Campbell, tanned, and wearing a grease-stained raincoat. Jack Olsen chatted wth Marian Rosen, Kim Paris and her fiancé; Gil Schultz, Paul Motard, Ray White and Ron Knotts were there, too.

Percy Foreman's young partner, Mike DeGuerin, was at the bench with Rusty, talking to the judge. Cindy had called him last night from the jail. Rusty wore his serious power gear: three-piece navy blue suit and favorite yellow foulard tie. David West entered with his two lawyers. The judge called them up to the bench. At 9:30 the judge turned toward Cindy Ray in the jury box and said politely, "Please come up here, Ms. Ray."

Now the expectant courtroom quieted down.

Cindy stood at the bench next to DeGuerin, who was just an inch or two taller than she. The judge read aloud an indictment for murder and solicitation of capital murder. Rusty requested no bail.

"Your Honor," DeGuerin said briskly, "she lives in Houston. She's never left Houston during this whole trial, when she was liable to be indicted at any time. She has no intention now of leaving Houston."

"Bond is set at $100,000," the judge said. Cindy wiped her nose and turned back toward the jury box, so that the photographers clustered at the courtroom door were able to catch her in their lenses for the first time.

247

The court then got back to old and nearly forgotten business: the motion to suppress the tapes. Both Gene and Rusty waived argument. The court ruled: "Ms. Paris was not a member of law enforcement. David West was not in custody. All statements by David West were voluntarily made. The court will admit the videotape into evidence and let the jury decide what was said. Any further business?"

"Yes, Your Honor," Rusty said, "I believe there is a plea."

Nettles, Leitner, and David West rose to approach the bench, the two lawyers flanking their client as if they were priests escorting him to the scaffold. Rusty's eyes shone.

Then it went quickly. David waived his rights to trial by jury, and Rusty moved to reduce the charge from capital murder to murder. Rusty solemnly read aloud a prepared statement by David admitting that he had murdered James and Virginia Campbell and requesting permission of the court to change his plea to guilty in the murder of Virginia. In return David promised to testify on behalf of the state, truthfully, in the trial of Cynthia Campbell Ray.

No one looked at Cindy, still alone in the jury box. Rusty had hoped she would crack, throw a tantrum. But she did nothing except let tears drip down her cheeks into the creases of her neck.

Leitner turned to David and in a loud, high-pitched voice that vibrated with swirling emotions of regret, relief and compassion, formally asked him if he knew what was happening.

"Yes, I do," David replied quietly.

He sounded dazed. You felt he didn't know at all. And perhaps had never known. Judge Azios then sentenced him to life in the Texas Department of Corrections.

The jury was called out, thanked, offered a lengthy apology, and dismissed.

It was like going to a bullfight and after the preliminary passes and the picadors and the *banderilleros,* seeing the matador pat the bull on the muzzle and the bull wag his tail and the two exit the arena like master and pet.

Where was the moment of truth?

———————

A jubilant Rusty arranged a press conference. Justice had prevailed, and he had won what he considered the most problem-racked case of his career. The gala event took place in a smaller courtroom in front of several dozen microphones and TV cameras, with Rusty center stage and the heroine, Kim Paris, at his left.

Earlier that day, in front of the press corps before the festivities started, Rusty had lashed into Dan Grothaus for printing the story of Kim's stint as a topless dancer. Now, in response to a reporter's question about her reaction to David's conviction, Kim had just said, "I'm relieved. Lately I've felt under a great deal of pressure and scrutiny. . . . David has done something very terrible. I feel sorry for him."

A reporter referred to Dan Grothaus's article and asked if she cared to comment concerning the speculation as to her background.

Rusty stepped forward as her champion. "Let me address that. Until today I had no idea that the *National Enquirer* was covering this trial. I am absolutely outraged at the article by Dan Grothaus that appeared this morning in the Houston *Post*. What is so outrageous is that *she* was put on trial! He talks about all kinds of things that I think are despicable, irrelevant, and improper, and she was in tears this morning." He began to grow more irate. "This day should have been something special to her! Solely through her efforts, a man was brought to the bar of justice for shooting two people three times in their bed, and some clown is writing about allegations that weren't even in evidence! This should have been her special day, and he nearly succeeded in ruining it with a character assassination."

The assembled press was not impressed. Houston media policy was timid and lightweight where the city authorities were concerned; Grothaus was one of the few outspoken critics. One reporter, referring to Rusty's preoccupation with *her special day*, said, "Sounds like an ad campaign for a feminine hygiene product, and he's mad because somebody said it smelled of rotten eggs." But Rusty was stubborn, and he believed that Kim was on the side of the angels. Grothaus said later, "I think he's half in love with her."

Rusty ended by suggesting to Kim that "she not even deign to respond to the allegations," and Kim nodded.

When did the state think Cindy Ray would go to trial? "In a few months, we hope," Rusty said. "As for the suggestions of incest between James Campbell and his daughter that came out on the tapes, I think we're going to find out they're totally untrue."

The press conference was over. As he left the room to return to his office, a strange mixed expression played across Rusty's face—one of triumph and relief, and yet also one of regret. He had come out a winner when he expected the worst, and it was enormously satisfying, but he had won in negotiation and patient lawyering and with a clever bluff, not in battle. The odds would have been against him in trial, but like any born battler he had still yearned for it, and he felt he would have risen to the challenge.

But now there would be a trial.

That's what he wanted, that's where he shone. And he *would* try Cindy Ray. No plea, no compromise. Now there would be full justice—and enlightenment.

————————

Gene Nettles, the loser, shrugged his shoulders stoically and said to me, "When you're dealt a hand like that, what can you do? Like the man says, 'Got to know when to hold 'em, got to know when to fold 'em.'"

He could live with it. He felt he and Leitner had saved a man's life, and you couldn't lose sleep over *that*.

Most praised him for a reasoned, lawyerly decision. Some believed he had been bluffed out of the pot and thrown down a winning hand.

But all felt that in the forthcoming trial of Cindy Ray, with David West on the witness stand spilling his guts as part of the bargain to save his life, there was a good chance that the truth about the Campbell family, for better or for worse, would finally emerge. And we would know what had happened that night—and perhaps even before that night—in the house on Memorial Drive. The truth would be laid bare. We might even learn the answer to a question that puzzled us all. David had never touched on it, not to Kim or anyone else.

A glove had been found on the living room carpet. Cindy's confidante, Gwen Sampson, had said: "She told me she left the glove so that there'd be some evidence." But was that true? *Had* she left the glove, and had that been her real reason? And in either case, why say so to Gwen?

The answer to that riddle, I believed, was at the core of the mystery of what had really happened.

22

On December 20 Cindy huddled, crying, in a holdover cell in the basement jail section of the courthouse. David paced in the next cell, between debriefings with Rusty, and when he realized she was there he said through the bars, "Cindy, I have to do this. They were going to give me the death penalty. I had to save my life."

She kept crying. David kept calling her name. Finally some inmate in another cell said, "Hey, man, leave the woman alone. You ain't helping her."

In the legal community there were still sharply mixed feelings about what David's lawyers had convinced him to do. "Once a prosecutor, never a defense lawyer," Sam Guiberson said, meaning that both Nettles and Leitner were prone to plea bargain and see things too readily from the district attorney's point of view. (On the wall in his office, Gene Nettles had a 1976 photograph of all the assistant district attorneys, including himself, Jim Leitner, and Rusty Hardin. It looked like a college fraternity photograph.) "But they did the right thing," Guiberson added loyally. "Texas juries will kill. It's the frontier mentality. The classic function of the defense attorney in a capital murder case is to see that his client doesn't die."

A victorious Rusty of course defended Nettles's action. "The hardest thing for Gene to do, with his ego, was plead the case. But he and Leitner were making a decision to save another human being's life. It's what Leitner wanted to do from the very beginning."

Gene said, "Rusty wanted me to come to him on my knees and beg for a deal. I'm not ashamed. I did it for David." But some new feelings surfaced. Gene gruffly apologized to Kim Paris for some of the things he had said to her when she testified. He also said one evening to me, "If he wasn't convicted, I think David would have killed again. He's a killer, more than anyone I've ever known. He tasted blood and he liked it."

Right after the plea Kim Paris asked Leitner if she could talk to David briefly. She cared about him, she said. But David said, "No thanks."

Kim asked Clyde Wilson for a part-time job. He turned her down on the grounds that her face was too well known in Houston; moreover, she'd never told him about her DWIs, which reticence he wouldn't tolerate in an employee, and she had badmouthed him too often to too many people. In January Kim flew to Los Angeles with Jack Olsen and Marian Rosen. When she returned she told Paul Harasim, a Houston *Post* columnist, "I could hardly sleep out there, I was so excited." She had met with Debra Winger, she said. "I want her to play me so bad in the film. I keep having this recurring dream where I see Debra going up to receive the Oscar for best actress, and then she calls me up on the stage and thanks me for doing such a good job. Hey . . . why not dream big?"

But in February, pregnant, unemployed, unable to marry because she still had a husband somewhere in California, too well known in Houston in a way that didn't entirely suit her, she moved back to her native St. Louis with David Borosov, the father of her baby that was due in April.

She got a part-time job for six dollars an hour working for a small detective agency, and she made plans to go to college and study finance. She waited for the movie contract.

Through his parents, since he was not allowed to profit from his crime, David West made an agreement with Jack Olsen to tell his story in return for a cash payment to offset the lawyers' bills. He and Kim Paris now shared, if not three kids and a house, the same authorized biographer.

David occupied an eight-by-ten cell on the fifth floor of the Harris County Jail. This part of the jail was given over to solitary confinement cells either for punitive or, as in David's case, protective reasons. His was a high profile case, and the protagonists of such dramas were often vulnerable to the marauding lunatics who make up the majority of inmates in county jails. Moreover, David was now officially a snitch—a witness against another defendant. Snitches were never safe.

He was not uncomfortable in the jail, a modern air-conditioned facility opened in 1983. A weak yellow-orange light burned in his cell most of the night, which David didn't mind: often he couldn't sleep, and the light was just strong enough to read by if you had young eyes. The cell had a bed, a toilet, a sink, even a tiny plywood desk balanced on lockers. He began writing notes for a novel about a NASA space shuttle that lands in Siberia. Three times a week he could work out on the roof or in the weight room, and then shower. The rest of the time he did pushups and situps, and took bird baths in his sink. He could make collect telephone calls. He was learning to jail; it was a way to live.

On Super Bowl Sunday there was a stabbing in the shower room. After the stabbing the unit was cut off from population. Telephone calls were limited to two a week. No more workouts on the roof, and food was shoved into his cell through a steel slot. David grew demoralized. He paced the bare concrete floor. He filed a cop-out slip to be put into general population, and finally on February 18 his request was granted. He was transferred to a special tank that housed a dozen men either convicted of murder or awaiting trial for murder. After a few days in there, one Chicano said to him, "You're a nice guy, but we're all facing the death penalty because of snitches. We advise you to go back to solitary, man, before you get killed."

David quickly filed another cop-out slip and returned to solitary, where he huddled like a pack rat in his hole. What would he do when he got to Huntsville? Murderers were put in the tough Ellis Unit. Even

252

if Rusty could circumvent that, half the men in Huntsville were there because a co-defendant had snitched on them in order to cut a better deal for himself, as David had done. Snitches were regularly stabbed or turned into passive homosexual punks.

He began to lie awake at night thinking about that.

In late February he called Ginger Casey of Channel 26 to tell her that he was frightened, and also that he couldn't talk to her anymore. Gene Nettles had forbidden it. In the course of that conversation Ginger told him that she and Dan Grothaus had ended their affair. David said quickly, "Did it have anything to do with me?"

Ginger realized then that she and David had differing views of their relationship. But she had never led him on, and she had broken no promises to him.

He wrote her a letter in which he further explained his position about communicating with her. He knew that Ginger and Dan and I were friends. He blamed me for having "betrayed" him by producing Paul Whitfield—that was the final reason he had caved in and pled guilty. "It would be naive of me," he wrote to Ginger, "not to consider you a direct conduit to Clifford and I do not intend to be a pawn in any more of his Machiavellian manipulation."

He had viewed me as a friend, and he believed I had been disloyal— "gone over" to Rusty Hardin's side and persuaded Whitfield to come out of the cold and administer the coup de grace. It didn't help that neither Nettles nor Leitner had ever showed David a transcript of the tape made at Renu's, in which Whitfield had said, without any encouragement from me, "I'd like to talk to Rusty Hardin."

I was upset. I went to Jim Leitner in his office, and he confirmed: "The Paul Whitfield testimony was the killer. When you told Gene, his feeling at that point was that all hope is lost. That night he talked to me about it for a long, long time. And then David caved in. He said afterward, 'Whitfield's the straw that broke my back.' But don't feel badly," Leitner said to me. "It was all for the best. I worked with him constantly to try to convince him of the moral and Christian wrong he had done."

"Why didn't you show him the transcript of the tape I gave you, the one we made at Renu's?"

"There wasn't time. Maybe we forgot."

"All right, it's done. But will you do me a favor and talk to David?"

He agreed.

Leitner thought to run for a vacant judgeship, but just before the filing date his wife talked him out of it. By the end of January he was defending two newly accused murderers and a rapist. In February one of his clients got ninety-nine years. Leitner became depressed.

David West's fate seemed to have been decided. I waited impatiently for the spring and for Cynthia Campbell Ray to paw the sand and for Rusty Hardin to approach in his suit of lights, cape and sword in hand. . . .

Mike DeGuerin was a temporary acquisition, for the day of indictment only. After hearing Cindy's plea of indigency, Judge Azios appointed a new lawyer named Kent Schaffer—thirty-one years old, Houston-born and Jewish, scrappy, quick-witted, and cosmopolitan. A trial lawyer who specialized in felony cases involving drugs, he charged between $1,000 and $10,000 a kilo, depending on the substance. If you were accused of possessing five kilos of cocaine and needed Kent Schaffer to fight for you, the fee was $50,000. He himself smoked cigars.

Schaffer liked the idea of defending Cindy Ray. "The state," he proclaimed, "has a psychopath who's trying to screw a topless dancer. Those are their two witnesses. Not a good case for them. I can win it."

After some early visits with his client he worked out a theory and explained it to me. "David West wanted to impress Kim Paris with how slick he was in concocting what *she* had labeled 'the perfect crime.' He also needed someone to share the accumulated guilt. So he invented all that crap about Cindy doing it with him."

"Why did he kill the Campbells?" I asked.

"To revenge what he thought they'd done to Cindy, and to help rehabilitate her, and because he was a frustrated Marine Corps killer who'd never seen combat. But Cindy didn't know anything about it until afterward. Then he told her what he'd done and threatened to shoot her, too, if she ever went to the police. That's why she left him. He's been threatening to kill her ever since."

Schaffer said publicly that he would never plea bargain. "She didn't do it, so I'm going to plead her not guilty. As for West, he's a snitch. If a client of mine decides he wants to turn state's evidence, I tell him to hire another lawyer. A snitch is a despicable person. And on top of it, *this* snitch is a nut and a liar."

Rusty smiled and replied to the media, "I understand that Mr. Schaffer has to make such obligatory remarks."

After a couple of weeks Schaffer told me that he had only one major obstacle in the way of his winning the case. The obstacle was named Cindy Ray. She was a psychological mess, a true paranoid. She kept calling him, and she shouted insults at him on the telephone. She shouted at his secretary, too, and at his twenty-three-year-old Acapulco-born wife, Nancy. On Super Bowl Sunday, while Schaffer drank Stolichnaya and watched the Bears maul the Patriots, Cindy called him seven times at his home. He took the first call, and after that Nancy kept repeating, "I'm sorry, he went out. . . . I'm sorry, he's still out." With his own funds Schaffer hired another lawyer and friend, Deborah Gottlieb, to sit second chair, and Cindy called Gottlieb and shouted at her, too.

Gottlieb began to woodshed Cindy—rehearse her in testimony and demeanor—but it was a torturous process. Cindy questioned everything. "*I'll* make the decisions," she said. Gottlieb found her quick and intelligent, but also a nitpicker and remarkably stubborn. During one visit to the jail, Gottlieb tried to show Cindy an appropriately modest way to use eye makeup and rouge. Cindy balked and said, "You're a complete asshole." Gottlieb walked out. An hour later Cindy called to apologize.

The next day she called Gottlieb again and screamed, "I want you down here *now!*"

From mid-December until late February she fought Schaffer on everything—what she would wear to court, what she might say in a prepared statement, who they should call as witnesses. He wanted her to lose weight, but she said no: didn't he understand she was under too much stress? She then admitted that when new prisoners came into population at the jail, often too upset to eat, she would grab their food and gobble it, too. To his horror Schaffer realized she was *gaining* weight.

One day he mused aloud over the possibility of her testifying on her own behalf, and she whimpered, "No, I can't do that, Mr. Schaffer. You'd have to be made of concrete to face that Rusty Hardin." A few days later he said, "I've thought it over, Cindy, and I agree with you," and she hunkered down and spat: "I've changed my mind, Mr. Schaffer. Don't try to muzzle me!"

He asked her to tell him about her childhood, and she said, "What's that got to do with my case?" He convinced her he needed to know in order to defend her properly, but then she broke down and wept and told him she was too tired to talk anymore. Incest? "Under no circumstances will I discuss that, Mr. Schaffer. I refuse to ruin my kids' lives."

She wanted to control her case, her destiny. For God's sake, didn't she have that right? "No," Schaffer said, "that's not how it works. *I* control your destiny. You have to trust me. You don't know anything about the law."

He worried about the incest issue. If he raised it in the trial, the jury might be more sympathetic toward her, but it also provided her with a motive for murder. And Texas juries were peculiar—incest was not that uncommon in rural areas, not that loathsome a concept. (Schaffer liked

255

to tell the old Southern story of the youth who says, "Paw, ah cain't marry Debbie Sue." "Why not, Joe Bob?" "She's a virgin, Paw." "Ah understand, son. If she ain't good enough for her own kin, she sure ain't good enough for ourn.")

Cindy's paranoia had convinced her that Rusty Hardin was out to get her, that he had political ambitions and this case was his stepping stone to the state capital, and therefore Judge Azios kowtowed to Rusty. Since the judge had appointed Kent Schaffer, it followed that Schaffer would do what the judge told him to do, and that was to let Rusty have his way with her. Azios was up for reelection in November and had first to get through a primary. In January Schaffer had the flu, and it turned to pneumonia—he later flew to Mexico for a week to recover. But during the flu siege he got out of bed to attend a fund-raising dinner held for Judge Azios, quite by coincidence, at Fat Ernie's restaurant, where Makhlouf worked as a waiter. Makhlouf was friendly to Schaffer: didn't spill chicken gumbo in his lap, gave him a second helping of chocolate mousse. Gene Nettles and Lyn McClellan were at the dinner, too.

The next morning Cindy called Schaffer at home. "I thought you were supposed to be sick. My husband says you look fine! And what are you doing hanging around with Mr. Nettles and Mr. McClellan?"

It was a cabal. They were all against her. Cindy remembered what Roy Beene had said about getting the judge to fire a court-appointed lawyer. She began telephoning other lawyers to ask if they thought Schaffer was doing a good job, and would they take her case?

Schaffer filed for a change of venue to Galveston or McAllen on the Mexican border, where fewer people had formed an opinion about the case. On February 24, with Rusty arguing against it, the motion was denied in court. Cindy then handed the bailiff a note saying that she wanted to talk to Judge Azios about his hiring a new lawyer for her.

The judge called her and Schaffer to the bench, read the note aloud, and asked pleasantly, "Ms. Ray, tell me why you're dissatisfied with Mr. Schaffer."

Cindy hung her head.

The judge said, "You have to give a reason, Ms. Ray." She muttered something under her breath. He said, "Please speak up."

She squared her thick shoulders under the green-checked prison smock, looked up, narrowed her eyes, puffed her cheeks like an adder, and yelled at the judge, "He wouldn't come to see me! He ran away to lie on the beach in Mexico when I needed him! And he won't accept my phone calls!"

It was a new Cindy: red-faced, fists clenched—exactly the image that Schaffer had feared might manifest itself in court during the trial: that was why he and Gottlieb had spent so much time trying to calm her and prep her.

The judge said gravely, "You can't just change lawyers like that, Ms. Ray. If we permitted that, we'd have total confusion around here. And your lawyer can't hold your hand every day. He has other clients, you know."

"I didn't ask him to hold my hand," Cindy said impatiently.

"He can't see you every day, either."

Until today Cindy had been a sniveling wreck, sitting in a huddled mass. Now she had on her battle gear. She snarled, "You keep saying that, Judge. We appear not to be communicating."

The judge looked puzzled, a little betrayed. He needed help. But it wasn't coming from Kent Schaffer. "If she feels that way," Schaffer said, fed up, "I think I should be off the case."

The judge announced that he'd hold a hearing and make a decision four days hence.

The next day, February 25, Cindy wrote a handwritten letter to the court, apologizing for any slurs she may have cast on Schaffer and requesting that Judge Azios rehire him. "I was emotionally upset," she wrote, "when I did not receive the Change of Venue. I regret the mistake I made in firing him, not only was it a embarrasement to him, but a inconvience to the Courts [sic]. . . . " She also misspelled the judge's name and Schaffer's name.

She called Schaffer three times that day but he refused to accept the calls. He had been fired, he thought. Cindy reached Nancy Schaffer at home and begged her to influence her husband. "I'll be good. *Please, Mrs. Schaffer.*"

That evening Makhlouf appeared outside Schaffer's office as he was leaving for home, asking: "Why did you quit on my wife?" Schaffer tried to tell him, but Makhlouf kept shaking his head in disbelief.

"She gave me back my senior ring," Schaffer summed up.

In the morning Judge Azios called Schaffer into his chambers and waved Cindy's handwritten apology under the young lawyer's nose. "She also says in the letter that you've 'given consent' to represent her again. Is that true, Kent? And do you want to?"

"It's bullshit," Schaffer said, "and I don't want to."

"You've lost heart?"

"No, Judge, I've lost the ability to get things done."

"Did she have any other reason why she wanted to get rid of you?"

"There's one she never came out with to you," Schaffer said. "She has no faith in anyone under forty. And she also thinks that every lawyer she ever had has screwed her. The others took all her money, and Roy Beene took her house. She's been indicted for murder on the word of a psycho-pathic killer. Maybe, if you think about it, she has good reason to be paranoid."

"All right," the judge said. He explained that it might imperil the validity of the trial to keep Schaffer on the case after Cindy had said so vigorously, in public, that she didn't want him. She had changed her mind, true, but she was the kind of mixed-up woman who could change it again, and the court would wind up with mud in its eye. He said, "I'll have her come in here on Friday. I'm going to listen to everything she says, very carefully. And then I'm going to give her the *chingada*." He smiled benignly. "If you don't know what that means, ask your lovely wife."

"I know what it means," Schaffer said sadly.

On Friday, in court, while Cindy Ray wept at this turn of events, the judge postponed her trial until June 3 and appointed two new lawyers to represent her. He asked one of them to take the case; the other came to the court and asked the judge.

The man he asked was Allen Isbell, a Church of Christ minister living in Galveston. Oklahoma-bred, he was forty-eight years old and known as a low-key, even-tempered jurist, calm to the point of serene. Some thought him excessively formal and reserved, but for the most part that was evidence of their prejudice against the clergy mixing in the law. Isbell's specialty was appellate work: cases already lost, where there was a technical chance for reversal. It was book work, drudgery to most criminal lawyers, but not to a scholar whose background involved re-search and reading, and Allen Isbell was such a scholar. Judge Azios believed that Isbell was also a fine attorney and a stubborn battler. He could handle the case.

The judge had one unusual request. "I'd like you to say yes or no to me before you meet your client."

Warily, Isbell agreed. He had never refused a court-appointed case in his life, no matter how low the fee, on the principle, as he put it, "that everyone deserves as good a defense as possible." Allen Isbell may have been reserved, but he was not lacking in ego.

The man who asked the judge if he also could represent Cindy was named Randy McDonald. He had got wind that one lawyer had been appointed but that the court was having trouble finding a second one. They'd all heard about Cindy Ray's habits as a client.

Randy McDonald didn't care. He was thirty-four years old, sandy-haired and blue-eyed, from near San Angelo in the boondocks of West Texas. He taught a course in criminal trial advocacy at the Bates College of Law at the University of Houston, and another course in trial simulation at the Thurgood Marshall Law School at Texas Southern University, and the previous June he had been elected chairman of the board of the Harris County Criminal Lawyers Association. In private practice for only three years, before that he had been a competent Harris County assistant district attorney under the tutelage of Rusty Hardin. And like everyone else, he deeply wanted to whip Rusty's ass in court. They were all gunfighters and Rusty was still the untouched sheriff of Dodge City. The David West plea was now seen as a brilliant coup.

Motive enough, the judge decided, to help defend Cindy Ray, and he said, "Okay, Randy. You sit second chair to Allen Isbell."

McDonald and Isbell met with Kent Schaffer for two hours. Schaffer told them about the stormy telephone calls and the abrasive visits, and said, "I've defended big dope dealers and rapists and a guy who killed his wife, but I never in my life as a lawyer had a client who gave me as much trouble and backtalk as Cindy Ray. If you ask her a question, she'll argue with you. You didn't have to state an opinion or make a request of her—*just ask a fucking question!*"

Allen Isbell frowned; he respected Schaffer, but as a Church of Christ minister and the son of a minister he had strong feelings about obscenity. He had heard about the nature of the language in the Kim Paris–David West tapes. He was not sure how he would deal with that.

But now he understood the judge's peculiar request that he take the case before meeting the client.

He and Randy drove over to the jail. Seated together at a table, Allen Isbell said calmly, "Ms. Ray, let's set guidelines at the beginning of our relationship. I'll visit you once every week until trial in June. You can call me once a week at my office. Never at home. Is that acceptable to you?"

Shaken by what she perceived as the so-long-honey-it-was-nice-to-know-you exit of Kent Schaffer, Cindy Ray murmured, "Yes, that's acceptable, sir."

After the meeting Randy McDonald walked Isbell to his car. "She likes you, Allen."

"She's stuck with me," the minister sighed.

"No—I get the feeling she doesn't trust *me* because I'm young, which Schaffer thinks was part of her problem with him. But you're older. She sees you as a father substitute."

It took Allen Isbell a few seconds to grasp the implications. Then he began to laugh wildly, and for several minutes he couldn't stop. He didn't want to stop. He sensed that it would be his last bout of laughter for a long time.

———————————

The new defense team's honeymoon with their client lasted exactly one session. Then she turned uncooperative and looked askance at them from the corner of her narrowed eye in the same way she had done at Kent Schaffer: with the certainty that they didn't believe a word she said, didn't give a damn about her either as a human being or an unjustly accused defendant, and were about to sell her down the river to Rusty Hardin and ship her to Gatesville, the women's prison. Allen Isbell said, "I don't know if I've ever met anyone who had a lower opinion of herself. She's a complete product of her upbringing and environment, a true victim. I'm going to help her in any way I can."

He considered the option of pleading her insane—hard to win in a Texas court. It required an expert psychiatric opinion. Cindy flatly refused to see a psychiatrist.

Scratch *that* option.

In February Rusty Hardin suffered what he called "the most disappointing verdict I've ever been a part of." He had helped prosecute a well-publicized case where a two-month-old baby had died of dehydration as the result of diarrhea. Although he asked the jury to convict the parents of first-degree injury to a child, punishable by a maximum sentence of ninety-nine years, the panel in Judge Doug Shaver's court convicted the mother—whom the defense characterized as "ignorant"—of a misdemeanor neglect charge, so that with time served she walked out that same day a free woman. The father was sentenced to ten years in prison and a fine of $5,000. Rusty told the jury, "We have to accept what you do, but God Almighty, how could you do it?" He told the press that he was "heartsick." He blamed himself for not communicating properly with the jury.

In the Cindy Ray trial he vowed he would make no mistakes, especially in picking and instructing the jury.

One of Allen Isbell's conditions for taking the case at such short notice was full access to the prosecutorial file. Such access, except for exculpatory material, was a friendly favor and not an obligation on the part of the state. But when Isbell and McDonald finally settled down at a conference table in the District Attorney's Office and opened the manila folders that Lyn McClellan dropped in front of them, they had the feeling that a great deal was missing. How could they check? There was no master list of interviews and statements. They couldn't ask Gene

17.
Brenda Palmer, March 1987. *"She's spoiled,"* the judge said. *"Sometimes I even carry her machine for her."*

18.
Judge A. D. Azios. *"Don't characterize me as compassionate. If a man's violent and I smell no remorse, I give him* la chingada.*"*

Kent Schaffer, December 1985. *"The state has a psychopath trying to screw a topless dancer. Not a good case for them. I can win it."*

Pete Justin. "That's the man I need, Cindy decided."

21.

Outside the Harris County Courthouse, November 1985. Left to right: Gene Nettles, Jim Leitner, the author. *"If you want to help us, get us a witness!"*

The defense team, left to right: Allen Isbell, Randy McDonald, Rick Brass (in Allen's office). "They were in a duel with Rusty Hardin, and he was the champion."

22.

Assistant District Attorney
Rusty Hardin. "Not so
much the attorney for the state as the attorney for the victims." 23.

Kim Paris and Lyn McClellan. *"I think they ought to be executed the same way they killed the victim."*

24.

Nettles or Jim Leitner, for they still represented David West, now the prosecution's star witness, and were reluctant to part with any information. They asked Kent Schaffer, but he had seen only what they had seen.

Who could they go to? Who knew every detail of the case and had more paper on it than anyone else in Texas other than Rusty Hardin? Schaffer told them there was only one person.

So once again I found myself more of a player in the game than just an observer. And once again there were repercussions that I couldn't foresee, and would come to regret.

But I made the first telephone call to the new defense team, for if I was going to report accurately the inside story of Cindy Ray's trial I needed to have the same friendly relationship with them that I had had with Nettles and Leitner and still had with Rusty.

In March Randy McDonald and I perched on bar stools at Pearl's Oyster Bar in Montrose. He was reticent at first, as lawyers always are, then gradually he opened up. He seemed fixed on the deep family background in the case. Sexual abuse was the key—unlike Rusty, he believed it had happened. Why had Virginia Campbell hated Cindy? Was it possible that Cindy wasn't Virginia's child? Randy's theory turned on David West's emotional bullying of Cindy, to the point where he killed her parents with Cindy as a reluctant, protesting hanger-on.

Makes some sense, I thought. I reminded him that in speaking to Kim Paris of his relationship with Cindy, David had said, *"I'm her Svengali."*

"How do you know that?" Randy asked.

"It's in Kim's notes to Denise Moseley and P. M. Clinton."

Randy hadn't seen the notes, hadn't known they existed. They weren't in the files that Rusty had let them look at. I gave him a xerox of my copy.

On March 25 I met Allen Isbell for the first time. Not as somber a man as I'd been led to believe, he was tall. with a solid, Roman senator's face, courteous and gentle-spoken, a wry humor peeking through the surface gravity. He was married, with a grown son and daughter. He had gone to college at Abilene Christian and taken his master's in philosophy at Rice—"I studied German philosophers," he said, "until I didn't know what they were saying"—and been a full-time minister until the age of thirty-four, when he went to law school at the University of Houston. "A midlife crisis ten years too early," he termed it. "The ministry is a young man's game."

Allen lived in Galveston, where he preached at the Broadway Church

261

of Christ and taught the adult Bible class. Most ministers, he said, were prosecution-oriented, believed in law and order, an eye for an eye. "As a lawyer, I surprised myself by not becoming a district attorney. But apparently I was a maverick. And rarely a joiner."

I liked him immediately, and we discovered something in common. Growing up in Oklahoma, which had no major league baseball team, Allen had cast his boyhood loyalty afar and come to root for the old Brooklyn Dodgers. Growing up on the West Side of Manhattan, so had I. So we had a brief discussion about Carl Furillo's rifle arm and Jackie Robinson's ability to steal home. Of such naive stuff, sometimes, friendships are born.

Allen told me he was unhappy at the short amount of time he and Randy had to prepare a major murder case, and so he was also enlisting the aid of his younger partner, Rick Brass. They had met in 1978, when Rick was a student in Allen's practice court class at the University of Houston's Bates College of Law. Rick, who was thirty-seven, liked to smile and say, "I've had four marriages in my lifetime, but only one law partner."

With some embarrassed reluctance Allen said to me, "I know you're friendly with Rusty. If we all talk freely in front of you, how do I know that you won't pass information to him?"

"I give you my word. One Brooklyn fan to another."

"That's all I wanted." He was relieved, and I was gratified.

One evening I took the three defense lawyers to Rudyard's British Pub, David West's old hangout with the Urban Animals. Randy observed that some bars paid fortunes for decor and advertising and couldn't draw half the crowd that Rud's did, with its dark and dingy walls, its scruffy atmosphere, and no mirror in the bathroom, where, among the scrawled graffiti over the urinal, Randy found, *"Want to know how to make Campbell's Soup? Ask David West."*

Randy ordered a Coors, but the bartender laughed at him. Other than on draft, Rudyard's only served imported bottled beers and ales.

Allen showed me the list of possible state's witnesses provided by Rusty. He didn't yet know who many of them were. Wickie Weinstein's name wasn't on it, but that night in Rudyard's we talked for a long time about Wickie. I mentioned what Paul Whitfield had to say about the fate of the .45 that had killed the Campbells. At that time I didn't yet know how much the threat of Paul's testimony had affected David West's decision.

Allen raised an eyebrow. He'd never heard of Paul Whitfield. Paul's name and an account of what he had told Rusty on that windy December night were missing from the state's file that Lyn McClellan had shown to the defense.

"You ought to talk to Cecilia West," I said. "She loves to talk. Duval always tries to shut her up, but if you call on Tuesday or Wednesday he's at work, and she'll invite you round."

That was exactly what happened, and Randy and Rick visited Cecilia. It was dark in the house for the first fifteen minutes they were there—then Cecilia needed some light, and raised a blind. The lawyers saw what a mausoleum it was.

Cecilia was reluctant to talk about David, but happy to discuss Cindy. To the lawyers' surprise she wasn't bitter at all about the woman who had supposedly led her son to commit murder. "Cindy was like a puppy," she said. "Warm and loving, but no code of ethics. If she borrowed something from you, she never thought about returning it, like a puppy who messes the rug and has no concern over it unless you scold him. And she had no interest in money. If she had a million dollars she'd go through it in no time at all. And if she didn't have a dollar it wouldn't be any worry."

She told an interesting story of what had happened to Cindy in the summer of 1982. "Cindy and David lived together less than a month after the murders. During that month she called me three or four times a day, sometimes for an hour at a time. She had started to drink. She deteriorated to the point where she could barely carry on an intelligent conversation. I didn't hear about her leaving David for some days, because he was so hurt and shaken. In fact, I'd say grieving. That went on for about six weeks, at least, before he started seeming to pull out of it. He would talk to me on the phone, or come over occasionally, but nowhere near as often as before. I didn't hear from Cindy at all during that time. Finally she called me and apologized—she was so apologetic always about everything. She told me she loved me, but didn't tell me where she was, or what she had been doing. I found out later that she had moved back into the apartment on Kingston and was trying to drink herself to death. Then in October she had a complete breakdown. She was terrified she couldn't lock the doors over at her apartment, so she fled from there. She called again and I said, 'All right, you can come here.' She was dirty and smelly—the first time I ever saw her like that. She slept on the couch in our living room. In the middle of the night she got up and told me she had to leave. I managed to hang on to her until it was daylight. Meantime she had drunk up every bit of alcohol in the house—beer, wine, bourbon, everything. That was when she called Gwen Sampson and said. 'Come get me.' "

When they left the gloomy old house on Kipling, Randy said, "Maybe we can use Cecilia as a witness, to back up the theory that Cindy left David because he was threatening her, and the reason he was so upset at her leaving was that he feared she'd go to the police."

David for the state. His mother for the defense. Interesting, Rick Brass thought.

David called Ginger Casey again: he wanted to see her. He had become dependent on her, he admitted, and he missed her. That worried her, but she drove down to the jail on Sunday morning, April 27, and visited him for nearly two hours. David said calmly, "I understand now what happened with Clifford and Paul. I'm not angry anymore."

During that visit he talked at length about Cindy. She had been a damsel in distress, he said, and he had been her knight. On that day last December when he'd pled out, he was only aching to tell the world: "She was once full of promise, and beautiful. Not this blob. I did it for the woman she *was*." He'd had to save her.

"After the murders," he said to Ginger, "Cindy freaked out. It was a bad day. I suggested she go into psychiatric care, but she was afraid they'd commit her to an institution if she did that." The subject of money never came up until then. "She said to me, 'I'll give you half of whatever I get.' She thought it would only be about $50,000. I agonized over that. . . . "

He added something that puzzled Ginger. At trial, he said, he feared his attitude that Cindy didn't deserve severe punishment might get in the way of his testimony. When Ginger asked him to clarify that, David backed off. "I've probably said too much already," he sighed, smiling at the new object of his affections.

Did it mean that he was exaggerating, or even lying, about Cindy's involvement? Later, Ginger quoted him to me, and I was puzzled, too. Nothing in this case was simple or obvious. Absolution, yes, but what about sheer survival? If David was a psychopath, could he be trusted to remember what had happened? Could he be trusted to even *know*?

One of the first things Allen Isbell asked his new client was, did she want to plea bargain? "Under *no* circumstances," Cindy said. "I had nothing to do with the murders of my parents. I want to fight."

All right, he said firmly, they would do that. They would fight to the end—whatever that might be—to prove that David West was lying and Cindy was not guilty.

PART III

TRIAL

23

Summer in Houston begins in May. The pavement heats up, the fresh air of spring hazes over. Sweat drips, and central air conditioners work full time. The murder rate climbs.

Rusty elected to try Cindy Ray for the murder of her father, not her mother. The original probable-cause warrant had named her mother; but now, under the Texas "speedy trial" statute, too much time had elapsed. Jury selection began on Tuesday morning, June 3, 1986. I was there, and I was boyishly excited. I had waited a long time for a real trial.

The wooden spectators' benches in Judge Azios's courtroom had been cleared for a panel of sixty jurors, of whom twelve and an alternate would be chosen. At 10 A.M. Keith Goode, one of Judge Azios's new bailiffs—a Texas Pied Piper costumed in a skin-tight tan uniform, a .357 Magnum stuffed in a shiny brown cowhide holster at his hip—shepherded the panel across the street through the ovenlike morning heat from 403 Caroline. They had been sworn in en masse, promising to uphold the laws of the State of Texas and do their duty as jurors if selected to serve. Now, a herd dumbly clustered at the gates of a slaughterhouse, they shuffled their feet for twenty minutes in the hallway by the bank of elevators on the eighth floor. Keith watched over them. ("Courthouse work," said one of the other bailiffs at the trial, "is the Club Med of custodial law enforcement.")

Ushered into the windowless, fluorescent-lit courtroom, the sixty men and women were led by the squeaky voice of Bettie Conway, deputy district clerk of the court, in the taking of the oath of voir dire: to speak the truth, the whole truth, and nothing but the truth. The oath was a ritual, and no one then, observing these ponderous beginnings of *The State of Texas* v. *Cynthia Campbell Ray*, could be blamed for failing to guess its significance in the trial about to unfold.

The chosen citizens of Harris County knew right away that this was no simple case of cocaine possession or common heat-of-summer murder in the *barrio*. Everyone in the courtroom—lawyers, journalists, the judge, and the bailiffs—was staring at them with an intensity that passed beyond the borders of rudeness. The jurors—technically, at this stage, they were not yet jurors, just veniremen (from the Latin *venire:* make to come)—had done nothing worse than register to vote in the last election, thus qualifying them to appear on a central list provided by the tax assessor's office, from which their names were randomly selected by computer. But now, as one of the jurors said later, "We felt like we'd just come off a slave ship from Africa. We wouldn't have been surprised if the lawyers had opened up our mouths to inspect our teeth."

The lawyers had blank sheets of paper prepared, with the numbers one to sixty inked in. Allen Isbell, rimless half-glasses perched on the tip of his nose, sat at the defense table next to Cindy Ray. She wore a navy blue suit, a white shirt, and a big flowing navy blue tie, so that with her pallor and sparsely applied makeup she could have passed for an overworked, overweight young lawyer herself. Overweight, of course, was a euphemism; she probably tipped the scales somewhere between 250 and 270. (And yet, according to Allen Isbell, she had finally begun to lose weight.) She wasn't yet in Lyn McClellan's class, but she was certainly what he had once dubbed "*large* large."

All beef to the heels, Cindy's legs under the counsel table were splayed out awkwardly like a giraffe drinking at a water hole, ankles bent inwardly at girlish angles. She presumed at the time that all but the upper half of her torso was safely out of sight under the table, but if you were in the jury box you could see it all. She raised one hand to her mouth and coughed harshly.

Isbell's bright young partner, Rick Brass, stood off to the left, a gold bracelet hanging from a French-cuffed wrist. Randy McDonald had the flu; he looked ill, but he was there anyway. To get a different perspective, he rocked back and forth in a swivel chair in the second row of the jury box.

Rusty Hardin was now going after his hundredth straight conviction in a felony trial—his only failures to win had been two mistrials and the one reduced offense in the "Dead Baby case." Crisply dressed in a cream-colored summer suit and yellow paisley tie, he placed himself in an unobtrusive spot two seats down from Randy McDonald, while Lyn McClellan was squeezed with his customary stoicism into an armchair at the state's table. Two young assistant prosecutors from the District Attorney's Office, Melinda Meador and Leslie Brock, leaned forward on the edge of their seats, pens poised above legal pads. The print and TV reporters were scattered around the edges of the courtroom.

With all those analytical eyes boring in on them, not one of the waiting jurors coughed. And none smiled. Clearly—and suddenly—this was serious business.

Judge Azios began by introducing himself and the lawyers, and then asking the jury panel if any of them had heard of "the Cynthia Campbell Ray case." Fifteen hands were raised.

The judge set out the basic facts: James and Virginia Campbell had been found in their home in the Memorial section "on or about June19, 1982, allegedly shot to death." And then in February of 1985, he said, a private detective named Kim Paris had befriended a young man named David West . . . and so forth.

Exactly forty of the sixty jurors, their memories refreshed, now raised their hands. The other twenty were dismissed and told, with the judge's usual optimism, to return at 2 P.M. The judge and the lawyers then turned their communal attention to the forty who remembered the case, and they were questioned one by one on a specific issue: "Would your memory of what you read in the newspapers or watched on television make it impossible for you to come to a verdict based solely on the evidence heard in this courtroom?"

Claude Emory, sixty, said, "I thought it was pretty slick the way the girl done it." There was some confusion for a few moments until Rusty brought out that he was referring to Kim Paris. A young fellow named Ernest Irving, who wore a blue suit and carried the *Wall Street Journal* under his arm, also remembered Kim; he used the word *entrapment* in referring to what she had done to David West, and he was the first juror excused for cause.

The problem was: how could you *not* have known about the case back in February and March of 1985—"Daughter No-Billed in Parents' Death, but Is Still a Suspect," and then again this past December— "West Pleads Guilty: Murderer Vows to Testify Against Ex-Girlfriend." The story was nearly always the lead item on the local TV news. If you didn't know about it you would have had to be singularly uninterested in the world you lived in. Who would want such an ostrich or simpleton as a juror? And if you had known of David's confession to Kim, and then his deal with Rusty Hardin that brought about Cindy's indictment, and if you were human and *had* formed an opinion, how could you now promise to eradicate it from memory, giving weight to no recollection, no chance remembered phrase from the TV news, no subconscious leaning *at all?* You would have to be a remarkable and superior person, a Solomon.

Rusty Hardin said, "The system is fallible, but it's the best we've got. We have to live with it."

The first moment of drama in *Texas* v. *Cynthia Campbell Ray* came shortly after 11 A.M. during the voir dire on the publicity issue. There was a flurry in the courtroom, and Allen Isbell asked permission to approach the bench. He told Judge Azios that Wickie Weinstein, subpoenaed by the defense as a reluctant witness, had quit his job that morning and flown to Miami, Florida. From there he was believed headed for the Bahamas.

"Flown the coop, Your Honor!"

The judge struck the bench with his fist. Declaring a recess, he stormed backstage toward his chambers, muttering to himself, the lawyers crowding after him. The absence of a key witness for the defense could lead to a successful motion for a mistrial. If he granted the mistrial, A. D. could be accused of weakness; if he denied it, he might be reversed by an appellate court. He smacked a fist into his palm and muttered, "If we can't find that mother . . . "

Deputy Larry Pollinger, the judge's process server, explained to the cluster of lawyers that Wickie had slouched into court early yesterday morning in response to the subpoena. He wasn't happy at the idea of testifying, but when Larry said, in that faintly smiling deadly manner that cops do so well, "Wickie, you have no choice," Wickie smiled back beatifically and said, "Hey, no problem! I'll call in every morning between eight and nine, right? And you can tell me if you want me that day, right?"

"The bastard shook my hand and looked me right in the eye when he said that," a mildly embarrassed Larry recalled. He had waited until 10:30 A.M. for Wickie's phone call. It didn't come. He sped over to the messenger service office where Wickie now worked. Wickie was gone.

"He asked me for a paycheck this morning," the office manager said. "Told me he had to catch an eleven o'clock flight to Miami."

With a sick feeling Larry remembered that after Wickie had seen the photograph of Larry's sloop on the wall of the deputy's small office, he

270

had mentioned that one of his Montrose pals had a ketch in Key West and was thinking of sailing it over to the Bahamas. Larry called the airport and confirmed that Continental 106, with a Mr. W. R. Weinstein on board, had taken off on time from Houston Intercontinental, due to land in Miami at 1:15 P.M. Houston time.

In court now, Randy McDonald contacted the Warrants Division of the Harris County Sheriff's Office, who listened carefully to the circumstances and then explained that they were sorry, but they couldn't extradite.

"Why not?" Randy asked.

"He hasn't committed any crime."

Rusty made a short speech in Wickie's favor, ending with, "He's never lied to me," but nevertheless picked up the telephone and tried his luck. It was predictably better: he got the Warrants Division to agree to teletype the Dade County Metropolitan Police at Miami International Airport. Rusty faced the three somber defense lawyers in the narrow hallway outside Larry's office. "That's the best they can do. They won't put his name in NCIC,* unless y'all want us to wink at the law and create a crime that doesn't exist. Miami doesn't have any jurisdiction . . . but they've agreed to escort him off the plane and have him call me."

"If the state wanted him here," Allen said in an aggrieved voice, "you'd get him here."

"And if he won't come," Rusty added, ignoring Allen's remark, nodding his head up and down like an old professor, "I'm going to be fascinated by how you'll prove that he's a material witness. I can only see it if you're going to use him to impeach David."

"That's a judgment call," Allen Isbell replied cryptically.

Rusty was fishing for anything he might learn about the defense strategy, and when Allen didn't say anything pertinent, Rusty realized he had hooked a playable fish. He began to worry a little.

The truant witness and former Urban Animal called collect at 1:50 P.M. from a telephone booth at Miami International Airport. A stony-faced representative of the Dade County Sheriff's Office stood a few feet away, leaning against a concrete post, thumbs hooked into his cartridge belt . . . just observing. While everyone eavesdropped as best they could, Rusty talked to Wickie. He told him he'd done a foolish thing. No harm would come to him if he flew back. The State of Texas would even pay

---

* If they wished, HPD could enter a name into its computer and call up information from the National Computer Information on Crime (NCIC) data banks, or the Justice Information Management System (JIMS), to determine if a suspect—or any citizen—had a record or an open warrant anywhere in the United States. But they had to have a legal reason to do so.

the round trip air fare. "Shoot straight, guy," Rusty said. "It's the better way."

No one in Miami or Houston had really explained Wickie's rights to him. That wasn't their job or, technically, their obligation. Wickie could have thumbed his nose and gone red sails in the sunset to Nassau, and nobody could have done anything about it. But Rusty was a persuasive man. His words carried moral weight. One day Wickie would want to come back to Houston—and why make enemies among the powerful? He agreed to fly back that evening.

Randy McDonald said, "I want him arrested when he gets off that plane."

Rusty, back in the courtroom, pleaded to Judge Azios that an arrest would violate the spirit of his having "talked Wickie back."

"You'll vouch for him, Mr. Rusty?" the court inquired.

The prosecutor's blue eyes blinked rapidly. "I didn't say *that*, Your Honor."

———————————

Wickie, aspiring ship's carpenter, in his worn blue jeans and sweaty gray T-shirt, stood with his slight slouch before Judge Azios at 8:30 the next morning. The forward half of his scalp had been recently shaved, and the hair was just starting to grow back; the aft portion sported long brown curls. Anyone susceptible to visual clichés felt that he carried an aura of calm and irrefutable menace.

Allen demanded that the judge set a $20,000 personal bond on Wickie, so that it would become a criminal offense if he took off again for Key West, and this time he could be legally extradited. Lyn McClellan strongly objected. No one twisted the man's arm to be here, Lyn argued.

"He's a liar," Allen said, "and he can't be trusted."

Lyn's belly heaved, and his little eyes sparkled. "He's *your* witness, isn't he, Mr. Isbell? You have to vouch for his credibility!"

Allen blushed. In the flow of his anger he had forgotten that detail.

"Request granted," Judge Azios said. "Bond set at $20,000." The judge was still annoyed that the authority of the court had been insulted by Wickie's flight, and his trial imperiled, and his deputy made a fool of. He glanced over at Larry Pollinger. Larry nodded with satisfaction. Way to go, Judge. Give him the *chingada*.

Wickie's smooth face twisted slightly. He was stuck in Houston for the duration, unless he wanted to risk becoming a fugitive.

"He's learning the law of the jungle," Randy McDonald said later. "Monkeys don't fuck with elephants."

272

By 10 A.M. that Wednesday the limited voir dire on the publicity issue was completed, and from the original sixty a pool of forty-seven eligible jurors had been culled who affirmed that whether or not they'd heard details of the Campbell murder case before this moment, they were now absolutely capable of reaching a verdict based solely on the evidence they would hear.

The whistle blew, and the main voir dire began. The judge said: "It is vital for all of you to understand that Ms. Ray is presumably innocent of the charge contained in the indictment. That presumption of inno-cence will last throughout the trial, and it cannot be taken from her unless the State of Texas proves beyond a reasonable doubt, to the satisfaction of all twelve jurors, that she is guilty as charged. When both sides have rested," the judge continued, "I will read the charge to you. I will define certain words, but there's one expression I will not define, and that is *'beyond a reasonable doubt,'* because in Texas we don't have a definition of it. If I were to give you a definition, I would be violating the law. You can create your own definition. Because you jurors will be the judges of the facts and credibility of the witnesses. I will be the judge of the law, but not of the facts."

He reminded them that the defendant in this case, or any case, didn't have to testify, and if she didn't they were not to hold it against her. "It's her sacred right, that we all have in the United States, and in Texas, not to testify when accused. If Ms. Ray chooses not to testify and if, during your deliberations, one of you brings up that fact, the others have the obligation to say, 'Wait a minute, hold on there! We dare not even *consider* that, or we're violating our oaths as jurors.'"

Rusty took over. Alternately grave and chummy, the words flowing like molasses on a June morning, which it was, he ticked off his points.

"Let's visit together a while on this issue. . . . "

"If you saw me drop this pen . . . " And then, "A jury is essentially a group of strangers who have to decide whether or not something hap-pened based on what other strangers tell them." Old hat: everyone but the jury had heard it a dozen times or more. But it was still a treat to listen. Rusty was so articulate, so bright with charm. This was how lawyers were meant to talk, with or without the gentle Texas-by-way-of-Carolina accent. He would have been as persuasive on Foley Square in Manhattan as he was on San Jacinto Street in Houston. This was no jaded bull once again boringly defending his right to provincial king-ship; this was a hardy new buck rising up to seize the day.

He explained that motive was not something the state had to deal

273

with. "We don't have to prove," Rusty intoned, with a light chuckle at the absurdity of the thought, "what the killer or killers were wearing, or even what they were thinking . . . just that they *did* it."

Cindy Ray coughed raggedly in what seemed to be pain, and Rusty glanced at her with the full candlepower of his moral disapproval. No smiles, no jokes. This woman was evil. She was not going to have the chance to get friendly with him the way David West had.

Rusty then brought up a theme with the panel that led to his first open argument with Allen Isbell.

"I'm sure y'all have thought seriously about the idea of giving the defendant in this case a fair trial, but how many have thought about giving the *state* a fair trial?"

This was one of Rusty's favorite approaches during voir dire. It seemed so sensible, and he was so firm in his presentation, that he had never been challenged on it before. But Allen Isbell objected aggressively —more aggressively than anyone would have expected: "Your Honor, the State of Texas isn't on trial. I want the jury to know that if they give Cynthia Campbell Ray a fair trial, the state by definition will *also* have had a fair trial."

The lawyers were called to the bench, and after some heated discussion, the judge sustained Allen's objection. First blood had gone to the defense.

That will piss Rusty off, Randy McDonald thought. Good.

But Rusty was a man who, if the front door was slammed, went round to the back door; and if the back door was locked, he tried the windows; and if the windows were barred, he would haul out a sledgehammer.

"How many of you think of the rights of victims?" he asked the panel, and went on from there to make his point.

He dealt with the law of parties. "A person who aids or assists or encourages a person to commit a crime, or attempts to do so, is just as guilty as the person who commits the crime." He paused significantly. "How many feel that's unfair?"

None did.

"Anyone have a problem in concluding that a person who assists a trigger man is just as guilty as the trigger man?"

None had a problem.

"Anyone feel uncomfortable at the idea of one accomplice in a crime testifying against another?"

One man raised his hand and said, "I would have to question his credibility." Lyn McClellan, Melinda Meador, and Leslie Brock marked big red X's on their list; this bold juror would be struck by the state.

But Rusty said enthusiastically, almost gratefully: "You're right to

274

think that way! Because usually an accomplice testifies in return for the promise of something, and that's why the State of Texas requires corroborating evidence. Now I'm telling you up front, there's an accomplice coming down the pike. It's no secret that David West cut a deal with us, that he agreed to plead guilty back in December and testify truthfully in this case in exchange for our dropping the charge of capital murder against him. I concede that there isn't sufficient independent evidence to convict, and if you don't believe David West's testimony"—here Rusty leaned forward across the lectern, cheek bones flexed, jaw and lower lip thrust forward—"you're going to have to walk the defendant out of here."

On that reverberating note the judge declared a break for lunch. The battle plan could not have been more clearly stated. The war would be decided on the credibility of the chief witness for the prosecution.

In the afternoon Rusty told the prospective jurors that there might be contentions in this case of improper sexual conduct. "Anyone feel so strongly about sexual allegations that the suggestion itself would make them believe it?"

No one raised a hand. But a certain sharper sense of attention could be felt on the part of the panel. Sex had entered the courtroom. Color it titillating.

Rusty raised the issue of punishment, "should Ms. Ray be found guilty." It would be up to the jury to levy it, he explained, and the possible range was five years probation up to life in the penitentiary.

"Anyone who couldn't consider as little as five years probation for the crime of murder?"

Probation? For *murder*? Hey, hold your horses, State of Texas. About eight of the forty-seven potential jurors slowly raised their hands.

Rusty clucked his tongue. "What about that case in Florida a while back, where a seventy-five-year-old man pulled the plug on his seventy-three-year-old wife who'd been in the hospital with cancer for six months, and she was in *agony*? That was legally the crime of murder. He had to be indicted. It'd be the same in Texas. Anyone really feel they couldn't consider five years' probation in such a case?"

Upon reconsideration, all the jurors agreed that it would be right and proper. You could see in their expressions that they were impressed with Rusty's compassionate logic. He was a seeker for justice, not retribution.

"If the jury finds Ms. Ray guilty," he said, turning the coin over, "the State of Texas will be asking for a life sentence. Anyone here, because of religious or moral scruples, who couldn't consider sending someone to prison for life?"

No one in the panel admitted to any such scruples. Rusty questioned a few of them individually. A frizzy-haired blond woman in the first row said, "Absolutely no problem."

Allen Isbell, Randy McDonald, and Rick Brass each put a red X next to her name.

"Anyone here ever been the victim of a crime?"

About fifteen of the forty-seven Texans raised their hands. Rusty patiently listened to their tales of burglary and assault and near-rape, and then asked if that experience would prejudice them one way or another in this case. Would they still be able to reach a verdict based solely on the evidence? Of course they would.

"Anyone here have any family members who've been accused or convicted of a felony? Any of you feel that this might prejudice you one way or another in this case?"

A handful of jurors raised their hands during different stages of Rusty's line of questions. He quizzed them closely; his three assistants took notes. Some received x's.

At three o'clock, Rusty finished. He had taken a great deal of time, but he knew how vital it was to select a proper jury. In the end they would be the most important players in the cast. They would have the curtain line.

Allen Isbell's turn came. This was the first opportunity for most of the courtroom observers to see him in action. An appellate lawyer, he was expected to be on the dull side. He was certainly a contrast to Gene Nettles, who had been so eager to lower his lance in the lists against Rusty Hardin last December: Allen lacked the brooding handsomeness, the scouring voice, the penetrant dark-eyed gaze, the charisma. On the other hand, watching him, I felt: this is *the law* speaking.

And he surprised everyone, except the judge who had appointed him. He asked the panel if serving on this jury, in a trial that might last as long as two to three weeks, would cause hardship for anyone. A woman said that if it took that long she would miss a planned trip to New Orleans for a regatta.

Allen modestly smiled. "For Mr. Hardin's benefit, will you please tell me what that is?"

Amid the laughter, Rusty, seated now in the jury box, jumped to his feet, took a little bow and said, "I've been recognized as a public employee." He drew a laugh from that, too. No way that Rusty was about to let Allen upstage him.

More soberly, Allen went on: "We're not going to contest the elements of the crime, only Ms. Ray's involvement in it. Gruesome photographs will be introduced by the prosecution and can fill you with such outrage that you may have prejudicial reactions. Are there any of you, because of experiences in your own life, who might tend to do that?"

No one raised a hand. These were Houstonians; violence filled the pages of their newspapers and the TV screens in their living rooms. They were Westerners, the spiritual descendants of Davy Crockett, Cochise, Billy the Kid, Santa Ana, and Gary Cooper in *High Noon*. Blood in Texas—white, Mexican, Apache, presidential—had flowed for more than a century. Bring on the photographs.

Ms. Ray might not testify. "I'd like to remind you," Allen said, "that when Pilate accused Jesus and Jesus said nothing, Pilate said, 'You're not responding!' So too with the law here—there is no obligation for the defendant to respond to any accusation. Does anyone have a problem with that?"

The frizzy-haired juror in the first row raised her hand and said, "I think if a person's innocent, he or she would want to testify."

Allen parried. "A person might not be a good witness. If they'd cross-examined Jesus, He'd have had to admit that He hadn't held a steady job for three years."

That drew a laugh. It also gave Allen a certain standing with any prospective juror who went to church or believed in the Good Book. They didn't and wouldn't know that he was a Church of Christ minister, but he'd given them a hint that more than a secular morality would be required of them.

At 4:45 the voir dire ended. The lawyers retired: Isbell, McDonald, and Brass with their client to the jury room; Hardin, McClellan, Meador, and Brock to the judge's chambers, sans the judge.

The procedure now was not so much selection as elimination. Each side was permitted eleven strikes, which meant that eleven names could be written on a sheet of paper by the defense and eleven on another sheet of paper by the state. After those twenty-two names were crossed from the master list, the next twelve names became the jury, and the thirteenth name was designated as the alternate.

Now came speculation, warm debate, attempted clairvoyance—even some forensic gambling.

Although they steadfastly denied it, the District Attorney's Office of Harris County had profiles of what they considered "typical state-oriented jurors." If you were over forty, Texas-born, a Republican, and a blue collar worker, you could be counted on to vote for a life sentence for just about any crime the far side of jaywalking. Retired folks, civil servants, and Lutherans were killers. Schoolteachers were good—they understood the basically shiftless nature of the average young defendant, and who had ever pulled the wool over his high school math teacher's eyes with a plea for mercy? Clergymen, farmers, young white males, and older black women were also favored by the prosecutorial forces. Lawyers, college professors, and architects were generally excluded: too intelligent. (But the defense attorneys disliked them for the same reason.) Accountants, scientists, and most engineers were almost automatically struck by the state: too hard to please when it came to a supposedly logical chain of evidence.

In addition, as I knew, Rusty liked women on the jury. And he wanted people with whom he had good eye contact. It had to *feel* right.

A woman named Sheryl Henderson, as a potential juror, presented an interesting problem. She was an unmarried, twenty-six-year-old, self-employed private investigator who mentioned during voir dire that she specialized in divorce cases. Was that a plus or a minus for the state? Rusty couldn't make up his mind, but in the end he decided that the defense was bound to get rid of her; it was therefore foolish for the state to waste one of its eleven precious strikes on Sheryl Henderson.

The defense was snarled over the selection. The major knot was Cindy Ray, who was in on the decision, for it was her life at stake. "I get very negative vibrations from that one," she would say, or, "That one looked at me in a mean and vengeful way. I won't have her."

Allen Isbell sighed and looked to the Lord for an answer.

"Let *us* prepare a list first, Cindy," Rick Brass said soothingly, "and then we'll show it to you for approval." Rick was a practical man who could be counted on to come up with time-saving solutions.

But the lawyers also disagreed among themselves. Julia Carr, a tall, thin, forty-four-year-old gray-haired woman, a service rep for Southwestern Bell Telephone, was she who looked at Cindy "in a mean and vengeful way." She had served on two previous juries and had sharply announced that the last one had been "hung up eleven to one. And *I* wasn't the one." Meaning: you can count on me to speed up the process.

"Give Rusty twelve of her," Randy said, "and he won't have to present any evidence."

Allen Isbell felt that Julia Carr was a possibly cantankerous personality, exactly the kind who might take such an immediately rigid position as to irritate other jurors and polarize the panel. Allen was not as sanguine as Kent Schaffer had been about winning. Since Cindy did not want to testify, Allen was already thinking that the best he could do for his client was to hang up the jury. That would be a victory, although Cindy wouldn't see it that way.

"I have a feeling," he said, "that if we let two dominant personalities get on that jury, like Julia Carr and the minister, they're bound to take opposite sides."

"The minister? You *want* him?" Rick Brass had already scratched a thick black line through the name.

Ministers, as Allen had told me, were generally anathema to defense attorneys, particularly in cases that involved violence, although they were sometimes lenient in the punishment phase of murder trials. But this minister—a bearded, well-spoken man named Randy Uselton, thirty-four years old, born in Carbondale, Illinois, a Harris County resident for only nine years—was a leader of the Houston Covenant Church, a small Protestant sect. In the voir dire Uselton had said he wasn't a devotee of vengeance; he believed in rehabilitation. "If he was a Baptist minister, or Church of Christ, like me," Allen said, bringing his special knowledge to the situation, "I wouldn't touch him with a cattle prod. But the Houston Covenant Church is a maverick church. He has to be an independent thinker, a stubborn man. I kind of like that."

Besides, Allen reasoned that if the jury couldn't make up its mind when it came to deliberation, and the majority were in favor of a guilty verdict, the minister would protect the dissenters. He would be a shielding influence. That's what ministers did.

And besides *that,* although Allen didn't mention this to his fellow lawyers, the minister wore loafers without socks. Allen wasn't sure why, but he liked that, too.

"If he decides our client isn't guilty, neither heaven nor earth is going to move him off that spot. Let's risk it."

If only one woman on the jury had suffered sexual abuse as a child at the hands of a father, she might tip the scales toward leniency in the punishment stage. Allen focused on Mary Kloss, a thirty-seven-year-old secretary at the Mosbacher Energy Company. She was either single or divorced, he wasn't sure. Another woman, Lydia Tamez, was twenty-nine, unmarried, no children, a salesperson for Philips Medical Systems.

Long shots, he realized. But who knew? And who knew about Sheryl Henderson, the young private investigator, who on her jury questionnaire had written "no religious preference"?

"A private eye works with the police," Randy McDonald pointed out.

"The state will strike her," Rick Brass said, "so why should we bother? Rusty won't want a juror who can see how flimsy his evidence is."

Allen sighed. He didn't think the state's evidence was that flimsy.

The triumvirate marked out their eleven strikes, conferred once more with Cindy—she objected to the minister's presence, but didn't make a stand on the issue—made a couple of changes to please her, then at 5:30 announced to the bailiff that they were ready. The state had been ready ten minutes ago.

In the courtroom Bettie Conway took the two lists of strikes, had the judge sign them, and within a few minutes had compiled a final list. There were nine women: Mary Kloss, the secretary; Lydia Tamez, the sales rep for Philips; Gwendolyn K. Beagle, a schoolteacher; Marcellee Ivey, forty-seven, retired from the Veterans Administration; Carlette Thomas, a twenty-three-year-old cafeteria worker; Jane C. McBunch, thirty-eight, a married mother working for Celanese Chemical; Melanie Wheat, twenty-three, single, in insurance; Julia Carr ("a state's juror if ever there was one"); and Sheryl Henderson, the private eye whom both sides had assumed would be struck by the other. Thomas and Beagle were the only black jurors.

The three men were Mark Vandervoort, twenty-three, born in Washington State, a salesman for a tubular steel company; Otho J. Bell from Arkansas, a burly forty-nine-year-old restaurant manager with a tattoo on his right arm; and the Reverend Randy Uselton of Cypress, Texas, the northernmost outpost of Harris County. The alternate juror, should one of the twelve fall ill during the trial, was Clem E. Denton II, an unemployed air conditioning repairman.

The state was surprised that the defense had struck neither Reverend Uselton nor Julia Carr. The defense was surprised that the state hadn't struck Lydia Tamez, who was single and Cindy's age. Both sides were surprised and a little worried that the other hadn't struck Sheryl Henderson, the private eye.

So was Sheryl Henderson. Even before the panel had left 403 Caroline she said to one of the other jurors, "This is a waste. No one pays me for my time if I don't work, so I don't want to be on a jury. And *they* don't want me, either, because I'm a P.I. and I know all the cops. I've been called twice before, and I was struck both times when they found out what I did for a living."

When she was selected this time, she remarked to one of the other jurors, "Hey, they must've made a mistake!"

The sockless minister, Reverend Uselton, said much the same thing the moment the jury was left alone to introduce themselves to one another. "I never *dreamed* they'd pick me," he said. "I was totally unprepared for it."

But the horse was bolted from the stable; it was too late for anyone to close the barn door. In his most cordial manner Judge Azios told the jury that besides being paid six dollars a day they would be taken to lunch each day by the bailiff, and that from now on they were not to watch the local TV news or read the newspapers unless they were censored first by family or friends. He ended by saying, "You are not free to discuss the case with *anyone,* including yourselves, until the time comes to deliberate." He told them to be in court the following morning, Thursday, June 5, to begin hearing evidence.

Trial, at last.

24

For the first day of testimony, the jury and the spectators in the crowded courtroom might have been forgiven for believing they were involved in what Sgt. Mike St. John had once called "The Case of the Surgical Glove."

The day began almost casually with the swearing in of the jury and then the reading of the indictment by the prosecutor. Standing, Cindy Ray spoke a clear, fervent, "Not guilty." Judge Azios then "invoked the rule": all potential witnesses were sworn in and told to leave the courtroom and not discuss the case with anyone. "If you violate this court's instruction, you will be held in contempt." Cecilia and Duval West were there, but Cecilia had been subpoenaed as a witness for the defense and now had to leave. (Until then she had kept me and other reporters at bay by saying, "Please don't come any closer. I haven't had time to brush my teeth.")

Rusty immediately provided the assemblage with another mini-drama. He had been eyeing Cindy Ray's husband, Talal Makhlouf, ever since the voir dire began. More to the point, he had been *seeing* Makhlouf for nearly six months, but not in a way that suited him. Since Cindy's arrest Makhlouf had attended all three trials where Rusty had served as prosecutor, including the "Dead Baby" trial. He had taken a seat in the back row among the spectators and just watched. His brooding gaze rarely left Rusty. He carried a little black bag with him all the time. No one knew what was in it, but it had an "S" on it.

"He's gonna find a telephone booth and change his clothes," Rusty joked.

But Gil Schultz said quietly, "This guy's dangerous."

What do terrorist look-alikes carry in little black bags? After some tossing and turning on May nights, and a glance at his ragged red eyes in the shaving mirror, Rusty finally decided to take action. As soon as the rule was invoked and the witnesses formally banished, he pointed Makhlouf out to the judge and asked that he too be sworn as a witness and then ejected from the courtroom.

Makhlouf was sworn in. "Why do I have to go?" he demanded.

The judge sent the jury to the jury room—it would be the first of many trips during which, as he explained with a charming euphemism, "we have to attend to an administrative procedure."

Allen Isbell quickly came to Makhlouf's aid, although by then he was almost as worried as Rusty about the little black bag. Makhlouf had not been friendly to Allen; he mirrored Cindy's paranoia when he expressed his misgivings with the way the defense team was preparing the case. Cindy had become enraged a few days ago when Allen had asked her questions about the light switch in the Campbells' bedroom—"You're implying that I was *there!*"—and injury was added to insult when the Houston *Post* quoted Allen that "her presence at 8901 Memorial wouldn't necessarily make any difference to the defense we intend to use." On Monday morning, before the voir dire began, Makhlouf stopped Allen by the stairwell in the courthouse corridor and told him that in his opinion they were actively conspiring to further Rusty's political ambitions, and he might not be able to do anything about that, but in Syria they'd know what to do.

Allen had to bite his lip not to snap back. He walked away without replying.

But now, in front of the judge, with the jury still absent, Allen said, "He's her husband! The state can't call him as a witness against his wife!"

Rusty played his hole card in this poker hand. In a conference held at the bench, he told Judge Azios and the defense team that he wouldn't mind challenging Makhlouf's status in the United States if he cared to claim testimonial immunity on the basis of his marriage. Hands behind his back, rubbing his thumbs together steadily, Makhlouf turned a dark charcoal look on Rusty Hardin that any Third World citizen would have recognized immediately as the Evil Eye.

"I will go," he said calmly to the judge.

Not quite. For the rest of the trial he stood outside the courtroom in the hallway by the elevators, wearing his inevitable chinos and blue shirt. He talked to no one other than the three defense attorneys. Sometimes he walked with them through the hot morning on their way to lunch. His little black bag was still tucked under one arm. It had been rumored that his marriage with Cindy Ray was one of convenience: she needed an ally in life, and he needed an American wife because his student immigration visa had expired and he was in danger of being repatriated to Syria. But he had been unhappy when she had filed a petition for divorce in late 1984, and pleased—he told Tim Lewis, his lawyer—when her civil suit was dismissed for lack of prosecution. He was in the corridor outside Judge Azios's courtroom every day. Was this evidence of love?

Tim Lewis said, "She's all he's got now, and he's all she's got. Is that love? Maybe it is."

A criminal trial is like a nineteeth-century Russian novel: it starts with exasperating slowness as the characters are introduced to a jury—then there are complications in the form of minor witnesses—the protagonist finally appears, and contradictions arise to produce drama—and finally, as both jury and spectators grow weary and confused, the pace quickens, reaching its climax in passionate final argument.

Rusty, wearing a dark blue suit, made his opening statement to the jury. It took only fifteen minutes. He was not at all inflammatory. Repeatedly using the meticulous phrase, "we expect the evidence to show," he outlined the state's version of what had happened from June 19, 1982, up to the time of David West's guilty plea on December 11, 1985. "We expect the evidence to show that he received in this court a life sentence, that in return he agreed to testify truthfully in the trial of Cynthia Campbell Ray, and that another capital murder charge to this day is still pending against him."

When Allen Isbell objected to the implication that David West *would* tell the truth in the trial, Rusty graciously clarified what he meant. "I'm not saying that he will testify truthfully. I'm saying that's for you, the jury, to decide."

Again, the issue was clear. Rusty seemed willing to throw all his prosecutorial eggs into one basket, a basket balanced in the hands of a man he had repeatedly called a psychopath. It was a bold move, and I wondered if it was a reckless one. I knew that Rusty, even with his powerful moral scruples, had come to like David. Had *like* metamorphosed into *trust?* That might be an irreversible error.

The judge asked if the state was ready to call its first witness. Rusty called William G. Rhodes, an emergency medical technician (EMT) who drove the Fire Department ambulance that reached the murder scene at 4:13 A.M. on June 19, 1982. Rhodes was a man of thirty-two with dark curly hair, a big mustache, and a pleasant demeanor. He was at the end of a double shift and admitted to having been awake for more than thirty hours. Nevertheless he was coherent, and there was a boyishness about him that made him seem sincere. He testified to seeing the bodies, the spattered blood, and the bullet casings, and to checking for a nonexistent carotid pulse in both victims. "After that we went hastily down the stairs. We were scared. We decided we could be in tremendous danger—the killer might still be in the house or on the grounds."

He offered a description of the surgical glove lying on the carpet inside the open front door. Rusty, of course, was laying a foundation

283

for what he hoped would be the climactic moment of the trial, when Gwen Sampson took the stand and repeated the story she had told in October 1982 to Gil Schultz: "[Cindy] said she took a glove off. She told me she left the glove so that there'd be some evidence and perhaps they could trace it back."

Allen Isbell knew that. He had to derail that freight train.

Rusty then asked that the jury be retired once more to the jury room, and when they had exited he requested the court's permission, as each witness testified, to play for the jury the appropriate parts of the HPD videotape of the murder scene. For example, if Rhodes or anyone else described the surgical glove, Rusty would fast-forward or rewind to a still shot of the glove on the video and ask, "Was that it? Was it in the same place when you saw it?"

Allen Isbell objected. This wasn't a quiz show on prime time. Judge Azios said, "Let's see the video, Mr. Rusty, without the jury present. Then I'll rule."

Lyn McClellan, as in the David West pretrial, padded in behind a nineteen-inch Magnavox TV with a VHS hookup, all on wheels, grunted it into place and played the video for the judge, the lawyers, the defendant, and the media. The age of television! You wondered if the program would be interrupted for commercials and newsbreaks.

The twenty-one-minute tape showed the sparsely furnished living room and den, the assumed window of entry in the den, the surgeon's glove lying on the nubbled green carpet inside the front door; and then, hand-held, with cops muttering, "Watch out for the cable, ya goon" on the sound track, it marched up the stairs as David West was supposed to have done with Cindy, then peered diffidently into the bathroom—it looked like anyone else's bathroom in anyone else's house—and finally, climactically, slid into the Campbells' bedroom.

Here was horror. It was particularly harrowing because it was so domestic. Virginia's old slippers were tossed on the floor, Jim's rumpled brown trousers flung on two suitcases stacked by the wall at the foot of the bed. The two suitcases were probably the ones the couple had taken to Europe—they had been back in Houston nine days and still hadn't put them away. These were not fastidiously organized or even tidy people. Just folks like us, the video proclaimed. The television stood atop a chest of drawers. Books were piled on Jim's night table. A white rotary telephone sat on Virginia's night table. At the foot of the bed, on the floor, were the carelessly tossed quilts and pillows that had made up a bed for the two boys.

Virginia lay on her side, arms dangling, mouth agape, face shattered by two bullet holes. Her shortie nightgown was not long enough to cover her buttocks, and she wore no panties. It was faintly obscene. I the two boys slept at the foot of the bed on the floor, one couldn't help wondering why she was so immodestly clothed.

Jim also lay on his back on top of the quilt, in his mauve shirt and baby blue shorts, the one brown eye staring blankly into the probing camera lens. The other eye socket was smashed, encrusted with blood. Blood spotted the ceiling, both lamp shades, the yellow drapes and headboard, even the drawn window curtains and the mirror on the far wall.

Duval West, father of the formally confessed author of this carnage, sat at the back of the courtroom, blinking through his thick eyeglasses at the video. He seemed unmoved by what he saw. But that had always been what the Wests communicated: a sense that all this was happening elsewhere, and they were watching it on television. If their son was involved it was as an actor, not a character. What should they do—wring their hands and utter dire prophecy? You didn't do that when you watched television. You just watched.

So did the daughter of the murdered couple. Cindy sat with a pencil in her right hand, swollen left cheek resting on clenched right fist. She was dry-eyed. Twice she started to write or doodle on a yellow legal pad . . . then stopped. When she doodled, Rick Brass noticed, she drew large, tearful eyes.

"We don't contest the identity of Mr. and Mrs. Campbell," Allen Isbell said, when the video was finished, "or that David West shot them. Therefore the scenes upstairs have no probative value. I can understand showing the window, the glove—but the rest, when they zoom in on the bodies, will only inflame the jury. On that basis, we object."

Rusty countered by arguing that introduction of the video was critically important in the assessment of whether or not David would be telling the truth when he testified. And he pointed out that defendants, under the law, are never insulated, and should not be insulated, from the horror of their acts.

But it hadn't been proven that it was her act, Allen rebutted.

Judge Azios overruled his objection. The jury was brought back in and shown the video.

They watched attentively. They rarely moved, and no one glanced at Cindy Ray, who still sat without expression, although now and then she offered up a dry hack of a cough. But this time, while they watched the action on the screen, she looked steadily at them—her first chance to do so without eye contact. Finally, when the video was over, the minister and Juror Jane McBunch, a young woman with sculpted blond Joan-of-Arc hair, briefly stared back, and with matching impassivity.

Cindy turned her head away.

During the lunch break the defense lawyers discussed this coolness of attitude. Would the jury see her as callous and soulless, or simply as lethargic and benumbed? "She isn't any of those," Rick Brass said. "She's tuned out because she's seething."

At lunch they also discussed a new problem. Cindy had told Rick that she had made up her mind about the defense getting into the area of sexual abuse, either on cross-examination of the state witnesses or direct examination of its own witnesses. It would be too hard, she said, on her children. They would have to live with it when they were men, when the question of her guilt or innocence would be, if not forgotten, then no longer at issue.

Now Rick laid out Cindy's final position for the other lawyers. Allen turned to Randy and said, "What are we going to do if she's serious and she sticks to it?"

"Ask her how much time she wants to serve," Randy said.

Allen Isbell took Rhodes, the EMT, on cross-examination. To the slight surprise of most onlookers, Allen produced a set of HPD's color photographs of the murder scene. The defense team had possessed the photographs for more than two months. Randy and Rick had studied all of them, but Allen had declined the opportunity until early this morning, and even then he was reluctant to look. He hated the sight of blood and violence. In court, when he spread them out, he felt nauseated.

Now he asked that the photographs of the glove on the carpet be placed into evidence as exhibits for the defense.

For the *defense?* That puzzled us all. Then I realized that Allen was trying to defuse the Power of The Glove. He hoped the jury would think . . . wait a minute . . . whose side is this glove on?

On direct examination Rhodes had said he and his partner had entered the house through the back door, which led to the kitchen.

"You parked at the head of the driveway?" Allen asked.

"Yes, sir."

"Why did you do that? Why not drive all the way in?"

"It was dark, and the ambulance is wide. The driveway was pretty narrow, and we thought we might have to leave in a hurry."

Rusty had introduced into evidence a diagram of the house. Allen showed it to Rhodes. "Then why not go in the front door? It was a lot closer, wasn't it?"

"It looks that way."

Allen was subtly trying to make the point that if they had gone into

286

the house by the front door *then*, they might not have seen a glove inside the door—that the glove had been dropped *later*. By whom? Probably by the same person who'd led them into the house through the distant back door. Draw your own conclusions, members of the jury. Who else was there?

"Did J. W. Campbell tell you he'd been upstairs and seen the bodies?"

"Yes, or words to that effect."

"J. W. was with you when you first came in the house by the back door?"

"Yes, with me and my partner."

"Did he go up the stairs with you to the second floor to view the bodies?"

"No, sir."

"After that first meeting with him downstairs, when did you next see J. W. Campbell."

"I never saw him again."

"Pass the witness."

Clever, I thought. Plant in the jury's mind the possibility that J. W. was a villain, that perhaps Cindy had been framed. Don't accuse him— let the jurors work it out by themselves.

Rusty took Rhodes on redirect examination.

"Mr. Rhodes, was that glove there all the time, from the moment you first walked into the house?"

"Yes, sir."

"Did it come from you or any EMT people?"

"No, sir, it didn't."

But no matter how hard Rusty tried, he couldn't establish with this witness that J. W. hadn't placed it there earlier.

Allen had no more questions. Rusty asked the court, "May the witness be excused?"—and, with a sympathetic smile, he added, "To go to bed." It was a nice touch; it personalized the EMT, made him brave and conscientious and excused any slight fuzziness in his testimony. It was typical Rusty, Allen thought, and you had to guard against it, and yet, how could you?

Next came Officer M. E. Meaney: also young and sincere and good-looking, with ten years' experience in HPD. These police officers might have been supplied by Central Casting in Hollywood. The jury would like them and trust them and remember them.

In 1982 Meaney had been a night shift officer at the North Shepherd substation. At 8901 Memorial he had noticed the glove before he went

287

upstairs. Yes, the glove looked just as it did in the video. Nothing was disturbed.

Rusty passed the witness.

Allen handed Meaney a piece of paper. The police officer agreed that it was his one-page official report on what he had observed on the morning of June 19, 1982.

"And didn't you write in that report that the EMT *told* you the front door was open, and *told* you that a surgical glove had been found there?"

Meaney studied the report and grumpily admitted that it was so. He hadn't actually seen The Glove himself.

Allen smiled, meaning: Ladies and gentlemen of the jury, don't automatically believe the first things you hear from these handsome, mustached officers of the law. They can goof up, too. Kindly remember they are employed by the State of Texas.

Rusty, annoyed at the setback, called Sgt. Wilson, photographer for the crime scene unit back in 1982, and the first thing he did was hand Wilson a Kleenex to get rid of his chewing gum. Thus unburdened, Wilson said, "Yes, I walked through the front door, didn't move or touch it. . . . I noticed a latex surgical glove."

Rusty's *son et lumiere* show continued with aerial photographs of 8901 Memorial and the neighborhood, and he asked permission to show Wilson's color photographs of the bodies. Granted. And so the jury was treated to a second round of Jim Campbell's red eyehole and Virginia's bloody nightie. No one flinched. But no one smiled either. The still photographs didn't flash by the eye as the video had done—you could study them, and in their brutality they were awful. The bodies looked embalmed.

Sgt. Wesley C. Sheldon, HPD's latent print examiner, an authoritative man with sixteen years' experience, then took the stand, and produced The Glove itself. It was darkened to a dark orange-pink fleshlike color from chemical treatment and age. HPD had never been able to lift a single fingerprint from it. (The jury must have wondered then how on earth it was of any significance in the state's case against Cindy.)

On that gloomy note for modern hi-tech criminology, the first day of testimony ended.

"The jury was bored," Allen concluded, on the way back to his office with Rick Brass and Randy McDonald. "They didn't know what was going on."

But Rusty on the way back to his office was satisfied. He was building his case with painstaking precision, hammering the nails one by one into the coffin of Cindy Ray's life sentence.

25

At 9:50 A.M. on Friday, June 6—the forty-second anniversary of D-Day and the second day of *State of Texas* v. *Cynthia Campbell Ray*—the air conditioning failed in Judge Azios's eighth-floor courtroom. Or, according to some observers, the body heat in that windowless cube simply overwhelmed a system that was weak at best. There was nothing above the courtroom ceiling except the merciless Gulf Coast sun. But as in that other business so akin to that of law, the show must go on.

Judge Azios began the day by swearing in a new lawyer, Edna Schneider. He read the oath, she plighted her troth to the Texas Bar by saying, "I will," and then everyone applauded politely and went back to wiping the ooze from their foreheads.

A pungent odor began to waft through the courtroom.

"Is the state ready?"

"State's ready, Your Honor," Rusty Hardin said brightly.

"Defense ready?"

Today Cindy Ray wore the second of the two suits that she had available for the trial. This one was mocha in color. Someone had told the defense team that it softened her appearance, and that the navy blue she'd worn yesterday was a harsh color.

"Ready, Your Honor," said Allen Isbell.

The judge, ignoring his fifteen-inch black oak gavel in favor of the clenched fist, pounded on his desk and ordered young Keith Goode to bring in the jury. When they were seated in the airless room, Rusty called his first important witness to the stand. Yesterday had been mere prologue. Now we were to close in and confront the murder itself.

Maria Bravo Gonzalez was about four feet nine inches tall, mostly bosom and buttocks with no sign of a waist, brown as pumpernickel under her royal blue dress, and constructed like a squat Mayan pyramid. She had a square face that might have been lifted from one of the friezes at Chichén Itzá, and on top of it was clamped a pair of heavy black horn-rimmed glasses. Her expressions ran the gamut from stolid to grave. She claimed to speak no English, so she was given the services of a court interpreter, Linda Hernandez. Hernandez not only translated Maria's Spanish but made every effort to reproduce Maria's considerable emotive output.

"Please state your name."

289

"Maria Luisa Bravo de Gonzalez." She had a strong voice that hardly needed the microphone provided for the witnesses.

"And, Maria, how old are you?" Rusty inquired.

"Sixty-two, Señor."

Although it didn't come out in testimony, I learned later from Maria that she had been born in Monterrey, Mexico, had been married forty-five years ago to a man long since vanished, and—this was unusual for a Mexican woman of her generation—had only one child, a son living in Monterrey, and five grandchildren. She had left school and gone to work at the age of nine. For the past three years she had been employed as a housekeeper by Martha Ann Traylor, a married real estate salesperson with two children.

"How long have you been in the United States?"

"Fifteen years, Señor."

"And why did you come here fifteen years ago?"

"*Por necesidad*"—which the interpreter translated more modestly as, "To work."

She cleaned houses, and in September 1977 she was employed by James and Virginia Campbell at a salary of seventy dollars a week plus room and board. They were very good to her, she told the jury. "I was mostly a babysitter for the boys, Matthew and Michael."

"What were the boys like?"

"*Muy buenos.*"

"What was Mrs. Campbell like?"

"Oh! *Muy buena!*"

"Were you close to her?"

"I was her great friend."

"What was Mr. Campbell like?"

"*Muy bueno.*"

"What was their relationship with the boys?"

"*Mucho amor.*"

On Fridays and Saturdays, Maria explained, the boys (she called them "*los chamacos*," which might have been translated by Hernandez, but wasn't, as "the kids") would sleep on the floor of the Campbells' bedroom upstairs. They would watch monster movies on the VCR.

"Did the boys always sleep in the same spot?"

"Yes, but sometimes Matthew would curl up on the bed next to Señora Virginia."

It flickered through my mind that if eight-year-old Matthew had curled up next to Señora Virginia on the night of June 19, 1982, he might have been shot, too. Then I realized—or decided—that if Matthew had been there in the bed, David West probably would not have been able to pull the trigger, but would have cut and run, and we wouldn't be here. In such casual and seemingly accidental ways are human fates decided. It was a frightening thought.

The lawyers approached the bench for a private conference with the judge, and Maria heaved big sighs to let everyone know her ordeal. She was sweating. So was everyone else now. The courtroom air was markedly fragrant.

Rusty showed Maria photographs of the Campbells in years past. Maria's eyes grew damp. The photographs were entered into evidence for the state and passed to the jury.

"Who took most of those photographs?"

"My Michael," Maria said, wiping her eyes with a white handkerchief.

Rusty then led her to that time in early June when the Campbells were in Europe and Cindy Ray paid a visit to Memorial. It was a Tuesday, about six o'clock in the evening, still sunny and bright and warm. Michael was in Austin with his Aunt Michelle; Matthew was at home. Maria first noticed Cindy from the window of her apartment over the garage. Cindy was outside the house: "Checking windows . . . about seven windows. I saw her checking the windows at the boys' room. Trying to lift up the window. One time for each window. But they were locked. They wouldn't pull up."

Rusty brought her waddling out of the witness chair and placed her directly in front of the jury box to demonstrate just how Cindy had done it. The jury watched with as much fascination as if she had been lifting ten-kilo gold bars.

Allen Isbell grew a shade paler. This was devastating testimony. Here it was, only the first day of the trial, and it seemed already proved that the defendant—their own daughter!—had helped plot the murder of her mother and father *weeks in advance*. Allen began to grind his teeth. His turn would come, but would it be in time?

Cindy's eyes, big and watery, were fixed on Maria, who stood with her arms crossed protectively on her bosom, as if to fend off evil.

Rusty calmly asked Maria, "Did you do anything when you saw Cindy trying to lift the windows?"

"Yes, I came running down the stairs from my apartment over the garage. I said, '*Cindy, Cindy, no es bueno!*' She was then trying to get into the window of the boys' room. She became frightened and surprised, and said, 'It's okay, Maria.' "

Cindy spent that night in the house, Maria said, and left the next morning. Two days later, on Thursday, June 10, the Campbells returned from Europe.

"They were in a very sad mood," Maria said.

Rusty declined to inquire why; he didn't know the answer and wasn't able to risk the question.* He asked, "When did you next see Cindy?"

"The next day, Friday. Cindy came to get money from her mother for food."

"Did she often come for food like that?"

"About once a week. The Señora† would take her to the store and buy her everything she needed. Or when she came to the house she would give her canned goods, cheese, chicken, bread, cookies."

"That Friday, the day after the Campbells returned from Europe . . . how did the visit end?"

"The Señora took her to her apartment. It was late, almost dark."

"And how did Mrs. Campbell appear when she got back?"

"Very nervous and very sad. She cried a lot. She no longer smiled. Nothing mattered anymore. She said, 'What will happen to the children?' "

Allen objected. That was hearsay—quotations from other than witnesses, inadmissible as testimony. Maria had been cautioned not to repeat anything that had been told to her by anyone except Cindy, who, as the defendant, was theoretically capable of rebutting testimony. Judge Azios sustained the objection, instructing the jury to disregard Maria's quotation of Mrs. Campbell.

Rusty swiftly said, "Thank you, Your Honor," as he always did when Judge Azios sustained a defense objection or overruled one made by the state. No one could ever tell whether it was routine politeness or a sincere respect for the judicial opinion.

And indeed, despite the judge's adverse ruling, Rusty had another way to get where he wanted to go.

"How long," he asked Maria, "had Mrs. Campbell been nervous and sad, and crying a lot, as you described her?"

"A little over a year."

"Was she having a particular problem with any person?"

"Objection," Allen persisted. "It's vague, and he's leading the witness."

"Sustained," said the court.

---

* Similarly, on cross-examination, Allen Isbell was also afraid to ask the question. And so we never learned why—if indeed it was true—the Campbells were "in a very sad mood" upon their return from Europe. It was an interesting commentary on the nature of the truth allowed into evidence: it must be *safe* truth for at least one side.

† This phrase in Spanish, "la Señora," was always translated literally by the interpreter as "the Mrs.," which missed the respectful flavor and intent of the term. In this context it really intends "the lady of the house."

"Thank you, Your Honor." And then, to Maria: "How would you describe Mrs. Campbell's relationship with Cindy that last year?"

"*Mala*," Maria answered. ("Bad.")

"What was Cindy's attitude to her mother?"

"She would come into the house angry, and argue with the Señora."

"You heard the arguments? What were they about?"

Allen objected again. Hearsay, and it required the drawing of conclusions. Judge Azios sustained.

Rusty asked Maria, "Did you hear them argue that Friday?"

Wearily Allen objected: this time he took a new tack. "She said she spoke only Spanish."

"Sustained."

But it wasn't good for Cindy. No matter how many times Allen objected and the court sustained his objection, the jury was getting a picture of a mother–daughter relationship far from the pages of *Family Circle*. And why didn't the defense want the jury to know what the mother had said? What revelation did they fear?*

"Did you see Matthew," Rusty inquired, "when they returned from taking Cindy to her apartment that Friday?"

"No, I saw him the next morning at 6:30, when I went to work. In the kitchen. He was crying, and nervous. He was waiting for me."

"Now don't tell us what he said to you," Rusty instructed, "because that would be hearsay. Do you understand that, Maria? You can't repeat what Matthew told you."

"Yes." (Her intonation and body language seemed to be saying, *But I would like very much to tell you, and you would learn a lot.*)

"Later that morning, tell us how Mrs. Campbell appeared to you."

"Sad, with teary eyes . . . "

Rusty then brought her up to Friday, June 18, the day preceding the night—technically, the morning—of the murders. Maria had checked all the downstairs windows that afternoon, and all were locked. She went to bed about 9:30 P.M. The boys were going to sleep upstairs with their grandparents. They referred to them as "*sus padres*," she explained— "their parents." They called them "Papa" and "Mama." Again Rusty did not ask why.

It was a hot night. There had been no rain.

" . . . I was awakened by the gunshots."

---

* Maria's claim—despite her insistence that she didn't speak or understand English—was that Cindy had overtly threatened her mother. Maria also maintained that Virginia Campbell had confided to her that Cindy had said, "I'll kill you." (Again, it was pertinent that Virginia Campbell by all accounts spoke no Spanish.) None of this hearsay ever got into evidence.

293

The courtroom grew unusually quiet. Trial spectators learn to sniff upcoming drama. They sensed now that Maria's peasant sincerity would not fail their expectations.

"I was falling asleep when I heard the shots. I don't know the time, I don't have a watch. I sat up in bed. I got up and looked toward the Campbells' bedroom. Their light was on. I seemed to see a lot of smoke in the room. After a while the children came out, frightened, and screaming. I heard the kitchen door slam. I turned on my light."

"And then?" Rusty said.

"*Fué terible!*" Maria cried powerfully into the warm courtroom. ("It was terrible!")

"What did the boys say?"

"I can answer?"

"Yes, you can answer."

This was an example of *res gestae,* the thing speaks—an exception to the hearsay rule. *Res gestae* is defined in the law as an "unthinking, unplanned utterance made in the heat of the moment, where the likelihood of it being untrue is remote."

" '*Mia, Mia . . . open the door! Our parents are dead!*' "

Rusty asked softly, "And then?"

"They cried out, 'Our parents were killed by gunshots by some bad men!' Excuse me"—Maria quickly corrected her remembrance, which had instantly electrified those of us who knew of Wickie Weinstein's undefined existence in the drama—" '*one* bad man.' "

She went on: " 'They've killed our parents! They're full of blood!' I opened the door . . . "

Maria began to sob and shake, then looked up at Rusty and the jury. "Excuse me . . . I can't hold myself back . . . "

Rusty's milking it for every tear he can, Allen Isbell thought, and you couldn't blame him. The defense attorney rose slightly from his chair and said, "Perhaps, Your Honor, this is a good time for a break."

The court agreed. Body odor hung like a noxious cloud under the fluorescent lights. Most people fled the courtroom to breathe the cooler air of the corridors. Allen kept grinding his teeth.

But after the break Maria picked right up where she had left off.

"The boys said, 'Our parents had a lot of blood on their breasts!' Michael spoke in English. Matthew spoke in Spanish. '*Papa, Mama—muerto!*' ('Dead!') He said it many times! He was hitting the door, pulling on the screen! He was frightened! I opened the door quickly and drew them into my arms. Matthew wanted an ambulance, but Michael said, 'No, they're dead! *Police, police!*' I held them, changed their clothes, gave them water and sugar. They had made peepee in their pajamas.

When they were calmed down, I told them to call Señor Campbell's brother . . . "

Maria then recounted what happened after J. W. and his wife Brucene arrived. At first, under Rusty's questioning, she didn't recall any Spanish-speaking detective or police officer talking to her. Then she remembered, and also remembered making some kind of statement down at Police Headquarters. In Spanish? She wasn't sure. That was after the burial.

"Over the last years," Rusty asked, "how did Mr. Campbell get on with Cindy?"

"Very well," Maria said.

"Were you present at any arguments between Mr. Campbell and Cindy?"

"No, I never saw any problems."

"How did her father treat Cindy?"

"Very well."

"How did her mother, Mrs. Campbell, treat Cindy?"

"Very well."

"Do you see Cindy in the courtroom, Maria?"

"Yes."

"Would you point her out?"

"Objection!" Allen scrambled quickly to his feet, beating Maria to it; she was eagerly on the rise. "We're perfectly willing to stipulate that she knows Cindy, and that Cindy's sitting right here next to me in the courtroom. There's no necessity whatever for the witness to point a finger."

The judge sustained the objection, seemingly robbing Maria and Rusty of the dramatic moment; but as we were soon to see, it was merely a postponement.

"Pass the witness," Rusty said.

Now came the turn of the defense, and Maria hunched down into the witness chair.

Counsel was called to the bench. It was 4:40 P.M. on a Friday, and the air had grown seriously offensive to the nostrils. After a brief discussion the judge struck his fist on the desk and adjourned the court until 10 A.M. on Monday, when, it was hoped, the air conditioning would be working again.

Allen Isbell lived in a spacious brick house on Galveston island, fifty miles away; he kept a comfortable *pied-à-terre* on Main Street near downtown Houston. He went home only on weekends. In the early morning he tried to run five miles at the indoor Houston YMCA track. He did his best thinking then, he said. Randy McDonald ran, too, but he thought mostly about how he could have won cases that he had lost.

During the Cindy Ray trial, which he characterized as "the most intense in which I've ever been involved," Allen gave up his weekends at home. His co-minister back in Galveston filled in for him at the pulpit on Sunday mornings while Allen went to church in Houston at the Pecan Park Church of Christ. His wife, Mikey, drove up to the city to observe several days of testimony, and his parents came down from their home in Fort Worth. Neither Mikey nor the elder Isbells had ever seen Allen in trial. Mikey had been a schoolteacher, only recently retired and now devoting her energy to the renovation of their home a mile from the Galveston sea wall; she was turning part of it into a pension called Michael's Bed & Breakfast. She had always been the organizer and mechanic of the family. If the lawnmower broke, she fixed it. Allen, brawny in his youth, did the muscle work, the mowing and raking.

On Sunday afternoon, an oppressively hot day, while most of Houston either rested or sat in front of their TVs watching the hometown Rockets get whipped by the Boston Celtics in the NBA championship, Allen drove out to see Rick Brass in Spring, a suburb north of Houston Intercontinental Airport. Rick lived there with his wife, Leslie, and his collection of guns and Americana.

Randy McDonald came with his wife, Jill, a civil lawyer born and brought up in Setauket on Long Island. As Leslie Brass opened the front door, Randy and Jill glanced down, then stopped short, for a plastic surgical glove lay at their feet on the carpet. They began to laugh. Rick said solemnly, "Cindy sent it over so we wouldn't forget about her."

After Allen arrived, Rick opened some bottles of strawberry beer and Leslie began to barbecue steaks. The lawyers settled down to plot the tactics and strategy for the upcoming witnesses.

They were in a duel with Rusty Hardin, and he was the champion. They realized that the fate of their client might depend not so much on the facts, the truth, but on which of the lawyers in the courtroom was the more clever.

Tactics was a relatively simple matter. By whatever means available, the defense had to attack the credibility of the state's witnesses. Randy McDonald would do the honors with Maria, and also handle Gwen Sampson. Allen would do the critical cross-examination of David West.

Strategy was a knottier problem. Defensive strategy had to give the jury an alternative theory to guilt: a theory to inspect, to grasp, and, finally, to *believe*.

David West, the accomplice-witness, was going to say, "I killed Cindy's parents. Cindy helped me do it." Gwen Sampson, the corroborating witness, would add, "Cindy told me later that she did it." And Rusty Hardin was going to conclude, "Therefore, under the law, she is guilty." What was the defense going to offer as the alternative theory?

They had two broad choices. David forced Cindy to aid him—he was the evil "Salino" in her tale to Gwen Sampson. Afterward he said: "If you tell, or don't alibi me, I'll kill you."

Or: Cindy wasn't there at all. David killed the Campbells on his own initiative, to avenge the sexual abuse at the hands of her father and her mother's refusal to put a stop to it, and to free her from their malignant influence. Then, just as in the first theory: "If you tell, or don't alibi me, I'll kill you." Did David have an accomplice? Who else but the owner of the murder weapon? His paramilitary pal, Wickie Weinstein. To that end, Paul Whitfield's testimony became vital. The irony, of course, was that whereas in David's aborted trial Paul's statements would have aided the state in a conviction, they now reversed their import and aided the defendant's quest for an acquittal.

But in the second line of defense, if Cindy *hadn't* been there, why had she told Gwen Sampson that she *had*?

That Sunday the three lawyers pondered, but they had been pondering since early March and still hadn't made a choice between the two alternatives. Cindy had told them, "I had nothing to do with it. David is lying." Was that true? They didn't know. Would the jury believe it? They didn't know that, either.

The lawyers debated into the evening. Their heads began to pound.

Finally a weary Allen Isbell said, "I think, whether we like it or not, we have to go with the second defense—she wasn't there. It's complex, it's going to be more difficult for the jury to swallow, *but that's what our client says is true*." He sighed. "And if all goes well, we've got the good doctor to back it up."

He was not referring to a physician but to Dr. Rob Owens, a former staff psychologist for the Texas Department of Corrections who now had his own private counseling service in Houston.

In late May Allen and Randy had attended the monthly luncheon of the Harris County Criminal Defense Lawyers Association, where Dr. Owens that day had lectured on his work in predicting recurrent violent behavior. Randy in particular had been impressed and said to Allen, "I have an idea. This psychiatrist could be an expert witness for us."

"About what?" Allen asked, puzzled.

"Let's ask *him*."

Randy contacted Dr. Owens and explained the problem at length. "How can we use your expertise, Doctor?"

Dr. Owens thought it over and came up with an interesting idea.

"Perhaps I could sit in on the trial and observe Mr. West," he said, "and develop a psychological profile, and come to certain conclusions about what a person of his specific psychological profile could or couldn't do ... and perhaps there might be some discrepancies between my analysis and his sworn testimony."

"You mean you could prove he was lying."

"Not prove it, but shed some significant doubt. If indeed he *is*, in my opinion, lying."

Randy reported to Allen, who said, "Sure, let's try it." They went to Judge Azios and asked permission for Dr. Owens, whom they might later call as an expert witness, to attend that part of the trial where David West testified. The judge agreed. Allen then asked Cindy if she would let Dr. Owens interview her. Cindy refused. Each time Allen or Rick asked her, her eyes blazed and her voice deepened to a witchlike rasp. "If you think there's something psychotic about me," she barked, "you shouldn't be representing me. I've told you nothing but the truth!"

"I'm hoping," Allen said now, at the Sunday meeting, "that Dr. Owens will be able to say that David's the kind of nut who would have to lie and implicate Cindy in order to save his cracked sense of honor. If so, Owens will be our key witness. Otherwise, with the 'duress' defense, we haven't got a single witness of our own—we just have to argue from what *their* witnesses say. And that's weak. So let's do it Cindy's way, and use Owens as a cleanup hitter. For now, she was not there on the night of the murders. If we see we're getting in trouble . . . we'll rethink it."

26

Over the weekend violent rain struck Houston and tornadoes ripped through outlying parts of Harris County. Thunderheads with anvil tops crowded the horizon all day, and lightning cut the darkling air all Saturday night. The skies were ominously chocolate brown all of Sunday, even after the rains drifted westward toward New Mexico.

Maria Bravo Gonzalez grimly busied herself doing the family laundry that she would normally have done on Thursday, the day she had waited outside the courtroom to testify, and Friday, the day she had in fact taken the stand. On Saturday afternoon when she was paid by Señora Traylor, Maria expressed surprise that she hadn't been docked two days' pay for her time in court. Tears came to her eyes when Martha Ann Traylor told her that wouldn't happen.

The tears and the rain dried by Monday morning, and at 10:30 A.M., before a packed house—for all Houston was fascinated by this trial and awaiting its outcome—a stony-faced Maria thumped down into the witness chair, prepared to face her own auto-da-fé of ordeal by cross-examination. She was positive that the Inquisition had come to Texas.

Randy McDonald rose slightly in his chair, smiling with the optimism of youth. "How are you this morning, Señora?" he said in his most soothing voice.

"Muy bien," Maria muttered. She wasn't fooled—he was her Torquemada.

"What would be the proper way to address you, Señora? I'm not familiar with Spanish names. Would it be Señora Bravo? Señora Gonzalez? Or should I say Señora Bravo de Gonzalez?"

"Gonzalez or Bravo, it's the same." *(You're out to get me, so what's the difference?)*

She refused to look at Randy at any time during cross-examination. There was nothing he could do to catch her eye. He was her enemy, that was that. He would try to trick her and make a fool of her. She stared straight ahead in the general direction of Rusty Hardin, praying to absorb some of his strength across the fifteen feet of humid, unmoving courtroom air that separated them.

Over the weekend, the air conditioning had not been fixed.

"Prior to Friday, the day you testified on direct examination, Señora Bravo, you talked to Mr. Hardin, did you not?"

Maria, in a panic, asked, "Who is this Mr. Hardin?"

Randy had to show her who Mr. Hardin was.

"Oh. Him. Yes, I talked to him."

About this time the interpreter cleared her throat a few times, and Rusty stepped quickly out of the courtroom, reentering with a glass of cold water. He gave it to Ms. Hernandez. Members of the jury nodded approvingly. Nice of Rusty.

Randy McDonald asked Maria, "Did you talk to Mr. Hardin, the assistant district attorney, on more than one occasion before you testified? And did you talk to Mr. Hardin about the same things you're testifying about?"

Looking gloomier by the minute, Maria nodded.

The judge said, "The court reporter doesn't have a 'nod' button, Mrs. Bravo. Please answer yes or no."

So he was against her, too. He had sold out to the gringos.

Maria grunted, "Yes."

Randy then refreshed her memory regarding her written statement to Sgt. Mosqueda, the police interpreter, at HPD Homicide on Tuesday, June 22, 1982. The defense was heading toward several contradictions:

299

in her testimony Friday to the jury Maria had said she'd suddenly come down the stairs from her apartment and caught Cindy in the act of checking all the windows; whereas in her sworn statement to Sgt. Mosqueda, only three days after the murders, she had told a more complex tale of hearing a car enter the driveway, a car that she identified as belonging to David West, and then, when she emerged to investigate: "I saw Cindy along the side of the house by the window of the boys' room. . . . The next morning, Wednesday, I walked around the house and I saw that the window of the boys' room was left wide open. This was when I came to realize that Cindy was going to get into the window that night, but I saw her."

Now, in court, Randy quoted her sworn recollections of June 22, 1982. He noted that there was no mention in her statement that Cindy had been "checking" or even touching any of the windows.

Statement? What statement? Maria told Randy that she remembered going down to Homicide with the Campbell sisters, but she'd had a headache that day. She had been nervous. She wasn't aware that this man Mosqueda had typed out anything in English and that she had signed it.

Patiently, Randy produced the four-page typed document with her signature at the bottom of every page. But she still didn't remember Mosqueda reading it to her, not in Spanish and certainly not in English translation. No, she hadn't sworn to anything.

Randy showed her the signatures a second time.

"So much time has passed," Maria said, sighing, "that I can't remember so many things."

Satisfied with that admission, Randy came about on another tack. Would it have been *physically possible* for Maria to have seen Cindy tampering with the windows of the den? He showed her the state's carefully prepared scale diagram of the house and grounds. It was clear right away that if she had been standing on the staircase leading to her apartment above the garage—which is what she had testified to on Friday—the angle of sight did not allow her to see what she said she had seen. Randy decided to let the jury—the group of thirteen was very attentive at this stage of the proceedings—draw its own conclusions. It was obvious, wasn't it, that Maria was confused and that she wanted to help the prosecution far more than she wanted (or was able) to speak the truth?

Randy then got out his 12-gauge and began peppering the witness with random buckshot. He kept quoting from her sworn statement to Mosqueda, and Maria kept replying, "No, I didn't say that." Then he would show her the phrases and her signature. Maria mopped her forehead with her handkerchief.

Finally: "Did you tell the detective that the boys had a habit of unlocking the windows at times?"

"Only theirs."

"And on the night of the murder, you said, you were awakened by gunshots?"

She grunted, "Yes."

"But didn't you tell Sgt. Mosqueda: 'Around 3:15 I heard a loud noise. A window slamming'?"

"Before the shooting, yes."

"And then you saw the smoke in the room?" (That would have been impossible, for the thick yellow curtains were drawn.)

"It seems to me that it was smoke," Maria said miserably. "I was so scared."

Randy hammered on, getting her to describe which way the door opened into the Campbells' bedroom, and where the light switch was on the wall—"So that if the door was shut, all I or anyone would have to do is open it and flip on the switch if I wanted light? Like this?" In front of the jury box, Randy demonstrated. The import was that David West could have done the same thing, flicking the light switch with his left hand and holding the .45 in his right hand. He didn't need a helper.

Maria said that was so.

"Did you tell Sgt. Mosqueda"—Randy bent his gaze to the statement, so that Maria groaned audibly—"that 'Cindy was a girl who respected her parents'?"

"Yes," Maria said, "but—"

"Pass the witness," Randy said.

Now began that legal back-and-forthing which is so confusing to the layman who has only seen courtroom battles on TV or read about them in Agatha Christie novels. Rusty had taken Maria on what was called direct examination (she was "his" witness), and Randy had subjected her to cross-examination. The rules of evidence were such that, with some exceptions, cross was barred from delving into areas of testimony that had not been brought up on direct. But following cross, the attorney who had "sponsored" the witness (in this instance, Rusty) was allowed a *re*direct examination, to clarify and explain any new areas conjured up by cross. And if by chance or design some additional virgin territory was invaded in redirect, a *re*cross was allowed in that area, and possibly even in adjacent areas if the judge adopted an attitude of "in-the-interest-of-truth-let's-find-out-everything-we-possibly-can." And then, again, if by chance or design . . . and so forth, until a final exultant "pass the witness" and a merciful "no further questions" had been uttered, and the battered, mentally raped witness was excused and allowed to stagger homeward.

The process made for some interesting tactics. Lawyers often say of opposing counsel, "They *opened the door,* Your Honor, to an area of testimony hitherto closed. Now we're entitled to step inside and explore what's in there."

So lawyers tread carefully when they're not sure what lies around the corner, and don't ask some questions to which they would very much like answers, for fear of opening up the wrong door. And some lawyers adroitly lure the opposition to place their fumbling hands on forbidden doorknobs and give powerful shoves.

After lunch, Rusty took Maria on redirect. He began by establishing their relationship, indicating to the jury that he hadn't been patronizing. "Do you mind me calling you Maria?"

"No, Señor." *(Thank God you're back.)*

"Do you recall Mr. McDonald asking you about your signing and swearing to the statement you gave to the police on June 22, 1982?"

"I don't know who is Mr. McDonald." Maria lost more brownie points; clearly she possessed a selective memory.

"Mr. McDonald is the man with the power-red tie over there," Rusty said, waving his hand toward the defense table.*

Rusty continued by challenging the verity of Maria's 1982 statement to Sgt. Mosqueda, and Randy objected on the grounds that Rusty was trying to impeach his own witness—another forensic no-no. Sustained. But Rusty, after he'd said his customary "Thank you," blithely continued on the same tack, trying to get Maria to tell the jury that when she'd dictated the statement to Mosqueda she was upset and frightened. Again Randy objected. Judge Azios, perhaps in the interest of fairness—"one for you, and one for *you*"—told him to go ahead.

Maria to Sgt. Mosqueda: "[A few days before the murders] Mrs. Campbell said she had many problems with Cindy and that Cindy wanted to move back. Mr. Campbell said that if Cindy moved back, he would move out. And I said I would move out, too. But Mrs. Campbell said, 'Don't go, Maria, because you and my husband mean more to me than Cindy, because Cindy was trouble.'"

Rusty asked Maria, "Did you go anywhere with Mrs. Campbell on the last day of her life?"

"Yes, to the stores in Memorial. We came back around nine. Señora

---

* Rusty had worn a red tie the day before, and Maureen Earl, an English screenwriter attending the trial, had told him banteringly that the color red was a psychological indication of power, used conspicuously now in Los Angeles for taking key meetings.

Campbell grabbed my arm and wanted me to stay in the house with her. I went to my apartment, to bed."

"Did you see Mr. and Mrs. Campbell again?"

"I never saw them alive again. . . . "

"Pass the witness."

"No further questions," Randy said. He didn't see what more he had to gain.

Maria began to weep.

"You are excused, Señora Bravo," Judge Azios said, "and thank you. You can leave the courtroom, or you can stay as a spectator, whatever you wish."

Rusty escorted the unhappy woman from the witness chair, diagonally across the front of the courtroom, toward the back aisle that would lead to the door and the comforting arms of her employer, Martha Ann Traylor, who had brought Maria there and was waiting to take her home. Rusty, five feet nine inches tall, dwarfed Maria; she was nearly a foot shorter than he, although quite a bit thicker, and probably outweighed him. A turtlelike waddler, she rocked from side to side as she moved. Her white handkerchief was pressed to her face to stifle her sobs.

The exit route passed inexorably behind the counsel table, where the defendant sat squeezed between Allen Isbell and Rick Brass. In the malodorous courtroom Cindy had been impassive throughout Maria's testimony, sometimes leaning pensively on her left fist, sometimes sitting glumly with folded arms. Her back was to Maria now. She didn't turn around.

Still sobbing into her damp handkerchief, Maria reached Cindy. Looking down, she halted briefly . . . Rusty seemed to loosen his grip. . . .

Maria lowered her hands. Loudly and clearly, she cried in Spanish, *"Qué mala eres, Cindy!"*

It meant, *"How bad you are, Cindy!"*

In the hubbub Rusty hurried Maria into the grasp of Martha Ann Traylor and out of the courtroom. Then he hurried back. Allen Isbell had sprung to his feet, vigorously complaining. Reporters and spectators were turning, talking, jostling—"What'd she say? Do you understand Spanish? Did you hear her?"

Judge Azios pounded his desk. "Members of the jury, I didn't hear what she said. If you did, you are not to consider it! If you speak Spanish, and you understood, don't tell the others! Is that clear?"

Declaring a Brenda-break, he rushed from the bench toward the hallway backstage. Just between the holding cell and the prisoners' wooden benches, the agitated lawyers caught up to him. Allen Isbell was already murmuring, *"Mistrial,"* when Judge Azios turned angrily—on Rusty, not on Allen.

"She did it intentionally," he fumed.

"You heard her?" Rusty asked. He was sure the judge had said exactly the opposite to the jury.

"Yes, I heard her! She was acting!"

I had squeezed in among the lawyers. "You believe that, Judge?"

"Fuckin' A," His Honor snapped.

"No!" Blotches of color flew to Rusty's cheeks. He loved Maria and was going to defend her no matter what. "She's a human being! She's been a basket case for three days!"

"That sonofabitch!" Jaw to jaw now with the prosecutor, the judge heatedly said: "She passed that way behind Cindy four or five times before this! She managed to restrain herself all those times, didn't she? Why didn't she do it one *more* time?"

Allen Isbell blandly repeated, "I'm going to have to move for a mistrial."

"Well, wait a minute," Judge Azios said, regaining his composure. "Let's back off and be calm. Let's see what we can do."

In court once more, Allen stood and asked permission to query the jurors as to what they had heard and understood of Maria's outburst.

"State has no objection!" Rusty thundered.

Once again in control of his courtroom, Judge Azios sent a written note to the jury room, asking for the names of those who understood spoken Spanish. When the jury's note came back via the bailiff, the judge groaned a loud "Oaoaoagh!" and theatrically put his head in his hands. No less than seven jurors had signed their names to the list.

One at a time those seven jurors were led in and took the witness stand, under oath. The first, Lydia Tamez, spoke Spanish fluently; her parents had been born in Mexico and it had been her language as a child growing up in Houston. "I heard some of it," she said. "I thought I heard her say, *'Muy mal'*—very bad."

Three other jurors heard much the same thing. Judge Azios, as each recounted his or her version, asked if what they had heard or observed would in any way affect their verdict, and each replied, "No." With the utmost gravity he instructed them to disregard any outbursts and reminded them all that "your verdict must be based on the law I give to you, and the evidence."

Nevertheless, when the last juror left the courtroom, Allen Isbell rose and formally claimed that the outburst of the witness was too much to overcome, even with the court's well-meaning instructions. He moved for a mistrial.

"Motion denied," the judge said to Allen, who was pleased at the outcome, since he now had possible grounds for reversible error in the event of a guilty verdict.*

From midafternoon of that day until 4 P.M. the following day, Tuesday, the jury heard testimony from three of the four Homicide sergeants who had investigated the murders on Memorial Drive. Carl Kent—brawny, Brobdingnagian, his mustache freshly shaven, in a brown tweed sport jacket—was crisply authoritative, a master of cop jargon.

"Sgt. St. John and I got the assignment at zero-four-thirty-five hours on 19 June 1982. We arrived at 8901 Memorial at zero-four-fifty-five hours. The complainants were upstairs in their bed . . ."

Yes, there was a single surgical glove lying on the carpet just inside the front door.

After talking to the maid, Kent and St. John had gone hunting for Cindy Ray. "We drove to 2301 Kingston. We wound up in apartment number four, but we didn't find her there."

"That was Cynthia Campbell Ray's apartment?" Rusty asked, casually.

"Yes, sir."

"What was it like? Can you describe it?"

"It was—"

Not fooled for a minute by Rusty's lazy tone, Allen leaped up to object. It was irrevelant, beyond the scope of the testimony. This was a major objection, and one he intended to fight for and repeat, for he dreaded the impression that a description of Cindy's physical life style would make on the jury, all of whom—particularly the younger professional women, like Tamez, Beagle, McBunch, and Kloss—seemed fastidious and eminently respectable. He imagined their kitchen surfaces ashine with Fantastik, their hall mirrors spotless with Windex, their toilets gleaming with Tidy-Bowl. Allen had listened to several graphic descriptions of Cindy's apartment. How would the jury deal with a woman who lived in a rat's nest with dried urine all over the floor?

"Objection sustained."

---

* "Reversible error," as opposed to "harmless error," is a judicial error of judgment arising during trial, of such serious significance that it mandates the reversal of a guilty verdict by an appellate court. Since no one can be tried twice for the same crime, only the defense can claim reversible error.

Allen would have argued on appeal that the judge's failure to declare a mistrial because of Maria's outburst was reversible error.

Relieved, Allen sank down. Rusty passed the witness to the defense.

Kent, in direct, had been asked questions about his interview of Robert Harris, Jim Campbell's office partner, and had said, "I asked Mr. Harris about Mr. Campbell's problems, and he volunteered information." In cross-examination Allen now tried to find out what Harris had told Kent about "Mr. Campbell's problems."

"Wow!" Rusty jumped up, sputtering. "That's hearsay and he knows it!" He went on to explain to the jury what hearsay was.

The first of many arguments began: Rusty demanded it be continued up at the bench, where he vigorously objected to the hearsay, and Allen, loudly and with equal fervor, said, "He makes all the speeches in front of the jury, but when I want to give my view of a legal issue, he wants to come up to the bench and be quiet about it. I resent that. I'll be happy if he'll cut out his sidebar remarks and his antics."

By the end of the day, as with Rusty and Gene Nettles, prosecutor and defense attorney were barely on speaking terms. Allen understood how good Rusty was, how dedicated and disarming and intimidating, and if it required open hostilities to keep him in check, so be it. Allen was as determined as Rusty to win this case and see justice done.

Sgt. Paul Motard came next. He recalled that on the Sunday morning after the murders, Cindy was shaking, and smoking a lot. On June 22 Motard and Gil Schultz babysat Michael and Matthew for three hours while the rest of the family attended the funeral. "The boys were jitterbugging around," Motard testified. "They couldn't stay on one subject."

After the funeral the four Campbell sisters and David drove down to Police Headquarters. No one had asked David to come. Motard was surprised to see him there.

"We immediately talked to Cynthia Ray. She was calm, quiet, soft-spoken, only talked when spoken to." Motard gave a curious weight to those phrases, as if there was something mighty suspicious in her attitude. "Her statement was freely given—if she hadn't given it, we would have let her go. We gave her warnings. We wanted her to know she was a suspect."

"How did you take the statement from her?"

"I typed. She sat on the opposite side of the desk."

"How did she appear?"

"Calm," Motard said. "Deadpan, like today"—he nodded across the steamy courtroom at the immovable Cindy—"with maybe, at one point, a tear in her eye. She wasn't angry a bit, or indignant. Just said, 'Okay.'"

Again there was a clear implication in Motard's tone that such behavior was only one short step away from a full confession of capital murder.

Cindy's alibi statement was submitted as state's exhibit #42. Standing directly in front of the jury, Rusty read to them aloud. *"I thanked my mother, told her that I loved her . . . David and I went on home and slept for a while and we got up around 3:30 or 4 A.M., I think."* Rusty read David's statement to the jury, too. *"When we got up, it was somewhere after 3 A.M. It was around 3:30 A.M. when we got to the party."*

On June 25, Motard related, he and Gil Schultz paid a visit to David West's house on Vermont, looking for Cindy Ray. After that, Motard said, despite certain statements made to Homicide in October 1982 by a woman named Gwen Sampson, they never felt they had enough evidence to arrest Cynthia Ray or David West. Not until Kim Paris came along.

Motard then detailed, from HPD's point of view, the events of those two nights in February when Kim had extracted the confession from David. Before the second night's taping began, Motard related, he made a suggestion to Kim that she tell David "Cindy had already received her portion of the estate and was denying him his fair share." The purpose was "to incense David to the point that he would get Cindy to admit that she was a part of it."

But it didn't work. And after David was arrested they wanted Kim to call Cindy and tell her that he "needed the money that Cindy had promised him from the inheritance." No answer to the phone call. They grew nervous and sent Sgt. Kent to arrest her.

During lunch the semi-retired engineer, Duval West, broke his long silence about his son's role in the Campbell murders. He requested a meeting with the press corps.

By the bank of elevators, under the harsh lights of the TV cameras, with pens flying across notepads, Duval protested the implications of Sgt. Motard's testimony. "All that business of 'denying David his fair share,' and needing 'the money that Cindy had promised him from the inheritance'—that's nonsense. My son David pleaded guilty to murder" —he smiled a little, blinking harder than usual—"not capital murder, not murder for hire. Just murder. And Cindy's being tried for murder, not capital murder. There's a distinction, and I want to point it out."

It was a sad argument. The media knew, and Duval knew—and the media knew that he knew—that the only reason David had been convicted of "just murder" and hadn't been tried for capital murder was that he'd struck a bargain with the state in exchange for his testimony against Cindy.

None of the reporters challenged Duval. They respected his paternal needs. They did seize the chance to ask him a few more questions, but Duval declined to answer. He had said his piece and they'd get no more from him. They quoted him accurately in print, and that evening, on the five o'clock news, he had his brief moment in the descending sun as the loyal father of a murderer.

The cross-examination of Sgt. Motard was rapid, terse, and of far more significance than anyone would realize until much later. It opened a door that neither the defense nor the prosecution saw. There it was, swaying in the breeze, creaking and banging—and no one knew it! Had either of the lawyers swung it open and peered inside, the outcome of the trial might have been different.

Allen said, "You describe Cynthia Ray on June 20, 1982 as 'nervous, shaking a bit, and smoking a lot.' Now that's not unusual for someone whose parents had been murdered, is it?"

"No, sir."

"You describe Cindy on June 22, the day she gave the written statement to you, as 'quiet and soft-spoken.' People who go to funerals are often quiet and soft-spoken, isn't that so?"

"Not quite in the same way," Motard drawled.

"You called her 'deadpan.' But you don't know what's in her mind or emotions, do you?"

"No," Motard admitted.

"She might be all torn up inside, might she not?"

"It's possible," Motard said.

"Isn't it your experience, Sgt. Motard, that people handle grief differently, on the outside?"

The Homicide detective had to agree with that.

"Cynthia Ray told you voluntarily that she saw her mother at 10 P.M. Friday night, six hours before she was murdered, didn't she?"

"Yes."

"No one else could have told you that, right?"

"Possibly not."

"*Did* anyone else tell you about that?"

"No."

"So you might never have known about it but for that, isn't that so?"

"It's possible," Motard said stubbornly.

308

"You took statements from all the Campbell sisters? And you told Cindy that there were many suspects?"

"Sgt. Schultz did."

"If you say to a citizen that 'you're a suspect,' what is the appropriate reaction? Should they act nervous or calm?"

Motard said, "I think an innocent person, a falsely accused person, would be indignant. They normally do that."

Allen then once again brought up the subject of James Campbell's problems with business associates and asked Motard what he knew about them. Once again Rusty objected: "I remain deferentially dumbfounded at this continued request for hearsay information!"

The judge overruled this flash of rhetoric.

"Let's jump ahead to Kim Paris," Allen said. "Didn't she promise David West love and marriage and three kids if he'd confess that he and Cynthia Campbell Ray murdered her parents?"

"Objection! Hearsay!"

"Sustained!"

"Pass the witness."

The veteran Gil Schultz came next. Schultz kept notes in his lap and cleverly looked at them from time to time without the jury noticing. Rusty moved him rapidly to February 1985 and the intrusion into Sgt. Schultz's life of Kim Paris. During the last moments of Motard's cross-examination Rusty had sniffed out an interesting possibility. Allen Isbell, in asking Motard what Kim had promised David West in return for a confession, had begun to open the door to admission of the February 20–21 tapes. Rusty would have been delighted to get them into evidence; he had begun the trial thinking there was no way. Now it occurred to him that in time he might bait a trap, might lead Isbell to the door and see if the defense attorney could resist opening it.

"What was your first opinion of Kim Paris?"

"That she was a squirrely girl," Schultz said. "I was very skeptical."

"How did you treat Ms. Paris?"

"Very harshly," Schultz admitted, hanging his head and coloring a little so that those of us who had followed the case since its inception felt a distinct sense of *déjà vu*. It was not an illusion. Rusty was replaying his little game during the pretrial testimony at the David West trial.

"Did you meet her again on February 19, the evening you all decided to try to tape David West?"

"Yes, and I was still skeptical."

309

"Did twenty-four-year veteran Police Officer Gil Schultz think anything was going to come out of that?"

"Just lack of sleep," Schultz said wryly.

Kim took off in the car with David, he recounted. They lost her. She was driving around in circles. Coming along Westheimer, Kim made a sudden lefthand turn, an illegal turn to boot. "All this," said Schultz, "reinforced my skepticism."

That drew a laugh.

"Did Sgt. Gil Schultz ever eat crow?" Rusty asked, grinning.

The jury grinned, too. They all knew this tale from current Houston folklore. They were like children listening to an oft-repeated and much-loved bedtime story. It didn't matter that they knew how it turned out.

"Yes, sir, I'm afraid I did," Schultz said manfully.

"Oh, by the way," said Rusty—and you knew from the casual "by the way" that something important was coming round the bend—"yesterday, at my request, did you revisit 8901 Memorial?"

"Yes, sir, I did."

"At my request, did you go to any place out there on the premises to check the view?"

"Yes, sir, I went to the garage apartment located at the rear of the house." To the maid's quarters, and he looked from there to the windows of the house below. He couldn't see the den window that was opened on the night of the murders, but he could see *one* of the bedroom windows Maria had claimed Cindy had been fooling with a week before the murders. His testimony was oddly imprecise and inconclusive, but he managed to give the impression that Maria could have seen what she claimed to see.

Rusty passed the witness. Allen Isbell wasted no time. During the lunch break Rick Brass had driven to 8901 Memorial to videotape the premises ravaged by the weekend storm and draw some lines of sight. He came back with an interesting report.

The softspoken Church of Christ minister showed once again that he had some sharp laic teeth. "Yesterday, Sgt. Schultz, when you visited 8901 Memorial, were you aware that someone had gone out there and cut the foliage?"

"Excuse me!" Rusty cried. "I'm going to have to object to that question until there's some evidence of it!"

Undaunted, Allen shifted his ground slightly. "Did you *see* that the trees and shrubbery had been cut?"

"No, sir."

"No limbs were cut?"

"I didn't see any."

310

"Sgt. Schultz, we're talking about *yesterday*, not 1982. Didn't you see it? Wasn't it obvious?"

"No, I didn't observe the limbs of trees." Schultz's tone bordered on surly.

Let the jury wonder why, Allen thought. He was building his closing argument against Maria's claim that she had seen Cindy checking the windows.

"From what Sgt. Motard testified," Allen said, "am I correct in thinking that the February 21, 1985 story given to the media of David West's arrest—which many thought was a police goof-up—was in fact part of a plan?"

"Yes," Schultz said.

"It was leaked deliberately to radio and television?"

"That's correct."

"And it was for Cynthia Campbell Ray's benefit?"

"Correct."

"Weren't you afraid she'd split for Tijuana when she heard of his arrest?"

Schultz saw the trap, would like to have swerved around it, but it was too late. "It happens," he mumbled.

"But she didn't, did she?" Allen concluded exultantly.

"No."

Schultz was then excused. It was a nice moment for the defense—a minor high point. Something for the jury to chew on. Allen felt a small surge of optimism. It didn't last long. Without even a break, at 4:15 P.M., even though it was late in the day, Rusty elected to bring his star out of the dressing room. It was time to fulfill the December bargain.

"The state calls David Duval West."

27

Center stage at last. He had grown his beard, shaping it so that the round white baby jowls and soft chin didn't show. Long, well-groomed, healthy-looking brown hair shone, and now that he was a state's witness he had been allowed to acquire a little color in his face. Navy blue blazer, off-white shirt, boldly striped tie: what the well-dressed confessed murderer rarely wears. Challenge tends to bring out the best of a man's style.

Center stage, the fluorescent lights glaring down on him. No room to glide into protecting shadow. Shoulders back, chest out, belly in.

We're looking for a few good men. . . .

Jim Leitner, still David's lawyer and now his mentor in Christ, said to me later, "I know you think David reveled in it. You really don't understand him. He was ashamed of what he'd done. It was a show, yes . . . but not one of bravado and charm. From start to finish it was a gut-level effort, and it tore him apart inside. Not only what Allen Isbell did to him, but what Rusty made him do. I'm telling you—believe me—he *hated* it."

But in the end I came to disbelieve that. Because in the end I learned something that Leitner didn't know.

"How old are you, David?" Rusty asked.

"Thirty."

"Where are you presently living?"

"Harris County Jail." (Accompanied by the first tentative curl of the mouth into a self-deprecating smile.)

"Where'd you grow up?"

"Right here in Houston. In Montrose. On Kipling, where my parents still live."

"Are either of your parents here today, David?"

"Yes, my father is in the courtroom." David pointed toward the third row. A few heads turned. Did Duval West behind his bottlelike glasses blink a few extra times to acknowledge his public introduction? There was always that fixed smile on Duval's face . . . that impression of ethical vacuity.

Montrose Elementary School—Lanier Junior High—Lincoln High. Familiar names to jurors and spectators. A local boy: everyone's son. Marine Corps at the age of seventeen, out at twenty-one, then to Europe for the grand tour—home, and worked odd jobs for a while—matriculated at St. Thomas in 1979: "I have sixty-five hours toward a college degree."

"Where were you living then?"

"At 1409 Vermont."

"Who owned the house?"

"The bank and I." The second scant smile, a hair bolder than the first.

312

Two or three of the jurors timidly smiled back, feeling an unwanted kinship with this murderer, for they also shared ownership of their homes with the bank.

"And while you were there at St. Thomas, studying, did you meet a young woman named Jamie Campbell?"

Jamie was seventeen then, David said, and he was twenty-two. Just friends. He visited her a few times in her parents' home in Memorial. He didn't know then that she had a sister named Cindy. He didn't meet Cindy until one day in the fall of 1980, with Jamie, he walked into Crooker Center, the student union building on the campus of St. Thomas in the old downtown residential area of Houston. Cindy, who had just entered the university as an art student, was sitting in the cafeteria. She was at a table where David usually met his friends. He noticed her right away.

"Sure I know her," Jamie said. "That's my sister."

With some reluctance, it seemed to David, Jamie introduced them.

Cindy struck him as a withdrawn, timid young woman. "She literally wouldn't look you in the eye," he told the jury. "She had long hair covering her face. She was all huddled over." He was somehow touched by her. The species needs to reproduce, and nature provides the stimuli and the knotting of the inner organs that we translate into the shimmering language of love. These preludes to mating are a matter of chemistry coupled with indefinable mystery. But they are recognizable.

"Will you show us, please, David, how she was huddled over?"

Show, don't tell. A basic dramatic principle. Rusty: what Hollywood calls the *auteur*. He was fighting to prove the credibility of a murderer. Not an easy task. But a worthwhile one, because only by succeeding could he do the right thing and achieve justice. In the witness chair, David hunched his shoulders together, crossed his arms protectively as high school girls do when their breasts begin to grow, and bent over into a sitting fetal position. "Like that."

"Was she overweight?"

"Less than now."

An innocent and respectful question; a polite answer. No one knew that it was the beginning of a chronicle of fluctuating poundage perhaps unique in forensic history. At a trial it's often difficult to see the broad vistas and serpentine trails that later, by whatever quirk of altered focus, will be memorable. By the end of this trial everyone in the courtroom, with a guffaw or just a cynical grin, would be able to quote often precise statistics on Cynthia Campbell Ray's weight at any given time from early adolescence through ripening womanhood. It became a running joke among the media. And yet it was another one of those concepts that by the end of the trial was to be of critical significance. But no one grasped that then.

She was living then with her parents, a refugee from a youthful marriage that had just collapsed. She was an artist, had studied at the Art Institute of Houston. She was good, David believed. And she had a talent for acting, too; she told him that one of her goals was to be an actress. After he got to know her well she often ad-libbed Shakespeare.

But in this early stage of friendship she was timid and shy. In that era he constantly tried to draw her out, even to the point of leaning over, spreading her hair, and saying, "Hello, is someone in there?" He demonstrated this on the witness stand, smiling more openly now at the jury, glad to recapture the moment because it was a tender one, deep-seated in memory, the fragile beginning of rapport that would lead to love, and from love to anger, and from anger to murder. And a few jurors smiled back. They knew the power of the onset of love. All had been there. Most seemed to have survived.

Gradually, as he got to know Cindy, she became friendly.

"When did you first see her alone, David, other than in groups of your friends?"

"Well," David said, trying to paint in a little background to the event, "it quickly became apparent to me that she and her sister Jamie didn't get along. I saw animosity demonstrated by Jamie—"

"Stop." Rusty interrupted firmly, like a movie director on a first take. There was no prepared script between him and the star witness. He hadn't coached David other than to go over the story in detail on several occasions and then, after the final debriefing, say, "Keep to the facts. Don't speculate. Just remember—your overriding obligation to me is to tell the truth."

He had a rock-hard belief that David had always told him the truth and would not veer from it at the trial. But there was pertinent truth and confusing truth, just as there were friendly facts and unfriendly facts. Rusty did not want to hear about conflict between the two youngest Campbell sisters: that would be confusing and unfriendly. He wanted only to hear the answers to his questions. Like any good lawyer, those answers were in his mind even as he asked the questions.

His voice hardened perceptibly; for the first time, with his star, he lazily cracked the whip.

"My question, David, was: 'When did you first see Cindy other than in groups?' "

"She and Jamie didn't get on," David said stubbornly—he was on the path toward absolution, determined to get it *his* way, and tell *his* truth —"and Jamie acted in a derogating manner to her." He hurried along, despite the fire and lightning spewing and crackling from Rusty's blue eyes. "I commented on it and Cindy said, 'Well, that's an old program. I never got along with my family.' Cindy didn't drive, and what had happened was that one day, Jamie, with no provocation, wouldn't give her a ride to school. It was sort of a Cinderella story. It was the rest of the family against her, she said."

Now Rusty didn't have much choice. Beyond a certain point, however annoyed he might be, he could not challenge or cudgel his own witness. He made the best of the mild betrayal, figuring that in the end he could make it work *for* him, like an unforeseen detour in the road that gives you a surprising view of where you're going. And at worst he could signal the judge that he wanted a break to go backstage and flay his witness alive.

"That's what *Cindy* told you."

"Yes," David said.

"When did she first tell you that?"

"A few months after I met her. Call it late 1980."

"And you had already met the family? What was your reaction to them?"

"My reaction . . . well, their general attitude was suspicious and defensive and . . . not at all normal. I got a feeling of"—David chose the word carefully—"shiftiness."

Rusty sighed. This skirted anarchy and bordered on insubordination. "You met them often?"

"Occasionally. Not often."

Rusty reluctantly backtracked. "Why do you say 'shifty'? What do you mean by that?"

"Well, they were just not your normal, average, straightforward—" Wondering how far to go, gazing into Rusty's obdurate, unamiable eyes, David hesitated. "There was a defensiveness," he concluded, lamely.

"A wariness? A caution? A skepticism?"

"Yes."

"And you translated that to be 'shifty'?"

"Well . . . yes."

Satisfied that he had momentarily repaired any damage to the Campbells' image, Rusty relaxed his expression and went on. What happened, he asked David, toward the end of 1980, after Cindy's claim that Jamie wouldn't give her a ride to school anymore?

"She was neglected," David said. "She was taking emotional flak from all sides. She painted a picture that was pretty bad. So I had this big house in Montrose, with a spare bedroom, and it was within walking distance of the school."

David offered her the room. No hidden clauses, no expectations on his part. Furthermore, he would help coach her into physical fitness. She knew nothing about nutrition or health or even makeup. He had the impression that in her midteens she had been slender and very attractive, but in recent years had fallen apart. A serious collapse. She had a terrible self-opinion and self-image. Never had been able to hold down a job, just couldn't handle it. David told her it was vital to take some positive steps: work on her appearance, her weight problem, and live in a way— as his guest in the ramshackle, easygoing house on Vermont, with a room all her own—that would allow her to study and go to school without the negative distractions of a bad family life.

At first she was skeptical. No strings attached, he promised, but that was hard for her to believe. Finally he convinced her by saying, "Look, Cindy . . . I don't like overweight women." That was true, he told the jury.

And she believed him and wasn't insulted. She appeared grateful for his candor, and of course for the offer of the room. In December of 1980 she moved in.

"My original intention was just to help her out," David said. "Sort of like picking up a stray dog."

He often glanced at the jury during his testimony, and he did so after saying that. He seemed to be hunting for impressions, reactions. He wanted to be liked, appreciated, *understood.* But a few jurors' eyes had turned slightly cool. David must have realized that "a stray dog" hadn't been a good choice of phrase. And if you factor the beginnings of love into the story, it was an inaccurate description, unless of course you were the kind of person who could only love a stray dog or the human equivalent. He wouldn't use that one again.

"I provided her with a place to stay. I coached her in physical fitness. I taught her how to watch calories, all about low grease intake, taught her to eat a lot of vegetables and drink a lot of fruit juice, take proper exercise . . . I myself was lifting weights, and I ran. I taught her about mental discipline, how you have to take yourself up by your own boot-straps. You have to feel good about yourself. I taught her that looking good and feeling good are interdependent—a very close-knit cause-and-effect relationship."

One or two jurors bobbed their heads up and down. That made sense. It was certainly better than how you'd treat a stray dog.

"So she began to lose weight," David said. "And she started grooming herself better."

"How much did she weigh when you met her?" Rusty asked.

"I seem to remember that she told me she was up around 180 pounds."

316

Rusty inquired as to how much she lost, in that second stage of their companionship, her residence at the house on Vermont, and David replied, "At the peak—six to eight months after we met—she weighed 127."

Gradually he began to see her—surely approaching 127 she was no longer in the dreaded category of *overweight*—as a sexually desirable woman. No longer just a protégé, or "subject," as he termed it. She was the frog princess, Cinderella unveiled, and she turned into woman and friend. She not only became more positive and outgoing, he said, but smarter. The brightness of intellect, the droll wit, had been there all along, but cowered unseen. By means of her physical metamorphosis she dissolved a mental block. She bloomed.

It was an attractive theory—body and mind intertwined, new bodily health giving rebirth to mental health and acuity—and David presented it from the witness stand with considerable zest and a forthrightness that he managed to couple with modesty. He didn't seem to be boasting. He was well-spoken; this was not the David of the tapes. He had some wit himself, if you gave him room. He could charm you. And slip past while you were trying to catch hold.

Would the jury be charmed? Were they thinking, "How could this pleasant, self-effacing and piquant young fellow be a *murderer?* Surely there's some mistake. If not a mistake, a tragedy. . . . " Or were they thinking, "He's sick. He's a rattlesnake in blue blazer and striped tie. It's all calculated for effect. I had better be on my guard!" Or were they confused by those alternatives, as so many others had been in the past?

" . . . Then we became romantically involved."

Rusty asked, "How else would you describe your relationship, David?"

After a pause, David responded quietly, "I was in love with her. I was totally committed."

"Who did you view as in charge of the relationship?"

"Oh, I was," David said. "No doubt of it."

Taking notes on his yellow legal pad, Allen Isbell was pleased to hear that sharp certainty. He underscored the words: *"No doubt of it."*

David drove her everywhere, to school and to work. He got her a job as receptionist in a company where he worked part-time at night as a security guard, but she lasted only one shift. She said that the supervisor made a pass at her. She quit, and so did David. He got them both jobs waiting table at the Lone Star Comedy Shop, a new Montrose restaurant. Business was slow, and two weeks later they were laid off.

"What did she tell you about her parents?"

Not much, at the beginning, other than that her father had clawed his way up from an impoverished background in rural Tennessee to a position of power and affluence in Texas. She loved him. She wasn't that fond of her mother but wouldn't say why. Her sisters had always mistreated her, laughed at her because she was fat. In early 1981, David said, the extent of Cindy's inhibitions, previous and still operative, began to dawn on him. Although at St. Thomas he was an art major, he had also taken several psychology courses; he was not by any means an expert in the field but nevertheless he considered himself to be knowledgeable and objective. He had traveled, he had lived a little. He was able to analyze. Cindy seemed to show what he thought of as "the classical signs of sexual abuse at an early age." Certainly he sensed there was something "latently wrong." She had flashed an abnormal fear of sex, he said, even when he was just her life-style mentor and health guru, long before he had approached her with the intent of carnal knowledge.

"She equated being a good girl with abstention from sex." She acted almost like a little girl. He smelled an early, unpleasant experience. He had no idea what it was or with whom.

But he said to Cindy, "Something must have happened to you."

At the defense table, Allen Isbell blinked a few times and resisted the urge to rub his already reddened eyes. He thought he knew where this was going, but it didn't seem possible. Rusty was no fool. He wouldn't dare.

"Did she always talk the same way?" Rusty asked.

No one in the jury box, and few people in the courtroom, understood what he meant by that question. But David understood it perfectly.

"No, she didn't."

"Did she talk in more than one voice?"

"Yes. Several."

"Can you describe them?"

"Well, there was a little girl voice. That's the most memorable. It's . . . hard to describe it. No, I don't think I could mimic it."

Rusty cajoled him to do so—he had imitated the voice before, in the privacy of the District Attorney's office—but David flushed. It would demean him, slash at his masculinity. He was a leading man, not a clown.

"Can you take a stab at it?" Rusty begged.

David defied him. "No, it's hard to do."

All right. Graciously, Rusty withdrew. He paced a bit, regained his posture of authority, while at the same time he searched his memory.

"When did the most blatant changes take place?"

"In bed," David said. "Her eyes would take on a glazed look. She would talk like a little girl. She would call me 'Daddy.' "

A hush came over the courtroom.

318

"What did she tell you then, in early 1981, about her father?"

That he had been having an incestuous relationship with her, David said, since she was twelve or thirteen years old. It started one evening when her mother and sisters were somewhere else. She was brushing her hair in front of a bathroom mirror, wearing a nightgown. Her father walked in behind her, told her she looked very pretty, stroked her hair, began fondling her nipples—

"At that point I didn't want to hear anymore," David said. "I got very angry."

Allen Isbell could hardly believe what was happening. *This was the heart of the defense position*—that Cindy had been so incestuously used by her father, with her mother in the permissive role as conspirator and punisher rather than protector, as to incite David, *on his own and without Cindy's knowledge*, to slay them for the evil dragons that they were. Cindy had vetoed any mention of sexual abuse. It was her right—it was her trial, her life. But Allen had fretted: how could he get round the prohibition? Now, in the opening hour of David's testimony, Rusty was doing the job for him!

That door wasn't open a crack; it was torn off its hinges.

During all this, Cindy never moved or changed her blank expression. Perhaps there was a slight narrowing of her eyes.

Clearing his throat, Rusty asked David if she had claimed there were actual sexual acts with her father.

"Yes, she did."

"Over what period of time?"

"I'm not sure. Years."

"How often? Did she say?"

"I got the impression it was six or more times."

It wasn't easy for her to talk about it, David said. Her confessions to him were not glib. They were wrenched from a twilight domain deep, deep inside her.

"Did she say anything to you about her children?" Rusty asked.

"She said that her oldest child was her father's child."

No one dared cough or clear a wet throat. The only sounds were the smooth slur of ink on paper as reporters' pens fled across the narrow pages of their notebooks.

"Did you believe her?" Rusty asked briskly.

"I didn't know what to believe. I thought it was possible, but the time frames didn't jibe quite right."

Vital as it seemed, Rusty just bobbed his head and let this slide; he wasn't ready for it yet.

"What was your reaction when she told you that her oldest son was her father's?"

"Revulsion. Disgust. Anger."

"When she told you about her father and her supposedly incestuous relationship with him, was that before or after you started a physical relationship with her?"

"Before. Probably over a month before. . . . " Rusty nagged him a little more, demanding precision. "I don't know exactly when. I didn't have a log book. Maybe it was around Christmas of 1980."

According to Cindy, Rusty asked, did her mother know what was going on?

Allen Isbell leaned forward, pen poised. *Say yes, David.*

"Yes," David said. "She did, and she resented Cindy for it. The mother was jealous. The mother had treated her badly all her life."

Allen still found it hard to believe that Rusty was doing this. Twin spots of color appeared on Allen's sallow cheeks. His delight began to change to suspicion.

Rusty asked David if Cindy ever gave examples of that bad treatment by her mother. Yes, indeed. Once when she was very young she was swimming in a lake somewhere. The family may have been on a vacation. Cindy hadn't yet learned to swim. Suddenly she found herself in deep water, she couldn't stand up, she thought she was drowning. She cried out in panic and turned for help . . . but her mother, nearby, just watched her . . . just watched it happen. "She was going down for the third time."

A man saved her life. A stranger. Only then did her mother respond to her terror and approach her.

"She remembered this clearly?" Rusty asked, as fascinated as everyone else in the courtroom.

"Vividly, apparently."

"How old did Cindy say she was when this happened?"

"About four."

Rusty looked up quickly at the judge, then for a brief blank moment at the jury, then back at the judge again. It was after five o'clock—time to refuel. The judge declared the court in recess until tomorrow morning.

———————

A good trial lawyer learns early in his career to focus his perceptions not only on adversary witnesses but on the jury's reaction to them. Allen

Isbell had studied the jurors intently throughout the testimony about the sexual abuse. One man had turned pale. One woman had put her hand to her mouth when David so vividly recreated the moment of Jim Campbell's first touch on his daughter's nipples. Her body language said, *Don't say such a thing out loud.* The jury had seemed sympathetic to Cindy. Who wouldn't be?

Allen returned to his office that evening at six o'clock still wondering why Rusty had let the issue into evidence. He theorized finally that over the weekend Rusty had snapped to the probability that his star witness wasn't going to go along with him on murder-for-hire as laid out in the prosecution's opening statement to the jury. Maybe they had argued about it and Rusty had threatened: "If you don't testify to the truth, you'll be facing a charge of capital murder for killing the father!" And maybe David had replied, "That's the truth as *you* see it, Rusty. But it's not what happened. So go ahead and prosecute me. I won't lie."

Wishful thinking, Allen decided. Nobody bullies Rusty into anything. And Rusty would not encourage a witness to lie.

Indeed, at the end of the day I asked Rusty why he had done it. Lounging against the wooden bar in the courtroom, jacket slung casually over his shoulder in the heat, lips parted in a boyish grin, he shrugged and said, "That's what I teach in the seminars to the young D.A.s. Lay it all out in front."

And he had a plan. The charge of sexual abuse was there, like a fire deep in the hold of a ship, sending wisps of smoke and acrid smells curling to the deck, a throbbing menace, and it had to be put out or dealt with lest it explode and without warning roar up hidden passageways to sink the entire vessel. He intended to deal with it and put it out forever. There was no fire, he believed, only the report of fire. She had concocted the charge to justify murder for money. And he would use the lie to destroy her.

28

The benches in front of and behind the bar, even the back rows of the spectators' benches, were jammed with lawyers and young assistant district attorneys who had come from all over the courthouse. They snatched an hour between pleadings or the writing of briefs; some came for the whole day. They had heard what was going on.

Dr. Rob Owens was there, too, taking notes.

For six more days in that hot courtroom David West testified. It was courtroom drama at its solid best, not in the Perry Mason style of eleventh-hour revelations, but in the way that lawyers love and learn from. Rusty's three-day direct examination of a major witness who had committed a brutal killing was a brick-by-brick erection of what seemed an unassailable fortress. And it was followed by one of the most skillful cross-examinations ever seen in the Harris County Courthouse—and the Harris County Courthouse, home field of Percy Foreman and Racehorse Haynes, had seen many.

———————

On Tuesday, as the second day of David West's testimony got underway, Rusty began to develop his principal theme. A bit of an overture, then the faroff but clear cry of a hunting horn, signaling a melody yet to come. . . .

David, as soloist, opened this second movement by again explaining to the jury how he felt about James and Virginia Campbell as a result of listening to Cindy's tales of villainy and woe. Clearly the parents were the root of all her problems. (Who didn't have at least one friend of whom, to some extent, that was not true?) They were, in his words, "revolting perverts." That belief never changed, he said, during his entire two-year relationship with Cindy.

To bolster her thesis she told him a dozen stories. She had a talent for singing—even now, David commented, she had a beautiful singing voice. She was six or seven years old, at a family gathering. She sang, and an uncle praised her for it. Virginia Campbell became so angry at the favorable attention being paid to the least favorite of her daughters that she snatched Cindy out of the living room. "Upstairs! Go to your room!" And forbade her to sing in public again.

Another time her mother locked Cindy in a closet for some unknown transgression and told her, "You'll have to knock to get out. You'll have to knock *hard*." And then: "Knock *harder*." Cindy knocked until her knuckles were raw and bleeding. . . .

"And when this supposedly happened," Rusty asked, "how old did she say she was?"

Keen ears heard the hunting horn.

"Eight or nine," David recalled.

Another time, for some other forgotten childhood sin, she was locked all day long in a bathroom. Maybe even overnight.

"And did she say how old she was at the time?"

"Nine or ten," David said.

Another tale had to do with what he characterized as "hygiene." At some prepubescent age, probably eleven, her mother began to force her to douche regularly. If she didn't, she was screamed at and humiliated. Ultimately, locked up. The dreaded bathroom again.

"What was your reaction when she told you that, David?"

"Normal anger."

"By early 1981, David, how would you characterize your opinion of the Campbells?"

"Based on what I had to go on, I thought they were pretty disgusting people."

Rusty thought for a few moments, then in the labyrinth of his knowledge seemed to find what he was searching for. "When Cindy first told you about her father supposedly being the father of her oldest son . . . did you believe it?"

"It was such an astounding statement—why would anybody say such a thing if it wasn't true?" David seemed to wait for an answer, and many in the courtroom imperceptibly nodded in agreement. He went on: "I was sort of bowled over by this whole thing all at once. She was so obviously extremely screwed up that I believed it."

But then later, he said, he questioned it. "For one thing, the dates didn't match up very well. Her older son was then eight. She was twenty-five. And she told me her father had got her pregnant in early adolescence, approximately twelve or thirteen. It was supposedly her first sexual experience, when she was first physically developing. Of course I didn't give her a third degree about it—I was pretty shocked. But it mathematically does not match up."

That was clear to anyone who bothered to make the calculation. (Unless David remembered it wrong, or had become confused when Cindy had told him.) Rusty allowed the arithmetic to penetrate a bit.

In early 1981, according to David, she continued these revelations to him, and for the most part, with the fundamentalist faith of a lover, he continued to believe her. "Her health and attitude were improving, snowballing, getting better and better." By then she had moved in, taking over the empty downstairs bedroom. One evening he cooked his favorite lamb stew, with liberal dousings of thyme and garlic, and they were talking, drinking good old Gallo Hearty Burgundy, lounging on the Naugahyde sofa that he'd bought at a garage sale when he furnished the place. Somehow the subject rose up again, like a shark's snout in bloodied waters: her scornful sisters, her cruel mother, the rapacious father with the strolling fingers. Oh! Cindy-rella!

Clenching a fist with impotent rage, David breathed to her, "God! If someone had done all that to me, I'd want to kill them."

A little shocked, Cindy said, "I couldn't do that."

He regrouped. "I meant, if I had one parent who, well, shit, *screwed* me, and another who locked me up in closets and beat me, I just couldn't take it! It's so terrible. So unfair. I'd have to strike back. Do *something.*"

———————————

In the spring of 1981 David introduced her to his own mother. They became friends. Cindy would say to David, "Let's go over and see your Mom." Cecilia West, mother also of an estranged forty-year-old daughter by a previous marriage, felt pity for Cindy, but liked her sense of humor and thought she was a sweet girl. The two women developed a relationship that excluded the man who was son to one and lover to the other. Cindy never told David many of the things his mother told her, and Cecilia was equally discreet.

"And how did you see yourself during this period?" Rusty asked.

"Friend—teacher—coach. Like a big brother. I was Henry Higgins."

On his yellow pad Allen Isbell wrote that name down and underlined it.

She responded, David said. She changed. He succeeded in forcing her to recover from the negative impression that her parents had given her of herself. He was the author of a splendid transformation.

"After a point she became extremely attractive. It was a relationship that had different angles to it. I had complex feelings, but by spring of '81 you could say I was totally committed. I was in love with her, as much as you can be. She seemed to return my affections."

Such an antique phrase. He said it wistfully, with feeling, with a remembrance of things past that can ne'er be retrieved or repeated. Everyone in the courtroom responded to it. All believed.

" . . . She said she loved me."

"How did you feel about yourself then, David?"

"I felt good. I was a veteran, going to school, in love with someone who was sweet, kind, intelligent, talented."

Everyone could see him that way, because, had he not been a confessed murderer, had the former object of his wrecked love not been sitting in the defendant's chair accused of parricide, he would have seemed the quintessence of decent, questing, palely romantic youth. Murderers do not wear signs proclaiming their capability. Psychopaths can look you in the eye.

But it was Rusty, not David, conducting this concert. David was only the first violinist. Rusty waved his baton and introduced a new theme: death impending.

324

"Did you view yourself then as a violent person, David?"

No, although he had been raised in a fairly rough neighborhood and wouldn't take guff from anyone. Yes, violence was right in some situations. But he didn't think he had the right to take a life. He didn't view himself as a killer. "Not unless I was a soldier in combat, or a policeman." His reaction to Cindy's ongoing lament of her childhood—*"if someone had done all that to me, I'd want to kill them"*—was a normal reaction, he explained, the kind of impassioned hyperbole you blurt in the heat of an emotionally charged conversation. He didn't mean it. It was a primal scream. No talk of following through.

The love reached a zenith, flattened out, began to curve downward. (Everyone could identify with *that*.) The honeymoon was over. She couldn't hold down a job. She made no effort. David was supporting her. He tried to define the nature of the malaise and concluded that she had reached a plateau and was stagnating. He was pushing and pulling, whittling and shaping, and she was just letting it happen, hanging there as dead weight. She didn't want to take the final step, whatever it might be, that would lead to true self-sufficiency. Or perhaps, he noted, he didn't want to see what that step had to be.

"I thought I needed to make her mad, so I began needling her. She reacted strongly. We argued. She said I was overbearing, jealous of her looks. Guys played up to her all the time now and she couldn't handle it. She would choose not to perceive a pass as such. I said, 'Cindy, so-and-so, who comes on so friendly, just wants to get into your pants.' And she was shocked at that. She'd say, 'You're dirty-minded!' I viewed her as basically afraid of sex, and so she couldn't, or wouldn't, realize what was happening. In order for her to be uninhibited sexually with me, she had to"—he groped for the word—*"change.* The normal Cindy wasn't capable of a normal physical relationship."

"In order to have a normal physical relationship, whatever that is," Rusty inquired, "what kind of person would she act like?"

David colored a little. Despite his impressive vocabulary, and his later declarations to Kim Paris that he loved her "body and fuckin' soul," he was still something of a prude when it came to discussing what lovers did on mattresses behind closed doors.

"Extremely uninhibited," he said.

Rusty wanted more. He brought up the subject of Cindy's little girl voice. What other kinds of voices did she use?

"Accents."

"What kind of accents?"

"French. Italian."

"Did you ever hear the name Gabriela?"

David seemed to balk there, but finally remembered that it was a name she used, a way she thought of herself, almost "a Sicilian whore." This was also the beginning of what David later characterized as Cindy's "Italian period." She told him that a while ago in some Italian restaurant she had been introduced to a man named Salino, a middle-aged mafioso. He took a paternal interest in Cindy. He had some younger henchman who lusted after her bones. For a while Salino and some members of his mob hid out in Cindy's Kingston apartment. Black limousines came and went. There were guns.

David dismissed most of this as a fantasy.

She began to think of using Gabriela as a stage name, David said. She still wanted to be an actress, and she took drama lessons at St. Thomas. She sometimes spontaneously performed roles; her favorite was the death scene from *Romeo and Juliet*. She liked to go to The Comedy Workshop in Montrose, a club that featured stand-up comedians and once a week, on what was called Animal Night, let amateurs perform. David never saw her on the stage, however. She was too shy to abide him there.

"Then an incident occurred," David said, "in the summer of '81. She was saying that I didn't like her newfound persona, which was the opposite of true, although I did think she was moving too fast now in a certain direction. But she thought I was being possessive."

It was Animal Night at The Comedy Workshop, June 1981. She was scheduled to go on that evening, but as usual she asked him not to watch. He dropped her off at the club. "Pick me up at 10:30," she said.

He showed up on time, parked, and went to the stage door. Cindy was in the greenroom, where performers and admirers and media people can cluster—and they were clustered there, praising her. She was offering a private reprise of her act. Approaching, David heard the applause. He entered, waved hello, let her finish, waited a few minutes, then said, "Let's go."

"I want to stay a while," Cindy begged.

Twenty minutes later she still wasn't ready to leave. An impatient David said, "I'm not your chauffeur. I don't hang around at your beck and call. Are you ready or not?"

"I'm enjoying myself. Without you," she said, arching a painted mid-night-black eyebrow. "Is that a crime?"

Who among us, with lover or spouse, on one side or the other, hasn't had such an argument? You could see nods all over the courtroom.

But he still had the wand of power and she left with him. It was just after eleven o'clock. The argument continued outside in the parking lot in the sticky June night, and then in the car, driving toward home. She told David again that he was oppressive, jealous. He yelled back at her; she yelled at him. He had to stop at a red light near Shepherd Drive, and she twisted the door handle and jumped out of the car. *Hey, wait . . . where are you going? Far from you! Get back in! Fuck you! Fuck you, too —get back in, bitch—I'm taking you home! Get lost, you creep! And leave me alone!*

He followed her, she striding on the sidewalk, high heels cracking like gunshots, he at the wheel of his Mustang, cruising slowly down Westheimer, until she reached a house where a party seemed to spill out on the lawn. The door to the house was open.

Cindy darted inside among the partygoers. From David's point of view she seemed to be talking nonstop—

"She gave me the visual impression that she was acting scared. Like, 'Help me, help me!' I was mad, because this was ridiculous. There was no violent aspect to it at all. She was causing a scene, irrationally, laying all this jealousy at my doorstep, which wasn't true. A big public scene, giving them the impression that I was some sort of beast. I find public scenes very embarrassing," he confided to the jury.

"I sat there for several minutes. It wasn't right that she was doing this. I put my car in park. I didn't know whose house it was or who these people were. I could hear music and see a lot of people standing around, but I didn't know what I was walking into. I had a gun, a .38, under the seat of my car. I got the gun out and put it in my back pocket, where it was visible—it wasn't concealed—and I went inside to get her."

He said this as if it was quite normal to bring a pistol into a party where you didn't know the people.

He reached her and said, "Cindy, come on." The argument began again. But this time there were strangers present. David said to the partygoers gathered round, "You really don't understand what's going on. We're just having an argument. She's in no danger." (Had they seen his gun? He'd said it wasn't concealed.) He was calm and reasonable, he recalled.

A woman butted in: "She doesn't have to go with you if she doesn't want to."

"We argued," David told the enthralled courtroom. "I didn't know this woman at all. She said, 'You're not going to take her out of here!' —meaning Cindy. I started to take her out, and the woman pushes me. And as she does, she grabs hold of the front of my shirt, which was a fairly expensive Oscar de la Renta shirt, and tears it down to my waist. I got very mad. I figured, what's good for the goose is good for the gander, so I took hold of her dress and I tore it down to her waist." He smiled, a bit embarrassed, perhaps remembering the bared white breasts.

327

The courtroom was very quiet now. David wasn't quite picking up on the vibes, or he might have stopped, or cooled his narrative.

"So, at any rate, then we left, and that was it. No, wait, excuse me, excuse me"—his memory became vivid. "Then she, this woman at the party, screamed and insulted me, and lunged at me, like this"—he raised both hands in a catlike, clawing gesture—"with her sharpened finger-nails, going for my face. I had to think pretty quickly. I didn't want to hit her, so I poked her in the eyes." He demonstrated with his right hand, stabbing out swiftly, index and middle fingers extended. "Which stopped her."

I didn't want to hit her, so I poked her in the eyes!

"Her *eyes?*" Rusty asked. This was unrehearsed. Rusty didn't know where to go with it. And he was no longer sure where it was going.

"Yes."

"In your view that was better than a hit?"

"Yes, it was."

Then David chuckled. His chuckle was that of a naughty boy owning up to an escapade. (I probably shouldn't have done it. It wasn't *that* bad, but I guess it would have been better not to do it.)

It was a remarkable moment, in that quite a few of the spectators, jury and onlookers and media and visiting lawyers, laughed, too. Laughter is contagious; it hides embarrassment and less acceptable emotional displays. No one likes to confront a sociopath; it's *scary*. They didn't know how to react, so they mimicked what they saw. And when they laughed, it made David chuckle all the more.

But it was hastily concluded. The courtroom grew sober. Those who had laughed either made a dutiful intellectual effort to assess their reaction, or tried to forget it . . . and David resumed the narrative. He took Cindy home to her apartment on Kingston. "That was it." They broke up that same night.

Over a period of time she moved her things out of his creaky old house on Vermont. He still loved her, and he missed her, but the big love affair of his life had come to an end.

The judge declared a Brenda-break. David went back outside the holding cell to read *The Good News Bible*.

The love story was concluded. Now, properly prepared, we could go on to the murder story.

———

Rusty showed David two contact sheets of photographs of Cindy taken in the spring of 1981, before their June breakup. David said he had shot

328

them downtown in Tranquility Park. She was relatively slim in the photographs: about 135 pounds, he estimated. At Rusty's urging he picked out the ones that best showed the Cindy he knew and loved. They were entered into evidence as exhibits for the state.

". . . When we broke up, I didn't see her for a long time. No, I wasn't supporting her. I kept on missing her. So in September of 1981 I called her up."

He was working as a bartender at the time, making fifty dollars a night at an English-owned pub in Montrose called the Ale House. At his invitation—David told the jury—Cindy came to see him there. She stayed for a couple of hours. She had gained some weight. To about 145, he guessed. (The graph went up and down, like the stock market then.) Lack of discipline. At first it was a pleasant reunion, but then it quickly degenerated. She began an intense conversation with a man sitting on the stool next to her, and she ignored David behind the bar. For about thirty minutes this went on. David had never seen her come on that way to anyone else. Blatant, and from his point of view, pitiable. When she wrote out her telephone number on a slip of paper and handed it to her new slavering friend, David interfered. He was direct, forceful, not loud. "Give me that number," he said, extending his hand.

The man wanted to know why.

"Because I invited her here," David said.

He didn't know what he would have done if the man had refused. But the intruder gave the paper back and left the bar.

Cindy claimed that David had misunderstood. "I didn't mean anything. I wasn't coming on, I was just being nice to that guy."

"Bullshit. You don't know what you're doing! Or saying!"

She kept drinking. "I gave her the beers free," David recalled, "and she proceeded to get really drunk. It got to the point where she demanded I keep it up. I said, 'Hey, wait a minute . . .' and it got out of hand. It was a scene again. I had to throw her out. She treated me rudely, as if somehow I was being unfair, like I owed it to her to give her free beer. She was loud and obnoxious. I told her I was totally disgusted and not to worry, I'd never call her again."

And he didn't. It was finished. He was free. Or so he thought.

Eight months later, in early May of 1982, she called him. Crying, almost hysterical. She needed help. Two men were living in her apartment—they had been there for three weeks. She'd allowed it because they were friendly and nice, from the East Coast, and they had no place to stay. Now one was making sexual advances, and neither of them would leave. They were threatening her physically.

"I didn't want to know any more details," David testified. "For me at this point the relationship was over. But yes, I was still in love with her. And she asked me to get rid of these guys. She said they were street people, and dangerous. A friend of mine, Jim Daggett, and I went over there.* I had a pistol, he had a shotgun. We set their belongings out in the hallway. They came back and banged on the door. Cindy told them to go away. We deliberately made enough noise in there to where they knew she wasn't alone. The guys argued through the door a little bit, and then they picked up their stuff and left."

Rusty asked if David knew from his own personal knowledge whether Cindy was having a "personal relationship" with either one of them. No, he didn't think so.

"Did either of the two people ever threaten her while you were there?"

"No."

"After you evicted these two men from her apartment, when was the next time you saw her?"

"When she showed up on my doorstep one afternoon in late May of '82."

The courtroom listened carefully. We were drawing close to June 19, the fateful date.

Describe her then, Rusty said.

"She had gained a lot of weight, and she was just about at the point where she'd been when I first met her." She topped 200 pounds, he estimated. Hard to say by how much.

"Compare her to the way she looks now," Rusty suggested.

"She looked worse then, although she weighs more now."

In the courtroom, Cindy Ray coughed deeply. She hated discussions about what she called her "weight problem."

"She was barefooted," David continued, "with no makeup, and her hair was unkempt. She was acting along the lines that she did when I first met her. Also she was curled up in the fetal position." At Rusty's bidding, he demonstrated.

And his first reaction, before she said a word, was, *Oh, no . . . she's back again. And she's totally fallen apart.* He acted, he remembered, "a combination of disgusted and I-told-you-so."

"When she showed up on your doorstep," Rusty said, with portent, "did she have something she wanted you to do?"

David hesitated.

"Just answer yes or no," Rusty said.

But David was still his own man. His manner was firm and calm. He

---

* The District Attorney's Office, HPD, Gene Nettles, and the current defense team had all searched for Jim Daggett and never found him.

waited a moment and then said, "I don't think yes or no would be a proper response."

It was hotter than ever in the courtroom now, and more packed than ever. It was like a Southern courtroom in an old black-and-white movie (*To Kill a Mockingbird* comes to mind), people fanning themselves with folded newspapers and plastic fans and lace fans from Mexico, and sweat beading the faces of lawyers and jurors alike. And yet no one was about to leave now. They sensed what was coming. In sworn testimony David had brought us through time, and now we were just two or three weeks away from carnage.

29

After a while they went inside the house. She was acting beaten, she was chain-smoking. She was contrite, regretful that she'd ever left him.

"Look at you!" David cried, shocked. "You've fallen apart!"

She couldn't shift for herself, she told him, and she'd had to go back to her parents for support. *"And they did it to me again."*

"You mean your father?" he said.

"Yes."

"And your mother, too?"

"Yes."

He felt shock, horror, helplessness. He took her statement to mean the worst. Her father's incestuous invasions—her mother's workaday torture as a means of vengeful punishment. Daily mental slights and jabs. The details always sickened him, and he was afraid to ask for them.

Leaning against him, she murmured, "Do you remember when you said you'd kill them?"

He remembered his outburst. *"I just couldn't take it. I'd have to strike back. Do something. . . ."*

"Well, I think you're right," she said softly. "We ought to."

"I didn't volunteer," he pointed out.

"You know that I couldn't do it," she said. "But you could. It's the only way I'm ever going to be free. They're always going to be there—they're always going to be messing with me—they're always going to be after me."

That reached a responsive chord. He knew that *they* lay at the root of her troubles. Previously, when she had told him her tales it had angered

331

him, but he had figured, what's past is past. The thing for her to do was try to forget about it and live her life, put herself back together, reinvigorate and get healthy. But now she had told him that it was happening all over again.

He told the silent courtroom that he could never remember what he replied in response to that first overture.

He recalled that she spoke faster than normal, as if she was desperate. "Think of what they've done to me. You know they deserve it."

To that he replied, "Yeah . . . they do."

A little later, as she continued to importune him, he said, "Let me think about it."

Heavyweight sighs came from David during this part of the tale. He disliked reliving that part of May and June of 1982: the choice, the decision, the moment when all went askew, flatly wrong. "I had talked to her before," he continued from the witness stand, "in late 1980 and early '81, when she first broached the subject of what her father had done to her, about getting help. I thought about it again. Going to the authorities, if nothing but the D.A.'s Office."

That drew a friendly grin from Rusty, so David, with the pressure easing off, tried to top it, and did, easily. He chuckled. "Last resort, you know."

Rusty laughed aloud. From the counsel table Lyn McClellan guffawed; his white shirt rippled like a parachute catching the wind. The whole courtroom joined in. The wonder was that David didn't rise from the wooden witness chair to take a bow.

But he didn't go to the authorities because she had told him back in 1981, and now again in May of 1982, that her father was a powerful lawyer. Jim Campbell knew underworld characters. (*"He'd bring bizarre people into our social circle, like a private detective named Dudley Bell who's in the penitentiary now."*) Once Cindy had run away, and when Daddy got her back he threatened to have her put in an institution if she ever told what had happened. So there was no way, David explained, that she could ever use the system to get something done against him. He had once run for district judge; even though he'd lost he was too much a part of that system.

After she asked him to kill them, he thought about alternative ways of handling it. Maybe he could rough Campbell up. But in the end that seemed so primitive. Confront him? Go to the police? With Jim Campbell's ability to bring power and money to bear, that could become a disaster.

332

For a couple of days he thought about what she had asked of him. His position was still that he hadn't volunteered.

But he knew one thing: they deserved it.

Rusty asked flatly, "Why'd she say her parents had to be killed? For the reason you mentioned? 'It's the only way I can be free'?"

"Yes, her mother's continuing mental torture, on top of what her father was doing."

"Did you believe her?"

"Yes, I did."

"Did you agree with her?"

"I did. . . . She was an emotional invalid." And if she was sick, *they* were her disease. Cause and effect could not have been more clearly diagrammed.

"Did you begin to think of the murders in those terms?"

"Yes. And each day she asked me if I'd decided."

"Were y'all having any type of physical relationship at that time?" Not: Did you go to bed with her? Did you have sex? Did you make love? The prosecutorial prudery struck a discordant note in the dialogue, which until then had the quality of two old friends reminiscing and analyzing by a fire on a winter evening in a colder climate.

David said, "That evening she came back, we resumed it." Even he was becoming formal: they *resumed it.*

"How did she act during that encounter? Did she call you Daddy?"

"No, but she turned into the little girl again. Extremely submissive. She continued to act that way. She said to me, 'You were right—guys are all after it, after me. They're all SOBs, and you were right, I should have listened to you. You're the best thing that ever happened to me.' At any rate, I felt that I still loved her. And she'd come back. But this thing that I thought I'd worked her out of, she'd totally gone back into it again. She'd totally regressed, and it seemed to be for the same reason, because of her parents.

"Ultimately," he sighed, "I came to the same conclusion that she had, which was that for what they had done to her, and to keep it from happening any more, they should die."

During this part of the testimony David took heavy breaths. Clearly he was uncomfortable with his words and thoughts.

It took four days to decide. He was pretty sure that Jim Campbell was an animal, a rapist, a vicious manipulator of human beings. . . .

". . . But I was less sure about the mother. I didn't have the same amount of impressive evidence against her. I told Cindy that. She said, 'Think about what she did to me . . . the drowning . . . the bloody knuckles.' She was afraid of the dark, she had to have a night light. We were in my bedroom when this conversation took place, the second day

333

after she came back. I told her I was pretty much decided about James Campbell, but I had some reservations about her mother. I said, 'Tell me again what she did.' Cindy said, in a pleading manner, 'Remember how she locked me in the closet . . . when she slapped me and said, "Silence is golden." My mother would get into these moods like that . . . she'd say, "Shut up! I can't stand the sound of your voice!" ' And," David explained, "the day-to-day continual picking and jabbing. . . ."

The courtroom smelled of sweat and stale air. Caught up in the flow as much as anyone else, Judge Azios nevertheless said, "Excuse me, David, just a minute." He conferred with Brenda and yes, her back ached. So the court recessed for lunch.

I had lunch that day with Dr. Barbara Thelkins, a child psychiatrist at De Pelchin Children's Center, a Houston psychiatric hospital, and her husband, Ellis McCullough, who had briefly given legal counsel to Cindy Ray after the murders.

"Incest is a factor in nearly half the criminal cases I deal with," McCullough said. "If not at the root, then certainly a part of it."

Dr. Thelkins said, "Incest between father and daughter is far more common than most people are willing to realize. I've treated or seen over a hundred cases. We hear of it more now, too, because today we have awareness programs that get the victims to come forward.* Kids can be videotaped and that can be presented in court—they don't have to appear in person. It's almost the norm in lower-class Mexican-American families, and appears a lot in lower-class black families. But it cuts across all social and economic lines, and you have an extraordinary degree of secret tolerance and lack of guilt. The guy is accused of it, and he says, 'Why are people so upset? I pay my taxes.'

"It usually begins in the early teens, but sometimes starts as early as five, and very often around eight. The girl, in response to the question, 'How often?' will say: 'Well, in the mornings. And whenever Mama left the house.'

"It's common in such cases that Dad isn't doing it to Mom. And Mom generally denies the fact—that's on the level of alcoholic denial, the way a wife won't admit that the man she's married to has a drinking problem. She says to herself, 'I'm economically and emotionally dependent on him, so I don't want to know anything that could imperil the marriage.'

---

* In 1985 Harris County authorities handled between 100 and 125 incest cases a month, up from 25 reported cases a month in 1979. In 1986 there were approximately 8,000 incest offenders in the Texas legal system, either in prison, on parole, or on probation.

"The usual pattern is that when the father is accused, the child tries to defend him. The anger and hatred is against the mother, because the father and daughter achieved a closeness through the sex, or the closeness was there before and it helped give rise to the sex. And the deep resentment takes the form of: *'Why didn't my mother protect me?'* "

———————————

After lunch everyone resumed their places around the campfire, and David again took up the narrative.

"I told her I'd think about it." Despite his contradictory mention to Ginger Casey that the subject of money never came up until after the murders, he said to the jury: "The next day—I guess she thought I was taking too long, or trying to talk myself out of it—she said she might inherit some money when her parents died. She didn't know how much, or if any. But if she did, she'd give me half of it."

An anxious David leaned forward in the witness chair toward the jury, confiding in them. "That was a whole new aspect. I had to sort out how I thought about that. I had been thinking of the moral aspect, not the financial."

From the looks on their faces the jury seemed to understand. Yes, it did put things in a new light.

He went to his good friend Wickie Weinstein, to talk about it and to seek advice. "I asked him if he'd ever kill anybody for money."

Wickie told David that no, he couldn't. "And I said I couldn't either. I'd have to have a lot better reason than that."

Rusty asked why he chose Wickie as a confidant.

"Because he was an ex-Airborne Ranger, a reactionary paramilitary type, with whom you could discuss abstractly the subject of killing someone and he would not be dismayed."

David said yes, he owned a gun then, and he was a good shot.

What kind of shot was Wickie?

"Not as good. But for the most part," David continued, "I'd pretty well already decided that *if* I was going to do it, it wasn't going to be for the money. I still had some reservations. I went to Cindy again, after another day—this was also in my bedroom, the most habitable room in my house, and we were standing near the bookcase, and I said, 'Okay, tell me again.' She came up close to me and said in my ear, in a low voice, 'Well, think about what they did to me. How Daddy put his hands on me . . . how many times he's done it to me . . . and what that's done to me. And what my mother did.' " She repeated all the details of the claimed torture. She was close to him, whispering the litany.

What strange perversion, I wondered, was being revealed here? *Tell*

335

me again. Did it thrill David in some deep-reaching way to think of Jim Campbell's hands on the virgin nipples, with Virginia lurking elsewhere, letting it happen, beating her and jailing her in closets and bathrooms as punishment for her carnality? Did it strum some responsive chord in David's memory? Did some naughtiness in his own life become sinful, and the thought of that sin flower into poisonous guilt, and guilt require surgical expiation?

"I got mad," David said to us. *"I crossed over."*

To Cindy he said, "Okay, I think you're right. They deserve to die."

"Then you'll do it?"

"Yes."

"Do you really mean it?"

"Hey, yes, I'm not kidding. I said so, didn't I?"

Then it was only a matter of planning *how*.

"Brenda's tired," said the judge.

Break: as in a heavyweight championship boxing match, when the two behemoths are panting and hanging on each other's sweaty shoulders. Not just Brenda at her stenograph with cramped fingers and pained cervical disks, but David West and Rusty Hardin and Allen Isbell, and Cindy Ray, the cold-eyed listener, and the thirteen jurors on the edges of their seats. And the judge, too. His smile was forced now. This was draining. It was the stuff that nightmares are made of.

But before David would freely tell the waiting world how he had done it, a debt had to be paid to David, a promise kept by Rusty. *Noblesse oblige*.

Rusty had a captive audience now in the jury. And no one other than the TV reporters with their five o'clock deadlines was going to get up and leave the steaming courtroom until the last juicy detail was squeezed from the hot fruit of David West's memory.

Once again David took his place in the witness chair, ran a hand through his bushy hair, shaped his beard, and straightened his tie.

Rusty began immediately. "Was the money why you did it, David?"

"No. But I didn't refuse."

"Did you think you'd actually get some money out of it?"

"I knew there was a possibility."

"A certainty?"

"A certainty, no."

"How would you describe the impact of the possibility of money on what you agreed to do, and what you did?"

"Minimal," David said firmly.

"Was there any conversation between you and Cindy to the effect that if Cindy's father died, and Cindy's mother *didn't* die, there might not be an inheritance?"

"Yes," David said, frowning.

"Who said that?" Rusty demanded.

"I'm not sure. It was kind of between us. . . ."

Rusty challenged him: "If James Campbell supposedly committed the sexual abuse, why did Virginia Campbell have to die for that?"

"Because she let it happen," David said, as Dr. Thelkins had predicted at our lunch.

"Was the inheritance any kind of a factor in your killing Virginia Campbell?"

"Not in my mind."

"In Cindy's mind?"

Before Allen Isbell could object, David replied, "She didn't think she was going to inherit anything under a will."

Allen slid back down into his chair, pleased.

"If you had done it for the money," Rusty persisted, "what would that have meant to you—what *does* that mean to you—in terms of your own self-image?"

David, after a gloomy little pause in whose shadows you could discern the whorls of chaotic shapes, personal star systems of undefinable feelings, said with perfect timing, and a remarkable equanimity under the circumstances, "It would have been even worse than it is."

Rusty hesitated. Had the prosecution paid its debt to the informer? He looked to David for an answer.

David nodded almost imperceptibly. The cash drawer closed. Now he would go on.

Now that they had agreed to the murder, he took charge of the planning. "I'm not just your errand boy," he told her. "If you feel this strongly, and this is the only way, then you have to *be* there. I mean, it's your deal, this is all for you, not me"—because he could envision going over there to Memorial, or wherever site they chose, and doing the deed, and coming back to find her shrieking, "Oh, my God! You really *did* it? You took me *seriously*? But you didn't give me a chance to change my mind!"

That would have bankrupted him morally. So she had to be there, reassuring him that it was for her. No problem. During that week she clung to him like a tick to a collie.

As for tactics: he decided that the main thing was to keep it neat and simple as possible. No witnesses. A good alibi. A weapon you couldn't trace. In Texas you could buy a hand gun in almost any mall with just a Texas driver's license. The law said you could keep it in your home, but not anywhere on your person or in your vehicle where it was "accessible." But a recent purchase might be remembered.

He went to Wickie, with whom he had discussed murder in the abstract, looking for a .22, the kind of common hand gun that any burglar could have. But at that time Wickie owned only a .45, a Colt Combat Commander with a satin-nickel finish. David was leery of it. Most military .45s had been manufactured before World War I. Jamming was a problem, and they were loud. He told Wickie that he needed the gun "for an operation," something paramilitary.

Wickie asked no questions, David claimed. "And I never hinted to him that I wanted to kill someone."

But hadn't he, only a week before that, discussed with Wickie killing someone for money? How could Wickie not make the connection? David's lying, I thought.

Rusty didn't probe.

The two young men drove north together to a firing range on Treschwig Road and test-fired the .45—maybe twenty to thirty rounds. It seemed a reliable gun. Wickie was fond of it. David was satisfied.

He decided on the early morning hours, while his targets were sure to be asleep.

Most of the details they worked out on the first evening, in the euphoria of decision. It was four days after she had first asked him, and the Campbells were still in Europe. Popping another can of Heineken in his living room, David said, "You've got to go over there first and open a window. Because I don't want to go banging and crashing around trying to force a window open at three o'clock in the morning, and have your father come tearing down the stairs with his sawed-off shotgun and fuckin' blow my head off. And the lights. You've got to see about the lights."

David's Mercury Capri was in Gerry's Automotive for a valve job, and they had loaned him a gold-colored Cadillac. He dropped Cindy off at Memorial in the late afternoon of Tuesday, June 8, and she spent the night.

The next morning he picked her up. She said, "Maria saw me checking the windows."

"*What?*"

"She didn't know what I was doing. She's a stupid cow. Don't worry about it."

Unaccountably, David let that go.

338

They decided to dress in a way that would make them least recognizable. He knew how to plan and outfit an operation, taking into account worst-case situations. Olive drab military field jackets with big expandable pockets, gloves and masks—combat boots, so that if it was muddy from rain or even damp they wouldn't find a woman's footprints. She weighed as much as a man. He owned the field jackets from the Marine Corps—they had no identifying marks—and a knit ski mask that Cindy would wear. He bought a fiberglass goalie's hockey mask for himself at Skate Escape, a sporting goods store, and spray-painted it matte black.

Wickie Weinstein walked up to the side of the house while David was huddled there at work, spraying. Wickie watched him finish the job. Didn't ask what it was for, David claimed. Again I thought: *no way*.

Then David went to Southland Hardware and bought two pair of thin, transparent surgical gloves.

Cindy's hair was to be slicked down and pulled back. The idea was to be like two men, unrecognizable unless, somehow, someone noticed his missing finger. Cindy was excited and fidgety. Nervous and engrossed. It was an "intense" thing to contemplate, David explained in court, stalking the proper adjectives.

He told her to watch out not only for overhanging branches but for twigs and loose rocks and fallen limbs on the driveway at Memorial. Don't break any, don't trip over the big ones. In back of his house among the scrub he taught her how to walk in combat terrain, putting the heel down first, tentatively, feeling for good footing and no impediments, then rolling the foot slowly forward.

In court, Rusty asked him to demonstrate.

David stepped down from the witness chair and in his black loafers padded diagonally in front of the prosecution's table. The jury's eyes followed him the way spectators' eyes follow a running back headed toward the goal line. They were fascinated, respectful of the skills involved.

He told Cindy to mount the inside staircase close to the wall, where the steps would be best supported by structural timbers and least likely to creak. In a hostile house, in an unfriendly village—St. Lô, Koblenz, Vinh Lai—that's how you did it.

She paid attention, absorbing it all.

"Once we decided they deserved it," he summed up, "and had gone through all the philosophical figuring, then it was a matter of figuring out the most effective, trouble-free method of doing it."

Rusty said, "That's trouble-free for you and Cindy, not for the family, right?"

David blushed.

The Campbells were just returned from their three-week golfing and gambling trip through Central Europe. David chose a Friday night— "because it was a typical party night." Their alibi would be that they'd been to Rudyard's, then to bed, then to a party. They were afraid to rely on anyone other than themselves to verify the alibi at the exact time of the murder. It was risk versus risk; and this one seemed better. An imperfect alibi, David decided, seemed more natural, therefore less suspect.

They chose the hour of 3 A.M., in case the family stayed up on the weekend night to see a late movie. They assumed that the boys would sleep downstairs in their own bedroom.

Of course some suspicion would fall on all the daughters. The police would question Cindy, and she had to know what to say and how to act. They went over the story thoroughly. "The main thing," David said, "is not to act scared. It's okay to act upset, because you normally *would* be upset . . . but not scared. There's nothing you should feel scared about in that situation, see? If anything, *under*play it. Act stunned, bowled over, poleaxed."

She was under control, he thought. Working it out together, they pretended one person was the homicide detective. *"Where were you that evening, Ms. Ray?" "Well, what did you do at home for those two hours, Mr. West?" "Anyone else see you there, Cindy?" "How about you, David?"*

They went over it three or four times, trying to avoid using the same phraseology. "And there should be one or two minor discrepancies," David said, "because that would be natural."

He was pleased with the way Cindy was handling herself. She had no trouble keeping her lines straight.

They made one last-minute decision: to go to the house on the appointed night and make sure the den window was open. The murder should look like part of a burglary. Finding no money, or panicking for a reason that no one would ever know, one of the burglars cut loose with his .45. Give the cops a theory to grab onto, no matter how flimsy.

They drove to 8901 Memorial at about 9 P.M. Cindy jabbered all the way out—he had to tell her, politely, to shut up. *Concentrate.*

David waited in the car. His heart was beating erratically, and he tore at the skin in the crease behind his thumb.

Cindy came back in five minutes. She had seen her mother briefly and borrowed ten dollars. Her father had stayed upstairs. The window had been locked, she said, but on the way out she reopened it.

340

"You see?" David said to her. "That paid off."

They tried to see *E.T.*, but the line was all the way around the block. So on to the Ale House for a beer, and then to Rudyard's, where David discussed pit bulldogs with the bartender while Cindy hung around the dart players in the back and asked one of them, "How do you keep score?" Drink a couple of more beers. Their presence established, having heard of an all-night bring-your-own-bottle party going on in a house on Tuam Street, they left at 2 A.M. Home to the house on Vermont, which was just around the corner. One more cold beer. Get ready.

He slipped the .45 into a shoulder holster. Late that afternoon he had broken it down, cleaned it, oiled the rounds of ammunition. They put on the field jackets and combat boots. They walked slowly up and down the stairs one more time, to practice.

"Tie your hair up, Cindy."

He wondered, is there something we've forgotten about? Some silly detail, some blind spot? No, it was all worked out. Calm down. No superfluous talking. *Concentrate.* Get into the soldier mode.

"Let's wait a little while longer," he decided. "Let the after-hours traffic die down. Otherwise cops might still be out looking for drunk drivers. I don't want to be stopped."

He glanced at her. Does she want to bail out? All she has to do is say the word. But it's too late—we'd feel like fools if we backed out now: feel like children who had toyed with thoughts of dangerous games. And we are not children. We are adults, going to *do* this thing. Because they deserve it. Because it's the only way to free her.

About to leave, at 3 A.M., he smiled raggedly. His guts were trembling a little. He said, "This is it. This is your last chance. Are you sure this is what you want to do?"

As he had known she would, she nodded.

"Okay, let's do it," he said grimly, and they left.

From his brown leather briefcase Rusty Hardin produced a .45 automatic. It was smaller than most people thought such a gun would be. There was a neat, compact look to it, an efficient gray look rather than a mean black look.

"Is this similar to the weapon you carried?" Rusty asked, extending it toward the witness stand, butt first.

David grasped it with his right hand and studiously examined it. No snap decisions here.

"Yes, it is."

"Show the jury how you loaded the gun that night," Rusty said.

David squared his shoulders. He wasn't embarrassed; he looked pleased to be able to demonstrate some technical expertise. It occurred to me that David might have made a good teacher.

"You put six bullets in the gun"—he faced the jury, the .45 held in front of him, barrel aimed at the ceiling—"and one in the chamber. Like this."

"Did you have the safety on?" Rusty asked.

"Oh, sure."

"How does the weapon eject?"

"To the right, and back."

"How much ammunition did you have?"

"I took two magazines, or clips, as they're called, with six rounds each."

"And did Cindy have a weapon, too?"

"No."

"What was the plan when you arrived?"

"We were supposed to park the car on the street, cater-cornered to Memorial, walk up the driveway, climb in the back window, walk across the den and the living room, and then up the stairs. She first, leading me. In the bedroom she was supposed to turn on the lights and stand there with me. The plan was to shoot and run."

"How many times?"

"I don't know," David admitted.

"And if the boys woke up when you first entered the house?"

"We were going to run."

"And if they saw you . . . afterward?"

"With those masks, they wouldn't know who we were."

"You *did* discuss the boys?"

"Sure, but we decided they'd be asleep."

"Did Cindy ever discuss the possible effect all this might have on the boys? The shooting in the darkness? The death of their grandparents?"

David nodded thoughtfully. "She said the boys were mostly attached to the maid, and the grandparents paid very little attention to them, and they would get over it."

"Did you wear your masks while you were driving down Memorial Drive toward the house?"

David laughed at that idea. No, they didn't.

"How long did it take to get there?"

"Ten or fifteen minutes at most."

"And where did you park?"

"On a street called Chatsworth, I believe, just around the corner. Under some trees, in dense shadow. That's when we put the masks on."

In the courtroom it was exactly 5 P.M., a natural time for Rusty to glance up at the bench and signal that he had finished for the day. The planning stage of the murder was over. Tomorrow would come the deed. End of Act I: The Murderer as Lover. We were about to begin Act II: The Murderer as Murderer.

———————————

All day long Cindy had been surprisingly animated, her face twisting and changing expression. Clenching one fleshy fist below the table, she wrote steadily on her yellow pad. During the testimony, no matter how dramatic the moment, she had repeatedly whispered in Rick Brass's ear. That's a lie, she said. And that. And that. And that, too. It's all a lie.

30

On Thursday morning, June 12, David took the stand and picked up the tale where he had left off on Wednesday afternoon. Down the driveway in the darkness, heel-to-toe, walking carefully, he and Cindy reached the yard at the back of the house—hearts hammering, palms under the plastic gloves slick with sweat.

He nodded toward a window.

No. She shook her head firmly. Not that one, that's the boys' room. The other one—the den.

In the nocturnal gloom it took him about five minutes to remove the screen from the den window. He had no tool to do it, just his hands. Cindy stood beside him and they tried not to talk, not even whisper, and then only with her lips pressed warmly against his ear. The idea conceived in the planning stage was that during the operation they were not to do anything that required talking, because talking could give them away. The window screen, as he removed it, made a loud popping sound. He felt fear.

The den, swathed in black, was dark as a pocket. David had to push a couch away from the window, and the legs jittered across the carpet, making a light sound. They waited half a minute. He gave Cindy a boost and she clambered in first, offering David a hand to follow her. The air was stale and warm—no air conditioning. Her Daddy never could sleep in the cold artificial air. They let their eyes adjust until they could make out shapes and vague shadows, then brushed their feet off in case any gravel or dirt had stuck to the soles of the boots. Leave no evidence, David had said. The shells, that's all. Shells are mute.

Rusty asked him to demonstrate for the jury how he walked through the house.

In the courtroom it was eerie. You were with him there at Memorial Drive in the 3 A.M. darkness. You felt the subtropical heat and the stillness. The floorboards creaked inside the den, near the window. With David, you halted to listen. You stopped your breathing, as he did, to listen *better.* "When you do that, you can often hear your own heartbeat," David explained, "and you have to weed that out." You were glad to learn this.

You drew the weapon and took the safety off as you started up the stairs. Stick to the support wall—anticreak. Gun held high, in a two-handed grip, at the ready. No lights on, yet. Cindy's in the lead.

Hey! Why's she going *left?* Isn't it meant to be the bedroom to the *right?* Guess not. God, I *hope* not! But she's signaling, a keep-going gesture of the hand. An agreed signal. One of several.

Okay, *okay!* . . . Take it easy. . . .

At the door now. She's supposed to open it, flick on the light switch just inside the door on the left wall, then stand aside—

———————

Midway through Act II of *Macbeth,* after Macbeth has murdered Duncan and confessed his deed to Lady Macbeth, a drunken porter enters to deal with a knocking at the gate. Scholars celebrate the scene for Shakespeare's genius at comic relief of unbearable tension. Not long after Act II of *David's Testimony* began, comic relief was provided by two Harris County porters.

Just as David reached the point where Cindy was supposed to snap on the light, two workmen punched open the door of Judge Azios's courtroom and marched briskly in. Carrying their green metal tool boxes, they strode straight down the aisle and through the door that led backstage.

The defective air conditioning! We all realized it at once. Everyone sighed in gratitude.

A few moments later the workmen started to hammer and bang. The sounds weren't deafening; just loud.

Bang!

Rusty approached his witness again . . . then turned, and announced, with a smile, "I don't think this is going to work."

"Break!" The judge's fist struck the desk. He fled the courtroom.

344

In three minutes the repairmen were done. As soon as they appeared they were greeted with a vigorous round of applause from the spectators. The repairmen seemed puzzled. They trooped out as briskly as they had come, oblivious to what might have been taking place in the world of criminal justice.

The bailiff called for order, Judge Azios reappeared, and David took the stand again. But somehow the sharpness had been rubbed off the fine edge of the drama. And perhaps, for that same reason that Shakespeare had understood when he bade Macduff and Lennox knock and the rowdy porter lecture them on drink and lechery, murder was less horrifying now. More bearable and workaday. Paradoxically, less forgettable.

"I was standing about here in the bedroom," David said, after Rusty had conjured up an imaginary door and king-sized bed in the space between the bench and counsel table. "My left foot must have been inches away from the boys. No, I didn't see them. It just looked like bedding on the floor, bedding that had been kicked off the bed." He shrugged.

"Cindy went in first. I had told her, 'Turn on the lights as soon as I get into position. And stand there.' " He turned confidingly toward the jury. This was something they had to understand or he had failed and his life sentence would be unbearable. "That's what the whole deal was about. It was for her."

At Rusty's request, he demonstrated his actions after she opened the door. He moved quickly to the foot of the bed, stood slightly to right of center, crouched in the approved shooting stance and aimed as best he could at the dimly lit head of the sleeping James Campbell. He said, "Hit it!"—and the ceiling lamp hanging over the bed blazed on. James, lying on his right side, began to turn. David aimed for the throat and squeezed the trigger.

The .45 swerved to Virginia Campbell, who had locked Cindy in the closet and bathroom until her knuckles bled. Her right arm came up as if to fend him off. The first shot at her was also a head shot. As it struck her, she convulsed.

But Cindy had fled the bedroom, he wasn't quite sure when. Vexed more than angered—it was vital now to concentrate—he alternated the other four shots. Two more head shots, then two chest shots.

"The idea was to kill them," David calmly told the jury, as he had told both Rusty and Kim Paris on other occasions, "not cause them pain or suffering. Just to remove them. I did that."

No further movement from the bed.

Rusty asked him to move the gun back and forth, pointing at the imaginary man and woman in the imaginary bed, saying "bang" each time he pulled the trigger.

"*Bang—bang—bang—bang—bang—bang.*"

(Twelve seconds, the Houston *Chronicle* reported. Eleven seconds, according to CBS-TV.)

"Then I ran."

Down the stairs, across the living room. The front door to the house was flung wide open. Yes, there was some light—ambient light, David called it: city light, starlight, whatever was filtering through the pine trees. He assumed Cindy was outside. He broke through the door into the damp of the morning and then realized she wasn't ahead of him. . . .

Wasn't *there.*

Jesus! God! Crunching to a halt, spinning, he fled back over the earth and gravel, mindless of twigs and rocks now, plunged through the open front door as into a malignant cave and saw a thick shape. She was crouched in a space inside the door. It was swarthy there, the sullen shadows stocked with spooks and goblins, every noise a megathreat, everything happening too fast.

He half-gasped, half-shrieked, "*What are you doing?*"

"I dropped a glove!"

Now, at last, the jury understood Rusty's early focus on the witnesses' descriptions of the glove.

"*Shit! Where?*"

"I can't find it!"

"Shitshit*shit!* Look for it! No, wait! Forget it! *Fuck the glove!* Come on!"

He ran, dragging her behind him.

He knew that surgical gloves were tight-fitting and made hands sweat. Back at Vermont he had helped her put hers on after squeezing into his own, worrying then about her sharp fingernails ripping through the tips. And freaking out now, thinking: what if the sweat inside the glove could be tested? What if they could get a hormone count and determine that it was a woman?

Trotting through the dull dark toward the parked car, he berated her. His voice rose: "You *dropped* it? What the fuck do you mean, you 'dropped it'? How could you drop the glove? They were tight on your hands! You *couldn't!*"

"I didn't mean to!"

"That's impossible!"

"*It was an accident.*"

A perceptive grainy yellow brightening of the air caught his eye. A car swayed round a bend of Memorial Drive. He knew its headlight beam would illuminate them. And it did . . . but the car didn't slow. It headed west. The morning wrapped them up once more in velvet-black folds. They reached the Cadillac.

David was fumbling in his pockets. His heart jittered and slithered against his ribs. "*I can't find the keys,*" he moaned.

To the jury he said, "In my typically organized manner, I had misplaced the keys." In response there came a low chuckle throughout the courtroom. Because they knew he *would* find them. He would get away. He wouldn't be stranded there and caught—that would ruin the story.

The keys were in his righthand pocket, where he always kept them; he had just missed them in the first wild grab and was looking everywhere else. But if he was panicky, Cindy was totally terrified.

He drove speedily down the winding curves of Memorial to Shepherd and took a right by what they called the Old Jewish Cemetery. The rest was planned, done by rote. He parked the car in the cloistered shadows and dumped the weapon, and boots, the gloves, nylon shoulder holster, ski mask, everything except his fiberglass hockey mask, all wrapped tightly in the field jackets, into Buffalo Bayou. He slung the pack out in the middle, where the current was strongest. The splash was sweet to hear.

"No, they've never been found," he casually told Rusty and the jury. "It was a good choice."

The fiberglass hockey mask would have floated. On the way home he stopped at an apartment complex and stuffed it into a dumpster.

———

It was time—in the courtroom of Judge Azios, in that other world where you could move about freely and feel comparatively safe in your bed at night—to eat lunch. "The jury will kindly return at 1:30," said the judge.

Still foul and oppressive and hot in the courtroom. What about the repairmen? Hadn't they done their job? Yes, of course they had, the judge politely explained, as inquiry was made. But their job wasn't to fix the air conditioning. Who had ever said it was?

The judge had an Old World sparkle in his brown eyes. He had known all along that the courtroom intruders were there to repair the smoke alarm in the hallway outside the holding cell.

———

How do you pass the hours after you've committed a murder?

Go to a party. The one on Tuam Street. Set up the alibi. A little bit of uncertainty as to time and place won't be bad. Leave some maneuvering room. David told the jury: "People were leaving the party to have breakfast at Perky's. Cindy was calm. We just picked at our breakfast—didn't have much of an appetite."

"Really?" Rusty's eyebrow arched.

David bowed his head slightly, acknowledging. *Touché*.

Rusty's questions came rapidfire now, and there was no longer a note of sympathy or connivance. David said, "No, Cindy never asked me how many times I shot them. She didn't ask any questions, that I recall. We were at my home by five-ish. Tried to relax, went over our alibi again. 'Okay, I saw Spike, I talked to him.' 'And I saw Scotty and Kathy— they'll remember me.' We turned on the TV, sat around. We went to sleep around 6:30 or 7 A.M."

"What was going through your mind, David?"

"I was extremely scared, but I realized that was one of the worst things working against me, and I had to fight hard to act calm. Try to stay in control. We got up at ten or so. Then we went to my Mom's for breakfast again, trying to act normal. I guess fairly successfully. We hadn't seen the papers yet. Then . . . I'm a little shaky on this . . . around noon we had coffee at One's-a-Meal. And then we went by Cindy's apartment on Kingston. I was supposed to be dropping her off. Her door was unlocked. The place had been ransacked by the police, although it was normally messy. Her grandmother came out—she lived across the hall —and she said, 'Cindy! Brace yourself. Your parents' house has been burglarized, and they've been killed.'

" 'What? *No!*' Cindy started crying. And she turned to me for support."

Rusty inquired coolly, "And did you give her support in her time of need?"

"Yes. What was I supposed to do?"

David had trouble remembering the aftermath. He seemed ashamed, and some of the spectators wondered why. He had presented the murder with such logic and detail that in context it seemed a normal event, and in all normal events there are natural progressions. If you killed someone, and didn't want to get caught—and what could be more natural than that desire?—you had to take certain steps. *David, we understand . . . so please, for God's sake, don't hang your head that way.*

The jury and the jammed courtroom were with him, urging him through it, wondering with him: how *do* you act after a murder? It was as if everyone wanted him to keep his cool . . . outwit the police, get away with it. At least for a while, until Kim came along. It was oddly satisfying to see him pull the wool over the eyes of the constabulary, whom we had already met in the persons of Messrs. Kent, Schultz, and Motard, and with whom, despite grudging respect, we had not fallen in love. David was the good guy; they wore the black hats and twirled their mustaches. And there was a strict forward progress that needed to be worked out to a conclusion: because, gifted with knowledge of the outcome, we could observe the young man sitting there—the existentialist antihero, tragic villain, what you will—and know that in the end he would reap the consequences and suffer his just deserts. He would be ensnared, jailed, tried; he would ultimately confess. He would wind up in this courtroom today. But until that hour, unless the coherence of the dramatic line was to be torn apart, *he must not be caught*.

On Saturday the remaining members of the Campbell family met at 8901 Memorial.

David said, "The early reports on radio and TV mentioned that the children were there when it happened. I thought that was a mistake. We didn't believe it. It was extremely tense. We were scared the whole time. But that's the way it was and we had to run with it. In the car on the way out to Memorial we discussed how Cindy would act. I had the easy part—all I had to do was be firm and supportive. We got there. The boys? They seemed to be holding up remarkably well. We were afraid that they'd be shocked and distraught, and instead they acted excited, like it was cops and robbers. Yes, that's how we perceived it. No one dwelled on how they reacted to finding the bodies."

Cindy cried at the funeral. Not massively, but she cried. Following the funeral David went with her to Homicide: "To give her support, and also I figured that sooner or later they'd ask me anyway."

A few days later he and Cindy picked up the boys at J. W.'s. "They didn't act afraid. They were a little reluctant, that's all. They were a couple of weeks with us, at my house. They were used to running wild. We tried very subtly to find out what they knew, like, 'Did you get a look at the burglars?' or, 'What did you see?' They said they hadn't seen anything."

"And how did Cindy handle having them over there at your place?" Rusty inquired.

"She tried the first couple of days, but she could hardly take care of herself. She wanted to be a mother but she didn't know how. The kids were used to being raised by the maid—they were more or less allowed to do what they wanted. I became responsible for them. But my house was in a perpetual state of being renovated, it wasn't a good environment for raising kids. So after two weeks we took them back to J. W. Campbell's house."

Mission accomplished. She was free, wasn't she?

_____

The relationship lasted six weeks more. The pressure of what they had done became overpowering, a corrupting shadow that darkened everything in their lives and blotted out any romantic feelings they had for each other. I wondered, why hadn't they anticipated that such a thing would happen? The murder would bond them, but it would also break their love.

One evening in late July, Cindy said wistfully, "I miss my mother."

David said, "Little late for that now, don't you think?"

She became irrational. They started getting on each other's nerves.

She left his house and moved to Kingston. Rusty, with David's tacit approval, skipped rapidly over this period in their lives, as if it was of no importance. He was heading elsewhere.

Cindy called David a couple of weeks after she left, he said, and told him she still loved him. But he wanted no more of it. "That's nice," he said coolly.

She told him she had a job with a family, the Salinos, as a live-in maid. He found out it wasn't true; she was still at Kingston. She called him again to reminisce. A long time ago, on Vermont, they were living downstairs and he had an upstairs tenant who complained about the noises they made during lovemaking. Bed squeaks and other squeaks. David had said gleefully, "Let's give him something to listen to that'll really freak him out."

She brought this up when she called him. The good old days. But the next morning David asked Southwestern Bell to change his telephone number.

The brother and troubled friend seeming to oust the prosecutor in him, Rusty asked, "Do you still love her, David?"

"No," David said.

"Are you sure?"

David thought it over a moment or two, then said, "Yes."

"Did you still love her at that time?"

"Yes, I did."

_____

Rusty asked David if he knew a man named Rory Lettvin. Yes, David had met him at Rudyard's. Tell us more about this fellow Rory, David. . . .

Cindy got David's new telephone number from Cecilia West. At the time of her next call he was aware that Rory Lettvin was living with her at Kingston. It was a strictly business deal, she said—Rory was supposed to pay her rent, but now he had welshed on it. And he was making sexual advances and wouldn't leave. With a strong awareness that this had happened before (he had done the same thing in May, with Jim Daggett as backup) David nevertheless went to Kingston in the early evening, alone this time, and talked to Rory—reasonably at first—and heard the other side of it: that Rory had invested money in repairs on the apartment, and in groceries, and by kicking him out she was being unfair. But it wound up in an argument.

"He became abusive," David said, "and I responded in a like manner. We started talking garbage to each other. I took a step toward him, and he tried to kick me in the balls. We got into a fight, and spun around, and I smashed his head into a plate glass window. It broke."

"The window?"

"Yes."

"And his head?"

"It didn't." David laughed, and so did the jury.

A bleeding Rory Lettvin left the apartment.

The Thursday afternoon was drawing to a close. Rusty moved David rapidly through Cindy's various legal and financial arguments with the family.

"She related to me that J. W. and Michelle had emptied out her father's safe deposit boxes and that J. W. was trying to embezzle money from the estate. She was trying to get him removed as executor. She was expecting a settlement of $25,000 cash and the fourplex on Kingston. She thought the estate was worth a couple of million, and that what was offered her wasn't a fair share. She also said she was receiving funds that would be charged against her at the final accounting. But she never spent much money. She dressed simply. She hadn't much interest in material things. She had a lot of expensive clothes in her apartment—mostly silk blouses. Never worn, just stuffed in drawers. I asked her why she didn't wear them, and she would get flustered and try to change the subject. . . . "

Rusty suddenly asked, "Now, sometime in late 1984, did you meet a woman named Kim Paris?"

David rendered his first impression of Kim: tall, hair streaked, offbeat, paramilitary, a pseudo-punk rock look, but good-looking. A new and definitely intriguing face on the Montrose scene. His roommate had brought her along to the Park Lane Tavern on Alabama.

"And your roommate's name was—?"

"Robin St. John."

"Sorry"—Rusty corrected himself—"your roommate's name *is* Robin St. John."

"No, he's not my roommate *now*," David said, and the courtroom laughed again.

Back in November 1984 Robin introduced him to Teresa. "I became extremely infatuated with her," David said. "No, I was not in love with her. Yes, we discussed marriage in an abstract manner."

(I remembered that with Wickie Weinstein he had discussed "abstractly the subject of killing someone.")

"I think I *wanted* to be in love. And I wanted a sexual relationship."

After establishing that David realized full well he had "gotten away" with murdering the Campbells, and the only thing he had to fear was telling someone he had done so, a seemingly puzzled Rusty asked, "What possessed you to talk to Kim about it?"

"It was a really heavy burden," David said. "I tried to justify it to myself, but essentially I still didn't feel right about it. I needed somebody to tell me they understood why I did it."

Rusty prompted: "It's not easy for you talk about this, is it?"

David's voice grew heavy. "No, it's not."

"Did you tell Kim some things that were not true?"

Yes. That on the night of the murders he had seen the boys in the room—in fact he only confirmed their presence when he got to Memorial at noon the next day, when the sisters told him, and the boys were yipping about it. That he'd had some idea of dealing violently with the driver of the vehicle that came round the curve on Memorial after he and Cindy fled—in fact, as he had testified, the vehicle never even slowed down. That he had switched license plates with another car in case his own was spotted—that was pure nonsense. He'd wanted to appear clever to Kim. Plus a natural leaning toward embroidery and drama.

He was shocked, he said, when he was arrested. Yes, he saw Cindy the next day, at Homicide, after her arrest. She looked pathetic. Totally fallen apart. And obese (264 pounds).

Rusty then established that David had been charged with capital murder and, after seven weeks of jury selection, had offered to testify to the truth in exchange for pleading guilty to murder and receiving a life sentence. Rusty asked him why he'd done that.

"I heard the tapes played in court. I had tried to sound like a tough guy, a macho guy, which was how Kim Paris presented herself, the sort of thing she wanted to hear. I related to her essentially the truth, but the manner in which I did it made it sound so heinous, so cold-blooded, and essentially gave the wrong impression, that I became convinced no other verdict would have been reached except death. I decided I wasn't left with a whole lot of options. Once the District Attorney's Office let me know that they would not be pursuing the death penalty in Cindy's case, I broke down and decided to go ahead and testify against her. I felt guilty in the sense that I had brought this upon myself . . . and I still felt that she was a victim, although I had come to question some of the specifics."

"I understand that," Rusty said glacially. "Did you want to testify against Cynthia Campbell Ray?"

"No, I didn't," David said quietly.

"Have you made any attempts to inform her of that since you agreed to?"

"Yes, I have."

"David, even as recently as today, did you speak to me about certain photographs of Cindy?"

"I said I'd like to have the black-and-white contact sheet of Cindy that I took back in 1981 in Tranquility Park, because I'd like to be able to remember her the way she was."

"Even after all this?"

"Yes."

From the desk in front of the judicial bench, where the marked exhibits were kept, Rusty picked up five color photographs—State's # 2, 4, 17, 21, and 22. They showed James and Virginia Campbell on their June 1982 death bed—he with one eye open, the other smashed by the bullet; she a mask of blood. Rusty fanned them out in front of David like a poker hand. "David, have you ever seen these before?"

"No, I have not."

"Is that how they looked?"

Stolidly, grumpily, David said, "They were in that same position, yes."

A pause followed, and the courtroom was intensely quiet, while Rusty made his slow way back to the prosecutor's table. He turned and asked, "Can you tell the jury how you feel about what happened on June 19, 1982?"

David waited a moment or two before he replied, "Horrible."

"Pardon me?" Rusty was suddenly hard of hearing.

"Horrible," David said again, bowing his head.

"Do you even want her to be convicted?" Rusty waved the photographs minimally in the direction of Cindy Ray, who sat at the defense table without motion or tremor, blank-eyed.

"*Want?*" David shrugged, smiled faintly. "It's hard to say. She deserves to be convicted. As far as what I want . . . it's complicated."

"On June 19, 1982, did Cynthia Campbell Ray aid, encourage, and assist you in the intentional and knowing killing of her parents, James and Virginia Campbell?"

"Yes," David said bleakly.

"I'll pass the witness, Your Honor," Rusty said.

Rusty had remarked earlier that when he finished with David he expected him to turn to the jury and ask, "Any more questions?" But now that the moment had come, David restrained himself. And there was no curtain, no thunderous applause. It was only the end of Act II. Allen Isbell had yet to brandish his dagger and enter from the wings.

Allen held a small press conference in the hallway outside by the elevators, usually an airless place, but now at least ten degrees less stickily warm than the courtroom. With the TV cameras silently taping, microphones thrust in his face and stony white lights illuminating the gravity of his expression and the pink edges of his eyes, Allen told the media: "Mr. West was not telling the truth. The truth is that Ms. Ray wasn't even there during the killings."

But later, in their office in the Old Cotton Exchange Building, Rick Brass said, "I think we're stuck with her presence. The jury believes him."

Allen nodded unhappily. Whatever his bravado before the media, he had to shift focus now and concentrate on the alternate defense of duress.

"Cindy won't like it," Rick said.

Allen said, "I think it's time we ran this trial as we see fit."

31

Allen threw the dice, and they came up "Be friendly." If I want David to trot down a path of my choosing, I have to make him feel that I like him and respect him. If I bushwhack him right away, he may freeze up.

Still no air conditioning the next day, and the courtroom was thick with bodies. Cindy Ray had a new hairstyle: tied up in a bun. David wore the same blue blazer and striped regimental tie. He looked perky, not at all fearful.

Good, Allen thought.

He began by introducing himself, and then asking politely about the many times David had talked about the case with Rusty ("four or five") —with Motard and Schultz and the D.A.'s investigator ("seven, could be six"), plus a trip to the bayou with Schultz and the HPD SCUBA team to hunt for the gun, which wasn't found. Then some more biography. David had studied art history and fundamental drawing and design at the University of Houston, and at St. Thomas he had taken courses in animation and photography. One of the reasons he had first been attracted to Cindy was her artistic talents. "Yes, I'm an artist, but Cindy is much better." He read a fair amount but did not consider himself well read. He had studied classical literature, but he preferred sci-fi, espionage, and adventure tales: "Real life adventures at this point seem more interesting than fiction."

Allen recalled David's remark that with Cindy he thought of himself as Henry Higgins, from Shaw's *Pygmalion*. Allen inquired, "What did Henry Higgins do? Who is he?"

"Well, at the time, I guess, he was what was known as an amateur psychologist, and he had made a bet with a colleague that through behavioral conditioning and training in etiquette and speech he could take anyone, even the most lowly flower girl, and turn her into someone so polished that he could pass her off as a fine lady. I saw the movie of the musical play, *My Fair Lady.*"

Allen began discussing the movie with David, and then the underlying philosophical concept.

Rusty was letting all this happen. Not a peep of an objection. He was captivated by the detail. Getting into David's mind seemed so easy. He really tries to tell you things, Rusty thought, in a way that few others do.

Yes, David admitted calmly, self-image was important to him. As he'd said before, he equated mental health with physical health. Like Henry Higgins and Eliza Doolittle? Yes, Higgins taught her to dress, to speak correct English; he drilled her in poise, made her read the newspapers. "Yes, I've read something about brainwashing." He was enjoying the dialogue, the exposure of his feelings and development as a thinker. "In the Marine Corps they tell you what can happen when you're captured."

Allen took him through his school years to the military academy in Bryan, Texas, where for practice exercises they used real guns but were denied real ammo.

Rusty objected now, on the grounds of relevancy. He saw how easily David was led off into dangerous waters, both shallow and deep.

"Overruled," the judge said.

"Would you point your rifles at other students?" Allen asked.

"Yes."

Then, at seventeen, with a school buddy, David joined the marines. "We wanted to prove we were men. At boot camp at San Diego they ran us into the dust, screamed at us. They wanted to scare us into exceeding what we had previously perceived as our limits." David was taught to kill and to reconnoiter an objective.

"Was that useful," Allen inquired, "when it came to sneaking up on the Campbells?"

"Any Texas boy who goes hunting knows how to do that," David said. That drew a laugh from the courtroom.

The Marine Corps saga ended with Headquarters & Services Company, Marine Barracks, Morocco. The primary duty was security, guarding a naval communications station. Not a dangerous posting, although there were some confrontations with native Berber tribes. They called these the Potato Wars—the marines guarded an antenna field of about a mile square, and seasonally the Berbers gathered wild potatoes there. On a couple of occasions David had to brandish his .45, but he never fired it. He had not then in his life ever fired a loaded weapon at a human being.

Allen asked—mostly for the benefit of juror Uselton, the young sockless minister, who now wore golf shirts every day to court—if David followed a moral system or was an existentialist.

David replied, more forcefully than Allen had dared hope, "No, I wasn't brought up to go to church."

Rusty objected. The judge said, "It's relevant."

Allen was pleased. He wanted the jury to doubt this man's word under oath. Now the minister-juror knew that David was a godless killer.

Attached to the garage at 8901 Memorial, David said, was a den, or playroom. He and Jamie and her friends would drink a six-pack of Heineken there. He met James and Virginia Campbell at that time, through Jamie, little dreaming that one day they would be his targets in the quest to free Cinderella. They seemed suspicious, as if searching for some ulterior motive. "And I really had none," David said.

Maria the maid was worse. She understood English fairly well but refused to speak it. (On balance, Allen was elated by this revelation.) She treated him brusquely and rudely for no reason. Blunt, obnoxious, no subtlety. A peasant. *"Jamie no está!"* she would screech, and slam the phone down. Or, if you came to the door, she'd grunt *"Espere!"*—wait! —shut the door in your face, make you hang there outside.

"I had a confrontation with her. We went upstairs one day to get something. She started bitching at me, badgering me, ordering me around. And she's a servant," he paused to explain. "This was in the spring of '81. It had been building up for a long time, and she was just *way* out of line. I had been asked to come upstairs. She ordered me around in a snotty, obnoxious voice. I used some strong language. I believe she went and complained to Mrs. Campbell, and I was asked not to come into the house anymore."

Had the jury understood the serious depth of his resentment? Not only at Maria the servant, but at Mrs. Campbell the domestic lawgiver? Allen wondered. He was on a good track here, and from the corner of his eye he could see Rusty's hands gripping the edge of the oak table.

Go gently, Allen thought. *Softly, softly, catchee monkey.*

He brought up the subject of Cindy's two boys, Michael and Matthew, living with the Campbells.

"They seemed to be pretty nice kids," David said. "The maid appeared to be the only one ever in charge of them. They would be running around, strewing things all over the place, and she would scream at them in Spanish. They would either ignore her or yell something back."

Allen asked why, in describing the Campbells, David in direct examination had used the word *weird.*

Never ask a "why" question to an adversary witness. He's liable to tell you, and you won't like it. A fundamental lawyer's dictum, but he had to risk it. And David had been gentled now, tamed beyond "adversary."

A big sigh came from the witness chair. "It was a combination of everything. Personal characteristics aside, their house was weird. It looks like a bunker."

Allen was thrilled. The choice of word couldn't have been better. If you're a psychopathic marine who's never had the chance to kill, and you come upon a bunker, what do you do? *You assault it.*

"In what way did it look like a bunker?" Allen said.

"Very ugly. Very expensive, but a big concrete block, with aluminum windows. A ratty blue rug on the floor. The general furnishings . . . it looked like they went to Tijuana to get them."

Allen chuckled, then asked, "Anything else you found weird about the family?"

"Well, one thing. The maid was an illegal alien, and they were paying very minimal wages, and just allowing her to stay in a grotty apartment behind the house."

"Did you find any irony that a lawyer would violate the law by hiring an illegal alien?"

"Yes. I suppose it wasn't a major violation of law . . . just kind of sleazy."

357

"Did there seem to be something that they were trying to hide? Did you get that in the atmosphere?"

"Yes, I did."

"In the fall of 1979, were you told by anyone, who you thought would have direct knowledge, what it might be that they were trying to hide?"

"Several things that a family would seem to want to hide," David said obliquely.

"Did Jamie reveal something to you one night, when you were having drinks at a bar called La Carafe, that was shocking?"

"Not when we were at La Carafe, no."

It was a bit like Twenty Questions.

"Would her being a lesbian be a reason why you felt maybe something was strange about that family?"

"Yes," David said.

Rusty stood up, distressed. "Your Honor, I'm going to object to the constant assassination of a family and ask that the jury be instructed to disregard the answer."

Allen calmly argued: "Mr. Hardin has repeatedly told the newspeople he personally doesn't believe there was any sexual abuse in the family. And I think I'm entitled to show, through witnesses, that here is a family —it's unfortunate, but it's true—that makes the story of the sexual abuse more reasonable to be believed than simply manipulation on the part of Cynthia Campbell Ray to try to get him to kill somebody."

"I'm just so disappointed," Rusty said, shaking his head sorrowfully at Allen, "that he's chosen to inject in the trial something that he knows, the court knows, the jury and everyone else knows, is improper." His voice began to rise. "For him to refer to anything that's said outside this courtroom is outrageous, and he knows it! I ask that he be instructed not to make such statements anymore, and let's resume this as a legal and proper trial!"

Allen immediately apologized for mentioning what Rusty had said to the media.

Rusty shouted, "And I object to him going any further! Could we now have an answer to my objection?"

"Objection sustained," Judge Azios said. There are judges who indicate their displeasure—and their prejudices—with a raised eyebrow, a grimace, an edge of sarcasm, an icy voice. Judge Azios used none of these devices. He said cordially but firmly, to both lawyers: "Let's proceed according to the rules of evidence."

Allen continued: "How did the Campbells treat their daughter Cindy, in your presence?"

"They ignored her," David said.

The weight question heaved up again. Asked to describe her appearance, David said, "She was about 180 when I met her, although she didn't look that heavy. But she was dense. I never weighed her. She wouldn't get on the scale."

He went on to relate that during the first stage of their relationship, before he became Cindy's mentor, she "never would sit at our level. She would insist on sitting on the floor with her legs curled up. If I offered her a chair she would tremble and say, 'No, no, no.' It's still my feeling, today, that she'd be beautiful if she lost weight." (Cindy, in the defendant's chair, seemed to sulk at yet another reference to her problem.) "I used to be fairly overweight myself," David explained, "and my own personal way of coping with it was that I considered the fat to be an enemy, and inculcated myself with a hatred of fat in general, and got rid of it. I was never impolite to someone because they were overweight, but I couldn't help but have diminished respect for their allowing it to be that way."

And when he met Cindy he thought, "What could have been the cause of this human mess?"

But if no one else saw the potential of this human mess, he did. "At first I thought there must be something behind this animosity between her and Jamie, but I never saw Cindy respond with a harsh word. I never saw her do anything or say anything about anyone that wasn't just sweet and kind. She displayed a good sense of humor. She was intelligent, friendly . . . and she had a beautiful singing voice. She patterned it after Barbra Streisand's."

"You call her your 'project' or 'subject,'" Allen reminded him. "Did you see yourself as her psychotherapist or psychoanalyst?"

"To some degree, yes," David said. "She was a passive person."

Allen suddenly asked, "Does Cindy have a bad scar? On her abdomen?"

David described it: "An old appendix scar, but doesn't look it. She told me that after the appendicitis operation, when she was convalescing at home, her father beat her with a strap." *

"Let's move up to May of 1982," Allen said, "when she knocked on your door."

David agreed that at that time she showed signs of regression. It made

---

* Cecilia West gave me a more detailed version of this tale, as related to her by Cindy, in which Jim Campbell found himself alone in the house with Cindy and tried to take her to bed. When Cindy fled from him and locked the bathroom door, he broke it down, then beat her with a belt buckle. The appendectomy stitches opened. A doctor had to be called, to whom the parents told the tale of a dog clawing at her while she slept on a sofa.

him angry. He described her then as "obese," with "a devastated emotional life." Yes, it appeared that every time she went back to her parents' house for any length of time, she regressed.

"They were ruining your creation?"

But David seemed suddenly irked by Allen's insistent reference to Pygmalion and Henry Higgins. He lifted his head and said sharply, "She had feelings. It's not just a matter that they were undoing some work of art. She appeared to be hurt."

On that note, since it was after four o'clock, Allen let him go for the day. It was Friday, June 13. The second week of the trial was over. "Have a nice weekend," the judge said to everybody, mopping his forehead.

On Saturday, with the thermometer at ninety-six degrees, Dr. Rob Owens, the psychologist, spent the day with the three defense lawyers in the sanctuary of Rick Brass's office, decorated with old *Saturday Evening Post* covers and a neon sign that said "Lawyer." The defense team asked whether their own evidentiary theories as to motive and behavior were consistent with Dr. Owens's psychological theories and the accepted body of psychiatric literature.

The psychologist leaned back into a leather chair and discoursed at length. Allen liked what he heard. After Dr. Owens left, Allen and Rick worked for an hour to develop an argument that would shoehorn the projected testimony into the rules of evidence. The problem was that Owens, although he was in court every day, listening attentively, had never spoken directly to David West. How could he testify as to David's psychological makeup and behavioral capacity? Would the judge allow it?

"The theory," Rick said to Allen, "is that Rusty asked the same questions that Owens would ask, and so are you asking them. David's giving the same answers that he'd give to Owens. *And under oath.*"

"It's worth a try," Allen decided. He sipped at an ice-cold lemonade.

Rusty, of course, would oppose with tooth and claw the admission of such testimony. And Rusty had been known to draw blood.

On Monday morning the courtroom air conditioning was still not working. Everyone theorized about massive body heat and the charge that Ted Poe, judge in the adjacent courtroom of his 228th District Court, had bribed the workmen to siphon off all the coolth allotted to the eighth floor of the old building. Judge Azios ordered a fan to be placed on a chair facing the jury box. When it was turned on it blew straight into the faces of jurors Wheat and Beagle. The judge and most of the media had observed on Friday that Beagle, the schoolteacher, was nodding off during Allen Isbell's cross-examination of the star witness, while Melanie Wheat, the young insurance agent, was chewing gum and staring blankly into a far distance, looking as if she was *ready* to nod off. Sometimes when there was a break and the jury didn't leave the box, she leaned over and giggled with the other young juror, Mark Vandervoort.

Rusty speculated on a developing romance—"Four weeks in that little jury room!" (As it turned out, he was dead right. Vandervoort had already approached Keith Goode, the bailiff, and asked if there was any reason he couldn't see Wheat in the evenings. Keith said, "Go for it. Just don't discuss the case.")

Allen realized he would have to pep it up. Sleeves in the courtroom were rolled up and wrinkled; pages of notes stuck together. Sweat shone on everyone's brow. Allen had to get this jury to listen and to doubt. He greeted David West cordially and began to rake up, seemingly at random, various stories that David had told the jury during direct examination by Rusty.

David admitted that yes, in early May of 1982, when he and his pal Jim Daggett had hurried over to Kingston to answer Cindy's call for help, they had been prepared to use their shotgun and pistol.

"What motivated you to go over there and do that?"

"The thought of the sexual advances was part of it," David explained. "But it's fair to say that I was once again coming to the rescue of a damsel in distress. And I was disgusted, because she couldn't handle things like that, and she knew she couldn't."

Again he described the fetal position in which he found Cindy— "timid and beaten, chain-smoking, pathetic"—on his doorstep in late May, or maybe it was early June. And this time his demonstration was far more visual than before; the jury rocked back and forth in their swivel chairs, chuckling. David's movements at such times were precise and uninhibited. And brief: David never milked it.

He admitted saying at a later date to Kim Paris that Cindy was "all nonspine, just a worm." And that "she had no balls."

Allen said, "Your reaction to this pathetic, timid, and beaten-down creature arriving on your doorstep, was . . . ?"

"Shock. Horror. Sadness and helplessness. It just seemed like after everything I did, as hard as I had tried and committed myself to her, and changed her for the better, it was all frittered away."

"But you were willing to take on the project again?"

"Against my better judgment. I still loved her. I couldn't abandon her."

Allen brought up the car-banging incident related to Cecilia, where Cindy had supposedly become hysterical and David had done "a thousand dollars' worth of damage" to the offender's body work. David confirmed all the details. But when Allen asked, "Isn't that when you decided to kill the Campbells?"—David said no, that wasn't so. Although Cindy's out-of-control behavior and her shrieks to her absent mother—"*I don't know what I've done, but please, stop it! I won't do it again!*"—no doubt had an impact on his decision.

"Didn't you tell Kim Paris, in December 1984, that Cindy regarded you as 'her Svengali'? "

He denied that. Then: "If I did, I don't remember it."

Sweating already, he shifted uncomfortably in the witness chair. The line of questioning harked back to the dilemma that the prosecution had faced as early as last December, when Rusty cut his deal with Gene Nettles. Who was the prime mover in the murders? Was there a possibility that David had coerced Cindy into aiding him . . . or that he was lying and had done it on his own? I wondered.

"You were in charge of the plans for the murders, weren't you?"

"Yes."

"Do you remember telling Kim Paris, 'I made her stand there with me'?"

"I don't remember that, no."

Allen brought out the state's transcript of the confession tapes and refreshed his memory. " *. . . the thing was that I made her stand there with me when I did it.*"

"Seems like I wasn't accurate," David said, seemingly chastised.

Allen then quoted several times from the tapes: but each time the minister-lawyer came to the word *fuck* he would instead say, "the F word," and when he came to "goddamn" he would substitute "the big-G word." A few people in the courtroom smiled, but no one laughed, and the jury as a whole seemed to reflect approval. (Allen's reason was simple: "I grew up in a religious family—there was no profanity at all. I never use those words. It would be out of character and unnatural for me to do so anywhere, including court.")

"When you were talking with Kim Paris about the shooting, you distinguished between 'personal mode' and 'soldier mode.' Can you tell me what that means?"

David shook his head. "To a large extent, that was just macho B.S. It meant that I had decided to do it. All the moral decisions had been made. Now it was just a matter of doing it."

"What was your plan of exit?"

"Just run out the front door."

Allen adjusted his half-glasses and peered down at the transcript. "You had emptied your gun. As you were running down the stairs to face whatever awaited you outside, you said to Kim Paris: 'I thought the,' and you used the F word, 'neighbors and everybody would be running out of the F-word houses . . . and as we were running across the road a car came around the curve, and we had the masks on, and you used the S word. I figured, well, if the big-G word car stops, I'll kill those MFs.' My question is: What if you had run into one of the neighbors whom you feared might have heard the noise? What would you have done with the empty pistol?"

"Run. It was only about a thirty-second sprint from the front door to the car."

"For both of you?"

"She didn't have any trouble keeping up with me," David said. The sweat seemed to spring afresh on his forehead.

I was waiting for Allen to ask how a 200-pound woman, "totally fallen apart," could keep up with him. But Allen didn't ask.

In the afternoon, mercifully, the judge arranged to move the trial next door to Judge Ted Poe's temporarily empty courtroom, where near-arctic air flowed uninterruptedly from the vents and cooled the brows of prosecution and defense alike. It was an identical mirror-image court-room to that of Judge Azios, with a big Lone Star State flag flying in the breeze behind the bench.

David was placed in Poe's blue-painted holding cell, on whose walls graffiti proclaimed, "Poe's Court of Western Justice" and "The Blue Room of Doom," and "Last Place You See Before TDC." (Poe wouldn't let the graffiti be erased.) David emerged and was led to the witness chair. Waiting for the proceedings to resume, he bent the mike to his mouth. "Testing, testing . . ."

Allen skipped ahead to when Kim Paris entered David's life, and then to the two nights in February 1985, when Kim, unknown to her would-be lover, was taping him.

"You've said that the Campbells deserved it." Allen quoted from the end of the first night of the tapes: " ' . . . they rated it. I don't feel like I've even compromised myself morally. I mean, I didn't do anything wrong as far as I'm concerned.' "

He then asked David an interesting question. Another "why" question, but he didn't fear the answer.

"If that's so, if they rated it, why was it a 'heavy burden' that you had to tell someone about—in this instance, Kim Paris—so that they'd 'understand why I had to do it.' ?"

It was key. David couldn't very well say, "Because I'm mentally ill," or offer an analytical self-portrait that would unintentionally satisfy those who believed he did have a moral screw loose somewhere. Lamely he answered, "Because . . . I felt bad about having killed *someone,* but at the time I felt that the Campbells themselves rated it, but looking back on it I didn't—even then, in looking back on it—I didn't feel good about having just gone out and killed someone, in general. . . ."

The quest for absolution.

"There was a certain degree of loss of innocence?" It was hard to tell by Allen's tone if he was being sincere and truly cared, or if it was a cruel irony. His face and tone never lost their solemnity.

"Yes, that's it." David seemed glad to agree.

"Do you remember referring to Cindy as 'an innocent person' ?"

"Yes, I probably did."

"The problem I'm having, David, is that if it was this heavy burden and you didn't feel right about it—why did you embellish the story and make it more ruthless than it really was?"

Calmly, as if it were the most natural thing in the world, David said, "Kim had made it quite clear, and I think it's quite clear on the tapes, that she had presented herself as a person who wanted to hear some real badass stuff, and so I was accommodating her."

Allen closed in on him. "You even embellished the story to show how clever you were, didn't you?" He offered the example of the false tale of the switched license plates. Now it was clear where Allen was headed. If David would lie about some things, *why not about others?*

David had no way to sidestep the implication. "That's correct," he said, starting to sound tired now that the afternoon was growing old.

"You tried to convince Cindy that the death of her parents was the best thing that had ever happened to her, didn't you?"

He hedged: "I don't remember that specifically."

"And in trying to convince her that it was the best thing, you told her that you did it for her, didn't you?"

"That's correct."

"And David, didn't you make Cindy feel that she was actually there because it was her deal? Isn't that where the idea of her being there originated?"

A weary David said, "No, that's not correct. She was physically present."

"Didn't you tell her that the only hitch was that as you were running out the door, you dropped a glove that had been in your pocket?"

364

"I didn't need to tell her that. She did it. I didn't."

Allen hammered: "And after telling her that you'd killed her parents, didn't you tell her that you would kill her if she told anybody?"

"No, that's not correct."

Allen thumbed through his transcript of the tapes and quoted Kim Paris: " *Did you seriously entertain thoughts of killing her?'* Meaning Cindy. And you said, *'Yes, yes I did.'* "

"I said that," David admitted.

"You were originally charged with capital murder, weren't you, David? One of the possible punishments was death by injection, is that correct? That's a frightening ordeal to go through, isn't it?"

"Yes, it is."

"Even a soldier fears the bullet that might get him, doesn't he?"

"That's correct."

"And it was your misfortune to be prosecuted by one of the very best, if not the best, that Harris County has, correct?"

"Yes."

"You have a lot of fear and respect for Rusty Hardin's ability, don't you?"

Fear? Respect? Pale words.

"Yes."

"You lost a lot of sleep in those seven weeks of jury selection for your capital murder trial?"

"Yes, I did."

Allen then passed to the jury a copy of special issue #2, the question as to future dangerousness, reminding them and David that if in last December's trial the jury in the second stage had answered yes to the question, the death penalty in the case would have been mandatory. He asked David if he had worried that the tapes might indicate a "state of mind toward violence."

"They could have," David admitted.

"And so you entered your plea of guilty because you thought the state was going to ram these tapes down your throat, correct?"

"That's correct."

"And you also knew that there were many more things, that never appeared on that tape, that would have pointed in the direction of you being a violent person, didn't you?"

"No," David said uneasily, "not that many."

"You were arrested and convicted for carrying a deadly weapon in Mexico, weren't you?"

David heatedly denied it, then remembered and laughed it off: just a souvenir knife, in Tijuana, and he'd slipped the cop ten dollars and was let go.

"Were you aware that Jamie Campbell was prepared to testify that you'd fired a gun in your living room a year before the murder?"

Rusty got up angrily to argue that such questions were impermissible and irrelevant. He pointed a finger at Allen, and said sharply, "He just wants to smear the man!"

No one even tittered. Rusty's inner conviction and persuasive power were so great that it only dimly registered that he was talking about the confessed cold-blooded murderer of two sleeping people. Getting *smeared!*

Judge Azios overruled the objection. "Go ahead, answer."

David said no, he wasn't aware back in December that Jamie was going to testify that he'd fired a gun in her living room.

Allen banged away at him. "You and Wickie Weinstein attacked Virgil Lee Johnson and hit him across the forehead with a baseball bat, didn't you?"

David denied it. I knew he wasn't lying; it had been a pickaxe handle.

"You got into this fight with Rory Lettvin and bashed his head against the plate glass window of the second story of Kingston, didn't you?"

Before David could comment, Rusty charged to his aid once more. How far back into David's life would this interrogative bullying go? What is the defense counsel doing, he demanded again, "other than just bringing everything he can to smear him?"

"I find it ludicrous that Mr. Hardin—" Allen began.

But the judge stopped him. "Just a minute. I don't approve the word *smear,* Mr. Hardin," he said instructively. "It's not a matter of smear. It's a matter of cross-examination."

"I see," Rusty said. "In that light, I withdraw my objection. I presume we've set the precedent that if *he* puts a witness up there, we can ask him anything." He thumped down in his chair.

Allen resumed: "Did you physically beat up a man for verbally insulting Lynn Roebuck?"

"Yes, I did," David said. "But not just verbally insulting. For following and threatening with two of his buddies, I did."

"Did you tell Kim Paris, after they repossessed your car, that you were going to go out and hire 'niggers' and kill whoever did it?"

"I may have."

"When you told Paul Whitfield that you had killed two people with the gun that you'd supposedly bought from Wickie Weinstein, you didn't tell anything about Cindy being involved, did you?"

"No, I didn't."

"Do you remember what you told Kim Paris you would do if you got caught? That you would make it appear to be Cindy's responsibility and no one would believe that you just did it on your own?"

"I might have said that," David murmured, "when she was asking me for some sort of assurance about Cindy."

"I'll pass the witness."

Rusty said on redirect: "Can you tell the jury, David, from the first time that you and I ever had any contact with each other, what my position has been as to whether or not you were violent?"

"We disagreed," David said cordially. "You said that I was, and I think I'm not."

"And indeed, since your plea of guilty, haven't you and I had extensive conversations about that very subject? And were you ever successful in convincing me that you were not a violent person?"

"I don't know. I guess not," David said regretfully.

The courtroom assemblage was thus given a fascinating glimpse into the developing relationship between the erstwhile defendant and current star witness with his prosecutor—a Texas Raskolnikov and Porfiry Petrovich.

David said, "I didn't want to be perceived by you as a killer for hire or an immoral, maniac sort of person. My perception of the Campbells was that they were totally evil, and at the time I thought it was morally right to kill them. I don't still feel that way."

"Why?"

"Because no matter how horrible someone is, people can't be permitted to just go and—even if they're a hundred percent right in their perception, they can't just be permitted to kill someone, because then people are going to be dying all over the place."

"Did you ever consider going behind Cindy to check out her story of sexual abuse?" Rusty asked.

No, David said, he hadn't. And no, neither Jamie nor any of the other sisters had ever told him of "the family doing anything nasty or immoral to Cindy."

"When you talked to Kim Paris about Cindy's role in the murders, that was before you had any reason to try to avoid the death penalty, wasn't it?"

"Yes."

Rusty then asked to have the jury excused, and when they were gone he set forth an argument in favor of admitting the Kim Paris–David West tapes into evidence. The door was open—the defense had already quoted from them extensively, and the thrust of Allen Isbell's cross-examination implied that David's testimony was false because, frightened of the death penalty, he had made a deal with the state. Therefore the state asked for prior consistent testimony: the tapes. Rusty concluded, "I think we have a right to show that he felt the same things before the State of Texas had an interest in him."

Judge Azios was willing, demanding only one thing. "Mr. Hardin, can you delete some of the boring parts?"

Rusty promised that he could.

Tomorrow morning, the judge said, he would make a decision.

———————

In the morning Rusty continued his argument that the defense had opened the door to the tapes. There was little that Allen could do except kick himself for having ever quoted from them in the first place.

In front of the jury the video was played in exactly the same way as during David West's hearing.

To what end? One began to wonder who was on trial here. Wasn't it supposed to be Cynthia Ray? It seemed more like David. This was his fifth day of testimony, and we *knew* he was the murderer—he had pled guilty, had been sentenced.

But the jury understood. The real issue in this trial was David's credibility. Cindy's life depended on it.

The tapes took all day. The jury was able to hear how David's voice had deepened since last February, how much more in control he was here in the courtroom than he had been with the woman he loved. (Or at least they *should* have heard it. Who could really tell what they heard, or how they perceived it? Most of the regular spectators *knew so much more than the jury*.)

During one of the breaks I wandered backstage and found David sitting on the wooden bench outside the holding cell, reading his Bible. Leitner wasn't there, and neither was the bailiff. David and I hadn't talked since December, and I knew through Ginger Casey that he had characterized me as Machiavellian, although later he had recanted and said he was no longer angry. Still, I wanted him to know exactly what had happened, and this was the chance.

"I understand," he said. "I didn't then. It was hard to take. I thought of you as a friend, and then you brought this guy in"—he raised a hand to stop me from interrupting—"I know now you didn't *bring* him, but I didn't know it then. And it was the straw that broke my back, that made me take Rusty's deal. But it's okay. It really is. It was all inevitable, I guess."

Strange: David and I each wanted the other's respect. We had bonded by our closeness during the autumn voir dire. No matter w̶ he said in court, no matter how much I learned of what he had done̶ still saw him not as a murderer but as a human being who had murdere̶ someone. There was a difference. In the light of that difference, this was my chance to ask him one of the things that had always troubled me— that raw question: How had he mounted the stairs that night and over-come what I still called conscience, the voice that in the back of the mind says, "You cannot under any circumstances do this"?

"I have a conscience," David said. "It was my conscience that led me to confess to Kim. I felt I should have done something earlier, when Cindy first told me what her parents had done. But I put it off. The second time, I had to do it. I thought, what kind of person am I if I don't act on my beliefs? Not just, 'How could I do it?' But more, 'How could I *not* do it?' I would have been immoral and a coward *not* to act. They were evil," he said doggedly, "and by removing them I could cure Cindy." He showed me a smile of despair. "I was a schmuck. I didn't realize how easily women manipulated me."

Still I didn't understand. His answer had been close enough to seem to satisfy the question, but enough off-line to make me feel that either he was remarkably clever or deeply blind.

The bailiff appeared, frowning at me for the intrusion on his space. I said goodbye to David and went back into the courtroom.

The next morning Rusty asked, "David, has this been easy for you?"

"No."

"I noticed that periodically you laughed during the playing of the tapes."

"That's correct."

"Why?"

David said, "Because it was extremely humiliating, and embarrassing, and that's just a defensive action. I mean, you either laugh or you cry. And parts of it were sort of ironic. They were actually funny."

Allen took David on recross. Earlier he had got David to admit that the planning for the murders began "only four or five days" before their commission; but to Rusty in redirect David had hedged on the accuracy of that time frame. Now Allen pointed out that if David had stuck to his story of "only four or five days," it would have effectively wiped out Maria's testimony that *ten days* before the murders, at his suggestion, Cindy had checked the downstairs windows at Memorial for possible entry.

ou've had a long time to prepare for this testimony, haven't you,
. West?" It was no longer *David*. "And you're looking at death from
his man if he doesn't like your testimony, isn't that true?" He gestured
toward Rusty at the counsel table.

"If he thinks I deliberately lied in order to mess up his case," David
said.

"You're tailoring your testimony to suit Mr. Hardin, aren't you?"
Allen said sharply.

"No, I'm clarifying the fact that I wasn't clear in the first place."

"You got the story of Cindy going to the house to check the windows
from reading in the newspapers of Maria's testimony, didn't you?"

David looked uncomfortable. Under a barrage of similar questions he
said, "No," and then "Probably," and then "I don't know about that
specific statement." Allen had now moved from calling him *"Mr. West"*
to an even colder *"sir."* As he cross-examined, he ranged back and forth
between the counsel table and the witness chair, sometimes coming so
close that you thought he was going to grab David by the lapels and
shake him. Allen projected outrage and revulsion. It was a startling
change from the friendly, sympathetic gentleman lawyer and part-time
Galveston minister.

"Did you have a powerful motive to lie to Kim Paris?"

"Yes," David admitted.

"In fact, you just told her a pack of lies!"

"A pack is a quantitative concept," David said. "I wouldn't say that."
He glared back at Allen now; he didn't like this.

"Did you lie a lot to Kim Paris about yourself?"

"I misrepresented a lot, I guess."

"When you met Kim you were making five dollars an hour as a delivery boy at A-1 Blueprint, isn't that correct, sir?"

"Yes," David said, coloring.

"And Kim is a pretty good-looking woman, wouldn't you say?"

"Fairly, yes."

"You're certainly more intelligent than a five-dollar-an-hour job, aren't
you?"

"I like to think so."

And so, Allen argued, you had to pump yourself up in her estimation,
and you made up the story of your coming into money from an old
girlfriend. And then, when you admitted to the murders, you were stuck
with that story, so you said that Cindy had agreed to pay you for committing them!

David's responses, whether yes or no, had become sullen.

"And when you confessed on the first night, 'I killed Cindy's parents,' didn't you think that would scare Kim Paris to death? And didn't she then say to you that she was afraid you might kill her? And wasn't it simpler to put her mind at ease, to assure her you're not a bloodthirsty killer, by saying that you didn't kill those two people because you didn't like them, *but because a girlfriend begged you to do it*? And to further explain why you stayed in contact with the old girlfriend, you said, 'She owes me a lot of money for the killing.' "

"I said that, yes," David admitted.

"And at one point Kim said, 'You know, we can have two kids and a third one on the way, and zap, Cindy turns you in and you're off to prison.' And you told Kim Paris, so that she wouldn't be worried about that problem, *'Remember, Cindy was there.'* Right?"

"That's what I said, yes."

"David," Allen said, exasperated, "tell the jury how they're to determine when you're telling the truth and when you're lying."

David said calmly, "Listening to me, and listening to the tapes, and deciding for themselves."

After a few more vexed questions, Allen said, "Pass the witness."

Rusty, on re-redirect, opened by nodding his head at Allen and saying, "Quite a different personality talking to you today, isn't it, David?"

That initiated yet another argument between prosecutor and defense attorney, and the judge instructed Rusty to cut out the sidebar remarks and move along.

Rusty then asked, "David, have I at any time asked you to match your testimony to suit any of my theories?"

"No."

"Pass the witness," Rusty said.

"No further questions," Allen said.

"Mr. West, you're excused." Judge Azios nodded at the bailiff, and then back to David with a brief little smile that seemed to mean: good luck, nice to have known you, even under these circumstances. Stay out of trouble and don't get killed in jail, and maybe I'll treat you to another cup of Nescafé in about nineteen years.

David smiled back. He thought the judge was a fine human being. On the way out his glance wavered across to Cindy and he shrugged, as if to say, "Sorry."

32

At this point Texas law required the state to produce only one more witness who would "tend to connect the defendant with the crime." After that Rusty could rest his case. The corroborating witness would be Gwen Sampson, Cindy's former friend and art instructor, and all the world knew it except the jury.

But Rusty understood human curiosity. Beyond that, he was thorough, and most important of all, he wanted to win *the right way*. Believing that the collective soul of the jury represented the American good citizen—for whom, in his bailiwick, he was chief interpreter and swordbearer—he wanted that citizen to make an intelligent and ethically correct decision based on the broadest possible knowledge. The law was servant, not dictator.

And he wanted the jury to know Cindy for what he had come to believe she was: a calculating destroyer not only of decent lives but of reputations, a frighteningly clever manipulator, a vicious murderess who had committed the most repugnant crime known to humankind, condemned by every civilization since our forebears grasped a baboon's thighbone and turned it into a weapon.

Rusty stubbornly refused to believe there had been sexual abuse by Jim Campbell or physical cruelty by Virginia Campbell toward their second youngest daughter. I disagreed. I thought that was Rusty's blind spot. But just as Allen Isbell and Randy McDonald represented the rights of Cynthia Campbell Ray in that court, so Rusty believed he represented the rights of the murdered lawyer and his wife. The whole Campbell family, in fact, was maligned by this obscene fairy tale of incest and near-drownings and bathroom lockups. Their parents could not unsully their own memories—Jim Campbell could not cry to the world from the grave: "I never touched her! I was nothing but a decent man and a good father. I tried to help that poor unstable creature every step of the way." Virginia could not protest that she'd done her best with a surly child, a quintessential bad seed—couldn't cry out: "Beat her? *Never!* Lock her in the bathroom? How could I? Bathrooms lock from the *inside!*"

Rusty would do it for them. It was his obligation, and he had a simple plan. Plow the most fertile ground. Her nature and that of her tales will become clear. Plow deep. Turn the earth . . . the jury will see the rot.

And so, to begin, as his next witness he called Rory Lettvin, the man whose head David had admitted to having smashed against a plate glass window.

Neatly dressed in a gray three-piece suit (his best, one sensed, and perhaps his only), Rory was twenty-five, with curly hair (no visible scars on his forehead) and a pleasantly deep, amused, Eastern voice. Born in Cleveland, he worked now as a part-time electrician and stagehand for the City of Houston, and he stated at one point in testimony that his ambition was to be a head carpenter on Broadway. He was already a performer; he seemed always on the verge of breaking into a stand-up comic routine.

Rusty wasn't interested in David's wreaking havoc on Rory's skull, or, for that matter, anything about Rory himself. It was Rory's perception and memory of Cindy that had brought him to this stage on the eighth floor of the Harris County Courthouse.

During the testimony of Sgt. Kent, Rusty had tried to get into the record a description of Cindy's apartment on Kingston, but Allen Isbell had thwarted him with a series of objections. Rusty rarely forgot and never gave up. Now, since Allen's cross-examination of David West had opened so many doors into the past, Rusty believed he could overpower the defensive objections to a truthful portrait of Cindy's life style and its attendant smells.

Rory Lettvin testified that in late September of 1982, three months after the murders, he was staying at David's house on Vermont, paying him thirty-five dollars a week for the privilege. One evening the telephone rang. Rory picked it up. Cindy Ray was calling.

"She said she was sick, and wanted David to bring her some soup. David wasn't there. I'd seen a picture of her on a bike, in David's bedroom. I told her I'd bring her some hot tea with Scotch in it."

Young Rory, only twenty-one then, went over to Kingston to meet the fate that was to bring him to this courtroom nearly four years later. "She was living in the upper lefthand apartment of the fourplex, facing the street. She was disheveled, lying in bed. I'd never seen anything like it. I stayed five or six hours and cleaned up the house."

"When you talked to her," Rusty asked, "did she give you any explanation of the condition of her apartment?"

"Yes, she did. Since the death of her parents she had not really been paying attention to her housekeeping, and David West had been doing a great deal of that for her."

"Can you describe the apartment?" Then, as Rusty had so keenly anticipated, he weathered the tornado of objections from the defense.

"Overruled."

Allen slumped down. He knew what was coming.

"Well . . ." Rory Lettvin took a deep breath.

"There was green and white carpeting on the floor that was full of pressed cat feces, and paint tubes that had been squished open so that the paint had dried in little piles all over the room. In one corner there were Styrofoam Popeye Chicken containers, stacked higher than my knee, that were probably one or two months old. Rotten food everywhere. A sink full of food cans, bits of food still in them. No garbage facilities whatever. She had a cat, a kitten, and the kitten had proceeded to take the entire bedroom and turn it into its litter box. There were some Chinese silk blouses and skirts and slacks from Neiman-Marcus all over the floor. The price tags were still on them—nothing under a hundred dollars. There were stains all over them. All the clothing smelled. I'd never seen so many clothes just ruined—over twenty blouses."

"How long did it take you to clean the apartment?"

"Four days."

After that, he moved in. "It became evident to me that Cindy wasn't capable of keeping up the apartment or handling anything by herself. I made a mutually beneficial arrangement with her—upon her receiving her inheritance, I'd receive a road box of tools in return for fixing the apartment and getting her to the point where she could carry on with her life." The tools he had in mind, he testified, were "worth ten to twenty thousand dollars." (For reasons that baffled me, neither the prosecution nor the defense questioned this figure.)

"How was it," Rusty wanted to know, "that after only a few days you knew she was coming into part of an estate? When did she first mention that to you?"

"The first night." Her sisters and uncle, she told him, were in cahoots to try and cheat her out of the estate. "She was under the impression that she was going to be coming into approximately a million dollars. She was never really clear about what she'd do with the money. . . . The first night she talked about her parents, who had been murdered. Shot. She said her father was a very sweet, congenial man who apparently traveled a lot—a loving, doting father—"

"That's the way she described her father?" Rusty said, open-mouthed.

"Yes, sir."

"Did she ever mention sexual abuse to you?"

"She mentioned that she'd been sexually abused at one time."

"Did she ever suggest that it was by her father?"

"No, sir."

She told Rory that she had a stepmother—her name was Virginia Campbell. "Apparently Cindy's mother had died when she was three or four. Virginia Campbell had then married Mr. Campbell. She had three daughters from a previous marriage. It was a sort of Cinderella story. There was the wicked stepmother and the three ugly sisters who would lock her in a closet for days on end. She told me that her stepmother would force her to eat her own excrement and wallow in it in a closet as punishment."

Almost collectively, the jury sucked in its breath.

Rusty said, "As she told you this, how would you describe her manner?"

"She appeared very calm and precise about it."

"Did you believe it?" Rusty asked.

"Very much so."

"You believed that stuff about being locked in the closet and having to roll around in her own excrement?" Rusty asked, amazed.

"Yes, sir," Rory Lettvin said, blushing.

"Did she tell you how often the wicked stepmother treated her that way?"

"Frequently."

"And did she tell you why the wicked stepmother did it to her?"

"It was out of spite, because her father doted on Cindy, and the stepmother felt that her own children were being neglected. The wicked sisters were trying to usurp her inheritance. She said her first sexual experience was that she had been raped, and that she had enjoyed it."

"Did she ever suggest or hint that it was her father who had raped her?"

"No, sir. She always spoke of 'my poor departed father.' My impression was that he was a very saintly man who was very seldom home, but when he was home he spent as much time as he could with her. She never told me anything about her real mother, her blood mother."

Rory Lettvin was into his performance now, even though it was non-Equity.

"At first, when I met her, Cindy was calm and rational. She gave me information in a clear, concise, controlled manner. But within three or four days she was crazy. I didn't see how any human being could function in society without being able to drive, without having a bank account, without any photo ID, unable to go to the store and go grocery shopping . . . she apparently didn't know how. She would walk up the block to Kojak's and buy Cokes and candy bars. I'm not a very well-educated person, but at least I understand personal hygiene. She didn't. She smelled. She didn't know anything of women's personal anatomy. I reached that conclusion because of the particular smell. I concluded that no one had ever taken the time to instruct her in that. I took it upon

375

myself to do it. And I tore the carpeting out of the apartment, did the dishes, the electrical work, and cleaned the bathroom. I also established a bank account for her at Texas Commerce Chemical."

"And did she mention David West?"

"She said she'd moved in with him after she'd finished art school over at St. Thomas. She was not in love with David. He was a friend who was constantly forcing his attentions on her, until finally one day he could take no more and he kicked the door down and had his way with her."

"She told you that?"

"Yes, sir."

"She told you that David West raped her?"

"Yes, sir."

"And you *believed* that?" Rusty asked.

"Yes, sir." Rory shrugged.

He then told the jury the story of his eviction by David, following an argument over Cindy's kitten continuing to foul the bedroom carpet that Rory had so diligently scrubbed. "I placed my foot on her rear end and gave her a shove, and said, 'Clean this place up now.' When David arrived he said I'd beaten Cindy up. He said, 'Pack your things, you're moving out.'" An argument resulted. "I told him to do something anatomically impossible, and he threw me out a window." The window was about eighteen feet above the ground. Rory's shoulder and buttocks were bruised, not his head.

He came back the next day to collect his things. "Cindy said, 'Last night was a bad dream. Why don't you move back in?'"

"Did you do that?" Rusty inquired.

"My mother raised crazy children, not stupid ones," said Rory, echoing one of the most common misconceptions among American youth in our time.

The jury laughed. Rusty passed the witness.

Allen had seen Rory Lettvin's name on the witness list offered by the state, but had been unprepared for the thrust of his testimony. He began his cross-examination cautiously.

No, Rory was not an Urban Animal, although he had first met David at Rudyard's Pub, where David used to bring his two pit bulldogs to the bar and sometimes fed them steak and beer. But David wasn't really so peculiar in comparison to the other people at Rudyard's. He at least had hair on his head. He seemed like a likable guy. Violent? "There were some rather drunk British gentlemen who came to the pub and proceeded to make some derogatory remarks about the United States. David biffed one of them out. He pushed a table up into his lap and punched him three times in the face. He acted vengefully. He was patriotic."

"Was Cindy fat when you met her?"

"No, she was a very attractive girl. She was at that point slightly overweight, but nothing that a little determination couldn't cure."

"Did you try any sexual advances with her?"

"Yes, in the beginning."

"Did you think she was crazy?"

"I didn't think she was crazy at first—just a slob of monumental proportions." But later, Rory said, he changed his mind. She was crazy.

On redirect Rusty asked him what he meant by the term *crazy*.

"Someone unable to make a rational decision. Unable to take care of herself. If someone didn't help her, she would die."

Exeunt Rory Lettvin.

Jamie Campbell came next, and her appearance caused a stir in the courtroom. Would the women of the family savage their bad sister? Did they really believe Cindy was guilty of murdering their common mother and father? Would there be outbursts of ineradicable hatred, or loyal protests of love?

From Jamie, neither. The kindest personal thing she said about Cindy was that "she always made me sandwiches after school." The nastiest things were that "she talked to my Mom like she was a maid," and "she glared at my Dad all the time when we were watching TV. She'd sing during the news, and he would say, 'Cindy, for God's sake, shut up!' She would look at you real mean."

The problem with Jamie was that she didn't seem to be quite with it. She was twenty-five years old, a pretty ingénue with straight brown hair. A copywriter, she said, for an Austin radio station. Wearing white slacks and a blue blouse, she looked like a younger, slimmer Cindy, but you could see from various bulges that in a few years, or sooner, she could develop what the courtroom now knew so intimately as a "weight problem."

But other things about Jamie were more remarkable than her weight. Her down-home cracker barrel voice was her most notable characteristic, and she seemed to have the attitude to match it. Igor Alexander, a magazine writer commissioned to write a story of how the media interacted with the principals in the case, threw up his hands. "Here's this hotshot urban lawyer," he said, "with a house in the Memorial area. All four kids go to college. Three speak decent English, but the fourth, this

Jamie—and she's the only one who spent a year in Switzerland—sounds like a throwback who never made it out of the pea patch back in Butcher Hollow. What's behind that?"

"Cindy is my big sister," Jamie explained. "We got along real good. She was real into art." Their mother "was real sweet." Their father "was a whole lot of fun. . . . When I was away at school I used to talk to them at least three times a week. I would have real conversations with my Mom, but Dad would get on the phone and bark. He also crossed his eyes behind my Mom."

With great patience, as though he were talking to a fascinating young woman at an uptown cocktail party, Rusty guided Jamie through her education—Hunters Creek Elementary, Alexander Smith Academy, the year in Switzerland, then U. of St. Thomas, and finally "a little tech school in Tennessee." Throughout her early childhood her parents slept in the smaller upstairs bedroom. All three of her older sisters shared the master bedroom in which her parents were later murdered. Jamie had no bed of her own; she crept in with whomever of her sisters would allow it. The sole downstairs bedroom—where Matthew and Michael lived in the 1980s—was reserved for Jim Campbell as his study.

A peculiar arrangement, I felt. No privacy for anyone except Jim. Didn't Rusty realize that? Wouldn't he inquire?

He didn't.

But he established that in the purview of Jamie's knowledge neither her father nor mother treated any of the daughters differently from the others, that her father hadn't sexually abused her sister Cindy, and that Cindy had never suggested he'd even touched her.

Cindy, she reported, had run away from home three times, the first time at the age of either thirteen or fourteen. "She was away a week or two. We went out every night looking for her. My Dad knocked on doors and showed her pitcher. Finally she called for money. She told me she ran away because the kids in school made fun of her, poked pins in her and tried to pop her like a balloon. Mom took her to Lane Bryant to shop, but Cindy didn't like it much."

The second abortive flight to freedom was six weeks later. Jamie didn't know the reason. Cindy stayed away more than a month and came back to Houston with a young man in tow. They lived in some other apartment, Jamie said. The sisters called him "Figgy," for figment—"because he was a figment of our imaginations. We never got to see him."

The third time she ran away, Cindy was sixteen. "Then I think she went to Oklahoma. She had a baby and a husband there. Both named Michael Ray. When she came home she talked funny—a new accent. Oh, yeah, she talked in different voices. Shoot, I don't know when that began. She had a little girl voice—pitiful little voice, she'd stick her little lip out, and seemed like she'd always get something after that. She had her scary voice, too, like *The Exorcist*. She'd act the death scene in *Romeo and Juliet*. She beat on her chest so much in rehearsal she developed a rash."

The boys, Michael and Matthew—"the little squirts," Jamie called them—came to live at Memorial. A couple of brief marriages followed the departure of Michael Ray, Sr., and then David West entered Jamie's life as a student at St. Thomas. "He popped up carrying a salad, and Cynthia and he met each other over the salad. She was a bit overweight. She had been pretty skinny. Her weight would be real little, and then it would go to real big, and then it would go back to real little. . . . First time I saw Cindy and David run into each other her little head dipped, she started talking real small in a little bitty voice, and didn't look up with her eyes. She acted pretty insecure."

Sometime in 1980 "they went to some kind of party, and Cindy asked to get to know him better. She called David where he worked. I was there when she called him and said he was real cute and she'd like to go on a date with him sometime. When she hung up she said he was really gross and he looked like a pig. She said, 'Have you ever watched that guy eat, Jamie? Looks just like a dog. You know, someone like that will do anything you tell 'em.'

"And I asked her, 'Why do you want to go out with him if you think he's so ugly?'

"She said, 'He'd be like a dog—just real easy to train.' "

In the courtroom there were a series of brief interruptions while the judge tried to get the bailiff to adjust the fan to cool the faces of as many sweating jury members as possible. Then Jamie told her captive audience of two incidents that she said occurred in 1980.

"At first"—after Cindy returned from her unhappy third "marriage" to Moe, and started to study art at St. Thomas—"she'd tell jokes to my Mom and make her laugh. Then she started acting mean and belligerent. She called her a bitch. She cussed her out. That was in the kitchen. Later she claimed we didn't like her. She cussed me, too, and I ran out to get in the yellow Suburbia, this car. Cindy kind of swung at my Mom—didn't hit her. She came close. I got mad and said I was gonna run her over and squoosh her. I had the truck right there. Then everything kind of relaxed. . . .

"Another time I was getting chewed out by my Dad for bad grades at St. Thomas. I cried, ran up to my bedroom, and Cindy was there. I said I couldn't believe how much trouble I was in. Cindy said, 'We'd be a lot better off without my father. I think I should kill Daddy, and I know

379

how I'd do it. It would work. I'd dress up like a man, and I'd wear big men's shoes or heavy boots and I'd leave footprints around a window and Marlboro cigarettes, and it would really look like a man did it.' I said, 'You're crazy.' She said, 'Well, we'd be a lot better off without Daddy. We could have whatever we wanted.' We had a little bitty linen closet outside of that room, and I heard a little thud in there, and that turned out to be my Mom. She was in there listening. I just got up and bugged out of the room."

Rusty asked, "When Cindy said all this, how would you describe her manner?"

"Pretty cocky."

"Did she appear to be kidding?"

"She said a whole lot of things like that, that never happened, so, considering it was her, yes, she could have been kidding."

"Did you take her seriously at the time?"

"No, I just thought she was really weird," Jamie said.

Jamie had last visited home in March of 1982. "Mom was nervous, afraid. Real sad, and she drank a whole lot of coffee. We watched *Airplane* together on the VCR. Dad laughed a lot."

Michelle called Jamie in June to tell her about the murders. Jamie flew up from Tennessee. "I talked to Cindy at J. W.'s house. She said she had to go, David was going to pick her up, and did I need any cigarettes. I saw them at the funeral. David was nervous. They weren't grief-stricken. She acted like it was just something they had to get over with. At the police station she made some jokes. I can't remember them—I was pretty out of it. But I didn't believe she'd killed our parents."

———————————

The next day, Thursday, was June 19, the fourth anniversary of the murders—a fact that was not mentioned publicly in court. I was aware of it, but my mind was focused primarily on a remarkable phenomenon: the air conditioning was working.

The jury filed into the courtroom. I noticed that half of them were dressed in blue. It was as if they had taken on a homogeneity—not so much twelve individual jurors, but *a jury*.

Randy McDonald opened the day by taking Jamie on cross, at which point her Butcher Hollow accent thickened even further and she professed extreme nervousness. After she had related a childhood incident at a supermarket checkout counter, Randy asked, "Were you able to count money at that age?" Jamie replied, "Ah kin hardly do that now."

After a while Randy wisely gave up.

25.
Roy Beene (with Harris County Jail in background). *"The strongest fiber in the world is a pussy hair."*

26.
Dan Grothaus. "He took one careful squint at Kim's changeable blue eyes and decided it was worth running a deep background check on her."

Ginger Casey. "He wanted to know there was a human being out there who cared."

Roy Beene at the fourplex on Kingston. *"If I get killed,"* he said to HPD, *"I want you people to know who did it."*

27.

28.

29.
Talal Makhlouf. *"She's all he's got now, and he's all she's got. Is that love? Maybe it is."*

THE MANY FACES OF CINDY RAY

Cindy Ray, December 11, 1985. *"She was an emotional invalid . . . totally fallen apart."*

Cindy Ray listening to David's testimony, June 1986. *"She said that her oldest son was her father's child."*

30.

31.

32.

Cindy Ray, July 1986. "I began to see the woman with whom David West had fallen in love."

Pete Justin and Cindy Ray, April 1987. "She pinched his thigh, hard, then kicked his shins."

33.

34.

▲Cindy Ray, April 1987. "A tearful Cindy wasn't something Rusty had counted on."

◄Cindy Ray in a photograph taken by David West in Tranquility Park, 1981. *I was totally committed.*

35.

36.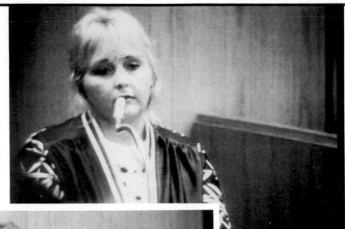

38.

39.

Top: Gwen Sampson testifying, June 1986. *"She said that he was with the Mafia out of Vegas."*
Center: Michelle Campbell testifying, June 1986. "She had inadvertently established that the bathroom *did* lock from the outside."
Bottom: Jamie Campbell testifying, June 1986. "The sole downstairs bedroom was reserved for Jim Campbell as his study."

37.

Michael Ray, Sr., June 1986. "It was the tale of a loser, and it darkened the day."

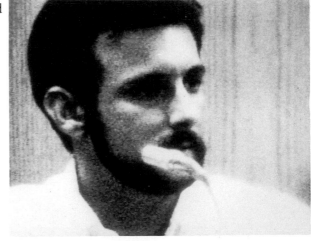

Paul Whitfield testifying, June 1986. "The ex-Marine was frightened of the ex-Ranger."

41.

Maria Bravo Gonzalez in court, June 1986. *"She's a loyal servant—it's a special Mexican mentality you have to understand."*

Wickie Weinstein testifying, June 1986. *"You've known all along that they were going to try to point the finger at you, right?"*

42.

Rusty took her on some redirect that made the sleepy jurors perk up.

"Jamie, do you recall Cindy having an appendix scar?" She did. "To your knowledge, did your father, James Campbell, ever beat her scar?"

Jamie laughed. "Big Boy, our German Shepherd—well, Cindy was asleep on the couch, and that Big Boy stuck his nose in her face. That woke her up. She jumped up and busted her stitches. She had to go to the hospital again."

"Did she ever tell you that her father had anything to do with the incident?"

"Nope."

On recross Randy asked: if that story was true, why hadn't her father, a skilled plaintiff's personal injury lawyer, ever sued the hospital for putting in stitches that were so easily undone?

Rusty objected, and the judge sustained the objection, but a perplexed Jamie was heard to mutter, "Gosh, I never axed him."

The cross had done nothing to damage Jamie's credibility, and at the end of her testimony, I thought, Cindy's in trouble.

Then Rusty surprised us all.

33

"The state calls Michael Ray."

Heads turned. Necks craned. *What did he say?* Would Rusty dare? A twelve-year-old boy? The alleged offspring of incest, the son of his mother on trial for the brutal murder of her parents and his grandparents? No, it would be too cruel. . . .

But Rusty showed an elfish smile and a purposeful glint in his eye, for down the aisle from the rear of the courtroom, like a father with a twitching bridgroom on his arm, came the bailiff, escorting a tall, stooped man in his late thirties with a mop of bright curly red hair, long muttonchop whiskers, uneasy woebegone blue eyes, and the defiant look of a trapped rabbit. He wore a sport jacket and a wide-collar sport shirt.

"State your name, please."

"Michael Charles Ray, Sr."

Rusty beamed like a magician who has doffed his black top hat, and behold, unbelievers—

As it turned out, Rick Brass, the night before, had received a tip from an undercover agent, working as a security guard, that the State of Texas was about to produce Michael Ray, Sr. as a surprise witness. The state had been hunting for him for a long time and had open warrants against him. But the state was not allowed any "surprise witnesses"—it was required to give to the defense a list of all potential witnesses, and Rusty had done that back in April. No new names had since been added. Rick, earlier in the day, armed with his inside tip, asked Rusty, who turned pink.

"His name *is* on the witness list." Rusty waved it in Rick's face. "There. 'Michael Ray.' "

"That's the kid!" Rick cried. "That's Cindy's son! It's listed there right above 'Matthew Ray!' "

"No, you just assumed that."

"Oh, Rusty, come *on!* He's got the same address listed as Matthew does—1601 California. That's J. W. Campbell's office. Are you serious?"

Rusty was, and there was nothing that the defense could do except swallow it and wonder how it would digest, reserving the right to lodge a protest and file an exception later.

Michael Ray, Sr. was originally from Ohio and had been living in Houston on and off for fourteen years. He volunteered right away that he'd had two back operations, the result of a work accident in the Marine Corps.

Another marine! Was this a theme of some kind?

"What's your line of work now?" Rusty asked.

"Anything I can do," Ray said. He clarified: he'd worked on tugboats, done die casting, been a fork lift operator, a septic tank installer, a line installer for grease traps—"just an all-around jack of all trades and a master of none." He was nervous, and he appeared to be frightened of Rusty. Any time he was able to he referred to his back operations and the resultant difficulties he encountered in working. He said "dis" for "this," and "den" for "then." He tried his best not to look at Cindy, who maintained her usual deadpan gaze, elbow on the table and a fist supporting her face.

Prompted by Rusty, he told a tale of a sorrow-laden life.

He had met Cindy up in Denver, in 1972, when she was seventeen and he twenty-four. He was "just hitchhiking around." In Denver, he said, he saw her running down the street, chasing an ex-boyfriend who was taking care of her after she'd run away from a girls' home. She was nearly hit by a car. Michael Ray rescued her. She was beautiful, with long hair. A clean, nice girl. Thin. About 120 pounds.

She didn't discuss her family at first. He told her not to keep looking for the boyfriend: *he* would take care of her now, if she would stay with him. They slept that night—not together, Ray stressed—at a crash pad set up by some religious group at a church. The next day they picked fruit and made twenty-five dollars each.

Her story was that her Dad had had a nervous breakdown and was in a mental hospital. Her mother was living with another lawyer. "She said the guy tried to have sex with her." She complained of that to her mother, who didn't believe her and locked her in a closet. The lawyer then convinced her mother to put her in the girls' home. "Then she ran away and met this man. . . . She said she loved her Daddy. Her Mom kept hitting her all the time. I didn't have no reason to question her at the time."

The young displaced couple, quickly bonded through love and loneliness and an obvious inability to master whatever it is that makes for a shipshape passage through life's tides and shoals, began to live together, and a few months later hitchhiked to Covington, Virginia, where Michael Ray got a job painting houses. Cindy was eighteen. She became pregnant. She called her mother for her birth certificate. She told Ray, "The bitch wouldn't send it up." But in October 1973 they were married anyway.

They moved to Tulsa, where he worked as a security guard. They were together all the time. She gave birth to the baby, Michael Jr.

Rusty Hardin asked forcefully, "Was there any way on God's green earth that James Campbell could be the father of your son?"

"Not unless he sent it by Western Union," Michael Ray, Sr. said, wooden-faced, drawing a hearty laugh.

Cindy became pregnant a second time with Matthew, and they moved down to Houston, to a room in the family manse on Memorial, then after three months to an apartment of their own in Sharpstown, a Houston area best known for its shopping mall. For a while Ray worked at a die-casting plant, until his father-in-law helped him get a job on tugboats in Galveston. No, Cindy never had a job. But she was levelheaded, clean, tidy. Her Dad treated her like the pet of the family, and "he treated me with respect." Ray never observed any evidence of sexual abuse or cruelty of any kind.

"I was away two weeks at a time. I came home, and she told her Daddy I'd been seen with a long-haired Mexican girl. It was a guy. I came back to find our apartment empty. Her father was there with separation papers. I signed two blank pieces of paper. They wouldn't let me see my boys. I went up to Oklahoma City and I hurt my back again. I went to the V.A. hospital, and that's when I called Cynthia to ask her how the boys were, and if I could come to see them. She said, 'No, you can't see me, and you can't see the kids. We're divorced.' That was the first I knew about it. She said I was supposed to pay forty dollars a week per child. After that I was transferred down to the V.A. Hospital in Houston, they had to do back surgery on me . . . later I was down at the Heights Hospital here . . . I had unbalanced equilibrium at the time . . . and when I was there James Campbell visited me and wanted me to sign adoption papers over to him. I didn't sign. I said they were my kids and I'm gonna keep 'em. He said, 'Okay.' He was nice. He always was a gentleman."

But under renewed pressure, the ailing father finally signed the papers. He had not seen his two sons since then. He had tried, "But Mr. Campbell threatened to have a peace bond put on me." *

It was the tale of a loser and it darkened the day. You could look at this thirty-eight-year-old man (married again now to a woman with eight children of her own) with his perennial aching back and his left-over-from-the-1960s muttonchop whiskers, and at Cindy in the defendant's chair, accused of murdering both her parents, and think of them at seventeen and twenty-four in Denver: in love, temporarily free, the world and its illusory rewards beckoning, and you could become cheerless and despairing for the human race at the way things work out, the way hope fades, innocence withers, lives crash.

Taking Ray on cross, the best Allen could do was get him to admit that he had never held a job for longer than seven months, that he couldn't remember the dates of his sons' birthdays, and that "I didn't pay no child support, and I still ain't paid none. But they're still my blood and flesh, and I still love 'em." He was a little hazy on dates, particularly during his marriage, and explained this by saying, "When me and Cynthia was divorced, I tried to forget everything."

Cindy whispered in Rick Brass's ear. Rick whispered to Allen, who asked Ray, "Didn't you tell Mr. Campbell that if he gave you $5,000 you'd sign the adoption papers?"

"No, sir."

"Do you think he pulled a fast one on you?"

"No, sir, I don't believe James did, but I think my ex-wife did."

During the break Allen decided that he would not protest against Rusty's listing Michael Ray, Sr. as Michael Ray. Because it hadn't turned

---

* A peace bond, in Texas, is a complaint sworn to before a justice of the peace which orders a third party to keep clear and not "breach the peace" by bothering the complainant. They are popular among separated couples.

out badly at all, Allen now felt. Incest had now been mentioned by Cindy when she was only seventeen years old. Denied, of course, but the point was that she had started talking about it even then. Never mind that the stories she told to David West, Rory Lettvin, and her first husband were dissimilar, confusing, and in the area of fantasy. How else would a seventeen-year-old girl—in 1972, before such subjects were discussed in the Sunday supplements and displayed in television movies-of-the-week—reveal such a horrifying tale to her potentially shocked peers?

Allen thought, if I can squeeze one or two points out of each witness that I can use in final argument, that's good enough for me. Let Rusty bring on a battalion of witnesses.

And that was what Rusty seemed determined to do in his effort to prove that Cindy Ray was a congenital liar. He called Michelle Campbell to the stand.

———————————

Michelle, the oldest Campbell sister, was a short-haired, roly-poly woman of thirty-six. Her cheeks looked as if she had stored enough nuts in them for a Northern winter. Exuding a tranquil self-satisfaction, she told the court that she had a B.A. in sociology, a terminal master's degree in photography, and currently taught photography at St. Edwards University in Austin. Never married, childless, she spoke with clarity and pleasing emphasis, as if she had been witnessing in criminal cases all her life.

The thrust of her testimony, coupled with Jamie's, was the most damaging so far to Cynthia Ray. Michelle's words painted a portrait of a healthy, happy, altogether normal family. They took vacations together to Acapulco and Colorado. There just *couldn't* have been any sexual abuse. Her father was a good man.

Now it was clear where the family stood. This is where Rusty had been heading all along when he allowed the cartoonlike versions of incest and cruelty into evidence. None of the nightmarish tales that Cindy had told to Rory Lettvin, David West or Michael Ray, Sr. were true. No one was locked up in a closet, or anywhere, Michelle said. Oh, yes, once: Cindy, in a bathroom, for some unnamed transgression. She was four. "She said she'd give my mother a nickel if she let her out. My mother laughed, and let her out."

But I realized that Michelle had inadvertently established that the bathroom *did* lock from the outside. Who had put the lock there? And why?

Ask her, Rusty.

But again he didn't.

Had Cindy nearly drowned when she was a child? Michelle remembered a family outing at a lake near Huntsville. Cindy was wading in shallow water when she stepped into a hole. "We didn't really see. She grabbed a man standing nearby, and he pulled her out. She was five or six. We were all upset. I can't recall specifically my mother's reaction. My mother didn't like the water."

Virginia Campbell was "a very good mother, attentive to our needs, polite to my friends. She was very jovial. One of us always talked to her on the telephone on a daily basis. In Austin I spoke to her once or twice a week." James Campbell "was interested in me, welcomed my friends. We could ask him for just about everything. . . ." He was very attached to the boys, Matthew and Michael, treating them "like his own children."

They went to Las Vegas a lot, that was true, but not for the gambling. "They enjoyed the glitter, the shows, that sort of thing." Gambling? She smiled at the absurdity of the idea. Did they ever gamble in Europe? Calmly she replied that she didn't know, but she doubted it.

From now on—assuming that Jim Campbell's loyal best friend, Bob Harris, was neither a crazy nor a liar—I had to doubt either the accuracy of Michelle's memory or her probity as a witness. But Bob Harris hadn't testified, and so the jury had no way to suspect that Michelle's portrait of her father might be sugar-coated.

She told them that after the murders, when the sisters gathered to discuss the inheritance, "it was proposed that we try to be frugal, to take care of the two boys and pay Grandma's [Virginia Campbell's invalid mother] medical expenses. Cindy wanted to sell the house on Memorial. She wanted her money right then. She was upset at the idea of spending it on her kids. We said, 'If you don't want us to do it this way, please take them and support them yourself.' She took the children a week later. David West was with her. The older boy, Michael, didn't want to go. He clung to the door frame, screaming in terror. . . ."

After that: "Cindy's attitude was abrasive, quarrelsome, and acrimonious. She seemed to think we were all trying to cheat her. She had four to six lawyers, serially. Ultimately, she sued. We agreed to settle. We agreed Cindy would get $25,000 and the Kingston property." The other three sisters got Memorial and various acreage in other parts of Harris County, in Waco, and in Brownsville.

Then Cindy evicted the seventy-seven-year-old maternal grandmother from her apartment at Kingston. "Yes, I have personal knowledge of it —we'd been there four hours, moving her out, when Cindy blocked my path and wouldn't let me up there again."

In late 1982 Cindy signed papers that made Michelle the legal guardian of Matthew and Michael. Michelle said that Cindy never expressed any interest in the boys' upbringing.

On cross, Allen felt he was trying to climb out of a ten-foot hole with five feet of rope. He did manage to get Michelle to make the unlikely claims that the last four years she and Betty Ann had left the home on Memorial open "for the police investigation," and that the $200,000 from her father's insurance "all went to taxes." And yes, she'd heard that Cindy accused her and J. W. of emptying the safe deposit boxes. "No, it didn't make me have any ill feeling toward Cindy."

Did she still have Cindy's children? "I realized in September '82 that I would not provide a suitable environment. J. W. would be better. I live alone. I lived alone then."

Looking at his notes, Allen asked: "On June 24, 1982, did you call the police and say that 'Cindy got real mad about the property split and took the children'? "

"Yes, but I didn't call them about the quarrel. I called because the older boy was so scared."

Allen dropped that quickly. He went on to establish that the property on Kingston was worth $250,000–275,000, and that there was a good chance to win it back from Roy Beene. In that event, he asked, "Isn't it true that if this jury convicts Cindy, each of you three other sisters will get at least $83,000?"

"No," Michelle said, "that leaves out the lawyers' fees."

Allen let her go.

Michelle, smiling gently like a large Mona Lisa, walked slowly to the back of the courtroom and squeezed into a seat next to her sisters, Jamie and Betty Ann, and her brother-in-law, Richard Hinds. She watched the rest of the trial as a spectator. None of the sisters would talk to any of the media. Their expressions as they watched the proceedings would have won them many a hand in a poker game. They showed no anger or tears or animation. They were just there.

At the break I couldn't restrain myself. Randy McDonald hadn't been able to dent Jamie. Michelle had the aura of a serene Oriental potentate, but she carried a keen-bladed scimitar. These were Cindy's sisters. Why hadn't Cindy risen from her chair in fury or anguish, crying out in protest? Isn't that what an innocent person would do? I said to Allen, "Why don't you give her a handkerchief full of raw onion?"

Allen offered me a wan smile.

"At least," I said, "she could groan, or thrash around a bit in her chair when these witnesses hack at her. She'd be humanized."

"I don't dare let her react in any way," Allen said finally. "We have no idea what would happen."

Rusty called the Harris County medical examiner, Eduardo Bellas—a gray man in his sixties, with a flavorful Cuban accent—for the purpose of establishing the high probability that the shots that killed the Campbells were fired from a standing position at the foot of the bed. The point was that if David stood at the foot of the bed to fire, he was nowhere near the light switch and someone else would have had to be in the room to flip it on and illuminate his targets.

Rusty was plugging holes, hammering nails. And yet, Allen Isbell realized, three weeks of trial had passed—it was now June 20—and the state had yet to set forth a fragment of evidence that "tended to connect" Cindy with the crime. Not one of the state's witnesses could be viewed as unbiased. Where was the case?

That afternoon the air conditioning gave up again. The courtroom smelled like sweaty sneakers. At last Rusty called the state's final and climactic witness—Gwen Sampson.

Big and busty, wearing a blue and white smock, she limped slightly and swung her buttocks in an odd upward manner as she made her way past the defense table. She had had polio as a child. She was a pretty woman, blond and blue-eyed, with a twang in her voice like that of a treble guitar chord plucked once too often. Back in October 1982 she had told Gil Schultz that she was self-conscious about what she thought of as her "Texas drawl" and had done some work on trying to improve it so she "wouldn't sound so Texan." She was a native Houstonian, an artist. That was the key: you felt, despite her bulk and her chalk-on-blackboard accent, that she was a subscriber to a more delicate and genteel world than that of this whiffy courtroom with its tortoiselike determination to get at the truth of a grisly double murder.

She seemed a little shocked that she had to give her address, and even more so, her age: "Thirty-eight."

Currently she worked for her mother's insurance agency. In the 1970s, however, she had taught painting and photography at the Houston School of Commercial Art in Montrose, and in 1977 she met a part-time twenty-one-year-old student named Cynthia Ray. "She had her hair down and wore a sweatshirt and jeans. She was very talented—I thought she had great potential in the fine art line. She painted pretty ladies."

Cindy was still at the school when Gwen quit in 1980 to open a darkroom in her home. They began to develop what Gwen termed "a social relationship," and thereafter became close friends. Gwen thought of her as a kind of younger sister. Cindy was living then with Maurice Lambert, whom she called "Moe the Shmoe." They had an apartment in the suburb of Spring Branch. He beat her, Cindy said. "I picked her up once," Gwen related, "and she was messed up, but I didn't see bruises." She would ride the bus to Gwen's home in southwest Houston once or twice a week to visit.

After about six months Cindy began to talk about her parents. It was the basic story the courtroom had already heard, with a few added twists: her father, who had sexually abused her and fathered her first child, still made passes at her and tried to get her to sit on his lap, which bothered her, although sometimes she thought it wasn't so bad because at least he loved her. But her problems were more with her mother, a cruel woman and a lesbian who made approaches to her and hit her because she was jealous that Daddy loved her better. The mother beat her with a coat hanger and a hairbrush and would lock her up for hours.

She had a nickname for the mother—"the Old Hunchback." Later, when she left Moe the Shmoe and moved from Memorial to the apartment in the fourplex on Kingston, her maternal grandmother, who also lived there, answered the door in a thin negligee and made passes at her dates. Her younger sister Jamie was retarded and had to be put in special schools for socially backward children, including one in Switzerland. She couldn't function. Her oldest sister, Michelle, was also a lesbian. The next one, Betty, was a drug addict and had brain burnout. "A total jell, as in Jell-O." Betty's husband was also into drugs.

Her mother got nose jobs for the other sisters but not for her. A group rate. The problem was an inherited family trait; there was double cartilage at the end of the Campbell nose, and if it wasn't fixed they'd all wind up looking like Karl Malden.

Gwen said, "This came up often in conversations we had in my darkroom. She was quite open. I liked her, and I felt sorry for her. We spent two years together in my darkroom. She would sit crumpled and beaten, like a little puppy that's been mistreated, cowering in a corner."

Gwen was married and had two children. Once, during that period, she and Cindy went out to a club: "Girls' night out," Gwen termed it. Gwen was trying to make Cindy feel more confident, make her feel there was a good friend she could count on. But Cindy, normally so shy, had a couple of drinks and became "boisterous." Two men came up to them.

"Cindy basically propositioned them, very loudly. Almost like a street-walker."

In 1981 Cindy underwent a physical change. She began to lose weight, began lifting weights and taking vitamins. She was vivacious and cheerful—"She looked great." No, Cindy didn't at all attribute it to David West. He was madly in love with her, Cindy said, but he mistreated her, pushed her around and beat her. They lived in separate rooms in his house. He was a chauvinist and she had grown to feel revulsion for him. She had a nickname for him: "Pigface."

Then, in early October of 1982, a few months after the Campbells' death, Cindy called Gwen. She had been staying with David West's parents, but Cecilia West—formerly "a delightful, well-educated person who was disappointed in her son"—had begun to mentally harass her. She needed to get away from Mrs. West to a place where she would be at peace, and safe. The Mafia was after her. They were looking for her because they were involved with her parents' death, and they had heard her vow that she wanted to get the person who had done it.

Gwen's unemployed husband, Don Sampson, didn't like Cindy and didn't want her staying in the house. But Gwen said, "She's my friend."

Into the Sampson household, with Gwen, Don (by Christmas he would be gone, en route to ex-husbandhood), fourteen-year-old Jeff (who would die three years later in a motorcycle accident), seven-year-old John, and a trio of dogs and cats, came the fugitive from Cosa Nostra. She stayed in the den, on a day bed. A week later Gwen decided to kick her out. She was hooked on Valium. She woke up drunk and went to bed drunk. She made messes. The end of her tongue was black with some strange fungus. She complained that Gwen's husband "dropped his drawers" in front of her. "She was *goofy*," Gwen said.

Worse, one night at 2 A.M., awakened by Jeff's cries, Gwen rushed into his room and found Cindy on or between his sheets, rolling back and forth and saying, "I'm not going to be another notch on his bed!"

A star-crossed friendship. Cindy had to *go!* Another "girls' night out" was arranged. Gwen took her to dinner at Felix's Mexican restaurant. Meanwhile Don and Jeff packed Cindy's bags and hauled them over to the apartment on Kingston.

At Felix's the "girls" ordered guacamole and chicken tacos and began drinking beer. The food hadn't come yet. Tears welled up. Cindy said, "*I was there, you know.* . . . "

Gwen's puzzlement lasted only a second, after which, she claimed, she knew exactly what Cindy was referring to. Cindy explained that her Italian Mafia boyfriend, "Salino, a high roller out of Las Vegas, had told her he was going to kill her parents to make her well." That way her father and mother could no longer abuse her, and she could lead a normal life. Cindy mimicked a New York Italian accent halfway between *The Godfather* and *Guys and Dolls*. "I'm-a gonna make-a you well, I'm-a doin' dis for-a you."

"She told me how it was planned and executed," Gwen said.

Gwen kept telling her to please shut up, she didn't want to hear it, but Cindy kept talking.

She and Salino had gone to the house when everyone was asleep. He seemed to know the floor plan better than she did; she didn't know her children would be there, but *he* knew. They had worn men's clothing and heavy shoes, and gloves, and their faces were covered so that neither one would be recognized. She panicked for a moment when she saw her children there at the foot of the bed. She turned her head away. She didn't see it, but she *felt* that her mother's body jumped when the bullets struck her. She was standing in the room next to Salino.

Horrified, Gwen asked, "How could you just *stand* there?"

"He held a gun to my head."

"Why didn't you run? Or scream?"

"I couldn't. He would have killed me, too."

Leaving, she dropped a glove, to help the police so that they would eventually find the killer.

The jurors nodded; this corroborated David, at least as far as the act was concerned.

Gwen was a clear, concise witness, seemingly sorrowed by the necessity of her presence. Rusty asked her, "Do you know if she had a friend named Salino?"

"No, I don't know."

"Did you believe all this?"

"I believed it enough so that I called the police very shortly thereafter, because I was afraid I would get shot."

"After you had your conversation that night, what did you do?"

"She looked at me across the table and said, 'You're taking me home, aren't you?' I said, 'Yes, I am,' and I walked her back to her apartment on Kingston. She was hysterical. She laid on the bed, her eyes rolled up in her head—she screamed, 'I'm dead! I'm gone now, they're going to get me!' I said, 'I'm very very sorry for you, but I have my own life to live.' "

A week later, Gwen called J. W. Campbell and told him the story, and J. W. called Gil Schultz.

"Then, later," Gwen said, "I called Cindy. I told her I had a peace bond out on her, and that I'd told the police what she'd told me. So I said there was no need to bump me off for fear I'd tell, because I'd done that already."

"How did she react to that?" Rusty asked.

"We just laughed and discussed Schultz and Motard. Schultz was the bad guy, she said, and Motard looked just like McCloud on TV."

Rusty brought up a statement supposedly made by Cindy to Gwen before the evening in Felix's restaurant. She had said at that time that she'd been with David West the evening her parents were killed.

"Did she indicate to you in that conversation," Rusty asked carefully, "how much of that evening she and David West had been together?"

"The whole evening."

Why, in Felix's, didn't Gwen ask about the apparent contradiction between that "whole evening" spent with David West, and her tale that Salino had killed her parents and Cindy had been forced to accompany him?

"I didn't *ask* her anything," Gwen replied wearily. "At that point I just wanted away."

"In later conversation, after that evening, what did you ask her?"

"We discussed who really was with her. I basically asked her to put my mind at ease about it not being Mafia. She told me that really it hadn't been Mafia, that it was someone else, and then gave me a clue as to who the other person was."

"How did she do that?" Rusty pressed.

"I can't remember. I have an absolute block on that. But it was an indication that she had been with Pigface."

Rusty said, "Pass the witness."

It was five minutes to four. Judge Azios once again wished everyone a good weekend. There was no way that Allen Isbell could complete his cross-examination before the downtown parking lots closed.

That cross of Gwen would be vital, but Gwen struck me as someone who couldn't be shaken, who would become more and more stubborn if she was placed on the defensive. Cindy, I thought, you're sunk now.

Over the weekend I finally remembered who Salino was—an awareness of the name had been nagging me for months. In *The Sting,* the 1973 Academy Award-winning movie with Paul Newman and Robert Redford, the female assassin who sleeps with Redford and then tries to kill him was named Salino. It hadn't come out in the trial; no one had ever put two and two together and come up with five.

34

Cindy had private little names for herself, like "Gabriela" when she was feeling sexy, or "Elmo" when she was feeling obese, ugly, bad. Few knew of them.

392

David West, back in his cell in the Harris County Jail, had Jim Leitner keep him up to date on the proceedings in the court. When David heard about Gwen Sampson's testimony he hunted down an inmate who was due to make an appearance on Judge Azios's Monday docket. The inmate would be in the holding cell backstage. It was possible for prisoners to talk to each other there.

David told the man to tell Cindy: "Pigface says hello to Elmo."

On Monday morning, June 23, the jury filed in. The dominating dress color today was yellow. They were definitely a close-knit group who thought alike.

Since early April Randy McDonald had been preparing for the cross-examination of Gwen Sampson. If the jury had believed David, and now believed Gwen, there was no hope. Randy approached the witness stand, cold-eyed and determined.

He brought out the fact that, despite her altruism in taking Cindy into her home back in October of 1982, Gwen had required in exchange that Cindy give her the only possession she brought with her, a Magnavox TV from Memorial. To Randy's surprise, Gwen, with a twitching smile, volunteered that she had asked for a notarized bill of sale. She typed the paper at her real estate office, stated that the TV was in exchange "for rent," demanded that Cindy sign, and then, as a notary public, she herself witnessed the signature.

Randy chipped away. Hadn't Gwen lied to Cindy to get her into Felix's restaurant on that October evening in 1982? Wasn't the purpose of the outing to get Cindy to drink? You said she wasn't drunk that evening, but didn't you say that when she was with you at your house she woke up drunk and went to bed drunk? And that evening, weren't you focused totally on getting rid of this person?

To all those questions, Gwen nervously replied with a flat "yes" or "that's correct."

And hadn't she reported to the police back in 1982 that Cindy said, "Salino made me dress up like a man, he made me go with him . . . and he pointed the gun at my head and said if you say anything or tell anybody I'll kill you next"—meaning that he would kill her? And hadn't Cindy claimed that Salino said he was doing it for her, and would make her well?

That's correct. Yes. Gwen seemed uncomfortable with these answers.

"Now," Randy asked, "not one thing about those statements indicates anything that Cindy actively did, does it?"

"No."

"It also indicates that Cindy was not a willing participant, doesn't it?"

"No."

"It doesn't indicate that? When someone makes you dress up in an unusual way and points a gun at you?"

"I have difficulty with yes or no answers," Gwen replied.

In a brief redirect Rusty asked why she had taken the TV from Cindy. Gwen explained, "She didn't want to keep the TV in her own apartment, because she said it had her parents' brains all over the screen. So I asked her to sign a paper. She was always saying that people took things from her."

In the restaurant: "No, Cindy was never drunk. She was very calm when she started . . . but then tears welled up in her eyes, and she got louder. . . . "

Finally, when both sides announced they had no more questions, Gwen sobbed, put her head in her hands, and was led out of the courtroom by the bailiff. Had it worked? Did the jury believe her? *I* wouldn't have, I thought. I didn't trust her.

_____

After lunch, at 1:30 P.M., Rusty rose and said, with a confidence that I wasn't sure he felt: "Your Honor, at this time the State of Texas rests."

The jury was excused in order for Allen Isbell to make several motions. To begin, he reurged the court to allow David West's testimony that Jamie Campbell had told him she was a lesbian. He argued that it was pertinent in a depiction of the family as a breeding ground for sexual abnormalities and the entire question of sexual abuse of the defendant by her father.

"Denied," Judge Azios said.

Allen's next try was more complex. The state had sponsored exculpatory evidence in the person of Gwen Sampson, who had quoted Cindy as having said that she was forced to be there under threat of death and that she left evidence (the surgical glove) in the hope the killer would be caught. This was not disproved by the state beyond a reasonable doubt. Furthermore, in the tapes with Kim Paris, also sponsored by the state, David West had reaffirmed that he forced Cindy to accompany him. In courtroom testimony the state was using a discredited accomplice-witness (David) to corroborate the very witness (Gwen) who had been brought in to corroborate David: a tainted circle. As a matter of law, Allen said, an acquittal was called for.

Rusty claimed that the defense was playing "silly little word games." The judge overruled Allen's motion. "Is the defense ready to present its case?" he inquired.

"Yes, Your Honor," Allen said, restraining a sigh.

———————————

Rusty was aware that Gwen hadn't come off as a sympathetic or altogether believable witness. He had rested his case simply because there was no one else to put on, nothing more to do.

But the trial was hardly over.

Prosecutors, as a rule, build cases rather than try to tear them down, and their training tends to develop those skills that are required for direct examination of friendly witnesses. They are not as skilled at cross-examination, and some of them approach it worriedly. Rusty was an exception. He gave lectures and seminars on the subject to all the young assistant D.A.s in Harris County. This was the part of the trial that he relished most. It was search and destroy, and he looked for every opening in the brush. He showed little mercy to the defense attorney, none whatever to an unfriendly witness. He could be patient and probing, or barbed and mocking, or bruising and deadly. Whatever it took.

Outside in the crowded hallway by the elevators, the witnesses for the day gathered. Wickie Weinstein was there, and Melanie Edgecombe, and the newly married Paul Whitfield with his wife, Lynn Roebuck. I said hello. They were polite, but deep in conversation, and then Wickie and Paul went off together to the privacy of the men's room.

———————————

The defense called Sgt. C. T. Mosqueda, the Chicano officer who had interviewed Maria Bravo Gonzalez the morning of the murders and then, on June 22, 1982, prepared the translated statement that she had signed.

Maria had claimed she caught Cindy tampering with the windows at Memorial the week before the murders. The defense team was determined to show the jury that she was either lying or mistaken. It was vital to their fallback argument of duress that Cindy hadn't been a willing participant as early as June 11.

Randy McDonald took Mosqueda on direct. He got Mosqueda to quote from the signed statement, in which Maria said no more than, "I saw Cindy along the side of the house by the window of the boys' room. I asked Cindy what she was doing here and she did not say nothing. I told Cindy that it was best for her to come during the day than at night because if something happen she would be the blame [sic]."

Mosqueda, short, black-haired, and olive-skinned, was a decisive witness. But Rusty started right in on Randy McDonald, objecting to anything that even had the faint aroma of a leading question or that required the witness—in this case, an increasingly confused Sgt. Mosqueda—to change his mind or even refine his previous answer. A leading question is one that already suggests an answer, such as, "Isn't it a fact, Sgt. Mosqueda, that at 1130 hours on June 22, 1982, you began typing your report?"—and leading questions are limited to cross-examination. A cross-examiner not only *may* lead an unfriendly witness, but is taught to do so. A skilled cross-examiner will spin out whole paragraphs with a fluency and breath control to befuddle even the most concentrated of witnesses, and then, having reached the final question mark, demand *"a simple 'yes' or 'no', sir!"* because that is the most effective way of keeping an adversary under control, and control is the key to effective cross.

In direct examination, however, leading questions are forbidden. In direct the lawyer controls a friendly witness by asking, in effect, "And what happened *then?*" For if he has a rapport with the witness and has prepared him correctly, he knows the answer.

"Object!" Rusty cried. *"He's leading him!"*

"Object! He's not on cross now!"

"Your Honor, there! *That's another leading question!* I most respectfully request you ask counsel for the defense . . . "

"Object! He's trying to impeach his own witness!" *

Judge Azios nearly always sustained Rusty's objections. When he occasionally overruled one, Rusty immediately began to explain to him why he was wrong to do so. When Randy or Allen tried to interrupt Rusty, to point out that the judge had made his ruling and that was supposed to be the end of the matter, Rusty paid scant attention. He was at war and he would take every inch of territory where he could plant his size nine oxfords. He became alternately angry, scornful, and amused. His *joie de vivre* and love for a good fight dominated the courtroom. He hopped up and down, he charged forward to the bench, he made swift, caustic remarks to the defense table, he shrugged and looked to heaven on the rare occasion that the judge reprimanded him. He was a one-man band. I loved watching him work. I would want him as *my* lawyer.

---

* A lawyer who has called a witness to the stand is said to "sponsor" him. In June 1986 the Texas rules of evidence were such that, with certain exceptions, the lawyer could not challenge or impeach the testimony of a sponsored witness—that privilege was reserved to the cross-examiner. On September 1, 1986, the rule was changed: a lawyer who called a witness to the stand could try to impeach him.

By the time Sgt. Mosqueda was excused few people could remember what his testimony had been all about.

Former Homicide Detective Michael St. John—he had realized his ambition and was now a practicing civil lawyer—was the next witness, and he testified that the foliage at 8901 Memorial had been far more dense in June of 1982 than now. No one was sure if the jury got the point: that it would have been impossible for Maria to have seen what she said she saw from the spot where she said she was standing.

St. John stepped down.

Then the defense called Wickie Weinstein.

———————————

Racehorse Haynes once said, "I continue to dream of the day when I am cross-examining a witness and my questions are so probing and so brilliant that the fellow blurts out that *he*, not my defendant, committed the foul murder. Then he will pitch forward into my arms, dead of a heart attack."

Allen did not quite expect that to happen. But he was determined to show—or insinuate, or charge if necessary—that Wickie, not Cindy Ray, had helped David West kill the Campbells. If he could do that, and if the jury believed him, he was sure that they would at least hang up and be unable to reach a unanimous decision. And that would be a victory, for a hung jury sets a precedent. The trial following it, if there is one, often has the same result. After that, any intelligent and ambitious prosecutor gives up.

Allen plunged in confidently. He knew that Wickie was a hostile witness who would undoubtedly lie, but he also knew that Paul Whitfield waited in the wings ready to expose the truth.

———————————

Handsome, well-muscled under a gray long-sleeved shirt and jeans, Wickie was still crewcutting the front half of his hair and letting the back half grow in luxurious brown curls. He looked like a contemporary punk version of James Dean—a little surly, more than a little dangerous. He had an actor's voice, too: modulated and lilting, with a relaxed delivery.

Nearly everyone in this cast was either a former combat soldier or some kind of actor, I thought. Or both.

Allen got Wickie to recite a little autobiography: born in New Jersey, quit school after the ninth grade—served in the U.S. Army, "Company G, 143rd Infantry Airborne Rangers, Long Range Reconnaissance Patrol" (he reeled that off as though he were being questioned by a drill sergeant), enlisted in October 1978 and out on November 5, 1980. No, he'd never seen duty outside the continental United States, and yes, it was true that he'd told the opposite to quite a few people. No, he hadn't been a volunteer in Central America—

"Object!" Rusty jumped up. "He's clearly trying to impeach his own witness!"

Allen went to the bench and argued to Judge Azios that in this instance he had the right to impeach his own witness, within limits, since his witness had proved hostile by taking off to Florida without advising the court and had been dragged back against his will.

The judge agreed, overruling Rusty's objection.

"Did you ever tell anyone you were in combat?" Allen asked.

"Maybe I did, maybe not." Wickie spoke blandly. "I drank a lot back then. I was confused. Maybe I had to bring that up to make it all worthwhile."

He had been living at 1409 Vermont at the time of David West's arrest, but only for six weeks or so. He was down on his luck then. Yes, he had read mercenary magazines like *Soldier of Fortune*. But he hadn't owned any copies. And he had never volunteered anywhere as a mercenary or expressed the desire to do so.

Allen brought up David's statement that he had gone to Wickie in early June of 1982 to discuss "an operation." Wickie couldn't remember it. An operation? Some kind of surgery? He didn't remember that phrase.

"No, he didn't tell me he was going to murder someone. We just discussed murder in the abstract."

The phrase hung in the air. David had used almost the exact words. Allen waited a moment.

"Do you do that often with your friends?"

"No, I do not," Wickie said patiently.

"Did you sell him a gun?"

"Yes, a .45 automatic. About two weeks later."

He admitted that in the summer of 1984 he and David had argued with a man named Virgil Lee Johnson over the return of some tools supposedly stolen from their friend, Robin. Wickie took a knife away from Virgil Lee, who had tried to attack him with it. Then he and David split open Virgil Lee's head with a pickaxe handle (not a baseball bat). David, I remembered, had denied it all.

Wickie, slouching on the witness chair, looked more and more to me like a man who might have helped David murder the Campbells. Had Cindy taken part, or not? Could David's story include a monstrous lie?

I didn't know. But I felt with all my instincts that something was wrong and askew in the way he had told the tale.

Allen asked Wickie, "Did you help David West dispose of the .45 you sold him?"

"No, I did not."

"Did you tell Paul Whitfield that you and David disposed of the gun together?"

"I'm not sure."

"How can you not remember?" Allen demanded.

"I don't know," Wickie muttered.

"Let me ask you this. Did you come to later learn that David West had killed two people with that gun you sold him?"

"Yes, I did."

"Explain to the members of the jury how you can't remember whether or not you told Paul Whitfield that you helped David West dispose of the gun after the murder."

Wickie frowned. "Would you repeat the question?"

Allen did so; then Wickie said, "I drank a lot in those days. I went to AA. I had periods of blackouts." Wickie slowed his pace, seemed to pick his words more carefully. "I drank for three years at least eight pints of beer a night. I was on heavy drugs—I smoked pot, at least eight or nine joints a day." He then offered a list of the pills he was taking in those days that made one wonder how, if it was true, he could even remember their names. "There are lots of times," he concluded, "that I cannot remember what I was doing."

If the jury would buy Allen's thesis—that Wickie and David threw away the .45 together—it would physically separate Cindy from David during the crucial hour on the night of the murder, destroy David as a credible accusatory witness, and crack the foundation of the state's case. It was potential dynamite for impeachment of David.

But Wickie refused to light the fuse. He hadn't told Paul Whitfield anything. He couldn't even remember where he was in mid-June of 1982. He had these blackouts, see?

For the better part of an hour—on cross, redirect, and recross—Allen and Rusty flung Wickie back and forth like a football, Allen trying to elicit an admission from him, Rusty trying to fortify his lack of memory and get the judge to end what Rusty claimed was harassment.

On cross Rusty asked him, "Are you nervous, Wickie?"

Yeah, he was nervous, he said.

But he hid it well. He was seen by onlookers as stolid, calm, surly, stubborn, scary, and, above all, evasive; but no one except Rusty saw nervous.

"You've known all along that they were going to try to point the finger at you, right?"

"Yeah." He had testified before the grand jury and been concerned then that it might look as if he was involved. He was afraid that David West or someone else might name him. It was frustrating—he couldn't ever remember where he was on June 19, 1982. He *still* couldn't remember. He'd gone up to Hazelden in Minnesota to dry out, and only after that had he started remembering things.

But not everything.

Rusty asked, "Did you help David West dispose of the gun?"

"No, I did not."

"Did you help David West kill the Campbells?"

"No, I did not."

When his turn came again, referring to the so-called blackouts, Allen asked him, "But as far as you know, it *may* be true that you told someone that you helped David West dispose of the murder gun?"

"I can't say that I didn't, but I don't believe it's true," Wickie answered.

"So that if Paul Whitfield said you did, you have no memory or no way of refuting it?"

Wickie, seeming to enjoy the role of the persecuted scapegoat, and knowing that Rusty was out there to block or even clip for him, smiled slightly and said, "I have no way of refuting it."

"Why don't you want to testify?"

"I don't want to be involved. It's something I'd like to forget."

That seemed like an honest statement. But *what* did he want to forget?

Rusty got him back on recross and asked: "Wickie, would it make sense to you for David West to tell somebody else that Cindy was involved in the crime in order to save you?"

"I wouldn't know," Wickie replied, and then, offering some flavorful food for thought that certainly wasn't on Rusty's menu, added a curious non sequitur: "David is a pretty moral person. Even though he goes in and shoots someone, he still, in my mind, did that because he thought it was right."

Allen had no further questions. He had expected the denials, but now he would rip them into tatters. He called Paul Whitfield.

———————————

Paul wore a white shirt and clean jeans. He was a thoughtful witness. Once again the judge had to explain that Brenda didn't have a nod button.

He had known David West and Wickie Weinstein for about three years, Paul said.

No, Wickie hadn't had any conversation with him about a gun he'd *sold* to David. "But he mentioned a gun that he had *loaned* to David."

That made a few jurors cease their 4 P.M. yawning. Paul went on: "He had loaned it to him for protection purposes, from what I understand . . . and it ended up Dave had killed a couple of people with that gun."

I nodded. Paul was on track. The jury was interested.

Allen continued: "And did Wickie Weinstein tell you that he helped Dave dispose of that gun?"

"Well, I'm not sure if he said that he *helped* him. It was . . . that he was upset that Dave had used it to kill somebody, and they had thrown it in Buffalo Bayou, because he didn't want to get it traced back to him or have any involvement."

Now Allen frowned slightly. "The words he used were that 'they had thrown it in Buffalo Bayou'?"

"I can't really be sure of the exact words he used," Paul said.

Come on, Paul. What's the matter with you today? I wanted to get up there and jab him in the ribs to wake him up and refresh his suddenly failing memory.

Angrily Allen asked if Paul hadn't told other people that Wickie had admitted to helping David West throw the .45 into Buffalo Bayou?

"I had conversations before with a writer, but I'm not really sure what was said. We had quite a few drinks."

"Is your memory today—" Nonplussed, Allen broke off, then resumed: "Did Wickie Weinstein tell you that he and David disposed of the gun?"

"I don't really remember who he said had disposed of it."

"If you told the writer something else, was it just because you were drunk?"

"I can't really remember what I told the writer. Like I say, I was drunk. I had quite a few drinks that evening."

No way, I thought.

And Allen felt it all slipping away. He realized what had happened. He didn't know if it had happened today in the hallway, or before Wickie had fled to Miami, but he was dealing with a witness who had been tampered with and suborned. With barely suppressed indignation he asked Whitfield if he "recognized Mr. Randy McDonald, who's sitting in front of you, and Mr. Rick Brass"—and hadn't he met with them in early June?

Yes, he had.

"And did you not tell them that Wickie said, '*We* disposed of the gun in Buffalo Bayou'?"

But Paul Whitfield said, "I told them that 'they' had thrown it away, or 'we' . . . I wasn't really sure which way it was . . . 'they' or 'we' or what."

"That conversation was less than two weeks ago, correct?"

"Yes, sir."

"*And you can't remember what you said two weeks ago?*"

Rusty jumped up, sputtering. "He's trying to impeach his own witness. . . . Mr. Isbell knows the rules. . . . He knows he can't do that!"

"Sustained."

At the bench, Allen argued strongly that the witness had said something quite different to defense counsel in pretrial investigation, and the rules of evidence allowed the impeachment of his own witness when counsel was thus—to use a mild word—"surprised."

Learning this, the judge reversed himself and overruled Rusty's objection. "Go ahead," he told Allen.

Trying to appear calm, Allen said, "You were sitting there in the jury room with Randy McDonald and Rick Brass—"

"Yes, sir."

"—and, once again, did you not say to them that Wickie, in his conversation with you, said that '*we* had disposed of the gun by throwing it in Buffalo Bayou'?"

"I'm saying that I said 'they' or 'we.' I'm not really sure, and I can't be positive exactly what Wickie said."

"Can you be positive about what *you* said?"

"I just told you. 'They' or 'we,' I can't remember."

In disgust, Allen passed the witness. Otherwise he felt he would have leaped at him and tried to throttle him.

Rusty was quickly up, like a middleweight coming out at the bell and moving in for a good solid tattoo that would end in a knockdown.

"Just so the record's clear," Rusty said to Paul, "the writer you're speaking of in the context of that meeting in the bar is Clifford Irving, who's somewhere here in the courtroom?"

"Yes, sir."

I didn't like this at all.

"Mr. Irving came to you and had conversations with you about what you knew in the case, is that correct?"

"Yes, sir." Now Whitfield snapped off his answers like a good marine.

"By the way, who was buying the drinks?"

"Clifford was."

True enough.

"He paid for all those drinks you had? Do you have any idea how many?"

"A half dozen or so, at least."

"Now, after that conversation, did you meet with me? And was that in my office during jury selection in the David West case, to discuss this very thing?"

"Yes, sir."

And then, to my astonishment, Rusty said, "You told me, as much as nine months ago, didn't you, what you just told Mr. Isbell?"

I remembered the night meeting at the District Attorney's Office. *Not true, Rusty.*

"Yes, sir," Paul responded.

"Did Wickie tell you that *he* helped David throw the gun in Buffalo Bayou?"

"Not that I can remember."

"But isn't it true, Paul," Rusty trumpeted, "that you've had a lot of people *wanting* you to say that Wickie helped throw the gun away, including this set of attorneys?"

A white-faced Allen leaped up to object to the form, the content, and the insult of the question. Judge Azios overruled the objection.

"Seems like everybody's been trying to get me to say that," Whitfield drawled in an echo.

Satisfied that he had scotched the snake, Rusty passed the witness.

Poorly masking his fury, Allen managed to establish that none of the defense attorneys had ever asked Whitfield to say any particular thing. Then, scornfully, he asked, "Are you afraid of Wickie Weinstein?"

"No, sir." Paul smiled coolly.

It was five o'clock. The judge adjourned, but told Paul Whitfield not to leave town, and to keep himself available tomorrow. The judge was an old hand, and he could already sniff the consequences. In that, he was one up on me. I was angry enough to take a bite out of an axe blade. I had no idea there was more to come.

35

Rusty was doing the Lord's work, but I went home from the courtroom that afternoon with the suspicion that the Lord would not approve. Rusty so badly wanted to convict this woman that he had

forgotten what Paul Whitfield had told him. Not for one minute did I believe Rusty was deliberately lying: he had simply brainwashed himself. It was the same inner conviction that allowed him to bridle at Allen Isbell's attempt to portray his star witness, the confessed murderer of two sleeping people, as a violent and out-of-control lunatic. *(He just wants to smear the man!")*

Beyond that, once my temper cooled, I was enraged all over again by the memory of Whitfield's yarn of my having gotten him drunk and feeding him "at least half a dozen drinks" in a bar. That was a lie—but how and when to prove it? I remembered the old Gypsy curse: "May you have a lawsuit in which you know you're in the right."

Allen Isbell telephoned me that evening. After I'd finished analyzing Rusty's memory lapse and grousing about Whitfield, he said, "Why don't you testify that Whitfield lied?"

"I'd love to," I said, with fervor. "I'd love to pillory the sonofabitch. But I've been there at the trial, I heard his testimony. Isn't there a rule against that?" I was sure there was. I *hoped* there was.

"In a special instance, the judge can give permission."

It had turned out to be fun to testify during the November jury selection, but I didn't think that would be the case this time. Face Rusty on cross in a murder trial? I shook my head. (But a seductive voice whispered in my ear: *"Jump in."*)

"I don't want to be a witness," I said. "I didn't come here to take sides. It's ridiculous."

"It's up to you," Allen said judiciously.

Then I realized that I knew part of the truth which otherwise would remain hidden from view. If I told the truth, I had nothing to fear. No one would be hurt. I would be one of Rusty's good citizens.

"I'll do it," I said, still reluctant, "if the judge agrees to let me stay for the rest of the trial—and if I can come up with a piece of hard evidence so that I don't get up there and look like an idiot."

"What evidence?"

"You'll see. I may still have it. Let me try to find the damned thing. If I do, I'll tell you what it is."

Allen wondered aloud if Dan Grothaus would testify to what Whitfield had said at our two meetings.

"I doubt it," I said. "He's a reporter. He has to protect his sources. But I'll sound him out."

Dan had not been covering the trial. When I called he was just filing his day's story in the news room of the *Post*. He surprised me by saying that since his source was already revealed there was no longer any journalistic privilege he needed to protect. Still he hesitated, reluctant, as I was, to doff the hat of neutrality in favor of the combat helmet that a

witness inevitably wore. He would discuss it with his city editor, Tom Nelson.

He called back in half an hour and said, "I'll do it."

Here we go, I thought. Into the valley of death rode the six hundred.

There remained Whitfield's lie about the "half a dozen or so drinks, at least." I felt seriously provoked. Just before midnight I began to hunt through my randomly scattered accumulation of memoranda, notes, transcribed tapes, and tax receipts. Like Judge Azios, I was not a neat worker: unlike him, I didn't know where everything was. Considering the heaps of paper that faced me, I didn't expect to find the object of my quest.

The gods are cruel. To test us, now and then they grant our wishes.

I called Allen early in the morning, before he went off to run at the Y. I had found what I was searching for.

Allen met with Grothaus in his Old Cotton Exchange office at eight o'clock next morning. They walked to the courthouse under a hazed sky in heat that was rapidly building toward the usual ninety-five degrees. In court, with the jury not yet seated, Allen announced that he intended to recall Paul Whitfield as a witness, then Dan Grothaus, and then, perhaps, me. He waited for an objection from Rusty. Rusty just shrugged.

Judge Azios agreed that if I absented myself from the courtroom during today's testimony of Whitfield and Grothaus, I could testify afterward and attend the remainder of the trial. I was locked in. I realized then I'd been hoping there would be a problem and I could gracefully slip out of it. I still wasn't up to snuff as Rusty's basic good citizen.

"Relax," Allen said casually. "I don't know yet if I'll need you."

I arranged with John Makeig, the *Chronicle*'s court reporter, to look at his notes at the end of the day, and I went out into the corridor. Melanie Edgecombe stepped out of the elevator. She had her blond hair cut in a short punk style so that it stood up like the spikes of a yellow sea urchin. I asked her if she had heard Wickie's testimony yesterday. Yes, she'd been here. Wouldn't miss it for the world.

"What did you think of it?"

"He's a world-class compulsive liar," Melanie said.

"Did you hear Paul on the stand?"

"He lied, too. He and Lynn told me the same story they told that lawyer, Isbell—that Wickie and Dave threw the gun away together that morning."

"And did Wickie ever confirm?"

She grew wary. "You know Wickie. One day it's this, the next day it's that."

"So why is Paul lying?" I asked, annoyed.

"Are you kidding?" Melanie raised her canary-colored eyebrows. "He's scared to death of Wickie. Do you blame him?"

The bailiff called for order, and she went into the courtroom to find a seat.

———————————

Grothaus and I stood sweating in the packed hallway, debating why the first-place Houston Astros couldn't yet draw a home crowd of more than 15,000 fans. We were buffeted to one side of the elevators by a bailiff who was trying to guide a new jury panel into another courtroom. They had the suffering deadpan look of a herd of cows.

Meanwhile, in Judge Azios's courtroom, Paul Whitfield took the stand a second time. He continued to deny that Wickie had ever said to him, "*We* threw the gun away."

On cross with Rusty, Paul again fudged about what he had said during the visit to the D.A.'s Office on December 6. Rusty asked him: "Isn't it true that [Grothaus and Irving] wanted and expected you to involve Wickie Weinstein?"

"Yes, sir, it sure seemed that way to me."

It took twenty minutes, and then Paul scooted out. A bailiff appeared and called, "Mr. Daniel Grothaus!" I stayed in the corridor, pacing. I wanted a cigarette.

Grothaus's testimony created the first uproar of what was to be a tempestuous day. If the trial was a war and the courtroom a battle zone, the creed of such combat is: if you're not for me, you're against me. Grothaus, by testifying for the defense, was not for Rusty. But Rusty had known that last December when, in defense of Kim Paris, he had characterized Grothaus as a "clown" who had written a "despicable" article about Kim on "her special day."

Allen began by allowing Dan to recite his credentials as a local reporter with the *Chronicle* and now the *Post*.* Then Allen moved to Dan's

———————————

* Grothaus was a week away from receiving an Emmy nomination for writing and producing a 1985 TV documentary on PBS called *Child at Risk,* a portrait of pedophiles (adults who seduce children into sexual relationships). In August he won the Emmy.

406

first meeting with Paul and Lynn. Whitfield's exact words—taped by Grothaus—had been: "I've had both of them telling me that David had shot somebody and got the gun from Wickie and they had to get rid of it. . . . Wickie told me it had to happen, because it was his .45. He had to throw it in the river. He didn't want anything to get traced back to him."

"Pass the witness."

Rusty wasn't fazed. With eyes like blue stones, he massed the Lord's cavalry and attacked. What right did a working reporter have to gather material for a book writer? How much did Grothaus stand to make if that book became a best-seller? Wasn't he sacrificing his professional ethics in favor of monetary gain? How could he write objective news reports of the David West trial when he was actually under contract to someone else? Wasn't he cheating his readers? Did his employers at the *Post* know what he was doing? Did Grothaus know his material—"Your work product!" Rusty cried—was being made available to the defense team in this case? Wasn't that the shoddiest sort of journalism?

Rusty's words snapped like whiplash. Grothaus kept calm, but he was distressed. He didn't feel he'd done anything wrong, and yet Rusty Hardin, enjoying prosecutorial immunity, seemed determined to humiliate him. Grothaus couldn't fight back.

Allen Isbell rose twice to object that the questions were badgering and irrelevant. The judge ordered both lawyers to approach the bench. Allen said sternly, "This man is here as a witness to testify about Wickie Weinstein's involvement in the murders, and he's being asked constantly about a *book contract*. That's ridiculous!"

It was germane, Rusty countered. Yes, certainly he was trying to discredit Grothaus as a professional journalist, but that was in order to discredit him as a witness. He was within his rights as a cross-examiner. He didn't say it, but he was also within his ethical rights, he believed, as a lawyer in an adversary proceeding.

Judge Azios overruled heated objections by the defense.

Ordered to respond, Grothaus stated that his bank account would hardly soar as a result of his occasional contribution of research and introductions: he had been paid a flat fee of $500 by me, and would be paid $500 more in about a year's time. The city editor of the Houston *Post* had been aware of every detail of his arrangement; the paper had no objection. And no, it hadn't in the least affected his objectivity as a reporter. As regards some of his research material being shown to the defense, it was common practice for journalists to trade off information with attorneys on either side of a case for an edge in information in return.

(What he really wanted to say to Rusty was: "Whitfield's surfacing last November was what caused David West to cave in, so you profited a lot more from my 'work product' than the defense ever did. Remember?")

But Rusty gave him no opening, and Dan kept his mouth shut.

Rusty hectored away. Wasn't Grothaus's "excessive interest" in Kim Paris last summer the result of his desire to get more smear material for a hot book that would make him rich? "And so you wrote a story about her being a topless dancer that made her cry on what should have been the happiest day of her life, didn't you? You couldn't wait to get that information into the newspaper, whether or not it was true or relevant, could you, Mr. Grothaus?"

Allen objected and was finally sustained. In a huff, as if he'd gotten his hands dirty, Rusty turned his back. "Pass this witness."

Allen asked only a few choice questions on redirect.

"Mr. Grothaus, is there any personal animosity between you and Mr. Rusty Hardin?"

"You'd have to ask Mr. Hardin that," Grothaus replied.

"On December 11, 1985, the last time you saw each other in this courtroom, in front of a dozen reporters, did Mr. Hardin have something to say to you that was particularly memorable?"

"Yes, he did."

"What were the last words he said to you that day?"

"He said, 'Grothaus, you're nothing more than a fucking sleazebag.' "

A few of the jurors, including the minister, winced.

Dan Grothaus was excused, and left the courtroom. Rusty sat down to confer with Lyn McClellan, but his lips were drawn tightly across his teeth. He knew the jurors were upset. And at that point, as if to rub fresh pepper in a bleeding wound, Allen Isbell said, "The defense calls Clifford Irving."

That morning I had stood in front of the mirror like a prima donna. Should I wear a suit and tie? Would I look respectable and be more convincing that way? Well, no matter—I didn't have a suit in Houston. I had a blue blazer and a pair of gray Hush Puppies, but I hadn't worn them since the David West voir dire. In the pungent heat of court for the past three weeks I had worn bush shirts, cotton khakis, and old running shoes. (*"Now* you look like a writer," Rusty had said—although one hot evening, carrying my Spanish straw shopping bag over my shoulder, headed for my car in the cheap two-dollar parking lot, a bum sidled out of an alley, fell in step with me, and asked, "You goin' to the mission, too?")

I'll compromise, I had decided. Clean khakis, a short-sleeved sport shirt with buttons, and my *new* running shoes.

I looked out over the crowded trial courtroom from the witness chair. The jurors all stared at me with open curiosity; they had seen me for those three weeks in the courtroom. In the newspaper accounts that they weren't supposed to look at they had read that I was writing a book about the Campbell murder case.

"After Dan Grothaus made the introduction, how many times did you meet with Paul Whitfield?" Allen asked.

"Three times," I said.

"Do you remember the dates?"

I looked at my notes. "November 25, December 4, and December 6. All in 1985."

"Where did you meet him the first time, on November 25?"

"At the bar of the Grand Hotel, Westheimer at the Loop."

"Who else was present?"

"Lynn Roebuck. She's his wife now—then she was his fiancée. She came with Paul, and Dan Grothaus joined us after about half an hour."

"What did you discuss?"

"David's statements to Paul about the Campbell murders. And Wickie's statements to Paul on the same subject."

"Did you eat as well as drink?"

"Yes, there was a free hors d'oeuvre bar with oysters and egg rolls and cheese."

"Did Paul Whitfield seem sober when he arrived?"

"Yes. We met at six o'clock. He told me he'd come straight from work."

"Who paid for the drinks that evening?"

"I did. With a Visa card."

"No one else contributed?"

"No, they offered, but I paid it all."

"No drinks were paid for with cash, by you or anyone else?"

"None."

"Do you have the Visa credit card receipt from November 25 with you in the courtroom today?"

I produced the flimsy pink slip of paper I had dug out of my teeming file on my midnight treasure hunt, and a xerox of this creased document was entered into evidence. The total bill, including tax and before the tip, was $25.75.

"How much do drinks cost at the Grand Hotel bar?" Allen asked.

"I can't remember exactly. It's a good hotel. Probably two and a half to three dollars."

"What did you personally drink that evening?"

"Two vodka tonics."

"Did anyone *not* drink?"

"All four of us drank."

"Is there any way that Paul Whitfield could have had 'half a dozen drinks at least'?"

"No way at all."

That took care of Whitfield's credibility and my new label as a seducer of witnesses, and I felt better. Allen then asked what Whitfield had told us that evening, and I repeated his tale of Wickie's involvement. Then on December 4, when we four met again at Renu's Thai restaurant in Montrose, at my urging Paul repeated his account for the third time. By then he was a little nervous, I said, having grasped the full significance of what David and Wickie had told him.

On the evening of December 6, I testified, he told the story a fourth time in the Harris County District Attorney's Office, in front of Lyn McClellan and Rusty Hardin. I had my notes in front of me—four single-spaced pages I had typed the following morning, December 7— to confirm the highlights of the conversation. They said:

"Paul was reluctant to talk, nervous, knees shaking, smoked a lot. Rusty had a hard time getting him to be specific. . . . Paul clarified that Wickie told him 'we (meaning David and Wickie) threw the gun away in Buffalo Bayou.' Rusty had no comment."

That caused brows to furrow in the courtroom. If Rusty had heard Whitfield's tale, why was Whitfield denying he'd told it? And why was Rusty soliciting that perjured denial?

Let's find out, Allen thought, and threw me into the lion's cage.

"Pass the witness."

Rusty stuck out a claw and went for an artery. I was an enemy now. I stood between him and the conviction of a woman he believed was guilty of cold-blooded parricide. That wasn't the intention, and he knew that, but it was the effect, and the effect was what mattered. He would do what he had to do.

He ran through our friendly relationship during jury selection in the David West case, lunches here and there with him and with Nettles and Leitner, then focused on our November 26 meeting in the courthouse coffee shop just before the Thanksgiving break. "You came to me, didn't you, Mr. Irving, with the tale of a possible witness? You didn't name him, did you? And you asked me for something, didn't you?"

I had to own up, and I didn't feel happy about it. "I tried to do a little horsetrading," I admitted. "I wanted a look at the HPD offense report in the case."

"And what did I reply?"

"You said you couldn't give it to me. It wasn't your property to give. You gave your reasons."

The jury and the spectators leaned forward in their seats, fascinated. They were getting a look at what went on behind the scenes during a murder trial. The deals, the manipulation, the hunting for advantage. The trial had taken on a new look. This was all so *personal.*

"You tried to barter the production of a witness for a look at confidential information, didn't you?"

"I never had any control—"

"Just answer the question yes or no," Rusty said sharply.

"It's not a question that properly deserves a yes or no answer," I said.

A look of hurt invaded Rusty's eyes. "Your Honor, this witness is not being responsive to the questions."

Rusty had always taken advantage of the judge's easygoing attitude. He knew his man, and how far he could go with impunity. But after all this time, so did I.

"It doesn't serve any fact-finding purpose," I said, "to answer questions yes or no when both yes and no would be misleading. I told you in the courthouse coffee shop, after I asked for the police offense report, that I'd been bluffing. I told you I had no control over Paul Whitfield. I couldn't and wouldn't influence him to testify. I told you that, too. You asked me to be a good citizen and bring him down, and I explained that he'd have to come of his own volition."

Fortunately he didn't remember (he told me later) what I'd replied when he'd asked me to be a good citizen. Had he done so, I would have been sorely embarrassed.

Nevertheless, it was 1–0, favor of Rusty. We worked our way through time to the night that I'd come down with Paul to Rusty's office in the District Attorney's Building. Rusty carefully avoided asking what Paul had said in the meeting. He did ask: "What was my response after I'd heard Paul Whitfield's story?"

"That you probably wouldn't use him as a witness in the guilt or innocence stage of the trial, but you might use him in the second stage, the punishment stage, if we got that far."

"And did I say *why* I didn't think I could use him in the guilt or innocence stage?"

411

"You thought his information about the .45 was too nonspecific. Which made no sense to me then, although later I realized you were in the middle of cutting a deal and didn't need Whitfield. You probably realized that Whitfield's testimony could make problems for you in *this* trial."

Now Rusty's eyes had a hard blank look, the more menacing because they showed no emotion. But he should have known, from the way I'd testified last November in voir dire, that I was going to have my say. Lyn McClellan tugged at his sleeve and whispered something. Rusty turned back to me.

"Mr. Irving, have you ever been indicted for a felony?"

I had guessed this might happen. What I'd gone through fourteen years ago had nothing whatever to do with the matter at hand, but if you're a dedicated prosecutor fighting for a conviction in a major murder case, you impeach the credibility of a so-called hostile witness any way you can. I looked toward Allen Isbell for guidance. He remained stolid; he didn't jump up to object.

So I answered as flatly as I could, and gave a few requested details. What, who, and when. "The main events of the Hughes hoax took place in '71. The indictment was in March of '72—"

Now Allen flew to his feet, quills rising. *"Your Honor!"*

Judge Azios pounded on the desk. He understood. Allen hadn't known the date of that period in my life. Neither had the judge. Both had assumed that it was more recent. The only one who had known the date was Rusty, for we had discussed it at length that first time back in October. *("Fourteen years ago? That makes me feel old.")*

Rule 609 of the *Texas Rules of Evidence* forbids attempting to question a witness on felony convictions more than ten years old. Called the "remoteness" rule, it is the law in all federal and most state courts, and no lawyer can practice criminal law without being aware of it.

"Your Honor!" Allen Isbell all but stamped his foot with indignation. "The state has deliberately and improperly attempted to impeach the credibility of a vital witness for the defense! The jury has been prejudiced beyond repair. I move for a mistrial!"

A vital witness for the defense. How had this happened to me?

Judge Azios glared at Rusty, but he was not about to let nearly four weeks of courthouse labor go down the drain because of prosecutorial error or misconduct. Let the appellate court deal with that issue. Sternly he instructed the jury to disregard all testimony regarding the felony conviction of the witness. Motion denied! This trial would go *forward!*

In a zigzag motion, however, and amid storms and tantrums.

Rusty squared his shoulders and went back to work. What about my having given my work-product, and the work-product of Dan Grothaus, to Gene Nettles and Jim Leitner? Had I done that?

"I provided copies of certain interviews," I said, "ones that didn't contain privileged information, to Gene Nettles, where I felt the interest of truth and justice would be served, and where I made promises to do so. But I gave some to you, too."

Rusty said he hadn't asked me that, and I replied that I knew he hadn't, but I thought the jury should know all the facts.

That was impudent. Rusty bubbled like a stew overflowing the pot. "And the facts are that when you were finished with the David West trial, the outcome of which was a terrible disappointment to you, you opened your files to Mr. Schaffer, the first lawyer appointed to defend Cynthia Campbell Ray! And then when Mr. Schaffer was no longer on the case, you gave the same files once again to Mr. Isbell and Mr. McDonald—isn't that so?"

True, I said, I had done that, mostly because they didn't have the resources of the state and didn't have all the information necessary to conduct a fair trial. "You said to me, 'I'll always be interested to hear what you learn.' The defense lawyers felt the same way."

"So you, who went under the guise of a writer, a journalist, supposedly independent and neutral, *in fact became a player in the game, didn't you?*"

It was the first time Rusty had ever admitted it was a game, and I was so pleased with his admission that I just said, "Yes, if you want to put it that way."

He was satisfied, too, and he passed me to Allen Isbell for redirect.

Allen swiftly brought out the fact that as early as October Rusty had known the date of my felony conviction. Then he asked me when I had first given Kent Schaffer information about Paul Whitfield's claims regarding the disposal of the murder weapon.

"In February, when I found out that he didn't know that Paul Whitfield existed."

Out of control, Rusty jumped to his feet, yelling—more a cry of outrage than an objection. "The state's file had all the information on Whitfield and Lynn Roebuck! Kent Schaffer had two weeks to come view it, but instead he went to Mexico on a vacation!"

(Schaffer later said, "I went down to look at the file the moment they agreed. McClellan gave it to me and sat around and cracked jokes. I looked through it and said, 'This is *it*? You guys have to be kidding.' And there was nothing whatever in it about Whitfield or Roebuck.")

The judge ordered Rusty to sit, and Allen continued his redirect with: "Tell me, Mr. Irving, do you recall, shortly after we met, my telling you that the exculpatory evidence of Paul Whitfield's statements made to the state was not in the state's file showed to the defense?"

"Yes, I remember that."

"And didn't you find that strange?"

I had wondered about it, but I hadn't found it strange, because it had occurred to me that Rusty hadn't made any notes about the meeting— if he *had* made notes, his cross of Paul Whitfield in this trial would have been markedly different.

I hedged the answer and told the truth. "I wondered about it."

But by now Rusty's face was flushed a deep red. He believed that Allen was trying to impugn his veracity and question his ethics. He began shouting at Allen, and then at me. He looked as if he would launch himself across the table at whoever got in his way. Brenda Palmer was trying to take it all down, but Rusty was flapping a sheaf of papers against the table like a cudgel, and the noise drowned out most of what he was saying. The jury just stared. This was a good show.

I had a microphone in front of me. Upset for him now more than for me, wanting to help more than to hurt, I leaned forward and said, "Calm down, Rusty."

And Rusty calmed down, and sat down. He looked a little stricken at what he had done.

Allen was finished. Rusty decided not to try his luck at recross. I was relieved to step down—although, as all witnesses do, I instantly began to go over what I'd said and regret that I hadn't said this instead of that and that I'd left out *x* when he asked me *y*.

It was 11:45, and the judge mercifully called an early break. As soon as the jury was gone I walked straight over to Rusty and extended my hand in peace. He took it instantly.

"Free for lunch?"

"Sure. Let's go."

"Okay, you were right," I said, walking through the heat of San Jacinto Street on the way to the restaurant, "I got too involved and became a player."

"And I forgot that more than ten years had elapsed on your conviction. It may have seemed like a cheap shot, and I'm sorry. I didn't want to ask anyway, but Lyn kept prodding me. You didn't see that, but he was whispering to me all the time: 'Ask him, ask him.' "

A fall from grace, I thought. A seduction. It could happen to anyone.

"I'm too righteous," Rusty admitted. "It's a bad fault."

"You want to win."

"Of course I do. But the right way. You know that. And when someone questions my ethics, the way Allen did, I go crazy. I mean, when he asked if you thought it strange that he hadn't seen the Whitfield file—"

414

"I said I wondered about it. That wasn't responsive, but it was true."

"You're a nasty witness," Rusty said.

"And you're a nasty cross-examiner."

In the restaurant we argued about what Paul Whitfield had said or not said that night in Rusty's office. I was right: Rusty was positive that Paul hadn't said what I'd heard him say. It became like a marital argument: *"But you said . . . he said . . . no, what I said was . . . "*

And then we gave up, and split the bill, and went back to the murder trial. The sideshow—or, what most people mistakenly thought of then as the sideshow—was over. We could focus again on Cindy Ray and whether or not she had helped David West murder her parents.

36

Throughout the trial, Cindy had been losing weight with remarkable rapidity. The pounds almost seemed to drop to the floor each day, and I wondered fancifully if there would be an audible *plop*. That afternoon for the first time, as I concentrated on her, the pretty Cindy showed. I began to see the woman with whom David West had fallen in love.

And that same afternoon Allen Isbell turned to the character of the Campbell family and to life as it may have been lived at 8901 Memorial. He wanted to convince the jury that the tales of incest related by the defendant, no matter how diverse their plumage, had a fundamental basis in a one-bodied truth. Rusty had first raised the question and then, through the sisters and Michael Ray, had tried to show that Cindy was lying, using the horror story to wheedle sympathy and manipulate people—culminating in the fateful manipulation of David West.

Not so, Allen believed. And to that effect he called a slim, dark-haired young woman named Deborah Ferguson.

Rick Brass made his first formal appearance for the defense team, taking Ferguson on direct. A navy wife now, she testified that she had been a childhood friend of Cindy's. She had been fat as a child, much fatter than Cindy, so that when they played Laurel and Hardy, she played Ollie. They put on a show for the Fergusons and Campbells. Deborah's parents laughed at it, but the Campbells weren't impressed. They banished the children upstairs.

On another occasion Cindy said, "Let's play Psychiatrist." The girls played the game in the Campbells' bedroom. "I was the psychiatrist, Cindy was the patient. She lay on the bed, and I pulled the chair up by the bed. I said, 'What's your problem? Tell me all about it.' She said that her maid did really horrible things to her, locked her in the closet—nasty things, sexually nasty things. 'Molesting' is what I'd call them now—touching her and things you shouldn't do. She was really dramatic and acted it out real extreme. . . . "

"Did the Campbells have a maid then?" Rick asked.

"I never saw a maid while I was there."

Rusty took her on cross and got her to repeat the psychiatrist game tale. "I thought Cindy had a strange childhood," she told him, in conclusion.

"Tell me all the things that make you think she had a strange childhood," Rusty gently said.

"I just did."

Rusty's voice rose. "Are you telling the jury that this woman had a strange childhood based on what she told you when you played Psychiatrist, and based on her parents' reaction to your playing Laurel and Hardy?"

"That's right."

Rusty let her go, shaking his head from side to side theatrically, in wonderment. The jury understood.

A young woman named Vickie Miller was the next witness for the defense, and her testimony elicited from Cindy Ray her first visible emotional response of the entire trial.

Vickie Miller lived in Magnolia, Texas, about forty miles northwest of Houston, and today was her thirty-second birthday. She was a heavy woman, with a clear and pleasant country voice. Her initial worried attitude soon dropped away; her modesty remained. Married with three children, she identified herself as "a full-time mama." She exuded, like an earthy perfume, a palpable warmth, a dominating sincerity.

She was Cindy's close and only friend in the eighth grade, she said, when Cindy was fourteen. She had spent the night at Memorial three or four times, visited four or five more times. And Cindy had done the same at her home. "At my house she would smile and laugh," Vickie Miller said. "She had a beautiful singing voice, and she'd sing for us. [At the Campbells] it wasn't a normal household. Her parents and her grandmother never spoke to us. They ignored us. They were cold. They ridiculed her because of her weight. Cindy told me they were ashamed of her. They didn't love her. She felt unwanted. She never smiled or laughed when we were in her house. She wasn't allowed to sing. She said they had a rule: Silence Is Golden. She hated it."

416

Vickie Miller told her tale in such a direct manner, with such controlled sympathy for the fat young girl now become a woman accused of murder, that it cast a spell over the courtroom. When the narrative reached July of 1970, you felt you were there with her. We all strained forward in our seats to hear her words.

"Cindy began to get more desperate to get away from them. She wanted to run away, to Los Angeles, to become an actress. She decided to do it. We went to the bus depot. I went just for moral support. She was going to get a ticket as far west as she could go. But she got insecure, afraid, and she said she'd split the money and we'd go together. I felt so sorry for her that I agreed. Her money took us as far as Hallettsville"—that was about eighty-five miles west of Houston—"way out in the boonies, right out where the cows are. No stars, no moon. In the middle of the highway. In Yoakum"—another eighteen miles down the road—"I had a change of heart. I called my Mama. I came back, and my Mama was waiting for me at the bus stop.

"A week or two later Cindy called me. She was back in Houston. There was a lot of noise and hollering in the background. Next day she called again from St. Joseph Hospital—the mental ward. She asked me to visit her, but she told me to ask for another person or I couldn't get in. When I got there she told me the family were going to take her away because she had embarrassed them. A big male nurse then took hold of me and told me 'no visitors.'

"Then we moved away to Magnolia, Texas."

Six years passed before she and Cindy met again.

"But when she called me—it was 1976, March or April—she was happy and excited. She had two little baby boys she was proud of." Vickie Miller's voice broke a little, then rose, almost exalted. "It didn't matter if she was fat or skinny! She had two little baby boys she loved!"

The courtroom was hushed. Some of the jurors' eyes shifted to Cindy Ray. A remarkable thing had happened. Cindy's eyes were filmed with tears. The tears began to roll down her cheeks. She made no sound.

"We visited and talked," Vickie Miller went on. She wasn't watching Cindy weep, and she couldn't hear it. "She said her parents were proud of her for the first time. In early May I visisted at her house. She was living on Memorial again—Cindy, her baby boys, her parents. No husband. Cindy said her father had offered the husband money to go, and he took it and ran. The baby was in Cindy's lap. He was lovin' on her. He was crazy about her and she was crazy about him. For the first time her parents actually spoke to me. They were cordial. They'd never been nice to me before.

"I became pregnant. Cindy wanted to buy my baby her first present. She did, and it was a high chair from Sears."

Vickie Miller then broke down on the witness stand and cried. "Then I didn't see her for ten years," she concluded, checking her sobs. "Not until today. . . . " She finally looked at Cindy and saw that she was crying, too.

There weren't many dry eyes in the courtroom.

"Pass the witness," Rick Brass said.

What could Rusty do now? No lawyer in the audience wanted to be in his shoes. Not often does such a wholesome person as Vickie Miller testify in a murder trial, and if she does, the opposing lawyer is usually wise to say, "No further questions." The alternative—to try to cut the wholesome witness to shreds, to shatter her believability—can alienate a jury beyond repair. If it fails, it can lose a case that is already won. Lyn McClellan said later, "The first witness, Ferguson, was easy. Vickie Miller was a different ball game. I didn't know how Rusty was going to do it. I couldn't even see how he was going to *begin*."

But it would have needed Jesus Christ on the witness stand as a defense witness for Rusty to say at the outset of cross, "No questions." And even then Rusty might have probed to show that perhaps His memory of events had been clouded by the traumatic events at the end of His life.

Rusty thought, I represent the victims. If that means undermining the credibility of a witness for the defense, no matter how wholesome she is, I'll do it. I *have* to do it. I can live with it, because her vision isn't accurate.

I can ask her questions, he figured, until the cows come home. I'll let her talk. It's only a matter of time before she winds down and trips herself up.

Cordially, and with a show of respect, as if he were interviewing Mother Teresa for the *Ladies' Home Journal*, he took Vickie Miller back in minute and boring detail from her present life in Magnolia to her childhood in Greenville, Texas, where there were fifty kids in her entire school . . . took her grade by grade up to the meeting with Cindy in the eighth grade at Spring Branch Junior High in Houston.

"I was a newcomer," Vickie Miller confided.

Rusty probed: "Did you have something in common?"

"We were both fat. You kind of tend to flock with your own."

Rusty nodded warmly. He understood about fat people. "It was a tough time for you here in Houston at first, right?"

Vickie Miller shook her head decisively: no. "I was a little timid, but

I could always make friends. I had a swell Mama and an okay stepfather and three sisters and they all loved me. The second or third week, Cindy and I became friends. She helped me with a test. I made A on it, too. About a month later, after she visited me—because my Mama always wanted to meet my friends—I visited her."

"A long visit?"

"I went on Friday afternoon after school, and I stayed the night."

"Were Mr. and Mrs. Campbell there?"

"They came in later. They didn't speak to us."

"What did you and Cindy do together?"

"We talked. And she painted, beautifully."

"Did you eat dinner there?"

"We ate Metrecal. Right out of the can." Vickie Miller smiled, remembering it.

"How did you get home on Saturday?"

"My mother came in the morning to get me. We had a new baby. I had to help. My Mama was an apartment manager."

"You said the Campbells didn't speak to you and Cindy. Did they do anything strange?"

"They didn't *do* anything strange. Just ignored you. Never spoke to me or Cindy. Never said nothing."

Rusty slowly began to harp on the fact that she had spent only four sleepover nights at Memorial, and that she was a child, and that both the Campbells worked long hours at a demanding office job. Some people are "touchers," he said, and some are not: wouldn't you agree? She did. And Vickie's family were touchers—warm, openly affectionate —and that's what she expected from other families, wasn't it? And for a child she made some rapid value judgments, didn't she? And she didn't know what happened in the house when she wasn't there, did she, to account for certain behavior? She assumed a great deal, wasn't that correct?

"I formed my opinion by what I saw," Vickie Miller said, "not so much by what I heard. They gave me a cold, eerie feeling. They looked at her like they despised her. I could see it in her eyes that she was unhappy."

"*You could see it in her eyes?*" Rusty gave each word full weight.

He had been patient, and finally had found the wedge in the door that he needed. In the nicest possible way, he began to contradict and ridicule Vickie Miller. Let them hate me for a while, he thought, as long as in the end they see that this woman is coloring the truth with her need to be loyal. "You assume that these people don't love their daughter, and you assume that they're embarrassed by her, and you assume that they make fun of her because of her weight. Because she *told* you." And then: "Let's talk about the number of things you could see in her eyes. . . ."

Rick Brass objected steadily, but he was overruled.

The end result was like a prizefight where the final bell has tolled, the boxers have retired to their corners to have the blood stanched, the referee and judges have huddled to reach a decision, and already both sides claimed victory. Lyn McClellan crowed, "Rusty's cross was a masterpiece. All the odds were against him, and he won." More modestly, Rusty said, "I don't think the jury believed the last two witnesses." For his part Allen Isbell was concerned that the young professional women on the jury may not have liked "Vickie the Mama," but he commented privately, "Rusty went too far. Sure he cut her up, but it's like Muhammad Ali in his prime licking me with his fists. Not sympathetic."

Outside the courtroom Deborah Ferguson, the preceding witness, said, "Boy, he's mean!" Vickie Miller just said, "I felt bullied and demeaned by him."

Rusty said quietly and sadly to Lyn, "I had no choice."

Allen called one more witness to end the day. His name was Carson Elliot Watson, known as Ed—black-haired, bearded, with a string tie and a West Texas cowboy accent—and he testified that at approximately 3:55 A.M. on the morning of June 19, 1982, he and wife had been driving home from the Houstonian Club, where he worked as a security guard. He was driving west along Memorial Drive when he saw a car sitting on the shoulder of the road near Chatsworth Drive. It was a late model large car, and there was a man standing beside it, on the driver's side, who seemed to be hanging around, waiting for something or someone. "I saw him step around the car," Ed Watson said. "It appeared he'd been in the trunk. He was about thirty to thirty-five, six feet tall, a hundred and eighty pounds. But that's just a guess. I didn't get a good look at him."

No, Watson hadn't seen a woman in or near the car.

The next day Watson heard about the Campbell murder on TV, and he called the police.

Rusty took Ed Watson on cross. Yes, when he first spoke to the police he'd said the man looked to be about forty. Just a guess. Well-dressed, wearing a sport shirt. "No, not a motorcycle kid or an Urban Animal." No, he hadn't noticed any combat boots. No field jacket, no mask. Nothing in his hands.

Still the question lingered in the air: If it wasn't Wickie Weinstein or some other confederate waiting for David West to appear, who was it?

The defense called its final witness. Allen had always predicted that this would turn the tide of the trial. Dr. Rob Owens, if allowed to testify, could plant in the mind of the jury the crucial seed of reasonable doubt. The jury was told to take the morning off and show up at 1:30 P.M. Dr. Owens was not what is called a "fact" witness, who could testify about things that had happened or what had been said by the parties in the case; he was being proposed as an "expert" witness, which meant that, unlike fact witnesses, he could offer his opinions. But he had first to be heard without the jury present, so that the court could determine if indeed he qualified as an expert, and then if his expertise was relevant. If that was so, he would testify before the jury.

Rusty told Lyn McClellan, "This psychiatrist or psychologist, whatever he is, has never talked to David, so I don't think his testimony can be allowed." That morning Rusty had set aside to hunt for some rebuttal witnesses for the state. They agreed that the examination to test Dr. Owens's credentials would be Lyn's job. Lyn was pleased. He was glad to do something other than occupy an uncomfortable chair.

"If you come back in the middle of it," he said to Rusty, "you've got to keep your mouth shut. No kibitzing, no laughing."

"I promise," Rusty said.

"I don't believe you can do it."

"I'll bet you a lunch at Glatzmeier's."

"Done," Lyn said.

"Smirk and smile don't count."

The media was there, and so were the spectators—but no jury—when Dr. Owens took the stand at eleven o'clock in the morning. With Allen prompting, he offered his credentials. He was thirty-nine years old with a B.S. from Mississippi State and a Ph.D. in counseling psychology from the University of Mississippi, and he was licensed as a psychologist in the State of Texas. His internship for his B.S. had been served at Florida State Prison, and he then became a staff psychologist for the Texas Department of Corrections. Yes, he had counseled the sexually abused. In Houston he now headed his own private counseling service, called Lifeskill Resource Center, Inc.

Judge Azios nodded pleasantly. He seemed impressed.

Allen then recited a series of facts in evidence concerning Cindy Ray —her voice change during sex with David West; her calling him "Daddy"; her running away from home as an adolescent; her well-chronicled "weight problem"; her lies to Michael Ray, Sr. about her father's being in a mental hospital and her mother living with another lawyer; her statements to Gwen Sampson that her mother had consistently locked her in the bathroom and that she was "Daddy's little girl"; her statement to Rory Lettvin that her "stepmother" had locked her in a closet; evidence that at the age of eleven she told a friend that a nonexistent maid had locked her in the closet and tried to "do nasty things to her"—and Dr. Owens responded to each proposition by repeating, "It's consistent with the behavior of sexually abused children." Dr. Owens went on to point out that there were a number of common syndromes for sexually abused children: at first they rebel against the values of the family; then they deny the nature of the abuse, continue to seek approval from the family and blame themselves for what's happened, and thus become depressed; and later they act out the abuse in various ways such as sexual promiscuity.

Of course it's possible, he said, for a father to abuse more than one child, but typically the abuse is confined to the most vulnerable child. Also typically there is favoritism by the father to the abused child, and corollary resentment by the other members of the family. Other family members usually are unaware of what's going on, despite the often tangible signs.

In the midst of this analysis, Rusty entered the courtroom and took his seat at Lyn's side. But they had agreed that this was Lyn's witness.

Smirk and smile don't count. Rusty dug an elbow into Lyn's arm. For the rest of the morning he sat there at the counsel table, playing with rubber bands.

Lyn now heaved his 300-plus pounds to his feet and voiced a general objection to the testimony. What area of law allowed it as admissible? He pointed out that no testimony whatever in the trial *showed* sexual abuse; it showed only that the defendant had *told* people about such abuse. Dr. Owens's testimony was just a chintzy way of skirting around the defense's reluctance to put the defendant on the stand.

Allen swiftly countered that the state, not the defense, had thrown the issue of sexual abuse into the arena. If an expert could aid the jury in understanding the evidence, he should be allowed to testify.

"I want case law on this issue," Judge Azios declared, "and I'll withhold my ruling until I read it."

Dr. Owens then went on to discuss the second subject about which he hoped to testify: a diagnosis of the personality of David West. He had heard all of David's testimony, had read the transcripts of the tapes, and had interviewed Cecilia West. He had enough data, he said, to make a diagnosis based on the formulae in a diagnostic manual called DSM-III, the standard in the field.

Rusty smirked.

422

"What is your diagnosis of David West, Dr. Owens?" Allen asked.

"An antisocial personality. A sociopath or psychopath. A disordered person—very manipulative, intelligent, and creative. Appears altruistic, but is immature and callous. Lacks empathy." He defined empathy as "the ability to understand the quality of another's feelings." From that he deduced that David's stated motive for killing the Campbells—to free Cindy from their evil influence—was not consistent with his personality, because there was no evidence of empathy in David. (Rusty looked through the ceiling of the courtroom toward heaven.) Also of interest, the psychologist said, was the parallel between David's sexual relationship with Cindy and James Campbell's assumed sexual relationship with his daughter. The father is the lawgiver, the carer. He establishes a trust relationship with sexual distance. But in the case of incest that trust is exploited into sex. Ditto for David, her mentor who slyly became her lover.

This was all accompanied by charts and slides with hand-drawn boxes and labels that led from EVENT to PERCEPTION OF EVENT to SUBCON-SCIOUS EVALUATION OF THE PERCEPTION and then branched off in directions that were a trifle difficult to follow. Well, *I* couldn't follow them. From time to time my eyes slowly closed. Rusty and Lyn, in their seats, hid their faces. (Rusty said later, "It was like being back in the army. A slide show to belabor the obvious. The more they can confuse you, the happier they are.")

Melinda Meador, the neophyte prosecutor, slipped a note to Lyn that said: "Tell me, Dr. Owens—*was she, or wasn't she, there on June 19, 1982?*"

When Dr. Owens finished, Lyn argued that the defense was trying to put the chief witness on trial. They wanted to impeach David's testimony because he was a psychopath. "We won't object to Dr. Owens saying that David's a psychopath. We don't argue with that at all," Lyn said, somewhat surprisingly, "but it's irrelevant in this case."

"Bring me law and cases by this afternoon," Judge Azios repeated.

"You can take me to lunch now at Glatzmeier's," Rusty said to Lyn, after they were dismissed. "And let's pray the judge allows this guy to testify."

Hurricane Bonnie, working its way on a northwesterly course through the Caribbean and the Gulf of Mexico, was due to hit Galveston and Port Arthur by the next day. The weather in Houston was windy, gray, and ominous. As usual the three defense lawyers bought shrimp and avocado sandwiches and Diet Cokes at Bob & Linda's cafeteria restaurant, and Rick toted them in a big paper bag to Allen's office on the second floor of the Old Cotton Exchange Building. They spread the food across Allen's cluttered desk and listened to the weather report on Channel 26. Allen, whose house in Galveston had two-foot-thick reinforced brick walls, wasn't worried—he invited everyone down for the weekend. "The last hurricane was Alicia in 1983. Hardly rattled a pane."

But Allen looked jaded and run-down—he had the pervading pale gray look that often identifies a trial lawyer, and today he looked bleached. He didn't like the way the case was going. And it had gone on so *long*.

"The jury's tired," he said to Randy and Rick. He started to rub a reddening eye, then stopped. "I'm worried about putting Dr. Owens on, even if the judge allows it. I think Rusty could give him a hard time."

"Lyn's taking him," Randy pointed out.

"Lyn *took* him," Allen said, "when the jury wasn't there. Once they're in the box, the state can change lawyers."

"Owens is very well prepared," Rick Brass said. "He's psyched up."

They had woodshedded the psychologist, and he had observed Rusty cross-examining witnesses for a week. Although he knew that he was going to be peppered and skewered and flayed, he believed he could handle it. He had authority on his side; he wouldn't back down. Moreover, his testimony would make everything else fall into place. Without it, the defense would have to rely almost entirely on the logic of final argument.

But Allen was still pessimistic. Everything depends on the bearded minister who wore sneakers with no socks. He's an independent, Allen thought again. He and Julia Carr will clash. There's a Julia Carr in every congregation. Ministers have to be pleasant to them, can't say, "I dislike you," but in a jury situation they let loose their spleen. If it's eleven to one in that jury room, and he's the *one*, he won't budge. The jury will hang up.

He had another infecting worry. If the jury brought in a guilty verdict, they then went on to the punishment stage, which could bring Cindy anything from an unlikely five years' probation to a likely life in Gatesville. But Cindy's reaction to the verdict might doom her to the worst. She could make Hurricane Bonnie look like a light breeze. Everything was battened down inside her. Only yesterday morning she had muttered to Allen, "I still wonder if you're secretly working with Rusty."

What if she blew?

He didn't say that aloud, not yet. He would have to talk to Rick. With his rabbinical calm, if anyone could control her, Rick could.

Before things got underway once more in the courtroom, I decided to canvass those trial groupies who had been there from the moment of Rusty's opening speech over three weeks ago. Most of the onlookers were retired folks; it was an interesting way to pass the time. Retribution was high on their list of priorities. Their unanimous decision was that the defense witnesses so far hadn't proved a single thing. She was guilty.

"What punishment would you give her, sir, if you were on the jury and you had voted her guilty?"

"Life. She killed her mother and father, didn't she?"

I mentioned that response to Rusty when he returned from a fine seafood lunch at Lyn's expense. "Looks like they came for a hanging," I said.

"My kind of people," Rusty said, grinning so that I wouldn't mistake the remark for other than a joke. Then he asked: "What would *you* give her?"

I didn't hesitate. I had been thinking about it for quite a while now.

"I believe that the sexual abuse took place. She's a bona fide basket case. Five years' mandatory psychiatric care, in an institution, with the court having the right to extend it if she's not cured."

"We don't have that in Texas law," he said.

"You should."

Rusty just shook his head wearily.

At ten minutes to two, with the lawyers in place, the jury out and the cool air nicely flowing, the bailiff called for order. Judge Azios adjusted his black robe and glasses and said, "The court finds that Dr. Owens will be allowed to testify on both topics, child abuse and the personality of David West."

Lyn McClellan approached the bench and argued with vigor that Mr. Isbell was trying to seduce the court into an improper act. "You cannot impeach a witness through the expert testimony of a psychiatrist!"

The judge said impatiently, "I've ruled. Now let's move along!"

Allen then made an error. Because she had driven in from Porter, Texas, seventy miles away, he called Mrs. Nellie Wisdom to the stand, deferring Dr. Owens until later in the day.

Nellie Wisdom was the mother of Vickie Miller, Cindy's childhood friend who had briefly run away with her. Rick Brass took her on direct. A woman of sixty-three with short, gray hair, she was even heavier than her daughter. She wore a flowing rose-pink Hawaiian shirt decorated with palm trees.

She testified to the unfriendliness of Jim and Virginia Campbell. "I picked Vickie up at Memorial. They never brought her home. I would bring Cindy home, too, after she stayed at our house. We always went in the back door. I tried to engage the Campbells in conversation, but they'd turn their backs. I'd just stand and wait at the door. Cindy was happy at my house. They played like children do. At Memorial she was quiet, scared-like. As we'd go in the driveway she'd tighten up, like she dreaded to go home."

She told her version of how the two girls had run away in the summer of 1970. She was crazy with worry, but she got a call from Vickie, and went to the bus depot to meet her. She called the Campbells to tell them, and they also showed up at the bus depot. "When only Vickie got off the bus, the Campbells were mad. Not concerned," Nellie Wisdom remembered.

"Next week, one night at one o'clock in the morning, the Campbells came to my apartment. They didn't call. I was asleep. No one knocked or rang the bell. A flashlight in my face was what woke me up. At first I was frightened. What had happened was that Mr. Campbell had come round with a police officer and got the security guard from the apartment complex to open up our front door in the dark of night. He was looking for Cindy. They all came into my bedroom. She wasn't there. . . . Oh yes, they had my phone number."

Rusty was delighted that the defense had unexpectedly put on Vickie Miller's mother. He had done his homework and was ready to tell the jury what had really happened out there "where the cows are." After a little talk last night with J. W. Campbell, he had subpoenaed the records of St. Joseph Hospital. He had been thinking of recalling Vickie Miller, but now it wasn't necessary.

Rusty went over in detail with Nellie Wisdom her testimony about the Campbells turning their backs to her when she was in their home. It wasn't the Campbells, she finally admitted, but Cindy's grandmother. She had been snubbed a couple of times in the kitchen, had to wait for ten or fifteen minutes. Her complaint suddenly seemed petty.

Then Rusty pounced. "Mrs. Wisdom, when your daughter and Cindy Campbell ran away, did you know they were actually staying in a rooming house in Yoakum with a couple of guys?"

"No, they weren't."

"Are you sure?"

"No, I'm not sure—"

"What you know is what your daughter, who was happy at home, told you after she ran away with another girl, right? That's all you know, isn't it?"

426

"And my daughter didn't tell me no lies," Mrs. Wisdom said.

"I understand," Rusty said sympathetically. He had children of his own. "No one wants to believe a daughter would lie about something like that, do they?"

"No. . . ."

"You know as well as I do, don't you, that Cindy's uncle was looking for her and drove with Cindy's grandmother all the way to Yoakum to find out they were in a rooming house—you knew that, didn't you?"

"No, I didn't know that." Nellie Wisdom began to show the doleful, shaggy look of a musk ox.

"Wasn't Mr. Campbell upset with your daughter Vickie for having run away with Cindy, and then for having abandoned her in Yoakum after spending the night with these two guys?"

Nellie Wisdom protested: "My daughter and Cindy spent the night with a little lady in a rooming house in Yoakum. And then some nice guy gave her the bus fare home."

Rusty smiled broadly.

"The two of them," he summed up, "were on the road near Halletsville, out on this deserted country road—two eighth-grade girls run away from home. Two guys came along and gave them a ride—they stayed the night in a rooming house—"

"Not with those boys—"

"The boys stayed somewhere else in the rooming house?"

"Yes, sir."

"And, 'Mama, nothing went on, and nothing happened, and I'm sure glad to be back, and I sure wish Cindy hadn't talked me into running away with her.' Is that what your daughter told you?"

"You're right . . . but she learned something from that experience."

"What did she learn?"

Nellie Wisdom breathed with relief, thinking that the ordeal was over. "She learned that there's no place like home, and not ever to leave her mother again."

"But when you were talking to the jury with Mr. Brass, you just weren't going to mention, were you, that the Campbells, who were so upset with their daughter, were upset about their running away because they stayed with two guys in a boarding house!"

Over a flurry of objection and argument and the judge's trying to halt her, Nellie Wisdom cried, "They did not stay in a boarding house with two guys! It was a nice little lady!"

Allen was miserable. I should have been content with Vickie Miller, he realized. The mother was a mistake. Overkill. He tried to smile at Cindy and look confident, but she turned away. Now she *knew* he was in league with Rusty. There was just nothing she could do about it, yet.

At 3:15 P.M. Allen finally called Dr. Rob Owens to the stand. Rusty, fresh from his successful dissection of Nellie Wisdom, shot to his feet, just as Allen had predicted, and requested permission of the court to take Dr. Owens on voir dire—in this instance, sworn testimony in front of the jury to establish Owens's credentials as an expert witness. Although most of us thought that was what had been accomplished in the morning, the judge puzzled us by granting permission.

Dr. Owens was not a prepossessing figure. He had a thick body and short legs, and he couldn't keep his white shirt tucked into his trousers. But, facing Rusty, he squared his shoulders and thrust out his jaw.

And well he might. Rusty was on a roll, ready for a scrap. He began by asking what books or articles or papers the psychologist had written on the subject of child abuse.

None.

None?

None.

Well, what had he *read*?

Dr. Owens couldn't remember.

Rusty gave him ample time, but Owens only looked more and more befuddled. He was terribly sorry, but he just couldn't remember. He had a mental block. Not a single book? Not a single article? No . . . sorry.

From the defense table, Allen stared at the doctor, uncomprehending. Allen's stomach was churning.

He hadn't come prepared, Dr. Owens explained, to cite the authorities. Rusty took the risk and asked, What *had* he come prepared for?

"I came prepared to give the benefit of my academic experience in a general way."

In the Texas Department of Corrections he had been in classification, in diagnostics and evaluation. "No," he admitted, "there were no abused children per se at TDC."

The more flustered Dr. Owens became, the more he reverted to multisyllabic words and academic jargon. In earning his master's degree, had he taken any courses in child abuse? Well, his master's degree had been in the subject of rehabilitation.

"Of whom?"

"It was in the subject of location evaluation . . . it was a multidisciplinary degree."

"Does that mean you were studying the prison system?"

"It does not mean that per se."

"What does it mean"—Rusty tried not to smile—"*per se?*"

"Psychometric testing of individuals . . . modalities . . . identifying specific syndromes."

"Is that child abuse? Did you study child abuse for your master's?"

"If you're asking was there a specific course entitled 'Child Abuse,' no."

Ditto for his undergraduate work and Ph.D. As for his practice as a psychologist, no, it had never been devoted to child abusers or abused children.

In one long sentence, area by area, Rusty summed up Owens's preparation, education, and current expertise in the field of child abuse—or rather, his striking lack of it—and ended by asking: "Is that a fair statement?"

"I would perhaps object to one comment," said Dr. Owens, "but except for that, yes, that's a fair statement."

"What's the comment you object to?"

"I don't recall it specifically," Dr. Owens said.

"Thank you, Doctor," said Rusty, "I have no further questions."

The judge sustained the state's objection as to child abuse, meaning that Dr. Owens would not be allowed to testify on that subject. Allen was furious—at himself for his terrible misjudgment of Owens's qualifications and abilities, at Owens for making such an ass of himself, and at the judge for reversing his ruling made that morning—but there was nothing he could do. After Nellie Wisdom and now Dr. Owens, the defense presentation was suddenly ludicrous.

In the jury box, Reverend Uselton cracked his knuckles and looked stern.

Sensing it would end in disaster, Allen nevertheless began direct examination on Dr. Owens's diagnosis of David West. Once again Owens brought out his slides and diagrams—so that half of us in the courtroom began to yawn and nod off, while the other half seemed to fight against it—and then analyzed David West as an antisocial personality and sociopath.

Allen passed the witness, bent his head to the desk, and prayed a little. Rusty stood up. After a few idle questions he said to Dr. Owens, in a rapierlike voice, "By the way, will you tell the jury whether or not on June 19, 1982, Cynthia Campbell Ray helped kill her parents?"

Dr. Owens said, "I would have no way of knowing that."

As the debate wore on, Owens took on the look of a trapped fish, round eyes glaring nowhere. Prior to an answer he made menacing

grunts—*"Hum!"*—as if gathering strength for a counterattack. He might better have plunged to the safety of the ocean floor. Rusty, who had gutted him on the issue of his qualifications as an expert on child abuse, now fileted him on the issue of what he had to say about the personality of David West. Toward the end of it Owens was sodden with sweat. Rusty demanded to know if he thought David West was or wasn't telling the truth. Owens gave several roundabout answers but they added up to: "I don't know."

Desperate, Allen rose for redirect.

"Has it not been your private opinion, Dr. Owens, that Wickie Weinstein probably did the actual shooting? And David West was there, but he was the one who ran out of the house?"

Remarkably, Rusty didn't object. Then, in quite a few more words than were necessary, Owens said that it would be more consistent with David's personality for him to have taken Wickie with him rather than Cindy; that more than his stated motive of responding to Cindy's entreaties, it was probable that he killed the Campbells in anger because of what they had done to his masterpiece.

"Pass the witness," Allen said.

But it was time to quit. It was five minutes to six on Wednesday evening, June 25. In the good old days, when everyone believed the trial might last only two weeks, two of the jurors had made plans to visit family in other states this weekend. They were both flying out of Texas on Thursday.

Rusty asked for recross of Dr. Owens when court reconvened the following Monday morning.

37

A lawyer's nightmare: the collapse of an expert witness during cross-examination. Allen left the courtroom in a hurry, avoiding the reporters. Back in his apartment he showered, scrubbing off the dried sweat of the courtroom. He went across the street to McDonald's and ate some Chicken McNuggets and a chef's salad. Coming back home, he put a pot of coffee in the microwave. It's my fault, he thought. It's my responsibility. But he told me he was prepared. . . .

He slept badly. He woke at 6 A.M., made another pot of coffee and began work on a memorandum of law for the judge's charge to the jury.

430

Randy McDonald called at seven. "It was awful."

"I know," Allen said dolefully.

"But Rusty made a mistake."

"Yes?" Allen suppressed a desire to laugh; he was afraid it would come out as a giggle. "What was it?"

"He shouldn't have insisted on bringing Owens back on Monday for recross. Owens told me he's going to bone up all weekend. He'll have a complete list of journals, books, magazines, whatever there is on the subject. He'll be so prepared that Rusty won't be able to even dent him."

Allen sighed. "Owens thinks it's like an orals exam for a Ph.D."

On Saturday morning, with no warning, Cindy Ray telephoned me collect from the jail, ostensibly to get Allen Isbell's home phone number in Houston—which I foolishly gave to her. But then she unburdened herself for nearly half an hour. I didn't know why, other than that after my testimony she saw me as an ally. Was I? I didn't think so. I felt grievously sorry for her, but in an enclosed space I'd never turn my back.

I just listened. It was a remarkable experience, insofar as she never spoke to me in court, averting her eyes whenever I looked at her. (She told Rick Brass: "That man always *stares* at me. He makes me feel like a frog he wants to dissect.") Now she was a disembodied voice in my ear.

She fixed on Rusty Hardin. "That man's amazing. I think the most immoral people on earth are those who alter their perspective at any given time and choose what they're going to believe. I think he knows that I'm innocent. I think's he's insanely dedicated to his progression up the ladder to success. Strange body language, too, when he's really upset —it's even effeminate. 'Self-righteous' would be too simplistic. If you don't have a dragon, or you can't obtain a dragon, create one. . . ."

I didn't agree, but I was nevertheless impressed with the force of her belief and the way she expressed it.

She went on: "An awful lot of people have got up there and lied. Some of it was so ludicrous, so absurd, that it made me want to laugh. Some were blatantly lying and showing that they have bad feelings toward me that have nothing to do with why they're there. I thought a few of the people he put up there to lie made him look worse. Not only have they lied, but they've created a person who doesn't exist."

Her voice was clear, self-assured, and firm.

"Those girls, for example—my sisters—since we were very young have dreamed of a way to do something to me. Plus that apartment building on Kingston would be another motive. I think it became so

431

obvious that they were lying that it was more beneficial to me than if they *hadn't* gotten up there.

"Gwen Sampson lied. I have exactly the same nose I was born with. Did my lawyers tell you how mad that made me? (No, they hadn't.) A doctor took my money, $1,700, and did nothing. And I've never grown anything on my tongue. I did not try to molest her son. Exactly the opposite: I was the mother to him that she wasn't. And when that incident happened with Don, she hated me. Apparently it's a hate that lasted a lifetime. Gwen is so self-centered—trying to take my life away from me with those lies—that at one point when she was feeling sorry for herself because she was being badgered, she looked over at me for understanding and pity."

She spoke about her husband, Makhlouf: "A very intelligent man, a truly moral man. He's Arabic, not an Americanized Arabic with gold chains. He said if I spoke to you, you would change my words to suit your needs. I hope that's not true. You have to give me your word that you won't do that."

I did so.

She spoke of the unfinished oil portrait left behind at Kingston. "The portrait is of someone who doesn't exist. She's stronger than I am. And I'm a better artist than *that*. That was, I guess the correct term would be, half-assed. I've half-assed my way through most of my art work. I was as good at six years of age as I am now. If you'd met me at six you would have assumed I'd be better than I am now. I was more creative then. Something happens as you grow older, if you're not careful. . . ."

She spoke of prison. "They put me in the wrong tank, the one for child abusers, and left me there for three months. One time there were six women in it, one time fourteen. They had either been charged with sexual molestation of a child or murder of a child. Someone was trying to hurt you all the time. Those women, if you're shy and passive, try to do to you what they must have done to their children. When I first came in there I was very shy, and they thought, this is a dream come true. My cigarettes and coffee have caused me pain and anguish. You have to fight for your life over a pack of cigarettes. One woman kept me alert for twenty-four hours a day, and 'alert' has not been one of my virtues . . . I'm always somewhere else. And some of the police are on the mentality level of the inmates, a type of disturbed ego about authority. They wrote me up for possession of a bottle of makeup, noncommissary—which they never do, they just take it away from a girl—and I had to clean eight hours a day for five days. They had me clean every window on every squad room the first night. I didn't tell my husband. I didn't want him to worry."

And of her fate: "On the news they said I had remained stone-faced. I'd rather chop my leg off than cry in that courtroom. I don't trust people I don't know. You feel like you're giving something. The older I've got the more I feel violated by crying in front of a group of strangers.

"I'm innocent. It's not a gray area. I had nothing to do with the murders of my parents. I just don't think that's going to have much to do with what's going to happen to me at this point."

She ended by saying, "I appreciated what you did, and I wanted to tell you that."

"Thank you, Cindy," I said.

After she hung up I thought about her. I realized that I hardly knew her. One witness after another talked about her and dropped pieces into the jigsaw puzzle of her life. But each piece was colored and shaped with a personal perception. Each was filtered through another psyche, in turn an unfinished jigsaw puzzle. The puzzle that was Cindy Ray only *seemed* visible. None of us are grasped whole; the puzzle is never solved or finished. We only pretend that it is, or can be, because we are afraid to face the knowledge that a human life is a dramatic abstraction. No one can be known, only described, sensed, glimpsed. Why do we do what we do? I wrote once in another book: "You may look for motive in an act, but only after the act has been committed. An effect creates not only the search for a cause, but the reality of the cause itself." I remembered that now. It helped to make me humble in my quest to understand what had happened at Memorial Drive.

Monday morning marked the beginning of the trial's fifth week. It would be over this week, Lyn McClellan predicted. "Anything less than a guilty verdict will put me into serious shock." The jury would deliberate for less than a day, he said, punishment phase included.

How much time would she get? "The jury may reason that David got life and he pulled the trigger," Lyn said, "so they'll go easier on her. Fifty years, if they believe Daddy diddled her. But you never know. They may think, 'Hey, it was *her* idea!' In that case, if they had the legal power, they'd stick a needle in Cindy's arm—if they could find the vein."

It was quiet and cool in the courtroom. Rusty entered briskly, tanned from a weekend outdoors with his two sons, camping and playing softball. For the first time, the jury was late. So was the defendant. Finally she arrived, and Keith Goode unlocked her handcuffs with an audible click just five seconds before the jury emerged from backstage. He

433

seemed to take pride in the timing. Maybe the ultimate kick would be for the cuffs to fall away precisely as the first juror emerged but before that juror's eyes could focus.

Today the panel was in red. Cindy wore her cocoa-colored suit, and her hair was up. She had lost even more weight over the weekend, particularly in her face. I caught her eye and nodded; she stared through me again as at an impudent stranger. She wore eyeliner and heavy mascara. She looked surprisingly well, I thought.

A refreshed and confident-looking Dr. Owens took the stand for the recross. He was in shirtsleeves now, ready for a fight. He even grinned as Rusty said good morning.

"Doctor, do you wish to withdraw any opinions stated Wednesday at the break?"

Owens broke from the starting gate and fell flat on his face. "None that come to mind right now," he responded. "To be honest with you, I don't recall the exact wording that I used, and I'm thinking back to the media accounts of what was said."

Obligingly, Rusty laid it all out for him, to the point where Owens began to nod and sigh and say, "Yes, that's correct . . . that's correct, yes. . . ." Then Rusty began to flay him.

"Doctor, on Wednesday, when you implicated Mr. Weinstein, that stretched expert testimony to the nth degree, didn't it?"

"What I voiced was a personal opinion," Owens said, "that David played the role attributed to Cindy and someone else played the role that David attributed to himself."

Rusty wagged his finger at Owens's face. "And would you agree with me"—his voice rose—"that you got into a box with Mr. Isbell on redirect, on Wednesday, because he led you down a primrose path and got you to express an opinion concerning a witness that *you never even met! —you never even saw!—and you never even heard of! Wickie Weinstein?*"

"I believe, to be responsive—yes. . . ."

Rusty's water was beginning to heat up. "Dr. Owens, how often do you engage in this clairvoyance, where you sit and watch somebody talk, and reach a conclusion as to what they're like and what they're capable of?"

"I observe people on a daily basis."

In a powerful ringing voice, Rusty said, "Isn't it true that when you walked into this court Wednesday it was the first time in your professional career that you have ever been asked to render a psychological opinion and swear under oath about a person you've never interviewed personally?"

"That is correct," Owens said.

Finally, Rusty let the poor man go. After a little while, so did Allen. The judge was tired and fed up and called for an early lunch break.

At lunch in his office, Allen said to his fellow lawyers, "I didn't watch the jury this morning. Did you?"

"They were basically asleep," Randy said.

"Well, that's good. That's the best news I've heard all day."

Rusty had a few more cards to play in this penultimate round.

In the state's rebuttal, he put into evidence the medical record from St. Joseph Hospital, after Cindy Campbell and Vickie Miller had run away on the bus to Halletsville and Yoakum. Cindy was then fifteen years old. She was admitted to the hospital on September 2, 1970.

Rusty quoted from the record. "Patient had a 'mental problem.' Mother informed personnel 'that patient was rejected by friends because of obesity.' Patient said that she was 'picked up by a man in Yoakum and went to bed with him.' Patient describes herself as 'always been bad and stupid.' The record goes on: 'Failed first grade. Feels guilt about hurting parents. Poor self-image. Vows she is no longer mixed up. Increased frequency of rebellion against parents. Rich fantasy life. Hostile and rebellious until admission, then shy and sweet. Naive and vulnerable.'

" 'Diagnosis: adolescent adjustment reaction.' "

Rusty paused to let that sink in. *Just another adolescent adjustment reaction, folks.*

" 'Stable, supportive home.' " He looked swiftly at the attentive jurors, then finished: " 'Discharged September 15, 1970. Testing done was not adequate. Appointment to complete testing was not kept. Signed, R. Johnston, M.D.' "

He then called three rebuttal witnesses—Stella Sumbera, Deborah Moeller, and Ginger Hansel—all childhood friends of either Betty or Michelle Campbell, and now in their midthirties. Stella Sumbera was married and chewed gum on the witness stand; Deborah Moeller, blond and heavyset, had two children and was married to a banker; Ginger Hansel was an unmarried electrical engineer with Motorola in Austin. They testified that the Campbells "were kind, gracious individuals" who never treated Cindy differently from any of the other children. James Campbell was "outgoing, jovial . . . always made me feel at home . . . showed a lot of attention to us. He talked to us about records. He did the 'Monster Mash' dance for us. . . . When I first started dating my husband, I brought him over for approval." Virginia Campbell "was a

435

loving mother, softspoken, kind. . . . I could confide in her, and did. She made herself available . . . she seemed like everyone's mother."

A strange impression emerged from all this wholesomeness, which Rusty in his overpowering contrary certainty never saw. By neighborhood standards the Campbell house was not a large house. It had three bedrooms, and earlier testimony had established that until the arrival of the grandchildren Jim Campbell used the downstairs bedroom as an office. Michelle and Betty shared a bedroom with Cindy ("although sometimes Cindy slept on the old gray couch in the living room," Michelle said), and Jamie for most of her childhood crawled into a bed with any one of her older sisters in their communal bedroom.

Each of the three new female witnesses now testified that during their teens, over a period of many years, they spent major time in the Campbell home. Stella Sumbera: "Four days a week, two or three weekends a month." Deborah Moeller: "Five to seven times a week." Ginger Hansel: "Constantly, three or four times a week." Factoring in the various friends of Michelle and Betty who *didn't* testify—and Jamie's friends, and Cindy's friends such as Vickie Miller and Debbie Ferguson—I had the giddying impression of 8901 Memorial as a kind of densely crowded teen-age girls' club presided over by a devoted, unflappable, remarkably permissive, sweetly smiling mother, and a flamboyant father who, when not golfing or hustling pool halls in downtown Houston or conning free trips to the craps tables in Las Vegas, or out and around Harris County evading sheriffs and playing his other role of "Dirty Jim," clowned for these squads of adoring nymphets nonstop on evenings, weekends, and holidays. Lesser men might have been driven mad, or at least might have cut back on the frequency of these adolescent and ultimately nubile parties. Not Jim Campbell. America the Beautiful . . . or something else?

Offering other interesting insights into the past, Sumbera related, "Mrs. Campbell brought home yellow legal pads and Cindy would draw, draw, draw. It was nothing for her to fill a legal tablet in a day and say she was saving the nicest drawing for her mother. . . . She was a very pretty little girl with long hair curling at the ends. After Jamie was born she began putting on weight. She wasn't the center of attention anymore. Every once in a while she said hurtful things."

After Moeller said that "No, Cindy never complained about her parents," Randy McDonald—thirty-one years old, nearly of Moeller's generation—took her on what was his briefest and best cross-examination of the trial. For Maria Bravo and Gwen Sampson he had prepared extensively over a period of months. This exchange with Moeller was entirely extempore, but later it lingered in the memory.

436

"Your kids have read about child abuse, haven't they?" Randy asked.

"Yes."

"Isn't it true that other people never know about sexual abuse within a family? And you never know who to suspect? And when you and I were kids, it wasn't talked about?"

"I guess so," she said, looking annoyed.

Randy smiled. "There's no way you'd ever say anything bad about the Campbells, is there?"

"That's right," Deborah Moeller said flatly.

After the State of Texas closed its case, Rick Brass read to the jury from other parts of the St. Joseph Hospital medical record.

"3/31/66. At that time," Rick quoted, "G.U. workup was advised, but mother refused. Mother was not available for questioning. Patient had urinary frequency for several years, which had been ascribed by the mother to nervousness. Urologic investigation was recommended at that time but refused by the mother."

The defense then breathed a prayer and closed its case.

That afternoon Judge Azios announced to the jury and to the media that his charge to the jury, to be followed by final argument, would begin the following day, July 1, at one o'clock in the afternoon. He told the jury that they would begin deliberating at about four o'clock. "You will deliberate as far as you go into tomorrow evening, and since I can't predict how long you'll be deliberating, I suggest you bring your overnight kit in case you have to spend the night here. Not *here*"—he chuckled—"I mean in a hotel."

The judge then retired to his chambers with the lawyers to wrangle over the wording of the court's charge to the jury.

Allen Isbell said, "Judge, on the issue of duress, don't forget, they have the burden." He meant that since the state had introduced evidence of duress through Gwen Sampson's testimony—*"He held a gun to my head,"* Gwen had quoted Cindy as saying—they now had the obligation to disprove that duress beyond a reasonable doubt. And, said Allen, the judge was obliged to point this out in his charge.

"Nonsense," Rusty said.

"Go look it up," Rick Brass suggested.

"Darn right I will."

Rusty vanished. He returned an hour later, pink-eyed, shaking his head with astonishment.

"You're absolutely correct," he said to Allen and Rick. "I just read a manual that says any prosecutor dumbass enough to introduce duress through a state's witness should be drawn and quartered. Must have slept through that lecture when I was in law school. . . ."

He drifted out of the meeting, still shaking his head, leaving Lyn McClellan to finish up. After they were done, on their way back to the Old Cotton Exchange Building, Rick said to Allen, "Watch out for Rusty. He's smart enough to get whiskey from a peanut. He's got something up his sleeve."

38

"All rise!"

Few of us in attendance at the Cindy Ray trial had ever heard the bailiff's cry before, for it only came when the judge appeared for the first time, and that was usually at 8 A.M. But now it was 1:30 P.M., and Judge Azios in his black robes flowed forward into a huge, unfamiliar courtroom on the fifth floor. The ceiling was lofty, the judicial bench and spectators' pews were thick oak, and the black walnut-paneled sides of the courtroom were lined with framed oil portraits of robed Texas judges from decades past. These gothic premises belonged to Judge I. D. McMaster (who had been one of the prosecutors in the Lilla Paulus "Blood and Money" trial for the murder of Dr. John Hill), but today they had been made available to Judge Azios in order to accommodate the expected crush of spectators. The ambiance was somber and dimly lit. Like justice and the law in this case, I decided.

Thermometers in downtown Houston that morning registered ninety-seven degrees in the shade, and in the sun any tar in the street was a hazardous ooze. But in the shadowy courtroom it was thrillingly cool. There was an air of high expectancy, like that of an audience about to preview a potential Academy Award-winning film, or a particularly amusing Christian thrown to a favorite lion. This was the climax of the judicial drama.

Rusty had dressed in light gray with a yellow tie. He seemed spring-like and confident. Allen wore a black suit, a gray shirt, a dark striped tie: gravity itself. Cindy today had chosen her navy blue suit; her brown

438

hair was down on her shoulders, long and curly, freshly washed. A young courtroom artist was showing the finshed crayon drawings of sketches that she had been working on for several days. She had made everyone look like attractive All-American actors in a TV soap opera.

The jury was not yet in. A few reporters took up a pool on what color they would choose today.

Moss Thornton, broadcaster for KPRC, whispered to me, "Today you'll see 'the Rusty Shimmie.'" She explained that was what the press called "Rusty's shaking from top to bottom with righteous indignation during argument." It was memorable; it could be relied on to happen. It was the prelude to victory—in this case, his one hundredth in a row.

———————

Allen began by objecting to the standard procedure of final argument in Texas courts, wherein the state can make both the opening and closing speeches, sandwiching the defense in between.

"Denied," Judge Azios said, and then ruled that each side would be allowed total argument time of two hours.

The jury was led in. They wore blue.

Judge Azios read the charge.

"Members of the jury . . . the defendant, Cynthia Campbell Ray, stands charged by indictment with the offense of murder. The defendant has pleaded not guilty. Our law provides that a person commits the offense of murder if she intentionally or knowingly causes the death of an individual." He went on to define the law of parties, explaining that "a person is criminally responsible for an offense if she solicits, encourages, directs, aids, or attempts to aid the other person to commit the offense. Mere presence alone will not constitute one a party to an offense. . . .

"The witness, David West, is an accomplice, and you cannot convict the defendant upon his testimony unless you first believe that his testimony is true and shows that the defendant is guilty as charged, and unless you further believe that there is other evidence in the case, outside of the testimony of David West, tending to connect the defendant with the offense committed. . . .

"The State has introduced evidence in this case that the defendant was, at the time of the commission of the offense, at another place. [He referred to the "alibi" statements sworn to by Cynthia Campbell Ray and David West on June 22, 1982, at Police Headquarters.] The State, having introduced such evidence, must disprove that evidence beyond a reasonable doubt or you will find the defendant not guilty.

"The State has introduced evidence in this case that the presence of the defendant at the time and place when and where the deceased was killed, if she was present, was by duress. [This referred to Gwen Sampson's testimony that Cindy told her "Salino" had forced her, on threat of death, to be present during the murders.] An accused cannot be found guilty for any offense if she engaged in the proscribed conduct because she was compelled to do so by the threat of imminent death and serious bodily injury. Such compulsion exists only if the threat of force is such as would render a person of reasonable firmness incapable of resisting the pressure. The State, having introduced evidence of duress, must disprove this duress beyond a reasonable doubt or you will acquit the defendant and return a verdict of not guilty."

Allen nodded brightly, and Rusty restrained a frown.

The judge ended by telling the jury that after they retired they were to select a foreman, and during their deliberations they were to communicate with the court only in writing which they would give to the bailiff, Keith Goode.

It had taken eleven minutes. The judge said, "Mr. Hardin, you may open for the state."

———————————

"Time to romp and stomp," Rusty had called it in a murder case several years ago, just before he drove a pickaxe through a telephone book to show how much force could be generated by such a blow. He had a reputation for original theatrics. In the capital murder trial of a man accused of indiscriminately pumping fourteen shotguns shells into a Purolator truck before robbing it, he picked up the shotgun and dashed about the courtroom, punctuating his argument with *"Ba-room! Ba-room!"* In more than one rape trial he had flipped off the lights in the courtroom at an opportune moment, and in that terrifying darkness said to the jury, "Now, put yourself in the victim's place. . . ."

Today Rusty presented himself before the jury as if he were someone they had met long ago and might only dimly remember. He seemed shy, a trifle embarrassed. He smiled and said, "Hi." The jury members smiled back at him. They liked Rusty.

"I'm a little afraid to stand up here," he said, "because I'm the one who told you this case would take about two weeks. I don't think the lawyers on either side foresaw that David West would be on the stand for six days. You've been incredibly attentive and patient. For that I thank you. Not for jury service, because I think that's a duty. But I appreciate the fact that you were willing to serve."

440

He offered a mild warning: "Perhaps some of you have noticed that I tend to get a little excited. I've tried to control it, but it doesn't work, so I've given up trying. What I want to make sure of is that it won't affect your verdict. Your verdict must be based upon the evidence. . . .

"I want to go over the charge and put it into English. I suspect all of us can agree that the Campbells were killed intentionally and knowingly. The question is: Who did it? You have to believe what David said *as to the elements of the offense*—not everything he said. You don't have to go back there and swallow six days of testimony. For example, you don't have to decide one way or the other whether David West was motivated by money or by his beliefs about sexual abuse. You don't have to decide *why* David West did it. You don't have to decide *why* Cynthia Campbell Ray did it. You may have your own ideas, you may want to bat them around, and that's fine. But what you have to decide is: Did she, acting alone or as a party, intentionally or knowingly cause the death of James Campbell?

"It would be a violation of your oath—at this stage—to discuss punishment. The horror of the crime is not an issue now, although it may very well be if we reach the punishment stage. Just: *Did she do it?*"

He kept his distance from the jury, standing back about thirty feet, sometimes approaching to twenty feet, but no closer. (At one point Lyn McClellan stood up, heaved forward and snatched a blackboard from the trekking path. Rusty grinned to the jury and said, "I'm the kind of guy who trips on the way to his car.")

He talked about sponsorship of witnesses. "There is a rule of law which says: whichever side puts a witness on the stand sponsors what that witness says. And if, for instance, the state offers evidence that would help the defendant, then the state is going to be bound by the exculpatory evidence unless the state puts on other evidence that disproves it. For instance, we put on Sgt. Paul Motard, and through him we offered Cindy Ray's alibi statement to the police made back on June 22, 1982, as to where she was when it happened. 'I wasn't there,' she said. 'David West and I were together, and I didn't have anything to do with the killing.' If we didn't bring you additional evidence to show that she *did,* there's a rule in the State of Texas that says, 'Hey, you put that stuff up there—you didn't offer anything to contradict it—so you're bound by it.'

"But David's testimony disproves her alibi. We could have walked around that, but we laid it all out on the table to let you decide. We didn't put David up there as a choirboy, or for you to go home with, or to suggest he had an unfortunate childhood and it's just a mistake that all this happened. The state would have given anything in this case to have been able to try Cynthia Campbell Ray without having to rely on the trigger man's testimony. But there was no way."

(Cecilia West's mouth fell open. She looked dumbfounded when Rusty characterized her son as a "trigger man." Apparently she'd never seen it that way.)

Rusty then became the Lone Ranger of the Law, battling against a tripartite axis. "You should say to yourselves, 'Mr. Isbell, Mr. Mc-Donald, Mr. Brass: *What about the glove?* What about what she told Gwen Sampson—*that she was there?* Wait a minute, Mr. Isbell, Mr. McDonald, Mr. Brass—what about the fact that David West testified that he used the actual words, as to why he was going to kill them, as this mythical Salino did? And didn't they both give statements to the police, after the killing, that tied themselves together? And what about the fact that in 1980, a year and a half before Cynthia Campbell Ray urges David West to kill her parents, she was telling her sister Jamie she ought to kill her father, and she knows how she'd do it, and the way she would do it is dress up like a man, wear boots, wear gloves, and go through a window? *That's the way the killing was done!* Mr. Isbell, Mr. McDonald, Mr. Brass—isn't that corroboration?'

"The most delicious irony of all is that David West swore to you with conviction that once she talked him into killing them, *he* planned it, *he* came up with the gloves, *he* came up with the coat, *he* came up with the idea of entering by the window! She was so effective in persuading him to do what she wanted that she even somehow planted the idea in his head of how to do it, and she talked him into believing that he thought of it himself."

Voice rising, he trotted out a mixed equestrian metaphor. "One final thing, for now. Ask Mr. Isbell: 'Hey, guys, come on, which horse are you going to ride?' Make them pick a saddle and stay on it! Don't let them stand up here, as they come on in a threesome, and talk to you about different theories. Pause in your mind and ask, 'Okay, guys, are you going to ride that horse that says she wasn't there and didn't have anything to do with it, or are you going to get halfway there, then bring up another lawyer, dismount, and say, "Okay, my second horse, if you don't believe that first one, is—she was there, but she was forced by Salino!" Or, third horse: "She was there, but she was forced by David West!" ' " He paused dramatically. "Make them get on one horse and ride it!"

After using thirty-five minutes of his allotted two hours, he sat down.

It was the defense's turn. The triple alliance, as Rusty had promised, decided to divide its two hours of argument into one-hour slices—first Allen, then Randy—going on Allen's belief that (1) he didn't have that much to say; and (2) two hours of nonstop talking by any one lawyer could bore even the most sympathetic of jurors.

Allen rose and said: "Ladies and gentlemen of the jury, if we were somewhere other than America, the last argument by the prosecutor would have some weight. But in our law the burden of proof in all criminal cases rests upon the state and never shifts to the defense. We don't have to prove anything. We have one obligation. It's basically the same obligation that each of you have. *We have to show up.* Now I know there are some prosecutors who would like to change that. 'Let's make the defendant prove: were they there or not there? Were they coerced or not coerced?' But that's not what Judge Azios told you our law is. And after all the evidence is in, if there is a reasonable doubt in your mind as to: 'I don't really know if she was there—or maybe I'm persuaded she was there, but I have some doubt about whether she was voluntarily there or she was coerced'—if those questions still remain after four weeks of trial, Judge Azios tells you that our system, our law, says you must return a verdict of not guilty.

"Judge Azios, in his charge, has laid out the law for you. The state tried to prove that Cynthia Ray hired David West to kill her father and mother. That seems to be a very simple path to be able to pursue, but I think you can see after four weeks of testimony that it's not really that kind of case at all. It is a case in which we have exposed, for your consideration, the background of David West, and of Cynthia Campbell Ray, and we've had a look into the home life from which each of these people came. It's a psychological drama such as I have never seen in all my years of practice."

He moved on to the theme of the accomplice-witness. The accomplice-witness, he insisted, was always a corrupt source, to be viewed as discredited. "And we have something even more in this case," he said. "We have *bought testimony.* 'I'll give you back your life,' Mr. Hardin said to David West. What would a man give for his life? David saw that they'd stick a needle in his arm!"

He referred again to the judge's charge, which explained that the state had the obligation to disprove Gwen Sampson's recounting of what Cindy had said regarding duress. "The only evidence that would disprove it came from the mouth of the corrupt source, David West. That's *evidence?* I call your attention to the tapes of the conversations between Kim Paris and David West. Even at that time he said, 'I *made* her go in, and *forced* her to stand there!' "

He brought up the contradictory versions of incest and sexual abuse that Cindy had told to different witnesses. But how else, he asked, would a young and confused girl be able to deal with such a horrible event in her life? He talked about David West's view of Cindy Ray: "Just a worm . . . no spine, no balls." Was this female worm someone who could manipulate him into committing murder? He mounted the second horse predicted by Rusty Hardin: Did that worm *willingly* stand there in the bedroom at Memorial, *knowing* that David West was going to kill her parents?

Allen jumped back on the first horse and set forth the theory he had begun to touch on during his cross-examination of David West. "After he had said to Kim the first night, 'I killed her parents,' then he *has* to say, 'She begged me to do it,' because otherwise, how are you going to keep your new girlfriend around after you've said, 'Oh, by the way, I just killed my *last* girlfriend's mother and father'? How many women are going to stick around and say, 'Well, that's wonderful, I'm glad I ran into *you!* You're just the type of person dear old Dad told me he wanted to meet!'

"In other words, he had a strong motive for lying. He couldn't get in bed with Kim Paris without mitigating the admission of the awful act, and he did it by saying *'She begged me to do it.'* And then, of course, to be consistent, he had to repeat that lie here in court."

He talked about Cindy's personality and her lack of ill feeling toward her father which made it "unreasonable to believe that she would approve of his murder." He quoted the hospital reports that said at age fifteen "she was seriously concerned about how she had hurt her parents." He quoted David West: "The strange thing is that Cynthia didn't harbor resentment against her father." He talked about Gwen Sampson's noting that above all Cindy Ray wanted parental approval.

Allen said, "Think about how she was described in late May of 1982. Think about the incident in which a car has bumped them and Cynthia goes to pieces and begins to cry, *'Mommy, Mommy, Mommy!'* while David West is out there attacking the car with his bare feet doing a thousand dollars' worth of damage. If you were going to kill somebody —creep in the dark of night up to a room where a man had only two months earlier chased somebody out with a shotgun—would you take a person with you like Cynthia Campbell Ray? You might take Wickie Weinstein. You might go alone. But you wouldn't take someone who was liable to go crazy on you at any time."

He said, "Let me talk briefly to you about a series of witnesses. . . .

"We have Wickie Weinstein, the man who David West went to and talked about killing people, and who said, 'Well, if you're going to do it for hire, you shouldn't care whether they're good people or bad people.'

Wickie Weinstein, who sold or loaned him the gun. Wickie Weinstein, scheduled to come to court, splits for Miami. Why? There's a saying that 'the wicked flee where no man pursueth.'

"Paul Whitfield, who claims that everyone's been trying to get him to implicate Wickie Weinstein. We *saw* Wickie, and I don't blame Paul Whitfield for being scared to death."

But then, Allen pointed out, two witnesses testified that on several occasions, without benefit of coercion or any falsely claimed six drinks, Paul *had* implicated Wickie, stating that Wickie had admitted to throwing the gun away in Buffalo Bayou in company with David West.

"The prosecutor got very upset. *'The nerve of these people! Letting the defense know that there was a guy out there saying he was there with David West, disposing of the gun!'* Now, what's wrong with that? Here is Paul Whitfield being brought to the state, in person, to say Wickie Weinstein admits he was involved in getting rid of the gun with David West in Buffalo Bayou. Why don't they like that?

"Because it casts reasonable doubt on David West's story!

"It is unreasonable to believe that a woman was with David West. Remember Ed Watson passed by at 4 A.M. and says, 'There was a tall, six-foot man walking behind the car either toward the trunk or the driver's side, and I thought it strange that someone would be waiting there at that time of the morning, and I called the police and told them.' That wasn't Cynthia Campbell Ray or David West that he described!

"I don't care how good an actress she is. If she is as David West has described her just before the murders, it is impossible for her to have made the appropriate responses that were necessary."

Six weeks after the murders, Allen reminded the jury, David and Cindy broke up. A month or so later, according to Rory Lettvin, Cindy was totally disassociated from reality: the cats are leaving feces all over the floor of her living room. "Her house stinks of an emotionally disturbed person. She has gone into total mental and emotional collapse. And Gwen Sampson says that is also true in October of 1982. What has happened? I submit that she suspects, and learns, that David West, by his own means, of his own design, has murdered her parents. And he says to her, 'If you talk, I'll kill you.'"

Allen paused before the jury. "If David West looked you in the eye and said, 'I'll kill you,' you'd back off. You'd believe him."

He closed by quoting David West from the February 20, 1985 taped conversation with Kim Paris.

"I'll make it appear to be Cindy's responsibility. No one will believe I just did it on my own. I'll tell them, 'She's the one that offered me a contract to do it.'"

He sat down. In a theater, I would have applauded.

Randy McDonald stood up in his place and approached the jury. His chief purpose was to demonstrate that all of the state's witnesses had been coached and tampered with not only by the police but by the D.A.'s Office. Let the jury draw its own conclusions.

He called the case "the most complex *I've* ever been involved in" as either prosecutor or defense attorney, and predicted to the jury that "you will never in your life see such a conglomeration of different kinds of people." Rusty Hardin was the best prosecutor the state had, and yet "I suggest to you that *he's* the one who has to ride the horses. 'I had to put on a psychopathic killer. God, I hated it! But without him, the case is insufficient.' "

He was certainly not impinging on the integrity of Mr. Hardin, he said, who had never lost a felony case in the State of Texas. But you couldn't do what Mr. Hardin was trying to do. There was no proof.

On Maria, the maid: "When I was cross-examining her, she wouldn't even *look* at me!" And he pointed out the variance of her sworn testimony in 1982 with what she was now able to remember about Cindy supposedly testing the downstairs windows at 8901 Memorial. Maria had been brainwashed.

On Jamie: "How amazingly similar her quotes of Cindy were—*'I'd dress up like a man, and I'd wear big men's shoes or heavy boots and I'd leave footprints around a window'*—to what David West told Kim Paris and the District Attorney's Office three years later." That wasn't the result of Cindy's advance planning; it was a product of Jamie's desire to help destroy her sister.

On Kim Paris: "Remember, she was sent out not to implicate David West, *but to get Cindy Ray.*"

On Gwen Sampson: "She admits trying to get Cindy drunk, doesn't she?"

To defuse the effect of this witness-by-witness demolition, Rusty interrupted with the complaint that he couldn't hear. And indeed, Randy had been leaning on the wooden railing of the jury box, his back to the judge and the spectators. He stepped back two paces and raised his voice.

"As for Cynthia Campbell Ray, I know what Mr. Hardin is going to say, and I know you do, too. 'Cindy couldn't tell the truth if it came up and stared her in the face. She's told all these different tales about incest and sexual abuse. Not one of them the same!' But they *are* consistent!" Randy cried. "The consistency lies in the theme, not the specific details. They *all* deal with the abuse of a helpless, frightened teen-aged girl!"

He finished: "Remember, nobody but David West tells you that Cynthia Campbell Ray was there. You can't present this case like a ping pong ball between two witnesses: 'You corroborate me on this, I'll corroborate you on that.' Make Mr. Hardin show you how an accomplice-witness can corroborate the corroborator! It's the kind of case, ladies and gentlemen, where you have to connect up the evidence. And if it does not connect. . . you can't find her guilty."

Randy sat down.

Good, I thought. Impressive logic. It suddenly seemed that Rusty's case was not as powerful as I'd thought it to be. Against any other prosecutor, the careful defense arguments would win. But it wasn't "any other prosecutor." It was a man who had never lost and wanted to win this case more than any he'd ever tried.

It was his final chance to romp and stomp. He'd been quiet the first time, I realized—no "Rusty Shimmie." He was an orator, a battler. He represented the people and the victims. I leaned forward slightly in my seat. Give us a good show, Rusty. We've waited nearly half a year for it, counting the David West pretrial. We deserve it. Only you can do it.

He came out smoking, like a preacher at a Sunday camp meeting. "Cynthia Campbell Ray," he cried, "has had a true, full, fair trial! Cynthia Campbell Ray has had three excellent lawyers fighting for her, and a judge who made sure her rights weren't violated! James and Virginia Campbell had none of that, and to this day they and their memory have been blasphemed!" He stood near Cindy and pointed a finger. "This lady told numerous people that her father had fathered her oldest son! *I'm sick and tired,*" Rusty yelled, "*of the way that family has been blasted!*"

Rusty used no notes. He never prepared his closing arguments. He relied on his memory, his rhetorical skills, his visceral sense of right and wrong. Back along Memory Lane he took the jury, the judge, and the spectators, to 8901 Memorial, to the childhood of Cindy Ray and the ceaseless grief this difficult girl had caused her hard-working, concerned parents. That section of his argument ended with: " . . . and finally at the age of fifteen she decided to run away. She's so persuasive that she convinces a girl who, by her own testimony was, just, 'Leave It to Beaver'! I mean, the Brady Bunch lived at her house! And yet the Brady Bunch daughter was convinced by Cynthia Campbell Ray to run away when she was happy! She loved her mother! She loved her life! But Cindy convinced her to leave! And they get on a bus, and they go. This helpless, unable-to-cope, timid, shy young girl, Cindy Ray, was able to convince a friend, Vickie 'Brady,' who was so happy, to run away with her. And out there on the road she and Vickie 'Brady' moved into a rooming house. Remember the mother? 'My daughter's a good girl!' And then Cindy has, according to the medical records, a sexual experience."

Something was wrong. Rusty's anger dominated his performance, but I had the feeling that anger wasn't what was called for. No one was quite sure what Rusty was trying to prove, but he had a captive audience and no one was able to nudge him and say, "Rusty, get to the point."

But he must have smelled it, or else Lyn McClellan flashed a warning glance.

Rusty stopped in midflow, and said, "Rusty Hardin, why are you spending so much time on Cynthia and how she treated her parents?" He answered himself: "Because if I don't, no one else will. The defense has tried to blacken their names—"

Allen swiftly objected. "Sustained," Judge Azios said.

"One of the most striking things about this case," Rusty went on, trying to calm himself and focus on the logic of the evidence, "is how little it takes for some people to reach conclusions." He cited Cindy's various tales to different witnesses: the beatings at the hands of her mother, her mother's lesbianism, her mother's death and the advent of the wicked stepmother, the cruel sisters, the father in a mental home, the sexual abuse.

David West fell for all of them, Rusty said, shaking his head in grief.

"And by May of 1982 Cynthia Campbell Ray had reached a conclusion. She couldn't survive, couldn't make it unless she found some financial means to do it. And David West wasn't going to be able to do anything for her with what *he* was making. I would suggest that because of all the baggage she had carried with her all her life—this continued and increasing belief that she was a mistreated child, that her sisters were preferred, that people didn't like her because she was overweight, that she was incapable of enduring relationships with others, that it was impossible for her to take care of herself on her own—that in that respect David West was right, because David West, and no one else she had found, was her solution. If Salino did exist, he might be the answer, but he did not exist, and no one like him did. At some time in May 1982, or perhaps earlier, Cindy decided that she was not capable of coping for herself. She had developed from that six-year-old attractive child to a child who increasingly had demons created by others, and imagined mistreatment by others, and no matter how much her parents cajoled her and tried to do for her, sent her to school, sent her to the Art Institute, tried to amuse her, tried to help her, tried to get her to live at home—they could not get through the wall Cindy had built around herself. I think she decided they were no longer going to take care of her. You remember what Maria said, that a few days before the murders Mrs. Campbell said she had many problems with Cindy and that Cindy wanted to move back. But Mr. Campbell and Maria both said that if Cindy moved back they would move out. And Mrs. Campbell said, 'Don't go, Maria, because you and my husband mean more to me than Cindy, because Cindy is trouble.'

"There is no evidence, but you might well draw the inference that they had told Cindy they were going to stop giving her money. No more clothes, shopping, school. By May of 1982 Cynthia Campbell Ray decided she needed to kill her parents. She killed the people who gave her life. I can't think of a worse crime.

"And so she went to David West, who had once said, according to his testimony, 'God! If someone had done all that to me, I'd want to kill them. . . . I'd have to strike back.'

"And together they did." There was "corroboration right down the line." She had told Gwen Sampson that she was there at the scene of the murder—that Salino "did it for her, to make her free, to make her well" —that she left a glove—that they dressed up like men.

"We didn't know that," Rusty pointed out, "until David West told us. Did you stop to think about that? Until December of 1985, until after David West pled guilty, no one had any idea the killers dressed up like men. That's very significant. That's why they couldn't be charged after Gwen Sampson's statement to the police, because there was no corroboration for what Gwen said."

Then, again: "You don't have to decide *why* she did it, only that she *did* it. I suggest to you that the evidence is overwhelming. At the time of their deaths the Campbells had no way to know they were being killed by one of their own."

He stood by Cindy now. She was immobile, impassive, staring at the wall. Rusty's look mingled anger and scorn with pity and an immeasurable sadness. "You can't bring them back," he told the jury, although his gaze never wavered from Cindy's averted face, "but you *can* say, 'Shame on you.' "

He sat down.

———————

Amazingly, the trial was over. No more witnesses, no more speeches. I felt hollowed, cheated. Rusty's argument wasn't at all what I had hoped for. He had picked on Cindy Ray, who could no longer answer back, but in my view he had failed to disprove or even contradict what the

449

defense team had pointed out regarding the tainted circle of corroboration or the bias of the witnesses. Prosecutors, even the best of them, can have their bad days, can miss the point.

He'd had nothing up his sleeve at all. I should have known that. He had only his sense of certainty. And it appeared to have let him down.

———————

There was nothing left except the waiting for the jury to deliberate and bring in a verdict. I went up to Lyn McClellan and raised an eyebrow. He shook his head. "What do you think?" I asked.

"Between us?"

"For now, yes."

"It was the worst final argument I've ever heard Rusty deliver."

I believed him, but I was still shocked.

"Can you lose?"

Lyn laughed quietly. "This is Harris County. You kill, you pay. They'll be back in under two hours with a guilty verdict."

He saw the look of doubt on my face. "Want to bet on it, Clifford?"

"No," I said.

———————

39

The jury retired to the jury room. They were given a choice: they could deliberate now—it was 6 P.M.—or they could be taken to dinner and return to deliberate. Deliberate now, they replied.

They delayed twenty minutes, sitting in silence. They were waiting for the alternate juror. He had been dismissed, sent home by the court, but the other twelve didn't know it. He was part of the group; how could they start without him? Combing their hair, studying their fingernails, they waited. Finally, when they dared to ask where he was, Judge Azios explained that he was gone from their lives. They must begin deliberation. *Now*. Did they understand?

Yes. They elected a foreman—Reverend Randy Uselton, as everyone had foreseen.

The thirty-four-year-old pastor of the Houston Covenant Church said after the trial, "The last ten years of my life have been spent leading people, and keeping an atmosphere where people can reason together."

He was determined to do the same in the jury room, and he opened the proceedings by asking everyone to make their comments and state their opinions in turn, with no interruptions.

They were all on a first-name basis by now. "You speak first, Randy," Julia Carr said. She liked the minister.

Outside, about twenty-five people were scattered throughout the courtroom. Others had wanted to stay but had to go home: meals were thawing in microwaves throughout Harris County. The lawyers, of course, stayed, and Allen Isbell's parents, and Rick Brass's wife; and Makhlouf, allowed in for the first time now that it was over and there could be no more testimony, alone at the rear with his black bag, one of the bailiffs watching him all the time; and Betty Ann Hinds with her husband, and Michelle Campbell, with Ginger Hansel, her childhood friend who had testified, and Denise Moseley and her new husband; and Kim Paris, in from St. Louis, looking alternately forlorn and upset and confused, no longer the center of media attention *("I'll be the star witness, won't I?")*, heavier than she'd ever been now that she was the mother of a two-month-old baby; and the media crew, haggard and smoked out and fed up, most of them hanging out in the hallway, close to the telephones; and Brenda, the court reporter, having a *long* Brenda-break now, sitting in the last pew, laughing with a friend. None of these people intended to go home until the jury filed out of the locked jury room with its verdict.

The charged hum of conversation gave the courtroom the feel of an airline terminal. Those who remained had all bought their tickets with one form of currency or another. They were willing to wait the predicted two hours for takeoff.

Keith Goode came out. He whispered in Rick Brass's ear that after he'd led Cindy backstage, following Rusty's closing "Shame on you" speech, she was so upset that her period arrived. Sitting on the wooden bench outside the holding cell, she pounded a full ashtray, knocking it to the floor.

Rick went in to calm her.

The jury had been instructed to push the buzzer once if they had a verdict, twice if they wanted to ask a question, three times if they needed anything else. At 7:15, after they had been deliberating for forty minutes, a buzzer sounded—one short ring.

The reporters hurried back in. The quickest verdict ever remembered in a Harris County capital murder trial!

Keith, dispatched to the backstage regions of Judge McMaster's court where deliberation took place, returned with a written note. Sorry, folks: false alarm. The jury had forgotten the buzzer code. They wanted to see some of the exhibits placed in evidence: the alibi statements, the photographs of the house, Maria's sworn statement to Sgt. Mosqueda.

What was *that* all about? Quickly everyone expounded a theory. But no two were the same.

At 8:05 the jury sent a second note, asking to see the transcripts of the David West–Kim Paris tapes. At 8:25 they sent a third note saying they would like to listen to the tapes themselves, or see the video again.

"I don't know about that," Judge Azios said, and he looked suddenly exhausted. He crooked a finger at Keith. "Ask them if they'd like to retire for the night. Tell them they can start fresh at eight o'clock tomorrow morning."

Keith trotted back and forth.

"Yes, Your Honor, they would like that."

So at nearly nine o'clock in the hot July evening, the jurors, under stern orders not to discuss the case until they were once more back in the jury room tomorrow morning, were driven off by Keith to the Holiday Inn at Main Street and the Southwest Freeway. And everyone else went home, or out to dinner, or to a bar.

Word of the delay spread rapidly. Lyn McClellan shrugged—win some, lose some. The outcome was still not in doubt as far as he was concerned. In his cell at the jail, David, who had received word that the trial was over, now heard of the delay and began to bite the skin on the sides of his thumbs. Cindy's face was without expression, as if she didn't care or else was supremely confident and had known all along that it wouldn't go as Rusty Hardin, her nemesis, had predicted.

"This case has ruined my law practice," Randy McDonald said. "I've been away from the office for a whole month. My other clients think I've quit on them."

But he was in the courtroom at 8:30 on Wednesday morning, July 2, when the jury began deliberating again in the old familiar jury room of Judge Azios's eighth-floor courtroom. Judge McMaster wasn't giving up his luxury domain a second day to have people just hang around, which is exactly what everyone had to do now—the prosecutors, defense attorneys, reporters, and those courtroom groupies who had attended the trial and were determined to stick it out until the verdict. Witnesses

were there, too; they were no longer barred. A full cast, minus Davi
West, who waited in the Harris County Jail.

Cindy arrived, handcuffed, then at her own request was led off by
bailiff to the holding cell, so that she could smoke. Rick gave her a fresh
pack of Benson & Hedges.

Rusty and Allen showed up wearing the same pale blue seersucker
suits. Allen's face looked gray, and his eyes were pink as a rabbit's.

Not many realized that every day, before testimony began in *Texas* v.
Cynthia Campbell Ray, the judge had been at work for more than two
hours on his regular docket of cases. But he had fallen behind. Now that
the Ray jury was out deliberating, the judge could catch up.

A young, frightened Nigerian came before him, accused of aggravated
sexual assault on a fourteen year old, but there were extenuating circumstances, and his rotund, cigar-smoking, court-appointed lawyer had cut
a deal for six years' probation. The Nigerian's English was limited. Judge
Azios rapidly went through a list of standard and necessary questions.
He reached: "Are you suffering under the delusive hope that by pleading
'no contest' the governor of this state will grant you a pardon?"

"Yes," the Nigerian said.

The judge scowled. The fat lawyer gave his thin client a poke in the
ribs. The judge asked the question a second time. Again the shaking
Nigerian said, "Yes."

"Get him out of here," Judge Azios said acidly to the lawyer, "and
make sure he understands what's going on in this courtroom."

Backstage I heard the exasperated lawyer explain, as best he could, the
correct answer to the judge's question, and the reason for it. "Listen!
You've got to get it straight. This man can grant you freedom, or he can
put you in prison for fifteen years. He's like God."

The Nigerian came again before the judge, who peered down and
asked, slowly, "Are you suffering under the delusive hope that by
pleading 'no contest' the governor of this state will grant you a
pardon?"

"No, my Lord," the Nigerian whispered.

At 11:40 that morning the Ray jury was ready with a verdict.

No, wait . . . they *weren't* ready. They just wanted to hear some testimony.

They filed back into the jury box. Brenda Palmer took the stand, was
sworn, and in a voice meant to be flat and unemotional, and yet oddly
moving, read from her own electronic shorthand portions of Gwen

Sampson's direct testimony about what Cindy Ray had admitted in Felix's Mexican restaurant.

Most of the reporters reckoned the jury was nailing down a guilty verdict with Gwen's corroborating testimony. Randy McDonald said to me, "When a jury asks for direct, the defense is in trouble. When they ask for cross, there's hope."

The jury went to lunch. They certainly wouldn't want to deliberate much longer. The Fourth of July weekend began the following morning. Could that be a factor? Could it determine a woman's fate?

———————

One of the jurors, twenty-nine-year-old Lydia Tamez, took detailed notes on what everyone said in the jury room.

By early afternoon of July 2, the second day of deliberation, the jury was unanimously agreed that Cindy Ray had been present at the murder of her parents. As for David West—they *liked* him. Tears had almost sprung to a few eyes when, during the playing of the tapes, he had said to Kim Paris, "You've got my life in your hands now." He was hot-tempered, yes, but not evil. When they heard about him poking the woman in the eye, the general reaction in their minds was, "Bad boy, don't do that again." He had killed the Campbells out of misguided chivalry, for love and pity, not for money.

Rusty had sold them. Although they didn't entirely swallow every clause of David's sworn testimony in the courtroom, they were strongly disposed to believe what he had said to Kim Paris on the tapes, for at that point, they reasoned, he wasn't fighting for his life. And they believed Gwen Sampson when she reported that Cindy had said, "I was there, you know."

And there was the matter of the glove. No one understood why she had left it, and they *wanted* to know. She hadn't testified. Nevertheless, the glove clinched it.

There was, however, one other issue to debate. The judge's charge, which they had in front of them on the table in the jury room, told them that Cindy could not be found guilty *"if she engaged in the proscribed conduct because she was compelled to do so by the threat of imminent death and serious bodily injury. Such compulsion exists only if the threat of force is such as would render a person of reasonable firmness incapable of resisting the pressure. The State, having introduced evidence of duress, must disprove this duress beyond a reasonable doubt or you will acquit the defendant and return a verdict of not guilty."*

Allen Isbell, in his closing argument, had reminded them of the import of that charge, and that they were obliged to pay close attention to it. They understood.

In the smoke-filled little room, the jury quickly focused on such duress as the only possible defense. Wickie Weinstein may well have helped David throw the gun away and been involved far more than the prosecution was willing to admit—they toyed with that idea. But did that exonerate Cindy? No. They believed that she had been there.

Had she been willing, or had she been compelled?

Each of the jurors spoke in turn.

Randy Uselton quoted David West saying to Kim Paris: "I made her go." But the word *made*, he pointed out, doesn't relate to a threat of death. And although Cindy had said to Gwen Sampson, "He put a gun to my head," she had also said, "We planned it, we executed it." If she had helped plan and execute the murders, where was the duress?

"I didn't hear her say 'we planned it, we executed it,'" Sheryl Henderson said, puzzled.

"I didn't either, when she testified," Reverend Uselton said, "and that's what's so amazing. But I heard it now when the court reporter read her testimony back to us."

"That's right," said Melanie Wheat and Mark Vandervoort, remembering. They were the two young jurors who had been seeing each other during the evenings and, according to Keith Goode, visiting each other's rooms at the motel.

"She said, *'We planned it, we executed it'*?" Lydia Tamez knuckled her brow. "Cindy said that to Gwen? I don't remember her saying that. But . . . well, okay."*

Julia Carr, in perfect accord with the minister on this issue, said, "Cindy's past showed she was able to resist people."

Mark Vandervoort argued that there was absolutely no evidence of duress during the planning stage of the murders, "So we can't even consider it."

Carlette Thomas said, "I think if she had wanted to stop the murder from happening, she could have done it at any time."

Mary Kloss reminded the other jurors that David had said to Kim, of Cindy, "She begged me to do it," and that Cindy had told Jamie that David was a dog who would do whatever she wanted.

Gwendolyn Beagle thought Jamie was "a flake," and they shouldn't

---

* Lydia Tamez and Sheryl Henderson were correct in their doubts, Reverend Uselton's memory played him false. Gwen Sampson had not quoted Cindy as saying, *"We planned it, we executed it."* Gwen had said, *"She told me how it was planned and executed"*—a statement of significantly different meaning.

consider her testimony. But regarding duress, she agreed with Carlette: there was plenty of time before it actually happened for Cindy to have slid out of it.

Melanie Wheat brought up David's admission that *he* had first said, "You should kill them," but that two years later Cindy reminded him of it. To Wheat that seemed to smack of truth.

Marcie Ivey said, "I believe David when he says she talked him into it. David was risking his life if he didn't tell the truth—they can try him again for the murder of the mother. Can he fool Rusty Hardin? I don't think *anyone* could fool Rusty Hardin!"

They all laughed at that.

Jane McBunch said, "I think the *defense* proved Cindy's desire to kill her parents, because of the sexual abuse. That was her motive—revenge. All the witnesses say that Cindy was a liar, an actor, a manipulator. I think she was unhappy enough to kill her parents."

Sheryl Henderson, the private investigator, frowned and said, "But David definitely hated them. They'd ruined what he had accomplished. Cindy had no immediate financial reason to do it—her parents were already helping her. And if she was such an unstable person as she seems to be, how could she have made any contribution to the planning of such a thing?"

Otto Bell just said, "I don't see that there was duress. Too much testimony against it."

Lydia Tamez had no firm opinion yet. But she was thinking.

It was three o'clock. "Let me get this straight now," Reverend Uselton said. "Does anyone here think she's *not* guilty?" He looked directly at Sheryl Henderson.

Sheryl Henderson said, "Hey, I didn't say that. But so far I've got strong reasonable doubt."

The others seemed a little shocked.

"Anyone else?" Uselton said.

Lydia Tamez slowly raised her hand.

———————

The reporters were outside in the hallway, badgering the lawyers for statements. But the lawyers knew nothing. They were all restive, wondering, fidgeting.

At four o'clock the jury buzzed once.

Once. A verdict! The reporters hurried to their seats. The lawyers flew to the counsel table. The TV cameramen jostled for position at the door to the courtroom.

But again the jury had forgotten about the buzzing code. They wanted a coffee break, Rusty announced, smiling apologetically. What was taking them so long? This should have been over by now. Rusty walked out and across the hall to an empty courtroom, where he sat down in the jury box and made a steeple of his fingers as if he was praying.

Allen Isbell broke his silence.

"If the jury hasn't reached a decision by this evening," he said to me in the corridor by the elevators, "A. D. will send in what's called 'a dynamite charge.' In effect, 'We've wasted all this money on you people: are you going to force us to have another trial? Make up your mind *now.*' But then if they say, 'We can't,' he'll declare a mistrial. It's essentially up to him when and how to do it. There are no rules. So, yes, the Fourth of July weekend becomes a big factor. I think the longer they're out the more encouraged we are that at least some of them don't believe that the state's proven its case beyond a reasonable doubt. After a jury argument like Rusty gave, it would be very easy for a jury to be stampeded into a verdict."

"Are you hopeful?"

"Always hopeful. We just never know. Anything can happen, and it can happen at any time."

At 4:30, after the coffee break, the foreman of the jury sent out a message: Were their cars safe? And they wanted cigarettes.

Rusty spoke to the judge for several minutes, then left. "He's angry," Allen said. "The delay is an affront to him." Then Allen left too; he had a headache.

At six o'clock there were still twenty-two people waiting in the courtroom. All of the Campbell family had gone except Michelle, who sat with a fixed smile, moving her eyes but not her head to look at people. Kim Paris, chewing gum, sat talking to a Channel 11 reporter, claiming that she had been misquoted on last night's news.

Rick Brass said, "Usually around this time you get 'what-if' notes. 'What if we're hung up? What about change of clothes.' This is unusual. No communication. No more requests for evidence or law. Lyn went by the jury room—he says they're quiet back there."

At 6:45, having deliberated all day, the jury sent out a final note: they wanted to eat dinner and retire for the evening. They would resume at 8 A.M.

"I'm worried," Rusty admitted to me. "They're at loggerheads. If it's a mistrial, we'll try her again as soon as the courts allow. If it's a not guilty verdict, we'll try her for the murder of her mother." He smiled wanly. "As soon as my wrists stop bleeding."

At night in the privacy of her room at the Holiday Inn, on a long yellow legal pad, Lydia Tamez laid out the arguments for and against duress. The strongest point against the validity of the duress defense was Maria's testimony that a week prior to the murders Cindy had tested the downstairs windows, presumably for ease of entry. If Cindy had tested those windows as part of David's plan, she was involved at an early stage—and how then could there have been duress? Maria's credibility thus became pivotal. No one believed she was deliberately lying. But could she be mistaken? How was the jury to know? *

Lydia Tamez wrote: "If [Cindy] was willing in the planning stages, why would David not know exactly the outline of the house as far as windows, the layout of the floor plan, and which bedroom [the Campbells] were in?" For David had testified that in mounting the stairs, .45 clutched in his hand, *he had been surprised when Cindy turned left instead of right.* He was a trained marine; he would surely have known in advance where his target was located. "If I had been David and not been in the house for two years—and he had been upstairs only once—I would have made sure that Cindy would have drawn me a picture with the exact position of everything pertinent."

Lydia Tamez also asked herself, if David knew that Cindy had been seen by the maid, and *could* be seen by the maid at the den window, why hadn't he chosen a different window of entry? Was that significant?

Lydia wrote: "Evidence for Duress: David's personality was violent enough to force her (he was obviously violent: he killed two people). He was capable."

I don't believe he forced her, she decided. But I want to think about it some more.

Keith Goode, the bailiff, who had announced his intention to quit his job and go to law school, brought the jury in at 8:10 on Thursday morning, the third day of deliberation. He said to me, "They'll be at it all weekend. Take my word for it."

---

* All the jurors had completely missed the point—so carefully demonstrated by Randy McDonald, but unfortunately omitted in final argument—that Maria from her vantage point on the outside staircase could not have seen those windows, particularly before the police had trimmed the junglelike foliage.

"How do you know?"

Before he could answer Lyn McClellan warned him to keep quiet. Backing off, smiling, Keith murmured, "Bailiff's intuition."

But now there was talk in the courtroom that eleven jurors were in favor of guilty and one was holding out. The minister? No—Sheryl Henderson, the private investigator, the one who had thought she'd be disqualified in voir dire and whom both sides had assumed the other side would strike. I remembered that yesterday, when the jury had left for their coffee break, Henderson had led the way, physically separated from the rest. Her face was flushed and spotted with red dots.

Andy Williams, court reporter for the Houston *Post,* had heard some of the jury argument as he passed the jury room with Lyn McClellan. It was definitely Sheryl Henderson, they said. And Keith Goode was not so consistently tight-lipped. He revealed that last night during dinner at the Holiday Inn, Reverend Uselton had said to Julia Carr, "Well, she's got to be heard. You can't just run over her."

Allen Isbell shook his head gloomily. "I was hoping it was eight to four, or at least ten to two. Eleven to one is bad. The eleven will say to the one, 'Cry calf-rope!'" (Among Texas kids "calf-rope!" meant "I give up.")

But no one could take for granted that Lyn McClellan and Andy Williams had heard correctly.

Out by the elevator Allen nodded hello to an older lawyer passing by; he was stooped and gray-faced. Too many years of this, Allen realized, does that to you.

By nine o'clock it grew violently hot in the courtroom. The air conditioning had broken down again. "That will make them reach a verdict," one of the TV cameramen said. He bet five dollars with a reporter that they'd be out by noon.

There were five nonsmokers on the jury. Their eyes teared, and two of them coughed steadily. The air in the little room was blue-gray.

That day the debate had waxed warmly, but Reverend Uselton still kept order. No vote was taken. They weren't ready for a vote, the reverend believed. They were clearly in favor of guilty, but three or four on occasion still used the phrase "reasonable doubt." They began talking about "crossing the line." The line was that of uncertainty.

Duress was still the major issue. "Why didn't she do something?" Uselton asked. "Would she be under *that* much duress as to sacrifice her parents? And why didn't she say anything to the police afterwards?"

"You're assuming a stable and rational person," Sheryl Henderson said.

Lydia Tamez was impressed by that concept, and what it might imply, but the line of reasoning was too complex to deal with now. She had to listen to the others.

Jane McBunch said, "I think David would have kept much closer tabs on her if he had threatened her."

"David hadn't seen the Campbells in over a year," Julia Carr said. "Then Cindy shows up on his doorstep that May or early June. After that long a gap, how could he have been so mad at them that he would talk Cindy into killing them and then force her to help him?"

That was powerful logic, Lydia Tamez thought. It meant that Cindy was guilty.

"Why," Sheryl Henderson asked, "would Cindy voluntarily bring up the subject, and tell Gwen Sampson all that she told her, if there was no duress? If we believe her when she says to Gwen, 'I was there, you know,' why don't we believe her when she says, 'He held a gun to my head and he would have killed me, too'?"

And that was a good thought, too, Lydia decided, vacillating.

Julia Carr said keenly to Sheryl, "Have you crossed the line to not guilty? Because then let's just hang it up and go out there and tell them."

"No," Sheryl insisted, "I want to hear more."

Lydia Tamez realized that several of the jurors had been biased toward guilt before anything started—not just before deliberation started, but probably before the trial started. And certainly before it was finished. They tried with all their heart to be fair, but the presumption of guilt was too overwhelming. Rusty Hardin was brilliant and knew the law. He exuded such conviction—those jurors felt, Cindy *must* be guilty. Why else was she here? And even her sisters believe it! They must know things we don't know.

They began bullying Sheryl. Sheryl was the stumbling block. Sheryl was being unreasonable. The goal was, change Sheryl's mind. Amid a hazed mist of cigarette smoke the jurors bent their energies toward that goal.

At 10:50 Reverend Uselton sent a note on behalf of the jury: "Could we have a further legal description/definition/explanation of coercion and duress as to time frames, what occurrence and whether or not it had to exist throughout?"

460

A bit testily, the judge replied in writing: "Members of the Jury, you have received the law applicable to this case. Please refer to the charge and be guided thereby."

At 11:15 juror Marcie Ivey sent a note out asking for anti-allergy pills and medication against the effect of cigarette smoke. At 12:05 Jane McBunch sent a note out asking for five pair of underwear, fifty dollars cash, a swimsuit, and her Wrangler jeans with the 32-inch waist, a book to read, a carton of cigarettes, and a twelve-pack of Miller Lite.

I was leaning against the bench with another reporter. The judge read the note and groaned theatrically. *Five* pair of underwear? How long were they planning to deliberate? He suddenly remembered something: "My old army division is meeting in Amsterdam, Holland, tomorrow at 4 P.M. I've got to be there."

The other reporter took out his note pad.

"Don't write that down," the judge said, alarmed. "Can't you tell when I'm joking?" He turned to Brenda and said, sotto voce, "Book me on the first flight out."

At 12:15 the jury broke for lunch. Their expressions on the way out were grim. Rusty's heart sagged toward his navel. On the way back in at two o'clock they were cheery. Rusty grew hopeful. He paced the courtroom in his shirtsleeves.

Kim Paris came up to me in a corridor outside the courtroom. "I wish a hole would open up and you and Jack Olsen would fall into it. I know the two of you are in collusion! I'm not a bad person!" she yelled. "I've got a baby, a life, parents, and I don't want them reading all these false charges!" *

Finally, in the corridor, she yelled, *"And whatever you do, don't say I'm fat!"*

At 3:25 the jury sent a long note: they wanted to hear portions of testimony from Maria Gonzalez (direct and cross on the subject of her confrontation with David West), from David West (direct and cross on how Cindy convinced him to kill her parents), from Jamie Campbell (direct on Cindy's expressed opinions of David when she first met him), and from Gwen Sampson (cross on Cindy's confession to her in Felix's restaurant).

---

* For the record: On April 26, 1986, Kim Paris had written to me, and referred to "a tape-recorded interview of a disgruntled former roommate of mine" containing "numerous allegations about me which include the following: 1. That I am a lesbian. 2. That I am a cocaine addict. 3. That I am a thief. 4. That I am (or was) a prostitute. 5. That I was dishonorably discharged from the Navy." Kim went on to say that "EACH AND EVERY ONE OF THE ITEMS NOTED ABOVE IS FALSE, OUTRAGEOUS, INSULTING, HUMILIATING, DEFAMATORY, SLANDEROUS AND LIBELOUS IN THE EXTREME."

The judge read this and put his head in his hands. *What* was going on? How long, oh Lord?

At 5 P.M. two couples were found wandering through the courthouse, hoping to get married. No justice of the peace was available on the third floor at that hour, so Judge Azios took time out from his woes. In front of Rusty Hardin and Allen Isbell and the few media people who still remained, he married them. The JPs normally charged a thirty-dollar fee.

"My treat this time," the judge said.

_____

That night, in the cool of her room at the Holiday Inn, Lydia Tamez wrote:

"Assume Maria was telling the truth, and assume that Cindy was helping David and was under duress: Is it reasonable that when Maria confronted Cindy checking the windows a week before the murders, and said, 'No, no, Cindy, it's wrong!' Cindy could still not have freaked out?"

And on the night of the murders: "If she was in absolute fear of her life, why would she have not kept running out of the house? Why would she stop at the door? If she was in total fear, why would she be trying to find the glove? She told Gwen Sampson that she left it on purpose."

And, "If she was under duress, is it possible that she not only fooled Maria but she fooled the police when she was giving her statement?"

She looked again at her notes taken during deliberation in the jury room. *"You're assuming a stable and rational person,"* Sheryl Henderson had said. Well, yes. If she was unstable, that would mean crazy, insane. She wouldn't be on trial this way. Or the defense would have pled insanity. Some juror had remarked on that much earlier: "They must have tried to plead insanity and the law and the judge wouldn't allow it. That's why we're here."

But it troubled Lydia Tamez. She was awake until 4:30 A.M., writing and reasoning. "Hyped up," she said later. "And I had broken out with a rash of nerves, and I had never done that before, but maybe it was the smoking. So they got me some Benadryl during the night and that knocked me out."

_____

The next day, Friday, was July 4—the fourth day of deliberation. The tropically hot street in front of the courthouse was deserted. You could park by a meter without paying. In New York's Upper Bay, and on television through the country, the tall ships with white sails were sailing past the Statue of Liberty. The world outside the Harris County Courthouse still functioned.

Kim was in court, and Makhlouf, and five reporters, and a few diehard spectators who canceled their holiday plans. Outside it was ninety-four degrees. Inside, in its fashion, the air conditioning worked, pumping cool stale air.

Cindy entered the courtroom, wearing her dark blue suit, hands cuffed behind her back. She was smiling. She looked toward her husband and nodded affectionately. Maureen Earl, the English screenwriter attending the trial, said in surprise, "She looks pretty."

I had wanted to do something for a long time that no one else seemed willing to do. I went up to Makhlouf and, after a minute of polite conversation, said, "Do you mind my asking you what's in that black bag with the 'S' on it?"

Unsmilingly he obliged me by unzipping it and showing me his lunch, wrapped in plastic, and the white shirt and black pants he wore as a waiter.

Rusty strode out of the elevator. He had started smoking again. In the hallway, while I told him he didn't have to worry anymore that a terrorist bomb was going to explode, he puffed at his pipe, sending up clouds of sweet, amaretto-flavored smoke. But his expression was war-like; he wasn't concentrating on what I said.

He had discovered something about Sheryl Henderson, the private investigator, the rumored holdout juror. Her brother, one Buddy Wayne Henderson, had been indicted some months ago on a felony charge—aggravated assault, robbery, and auto theft—and was scheduled for trial next Monday. Yesterday afternoon the prosecutor in the case called a lawyer, Bob Scott, who represented the brother, to see if he was ready for trial. Scott said, "No. My client's sister has a tape recording of her brother's parole violation hearing, and I can't get it from her because she's on the Ray jury."

The prosecutor immediately called Rusty, who yelped in pain. Sheryl had failed to mention anything about her felonious brother during voir dire. Had she done so, Rusty almost certainly would have struck her as a juror, out of the reasonable fear that she might have undue sympathy for a defendant—*any* defendant. And that's exactly what's happening, he now decided.

"*That's* what's hanging up this jury!" he told me. He slammed his fist against a wall.

Throughout the morning and into the afternoon a substitute court

463

reporter read to the jury from Brenda's electronic tapes. The three men on the jury looked far more exhausted than the women. Otho Bell's legs shook, and he coughed badly. Sheryl Henderson had her hands stuffed deep into the pockets of her jeans. Her face had broken out again in a raw red color.

Intermittently, Rusty argued with the judge. "They're retrying the case," he said. "We're going to be here two or three days reading this stuff." Rusty had a personal reason to be upset: he was scheduled to fly on Monday to Florida with his wife and children, to visit with his parents for two weeks.

"I have to do what they ask," Judge Azios said.

"They need to be more specific," Rusty said. "The law doesn't require that we give them a license to chaos."

After lunch the jury retired again to the jury room, and then sent out a note asking for extra-strength Excedrin caplets.

"We don't have any available," the judge said to Keith. "Give them aspirin."

Keith said, "They specifically said extra-strength Excedrin."

Rusty, no doubt thinking of Sheryl Henderson, began to laugh hysterically. "Give them capsules!"

––––––––––––––

"So on Friday"—Lydia Tamez later recounted—"I told them what I'd been thinking, but I said I don't trust myself to make a final decision because of the fatigue and the Benadryl. I went to lunch with them. After lunch I fell asleep on the jury room floor under two jurors' chairs. I was sick. We were at a standstill, waiting for the judge and the court reporter to give us more material . . . so I just lay down on the floor."

After they had heard the last of the requested tapes, they went back once more to the jury room. I'm going to cross the line with the others, Lydia decided, and vote guilty. I just want to hear one last time what Sheryl has to say. I know she has a clear vision, but she just hasn't got it across to me.

"Cindy's not a stable person," Sheryl said. (She had first begun thinking about this possibility when Sgt. Motard had described Cindy as "deadpan" on the day of the funeral, and Isbell had said, "She might be all torn up inside, might she not?" Motard had agreed—that unseen door had swung open.) Sheryl also reminded the jury of Rory Lettvin's vivid description of Cindy's grotesque and filthy apartment, the description that Allen Isbell had worked to hard to keep out of evidence when Sgt. Kent had been on the stand. And then Lettvin saying: "I didn't see how any human being could function in society without being able to drive, without having a bank account, without any photo ID, unable to go to the store and go grocery shopping . . . she apparently didn't know how . . . [and she didn't] understand personal hygiene." Rory Lettvin had called her "crazy," and, prodded by Rusty, defined it as *someone unable to make a rational decision. Unable to take care of herself. If someone didn't help her, she would die.*"

And the weight problem. The sharp gains and losses that had been chronicled so carefully by Rusty Hardin—what kind of person could alternately starve herself and then pig out to such a drastic extent on junk food? Not a stable person. That was major irrational behavior.

The others didn't believe that. They saw Cindy Ray as a rebel and a liar, highly independent, a tough kid, an actress, and she'd sleep with anybody. Look at all those different stories she told! No two the same. All to get her way, to pry something out of someone else. Above all she was a manipulator.

"But the stories and lies are just more proof of her instability," Sheryl said. "And what they're hiding may still be true. I don't think she knew what she was doing. Remember how David described her when she arrived on his doorstep? How could a woman in that terrible shape convince anyone of anything? I think David convinced *her*. Why should we believe David when he says the opposite? Remember back in voir dire how Rusty prepared us? He said, "How many of y'all would not take the word of somebody just because he was the trigger man?" And we just about promised him we'd believe him! I bought it, for sure, at least until that time when he went out of control against that newspaper-man and the writer—he wasn't supposed to ask the writer all about his having been in prison, and he did, and of course it influenced us. Then I trusted Rusty less. I keep trying to feel that it's his true conviction that she's stable and she did it, but maybe he believes that because of the kind of person *he* is. It's like he's a salesman and what mattered was selling the product."

The other jurors sighed.

40

Suddenly, everyone began to believe the jury was going to hang up. Allen said to me, "*Now* I wish they'd deliver a guilty verdict. Because obviously they'd be lenient in the punishment phase." And Rusty said, to anyone who cared to listen, "I *want* them to hang up. I want to try this case again with a fair jury. I asked during voir dire if anyone had been arrested or had a relative who'd been arrested. That one juror lied. The State of Texas never stood a chance."

Rick Brass scratched his beard and looked at me as if the world had been turned upside down. "I've never in my life as a lawyer seen a situation like this."

At 4:30 the jury asked: "Can we hear a segment of closing remarks by the attorney?"

The judge replied: "The law does not allow that."

At 4:45 the jurors sent out individual notes. Melanie Wheat asked for her red jumpsuit. Lydia Tamez wanted shampoo. Mary Kloss wanted a message read to a friend: "Please feed the cats again. I owe you two six-packs for this one. Three six-packs if you'll change the litter box." Sheryl Henderson wanted a six-pack of Diet Pepsi, twenty dollars cash, and deodorant, and asked that Bonnie Henderson be told: "*I MISS YOU*. Happy 4th of July."

They also asked for more legal pads.

"I think we'd better take a vote," Randy Uselton said. He was jaded, drained.

Lydia Tamez said, "I'm not ready for that yet. If I have to vote now, I have to vote not guilty. And I'm still not convinced that way. I think she's guilty, but I haven't crossed the line."

There were murmurs of "My God!" and "Come *on* . . ."

Uselton said, "Let's everybody write 'guilty' or 'not guilty' on a slip of paper and fold it up and just throw it in this bowl." He passed the bowl, and they all scribbled quickly.

In the courtroom it was like a shipwreck. We were stranded on a desert island. The fluorescent lights blinked whitely down on the twenty-two survivors. There was no night or day in here. Everyone was a little giddy. Some brought in Pepsis and six-packs of cold beer. Rick Brass and his wife played Scrabble. One reporter set up a portable TV on a back bench, and everyone watched the five o'clock news report of the case.

At six o'clock the judge ordered Rusty and Allen to the bench. He wanted to call the jury out and poll them individually. Allen wouldn't agree. "If they're polled," he said, "it would exert subtle pressure for deadlock and a mistrial. The defendant wants this jury to go all the way to reach a verdict."

The judge decided to compromise, and at 6:20 he ordered the jury into the jury box. They looked wan and whipped.

"Members of the jury, you've been deliberating since about 6:15 P.M. Tuesday on July 1. You deliberated all day Wednesday and Thursday, July 2 and 3, and all today, July the 4th. Reverend Uselton, you're the foreman. I want to ask you a question. Don't tell us *which way* you're divided—that's not my question. The question is, numerically, *how* are you divided?"

"Ten to two," the minister said.

"How long have you been divided ten to two?"

"We were divided eleven to one, and now it's ten to two. Let me think when that happened . . . I'm not real sharp right now. Yesterday morning."

"Do you believe that continued deliberation will be helpful in reaching a unanimous verdict?"

"At this point, yes," the minister said firmly.

The jury then elected to quit for the day. After that none of us knew what to think, or how it would go. Did the minister mean that the two holdout jurors were ready to cross the line?

Once again, in her room, Lydia Tamez stared at the blank television screen and focused her mind. She was fresher now; she had showered and washed her hair and she felt keen.

Duress. Unstable. There was a connection. But how?

She cast her mind back to what had happened during the trial. Tried to see the faces of the witnesses. Tried to concentrate on what had been said that was clearly believable. They told all these stories of what Cindy Ray had said to them, and it was obvious—Rusty *made* it obvious— that they had been fooled. And were fools to have believed her. And so, of course, would we be.

Wait a minute. Maybe she was so good at fooling all these people not because she was a good actress, but because there was a basis for it: she really was messed up. We assumed that because there was no insanity plea she was stable, and then there's no choice but to assume that she was lying all the time.

David did it to make her well. He said that. Cindy said it, too. Maybe he was doing it to make her well *because she really needed to be made well.*

Lydia Tamez wrote:

"Is it reasonable that someone like Cindy, who is so in control and totally manipulating and such a great actress and fooled David into believing it was his idea all along, would live a life that showed such obvious signs of instability?

"Young girls don't run away for weeks without having serious reasons. It is inconsistent that everything was 'great' at home.

"Weight problem: she could lose it and gain it and lose it—not just a few pounds but an incredible amount of weight. Only if you starve yourself. Why would you do that unless you had an incredible need for approval or were a very insecure person?

"She can't hold a job. She can't function alone.

"She was only fourteen and already needed to be hospitalized in a mental ward. Something is wrong.

"This girl is not stable."

But does that make her *not* guilty? Well, Lydia Tamez thought, it would have to have an effect on the penalty. This girl is so *out* of it. She needs help.

She's desperate. David offers her hope, however sick his idea. She could have bought it: if not, I'll die. She's not capable of reason and she may have been under duress and not seen that she could have told her parents. She could have been there and still not been there mentally. If she was unstable, how could she have performed as she did in the week preceding the murders, and during the murders? No way. Not unless he prodded her, forced her, convinced her, threatened her. A combination of that. She reread the charge. *"Such compulsion exists only if the threat of force is such as would render a person of reasonable firmness incapable of resisting the pressure. The State, having introduced evidence of duress, must disprove this duress beyond a reasonable doubt. . . ."*

Was Cindy a person of reasonable firmness? Rusty would cry, "Of course she is! So firm that she conned David into believing *he* planned it!"

Lydia Tamez thought: Wait a minute, Rusty. You said from the beginning that without David you didn't have a case. You were seeking the death penalty for David until he caved in and cut a deal. Back then he was a psychopathic killer. What would you have done to David if he'd taken the stand in his own trial? What would you have made *him* look like? Now you needed him as a credible witness. You had to make him look good. Not a psychopath anymore. And you did it, you did a fabulous job of it.

You're a salesman, a great one. Sheryl was right. You sold us on David as a truthteller. You sold us on the logic that Cindy had made fools of all these people by virtue of the fact that they believed her, and therefore if we believe her we're fools as well. Brilliant. An incredible game plan. And what mattered was selling the product—winning. And if somebody got in your way you'd stomp on 'em any way you could. We saw that happen with the writer.

Rusty . . . what if the truth got in your way? If you're so intent on winning, would you be able to *see* it?

Start with the fact that Cindy's lying about her life with her parents, and you can make a great case that she's guilty. But if you get out of that mode, it doesn't work. Then, probably—or in the very least, maybe— she *wasn't* "a person of reasonable firmness."

On Saturday morning, July 5, the jury reconvened. "Who wants to speak?" Randy Uselton asked. Mark Vandervoort's hand shot up, then Sheryl's, then Lydia's.

Mark said, "I've thought about it from every angle, and I still believe she's guilty, because duress won't work"—and he explained why.

Then Sheryl said, "I've crossed the line. I have reasonable doubt. Up to now I was open to change, but now I can't change my vote. I have to live with this for the rest of my life. It's a matter of conscience."

Randy Uselton believed her.

"Let's pack it up," the others said.

"Hey, wait a miute," Lydia said excitedly, "*I've* crossed the line, too! I believe she's not guilty, and I have reasons, and I want to explain them to you. I think I can convince you, and it's important!"

But they didn't want to hear her reasons.

Randy Uselton snatched a pen and slowly, firmly, wrote on a sheet of yellow legal paper: "We are hopelessly hung up."

The jury sat once more in the box.

"Reverend Uselton," Judge Azios asked formally, "given time, is there a reasonable probability you can reach a unanimous verdict?"

"No, Your Honor."

"I'm going to ask a different question. Is there any one person among you who feels that, given more time, you can reach a unanimous verdict? Indicate yes by raising your hand, please."

No hands were raised in the jury box. Melanie Wheat and Mark Vandervoort looked displeased, almost disgusted. Sheryl Henderson was red-faced again, and seemed ready to cry.

With a long sigh, Judge Azios said gravely, "The court therefore finds that a manifest necessity has arisen to declare a mistrial. I want to thank you members of the jury very much."

But before anyone could react, before we could digest the full meaning of this—the waste!—Reverend Uselton asked permission to address the court. Taken aback, for this was not on the agenda, Judge Azios nodded.

The reverend rose. He knew that everyone in this courtroom now—judge, lawyers, Cindy Ray, reporters, and the few spectators—had a stake in the proceedings of the last five weeks, and beyond. We were a peculiar club, and our existence in this form was about to end.

He used no notes . . . he didn't need notes. His voice quietly vibrating with emotion, he addressed us all.

He said: "In the last five and a half weeks, we've been silent. You gave us the responsibility for an awesome task—to hear this case and make a decision on someone's life. This jury has given it absolutely everything we've got toward reaching a unanimous decision. And we could not. Today is the first day in my life that I ever used the word 'hopeless,' and I trust I'll never have to use it again . . . because it is the worst feeling I've ever had in my life."

The minister never once raised his voice or gave undue emphasis to a word. He was a speaker of enormous inner conviction.

"We've never for one moment taken our task lightly. And it is with deepest sorrow and regret that we have to make the statement that we could not reach a decision. Each and every one of you has touched our lives, and I want you to know that." His voice broke.

Half the jury had tears in their eyes. So did I, surprisingly, and many around me.

"This is a day," said the minister, "that we will never forget. If what I have just said were not so, I would owe you an apology, but I offer none. The thing that has impacted us the most is that when a crime is committed there are many people who have to pay. The Campbells paid with their lives. That's the highest price. I want you to know that *we* paid a price, too. But we do believe, with all our heart, that justice will prevail."

Having touched *our* lives, he sat down. The judge thanked him and the jury, and the murder trial was over.

I still didn't quite grasp the implications.

———————————

Rusty waited until Sheryl Henderson had come out from backstage and a bailiff was escorting her toward the courtroom exit. Then he crowded into the jury room with the other eleven women and men, where he told them about the felony charge against Sheryl's brother.

"Sheryl Henderson lied to me," he said bitterly, "and y'all were barking up a hopeless tree. Sheryl made up her mind before she heard any testimony, and if I had known I wouldn't have put her on there."

To the media, before she left, Sheryl had already emphatically denied both of Rusty's allegations.

"Wait a minute," Lydia Tamez said in the jury room. "Yesterday I voted not guilty, too. And I would have kept voting it."

"Because Sheryl convinced you," Rusty said.

"No, *sir*."

Rusty felt he had let down the Campbell family, and Kim. He had an obligation, and he had failed. "I'm just heartsick," he quietly admitted.

"That's because you're not listening to me," Lydia Tamez replied. "I crossed the line not because of what Sheryl said, but because I finally started considering the instability. You had us liking David, and even feeling sorry for him. And certainly believing in his credibility. You're the greatest salesman I ever saw in my life, Rusty! You ought to be a rich man, because you are *good*. But what you told us about Sheryl's brother had nothing to do with anything! I'm grateful that she was there, because she bought me enough time to come to my own decision."

Lydia Tamez walked out.

In the courtroom Cindy Ray showed the same lack of emotion that she had showed for the last five weeks. Allen Isbell said to us, on her behalf: "Cindy is relieved that *some* decision was made . . . that the jury couldn't *make* a decision. She considers that a vindication."

"The jury did exactly what the system wanted it to do," Randy Mc-Donald murmured, exhausted.

Lyn McClellan, who had a joke or a wry observation for every occasion, was unable to speak. He left the courtroom, shaking his head from side to side, as if he were in shock and might cry.

Rusty said, "Sheryl Henderson is *the* reason Cynthia Campbell Ray was not found guilty. We never had a shot, and didn't know it." He was going to ask the special crimes division of the District Attorney's Office to look into the possibility of filing criminal charges against Sheryl Henderson.

"And what about Cindy?" I asked.

"We'll try her again as soon as possible," Rusty vowed.

It was not over.

PART IV

JUSTICE

41

There is a story of a palace thief, caught red-handed. "Death," says the king, and asks for any last request. The thief replies, "If within a year I can make your monkey talk, let me go. If not, kill me." The king agrees. The thief's astonished lawyer asks his client, "How can you do that?" The thief says, "In case you haven't noticed, I'm still alive. Within a year the king might die. The monkey might die. There might be a revolution. Or . . . the monkey might talk!"

David West, in the Harris County Jail, contemplated his options. The moment that Jim Campbell first laid his fingertips on his daughter's breasts, the possibility of justice died. The mother had let it happen. David believed all that wholeheartedly.

It's enough that I have to pay the price, he thought. I don't want Cindy to go to prison for life. She doesn't deserve that.

He had fulfilled his obligation to the state. He had testified truthfully and nothing had come of it. They'd had their pound of flesh. *Where did it say he had to do it a second time?*

All right, all right . . . Rusty won't buy that. Not Rusty. But I can still refuse. I have that right, don't I? They can never take away your right to choose.

If he refused to testify again they could indict him for the murder of James, and they would have his voluntary confession made before Judge

Azios. But he could delay, appeal, appeal again, have Rusty subpoenaed as a witness to the confession and taken off the case (a jailhouse lawyer had told him it was called "a motion to recuse"), then hope for a less dedicated prosecutor with no personal interest because it wasn't he who had been betrayed.

And even if none of that worked, David understood how much the jury had liked him and sympathized with him. Another jury would be the same; they would see him as a man who made an aberrant mistake, was manipulated dreadfully by two women. They would know he was not a man who would have cause to kill again. In the punishment stage of the trial the odds would be powerfully in favor of a *no* to special issue #2, the question of future dangerousness. He would get life in TDC. He had that already.

Worst case scenario: if he was unlucky and they answered *yes* to future dangerousness, and for his temerity he was awarded death, he could appeal that, too. The appeals would pile up, take years. Men lived on death row for years. People forget. Somewhere in the criminal justice system someone might take pity on him, or admire his loyalty and sense of mercy, grasp the fact that he had done what he had promised to do and it was wrong to make him do it a second time.

Or the monkey might talk.

In the Harris County Jail throughout the summer, Cindy Ray bit her nails. Maybe they were low calorie nails, because she began to lose more weight. Everyone told her what a good job her lawyers had done for her, but it was not Cindy's nature to believe in others. It occurred to her that she had been only a single juror away from serving a life sentence. The retrial was set for January 20, 1987, since both Rusty Hardin and Allen Isbell had other commitments. But from the jail, while she waited, Cindy began telephoning other lawyers. Would they take her case? Did they think they could win it?

In late August Cindy called the Houston *Post* and demanded an interview. Reporter Mary Flood visited the Harris County Jail. Rick Brass was present, and he coolly told Flood he had advised his client not to talk to the press.

Cindy was well groomed and down to about 170 pounds. "I didn't have a fair trial," she said to Flood. "I was accused with only hearsay and lies." Rusty Hardin was trying to further his career at her expense: "Not only am I innocent, but I was made into a commodity." The state's key witnesses were coached into lying. "I feel Mr. Hardin tutored people very intelligently, but that only makes it more immoral."

476

Whenever Rusty wanted something, she said, "Judge Azios was pliable. All during the trial, even though I'm a layman, I could see that his decisions were outrageous."

As for the jury, the ten jurors who voted guilty hadn't been paying close attention. "These people felt they had the right to destroy a human life, and yet they only listened off and on. It was morally wrong for people to draw a conclusion when the majority of the ten were watching the clock the last hour before lunch."

In the forthcoming trial, she said, "I will take the witness stand, answer any questions, and vindicate myself."

In September, when Allen Isbell learned that Cindy had been on the phone to a good part of the Houston criminal defense community, he asked to be excused from the case. Request denied, Judge Azios declared.

But in early December, in her cell block, Cindy heard of a recent trial victory by a thirty-six-year-old lawyer named Peter Justin. An ex-con was found not guilty in the murder of a money-flashing cement truck driver who was stabbed nineteen times and killed during a robbery. The thrust of Peter Justin's defense discredited the state's witnesses, all of whom were friends of the victim.

Justin was hard-working, afraid of no one. Years ago, in a high-profile *barrio* riot case in Moody Park, he had represented one of six Chicano defendants charged with attempted murder of police officers. He won the only verdict of not guilty.

That's the man I need, Cindy decided.

She called Justin three times in one day, and finally he returned the call. The next evening he went down to the jail to talk to her.

She was used to Allen Isbell, the embodiment of solidity and solemnity. Pete Justin was fast-talking, tall, and gangly; with his bangs, long hair down to his collar, and big round John Lennon spectacles, he could have passed for the road manager of a successful rock group.

In the newspapers he had seen photographs of Cindy, and he had heard talk among his fellow lawyers—he expected an obese, slovenly, difficult woman. Instead he found Cindy down to a sleek 125 pounds. Her long brown hair was freshly washed and curly. She spoke to him with respect.

"I can pay you," she said. "My husband has saved some money. He believes in my innocence. If you do, too, I want you."

Two weeks later Pete Justin agreed on a fee of $2,500 plus expenses, with a promise of more to come. The money was insignificant; Justin liked the facts and the challenge. Judge Azios had no choice. He reset the trial for March 16, 1987, and dismissed Allen Isbell and Randy McDonald. Now it was Pete Justin's turn to take on the starring triumvirate of Rusty Hardin, David West, and Cindy Ray.

Justin plunged into the case, and like all the lawyers who had previously become involved, he quickly found the waters lapping around his ears, while underfoot the quicksand sucked at him.

In March I flew up from Mexico into stainless blue Texas skies, the weather on the cusp between spring and early summer. Like Judge Azios and Rusty Hardin, I had signed up for the duration. The judge looked older, a little grayer, a little more tired. We had become friends. I thought he fulfilled Socrates' classic qualities of a judge: "To hear courteously, to answer wisely, to consider soberly, and to decide impartially."

As for Rusty, late last summer yet another crisis had rippled the hitherto smooth momentum of his life. Since enlisting with the Harris County District Attorney's Office he had never thought to do any other kind of work, but now it gradually and uneasily occurred to him that he had two growing sons—Russell III, eleven, and Thomas, seven—who wanted to go to college and law school, and with the Reagan cutbacks in financial aid Rusty wasn't making enough money to accomplish that feat without some sacrifice. With Tissy he discussed leaving the D.A.'s Office and going into private practice in order to save money for his children's future education. Houston law firms would fight to get him. Or he could take the risk and practice on his own.

"I can probably make a couple of hundred thousand a year. Maybe not at first, but soon. And then, if I want to, if I'm able, I can go back—"

Young Russell overheard. When Rusty came to tuck him into bed that night, he said, "Daddy, if you left the D.A.'s Office . . . would your job be to keep people out of jail instead of keeping them in when they've done something wrong?"

"That's about right, son."

The boy thought it over a minute before he said, "Daddy, I don't need to go to college."

Then Rusty understood that he was condemned to prosecute until his hair turned white. If need be, Thomas and Russell would work their way through law school, as he had done.

Since then Rusty had been grinding away, teaching the young assistant D.A.s, and at the same time winning two major cases. Thomas

478

Grettenburg, known as "the Austin rapist," visited Houston on parole and raped two more women. Rusty prosecuted him and Grettenburg got life. Then Geraldine Swain, a nurse deeply in debt, wrote out a "Contract of Termination" and talked her seventeen-year-old son into having two of his friends kill her trucker husband for the insurance. She got life. Her son cried throughout his trial, but he received life, too. Rusty prosecuted both mother and son.

But a victory in the Cindy Ray case was the one he still wanted more than any other. He had put too much of himself into it to accept failure, and failure was what he had tasted. In the long saga of the Campbell murder case he had triumphed with David when he thought he would probably fail, and then failed with Cindy when he was almost certain he would be victorious. He had dropped the charges against Sheryl Henderson. Quick to use the word *heartsick,* this time Rusty felt real pain. If Cindy Ray ultimately walked away from what she had done, then justice had been too cruelly mocked. And how would the Campbell family feel?

On the first day of trial, outside the door to the courtroom, the prosecutor and I greeted each other with quick smiles. We were stubborn travelers on the same journey, and we both needed to know where it would end. We shook hands. But despite our lunch of reconciliation, our friendship had been tarnished by the events of last June, when I had testified against his cause and he had lost the case he so desperately wanted to win. Rusty had learned from the other jurors how his rage at me on the witness stand had been factored by Sheryl Henderson and Lydia Tamez into their decision. I stood as a symbol of his failure. He was polite to me and answered all my questions, but the warmth was gone.

Lyn McClellan was also in the courtroom when I arrived, but off the Cynthia Ray case. I asked him why, and with a swift grin he said, "Had too much fun the last time." He didn't care to elaborate. The assumption by most other lawyers was that he was reluctant to be associated with failure a second time. No one blamed him.

His place at Rusty's left hand was taken by Jo Ann Lee, a slim, personable young black assistant district attorney. She had been with Harris County for three and a half years and was number two prosecutor in the 232nd District Court. This case she considered a learning experience, since aside from exchanging ideas with her, she knew that Rusty would do it all. "That's okay," Jo Ann said to me, "he's the best."

The retrial began on schedule on March 16, 1987. Rusty and Peter Justin had agreed that this time it would be for the murders of both James and Virginia: double or nothing, and no reprise unless the jury hung up again.

Curtain up . . . again. I settled down to go through it all a second time.

Voir dire lasted three days. The new jury seemed a shade more blue collar than the one picked in June, possibly because there was a majority of eight men. Seven had been born in Texas. All twelve jurors had children. The jury included a golf pro, a computer software expert, a woman who described her occupation as "homemaker," an anesthetist, and a mail courier.

Following its selection, in the light of what he considered his disastrous experience with Sheryl Henderson eight months ago, Rusty ran a rap sheet this time on all twelve jurors and the alternate. The result stunned him. One of the older jurors, who had looked like a conservative rock, popped up in the printout with three misdemeanor convictions for theft, DWI, and assault. The juror had failed to mention any of these during voir dire. Now he explained the first one with "I got tired of standing on line in a supermarket, so I left." The last two, he said, were nobody's business but his.

Rusty kicked him off the jury, substituting the alternate.

Judge Azios had moved his court next door to where Ted Poe formerly reigned; it was a mirror image of his old courtroom, with handsome smoke-blue carpeting laid wall to wall. The air conditioning worked wonderfully.

The two lawyers afforded good contrast—Rusty, with his deceptively casual air, short but well-proportioned, somehow always seeming a physically larger man than he really was, sporting a new close haircut that emphasized the conservative side of his nature (although he wore a blue blazer and cream-colored trousers); and Pete Justin, nearly six feet three inches tall, lanky, mod, and free-flowing. "He looks like Lincoln without a beard," Judge Azios commented one night during the trial when we had dinner together. The spectators' benches were as packed as they were last time. Two of the majority jurors from the June trial, Melanie Wheat and Jane McBunch, were in attendance, and Rusty greeted them warmly. Asked by reporters why they had come, Wheat and McBunch gave a standard cool reply: "We have a vested interest."

None of the reporters could guess what would be the outcome this time. They had been too sure of a guilty verdict in June. The opposing lawyers of course oozed confidence—that was part of their job—and few could tell what they really thought. But there was no doubt that it would be an uphill battle for the prosecution.

Rusty brooded and twisted rubber bands, and in the last two weeks had chewed one Alka Seltzer after another for an upset stomach. Not only did he once again have to deal with the major problem of David's credibility—he now had to blunt the thorn of the duress issue. He agonized, remembering what had happened in the June 1986 trial. Most lawyers thought he had blundered then in allowing Gwen's testimony to bring in the words: "He held a gun to my head. He would have killed me, too." This time, ideally, from Rusty's point of view, it would be up to Pete Justin on cross to dig that out of Gwen's memory, so that the defense would have the burden to prove duress rather than the state having to *dis*prove it.

Rusty fretted. How can I do that? If I omit the duress concept, then when it's brought out on cross-examination it will look to the jury as if I've been trying to hide it under the carpet. That revelation might be too dramatic. They'll fix on it. They'll hang up again, or, worse, find her not guilty.

He didn't know what to do, and so he postponed the decision. It was an indication of his uncertainty.

———————

There were no surprises at first, unless you counted Cindy Ray's new persona. Dan Grothaus, now a writer-producer of documentary films for PBS, dropped in to the trial on the first day. Unprepared for what he saw, he blurted, "Hey, she looks *good*."

She was well made up, with a touch of rosy color high on her cheeks, and her long wavy brown hair was tied back neatly in a bun to show off a white, slender neck. She was uniformly slim except for swollen ankles —she said to Pete Justin, "No matter what I do, I can't lose weight in my calves. That's a family trait."

The only one unhappy with her weight loss was her husband, Makhlouf. Pete Justin told me, "He *likes* her fat."

She still had a hacking smoker's cough. On that first day she wore a single-breasted navy blue suit and a white cotton sweater. At Justin's request Makhlouf had gone out and re-outfitted her; he bought a dress and two suits, one on sale at Neiman-Marcus, and one at Lord & Taylor. Justin told him to return the one to Lord & Taylor. He didn't want the jury to get the impression that Cindy was an heiress. It was all right to have a good suit, but only *one*.

Trial testimony began on Monday, March 23. Makhlouf was in the spectators' section this time, minus his black bag, and no longer presumed dangerous since I had found his lunch where a hand grenade had been feared. Also at Justin's request, over his chinos he wore the single-breasted jacket of a dark suit. Justin wanted the jury to notice him and remark his loyalty.

Once was enough, and this time out I was determined not to be a witness. But there was no cause for worry, Justin assured me. Wickie Weinstein had moved to an unknown address in Oregon, and Justin had abandoned the Wickie-not-Cindy-was-there scenario. After a score of conferences with his client, Justin was determined to prove that on the night of June 19, 1982, in the upstairs bedroom at Memorial, Cindy had not been there at all.

The glove by the front door was established as before by Rhodes, the EMT, and then by Sgt. Kent. When Homicide's videotape was shown this time, and the bloody bodies on the bed filled the screen, tears rolled down Cindy's cheeks. Pete Justin was convinced that her cold demeanor at the last trial had hurt her badly. "*Let go,*" he said. And she did.

In cross-examination of Kent, for his final question, Justin asked: "Sergeant, as an experienced police officer, weren't you surprised at the crime scene by the way Mrs. Campbell was dressed?" He referred to the bare buttocks.

"Well . . . yes," Kent said.

Rusty glared at Justin and in redirect tried to defuse the effect by discussing the possible effects on clothing of a .45 bullet. But on recross, Justin said, "Despite all that, Sgt. Kent, didn't you still find the mode of dress—considering that two children were sleeping in the room—unusual?"

Kent said yes, he did.

Rusty continued to look reprovingly at Justin for a long time. The defense attorney stood up again and in the presence of the jury said coolly to the court reporter, "Let the record reflect that the prosecutor is trying to stare me down."

Then we knew that this was to be a different sort of courtroom battle from the one waged between Rusty and Allen Isbell. From the outset Justin clambered to his feet to object steadily to anything that smacked of hearsay or sidebar remarks or that was not exactly responsive to the question asked by the prosecutor. His long body bobbed up and down like a buoy in a heavy sea.

"Your Honor, I'm going to have to object to that . . ."

And that. And that, too.

"Your Honor, I believe Mr. Hardin's question calls for a simple yes or no answer."

The judge kept sustaining his objections.

Rusty was not intimidated, but by the end of the first day he was respectful of his opponent, and on his guard. He also seemed a little tired. He had been sleeping only four and five hours a night.

Wednesday, March 25, was Brenda Palmer's thirty-fifth birthday, and

Bettie Conway, the judge's faithful clerk, brought a chocolate-covered marble cake to celebrate. On the same day, a slow-moving Maria Bravo took the stand, wearing the shiny blue dress she had worn nearly ten months ago. Before her testimony began the judge had invited her into chambers to warn her about any outbursts or demonstrations.

On the witness stand, when Maria described the boys' terror upon reaching her apartment over the garage, Cindy again wept quietly. Rusty frowned; a tearful Cindy wasn't something he had counted on. He didn't like it at all. He saw it as a harbinger of perhaps even more unpleasant surprises.

A few fresh bits of information were drawn from Maria, particularly during cross. In June of 1982 Cindy had her own set of keys to the doors at Memorial. During an argument in the driveway, probably back in 1980, Cindy had once struck her mother a blow on the neck. That same year David West had spanked young Michael Ray, "very hard, two or three times, in the butt. And he called my Michael 'stupid and spoiled.' His eyes were always red. He stared a lot at me and the children."

Aside from this minor violence and excessive eyeballing on the part of an alien presence, Maria said, the Campbell household had been a model of tranquility. The only disruptive presence was Cindy's. None of the other sisters ever raised their voices to their parents. James and Virginia Campbell never raised their voices to any of their daughters. In the five years of Maria's residence there was not one single argument between husband and wife.

"Not one?" Pete Justin asked.

"No, sir, none."

"Señora Bravo, have you ever been married?"

"Yes, sir."

"Do you know what a marital argument is?"

"Yes, sir."

"And you never heard a single one in the Campbell house? You never heard them raise their voices to each other or to any of their daughters?"

"No, sir. Not once. They were a very fine family."

Maria left the courtroom in tears, but otherwise quietly.

David had a short talk with Rusty. Yes, you can refuse to testify, Rusty said. In which case we'll enter into the record of this trial your testimony in the last trial. And you'll be tried for capital murder. If not this year, then next year.

Rusty, if it was his last act on earth, would personally see to it that the result was the death penalty. You made a deal, David.

David sighed, looked into those unrelenting vigorous blue eyes, and made his choice.

"Are you before this jury voluntarily?" Rusty asked, when his star witness took the stand to begin the second week of trial testimony.

Almost as if he had been insulted, David raised his eyebrows. "Voluntarily?" He flushed, waited a long moment . . . then sighed: "No."

This was a different David from the man who had testified so jubilantly last June. In a three-piece suit he looked well: he had been working out, he had good color and had trimmed his beard into a well-shaped goatee. But he was morose, thoughtful, slow to answer. Each statement began with a sigh, then a "Well . . . " and then a decorous reply suffused with world-weary pain. No joking with Rusty and the jury this time. The theatrical rapport between murderer and prosecutor was gone. Last summer David had received absolution; he no longer had anything to prove or gain. The catharsis was complete. This was what Rusty had feared might happen.

". . . Jamie told me she was a lesbian, and she and Cindy told me their older sister was, too."

Rusty flushed with annoyance. He hadn't expected that. He certainly hadn't asked for it.

Backstage, at the first break, he reprimanded David. He added: "Don't think so much before answering!"

But David, when he resumed testifying, was still disobedient. He wasn't trying to charm the jury. Just trying to tell the truth as he saw it. If they didn't like him, that was too bad. Like Rusty, he was doing what he had to do. He went through the paces like a trained but sluggish bear. The planning—the murder—the aftermath. The direct examination took one and a half days.

The jury, listening carefully, never smiled. Rusty didn't like that either.

On cross, late in the day, Pete Justin faced a dilemma. If he worked too vigorously at impeaching David's credibility, he would open the door to the admission of the Kim Paris tapes as prior consistent testimony. He was convinced that the defense lawyers in the June trial had made an error in the cross of David by quoting from the taped transcript. That had led to the tapes being admitted into evidence, and the June jury had then decided that if David told the same tale when no threat of death hung over him, he must have been telling the truth.

But Justin nevertheless had to lead the jury to the conclusion that David was violent, a man whose credibility was flawed. He never tried to make friends with David. Instead he flew at him.

"You took an oath to tell the truth, and then you told us how you slaughtered those people, right? . . ."

"Didn't Rusty Hardin say to you earlier this morning, 'Stop thinking so much' ?. . ."

"Wasn't Mr. Hardin angry and upset about you mentioning the sisters' lesbianism? . . ."

"Didn't you hit the children even before you knew Cindy? . . ."

"It didn't take any guts to murder the Campbells, did it? . . ."

"After you had that argument with Cindy at The Comedy Workshop, didn't you follow her into a party with a .38 in your back pocket and poke a lady in the eyes?"

"Lady?" David smirked. "You can call her that. I'd call her a drunken, pushy woman."

Justin asked him to demonstrate exactly how he had poked her. David didn't seem embarrassed. The defense attorney and the murderer stood face to face in front of the jury box. Fingers extended, David tapped Justin sharply in the chest.

Justin said, "But you did it in her eyes, right?"

"Yes." David grinned up at him. "You care for a better demonstration?"

That echoed in the cool air for a long moment. Justin let the jury absorb it.

"You turned the light on, walked to the foot of the bed, and blew Mr. Campbell away, right?"

"Yes."

"David, did you understand what I said? *Look at me, not at Mr. Hardin! You* turned the light on, and walked to the foot of the bed, and pulled the trigger six times, isn't that right? And Cindy wasn't with you at all, was she?"

David backed off. "No, she was with me. I didn't understand you the first time."

David grew more sullen as Justin pecked and jabbed. Conspicuously, as he asked questions and received answers, Justin checked off notes on his various lists with a thick fluorescent pink marking pen. Rusty played nervously with a rubber band.

"You threw the combat boots away in the bayou? Does that mean you wore no shoes to the party? . . ."

"You can't remember whether you put a second clip in the gun? You didn't stop by the front door and reach into your pocket and put the clip in then? And drop the glove by mistake? . . ."

"David, do you think you're a psychopath?"

Rusty objected to that—"It's a potentially interesting discussion, but really irrelevant"—and was sustained.

485

David stepped down from the witness stand at the end of the second week. He looked worn out and relieved.

At the beginning of the trial Pete Justin had been sanguine enough to say to me, "I'll bet you a dinner at Tony's that my client walks."

"Goes free?"

"A hung jury or a guilty verdict, I pick up the tab."

"You're on." But then I thought about it a moment and said, "If she's found guilty, you'll be too depressed to go out and pay for an expensive dinner."

"No, I won't," Pete said.

He must have known something.

Everyone had warned him. Throughout the first trial Cindy had berated Allen Isbell steadily, insulted him, threatened him with malpractice lawsuits. She had said sneeringly to Allen, "You're appealing to the low mentality of the jurors." But Randy McDonald had shared Allen's role of target, and Rick Brass sat at both their sides as peacemaker. Pete Justin was defending Cindy solo.

When they first met, Cindy had said to Pete, with a shy smile, "I'm not very likable." Then, it seemed, she set out to prove it: she nagged at him, cursed at him, and threatened him. By the second week of trial, once her sisters took the stand, her agitation peaked. She began tugging at Pete's sleeve, whispering harshly in his ear.

Michelle Campbell looked to be the same weight as last July, so that her resemblance to her accused and now svelte sister was less distinct. Michelle's testimony hadn't changed, however, except that now she remembered a time in the summer of 1975, sitting on the living room couch, when Cindy had looked up and "started talking in a deep, strange voice and said she wanted to kill me, break every bone in my body and make me suffer."

Cindy printed large letters on her legal pad and thrust it in front of her lawyer. "ALL LIES!" When Michelle said, "We took my parents' carpets back to Austin that afternoon," Cindy interrupted Justin's cross-examination to insist sotto voce that it had been that *morning*.

During a break Justin said angrily, "The jury doesn't believe Michelle's tales of the happy Campbell family. But if you carry on like that, you give importance and even credibility to what she's saying. So will you please shut up?"

Cindy snarled at him, "When I tell you to ask a question, I want you to damn well ask it!"

He walked away. Later she apologized.

The next day her sister Jamie took the stand and added a new wrinkle to her recollection that back in 1980 Cindy had said, "I think I should kill Daddy" and had offered details about wearing heavy boots and scattering Marlboro cigarettes outside the window. Now Jamie also recalled, "She said she was going to leave a man's glove."

Cindy kept snarling in Pete's ear that Jamie was a bitch and a retard and an unprincipled liar. At the break she yelled at Pete again: "If they find me guilty and give me life, I'll kill myself within thirty days. You remember that, Mr. Justin!"

"You keep interrupting me during cross," Justin said grimly, "and you can start measuring your neck for the rope."

That evening she called him at home and said, "You're no good. I'm going to sue you and tell everyone you're dirt."

As the trial wore on he began to realize that she was unbalanced. Understanding that, you could deal with her, you didn't take her seriously. He threatened her with a competency test, and she was quiet the next day.

He decided that in the nearly four months he'd represented her he had yet to find anyone other than Cecilia West who had known her as an adult and liked her. He had searched—there was no one! And yet, if you didn't count murder, no one had ever accused her, in or out of court, of one overt nasty act. Crazy, manipulative, parasitic, filthy, warped, a pathological liar . . . all those labels, but not nasty or mean.

Except that she'd kicked Granny out of Kingston. But Granny was a spy for the sisters, Cindy claimed. Well . . .

I want to like her so that I can save her life, Pete Justin realized. My judgment may be a little clouded.

During the third week of trial Kim Paris stepped out of the elevator, flown in from Missouri by the State of Texas. She looked slim and attractive, with short dyed auburn hair and pink lipstick, more attractive than ever before. Sitting outside the courtroom with Debbi Johnson of ABC-TV, she discussed clothes and babies. She was friendly to me again. A declared happy mother, she was at last married to David Borosov, having secured an annulment from Jay Monson on the grounds that their marriage was never consummated. She was working as a manicurist in a St. Louis department store, hoping to finish a finance degree at a small local college and then go on to law school. "A big night now," she said, "is going for a beer while my clothes are in the dry cycle. The other night a guy next to me asked what I've been doing the last few years. I thought a minute. Then I just said, 'Skip it.' "

Last July she had fired her lawyer, Marian Rosen; but then in November Marian sued her for damages. Kim's answer accused Marian of "incompetence" and "gross negligence," and Kim immediately countersued for $6 million with charges of fraud, deceit, theft, and legal malpractice on Marian's part. She claimed that Marian had shortstopped her money from the Jack Olsen book and forged Kim's endorsement on $14,000 worth of checks. Marian denied it all. Olsen, Kim said, was also refusing to pay her. She had yet to make a dime out of the entire affair. "And if anyone deserves to," she asked, "shouldn't it be me?"

On the afternoon of April 7, Kim followed Michael Ray, Sr. ("Only if he sent it by Western Union," he said again, on cue) to the witness stand. It was the first time that the two chief women in David West's adult life had ever confronted each other. David wasn't there to see it happen. Cindy glared furiously. Kim, however, seemed barely interested in the woman whom she had once so passionately pursued. Kim's attention, like a child's, focused on the jury, and she kept smiling winsomely at them after she had taken the oath. She seemed to be trying to make friends. Pete Justin said later, "It took about one minute flat for two of the jurors in the front row to fall in love with her."

Fortunately for Kim, her credibility and past indiscretions were not at issue in this trial; she was there because Rusty needed her in order to get the tapes into evidence. Like Pete Justin, he understood that the prior consistent testimony was key to making David believable. He argued to Judge Azios that although defense counsel during cross-examination had made a staunch effort not to overtly impeach David's credibility as a witness, "you'd have to be a man from Mars not to realize that Mr. Justin asked a number of questions in such a way as to *imply* that David was lying, and therefore prior consistent testimony is admissible." Pete Justin in turn argued that as regards Cindy the tapes were nothing but hearsay.

The judge came down on Rusty's side; the tapes were in.

Officer Raymond White trundled out the three TV sets, and yet another jury and elbow-to-elbow roomful of spectators were treated to yet another showing, in flickering blue-and-white, of "Body and Fuckin' Soul."

Rusty was taking a calculated risk. Now Justin would recall David and try to portray him as a liar, a villain, a murderer, a psychopath. David would have to suffer the assault like a leaky craft in foul weather.

But not until another storm first buffeted the courtroom.

On April 8, the day the tapes were played, the relationship between defense attorney and client reached a crisis. With the jury out for their midmorning break, and Brenda about to abandon the stenograph, Cindy rose to her feet and demanded to make a statement. In a low and strident tone she objected to the introduction into evidence of the tapes; she wanted the court to know that "both the attorneys' arguments were incompetent and wrong." She had ordered Mr. Justin to discredit Kim Paris as a witness on the grounds that Ms. Paris was not a licensed detective at the time the tapes were made with David West.

"Mr. Justin," Cindy said angrily, "refused to follow my instructions."

She sat down. Justin kept his temper close-hauled, but after lunch, just before the jury returned, Cindy hissed once more in his ear.

He leaped to his feet. "Your Honor, this time *I* want to go on the record. Since this trial's begun, my client has been ninety-five percent uncooperative. On almost a daily basis, at least ten to fifteen times, I've been threatened with malpractice, with a lawsuit, and of being in cahoots with Rusty Hardin. She just did it again. I want her to go on the record right now with her complaints."

Cindy obliged. She growled, "My attorney has refused to speak to me or my husband since the trial started."

Pete cried in her face, "How many times have I spoken to you on the telephone?"

"Only for a minute or two," Cindy said.

"If it didn't last more than a minute," Pete snarled, "that's because you screamed and hung up!"

Judge Azios began to look embarrassed. He asked for order.

"I don't want to comment any further now," Cindy said, looking the judge straight in the eye, "but that doesn't mean I don't have any more complaints. And if I do sue him, it will be with another judge. You can run this trial in *your* unorthodox way, but I'll sue him in an orthodox court."

No one thought she meant a synagogue.

Pete Justin said, "Your Honor, now I want to call on her husband, Mr. Talal Makhlouf." He turned to the rows of spectators. "Mr. Makhlouf, isn't it true that you've urged your wife to sue me?"

Makhlouf, a rosy flush showing through his olive skin, stood up and said, "I don't wish to comment on conversations between me and my wife."

"Any more?" the judge inquired. "If not, let's try to get on with the trial."

That night Cindy called Pete at home, to apologize again, and they spoke for thirty minutes. "A cordial conversation," Pete told me.

489

The next morning she was at him, demanding that he not give credence to Jamie's testimony by cross-examining her.

"I'll do this my way," he said.

She pinched his thigh, hard, then kicked his shins a few times under the table. He kicked her back, once. (During all this supposedly unseen violent game of footsie he was cross-examining Jamie.) Cindy scrawled a note and passed it to him: *"I hate your guts."* Then another note: "I'm sorry."

He whispered something in her ear.

The trial had to be delayed forty-five minutes while Cindy Ray sat on the bench backstage, weeping.

_____

On the counsel table before him Pete Justin had computer printouts of discrepancies between David's testimony in both trials and a recorded statement made to Sgts. Schultz and Motard in the Harris County Jail on December 14, 1985, four days after the guilty plea. That statement had recently been offered to the defense only because a change in the Texas rules of evidence demanded its production; otherwise it would have sat in the dark of the prosecutorial file cabinet forever. And even now Rusty argued—but without success—that it was "work product" and not admissible as evidence.

It was a depressing hunk of dialogue. Here was David last December, purged, a budding turncoat, a murderer crossed over to the side of the angels and bearing aloft the banner of societal retribution, but still begging to be popular even with the cops he had described to Kim Paris as "petty little sick egomaniac fuckheads." He and Gil Schultz laughed and joked as equals; both were men with a secure future. "I really wanted to kill James," David confided. "Her I didn't feel that strongly about—not as much gut hatred." He showed an even more forgiving attitude toward Maria: "Even that bitch, I didn't want to kill her." Then, after describing Cindy as "a submissive little Oriental housewife," he went on to some intimate details of his relationship with the woman for whom he claimed to have killed two people in cold blood in order to cure her. "Our basic sex life was two or three blow jobs a day from Cindy."

Laughter followed. But at David's request Schultz clicked the tape off . . . then on again.

David took the stand again in this fourth week, looking pale and gray and tough, swaggering a little as he walked to the witness chair, and Pete Justin kept him there for nearly a day. Both David's voice and Rusty's voice rose in anger and protest. Pete whacked away.

"And you smacked those kids, didn't you, even before you knew Cindy? . . . "

"And you had no use for Maria and called her a whore, isn't that right? . . . "

"Who is Paul Whitfield? Did you ever tell Paul Whitfield that you killed two people with a gun you got from Wickie Weinstein? Did you ever tell him about Cindy being involved in the murder? You didn't bring Cindy in then, did you? You left that out because back then you had no need to involve her to save your neck, isn't that so?"

She was there, David kept saying.

"And didn't you tell Kim Paris that you were Cindy's 'Svengali'? You didn't? Let me read to you from Ms. Paris's notes to her employer. *'[David] knows which buttons to push with Cynthia and I have no doubt, him being as strong as he is, that in their relationship, she was manipulated.'* Oh, now you remember referring to yourself that way? And who was Svengali, David?"

"A magician, and a hypnotist," David said, and those phrases echoed, too.

David looked profoundly unhappy. But Rusty, on redirect, turned it around part way by getting David to admit that in his relationship with Kim it was he who had been manipulated. And so why should it have been different with Cindy?

The murderer as victim. Woman as the perennial evil femme fatale. Explosive stuff that in 1987 could easily backfire. Rusty made a note to touch on that and defuse it in final argument. There were only four women jurors this time, but he couldn't afford to alienate even one of them. He had learned his lesson.

Late that afternoon—the trial was in its fourth week now, threatening to run even longer than its June 1986 forerunner—Pete Justin met with Allen Isbell at the Old Cotton Exchange Building, and for two hours they discussed various lines of argument and defense testimony. In particular: Should Cindy take the stand?

Pete's original idea was that if the tapes got into evidence, then she was in trouble—and in that case, yes, she should testify. But now neither he nor Allen thought it wise. She would say, "I wasn't there," but Rusty would keep at her for days, and she might shatter like heated glass. And she wouldn't be able to deal forthrightly with the incest question, and would effectively portray herself as having lied to half a dozen former witnesses. In the process she would manage to insult everyone in the courtroom, including the jury. She *hated* this jury.

"The bottom line," Pete said, "is that I don't think the jury is going to believe that a former marine, a bright guy like David West, even if he's fundamentally cracked, is going to take someone he considers 'a human mess' along with him on a dead-of-night assassination of a man who keeps a shotgun next to his bed. Would it make any sense?"

"To know her," Allen said, "is not to take her with you."

"I think we're headed for another hung jury."

"It may well be that you can't ever get twelve men and women who'll agree on this case," Allen said. "If this jury hangs up, too, what will you do?"

He meant that Pete, as the attorney-of-record, would require the court's permission to be excused from his obligation to defend Cindy in yet a third trial.

Pete massaged his sore shins. "I'd have to decide which was my most disposable body part," he said, "and show the stump to the judge, and beg for mercy."

It was Gwen Sampson's turn to testify.

Rusty made his decision that morning in front of his shaving mirror. Open up the question of duress, or leave it to the defense to do it?

I have to risk it—gamble on being drawn and quartered if I lose a second time.

He still argued back and forth with himself. If Sheryl Henderson hadn't been a tainted juror, *I would have won that first trial.* The blunder hadn't really been with Gwen, it had been in voir dire. This time he'd made sure there was no Sheryl Henderson on the jury; therefore it followed that if he presented the case in exactly the same way, he would win.

He *had* to win. Two hung juries in a row, and the state inevitably backed down. The district attorney would not want to look foolish a third time. That kind of failure stained any political career. You were always remembered for it. As for the prosecutor: *"Rusty Hardin? Oh, sure, the one who could never convict that woman who murdered her parents."*

And so, on the Thursday afternoon of April 9, midway through direct examination, Rusty elicited exactly the same response from Gwen Sampson—

"Cindy told me that Salino had held a gun to her head, and that if she didn't stay there with him he'd have killed her, too."

Not a blunder this time, he hoped. A devilish necessity.

42

What does a jury believe? What have they heard? A trial lawyer is never sure. His knowledge of a case is long term and encyclopedic. He knows too many facts and his mind is crowded with too many statements that have never been placed into evidence. Truth, in a trial, is limited to what the law can bear.

In the warm noon of April 10, Pete Justin sat on a wooden bench in a shaded little park near the courthouse, trying to focus on what the jury knew as opposed to what *he* knew. Munching on a ham and cheese sandwich, he made his final decision about Cindy. She would not testify.

He had planned to put Cecilia West on, too, and then late yesterday afternoon she had told him a tale. In the spring of 1985, after Cindy had been no-billed by the grand jury, a Korean man, a friend of Cindy's, came by the West house one day with Cindy in tow: a mess, her hair so greasy and knotted that later Cecilia had to cut half of it off, and so smelly that Cecilia guessed she hadn't bathed in a month. She was bloated with fat, and drunk. She sagged out of the car and laid down like a hippopotamus in a puddle of water in the street.

Cecilia and the young Korean half-dragged, half-carried her into the West house, and then Cindy, in a sudden rage, leaped up and hit Cecilia —in the dusty darkness knocked her down to the carpet, nearly knocked her out.

How many other such tales did Cecilia have to tell? After hearing that one, Pete decided not to have her testify either.

That Friday afternoon he put on Steve Simmons, Cindy's former civil lawyer, who offered evidence that Cindy's 1984 lawsuit to remove J. W. Campbell as administrator of the estate was not motivated by greed and, indeed, had some legal merit.

On Monday morning he put Rick Brass on in order to have the jury study Rick's color photographs, taken last June, of the grounds at 8901 Memorial. They seemed to prove even more decisively that Maria, peering from her garage apartment through the junglelike summer foliage, could not possibly have seen Cindy checking the windows of either the den or the boys' room.

Then Pete Justin rested his case.

On Tuesday morning, April 14, Judge Azios charged the jury. To my surprise, Jo Ann Lee rose to open for the state. She had done nothing before except take notes. I didn't understand what Rusty was trying to do. Maybe create suspense, I thought, or appeal subtly to the black and the female jurors. Was it a sign of supreme confidence or ongoing uncertainty?

Jo Ann's delivery was crisp. She moved immediately into the arena on the duress issue, setting forth an ingenious and complex argument which no one quite grasped. There had been no duress. How could there be? Cindy said to Gwen that Salino had forced her to "be there." Not to participate, just *be there.* Therefore, since mere physical presence at the scene of a crime did not rise to the level of culpable criminal participation, duress could not be considered.

Cute, I thought. But foggy and off-line, and the jury would see through it.

As for David West: "The state will never contend that he's other than a cold-blooded killer, but no law says that a killer is also a liar. Don't get bogged down in the little-bitty things, the discrepancies in his story. He is, above all, *consistent.*"

She sat down. She had served up an appetizer, and the main courses were yet to come.

Pete Justin unfolded to his feet. He stood close to the jury, looking young, vulnerable, and intense.

"This," he said, "will probably be the most important decision you'll make for the rest of your life. You have to live forever with what you do today. The question you have to ask yourself is: Has Mr. Hardin presented enough evidence—enough *credible* evidence—to reach that magic spot where you're convinced beyond a reasonable doubt? For God's sake, *don't hold him to a lesser burden!"*

He moved inevitably to what he and just about everyone else had always seen and still saw as the major issue in the case: the character and integrity of David West. No physical evidence, he stressed, tied Cindy to the murders, only David's word—"the word of a man who saved his life by testifying against an old girlfriend." And what kind of a man was that? How could they possibly know? They hadn't seen the real David here in the courtroom. This fellow in the blue suit? No, no. That was an impostor! You had to imagine him in a mask and beard, as eight-year-old Michael saw him. You had to imagine him showing off to Jamie, firing a pistol in his own living room. You had to imagine him sleeping in a hammock in his bedroom.

"Think of it! If you met David in a cafeteria, or your daughter brought him home, *you wouldn't know!* You'd probably think ... what a nice fellow, what a bright young man. You can't put yourself in his mind. He's quick, he's clever, he's no dummy. That's what's so horrifying."

You can't believe him, Pete kept saying, because there's no way you can understand what makes such a mind tick, and the normal patterns of behavior do not include it. The normal standards of judgment are off base—"we're dealing with a sick mind." Only a sick mind could have killed the Campbells as David West did. A sick mind such as his has no conscience, no awareness of truth and falsity.

"Do you remember how David slipped up about turning on the light? I asked him, 'You turned the light on, walked to the foot of the bed, and blew Mr. Campbell away, right?' And he said, 'Yes.' That wasn't a slip-up! That was the truth! All he's got to do in his whole story to involve Cindy is change 'I' to 'we'! And that's what he did! If he's that quick to embellish all this stuff to Kim Paris, he's quick enough to make up Cindy's involvement. And he did! He said on the tapes, *I thought of everything.*'

"Think," Pete said, more slowly, "how David West would have been portrayed by Rusty Hardin in the capital case that never came to trial because they cut their deal. Imagine: *'A violent and vicious man . . . the prime mover in the murders . . . and a man, ladies and gentlemen of the jury, who you certainly can't trust.'* And you would probably believe it, as you may now believe that you *can* trust David—because Rusty Hardin could sell ice to Eskimos."

Rusty winced. Still top gun. Still they wanted to drill a hole between his eyes. And if he lost this one, they would have succeeded.

Pete Justin talked about Maria's hindsight in recalling that she'd seen Cindy checking the windows. "The maid didn't make that up herself. The maid got that from somebody. Ask yourselves who."

On Jamie: "She testified that Cindy told her she'd murder her father and leave a man's glove. She didn't seem to remember that detail in June at the last trial. Why not? Because it's a flat-out fabrication!"

On Paul Whitfield: "David somehow 'forgot' to tell him that Cindy had been involved in the murders. Ask yourselves why."

On the tapes: "They're horrifying, but it's always Kim Paris pressuring David to talk about Cindy."

He demanded to the jury: "Do we have *one* unbiased witness? *One* who doesn't have a cross to bear against Cindy?"

On the dovetailing alibi statement: "How long do you think it would take David West to commit these murders? In 3 A.M. traffic, even keeping within the speed limit—less than fifteen minutes to drive there, another ten or fifteen minutes to do it, and fifteen minutes back. Cindy's in bed, asleep, when all this happens. She wakes up. He's right there.

How does she know where he's been, what he's done? *His* alibi statement is a lie. *Her* alibi statement tells the truth!"

He finished with a plea for not guilty, and sat down.

———————

At three o'clock in the afternoon Rusty walked to a podium that had been placed to the left of Cindy Ray. Pete Justin, for this solemn occasion, had worn a dark blue suit and dark tie. Rusty, however, wore ice-blue seersucker, and it wasn't a particularly hot day.

Last July he had failed himself, the Campbell family, and the system he loved. Now . . .

———————

Rusty began quietly.

"I think Jo Ann said it all. I'm tempted to add no more. But if there's one thing that might have slipped by you, it's our responsibility to point it out to you . . . so let us proceed.

"I think there's a fundamental misunderstanding as to the purpose of the State of Texas. We are not presenting David West as an altar boy. We are not saying, 'Look, here's a poor misunderstood youth who fell victim to the wiles of a scheming woman.' I am not speaking of a femme fatale situation, where the woman leads the man on. Wrong. I'm talking about what I would suggest to you is the perennial—and thank God, very rare—bad seed. And it is a bad seed that sowed with men and women, with people who are naive and people who are sophisticated. And it is a bad seed that sowed regardless of the harm she did to others, for she armed the weapon and cocked the hammer that sent David West to kill her own parents.

"Even as you realize our burden is only to prove guilt beyond a reasonable doubt, every so often a fact situation comes along which leaves you with *no* doubt. I think after you were exposed to David West for all that time, there is no doubt in your mind as to what happened. Why, through the many witnesses, did we talk about Cynthia Campbell Ray and the stories she told concerning sexual advancement by others? Why did we talk about the different voices, the different personalities? Because you don't understand her, or what she did, or why she's guilty of murder, unless you look at that full picture. If an author wrote a book about her, portraying her as I suggest the evidence has shown her, *you wouldn't believe it!* You'd treat it as a work of fiction. . . .

"You might ask: 'Can a person do what she did, responding as bi-

496

zarrely as she did under such circumstances, and still be sane?' Do you remember in jury selection that I pointed out how sanity or insanity was not an issue in this case? Insanity is what's called in law 'an affirmative defense,' just like duress, and it has not been presented. So no matter how bizarre you may think her conduct is, insanity is not in the charge, and you would be violating your oath as jurors if you even discussed it."

He stood only a foot away from Cindy during all this, glancing at her now and then, as if daring a reaction. But she looked completely blank, nearly catatonic.

So far Rusy had been shoring up against a possible nightmare repetition of what had happened in the first trial. He was aware how poor his final argument had been back then in July. The personal events of that trial had rattled him, put him on the defensive. Not this time.

This time he didn't snipe at the defense lawyer. This time he avoided the trap of concentrating on Cindy's relationship with her parents, and he didn't romp and stomp in protest that the Campbell family had been blasphemed. He didn't counterattack by raging at Cindy's life style. Instead, coolly, logically, and inexorably, like the good Indian Guide that he was on weekends with his sons, he set out to hack a path through the tangled undergrowth of the evidence.

David West, he said, never understood the nature of the woman who was manipulating him—Rusty, with a wave of his hand, indicated the immobile Cindy—"because then he would have to face the cold and utter darkness of what he did. He recognizes now that by society's standards what he did was wrong, and he shouldn't have done it. And he feels bad about it, he says. But David West, to truly live with himself, will probably never be able to concede just *how* horrible it was. The day he faces, in that solitary confinement cell or in the Texas Department of Corrections, that she talked him into killing those people *for something that didn't even happen,* he will never be able to live with himself.

"I'm not going to tell you what to believe and what not to believe. That's your job. The law says this: If you believe David West as to this crime, as to how he did it, and as to her involvement in either aiding or encouraging him, then—since he is an accomplice-witness—you can only say she's guilty if there's any other evidence in this case that tends to connect her with the crime."

And there *was* other evidence.

First, Maria saw her at the window.

(Here Rusty couldn't resist; he glared at Pete Justin and said, "By the way, it is not *'the maid.' 'The maid'* has a name, like everyone else, and her name is Maria.")

Then: the crime occurs on June 19, 1982. A glove is left. No robbery, no burglary, no theft. Apparent entry through the window around 3:30 in the morning. "At the time, that's all the police know. Everything else that they found out in this case is through David West or through corroborating evidence. Where *he*"—indicating Justin—"keeps missing the boat is on the sequence of events. On June 19, 1982, do we have any idea that they wore masks or gloves? No. He wants physical evidence, but they made sure there *was* no physical evidence. Surely he doesn't mean to suggest that they benefit from the cunning of their own crime!

"When is the first time we hear anything about their wearing gloves? From Gwen Sampson. Plug that into your mind, and remember it, because it's corroborated by the fact that a glove was found inside the front door, and it will be further corroborated later when David West says, 'Cindy dropped one of her gloves.'"

Rusty paused reflectively. He was a logical juggernaut, but he was also, and always, an imaginative thinker, and you could see that something troubled him. Aloud, he asked, "Why did she do that? That is a true mystery. No one knows. We will all go to our graves never knowing why she left a glove."

He seemed then to glance at me. We had discussed it often enough. And he smiled, almost apologetically, before he went on.

"But on June 19, 1982, do the police know they wore masks? No. We find that out first from Gwen Sampson, when Cindy tells her that she and Salino covered their faces. And then David corroborates it. On June 19, 1982, do we know they dressed like men? No. Again we find that out from Gwen, and David later corroborates.

"Why was it important to hear Jamie as a witness? Because Cindy tells Jamie the same thing she tells Gwen Sampson, long before we ever knew these details: 'I think I should kill Daddy, and I know how I'd do it. Dress up like a man, wear heavy boots, leave footprints around a window, and it would look like a man did it.'

"Who made the plans? Who figured out the logistics? We know what she told Jamie. And she led David to the right window. He starts to go to the wrong window, but she pulls him away. Only *she* would know which was the safe den window and which was the unsafe boys' window.

"The way she went after the inheritance is also a form of corroboration. We don't have to prove why she did it, but I suggest to you the evidence shows complicated motives, one of which was the estate. Two days after the murders, she's there, saying to her sisters, 'You're not going to tell me what to do with my money!'

"Her conduct after the death, at the funeral, in the Campbell home, was exactly how David told Kim Paris that Cindy had agreed and rehearsed to act.

"Years later, David West makes the mistake of talking to Kim Paris, and she tapes him. On February 20 and 21, 1985, did David have any way to know what Gwen Sampson told the police? No, he did not. Does he have any way of knowing that the two homicide detectives who talked to Gwen and heard her quote Cindy about 'Salino' who would *'make her free,'* are the same two who are outside in a van listening to him tell Kim Paris that he killed Cindy's parents *'to make her free?'* No."

Rusty then quoted, in its entirety, David's long uninterrupted monologue on the first night of the confession to Kim, beginning with, "Look, the deal was she was going down the fuckin' drain," and ending with, "She fuckin' begged me to do it, and I wanted to do it, frankly. And she also offered me a lot of fuckin' money. . . . And the thing was that I made her stand there with me when I did it." It took Rusty several minutes, and he gave it a good reading.*

"That," said Rusty, "was before he'd ever heard about the police, before he knew Rusty Hardin from Adam. He implicates Cindy without Kim's prodding him at all. *He's telling Kim Paris, two years ago, exactly what he told you in this courtroom!*

"You should believe David," Rusty said, "because you've had a chance to listen to him. And if you believe him, you go to corroboration, which I've just laid out for you. The law tells us that only *one* piece of corroboration is necessary, not all of them. You don't have to buy the package. Just one item."

As for the defense crying that the December deal for a life sentence influenced David's testimony, the existence of the tapes destroyed that argument. "And I'd make the deal anytime," Rusty said, "because to watch David West get the death penalty, while *she* walks free, would be about as unfair as I can imagine. If she did not hate her parents, if she did not want their money, if she did not realize she couldn't live on her own once she could no longer leech and suck off the work and health of her parents—then David West, no matter how skewered his view of mankind, without her aid and her solicitation and encouragement would not have gone out and killed them. So I will not apologize to you for making a deal with him."

For the first time in any of the trials Rusty touched on what he called David's "Charles Bronson *Death Wish* mentality." He hesitated—for these were hazardous waters—then set sail. "What kind of guy is David, really? I don't know. Did you see, in this courtroom, even under oath, how anxious he was to please? That's tragic. That's sad, when anyone wants acceptance so badly. . . . "

Was the prosecutor about to fetch up on a reef and sink both himself

---

* The reader may want to look again at David's speech, which is on pages 214–15.

and the State of Texas? Would the jury realize that David's desire to please might transpose into a need to lie?

But brilliantly, and finally, Rusty tacked on by. "Only the truly evil, only the truly manipulative, only the truly wicked and calculating, zero in on such a personality."

He sat down.

The jury left to deliberate at 4:25 P.M. Remembering what had happened the last time, Judge Azios told them if a verdict hadn't been reached in two hours he would make plans to remove them to a hotel. "Push the buzzer once if you need anything, twice if you've reached a verdict."

That was the opposite from the jury deliberation over the Fourth of July weekend last summer. The judge thought it might change his luck.

The lawyers paced the courtroom. The reporters smoked in the hallway. Jo Ann Lee said, "They look like a serious and thoughtful jury. I'm confident that they'll find her guilty, but I don't think they'll do it this evening."

In one hour and forty-five minutes, at 6:10 P.M. on April 13, 1987, the jury marched out.

I could feel the beating of my heart as the jury foreman handed the verdict to Bettie Conway.

In a clear voice she announced that this jury had found Cynthia Campbell Ray guilty of murdering her parents nearly five years ago.

I let out a long breath. Pete Justin's face seemed to age. Rusty and Jo Ann Lee exchanged quick arm-hugs of triumph.

Cindy turned distinctly pale. Tears rolled down her face from suddenly red-rimmed eyes, but she said not a word.

The youngest woman juror, Kimberley Jones, began to cry. Then another juror—Martha Weems, the homemaker—bowed her head and sobbed. The judge told the jury that they would hear argument in the punishment phase at ten o'clock the following morning. Immediately thereafter, they would begin deliberation.

To the reporters and TV cameras gathered outside the courtroom, Pete Justin said, gloomily and bitterly, "Punishment in this case is a prosecutor's wet dream." But the jury could still hang up in the punishment phase. He knew that. Two of them had cried.

If they cried at home, tonight, there was hope.

43

The next morning, April 14, while behind him a raw-eyed Cindy blew her nose in wads of pink tissue, Pete Justin reminded the jury that Rusty had told them they could award her as little as five years of probation. He begged them, even if they felt they had to send her to prison, not to destroy the rest of her life.

Then Rusty rose again. He wore a tan summer suit and a striped tie, like an older Southern lawyer in a hot August courtroom with the fans turning. This air-conditioned courtroom was packed, more than thirty standees squeezed against the walls. They formed a true audience. He had triumphed so far, but it would be a hollow triumph if he didn't now follow through. He believed with an overwhelming, almost physically visible conviction, that the woman who sat in the defendant's chair deserved the most extreme punishment the law would allow. Had it been a capital murder charge, he would have argued with passion for the death penalty.

He said quietly, "I've had to live with this case for two years, and I want to get some things off my chest. It's a clean table now . . . no more files in front of the lawyers, no more boxes full of testimony and interviews. Now you talk about: what do we do with a young woman who decides to have her parents killed?

"Let's look first at the crime. If we're not careful, we can forget about the horror of what happened. He hesitated a moment. "Let's talk about the victims. Have you forgotten them? Maybe you have."

Deliberately he walked to the table that held the cardboard carton full of labeled evidence. He took a long time hunting through it, and then he extracted a stack of eight-by-ten color photographs. Kimberley Jones in the first row of the jury box looked a little nauseated, and tears began to form again in Martha Weems's eyes.

Not only Rusty's timing, but his concept, were both flawless. Like any skilled dramatist he understood the power of imagination. He looked up deliberately, and then into the jury box, and then he shook his head.

"No, not *those*. I'm not going to wave bloody pictures in front of you.

501

I think that's offensive," he said softly. "I think you remember the blood and the gore. I want you to look at *these.*"

He held aloft a photograph of James Campbell, smiling, alive, with his grandson Michael; and then a photograph of a laughing Virginia Campbell, with young Matthew. "I want you to look at a picture of a fifty-year-old woman who will never have a chance to be a grandmother again."

Rusty said, "Think of the Campbells in their late forties, with their own children gone. They're free to live as they please. And what happens to these two boys is more important to them than that freedom. They take them on in a second life."

He chronicled the Campbells' life with their third daughter. She runs away. What do they do? They cry. They hunt for her and find her. She runs away again. They find her again. "It's the nightmare all of us as parents have—a child we can't get through to. Be somebody, Cindy. Go to school. Get involved. But she runs away again. She marries a total stranger. She tells him her father's in a mental hospital and that her mother, who locks her up in closets, is living with another man who tried to sexually abuse her when she was a child. Nevertheless, her father, miraculously recovered, helps the young couple and invites them into his home, where they stay while the husband, down on his luck, looks for a job. Then they split up. She grows fat and she can't, or won't, take a job. She looks for someone else to take care of her.

"It's David West she meets. With one of the great classic male chauvinist approaches, he decides to 'make her over.' And first she convinces him he's succeeded, and then two years later she convinces him that he's failed and *they're* responsible . . . and he's got to kill them. I think one of the most chilling things I've ever heard, and ever expect to hear, is David's description of how Cindy convinced him to do it."

Playing the part of Cindy, Rusty leaned up against an imaginary David and whispered, *"Remember what he did to me? Remember how she locked me in the closet. . .?"*

He shook his head in grief at the thought of this monstrous deceit and the act that it had bred.

"This woman who called him Pigface, who says he's like a dog and you can train him to do what you want! The first night, they make love. David West thinks he's in charge. *She* knows who's in charge."

Rusty paused, and his tone became even more pained. If he could have, he would have cried, and bled.

"Think about what happened then. Think about planning the murder. Think about practicing walking heel-to-toe so you don't make noise in the driveway. Think about going to bed the night before, saying to

502

yourself, 'Tomorrow I'm going to kill my mother and father.' Think about the mind that goes about setting up the alibi, what you're going to say to the police afterward. Think about practicing an alibi for your own parents' murder! *Think about the mind that allows that to continue.*

"Then that evening they drive to the house. He waits in the car, and she goes inside. Think about going into the house where your children are—where they're being taken care of by their grandparents, because you can't or don't want to care for them—for the sole purpose of opening a window so that you and your boyfriend can enter in a few hours and murder those grandparents, who are also your parents. *Think about borrowing ten dollars from your mother.* Think about the kind of mind and heart that could ask her mother for money, knowing that within hours she'll be shot dead. *The heart and mind that could do that should never be unloosed on society again!* Doesn't that crime go to the very heart of what we are as human beings?"

A few jurors nodded. So did I.

"Think about her putting on the clothes and the mask. Think about, as she's getting ready to leave, David West turns to her and says, 'This is it. This is your last chance. *Are you sure this is what you want to do?*' And she nods. *Yes.*

"Think about being in the house. The house you came home to as a schoolgirl. The house you ate suppers and breakfasts in. I'm taking a man up to the room I grew up in as a child, to kill my parents, while they're sleeping. Do I stop? Do I say, 'Wait a minute.' No. What do I do if I'm Cynthia Campbell Ray? I open the door. Think about the children being there. Think about David having asked her, 'What effect do you think this will have on the children?' And she said, 'They're young—they'll get over it.'

"Do you believe," Rusty asked us, "that those children will *ever* get over what they're about to experience on the night of June 19, 1982?"

No, I don't.

"David West says, 'Hit it.' She flips the light switch, runs down the stairs. She must not have run too soon because she told Gwen Sampson, 'In my mind I saw my mother's body jump.' Do you remember David's description of how, with the first shot, Virginia Campbell's body convulsed?"

Rusty cried, "She *saw* her mother's body convulse!"

Behind him, the bones of Cindy's face pressed against her flesh. Her teeth were tightly clamped. Her eyes were half-shut, but they glittered with tears.

The rest of us in the courtroom barely breathed. Rusty had us. We were there.

And then: "David keeps firing, finishing the job. He runs from the room. He finds Cindy, and they drive away. The boys jump up. There's blood streaming down their grandparents' faces. They run to Maria."

Rusty crossed the courtroom swiftly to confront the defendant. He screamed shrilly into her face: *"Maria, Maria! Blood everywhere! Blood is everywhere! Mama and Daddy are dead! Maria!"*

He glared down at a white-faced Cindy.

" 'They're young,' " he said quietly. " 'They'll get over it.' "

He took a step back, as if afraid of contamination.

"Cynthia Campbell Ray that night took away the only parents those boys ever had. She took away, probably for life, those two little boys' sense of security. She took away her sisters' parents."

Rusty sighed. "I guess you could say, as David does, 'Hey, she's so bizarre, she's so screwed up—there's got to be something wrong! Something had to be there in her past to account for this.' " He shook his head. "Can't we ever reach a stage in this society where we can say, 'Look, no matter how hard or uncharitable it is to conclude, there are some people who should not be among us?' Perhaps it flies in the face of your religious or moral training, but aren't there just some people whom we don't have the right to take a chance on? Do we have to conclude, because she's got all these problems, that it's someone else's fault? That's what David West concluded: that because she was so bizarre, it had to be her parents' fault. *Why does it have to be that way?* You're not talking about a poor deprived child! She had every chance she wanted! She is a child who, for whatever reason, early in her life, was different. Sometimes we celebrate difference, sometimes we say it's wonderful to march to a different drummer, to be an individual. But other times it's frightening. It's . . . dangerous.

"You've got to realize this—folks, there are other David Wests out there. Do you really think, after what you've seen in this trial, that she's not capable of arming them? You bet she is. I suggest to you that she only have that opportunity with the people in the Texas Department of Corrections."

He reminded them then that in voir dire, when he'd asked if they could give a sentence of life in a proper case, they had all said, "Yes," and many had said, "No problem."

"If there was ever a case on God's green earth that cried out for a punishment of life in prison, this is it. I can't imagine, other than a mass murderer, anybody that impacted so many lives with so much horror, so much damage. Is it fair to give her less than David West? He committed a cold murder, no question about it. But David West would never have

504

done it if she hadn't convinced him. And he would never have done it even if going up the stairs she had said, 'Stop, stop! It is my family's home! *No!*' If she had done that, this crime would never have happened.

"And after that, she is the one person who kept her mouth shut. She spent the next three years trying to get the money." A weary, saddened Rusty said: "Do you want to look into the heart of Cynthia Campbell Ray? Look into the heart of a woman, who after she killed her parents, carted out the TV and the VCR with their blood on it. That's Cynthia Campbell Ray."

As in the last trial, he turned to her and said, "Shame on you." And said it twice more, and then he was finished.

––––––––––

After that, what could the jury do? After four hours of deliberation, they gave her a life sentence. Had I been a juror, I think I would have done the same.

Cindy wept without a sound.

Rusty squeezed Jo Ann Lee's arm, then strode back into the pews of his congregation, where he and Betty Ann Hinds embraced.

––––––––––

Was it really over? I was not a juror—thank God. I knew things that, through no fault of theirs, they did not know. There was no question that at some point I hadn't asked of myself and others, but the answers were still shrouded in shadows.

One question in particular tainted the air. Even in final argument Rusty had said, "We will all go to our graves never knowing why she left a glove."

Not good enough, I thought. The question of the glove was haunting. Something there suggested a path of thought no one had yet trod.

Judge Azios, a few hours after the verdict, standing in the lobby of the courthouse shorn of his black robes, looked slightly forlorn, alone, cheated.

He said to me, "Is that it? You're not just going, are you? Is that the way it ends?"

"I don't know, A. D."

I stayed in Houston a while longer, accepting the onset of the coming summer heat. In late April the temperature moved up into the nineties. I asked, I prodded, I made a pest of myself. I found it hard to let go. But I wasn't alone in that; everyone connected with the trials, with the exception of the Campbell sisters, seemed to have a need to share their abiding uncertainties, to talk over icy vodka tonics and through packs of cigarettes about David West, Cindy Ray, the Campbells, and life in the house on Memorial: to analyze, to speculate, to wonder about the complex human condition and the frailty of knowledge.

It was as if, while everyone accepted the verdict, and the rough justice of it, they didn't really believe that they knew the truth. There are levels of truth. We had only penetrated the skin.

The exception to disbelief and doubt was Rusty Hardin. He closed the book. The jury had declared her guilty. That's what juries were for. The system had worked. David . . . well, yes, there were things about his psyche we would never quite grasp. James and Virginia Campbell . . . who knew? Nobody was perfect. Let them rest in peace, blasphemed no more. Cindy? There had been no incest. She was trash, and evil. In final argument Rusty felt he had explained it all.

And yet even Rusty sensed that truth was far more elusive than he could accept. No one tells the pure truth, because in human matters there is only a stormy confusion of acceptable perception, bolstering, accusation, and deep denial, the mix hardening with time into what we call memory. Let anyone who doubts this read a journal kept years ago and compare it with the way that past is now remembered. Not that the journal will be free of deception—but it will be frighteningly different from memory.

And so . . .

A week after the trial I drove out I-10 to a hot, dusty part of East Texas that I didn't know, past the Port of Houston and Jacinto City to near a place called Channelview. I picked up Michael Ray, Sr. in front of a Mobil station on the access road, for he didn't want me to see where he lived.

I was surprised that he had agreed to meet with me. On the last day of his testimony I had given him my telephone number. He had called three times until he reached me; he must have needed badly to unburden. He was living with his second wife, Wanda, and her eight children. His telephone had just been cut off, he told me. His back was hurting— he couldn't lift more than twenty pounds. He was out of work.

We passed up Denny's and Burger King and went to a restaurant called Champs, on the edge of the freeway, to hear his version of the truth. But it was not the same version he had told in either of the two trials. On the witness stand, speaking of Jim Campbell, he had said: "He treated me with respect. He was nice. He was always a gentleman."

Ray didn't seem at all embarrassed now to let me know that he had lied.

He was a simple man, not bright or quick. From the beginning—he

506

said to me—to the point where it became an obsession, Jim Campbell had schemed to wrest his two children from him and Cindy. "He told Cindy that if she'd divorce me and live with the children there at Memorial, he would send her to art school, and give her anything she wanted. It was *him* who told her I was fooling around with another woman, and that wasn't true. He wanted my children for his own because he had no sons. He was a sneaky bastard. He was always smiling to your face but always scheming behind your back. That lawyer Isbell at the first trial asked me if I'd told Mr. Campbell that for $5,000 I'd sign the adoption papers, and I said no. The truth was that without my asking, James Campbell offered me $10,000 if I'd sign. He said, "I'll give you $5,000 for each kid." And I said, 'No, and you get out of here.' But he bribed Cindy, and he got them."

Ray only toyed with his food. He said, "Around the time I wouldn't sign the adoption papers, I got shot at twice in the dark, two different times, and it was in two different parts of Texas. It wasn't no accident. Who had reason to do that? Later when me and my wife Wanda split up for a while, J. W. Campbell was in touch with her about something, and he told her that his brother James had once hired a private detective to follow me. That guy's in jail now for attempted murder. So you can put two and two together, if you like."

Why, I asked, had he said none of this from the witness stand?

"I was grateful to James and Mrs. Campbell for taking care of my sons all those years. I made up my mind I wasn't going to do anything to hurt their memory."

But a few minutes later another reason popped out: he said that J. W. Campbell had promised him visitation rights to his two lost sons, once the trial was over.

"And have you seen them?"

"Every time I call J. W. he says they're out, or away for the weekend, or he's busy and could I call back later. And I do, and then he's not there. It don't seem fair. . . . "

No, it didn't.

Who else, I wondered, had lied, or shaded their testimony to suit their needs?

"You've hardly eaten," I said. His cheeseburger and french fries had grown cold on the plate.

"When I think about what happened to my two boys, I don't have no appetite."

I dropped him off by the Mobil station on the access road.

507

Collecting my bet at Tony's, with Pete Justin and his redheaded wife, Lisa, I ate oysters *maison*, a veal chop, and sweet chocolate torte. Pete wore a large diamond ring that he had never worn in court, and a gray silk sport jacket and ice-blue pants. He had lost eleven pounds during the trial, he said, down at the end to 164, which he hadn't weighed since college.

He told me that after the sentencing he and Rusty went back to the jury room to talk to the jurors, to find out what had moved them in their deliberations and what hadn't. Four of the eight male jurors said they hadn't really believed David until the tapes were played.

Rusty smiled. He had gambled and won.

The jury gave Rusty a present of a box of rubber bands, because he played with them so often during trial, and they gave Pete a new double-ended fluorescent marking pen to replace the pink one he must have worn out during the four weeks, checking off each question as he asked it. But the two women jurors were still red-eyed and teary. They asked the lawyers for some reassurance that they had done the right thing.

"Of course you did," Rusty said instantly. Then, when their eyes didn't clear, he realized they were really asking for absolution from Pete as Cindy's representative. They were the hangmen and they hadn't been paid a silver coin. Rusty withdrew.

Pete said to the two women, "You did well. It was a very hard case. You did the right thing. Don't lose one night's sleep over it."

They nodded and slowly began to lose their pallor.

Later in the day, outside the backstage holding cell, the bailiff was ready to handcuff Cindy and lead her downstairs and through the underground tunnel to the jail. Cindy turned to her lawyer, offering him a feeble smile. For more than a year she had only seen her husband through a bulletproof glass partition or at a distance in the courtroom. In her tank at the jail she had been among women whom she feared and distrusted. Without tears, with just an immense mournfulness, she said quietly to Pete, "Could you please give me a hug? No one has hugged me in such a long time."

He quickly clasped her to him. He felt her heart beating against his stomach.

That same evening Cindy called Lisa Justin and apologized for having been difficult, and disrupting their lives.

Lisa said to me in Tony's, "It was true. Pete reacted to that woman in some ways he never reacted to me. I was almost jealous, she could provoke him so."

———

508

Melanie Edgecombe visited David in the jail after the trial. Afterward, cautiously, for he was an old Montrose friend and she felt some loyalty to him even if he was a murderer, she told me part of the conversation.

"David killed the Campbells," Melanie said, "to prove himself to his peers—mostly Wickie. Wickie just kept egging him on. It was a rite of passage for Dave, because he was a flunky in that Urban Animal society. He thought the Campbells were bad people, and that made it easier." She hesitated. "You have to understand that Dave is weak-willed and basically a coward. Those are the people who do all the damage in the world. He didn't have enough self-confidence to do the killings on his own, so he had to get Cindy's approval and drag her along."

"He said that?"

"More or less."

"He sees what he's saying?"

"He sees it, and then again he doesn't see it. Depends on his mood."

"Did he lie under oath?"

"Not consciously, I don't think. Not like Wickie did." She hesitated again. But the trial was over. "You know, Dave was drunk when he did it."

"Drunk?" I was appalled. "How is that possible? How could he do it when he was drunk?"

"How could he do it when he was *sober?*" Melanie replied.

And drag her along . . . Those words stayed with me.

So many people knew different parts of the jigsaw puzzle. One night I met with one who knew a great deal about many things—an anonymous donor to my enlightenment. It was someone I trusted and believed . . . another person with a need to unburden.

"The dropping of the glove still doesn't fit," I said. "Compulsion to confess? Too simple. Because then later, when the cops arrested her, she *would* have confessed—it would have been blessed relief. But she didn't, did she?"

"Her official story was always that she wasn't there."

We would get back to that.

I explained my conclusions about David, that I didn't believe he had killed "to make her free." That was his rationalization, his way to haul a cowardly will to the brink of action. He didn't kill for money either, although I wondered if the lure of it hadn't seduced him more toward the definition of his desire than he could ever admit.

He'd told Wickie that he wanted to "bomb people out, clean up the trash in the neighborhood." In David's disordered mind, as he'd explained to Kim Paris, wasn't Jim Campbell just poor white trash from "some sleazy hick family in Tennessee"?

David, I said, couldn't be an Urban Animal because he didn't know how to skate, but he could do something better than skate, something Mad Military Mike and Wickie hadn't done, although they'd blown off a lot of steam about it. He could kill. He needed to do what the Marine Corps had taught him to do but never had given him the opportunity to do. Bernhard Goetz striking back in the New York subway, Rambo taking on half the North Vietnamese army, and Arnold Schwarzenegger in *Commando* were a few years in the offing, but the lone avenger mentality that would make them so popular was already in the air, a force in the mean inner-city streets. It wasn't retribution for violence to a loved one—David wasn't in love with Cindy in June of 1982. She was just the only woman who'd ever let him stay around, the only one who'd appeased him sexually without the embarrassing demand that he reciprocate by performing.

And the affair was over when he committed the act. You don't kill for a former lover unless you have a distinctly separate need. Rusty said to Pete and the jury after the trial, "I'm sure David would have killed somebody someday. In an argument, in revenge, to help a friend, or in self-defense. The need was in him. He was just waiting for a cause."

David found it easy to think of the Campbells as his cause because of what Cindy had told him they had done to her, but the reason he hated them, I believed, was that they had barred him from their house for paddling their supposedly spoiled grandson's bottom and cursing at their supposedly surly Mexican maid. They had overreacted. They'd had no right.

Assault the bunker.

Amid all his pedantic uncertainty the cutting edge of the psychologist's diagnosis of David West had gone almost unobserved: *"A disordered person—very manipulative, intelligent, and creative. Appears altruistic, but is immature and callous. Lacks empathy—the ability to understand the quality of another's feelings."*

"I got mad," David said. *"I crossed over."*

Mad at what? Nothing Cindy revealed to him in early June of 1982 was new information. David testified in both trials that *she had never specifically told him that either the sexual or physical abuse had begun again.*

The anonymous donor smiled, ordered another margarita from the bar, then turned back to me. "And so you think that the incest really happened?"

510

I nodded. "Running away from home at fifteen, all those tales to friends starting when she was seventeen—that's an abused kid crying out for help. I tend to believe the sisters when they say their mother didn't torture Cindy. So Cindy's apparently irrational hatred of the mother fits the pattern, too. Her parents support her to the age of twenty-six. Why? Because she's manipulative? No—because they feel guilty. Denial, denial. We deny what really eats at us."

"And where do you think Daddy screwed her, that the sisters weren't aware of it?"

It was my turn to smile. "He only used the downstairs room as his private office in those years when all four of his daughters were jammed together in the master bedroom. Why did he do that? In 1982, when the girls were gone from the house, there was an empty bedroom—he didn't use it as an office *then*. Why did he need a private office in his home when Cindy was living there, and none when she was gone?"

"Good."

"Now . . . tell me about the glove."

The anonymous donor sighed at my insistence. "First you have to understand what happened *before* she dropped the glove."

"She showed up on David's doorstep in late May. David took her in. Then she wanted to go back to her parents, but he said, 'No, you should kill them, like I once told you.'

"They talked each other into it. That's how such things happen. One person alone is not a prime mover. It takes two to tango.

"It was on—off—on—off. Cindy can't keep a plan for more than a day. She's so vacillating. You have to bear in mind, though, that her parents hated her. And she hated them. They took her kids from her. Her father wouldn't speak to her anymore, and she had really loved him.

"So David, furious at what's happened to her—and with his own flawed needs, as you pointed out—finally says, 'It's the only way to make you free.' He does all the planning—with Wickie's help, but she didn't know that until later. Checking the windows a full week before the murders, the way Maria tells it? No truth to that. You can't confuse Maria's depth of feeling with her accuracy. Remember, Cindy had a key to both doors."

(That explained something that had always puzzled me—and Lydia Tamez during the first jury trial. If Cindy had checked the windows a week before the murders, and Maria had chastised her for it, why then on the night of June 19 did David still dare to break into the house through one of those same windows? Now I grasped it. Maria had

511

probably seen Cindy walking near the windows—then, when she'd heard they were the point of entry, her mind had made a mighty leap, and she had pointed the accusing finger. Bad Cindy must have been checking them!)

"The inheritance was a factor. But neither one wanted to confront that factor head-on. Rusty was wrong as to Cindy manipulating David. It was the other way round. If you think about it, you'll see that Cindy had never manipulated anybody with any success at all, although she used to try with those different voices. And sex wasn't her weapon—they had a lousy sex life. David admitted that to Gil Schultz after he pled out, and Cindy's story is that what he really liked best was to masturbate while she undressed and laid in front of him, naked.

"David was emotionally weak, but still a lot stronger than she was. When they lived together he used her to buck up his ego. Later he was conned by Kim, but Kim was so purposeful, so much more attractive than Cindy.

"The night of the murders David and Cindy drank an awful lot, and he smoked a joint. He could still function.

"They had prearranged hand signals. Go left, go right. Crouch down. A yank on the elbow meant: abort the mission.

"She changed her mind halfway up the stairs. She tugged at his arm, told him not to do it. He ignored it. He was into what he called his soldier mode. He was turned on.

"She whispered, 'This is insane! I've changed my mind!'—but he wouldn't, or couldn't, stop. 'Too late,' he told her. He waved the gun at her. He went into the bedroom, alone.

"She freaked out, lost control, ran down the stairs—in panic, horror, fright, guilt—in her hysteria tore at her gloves, peeled one off, threw it to the carpet. Ran to the car, huddled on the floor in the back seat. She heard the shots from there.

"She was demented by then—in nightmare shock.

"David's 'slip' during the second trial was the truth. If you remember, he was asked: 'You turned the light on, walked to the foot of the bed, and blew Mr. Campbell away, right?' And he said, 'Yes.' "

(I understood. If the anonymous donor was accurate, this was the most hurtful part of the story for David's psyche—he couldn't face what had happened. So momentarily he told the truth, or forgot to lie: it came to the same thing.)

"He came out to the car on Chatsworth Drive and yelled that he'd kill her too if she opened up her mouth and didn't alibi him the way they'd planned. But he didn't really have to do that. From then on she'd lost it. From then on it was as if someone else had killed them.

"Gwen got her drunk. And Gwen was drunk, too, which accounts for a lot.

512

Gwen said, 'What do you think happened that night?' Cindy said, 'I don't know, but I can imagine. Sometimes it's as if I was right there. You know?' Later Gwen got that all twisted.

"Cindy's filth only started after the murders. After the murders she felt like she was a dirty person. She stopped washing.

"Think about that as a kind of unconscious expiation, an admission. . . ."

David had told Ginger Casey that he had wanted Cindy to go into psychiatric care, "but she was afraid they'd commit her to an institution if she did that," and then said that Cindy didn't deserve severe punishment. Now that tied in and made sense. So did his telling Kim that he was Cindy's "Svengali," and his discomfort on the witness stand when that was quoted to him. And so, for the first and only time, did the glove.

I asked the anonymous donor, "If David or Gene Nettles had told that version of the story to Rusty back in December of 1985, would there have been a deal?"

"No deal."

"In her trial, if Cindy had testified, and if she'd said all that, what would have happened?"

"At worst—if the jury believed her—a light sentence. At best, if David could be broken on the witness stand, probation or acquittal. If one of the parties withdraws from a criminal conspiracy and makes the withdrawal known to the other conspirators, that party is no longer culpable, even if the crime is committed. It's called renunciation. And what she did no longer measures up to the language of the indictment: '. . . intentionally and knowingly cause the death of.' "

"Then, for God's sake, *why didn't she testify to all that?*"

"The question only makes sense if it's applied to a rational person. Look how far she'd gone in the murder plan before she tried to back out. Look how feeble her refusal was. She could have grappled with David, she could have screamed to wake her parents. All she did was tug at his elbow, and then whisper, 'Don't do it,' and then she ran. Not a lot, is it? She'd gone much too far along the path of parricide, and she couldn't bring herself to admit, even to herself—not with any consistency, anyway—that she'd ever agreed to murder her parents or encouraged David to do it. You're talking about an emotionally unstable woman infected to the bone with guilt. She'd wanted him to kill them. But she had to deny that to herself afterward. For the most part, in her mind—don't you see?—she was never there."

Without naming the source, I ran that story by all of Cindy's lawyers, one by one. Barred by the oath of confidentiality between attorney and client, none of them could confirm. But only one denied it, and not with enough warmth to convince me.

On May 5, 1987, still at the Harris County Jail and awaiting transfer to the Huntsville complex, David called Ginger Casey to wish her a happy birthday. He reminded her that his own thirty-first birthday had been the day before. A fresh start, he hoped. He wanted to look ahead, not backward—he said he viewed what had happened as "a disgusting and sordid chapter of my life that I'd rather put behind me." Ginger was a little taken aback by the casual implications of that view.

Toward the end of the call she said, "Dave, there's a funny rumor circulating out on the street, that Cindy wasn't there when you pulled the trigger. That she tried to stop you. That at the top of the stairs she gave you the signal to quit."

For the first time in all their conversations David grew irate. "Why would you even *ask* me something like that? Do you think I'm stupid?"

"No, I don't think you're stupid—"

"It's ridiculous!" he yelled. "Just ridiculous! I'm insulted that you'd think I'd say one thing under oath and then another thing later! What do you want me to do? Get up there now and change my testimony?"

"Calm down," Ginger said.

She realized later that he had never actually denied the story.

A few days later Melanie Edgecombe received a letter from him in a neat, legible handwriting on white lined legal-sized paper. He was expecting to be moved any day to the Huntsville complex, where he would spend at least the next eighteen years.

The letter began, "Hi! How ya doin', cutie?"

And then:

I heard they had to put Cindy in the rubber room for a while because she freaked out. They let her out and she is better now.

You know her lawyers tried to make me look like some kind of fascist paramilitary fanatic, but *you* know I didn't ordinarily act like that. That was Wickie-talk for the benefit of Kimbo the Bimbo. I outgrew that garbage while I was in the Corps. I got tired taking orders from inferior people. Little men with little

514

minds. I was proud to be a Marine but sick & tired of bureaucratic stupidity & death-oriented dogma. There has to be more to life than that. It was all so negative & childish. . . .

I'll never know if Cindy's parents did any of that stuff to her or not, but I do know that even if they did, what we did wasn't right. I've realized, a little late, that you can't live for other people and can't right all the wrongs & injustices in the world. All you can do is try to carve out a little bit of peace & happiness and try to avoid as much of the cruelty & injustice as possible, instead of trying to meet it head-on & change it singlehandedly.

Although I'm not very religious there is a lot to be said for maxims like 'Judge not, lest ye be judged,' and 'Let he who is without sin throw the first stone.'

Well, I'm not doing much but reading and working out (I'm benching 275 lbs now) so everything is about the same. Hopefully I'll see you next week.

Later!

Love,
Dave

A month later, on June 5, 1987, in Judge Azios's court once again, with Rusty at his side—the faithful shepherd—he pled guilty to the second charge of murder that had hung over his head during both trials. He received a concurrent life sentence. The Texas legislature had just passed a law reducing mandatory prison time to one quarter of the sentence— it meant that David (and Cindy) could be eligible for parole in fifteen years rather than twenty. David might be free in the year 2000, when he would be forty-six.

If he lived through it. To a few reporters Rusty voiced his worry about David's safety because of inmates' distaste for snitches. "But I think most of them will understand that he was only testifying against the person who got him into trouble."

He and David shook hands. "Good luck," Rusty said.

"And to you, too," David said sincerely. "Take care of yourself. Don't work too hard."

When at last David had been taken away, a reporter asked Rusty what would happen if Cindy won her appeal for a retrial. Now that no more indictments could be leveled at David, why would he testify a third time? Rusty thought a moment and said, "I'd have no means any-more to compel him. But I have a feeling David would do the right thing."

David had been in solitary confinement for two years and four months. When Rusty left the courtroom that day he let out a heavy sigh and said, "I've been so trapped within this case that I can almost identify with him. I feel as if that two years and four months was my *own* form of solitary confinement."

I knew what he meant.

_____

On my way to Hobby Airport I cruised past the house on Memorial Drive—and stopped the car there on the shoulder of the road under the beat of the Texas sun. The house was still abandoned. Summer weeds had cracked the driveway into a jigsaw puzzle, and scrub swarmed at the walls. The riotous foliage of the oak trees cast an immense, gloomy shadow over whatever the eye could see. All seemed forsaken—plagued.

Was the den window still open? For a moment I was tempted to look. But I drove off to the airport.

PHOTO CREDITS

PHOTO CREDITS

About the Author

Clifford Irving was born in Manhattan, educated at the High School of Music and Art and Cornell University, and lived for many years in Europe. A one-time correspondent to the United Nations, and the Middle East, he is the author of thirteen books, including *Fake!* and *Tom Mix and Pancho Villa*.